# The
# Edinburgh Critical History
# of
# Twentieth-Century
# Christian Theology

The Edinburgh Critical History of Christian Theology
Series Editors: Russell Re Manning, Bath Spa University and Tom Greggs,
University of Aberdeen

The Edinburgh Critical History of Christian Theology presents the history of Christian theology in an innovative way with critical essays addressing the emergence and development of the themes and problematics that characterise each period. Particular attention is given to the diffusion of themes across disciplinary, geographical and historical boundaries, and to the changing practices of Christian theology.

A key concern of the series will be to explore the ways in which themes and clusters of themes can be traced within and across historical periods, leading to a new and informative way of conceptualising the development of Christian theological thinking. In so doing, a guiding methodological assumption of the series is that the history of Christian theology is one of a series of encounters and negotiations between traditions and contexts. The thematic *foci* of the volumes range broadly across creedal and doctrinal *loci* as well as historical particularities.

The Edinburgh Critical History of Christian Theology reflects on how the dominant themes and problematic of a period took shape, were developed, and were bequeathed to subsequent generations; enabling both a re-evaluation of the dynamics of historical Christian theology and a *ressourcement* for contemporary Christian theologians and critical thinkers.

### Volumes available
*The Edinburgh Critical History of Nineteenth-Century Christian Theology*
Edited by Daniel Whistler
*The Edinburgh Critical History of Twentieth-Century Christian Theology*
Edited by Philip G. Ziegler

### Forthcoming volumes in the series
*The Edinburgh Critical History of Apostolic and Patristic Christian Theology*
*The Edinburgh Critical History of Medieval Christian Theology*
*The Edinburgh Critical History of Renaissance and Reformation Christian Theology*
*The Edinburgh Critical History of Early Modern Christian Theology*
*The Edinburgh Critical History of Contemporary Christian Theology*

Visit the series webpage at
edinburghuniversitypress.com/series/echct

# The
# Edinburgh Critical History
# of
# Twentieth-Century
# Christian Theology

## Edited by Philip G. Ziegler

EDINBURGH
University Press

Edinburgh University Press is one of the leading university presses in the UK. We publish academic books and journals in our selected subject areas across the humanities and social sciences, combining cutting-edge scholarship with high editorial and production values to produce academic works of lasting importance. For more information visit our website: edinburghuniversitypress.com

Edinburgh University Press Ltd
The Tun – Holyrood Road
12(2f) Jackson's Entry
Edinburgh EH8 8PJ

Typeset in 10/12 Goudy Old Style
by Cheshire Typesetting Ltd, Cuddington, Cheshire
and printed and bound in Great Britain by
CPI Group (UK) Ltd, Croydon CR0 4YY

A CIP record for this book is available from the British Library

ISBN 978 1 4744 8884 6 (hardback)
ISBN 978 1 4744 8887 7 (webready PDF)
ISBN 978 1 4744 8886 0 (epub)

# Contents

# Notes on Contributors

**Andrew Atherstone** is Latimer Research Fellow and Tutor in Church History at Wycliffe Hall, Oxford (UK), and a member of Oxford University's Faculty of Theology and Religion. His research focuses upon the history of evangelicalism and Anglicanism in the nineteenth and twentieth centuries. His recent books include, as co-editor, *Making Evangelical History: Faith, Scholarship and the Evangelical Past* (2019) and *Transatlantic Charismatic Renewal, c.1950–2000* (2021).

**Jane Barter** is Professor of Religion and Culture at the University of Winnipeg (Canada). She has published several works of constructive theology, including *Thinking Christ: Christology and Contemporary Critics* (2012) and *Lord, Giver of Life* (2007). She also researches at the intersection of feminist theory and Continental philosophy of religion.

**Anthony Bateza** is Associate Professor of Religion and an affiliated faculty member in the Race and Ethnic Studies programme at St. Olaf College in Northfield, Minnesota (US). A specialist in Martin Luther and political theology, his research examines human agency, questions of race and identity, as well as moral formation, with particular interest in the virtue tradition and its liberative potential in the work of social justice. Recent works include 'Reclaiming the Legacies of Martin Luther and James Baldwin in Fighting Racism', in *Forgotten Luther II: Reclaiming the Church's Public Witness* (2019) and 'Reconciling Rapacious Wolves and Misguided Sheep: Law and Responsibility in Martin Luther's Response to the Peasants' War', in *Political Theology* 19:4 (2018).

**Daniel Castelo** is the William Kellon Quick Professor of Theology and Methodist Studies at Duke Divinity School (US). He is currently pursuing questions in the fields of pneumatology and Latinx theology. Most recently he is co-author of *The Marks of Scripture* (2019) and co-editor of the *T&T Clark Handbook of Pneumatology* (2020).

**Christophe Chalamet** is Professor of Systematic Theology at the University of Geneva (Switzerland). Among his recent publications: *A Most Excellent Way: An Essay on Faith, Hope, and Love* (2020), and, as editor, *The Challenge of History: Readings in Modern Theology* (2020). He is currently working on a renewed theology of covenant.

**David Grumett** is Senior Lecturer in Theology and Ethics in the University of Edinburgh (UK). His expertise includes twentieth-century French Jesuit theology and the liturgy. His books in these fields include *Henri de Lubac and the Shaping of Modern Theology* (2020),

*Material Eucharist* (2016), *De Lubac: A Guide for the Perplexed* (2007) and *Teilhard de Chardin: Theology, Humanity and Cosmos* (2005).

**Paul Hedges** is Associate Professor in Interreligious Studies at the Studies in the Interreligious Relations in Plural Societies Programme, RSIS, Nanyang Technological University, Singapore. He has previously worked for, or lectured at, other universities in Asia, Europe and North America. He researches, teaches, and publishes widely in such areas as interreligious studies, theory and method in the study of religion, contemporary global religious ideologies and interreligious hermeneutics. He has engaged in work beyond academia with the media, NGOs, faith groups and governments. He has published fourteen books and over scholarly seventy papers. His most recent books are *Understanding Religion: Theories and Methods for Studying Religiously Diverse Societies* (2021), and *Religious Hatred: Prejudice, Islamophobia, and Antisemitism in Global Context* (2021). He is co-editor of *Interreligious Studies and Intercultural Theology*, editor-in-chief of the Occasional Paper series *Interreligious Relations* and sits on the editorial board of a number of other journal and book series.

**Christine Helmer** holds the Peter B. Ritzma Chair of the Humanities at Northwestern University in Evanston, Illinois (US), where she is also Professor of German and Religious Studies. Her areas of teaching and research are German intellectual history, theology (including biblical reception, philosophical theology and systematic theology), Luther studies, Schleiermacher studies, critical theory, race and religion in sport, and women in higher education. She is the editor of numerous volumes, recently *The Medieval Luther* (2020) and *Truth-Telling and Other Ecclesial Practices of Religion* (2021), and author of *Theology and the End of Doctrine* (2014; also available in Korean translation), *How Luther Became the Reformer* (2019) and *A Constructive Theology in Conversation with Christians in Taiwan* (in Chinese, 2020). She is also the instructor of the free massive open online course (MOOC) 'Luther and the West'.

**Veli-Matti Kärkkäinen** is Professor of Systematic Theology at Fuller Theological Seminary, Pasadena, California (US) and Docent of Ecumenics at the University of Helsinki (Finland). A native of Finland, he has also lived and taught theology in Thailand, and continues participating widely in international ecumenical, theological and interreligious work. Among the almost thirty books he has written and edited, the most important projects include a five-volume series titled *Constructive Christian Theology for the Pluralistic World* (2013–17), which develops a full-scale systematic theology in a critical dialogue with Christian tradition, including global and contextual interpretations, natural sciences and four living faiths. He is a member of the Academy of Sciences in Finland and an ordained Lutheran minister (ELCA).

**Kirsteen Kim** holds the Paul E. Pierson Chair in World Christianity and serves as the Associate Dean for the Center for Missiological Research at Fuller Theological Seminary, Pasadena, California (US). Her research interests include intercultural theology – especially in India and Korea – pneumatology, theology of mission, and mission studies. She is an editor of the book series Theology and Mission in World Christianity (Brill). Among her numerous publications are *A History of Korean Christianity* (2015), *The New Evangelization* (2015) and *Christianity as a World Religion*, 2nd ed. (2016).

**P. Travis Kroeker** is Professor in the Department of Religious Studies and the Arts and Science programme at McMaster University, Hamilton, Ontario (Canada), where he teaches and publishes in the areas of ethics, literature, philosophy and religious thought. He is the author of *Christian Ethics and Political Economy in North America* (1995) and (with Bruce Ward) *Remembering the End: Dostoevsky as Prophet to Modernity* (2001). He has recently published the first of two book projects on political theology: *Messianic Political Theology and Diaspora Ethics* (2017) and *Literary Apocalypse as Political Theology* (forthcoming).

**Mark Lindsay** is the Joan F. W. Munro Professor of Historical Theology at the Trinity College Theological School, in the University of Divinity (Australia). A priest in the Anglican Diocese of Melbourne, he has taught in universities and seminaries across Australia, and in England. With a particular interest in Barthian and post-Holocaust theology, he has published three books on Karl Barth, a fourth on the doctrine of election – *God has Chosen: The Doctrine of Election through Christian History* (2020) – and is currently writing a major biography of Markus Barth.

**Rachel Muers** was appointed to the Chair of Divinity at the University of Edinburgh (UK) in 2022, having previously held posts at the University of Leeds, the University of Exeter and at Girton College, University of Cambridge (UK). She has published on a range of topics at the intersections of modern Christian theology and theological ethics. Her publications include *Keeping God's Silence: Towards a Theological Ethics of Communication* (2004), *Living for the Future: Theological Ethics for Coming Generations* (2008), *Testimony: Quakerism and Theological Ethics* (2015), *Theology on the Menu: Asceticism, Meat and Christian Diet* (with David Grumett, 2010) and *Modern Theology: A Critical Introduction* (with Mike Higton, 2012).

**Angus Paddison** is Reader in Theology and Acting Deputy Vice-Chancellor, University of Winchester (UK). His research and writing has focused on the theological interpretation of Scripture and includes *Theological Hermeneutics and 1 Thessalonians* (2005), *Scripture: A Very Theological Proposal* (2009) and edited volumes such as *Theologians on Scripture* (2016).

**Tracey Rowland** holds the St John Paul II Chair of Theology at the University of Notre Dame (Australia). From 2014 to 2019 she was a member of the International Theological Commission, and in 2020 she won the Ratzinger Prize for Theology. Her recent publications include *Catholic Theology* (2017), *Portraits of Spiritual Nobility* (2019) and *Beyond Kant and Nietzsche: The Munich Defence of Christian Humanism* (2021). She has also edited a collection of essays on *The Anglican Patrimony in Catholic Communion* (2021). Her research areas include fundamental theology and theological anthropology. She is the English subeditor of a forthcoming multilingual *Ratzinger Lexikon*.

**Katherine Sonderegger** is Professor of Theology at Virginia Theological Seminary (US). She is well known for her work in the study of Christian doctrine generally and the theology of Karl Barth in particular. In addition to many essays and articles, her recent publications include *Systematic Theology I – The Doctrine of God* (2015) and *Systematic Theology II – The Doctrine of the Holy Trinity: Processions and Persons* (2020).

**Elina Vuola** is Professor of Global Christianity and Dialogue of Religions at the Faculty of Theology, University of Helsinki (Finland). Her scholarship concerns Latin American liberation and feminist theologies as well as the relationship between secular gender studies and feminist study of religion. A long-standing interest has been the figure of the Virgin Mary and its relationship to feminist and liberation theologies. She served as an Academy Professor of the Academy of Finland in 2013–17, researching Finnish religious minorities from a lived religion and gender perspective. She has been a visiting researcher at the Departamento Ecuménico de Investigaciones in San José (Costa Rica); at the Women's Studies in Religion programme at the Harvard Divinity School (US); and at the Department of Religious Studies at Northwestern University in Evanston, Illinois (US). Her most recent publication is *The Virgin Mary across Cultures: Devotion among Costa Rican Catholic and Finnish Orthodox Women* (2019).

**Judith Wolfe** is Professor of Philosophical Theology at the University of St Andrews (UK). She has written widely on eschatology and other subjects in systematic and philosophical theology, as well as on theology and the arts. Her books include *Heidegger's Eschatology* (2013), *Heidegger and Theology* (2014) and the *Oxford Handbook of Nineteenth-Century Christian Thought* (with Joel Rasmussen and Johannes Zachhuber, 2017); she is currently editing the three-volume *Oxford History of Modern German Theology* (with David Lincicum and Johannes Zachhuber) and the *Cambridge Companion to Eschatology*.

**Philip G. Ziegler** is Professor of Christian Dogmatics at the University of Aberdeen (UK). His research interests include issues in modern Christian theology and the contemporary theological legacies of Karl Barth and Dietrich Bonhoeffer in particular. In addition to essay and articles, he is the author of *Doing Theology When God is Forgotten: The Theological Achievement of Wolf Krötke* (2006) and *Militant Grace: The Apocalyptic Turn and the Future of Theology* (2018) and the editor of *Eternal God, Eternal Life: Theological Investigations into the Concept of Immortality* (2016). He is co-editor of *The Oxford Handbook of Dietrich Bonhoeffer* (2019), *Christ, Church and World: New Studies in Bonhoeffer's Theology and Ethics* (2016) and *The Providence of God* (2009).

# Editor's Introduction

## Philip G. Ziegler

As Daniel Whistler observed in his own introduction to the *Edinburgh Critical History of Nineteenth-Century Christian Theology*, Christian self-reflection and doctrinal thought 'attained modernity in the nineteenth century, and this modernity was constituted out of anxiety over its own foundations'.[1] The twentieth century saw theology continue to grapple intensely with the searching intellectual challenges of modernity so crucial to those previous developments. This nineteenth-century legacy is evident in the continued preoccupation with theology's foundations and methods, with the consequences of the transposition of the study of divinity into the study of *homo religiosus*, with the propriety and significance of historical and hermeneutical critique to Christian self-understanding, doctrinal reflection and reconstruction, as well as with the fate of faith itself in a world increasingly secularised by social reorganisation under the prestigious tutelage of the natural and social sciences. In many ways the controlling images of the nature and tasks of theology cultivated in the hundred years following Kant's death continued to organise the theological imaginary of the century to follow.[2]

Yet, as one of our philosophers has aptly remarked, 'Much of twentieth-century history has been a very unpleasant surprise', populated with events that shock in virtue of both their scale and profound contradiction of the optimistic expectations previously cultivated by modern humanity.[3] And so the theological discourses and deliverances of the nineteenth century were themselves cut across, shaken and disrupted by the advent of further social, technological, political and intellectual revolutions throughout the course of the new century. It was undoubtedly a century in which Christian theology was provoked by its exposure to world historical events: the invention and prosecution of new and unheard-of forms of total war in Europe between 1914 and 1945 and its global entanglements and entailments; the Holocaust of European Jewry; the ideological reordering of geopolitics and accompanying 'cold war'; the simultaneous modulation of dissolving European empires into both the international order of the 'global village' and ravenous global capitalism amidst the emergence of a post-colonial 'majority world'; the first orbital vision of the earth as a 'big blue marble' and the dawning discernment of our age of the Anthropocene. This was also a century that witnessed the unprecedented globalisation of both Christianity and theological discourse in what was anticipated by many in the West to be the 'Christian century'. As Brian Stanley has written, 'The twentieth century may not have been the Christian century that missionary strategists hoped for in 1900, but it was indeed the century in which Christianity became more truly a world religion than ever before.'[4] In short, while the story of twentieth-century theology must be told as one of continuity with that of the century preceding, it must also be approached with an eye for the sheer novelty of many of its key challenges, opportunities and developments.

This volume offers an innovative conceptual survey of Christian theology as it developed in the twentieth century in relation to key historical events and transformative developments in intellectual and ecclesial cultures. As with the other volumes in this series, this volume re-examines a specific era in the history of Christian theology by tracing key concepts, problems and themes as they develop in context with explicit interest in new perspectives opened up by contemporary theology itself. The overarching ambition is to examine and represent the defining contours of this moment in the history of Christian theology so as to illumine the contexts, dynamism and complexities of its traditions. In this way, it hopes to offer a critical and creative *ressourcement* for contemporary theologians. The contributors to this volume together aim to enquire afresh into the preoccupations, problems, provocations and prospects of Christian theology in the tumultuous century just past and to ask anew about just what in this recent history matters and why. This introduction briefly sketches how the chapters that follow seek to understand and portray the complex and centrifugal dynamics of Christian theology in the twentieth century by a concentrated exploration of a selection of key themes, questions, movements and figures.

The opening chapter begins the conversation by thinking afresh about the way modernity itself is conceived in relation to the work of theology in the twentieth century. Katherine Sonderegger revisits the commonplace claim that modern science and critical historiography one-sidedly issue in an intellectual and cultural break with all that has gone before. With Thomas Huxley and the artists of the Vienna Secession as evocative points of reference, she thinks about and forward from the particular examples of Rudolf Bultmann and Johannes Weiss, to contend that the influential historical and scientific forms of thought that mark this period in fact show 'the modern' to be a notably plastic concept concerned with 'the dynamic *interplay* between the continuous and the interrupted, the stable and the ruptured'.

David Grumett then moves in the second chapter to address the closely related theme of 'tradition and innovation', considering in particular the way in which the theology of the last century wrestled with the notion of tradition itself in ways that funded influential insights into the dynamic, developmental nature of theological discourse. The opening section of the chapter engages the diverse perspectives of Orthodox, Roman Catholic, Anglican and evangelical theologians to just this end. From here Grumett goes on to explore several representative examples of the work of doctrinal revision undertaken by theologians from varied ecclesial and doctrinal traditions which demonstrate how in fact 'tremendous theological innovation' was funded precisely by renewed, critical and constructive engagements with the long theological tradition.

Angus Paddison's discussion of 'Scripture and criticism' draws the focus in even more tightly to explore the ways in which modernity's critical – and self-critical – impulses have played themselves out in the specific field of biblical interpretation. While biblical studies has of course continued to be a particular locus of critical historiographical endeavour, Paddison argues it was the emergence of 'ideological criticism' and its search for the covert operations of power at play in the work of texts and their interpretation which proved particularly vital to twentieth-century developments. Perhaps unexpectedly, the surfacing of 'interests' admits and accompanies efforts to theorise a consciously 'theological interpretation of scripture' which is ambitious to (re-)connect normative hermeneutical discussions with both empirical study of the actual use of the Bible in diverse church communities and the interdisciplinary conversation of the modern university.

In the fourth chapter, Christine Helmer critically examines the place of 'reason, method and system' in the practice of theology in the last century. The sheer methodological diversity of theology in the twentieth century perhaps belies the suggestion that this triad of concepts can or must be at the heart of theological practice and self-understanding. Yet, as Helmer argues, a family of institutionally regnant and influential accounts of theology developed in Germany during the early part of the century, and disseminated widely thereafter, have made much of precisely these concerns. Yet, during an era when theology's progress was marked by 'trauma and judgement, system and interruption, dialectic and resistance', as Helmer says, this received 'epistemic advantage model' came to be challenged by other, self-consciously 'contextual models' whose methods and modes of reasoning queried its privilege and systematic ambition.

The chapter from Tracey Rowland that follows explores what must be one of the most decisive marks of Christian theology in the twentieth century, namely the emergence and advance of ecumenism. Through a fulsome account of the history and specific contributions of Roman Catholic theology to the unfolding of the 'ecumenical century', Rowland demonstrates how key Catholic theologians and developments in Catholic theology – not least the *ressourcement* movement with its re-evaluation of medieval and early modern Catholic thought – funded ecumenical possibilities and gains, both doctrinal and institutional, that would have been unthinkable a century before.

Andrew Atherstone's essay on 'Fundamentalism and Evangelicalism' illuminates the two important theological and ecclesiastical phenomena named in its title by way of a close examination of the rather heated debates about them that took place in Britain after the Second World War. Here the English case stands *pars pro toto*, as an exemplary instance of the kinds of theological tensions and institutional concerns which arise more generally. Atherstone demonstrate that 'fundamentalism' together with the even more plastic 'evangelicalism' proved to be 'highly malleable and potent' theological categories in twentieth-century debates in which not only doctrine, but also intellectual and socio-cultural prestige were at stake.

As Mark Lindsay argues in his chapter 'Synagogue, *Sho'ah* and State', the twentieth century brought about 'a reckoning' among Christian churches and theologians regarding historic Christian antipathy towards Judaism and their willingness to tolerate or indeed cultivate anti-Judaic/anti-Semitic politics and policies. The unprecedented assault on the existence of Jews and Judaism in the Holocaust forced searching questions upon Christian theology in this regard – questions about supersessionism, Christian collusion with political interests, and about the ecumenism of 'Church and Synagogue' – whose import and consequence are by no means exhausted.

Modern theological reflection on human religion and world religions began in earnest during the nineteenth century, yet the massive globalisation of Christianity ensured it became a prominent and inescapable feature of Christian thought during the twentieth. Paul Hedges treats of this theme and of its importance in his chapter. Beginning with the theological construction of the concept of 'religion' itself, Hedges traces its complex evolution through the theological and ecclesiastical contexts from which have emerged, especially in more recent decades, formative impulses towards dialogue, comparative theology and a reckoning with the deep entanglement of religion not only with culture, but also thereby with contested colonial legacies.

The next several chapters consider the fate of central theological *loci* and doctrines. First, Daniel Castelo explores the fate of 'God' across the tumultuous history of the century, reflecting closely upon developments in both the God-haunted secular North

Atlantic world – home to debates concerning the nature of atheism, the abiding issue of theodicy, the surprising resurgence of Trinitarian doctrine and the contested status of received 'theism' – and the Global South, where the question of God arises amidst an 'indigenous discovery of Christianity' that is funding new and creative advances in the field of theology proper.

Next Veli-Matti Kärkkäinen traces the expansive importance of the 'Spirit' in twentieth-century theology as fuelled by the global explosion of charismatic and Pentecostal Christianity, the Trinitarian renaissance, as well as by the widening influence of Orthodox Christianity via its ecumenical engagements. In Western theology the theme proved crucial for integrating appeals to piety and experience in theological construction, as well as reconnecting with certain trends in the natural and human sciences; meanwhile, Kärkkäinen suggests the ubiquity of the Spirit in Pentecostal discourse is shifting theology as such in new directions that are also increasingly refracted through the perspectives of Christians and churches from the majority world.

Christophe Chalamet's chapter analyses the 'dizzying array' of Christological developments in the period that runs from the anti-dogmatic account of Ernst Troeltsch to contemporary reflections on the identity of the 'global Christ'. Once again, here the story is one of manifold, complex developments driven by a constellation of doctrinal, intellectual and social considerations. Time and again in this era, whether in Protestant, Catholic or Orthodox worlds, Christological doctrines orbit uneasily around the poles of divine distinctiveness and human solidarity. As Chalamet observes, even in the radically critical Christologies of recent decades, the abiding capacity of the figure of Christ to shape theology as a whole remains manifest.

Elina Vuola then takes up the task of tracking how the notions of 'liberation and freedom' have been reconsidered and developed in the course of twentieth-century theology. Central to her analysis are the diverse range of liberation theologies which emerged during the century and which have made servicing the struggle against interlocking schemes of political and social marginalisation and oppression programmatic to the theological task itself. Here theological subject matter and importantly also theological *method* have been radically reformed. As she argues in her analysis of key works and developments, liberation theologies have contended not only that practical liberation is central to Christian life and faith, but also that there are important religious dimensions ingredient in all such political and social projects that ought not to be neglected.

The question of the theological engagement with the world of politics remains central to the next chapter, in which P. Travis Kroeker examines the fate in the twentieth century of the concept of 'the secular' and its interrelation with 'the political'. Kroeker contends that, beginning with a formative exchange between legal theorist Carl Schmitt and Catholic theologian Erik Peterson, crucial debates about and creative receptions of Augustine became and remained central to political theology in the century. The ancient concept of the *saeculum* and its reconception amidst disputes about the nature and interrelation of Augustine's 'two cities' admits new conceptions of the nature and scope of 'the political' which he argues – by way of an extended close analysis of key threads of the debate and suggestion of the possibility of a 'messianic' Augustinianism – expand its reach beyond overly narrow concern with the mechanics of states and governance to include the fields of society, economy and increasingly also technology.

Kirsteen Kim's chapter then explores one of the decisively important phenomena in the history of both Christianity and Christian theology in the last century, namely the emergence of 'World Christianity' following the dissolution of European empires. As Kim argues, there has been a notable lag between the expansion of the churches of the majority world and the reception and integration of their distinctive questions, perspectives and contributions into existing theological discourse. Indeed, in the course of a detailed examination of the institutional and conceptual history of the churches and the rise of global Christianity, she contends that Western 'resistance' has been an impediment to the full theological flourishing of Christianity around the world and hindered its capacity to confront, thematise and address the pressing challenges of inculturation and interreligious dialogue that the reality of a 'world Church' enjoins.

In many ways the twentieth century was a uniquely war-torn century. In her chapter on 'war and peace', Rachel Muers considers the impact of the experience of modern warfare and the warring imperialism of 'Christian nations' in relation to sometimes radical theological reconsiderations of military violence in particular, and the received symbology of war and 'redemptive violence' in the Christian tradition more generally. Her exploration of key developments and debates in this regard takes as its crucial compliment a no less important discussion of the unfolding of twentieth-century theologies of peace and peacemaking, Christian nonviolence, as well as important reflections on the abiding entanglement of the concepts of peace and justice in more recent theological enquiries into the nature and prospects for reconciliation 'after war'.

Anthony Bateza's chapter concentrates on the nature and practice of 'Black theology' as a way of exploring the emergence of the theme of race and the realities of racial oppression as explicit *theological* concerns in twentieth-century Christian theology. Through the lens of a particular analysis of the development of Black theology in the United States, Bateza explores the way in which the challenge of this kind of theological work reaches beyond the demand for 'inclusion' or 'recognition' and instead stakes critical claims about the very *ethos* of the theological endeavour which, as he says, challenge 'the formal and substantive claims of Christian thought'. Again, as surfaced in other chapters, here both theological content and theological method are implicated in the fecund epistemic and ethical questions raised by the practice of Black theology.

'Sex and gender' are the central concerns of the volume's penultimate chapter, by Jane Barter. Her analysis of debates and developments around these themes in Catholic, Orthodox and Protestant theological traditions surfaces some of the most telling tensions in the theological sensibilities of the 'century of sex': between nature and construction, between the import of given sexual differences and the plasticity of human desire and identity. Barter suggests that fundamental challenges are posed to theology's wide investment in the self-evident quality of human sexual difference, not least by the theoretical 'queering' of gender and the deeply unsettling realities of sexual abuse within the life and ambit of the Christian churches.

Judith Wolfe concludes these explorations aptly in the final chapter with a discussion of the concept of hope in twentieth-century theology. If the 'crisis of eschatology' ingredient in the disruption of classical doctrine by modern reason were met in the nineteenth century in part by embrace of progressive understandings of history moved by a God immanent in the course of world affairs, the brutalising experiences of mechanised global warfare of the first half of the twentieth century funded something other. As Wolfe shows through a close reading of key European developments, the last hundred years have seen wide-ranging reconsiderations of the concept of history, of early Christian eschatology, and the doctrines of 'last things' and Christian hope that have been as critical as they have been radical. As she observes, this programme is far from concluded, since theology has 'not yet risen to the challenge' of confronting and responding to the eschatological and apocalyptic imagination of the previous century 'in relevant and distinctly theological ways'.

This introduction would not be complete without an expression of thanks to Daniel Pedersen for his assistance and, in particular, for preparing the index

## Notes

1. Daniel Whistler, 'Editor's Introduction', in *The Edinburgh Critical History of Nineteenth-Century Christian Theology*, edited by Daniel Whistler (Edinburgh: Edinburgh University Press, 2018), p. 2.
2. For a compelling account of this claim and discussion see George P. Schner, 'Metaphors for Theology', in *Theology after Liberalism: A Reader*, edited by John Webster and George P. Schner (Oxford: Blackwell, 2000), pp. 3–51.
3. Jonathan Glover, *Humanity: A Moral History of the Twentieth Century* (New Haven, CT: Yale University Press, 2000), p. 3.
4. Brian Stanley, *Christianity in the Twentieth Century: A World History* (Princeton, NJ: Princeton University Press, 2018), p. 11.

## Bibliography

Glover, Jonathan, *Humanity: A Moral History of the Twentieth Century* (New Haven, CT: Yale University Press, 2000)

Schner, George P., 'Metaphors for Theology', in *Theology after Liberalism: A Reader*, edited by John Webster and George P. Schner (Oxford: Blackwell, 2000), pp. 3–51.

Stanley, Brian, *Christianity in the Twentieth Century: A World History* (Princeton, NJ: Princeton University Press, 2018).

Whistler, Daniel, 'Editor's Introduction', in *The Edinburgh Critical History of Nineteenth-Century Christian Theology*, edited by Daniel Whistler (Edinburgh: Edinburgh University Press, 2018).

# 1

# Modern Theology in a Scientific, Historical Age

*Katherine Sonderegger*

'What is it that underlies change?', Aristotle asked, in one of the oldest reflections we possess on stability and novelty in creaturely life. What underlies, what subtends and supports the dynamic efflorescence of animal and human life within this island home? Famously, Aristotle answered his own question with his stubbornly elusive discussion of 'substance', a category that would subvent all change in concept and property, until the dawn of the modern era.[1] But we need not import 'substance' directly into our discussion of history and science in the modern era – that would undermine too plainly the championing of novelty that is a hallmark of the modern – but we will nevertheless need something in its place. For the modern world, in its historical, scientific and theological reasoning, is a place where the novel jostles alongside the enduring, and the focus upon the novel, the stark break and rupture with the past, the emancipatory and revolutionary – so strongly associated with modernism – will stand, all the same, shoulder to shoulder with the substantial, the memorialised, the inherited, the continuous and the ancient. It has been the stuff of textbook and popular saga to say that the modern erupted as a brutal overthrow of the *ancien régime*, an enemy of the aristocratic, the clerical, the traditional and enduring. But neither history nor science, for all their disruptive power, exists wholly as enemy of religion, nor have they, as magnitudes of human thought, emptied out or made otiose the worlds of cosmology, metaphysics and the Divine. Rather we might think of the modern, most especially but not exclusively the modern in the West, as a rather frayed garment of transformation *and* stability, of revolution *and* the *longue durée*. Indeed, the very idea of 'the modern' might be taken not as a synonym for the new, but rather as a placeholder for the dynamic *interplay* between the continuous and the interrupted, the stable and the ruptured.

This is not the story usually told. Any student of the unfolding rise of modernism in the West will remember the familiar story, the narrative of the modern as pioneer of rupture. Gotthold Lessing famously concluded his widely cited essay 'On the Spirit and Power' with a piteous cry (or was it mischievous?) for someone to ferry him across the 'great, ugly ditch' – 'der garstige breite Graben', a fully resonant term in German, with its echo of grave and sepulchre – that had opened between the facts, or 'accidental truths', of history and the perduring and 'necessary truths of reason' and of dogma.[2] On either side of this ravine lie the dismembered elements of older arguments of natural theology that rise up from the creaturely realm to touch the hem of the metaphysical, and to find in the events, the habits and flourishing of living beings the signs and effects of a Heavenly and Provident Lord. It was Lessing's proper anguish (or delight) to find *historical* events in themselves unable to bear the weight of dogmatic truths, and to claim, to his satisfaction, that one could never move rationally from contingent happening to necessary *ratio*. But students of this era can equally call to mind the rupture that is said to emerge from the spectacular brio of the physical sciences as they brashly encountered the teachings of the old religion. Galileo's furtive cry 'Eppur si muove' ('still she moves'), said to have been flung in the teeth of arrest and torture, seems the shining example of an empirical truth overturning and breaking in pieces the old necessary truths of dogmatic reason.[3] Far closer to home, we cannot but think of the great Charles Darwin, and the fate of his theory of natural selection in the hands of theologians, evangelists and prelates of all sorts.[4] It does not take a Richard Dawkins or a Daniel Dennett to tell students of modernism on the grounds of the old Christendom that the theory of evolution has become an enemy to some Christians, a much feared and respected opponent in the ring of public schooling and science instruction. William Jennings Bryan will suffice for that task.[5]

What animates this older account of the relation of religion to science and historical study is the conviction that the modern is the revolutionary, the transgressive, the avant-garde. This is an image zealously defended by the artistic and musical pioneers of the modern style, and by theorists, of many schools, who understand their principal work to lie in overcoming resistance to the demanding, the unwelcomed, the real. We might advert here to the famous Secessionist exhibition, held in Vienna at the febrile turn of the twentieth century. The painters, printmakers and architects who displayed their work in the newly built Secession Building (Secessionsgebäude) were rejected by the authoritative arts council of Vienna, and gladly took upon themselves the mantle of the avant-garde who braved bourgeois scorn to express the world that lies beneath and beyond convention.[6] The maxim inscribed on the newly built hall appears to clinch the Secessionists as the revolutionary cadre: 'Der Zeit ihr Kunst – der Kunst ihr Freiheit', i.e. 'To each age, its art – to Art, its freedom!'[7] Or, discursively closer to theology, we might consider the brash young Freud, who understood himself as 'a Copernican' of the unconscious, shattering the cosmology of the prim and the correct, erecting in place of the old gods who totter our 'god *Logos*' – science and rationality – which dares to confront and embrace the real, whatever its cost.[8] Another titan of the modern might seem to emerge in the work of the young Bertrand Russell, who considered early Cantor-style set theory to overturn and handily best all old, threadbare accounts of mathematics. All his long, fabled life, Russell seemed to delight in the badge of the modern: a pacifist when war-mongering was sweet; an atheist when religion was still held dear; a sexual fellow-traveller when marriage was still thought to be lifelong and exclusive to its members. Russell was all a pugilistic modernist could hope for: witty, urbane, wonderfully learned; his books on philosophy entirely his own affair; unafraid and thrilled by the chase. He seemed even capable of taking in stride his humiliating dressing-down by Wittgenstein – a man of no mean modernist credentials himself, and who was published, employed and saved by the philosopher he dared to scorn.[9]

Or consider, more fully now, the case of Thomas Huxley, the comparative anatomist who styled himself Darwin's 'bulldog', and who delighted in debates with all comers, most especially the Evangelical and Episcopal opponents of Darwinism.[10] With his fellow protagonist in the struggle, Herbert Spencer, Huxley painted the evolutionary dynamism of living species as a 'struggle for existence', or, in Spencer's more famous phrase, the 'survival of the fittest'.[11] For Huxley the polemicist, evolutionary competition surged all the way up to the very debates he relished and in which he excelled. 'The struggle for existence holds as much in the intellectual as in the physical world. A theory is a species of thinking, and its right to exist is coextensive with its power of resisting extinction by its rivals', Huxley boldly claimed, showing the modern theory in its most muscular form, fighting off 'extinction' from its 'rivals' and displaying, in its toughness, its 'right to exist'.[12] Thomas Huxley was in truth no rival or subaltern to Darwin; he was a consummate scientist in his own right, and a theoretician of biological development who made lasting contributions to evolutionary doctrine. Perhaps it is not entirely coincidental to his place within modernism that Huxley early on proposed a stark form of *rupture* within zoologic life: 'saltation' or 'leaping across' gaps in animal development, marking breakthroughs in adaptation, species identity and group survival. Saltation opposed a kind of 'gradualism' or continuous development, from ancestor to descendant, from earlier species to later, a thesis more attractive to Darwin and his more fluid conception of 'natural kinds'.[13]

Huxley seemed ready to leave his mark on modernism as avant-garde, too, in his coinage of the term 'agnosticism' to denote the proper openness and methodological parsimony of the scientist. The scientist has no prior commitments, no doctrinal constraints, on the work set before her or him; rather, the scientist follows truth wherever it may lead. In a full display of his polemic skills, Huxley unloads an arsenal of the most advanced German higher critical analyses of the Scripture – of which David Friedrich Strauss was, of course, a favoured champion – a withering account of his opponents' views, a witty survey of cruel or bizarre attitudes held by our ancestors, and in its midst, a stout defence of common-sense realism. He defines agnosticism in this revealing paragraph, buried in the midst of much debate-platform *élan*:

> Agnosticism, in fact, is not a creed, but a method, the essence of which lies in the rigorous application of a single principle. That principle is of great antiquity; it is as old as Socrates; as old as the writer who said, 'Try all things, hold fast by that which is good'; it is the foundation of the Reformation [no small allegiance is being displayed here], which simply illustrated the axiom that every man should be able to give a reason for the faith that is in him; it is the great principle of Descartes; it is the fundamental axiom of modern science [hence, 'methodological agnosticism']. Positively the principle may be expressed: In matters of the intellect, follow your reason as far as it will take you, without regard to any other consideration. And negatively: In matters of the intellect, do not pretend that conclusions are certain which are not demonstrated or demonstrable. That I take to be the agnostic faith, which if a man keep whole and undefiled, he shall not be ashamed to look the universe in the face, whatever the future may have in store for him.[14]

Note the way Huxley takes his milder 'agnosticism' into decidedly religious territory: it is 'scientific', yes; but it is also 'the foundation of the Reformation', idiosyncratically defined, and the near cousin to a ripe anti-Catholicism, exhibited in these debates and in many others. Huxley was all for causing embarrassment to the prelacy of his day who carelessly entered the ring with him – his was a fearsome intellect and took no prisoners in debate – and many materialists after him consider Huxley a true and undefeated champion against superstition and reaction.

Huxley, of course, did not stand alone: Christian theologians too saw that modern science and historiography appeared to change the entire doctrinal landscape. We might advert here to the theological generation raised on the First World War and its aftermath. These are great names – Paul Tillich, Karl Barth, Emil Brunner, Karl Rahner – but we might take as our initial spokesman the New Testament theologian and exegete Rudolf Bultmann. Unlike Paul Tillich, who served in the First World War as an ambulance driver, chaplain and solider, Bultmann was exempted from military service because of disability. But Bultmann's brother was killed in action, and he shared Tillich's horror at what unfolded in the vast killing fields of Flanders.[15] Christian theology, these young dialecticians said, had to begin again. It would be difficult indeed to exaggerate the cauterising horror of this war on the women and men who survived it. A European collation of empires and monarchies entered into this conflict, many direct descendants of one queen; after four years of brutal battle, few yards won or gained at staggering cost, new forms of government emerged on the other side of Versailles: republics in Germany, in Russia, of a sort; in Great Britain, a 'House of Windsor' and an empire now dubbed Dominions; and even in neutral Spain, within a generation, a deposed monarch, a fledgling Second Republic, and soon a caudillo, Francisco Franco. Rudolf Bultmann became a theologian under these suns.

In an essay that is perhaps the most widely read of his works, Bultmann confidently assured his readers:

> We cannot use electric lights and radios and, in the event of illness, avail ourselves of medical and clinical means and at the same time believe in the spirit and wonder world of the New Testament. And if we suppose that we can do so ourselves, we must be clear that we can represent this as the attitude of Christian faith only by making the Christian proclamation unintelligible and impossible for our contemporaries.[16]

Earlier in this famous essay, 'The New Testament and Mythology', he tied the attempt to maintain the old cosmology to a form of 'works-righteousness', the Lutheran epitome of sin: 'It is impossible', he tells us,

> to repristinate a past world picture by sheer resolve, especially a *mythical* world picture, now that all of our thinking is irrevocably formed by science. A blind acceptance of New Testament mythology would be simply arbitrariness; to make such acceptance a demand of faith would be to reduce faith to a work, as Wilhelm Herrmann made clear, one would have thought, once and for all . . . Criticism of the New Testament is simply a given with modern thinking as it has come to us through our history.[17]

Bultmann is pitiless in his catalogue of the discarded: 'stories of Christ's descent and ascent are finished';[18] so too are belief in spirits and demons, sacraments and the Spirit's Presence as recounted in the New Testament, original or birth sin, substitutionary atonement, resurrection, especially as a grace given in the Lord's Supper, indeed the end times, the Second Coming, the very notion of heaven or hell – all rendered incredible by the rupture of the modern world into human history.

In a particularly telling phrase, nearly an aside in this sweeping condemnation of the old, Bultmann says that

> the possibility that such a life [one not subject to death] should be created by a dead person's being brought back to physical life is unimaginable. If God creates life for human beings by any such means, God's action is evidently tied up with natural occurrences in some completely unintelligible way.[19]

What we see here is the firm conviction that the modern world we find ourselves in – the world of natural science, of critical history, of technology and its blind powers – has made the world of the Bible not 'strange', as the young Barth would style this, but rather 'antique', 'mythological' and, despite our most pious efforts, wholly incredible to modern thought. God's mighty working, bursting forth from a 'three-story universe', would be involved with the forces of the material realm in such a way that we could never in truth comprehend it, perhaps not even discern it. Just this makes it 'mythological': the story of the gods, making themselves visible under the conditions of creaturely life. What Bultmann called 'the Redeemer myth' was an externalisation of just this kind. A 'pre-existent' figure emerges from the heavenly realms, descends down among the children of the earth, and in its ascent back to the empyrean, shows itself to be a heavenly Redeemer, a Saviour figure of those left in the world of estrangement. Such, Bultmann thought, was the theology of the Gospel of John, a text he considered 'Gnostic' in its reliance upon such a heavenly incursion of Light into our dark world.[20] The mythological can no longer hold sway over the citizen of the modern world: it is now seen simply as a story, a narrative that belongs to the Pantheon and Valhalla, poetic perhaps, even stirring, but hardly a depiction of the real world and its workings. A stronger declaration of the modern as 'rupture' and 'novelty' could be scarcely imagined on the theological terrain.

Bultmann's solution, equally famous to his diagnosis, is a programme he entitled 'Demythologisation', a neologism no better in the German original (*Entmythologisierung*). Here Bultmann proposes a form of translation, whole world view into whole world view, where the cosmology of an old scriptural universe becomes expressed in the language of 'existence' – the existentialism or phenomenology of interwar Europe. Bultmann is keenly aware of the pitfalls encountered in earlier attempts to 'modernise' the faith once delivered. He knows, none better, that Adolf von Harnack foundered on the attempt to discover an 'essence' of the Christian faith that could be retained – a kernel, in the celebrated analogy – while the husk of the old was stripped away.[21] This Bultmann rejects as a force of piecemeal surgery, the lopping off of an arm to save the body. He rejects the 'History of Religions' school, the great historicists of the nineteenth century, and their focus upon *cultus* and a hieratic way of life. In their focus upon these 'external' rituals, they miss the profound claim laid upon human life by God. But the problem lies far deeper than this, Bultmann assures us. In an Augustinian move of real daring, Bultmann proposes that *everything* of the Christian religion – its cosmology, its Prophets and Apostles, its Saviour and saving truths, its habits of life and sacred ritual, its texts and variants – all will be taken on the inward journey, to become expressions of the crisis of human existence. This intimate, personal encounter with the inexplicable, inescapable demands upon each life is what Bultmann will call the *kerygma* – the Greek term for 'proclamation'. The aim of the programme of demythologisation is to recover and translate the proclamation of the gospel into the idiom of 'decision'.

We catch a glimpse of the radicality of this vision by considering just what Bultmann depicts in the call to decision about faith in Christ – in Bultmann's idiom, the decision under the 'Christ-event'.[22] Modern existence unfolds in a condition of 'desperation', 'thrown-ness' in Heidegger's evocative phrase. The meanings offered to human lives and nations under the old regime have crumbled in the trenches of the world wars; we now must *discover* a meaning, forge it out of the conditions of human and social life. Bultmann lived in an era when major programmes in philosophy – one thinks of Karl Jaspers here, or Martin Heidegger, or in the francophone world, Jean-Paul Sartre and Albert Camus – rivalled religion as sources of meaning-making, a kind of secular *kerygma*. Bultmann boldly acknowledges the question such radical secular programmes pose for Christian faith: is the Christ-event now superseded? The answer for Bultmann will never come directly by comparison between secular and gospel proclamation. To assume such an answer would be to live 'according to the flesh', that is, to find oneself secure in one's analysis of the world and one's place in it. No, this must be the crisis of *decision*: one must wager one's life on the unsurpassed deliverance of Christ, made present in the proclamation of the gospel. But Bultmann does allow himself a bit of what later commentators would call 'ad hoc apologetics'.[23] He believes that secular reason simply does not know the depths of modern despair and alienation. 'Human beings as such, before and outside of Christ, are not already in their authentic being – in life – but are rather in death.'[24] This is *fallenness*. The Christian proclamation of God's act in Christ discloses what philosophy cannot know: that we are not simply inauthentic in some region of our personal life, subject to tidying up by some analytic concentration; rather, we are 'utterly and completely fallen'. Our authentic being is not under our control; it is not 'disposable' to our manipulation. Rather we must receive our life from the Transcendent, to trust that 'faith as obedient surrender to God and as inner freedom from the world is possible only as faith in Christ'.[25]

Now, before moving on in our roll-call of intellectual modernists, we might pause a moment before Bultmann's sweeping programme of theological remaking. What should we think about this assessment of modern science and critical historiography by a citizen of advanced Protestant dogmatics? One element that the twenty-first century has exposed to us Western Christians is the myopic and narrow conception we have held of serious theological debate. For the twentieth-century Protestant sphere in the developed world, Germany and perhaps England just *was* the centre of dogmatic theology. It was a rare divinity school that did not have a germanophone theologian on its staff, and Anglican divines were considered exemplars of serious conceptual and revisionist theology. As someone raised in this world, and for whom Karl Barth is a father in the faith, I know how rich, how demanding, how exhilarating this small world of dogmatic theology can be. But we now all know how very small it is. Christians in other parts of the globe have quietly been turning on their electric lights, consulting medical and psychiatric specialists, and finding no difficulty at all in affirming the 'mythological world view' of the New Testament. Secularism – that great thesis of nineteenth-century European letters – has not unfolded as its pioneers imagined. It is not *false*, certainly: the secularism and religious indifferentism in some parts of the old Christendom is stunning and, for a religious believer, deeply troubling. But it is not uniform, even in Europe, and most certainly not the storyline of the 'new Churches', the vast army of the faithful in the continents of Asia and Africa.[26] It seems, then, that Bultmann's confident assertion of an unendurable conflict within the consciousness of the modern believer – the new breaking up and driving out the old – cannot be sustained. We may well wonder why that is. The crisis a sophisticated European such as Bultmann spied in the old faith seems conceptually and experientially, for many Westerners, a commonplace. So earnest a dogmatic theologian as Robert Jenson could speak of the Doctrine of Ascension as one that must avoid turning the Risen Christ into an 'astronaut jetting through outer space toward an invisible destiny'. Yet equally sophisticated African theologians can speak readily and realistically about demon possession, exorcism and Spiritual healing without losing their hold on quantum mechanics and the pharmacological practice of modern medicine.[27] It seems, then, that 'modernism' cannot be properly contained or exhibited only in a single, European form. There will be time for a fuller discussion of this salient lesson to be learned from global Christianity; but a placeholder can be registered here. The 'modern' itself is more plastic, more variable, more complex than the 'secular' or the 'avant-garde'.

We might also wonder, as we look back upon Bultmann's ambitious programme, whether the inward journey, and the pronounced emphasis upon 'decision', so redolent of existential meaning-making, has properly captured the distinctive world-embracing realism of the Christian faith. Much has been written on the individualism of Bultmann's theology, an element now widely considered noxious to proper Christian life in Christ.[28] But this seems to me to overestimate the place of the individual in Bultmann's thought, and to overlook the centrality of 'witness' in Christian discipleship. Demythologisation is a corporate programme in theology in its fundamental structure: we live, Bultmann argues, as citizens of the modern world; we cannot escape it; we are formed by it and move within it, intellectually and spiritually. What Bultmann advocates is a moment of personal recognition and acknowledgement of this citizenship – to bear its burden knowingly – and to affirm in its midst that the Christ-event liberates and heals us from our *Anfechtung* and *Sorge*. The principal worry, rather, is that Bultmann's focus upon the act of faith isolates Christian teaching from the world it is designed to teach, to understand and to love. Like Schleiermacher, Bultmann has reserved a distinct realm for the Christian faith, one undisturbed by the developments of modernism, but also unable, by axiom, to address it on the same level and through the same terms. We need not erase the distinction between faith and reason, or grace and nature, to see that the Christian teachings on creation, on humankind and its destiny, on providential guidance and sacramental grace, address the world of matter and of things: they refer to and denote the world.

We might finally wonder about the controlling category of 'myth'. Karl Barth famously advocated for a substitute notion, 'saga' or 'legend' or even 'poetry', as a corrective to 'myth', which he rejected.[29] Indeed, as Barth himself notes during the long course of the *Church Dogmatics*, a quiet debate with Bultmann flows continuo-like under the whole. Looking at this matter from our vantage, we may not find the conflict between Barth and Bultmann as inevitable as it seemed in their day; but this notion of myth remains a vital one in any encounter between an ancient faith and the world modernism has built. The central concern for Christian theology has to do with the major saving intervention of the Transcendent into the earthbound: the Incarnation of the Eternal Son. This is the plastic, local, visible and tangible Presence of Almighty God to this earth, and in Christian thought, it remains unsurpassed. 'God is *there*', Christians say, when gazing upon Christ, and for much of Christian history, this locution was intended in a straightforward, realist manner. The category of myth, when applied to the Bible, corrodes this central claim, as David Friedrich Strauss saw, long ago. It was Strauss, after all, and not the signatories to the *Myth of God Incarnate* that inaugurated the notion that Jesus Christ in dogmatic teaching belonged on the shelf with the *Iliad* and the *Ring of the Nibelungen*, yet another story of the heavenly gods visiting the realm of mortals.[30]

Now Bultmann is careful and cautious in his application of myth. Even in this brief essay we have been examining, Bultmann notes that demythologisation begins in the New Testament itself, notably in the Pauline epistles. The Apostle Paul pioneers the destruction of mythic security, the empirical and verified, and launches his hearers into a world of risk, of trust, of dispossession. Just this is why the doctrine of justification stands at the centre of Bultmann's constructive theology. But allowing the category of myth to stand unconstrained as a biblical and dogmatic analytic tool threatens Christology at its mainspring – the Word made flesh. The reluctance to speak directly about the Incarnate Word but rather about a 'happening' – the Christ-event – makes Christology an expression and extension of the act of preaching. We are *addressed* by the Word in the preacher's proclamation of Him, and it is *now*, the eschatological *now*, in which we receive Christ's claim on our lives. This is bracing stuff, a kind of revival in the heartland of Lutheran orthodoxy, but it leaves open and unprotected the crucial flank of Christian teaching: that the *kerygma* rests upon the historical event of the Incarnation. Here we see the true radicality of this vision of the modern: the *Christus praesens* may recognise the historical Jesus, but His dignity, as Eternal Son enfleshed, rests not upon a miraculous divine intervention but rather upon the proffer of the preacher and the unreserved decision of the hearer. Here the 'rupture' of the modern breaks through into the heart of the Christian mystery.

In his student days, Bultmann sat under the lectern of Johannes Weiss, a historian and exegete who again stands, for all his hesitancy, as exemplar of this transgressive mode of the modern. We turn to Weiss's agonised encounter with history now. A generation older than Barth or Bultmann, Weiss might be termed the high-water mark of the historical consciousness of nineteenth-century German theology. To his name belong major studies of the Apostle Paul, and the speculative explanation for the common teaching material found in the gospels of Matthew and Luke, the so-called Q source. He could write titles that might be mistaken for Bultmann's: *The History of Primitive Christianity*, and *Jesus of Nazareth, Myth or History?*[31] And through marriage he took up membership in one of the most prominent Lutheran movements of German high academic theology, Ritschlianism, founded by Weiss's father-in-law, Albrecht Ritschl.

Ritschlianism went far beyond the massive historical and dogmatic works of its namesake.[32] In the years before the First World War, this school brought together erudition, civic prominence, urbane German sociality and high bourgeois culture as an expression, complex yet unified, of modern Christian faith. In this broad sense, Adolf von Harnack was a Ritschlian, so too Wilhelm Herrmann, and so too the young, liberal Karl Barth. These men moved in elite intellectual and civic circles; they were that generation's public intellectuals, and it was not surprising to his peers that Harnack would know the German kaiser or would be relied upon to make a theological address – 'To the German Nation' – in vivid support of Germany at the outbreak of the war. It is indeed a mark of the secularism that suffuses the political systems of contemporary Europe – even of so religion-laden a political sphere as is the US – that it seems to us odd to envision a university theologian sharing the stage with a modern head of state. But not so the Ritschlians!

To be a Christian theologian was to be a bearer of German high culture, to speak to and for it, and to consider the Christian Idea the genius and ground of all humane society. This was *Kulturprotestantismus*, a form of Protestant faith that saw itself as the bedrock of civil society and also its flowering.[33] It took responsibility for it in a way scarcely imaginable to contemporary Western intellectuals, religious or no. Some present-day theologians may be tempted to smile at what might be considered a naïve and uncritical loyalty between Christianity and the world, as if these eminent theologians of the Victorian era just did not see how grotesque it is for the Church to be cup-bearer to empire and war. But such knowing dismissal does not come to terms properly with the sophisticated doctrine of history that animates the Ritschlians. They understood – and Johannes Weiss was a pioneer – that religion itself has and is a history; and that that history unfolds the growth and sociality of religion. Ritschlians understood, long before the post-structuralist age, that religion is a cultural form, a corporate *habitus* that swims in the tide of its era, borrowing and shaping in turn the idiom of social life. For Christians to participate in civic life, to lead it, is simply to act upon the religious dimension of historical being, to *realise* it. Christian socialism expressed this conviction from the left side of the aisle, but the aim was the same. The spiritual dimension of collective life must be articulated, clarified, strengthened for its task: this was the role of the intellectual in mass movements, left and right, atheistic and Christian, throughout the nineteenth century in the West.

The political expression of this world view was the theologian as civil leader; its intellectual arm was the *religionsgeschichtliche Schule*. The aim of this highly literate and fearless programme was to set out not simply the *background* or *praeparatio* for the Christian faith, but rather to see clearly the sharp contours of the Christian Idea as it has been formed by parallel movements, social and ideological. To the History of Religions School we owe the widespread conviction among twentieth-century theologians that the Greek 'mystery religions' shaped Christian views of sacraments, ritual and communal life: the Eucharist was a Christomorphic mystery cult. To this circle of analysis belonged the central category pursued by Johannes Weiss: eschatology, the end of the age. This is a Janus concept, looking back into the riches of comparative religious history, but also gazing forward, into a rupture with the past that Weiss himself found deeply alarming.

Like higher critics of his era, Weiss recognised that Jesus shared many of the traits, idioms and images of his contemporaries, the Jews of first-century Judaea. Faithful to the History of Religions School, Weiss compared the gospel teachings of Jesus with other prophetic voices of the era, including those texts that belonged on the far margins of the canon. By mid-century, the years of Weiss's teachers, Christian theologians had absorbed the shocks of radical Enlightenment historiography, and had found their own way to interpret, extend and receive the findings of the *Leben-Jesu-Forschung*, the historical investigation into the life of Jesus of Nazareth. Much of this rather delicate settlement can be found in Ritschl's own massive work on the Doctrines of Justification and Reconciliation: the Kingdom of God that Jesus preached is at base an *ethical* vision, a Beloved Community, that to Christian ears rises loftily above the clang of the competitors.[34] Weiss had been schooled in this tradition, and in many ways remained a proud alumnus. But in his slim volume *Jesus' Proclamation of the Kingdom of God*, Weiss travels far from his homeland.[35]

Delayed until the death of his father-in-law, this work exposed with relentless objectivity the break an honest accounting of Jesus' proclamation would require of His latter-day disciples. We are not surprised, then, to find Bultmann providing a foreword to the work, nor that he underscores the radicality of eschatological proclamation in modern theology: it is the seedbed of Bultmann's daring programme in Protestant dogmatics. What is so stern and uncompromising in Weiss's essay is its insistence upon *rupture*: the only proper historical understanding of the preaching of Jesus is apocalypticism. It is as though Weiss stands surety for the entire movement of modernism as avant-garde. For the very thought form of apocalyptic is of the breaking of the old order, the shattering of the cosmos and its settled evils, and the incursion of the new, the transcendent, as the final justice and reign of the God of Heaven. Apocalyptic thought is thoroughly ethical in this startling sense – that the victory of the Hidden God over the demons of this age will usher in the days of judgement, when all enemies will be routed and sent to unquenchable fire. But this is the ethics not of the elites, not of the settled curators of culture and state; rather, it is the explosive ethic of the dispossessed, the colonised, the subaltern. The Book of Revelation, the apocalyptic vision of St John, is ethical revolution of just this sort – vivid, alien, violent. Johannes Weiss became convinced in his analysis of the thought-world of first-century Judaea that just this form of apocalypticism dominated the vocabulary and social imagination of the Jews under the Roman Imperium.

Jesus of Nazareth was a son of his age. He too spoke of God's kingdom, he preached repentance as did the herald John the Baptist, he urged a fervent prayer for the kingdom to come, and he expected angelic armies, with battledress and trumpet, to announce its arrival, and that the world would pass away. *Jesus' Proclamation of the Kingdom of God* depicted a revolutionary Jesus, that is, and one of the colonised; but, Weiss cautioned, this was no *political* or *earthly* overthrow. Jesus rather was revolutionary prophet of *God's* kingdom, *His* work and approaching judgement, *His* breaking the bow and shattering the shield in the furious advent of God's own sovereign rule over the cosmos. Jesus was a *religious* figure for Weiss, a man not trifling with worldly affairs, its moral or social or political ordering, for all that was 'as if not', an order that would soon pass away. Indeed, Weiss tells us, Jesus came soon to realise that he must die in order that the Kingdom come; in some way inexpressible to his inner circle, his suffering would join in and escalate the urgent longing for God's in-breaking. And though merely a herald now, a teacher of parable and sign, Jesus would through his own terrible death be named and enthroned as Son of Man, the Judge of the Last Days. From Galilee to Jerusalem, then, the call Jesus issues is this: prepare for judgement! All will stand before Almighty God, and all the ethical commands, beloved of Christian moralists from St Bonaventure to Ritschl, were nothing more than time-bound 'rules of the road', temporary assignments until the Godly Reign come with power. The twin pillars of Ritschlianism – the inner confidence of one's childlike trust in the Heavenly Father, and the grace-given duty to build up a just and equitable society on earth – belonged not to the historical Jesus, to his vision or teaching, but to the aims of a subsequent literate and cultured cadre of Christian intellectuals. It was, in Weiss's famous phrase, an 'issuing of old coinage at a new rate of exchange'.[36] In Weiss's own words:

> Precisely from *Jesus' own standpoint*, his entire activity is *not* of messianic, but of pre-paratory character. It is evident from a great number of passages that Jesus thinks the establishment of the βασιλεία τοῦ θεοῦ will be mediated solely by God's supernatural intervention. Any human activity in connection with it thus is ruled out completely . . . Thus even he cannot intervene in the development of the Kingdom of God. He has to wait, just as the people have to wait, until God again definitively takes up the rule.[37]

So is settled in Weiss's mind the great question agitating the nineteenth-century higher critics, the 'messianic consciousness of Jesus'. Jesus is prophet, rabbi, herald; only in the end times will he become, and be recognised, as the Messiah, the eschatological Son of Man who will sit in judgement over the nations. Thus, the Kingdom of God does not reside on earth: it is not, in the idiom of a later generation, a 'realised eschatology'. Rather, it is the *coming reign*, the future advent that will shake the heavens and the earth, terrify the rulers of this age, and beat down Satan finally under our feet. With apocalyptists of every age, Jesus lived an inner life driven by this vision of the approaching end times; like the mysterious author of the *Didache*, he could pray 'Let grace come, and let the world pass away!'[38]

The signal mark of historiography here is *difference*: Jesus of Nazareth stands in a different age, obeys the idiom of a different thought-world, and hears the command of a distant and alien end time. The aim of historical research is to expose this difference, to make us feel its weight. We are to look across the centuries that divide us, and take full measure of this 'alien land, the past'. No more than any other modern citizen can the historian live in this alien landscape; ineluctably he or she has citizenship in the present age. But the act of writing history is the daring encounter with the strange, the 'not-ours', and the remarkable power of the human intellect to consider and inhabit the uninhabitable. We the modern can grasp that the ancient does not think as we do, nor populate the universe with the causal powers, structures and elements that compose our notion of the real. And yet we scholars of the past can think these thoughts that are not ours: modern historiography is just this.

Much has been written about problems of objectivity in the historical arts, and indeed the 'scientific' status of the historian's professional findings. To be sure there are puzzling lapses of self-awareness by a school of such heightened self-consciousness – we might think of Ranke or Gibbon or even Ritschl himself or at times the great Harnack – but in truth none of these historians of the modern era imagined that they arrived at a 'noumenal' history, untouched by the limits and insights of the historian. We can see just this in Johannes Weiss. He knows well that he is a *Dogmatiker*, and that this matter of the *kerygma* of Jesus of Nazareth is no bare object, lying open to his disinterested eye. Rather, he believes he can take this commitment *into account*; he can watch for it; indeed, he can take up his theological interests when the full historical analysis has been laid bare. But like a beachcomber who can distinguish jetsam from a native seashell, Weiss can see the alien and strange among the visionaries of the first century, and he can turn his attention to them, and imaginatively enter the artefact that is the past. This, Weiss believes, is what we *learn* when we place Jesus of Nazareth in his first-century milieu. He is inconvenient to us, and his manner is strange.

Now this very move, from the present to the alien past, is the alarming force of modernist historiography for Christian theology. It is what drives the *rupture*, the flair of the avant-garde. For Johannes Weiss knows as well as any other ecclesial theologian that *continuity* is what underlies the dogmatic tradition. This is not simply a backward gaze, as if Christian thought must reach some stable position, at the time of the Apostles, or the time of the Councils, and from there never change. It may be that some theologians of the pre-modern era imagined that such stasis was possible and indeed ideal, but it seems far closer to the historiography of Late Antiquity and European scholasticism to say that change took place in the midst of an always stronger unity, a variation that gave clues to the organic whole. We might think, for example, of the way in which Augustine or Cyril might express recognition of distinctive themes in Holy Scripture or in the writings of the early authorities: these would be expressed in terms of rhetorical idioms, variants in speech patterns. 'Holy Scripture often speaks this way', they would write, and then adduce examples across the canon that allowed for such unexpected elements within the reading of a larger whole. In the wake of greater interest in dialectic among the Schoolmen, Peter Lombard could cite competing authorities, or conflicting texts within Augustine's corpus, and make a 'ruling', a kind of adjudication of difference in the light of the strongest, most persuasive tradition. Thomas shows the greater cosmopolitanism of the high Middle Ages by noting the progressive unfolding of the truth: change was understood as Divine Truth 'leading human reason as it were by the hand' into a deeper and fuller recognition of Eternal Law. Many of these traits are scattered throughout Calvin's *Institutes of the Christian Religion*, where Holy Scripture is seen to speak in several idioms and at different levels, and the past warehouse of theological tradition can be rifled through in search of the 'sounder Schoolmen'. All these are pre-modern forms of 'speaking difference', but all in service of an assumed axiom, namely, that the Christian faith is a complex, integrated whole, continuous with the Apostles and martyrs and the blessed dead.

Against this we may return to Johannes Weiss's brief but trenchant conclusion to *Jesus' Proclamation of the Kingdom of God*. Here Weiss returns to that early, nearly parenthetic remark about theological currency, revalued, and issued at a new rate. He writes:

The results just summarized present peculiar difficulties for systematic and practical theology. Jesus' idea of the Kingdom of God appears to be inextricably involved with a number of eschatological-apocalyptical views which systematic theology has been accustomed to take over without critical examination. But now it is necessary to inquire whether it is really possible for theology to employ the idea of the Kingdom of God in the manner in which it has recently been considered appropriate. The question arises whether it is not thereby divested of its essential traits, and, finally, so modified that only the name still remains the same.[39]

The threat of equivocation solidifies the notion of difference which underlies the whole. Weiss early on lets us know that his findings have been costly to him: truth has led him where he did not wish to go. But now he struggles to find a path forward. 'Under these circumstances [a dogmatic theology untethered to apocalyptic], one will perhaps judge the connection of the modern dogmatic idea with the words of Jesus to be a purely external one. This is, in fact, the case.'[40] A stronger expression of *rupture* could not be hoped for. 'This is not to say', Weiss hurries on,

> that one ought no longer to use the concept 'Kingdom of God' in the current manner. On the contrary, it seems to me, as a matter of fact, that it should be the proper watch-word of modern theology. Only the admission must be demanded that we use it in a different sense from Jesus.[41]

Only! one might say.

Can Christian theology continue under these conditions? Can a dogmatic system built up on the person, teaching, parables and warnings of Jesus of Nazareth equivocate on his 'sense of the words'? Over this chasm Weiss throws a slim tether: we simply continue using these phrases, 'the Kingdom of God', the 'rule of the Father', the Lord's Prayer, all the while knowing that *we*, unlike Him, are invested in this world and seek transforma-tion *within* it. We 'realise the eschatological'; we announce the presence of the Kingdom on this earth. That this was an unstable and intolerable position for Christian theology announced itself in the radical programme of translation from myth to existential commit-ment, as we saw in Bultmann. But the matter of history – its force and volcanic disruption – must be faced by modern theology, even as the matter of science – its cosmology and novel account of natural kinds – must be acknowledged by a Christian world that has passed through its fires.

The modern, that is, must be taken up as a movement not only of *rupture* and of the avant-garde but also of the continuous, the organic and the ripened. We will not be able to grasp the explosion of the modern into Christian theology, that is, without taking full measure of difference, yes, and also of identity and growth. Modernism, in truth, contains both. Modern evolutionary biology is 'punctuated equilibrium' and 'saltation', yes, but also gradualism and conservation of type. Modern art breaks with everything of the old – 'To each age, its art – to Art, its freedom!' – yet it scours the past, notably the scorned past, for archetypes, primal patterns, fresh soil for deep roots. The modern looks forward *and* back, and though it presents itself often in martial dress, the modern also *belongs* to its past, extending and confirming and solidifying its membership in the cultural development of the West. The Annales School in historiography, especially as it was realised in Lucien Goldmann and Georges Lefebvre, and later Braudel, sought to anchor the study of the past in the deep continuities of human collective life, its *mentalité*.[42] This sketch is not the prominent face given to modernism, so I want to return to our exemplars of the modern to unfold the mystic chords of memory that tie the radical present to the past. Let me begin the defence of this thesis by returning to the most radical apostle of modernist difference, Johannes Weiss.

In *Jesus' Proclamation*, Weiss recognises, though with some reluctance, that Jesus proclaimed, from time to time, the *presence* of the Kingdom of God in the midst of the 'little ones'. 'In what sense', Weiss asks, 'does Jesus speak of a "presence" of the Kingdom of God?' To put it superficially, one might answer: in a paradoxical way. Here Weiss adduces the celebrated 'two-storey' universe that troubles the modernist conscience of Rudolf Bultmann. There is a parallel structure to the cosmos: events in Heaven, where God's will is even now being done, and events on earth, where the will of God will be done, but over many seasons and years, perhaps with resistance or violence, perhaps in a fashion utterly hidden to the proud and hypocritical. The great martial language of the apocalyptic enters in here: what is determined already in the heavenly places, will be done on the earthly plain, but only in tumult, battle and binding in chains the Strongman. Yet this is a form of *presence*, of the realisation of the Kingdom of God within the land and people of Israel. Weiss here makes a subtle but unmistakable move towards the Christology of the Church. He acknowledges that Jesus' exorcisms are 'signs' that the reign of the Satan is collapsing and his goods plundered. But this does not mean that the disciples or the crowd, following this wonder-worker, are now simply, and in themselves, the members of the Kingdom. No, the Kingdom of God still cannot be realised by any human effort or not belong to any school:

> Rather, Jesus [speaks of a Kingdom of God which is present] because *by his own activity* the power of Satan, who above all others is the source of evil, is being broken. But these are moments of sublime prophetic enthusiasm, when an awareness of victory comes over him . . . In such moments it may have become clear to Jesus that he knew and saw more than did these dull observers who still refused to notice any change in the course of the world.[43]

Here we see Weiss folding into this radical historiography a theme of continuity, of presence and of singular authority to the Man from Nazareth. The Kingdom is present in the midst of the suffering, but also in the midst of the skeptics and critics, because Jesus himself has acted on earth as God wills in heaven. Satan's thralls are liberated by the authority of this Preacher, and what will come at the close of the age has already touched the hem of His garment, and begun in His life work. Out of such material is born a 'two-nature Christology' and an acknowledgement that the heavenly realms are reached when a disciple stands in Jesus' Presence, and under his authority. Indeed, some of the major Christologies of the modern era, those of Barth and Pannenberg, draw on this particular dialectic between the Kingdom present and the Kingdom yet to come, each wedded intimately to the startling authority of Jesus, the Son of Man. We see here why *event* and *act* become central to modernist Christologies: 'if I cast out Beelzebul by the finger of God, then the Kingdom of God has come upon you' (Luke 11:20). The person of Jesus and His mighty deeds are joined in this proleptic in-breaking of the Kingdom under His hand. It is a short step from this exegetical position to a Christology in which the Divine and human natures of Christ are understood as 'history' or 'event' or 'principle in act'. Modern historiography has uncovered the *cosmological* dimension of the Person of Christ: he battles not flesh and blood but the powers and principalities, the godless forces of this age. The vivid appeal of a *Christus Victor* to generations raised on world wars underscores the *ressourcement* that modern study of the apocalyptic provides for Christian theology. In such Christologies, the element of difference is integrated within a larger organic whole, the Lordship of the Son of Man. A 'rupture' still explodes in the midst of theology – but this time between the *Kulturprotestantismus* of the bourgeois elite, and the dangerous memory of a Galilean preacher who casts out the Evil One and brings in His Person the Kingdom of God.[44]

The modernist oscillation between rupture and continuity can be seen in Bultmann as well. In the midst of his oracles about electric lights and motorcars stands his conviction that the New Testament *itself* teaches and inaugurates de-mythologisation. This is perhaps not a surprising move for a Christian theologian who is also an exegete. But it underscores the way in which modern historiography itself uncovers the patterns for its radical novelty in the texts and traditions of the past. Significantly, Bultmann does not search for such *ressourcement* within the gospels; following Weiss, he regards them as wholly mythological, apocalyptic and incredible. But the Apostle Paul emerges from this two-storey cosmos as the herald of an inward life, one built upon risk and trust and dispossession, the life 'in Christ'. Not surprisingly for a Lutheran theologian, Bultmann's exegetical taproot into the Pauline corpus gives rise to a form of the doctrine of justification: 'If by grace it is no more of works; otherwise grace is no more grace.' But just this is our point! To claim a modern form of the doctrine of justification in the letters of Paul is to see an organic continuity in the midst of all rupture, difference and repudiation. And this is not all. An intriguing parallel in historiography emerges in Bultmann's reversion to the Apostle Paul as demythologiser *avant la lettre*. The generation raised on Johannes Weiss puzzled greatly over what was called the menacing 'delay of the *parousia*'. Why did Jesus' prediction that the Kingdom of God would come within one generation – a prediction, it seems, palpably false – not deeply trouble the early Church? Where did the apocalyptic fervour go? Why do we not see this ornate mythological world view bristling out of second-century texts? Apart from the *Didache*, a document enigmatic in origin and provenance, the circular letters stemming from Clement or Ignatius or the Shepherd of Hermas seem to measure the seismic apocalyptic with not a single tremor. What is more, early Christian exegetes, who cite the gospels copiously, display no embarrassment that Jesus seemed to be wrong on this central teaching. Why might this be? Of course, such complex historical matters could not be settled in a brief essay of this kind! But might we consider both Weiss's and Bultmann's modernist moves towards continuity and development an element in the solution? Might it be, after all, a 'non-problem' just because the dominical teachings about the presence of the Kingdom, under Jesus' hand and authority, struck the early readers as being as important and foundational as the predictions of the near end times? Could it be that the sayings about the *ecclesia*, the council of Apostles and disciples, the great family of the last and least – could it be that those *logia* carried as much weight to early followers as the 'little apocalypse' in the Synoptic Gospels? This might be another way of pointing to Bultmann's other central text in his distinguished exegetical career, the Gospel of John. Perhaps this tradition, stemming, it seems, from Asia Minor, might have confirmed the Synoptic impulse of a Kingdom realised in Jesus' own presence? Might this be another way to express Bultmann's golden verse from Paul – not that we know Christ *kata sarka*, but rather that in Christ there is new creation (2 Cor. 5:16–17)? I speculate here; but if there is any weight to the suggestion, we would then find a de-mythologisation in both historiography itself and New Testament theology.

Let me suggest, more briefly, how the dialectic of innovation and conservation might apply also to our earliest examples of modernist rupture, the outbreak of radical art in

Vienna's Secession Building, and the outbreak of secular cosmology and biogenesis in the work of Darwin and Huxley. Thomas Huxley, we recall, began his scientific career persuaded that the fossil record could not support Darwin's eager acceptance of gradualism in the origin and descent of species. Huxley noted that early investigations of geological shale did not yield the kind of inter-species animals that Darwin's theory entailed. Later, and with great fanfare, the fossil deposits in Solnhofen in Bavaria produced the celebrated mixed kind of a feathered reptile, and in the American west, a mammalian ancestor to the horse, the Orohippus, each exhibiting some of the early, more general features of a larger, undifferentiated genus, and the hallmarks of a specific and more determined species. Huxley, always the orator and debater, relished displaying these finds, and announcing publicly the great confirmation of Darwin's theory of gradual descent of animal species. But such public defence of Darwin's views did not ease Huxley's continued worries over species formation, especially in the stubborn case of hybrid sterility.[45] Huxley's underlying concern in all his private exchanges with Darwin stemmed from his strong instinct for the *lasting*, the enduring, the stubbornly distinct. Function, or adaptation to niche, was not the only element in evolutionary doctrine; preservation and extension of form was another. Huxley was a comparative anatomist in all his ways, and for these explorers in the creaturely past, the *types* of creatures – radial or rectilinear or bivalve – spanned the many centuries of living beings on this earth, and can be seen as subtending all that changes and is made new.

Finally, let me end where I began: the eruption of modernist art in the Secession Building in Vienna at the dawn of the twentieth century. The Secession Building itself was the enactment and centre of the movement: starkly unadorned in its massive, block-like exterior, sleek and stylised, it seems the epitome of modernism in architecture. Yet a moment's lifting of one's eyes off the stern facade leads the viewer to an enormous golden dome – the unmistakable sign of the building as a whole – that speaks clearly of ancient architectural idioms, cathedrals, basilicas, but also 'pagan temples', Babylonian and Assyrian cultic arenas. The architect, Joseph M. Olbrich, not only belonged to the first generation of Secessionists, he aligned himself with the great builder of bourgeois Vienna, Otto Wagner. Indeed, Wagner himself spanned both worlds, designing the massive, monumental palaces of the expanded Ringstrasse, but also the celebrated Karlsplatz Stadtbahn station and the florid Kirche am Steinhof. Gustav Klimt moved fluidly between the avant-garde and the traditionalist, creating the icons of fashionable modernism – e.g. *The Kiss* – but also the strangely disturbing *Beethoven Frieze* for the Secessionist interior, and the hauntingly resonant and archaic *Pallas Athena*. We might say that the *Jugendstil* itself, standing at the birth of the 'terrible century', placed one foot firmly in the conservation of type – its advocacy of the Arts and Crafts Movement, its love of decorative and interior arts – and the other in the chasm opening wide between the stolid bourgeois and the daring experimenters of the chaotic unconscious. Perhaps the strongest symbol of this restless movement of the modern between the archaic and the revolutionary is the great financier and public citizen of *fin-de-siècle* Vienna, Karl Wittgenstein, father of the philosopher Ludwig. A more conscientious and unremarkable member of the bourgeois establishment could not be imagined – Karl Wittgenstein seemed everything a radical could scorn – yet it was he who underwrote the cost of the Secession Building, and it was in this family, these connections and vast wealth, that the rebel Gustav Klimt found his patron and his models for iconic paintings of women, the golden *Echtmoderne* of contemporary art.

Christian theology entered the modern age with twin forces at its side: science, most especially cosmology and biology, and history, most especially the self-conscious search for a scientific approach to the past. Up to and throughout the twentieth century, theology faced these forces with mixed success. At times, modern theology appeared ready to absorb wholesale the findings of scientific and historical researches; at times, a marked retreat and isolation from the threats of these newly emancipated and invigorated fields. Such ambivalence, however, is hardly to be remarked, as the modern itself can be seen more clearly as a force field drawing one forward *and* back, a revolution and a profound conservation over the past. Continuity and rupture mark Christian theology at its most vigorous and creative eras; and as it encounters these twin pillars of the modern, secular world, it must travel forward and back to find its faith resourced from its deepest wells, and equipped for a journey not yet taken, but only to be imagined. In all these ways, Christian theology at its best mirrors in creaturely idiom its own God, who is in all eternity, as Augustine taught, both ever ancient and ever new.

# Notes

1. Aristotle, *Metaphysics*, Book Λ (12), 1069a (ch. 1). For a remarkable and exacting accounting of this change, see Robert Passnau, *Metaphysical Themes, 1274–1671* (Oxford: Oxford University Press, 2013).
2. Gottfried Lessing, 'On the Proof of the Spirit and of Power', in *Lessing's Theological Writings*, edited by H. Chadwick (Stanford, CA: Stanford University Press, 1956), p. 55.
3. For the controverted phrase, and the trials associated with it, see Stephen Hawking, *On the Shoulder of Giants: The Great Works of Physics and Astronomy* (Philadelphia, PA: Running Press, 2002), primary readings on Galileo, and especially the introduction, pp. 396–7. See also Richard J. Blackwell, *Galileo, Bellarmine, and the Bible* (South Bend, IN: University of Notre Dame Press, 1991), for a full analysis of Galileo's encounter with Vatican theologians and exegetes.
4. See the magisterial biography of Darwin by Janet Browne, *Darwin: A Biography*, 2 vols (Princeton, NJ: Princeton University Press, 1996, 2003). For varying reception of Darwin's ideas by religious thinkers, see Alvin Plantinga, *Where the Conflict Really Lies* (Oxford: Oxford University Press, 2011) and Sarah Coakley, *Sacrifice Regained: Reconsidering the Rationality of Religious Belief* (Cambridge: Cambridge University Press, 2021).
5. Most famously Richard Dawkins, *The Blind Watchmaker* (New York: Norton, 1987); Daniel Dennett, *Darwin's Dangerous Idea* (New York: Simon and Schuster, 1995); for the irrepressible William Jennings Bryan, see George Marsden, *Religion and American Culture*, 3rd ed. (Grand Rapids, MI: Eerdmans, 2018), and for primary documents, Sheldon Norman Grebstein, *Monkey Trial* (Boston: Houghton Mifflin, 1960). Also perhaps David Livingstone, *Dealing with Darwin: Place, Politics, and Rhetoric in Religious Engagements with Evolution* (Baltimore, MD: Johns Hopkins University Press, 2014). Also, diagnostically, Andrew Dickson White, *A History of the Warfare of Science with Theology in Christendom*, 2 vols (New York: Dover, 1960).
6. See *The Vienna Secession: From Temple of Art to Exhibition Hall*, edited by Vereinigung bildender Künstler Wiener Secession, texts by Gottfried Fiedl and Otto Kapfinger et al. (Ostfildern-Ruit: Hatje, 1997) and Kirk Varnedoe, *Vienna 1900: Art, Architecture and Design* (New York: Museum of Modern Art, 1986). Also the superb study by Carl Schorske, *Fin-de-Siecle Vienna* (New York: Alfred Knopf, 1979).
7. It most certainly is Art with a capital 'A' in the second phrase!
8. So Sigmund Freud in his 'A Difficulty in the Path of Psycho-Analysis' [1917a], *Standard Edition of the Complete Psychological Works of Sigmund Freud*, vol. 17, James Strachey (ed.) (London: Hogarth Press, 1953).
9. See Ray Monk, *Bertrand Russell: The Spirit of Solitude 1872–1921* (New York: The Free Press, 1996) and *Bertrand Russell: The Ghost of Madness 1921–1970* (New York: The Free Press, 2000).
10. On this protagonist in the battle for evolutionary theory, Sherrie Lynne Lyons' splendid intel-

lectual biography, *Thomas Henry Huxley: The Evolution of a Scientist* (Amherst, NY: Prometheus Books, 1999), is essential reading, and the basis of this analysis.

11. See Herbert Spencer, *Herbert Spencer on Social Evolution: Selected Writings* (Chicago, IL: University of Chicago Press, 1972).

12. Thomas Huxley, *Collected Essays: Darwiniana* (London: Macmillan, 1893), p. 229.

13. Later Darwin appeared to convert Huxley on this central point – though with Huxley's distinctive 'structural' views intact – see Lyons, *Thomas Henry Huxley*, pp. 148–52.

14. Thomas Huxley, 'Agnosticism', in *Collected Essays*, vol. 5 (New York: D. Appleton and Co., 1902), pp. 388–9.

15. Paul Tillich, 'Feldpredigten 1914–18', in *Ergänzungs- und Nachlaßbände zu den Gesammelten Werken*, vol. 7, *Frühe Predigten 1909–1918* (Berlin: De Gruyter, 1993). Also see *The Shaking of the Foundations* (New York: Charles Scribner's Sons, 1948).

16. Rudolf Bultmann, 'The New Testament and Mythology', in *New Testament and Mythology and Other Basic Writings*, S. M. Ogden (ed. and trans.) (Philadelphia, PA: Fortress, 1984), p. 4.

17. Bultmann, 'The New Testament and Mythology', p. 3.

18. Bultmann, 'The New Testament and Mythology', p. 4.

19. Bultmann, 'The New Testament and Mythology', p. 7.

20. See Rudolf Bultmann, *The Gospel of John: A Commentary*, G. R. Beasley-Murray (trans.) (Oxford: Basil Blackwell, 1971).

21. Adolf von Harnack, *What Is Christianity?*, T. Bailey Saunders (trans.) (Philadelphia, PA: Fortress, 1986).

22. For indicative use and discussion of this term, see Rudolf Bultmann, *Faith and Understanding*, R. W. Funk (trans.) (Philadelphia, PA: Fortress, 1987), pp. 19–22.

23. See William Werpehowski, 'Ad Hoc Apologetics', *The Journal of Religion* 66:3 (1986), 282–301.

24. Bultmann, 'The New Testament and Mythology', p. 27.

25. Bultmann, 'The New Testament and Mythology', p. 21.

26. See David Martin, *On Secularization: Towards a Revised General Theory* (London: Routledge, 2005), Philip Jenkins, *The Next Christendom: The Coming of Global Christianity*, 3rd ed. (Oxford: Oxford University Press, 2011) and concise discussions in Bryan S. Turner (ed.), *The New Blackwell Companion to the Sociology of Religion* (Oxford: Wiley-Blackwell, 2016).

27. On which see Esther E. Acolatse, *Powers, Principalities, and the Spirit: Biblical Realism in Africa and the West* (Grand Rapids, MI: Eerdmans, 2018).

28. See, for example, John Macquarrie, *An Existentialist Theology: A Comparison of Bultmann and Heidegger* (London: SCM, 2012 (reprint)), p. 215.

29. Karl Barth, *Church Dogmatics*, vol. 3, part 1 (Edinburgh: T&T Clark, 1958), pp. 81–94.

30. John Hick (ed.), *The Myth of God Incarnate* (London: SCM, 1977). David Friedrich Strauss, *The Life of Jesus Critically Examined*, P. C. Hodgson (ed.) and George Eliot (trans.) (Philadelphia: Fortress, 1972).

31. Johannes Weiss, *The History of Primitive Christianity*, F. C. Grant (trans.), 2 vols (London: Macmillan, 1937); *Jesus von Nazareth, Mythus oder Geschichte?* (Tübingen: J. C. B Mohr, 1910).

32. See, for example, James Orr, *Ritschlians* (London: Hodder and Stoughton, 1903) and also A. E. Garvie, *The Ritschlian Theology, Critical and Constructive: An Exposition and Estimate* (Edinburgh: T&T Clark, 1899).

33. See F. W. Graf, 'Kulturprotestantismus', *Religion in Geschichte und Gegenwart*, vol. 4, 4th ed. (Tübingen: Mohr Siebeck, 2001), pp. 1850–2.

34. Albrecht Ritschl, *Die christliche Lehre von der Rechtfertigung und Versöhnung*, 3 vols (Bonn: Adolph Marcus, 1870), partially rendered into English as *A Critical History of the Christian Doctrine of Justification and Reconciliation*, J. S. Black (trans.) (Edinburgh: Edmonston and Douglas, 1872) and *The Christian Doctrine of Justification and Reconciliation: The Positive Development of the Doctrine*, H. R. Mackintosh and A. B. Macaulay (trans.) (Edinburgh: T&T Clark, 1902).

35. Johannes Weiss, *Jesus' Proclamation of the Kingdom of God*, R. H. Hiers (trans.) (Philadelphia, PA: Fortress, 1971).

36. Weiss, *Jesus' Proclamation of the Kingdom of God*, p. 60.
37. Weiss, *Jesus' Proclamation of the Kingdom of God*, p. 82.
38. *Didache* 10:6.
39. Weiss, *Jesus' Proclamation of the Kingdom of God*, p. 131.
40. Weiss, *Jesus' Proclamation of the Kingdom of God*, p. 135.
41. Weiss, *Jesus' Proclamation of the Kingdom of God*, p. 135.
42. See André Burguière, *The Annales School: An Intellectual History*, J. M. Todd (trans.) (Ithaca, NY: Cornell University Press, 2009).
43. Weiss, *Jesus' Proclamation of the Kingdom of God*, pp. 78–9 (emphasis added).
44. In twentieth-century Roman Catholic theology, these very themes are pursued together in the period after the Second World War by Johann Baptist Metz, *Faith in History and Society: Toward a Practical Fundamental Theology* (New York: Crossroad, 2007 (reprint)), where the 'dangerous memory' of Jesus funds pursuit of a Christianity and Christian theology freed from bourgeois conformity.
45. Darwin's triumphant letters about botanical experiments did not win over Huxley, who was much more preoccupied with skeletal structure than with plant morphology. No more did the 'Wallace effect', as it treated speciation but not the continuity of type – see Lyons, *Thomas Henry Huxley*, pp. 247–50.

# Bibliography

Acolatse, Esther E., *Powers, Principalities, and the Spirit: Biblical Realism in Africa and the West* (Grand Rapids, MI: Eerdmans, 2018).

Barth, Karl, *Church Dogmatics*, vol. 3, part 1 (Edinburgh: T&T Clark, 1958).

Blackwell, Richard J., *Galileo, Bellarmine, and the Bible* (South Bend, IN: University of Notre Dame Press, 1991).

Browne, Janet, *Darwin: A Biography*, 2 vols (Princeton, NJ: Princeton University Press, 1996, 2003).

Bultmann, Rudolf, *Faith and Understanding*, R. W. Funk (trans.) (Philadelphia: Fortress, 1987).

Bultmann, Rudolf, *The Gospel of John: A Commentary*, G. R. Beasley-Murray (trans.) (Oxford: Basil Blackwell, 1971).

Bultmann, Rudolf, *New Testament and Mythology and Other Basic Writings*, S. M. Ogden (ed. and trans.) (Philadelphia, PA: Fortress, 1984).

Burguière, André, *The Annales School: An Intellectual History*, J. M. Todd (trans.) (Ithaca, NY: Cornell University Press, 2009).

Coakley, Sarah, *Sacrifice Regained: Reconsidering the Rationality of Religious Belief* (Cambridge: Cambridge University Press, 2021).

Dawkins, Richard, *The Blind Watchmaker* (New York: Norton, 1987).

Dennett, Daniel, *Darwin's Dangerous Idea* (New York: Simon and Schuster, 1995).

Dickson White, Andrew, *A History of the Warfare of Science with Theology in Christendom*, 2 vols (New York: Dover, 1960).

Freud, Sigmund, 'A Difficulty in the Path of Psycho-Analysis' [1917a], in *Standard Edition of the Complete Psychological Works of Sigmund Freud*, vol. 17, James Strachey (ed.) (London: Hogarth Press, 1953).

Garvie, A. E., *The Ritschlian Theology, Critical and Constructive: An Exposition and Estimate* (Edinburgh: T&T Clark, 1899).

Graf, F. W., 'Kulturprotestantismus', in *Religion in Geschichte und Gegenwart*, vol. 4, 4th ed. (Tübingen: Mohr Siebeck, 2001), pp. 1850–2.

Grebstein, Sheldon Norman, *Monkey Trial* (Boston, MA: Houghton Mifflin, 1960).

Harnack, Adolf von, *What Is Christianity?*, T. Bailey Saunders (trans.) (Philadelphia, PA: Fortress, 1986).

Hawking, Stephen, *On the Shoulder of Giants: The Great Works of Physics and Astronomy* (Philadelphia, PA: Running Press, 2002).

Hick, John (ed.), *The Myth of God Incarnate* (London: SCM, 1977).

Huxley, Thomas, *Collected Essays: Darwiniana* (London: Macmillan, 1893).

Huxley, Thomas, *Collected Essays*, vol. 5 (New York: D. Appleton and Co., 1902)

Jenkins, Philip, *The Next Christendom: The Coming of Global Christianity*, 3rd ed. (Oxford: Oxford University Press, 2011).

Lessing, Gottfried, *Lessing's Theological Writings*, H. Chadwick (ed.) (Stanford, CA: Stanford University Press, 1956).

Livingstone, David, *Dealing with Darwin: Place, Politics, and Rhetoric in Religious Engagements with Evolution* (Baltimore, MD: Johns Hopkins University Press, 2014).

Lyons, Sherrie Lynne, *Thomas Henry Huxley: The Evolution of a Scientist* (Amherst, NY: Prometheus Books, 1999).

Macquarrie, John, *An Existentialist Theology: A Comparison of Bultmann and Heidegger* (London: SCM, 2012 (reprint)).

Marsden, George, *Religion and American Culture*, 3rd ed. (Grand Rapids, MI: Eerdmans, 2018).

Martin, David, *On Secularization: Towards a Revised General Theory* (London: Routledge, 2005).

Metz, Johann Baptist, *Faith in History and Society: Toward a Practical Fundamental Theology* (New York: Crossroad, 2007 (reprint)).

Monk, Ray, *Bertrand Russell: The Spirit of Solitude 1872–1921* (New York: The Free Press, 1996).

Monk, Ray, *Bertrand Russell: The Ghost of Madness 1921–1970* (New York: The Free Press, 2000).

Orr, James, *Ritschlians* (London: Hodder and Stoughton, 1903).

Passnau, Robert, *Metaphysical Themes, 1274–1671* (Oxford: Oxford University Press, 2013).

Plantinga, Alvin, *Where the Conflict Really Lies* (Oxford: Oxford University Press, 2011).

Ritschl, Albrecht, *The Christian Doctrine of Justification and Reconciliation: The Positive Development of the Doctrine*, H. R. Mackintosh and A. B. Macaulay (trans.) (Edinburgh: T&T Clark, 1902).

Ritschl, Albrecht, *A Critical History of the Christian Doctrine of Justification and Reconciliation*, J. S. Black (trans.) (Edinburgh: Edmonston and Douglas, 1872).

Ritschl, Albrecht, *Die christliche Lehre von der Rechtfertigung und Versöhnung*, 3 vols (Bonn: Adolph Marcus, 1870).

Schorske, Carl, *Fin-de-Siecle Vienna* (New York: Alfred Knopf, 1979).

Spencer, Herbert, *Herbert Spencer on Social Evolution: Selected Writings* (Chicago, IL: University of Chicago Press, 1972).

Strauss, David Friedrich, *The Life of Jesus Critically Examined*, P. C. Hodgson (ed.) and George Eliot (trans.) (Philadelphia, PA: Fortress, 1972).

Tillich, Paul, *Ergänzungs- und Nachlaßbände zu den Gesammelten Werken*, vol. 7, *Frühe Predigten 1909–1918* (Berlin: De Gruyter, 1993).

Tillich, Paul, *The Shaking of the Foundations* (New York: Charles Scribner's Sons, 1948).

Turner, Bryan S. (ed.), *The New Blackwell Companion to the Sociology of Religion* (Oxford: Wiley-Blackwell, 2016).

Varnedoe, Kirk, *Vienna 1900: Art, Architecture and Design* (New York: Museum of Modern Art, 1986).

*The Vienna Secession: From Temple of Art to Exhibition Hall*, edited by Vereinigung bildender Künstler Wiener Secession, texts by Gottfried Fiedl and Otto Kapfinger et al. (Ostfildern-Ruit: Hatje, 1997).

Weiss, Johannes, *The History of Primitive Christianity*, F. C. Grant (trans.), 2 vols (London: Macmillan, 1937).

Weiss, Johannes, *Jesus' Proclamation of the Kingdom of God*, R. H. Hiers (trans.) (Philadelphia, PA: Fortress, 1971).

Weiss, Johannes, *Jesus von Nazareth, Mythus oder Geschichte?* (Tübingen: J. C. B Mohr, 1910).

Werpehowski, William, 'Ad Hoc Apologetics', *The Journal of Religion* 66:3 (1986), 282–301.

# 2

# Tradition and Innovation

*David Grumett*

During the twentieth century, theological tradition was viewed in different ways. Some regarded it as a fixed and coherent set of doctrines and practices traceable back to a point in past time. Earlier in the century, doctrines might have been written down in neo-scholastic manuals, and the compilers of these manuals probably regarded them as containing unchanging, true theology, even if their critics did not. Others saw tradition as a developing body of doctrines and practices that are rooted in the past but are continually received and interpreted in the present. Closely linked with this was the notion that tradition is *lived*, through its connections with ecclesiology, liturgy, ethics and politics. According to the first understanding, tradition and innovation are opposed, whereas the second understanding takes tradition and innovation to be at least compatible, and at the most, identical. Many of the theological debates of the twentieth century were precipitated and perpetuated by competing conceptions of the relation between tradition and innovation.

In many respects, the stage for twentieth-century theology was set in the nineteenth century. When applied to Scripture, historical-critical method had undermined the belief that what was written on the page was a literally true description of past events, but in so doing had opened new space for constructive systematic theology. Developmental models of history – whether those of Darwin, Mill or Marx – had presented events as caused by different kinds of material factor, but readings of history as linear could be reframed and revised in a Christian theological context. Industrialisation had intensified previous social inequalities, opening a large new arena for social and political theology. Intellectual hostility to Christian claims would encourage theologians to discover a more confident and independent voice, rather than relying on the support of other intellectual disciplines. Against this backdrop given by the preceding century, important new conceptions and rereadings of tradition emerged, accompanied by innovative engagements with tradition. This chapter surveys these new conceptions, rereadings and engagements in three sections. Tradition has been a prominent concept in Orthodox and Roman Catholic theology, and the first section examines some understandings of it by key figures. A broad range of other theologians have critically engaged with received readings of doctrinal traditions, and these are considered in section two. Christian doctrine is always shaped by innovative engagement with tradition, and the third section appraises how a variety of twentieth-century theologians accepted some doctrinal elements while reworking others.

This chapter focuses on major theologians who, two decades past the twentieth century's end, may be judged to have produced enduring constructive work on core doctrinal themes that was situated squarely in that century. For ease of signposting, denominational subheadings are employed, even though the work of leading theologians invariably engages with a variety of denominational traditions.

## Conceiving Tradition

When theologians have worked within an institutional church with a strong sense of its historical continuity, tradition has often exerted a powerful influence on their work. In such a context, the conceptual understanding of what tradition is and what precisely it consists in has contributed to its theological influence, whether formally, through conciliar and magisterial teaching, or by informally shaping the way theology is undertaken.

### An Orthodox Approach

Orthodox theology has classically been rooted in Scripture, the Seven Ecumenical Councils (325–787) and the Church Fathers. Many Orthodox theologians have believed their role to be to conserve the ancient deposit of faith that these represent. This has presented a challenge for the constructive understanding of tradition, which can too easily be viewed as a defined body of teaching and practice that must remain unchanged forever. By extension, subsidiary traditions, such as particular liturgical ceremonies and folk customs, may also be regarded as unchangeable.

From 1917, Russia was ruled by a Communist government that persecuted the Orthodox Church. As a result, a Russian Orthodox community grew up in Paris. One of its key members was the lay theologian Vladimir Lossky (1903–58), who articulates a theological understanding of tradition that distinguishes it from both specific traditions and traditionalism. He uses 'traditions' in the plural to refer to particular determinations such as the details of liturgy, canonical prohibitions, iconography and devotional practice, and 'traditionalism' to describe folk and clerical practices that have been uncritically inherited and perpetuated.[1] In contrast, 'tradition' is, for Lossky, the 'unique mode' by which the Church receives the truth. Lossky likens tradition to a light that reveals content, and to a living breath that renders both words and silence audible. He describes tradition as

> the life of the Holy Spirit in the Church, communicating to each member of the Body of Christ the faculty of hearing, of receiving, of knowing the Truth in the Light which belongs to it, and not according to the natural light of human reason.[2]

By identifying tradition with the Spirit, Lossky does not place it in competition with the work of Christ. Rather, Christ and the Spirit have reciprocal roles in tradition, with Christ the Word becoming incarnate in Mary by the power of the Spirit, and the Spirit descending on her and the other disciples at Pentecost through the power and promise of Christ the Word. In relation to each other, both Word and Spirit exhibit a proper functionality.

For Lossky, tradition is thus a faculty of judgement in the light of the Spirit, representing the Church's critical spirit in determining which new forms of piety and dogmatic expressions should be taken into its theological and material life, and which should not.[3] Lossky recognises that tradition is dynamic, impelling the Church in its ceaseless renewal. For example, at the First Ecumenical Council (325), Christ was described as 'of the same being' (*homoousios*) with the Father. Before the Council, this now classic theological term had been employed only by figures like the Valentinian Gnostics, whom Irenaeus and Tertullian dismissed as heretics, and the Syrian theologian Paul of Samosata, whose doctrine and morals were condemned by Eusebius. The *homoousisos* language by which orthodoxy was safeguarded was therefore highly innovative. Nevertheless, distinguishing his view of tradition from that of many Roman Catholic theologians, Lossky insists that tradition, although dynamic, is not developmental. This is because tradition is a *mode* of knowing, which as such does not change. Although the truth may be expressed in new ways in response to new circumstances, the truth itself cannot alter or develop.

## Roman Catholic Approaches

During the first half of the twentieth century, the Roman Catholic Magisterium and most Catholic theologians defended a 'two sources' model of revelation. This presented Scripture and tradition as two consistent but distinct sources of revelation. In the years preceding the Second Vatican Council, however, this model was increasingly under attack. Ratzinger locates these contemporary assaults on tradition within a lineage stretching back to Martin Luther (1483–1546). Its detractors, he avers, appraise tradition as a 'human invention by which man hides himself from God or, rather, rebels against him in order to take his salvation into his own hands instead of hoping for it from the favour of the Lord which cannot be claimed or extorted'.[4] Implicitly refuting the principle of *sola scriptura* (Scripture alone), tradition represents the real, justifiable gap between Scripture and revelation.

Ratzinger and other reforming Catholic theologians of his generation accepted this critique of the 'two sources' model of revelation, informing the Second Vatican Council's dogmatic constitution on divine revelation, *Dei verbum* (1965), in which Christ is the sole source of revelation and is conjointly manifested in Scripture and tradition. Importantly, tradition was acknowledged no longer to be straightforwardly the possession of the Church, but as regulated by Christ. Within this revised theological context, Ratzinger identifies three distinct sources of tradition. First, the excess of revelation over Scripture that has already been described. Second, the form of revelation given in the New Testament, which is as Spirit (*pneuma*) and is therefore grounded in faith and unable to be objectified. The third source of tradition is the character of the Christ-event as the 'present and the authoritative enduring presence of Christ's Spirit in his body the Church', which entails the 'authority to interpret Christ yesterday in relation to Christ today'.[5] Accompanying these three sources of tradition are four strata. The first is the Father's gift of the Son to the world, which Ratzinger states means that the

> whole mystery of Christ's continuing presence is primarily the whole reality which is transmitted in tradition, the decisive fundamental reality which is antecedent to all particular explicit expressions of it, even those of scripture, and which represents what has in fact to be handed down.

The second stratum of tradition is its concrete presence in faith as the indwelling Christ. Third, the organ of tradition is the authority of the Church and of those who bear authority within it. Fourth, tradition also exists as 'actually expressed in what has already become a rule of faith (creed, *fides quae*), by the authority of faith'. Thus is laid out a dynamic setting for tradition, in which Christ is interpreted and mediated through the personal, the institutional and the historical.

In the twentieth century, most of the theologians who have accepted developmental understandings of tradition have been Roman Catholic rather than Orthodox. Catholic theologians have been more likely to see the development of tradition as a valid task, and even an essential task, in an era of rapid social and political change. For Yves Congar (1904–95), development is important because it entails activity rather than 'passive, mechanical reception'.[6] Congar considers doctrinal transmission from one period into another, identifying tradition as the principal instance of humans' dependence on others. Tradition, this dependency suggests, is fundamentally relational. Congar presents the active reception of tradition through Mary's 'perfect example of responsive faith' by welcoming the Word into her heart through the power of the Spirit. For Congar, tradition is the *time* of the Spirit, which is the time of the Church. It is, he writes, 'not the simple permanence of a structure, but a continual renewal and fertility *within* this given structure, which is guaranteed by a living and unchanging principle of identity'.[7] This principle 'concerns the relations between Christ and the Holy Spirit', with the Word founding tradition and the Spirit vitalising tradition as its 'transcendent subject'.[8]

Congar clearly distinguishes tradition from traditions. Tradition, he writes, has three aspects. First, it is the whole gospel or Christian mystery in any form of transmission, whether Scripture, creeds, the spoken word, sacraments, worship or customs, either as content or as act. Second, tradition is the interpretation or meaning that the whole community who lives and shares these forms, including both the laity and the clergy, gives to it. Third, tradition includes fixed expressions such as institutions, liturgy, art and customs.[9] For Congar, these three elements are ordered in descending priority. Like Lossky, he attaches greater importance to the doctrinal understanding of tradition than to its contingent manifestations. However, two significant differences are evident. The role that Congar gives to interpretation in mediating the doctrine and manifestations of tradition is absent from Lossky. Congar's insistence on the need for interpretation is influenced by his refusal of the classic Protestant notion that Scripture alone provides the basis of faith. Further, in addition to the category of 'tradition', Congar uses 'traditions' to designate normative determinations that, although not formally contained in Scripture, may nevertheless have a divine origin in Jesus, an apostolic derivation, or ecclesiastical endorsement. Such traditions may be permanent or temporary, and are mostly doctrinal or liturgical. Whereas Lossky strongly favours 'tradition' over 'traditions', Congar embraces both, thereby allowing a positive appraisal of elements of historic piety.

# Rereading Tradition

Alongside conceptual understandings of tradition have been reappraisals of its content by means of the detailed historical exegesis and retrieval of theologians, doctrines and movements. Because, as has already been shown, tradition exerts a normative influence on the content of current theology, this activity has often been undertaken for the overt purpose of reshaping that theology. Moreover, as will be seen, an objective of historical retrieval is sometimes to show that tradition is fundamental to theology in ways that are both acknowledged and unacknowledged.

## Roman Catholic Assessments

Because of his association with the *nouvelle théologie*, Henri de Lubac (1896–1991) might be presumed to have been hostile to received tradition. In fact, de Lubac himself uses 'new theology' and 'modern theology' to designate Thomist and Suárezian neo-scholasticism.[10] He views its propositional manualist approach as arid and hubristic because it fails to acknowledge the complexity of theological traditions, and presumes that theological knowledge is infallible and may be rationally ordered and accessed with ease. De Lubac dates the beginning of modern theology from earlier than is usually done, associating it with the concept of 'pure nature' articulated by the Spanish Jesuit Francisco Suárez (1548–1617), which he sees as illegitimately denying to nature any desire for the supernatural.[11] For de Lubac, the past is often reiterated in the present, with the Jesuit Pedro Descoqs (1877–1946), the Dominican Réginald Garrigou-Lagrange (1877–1964) and other neo-scholastics of his own generation reappropriating the work of Suárez and Aquinas. Lamenting the tendency to devalue the supernatural by failing to grasp its infinite qualitative difference from the natural, de Lubac writes:

> There can be no doubt that this is the direction in which a large segment of modern theology is tending, for, given its point of departure, it cannot logically do otherwise. It sees nature and supernature as in some sense juxtaposed, and in spite of every intention to the contrary, as contained in the same genus, of which they form, as it were, two species . . . Under such circumstances, the supernatural is no longer properly speaking another order, something unprecedented, overwhelming and transfiguring: it is no more than a 'super-nature', as we have fallen into the habit of calling it, contrary to all theological tradition; a 'supernature' which reproduces, to what is called a 'superior' degree, all the features which characterise nature itself.[12]

This excerpt's focus on the supernatural might suggest a concern with doctrine rather than with theological anthropology and epistemology. However, alongside the immanentising of the supernatural, de Lubac equally wishes to address the exaltation of the natural as a realm of autonomous human action and knowledge. In his view, this prepared the way for modern secularism by normalising the idea that humans may do good by their own natural powers unaided by grace.

De Lubac sees well beyond simplistic narrations of 'tradition' or expositions of 'traditional' doctrine. As has just been shown, he is alert to the unforeseen consequences of doctrinal development in spawning or giving impetus to new competing traditions. He is also keenly attuned to how texts are deployed to promote chosen ends, to the multiple twists and turns of reception history, and to the shifts in meaning that concepts undergo over time. When turning to the 'great traditional texts' of Augustine and Aquinas, de Lubac protests against the hermeneutic by which they were 'systematically brought down to a natural plane and their whole meaning thus perverted', and contends with a 'way of recalling certain aspects of traditional truth and leaving others in the shade'.[13] He calls theologians today to an attentive reading of texts that is sensitive to the hazards that accompany the pressing task of retrieval.

De Lubac's fellow Jesuit Karl Rahner (1904–84) also interrogated received scholastic understandings of key doctrines, opening new fields for theological debate by reflecting epistemologically on theological knowledge. Theologians, he recognises, necessarily deal in precise dogmatic formulae. Yet, regarding the assumption that any such statement may be certain and unchanging, Rahner writes in a programmatic essay that

> while this formula is an end, an acquisition and a victory, which allows us to enjoy clarity and security as well as ease in instruction, if this victory is to be a true one the end must also be a beginning. It follows from the nature of human knowledge of truth and from the nature of divine truth itself, that any individual truth, above all one of

God's truths, is beginning and emergence, not conclusion and end . . . The clearest formulations . . . derive their life from the fact that they are not end but beginning, not goal but means, truths which open the way to the – ever greater – truth.[14]

Formulae, for Rahner, are transcendent, both because of the nature of the mind and the nature of the quest for reality and truth, which always seeks a greater fullness. This means that theology seeks as well as finds, and forgets as well as progresses.

Turning to the Christology of the Council of Chalcedon, Rahner examines the neo-scholastic presumption that the council held in 451 on the opposite shore of the Bosphorus from Constantinople supports a single, univocal Christology defined in propositional terms. He concludes that it does not. Scholastic Christology, Rahner protests, has tended to portray Christ's humanity as an instrument of his divinity, thereby giving undue priority to the two Chalcedonian principles that the divine and human natures be without division (*adiaretos*) and without separation (*achoristos*). Humanity has been presented as 'merely operated and managed by the divinity, the signal put up to show that the divinity is present in the world'.[15] Yet scriptural notions, such as Christ's role as mediator, entail a greater degree of reciprocity between the two natures.[16] Moreover, and for Rahner at least as importantly, twentieth-century consciousness is more inclined to reflect upon Christ's humanity, giving due attention to Chalcedon's stricture that his divine and human natures be without mixture (*asynchutos*). For both these reasons, Rahner presents Jesus freely responding to God, with his free response made possible precisely because, in his will, he is simultaneously completely united with God and wholly differentiated from God. In Rahner's assessment, a latent monophysitism in modern Christology is thereby corrected, with unity seen as grounding diversity.[17] Although Rahner's methodology is more philosophical than de Lubac's, which is focused on historical exegesis, the two Jesuits are engaged in similar tasks of critical and constructive retrieval.

## An Anglican Assessment

Like de Lubac, the Anglican theologian and bishop Rowan Williams undertakes a reread-ing of a key theological debate from the past with an eye to contemporary implications. Examining the doctrinal controversies of the fourth century, he contests the standard view that Arius was nothing more than a heretic, while Athanasius was the heroic guardian of doctrinal orthodoxy. Rather, Williams shows, tradition is equivocal, with neither party to the controversies entitled to claim a monopoly of truth. In his doctrine of God, Arius insisted that God was the sole originating principle, begetting the Son out of nothing by the undetermined exercise of free will. God was therefore mysterious to humans, while the Son was, like other humans, not himself part of God but manifested a knowable likeness to God.[18] However, Athanasius' description of the Son as 'of one substance' (*homoousios*) with the Father was vulnerable to an incarnational triumphalism. In contrast, the 'mode' of salvation that God offers is through vulnerability and mortality, by which the Son shares the life of suffering humans and dies on the cross. This modality of salvation needs to be recognised as 'intrinsic to its authoritative quality and as requiring its own kind of obedience'.[19] In practice, triumphalism may justify unscrupulous polemical strategies and ecclesial authoritarianism.

At the end of his study, Williams reflects on its implications for understanding tra-dition. Arius and Athanasius both saw themselves as guardians of traditional doctrinal formulae drawn from Scripture and Church teaching. Indeed, Arius was in one sense more traditional than Athanasius, wishing to conserve inherited doctrinal language unchanged. However, in changed times, Williams argues, mere repetition could not preserve orthodoxy:

> By the 360s – as Athanasius had seen – it had become necessary to choose what *kind* of innovation would best serve the integrity of the faith handed down: to reject all innovation was simply not a real option; and thus the rejection of *homoousios* purely and simply as unscriptural or untraditional could no longer be sustained . . . It became necessary to say new things and explore new arguments, even while still professing to make no changes in the deposit of tradition.[20]

Athanasius, Williams continues, sees that the 'break in continuity generally felt to be involved in the credal *homoousios* is a necessary moment in the deeper understanding and securing of tradition', which needs to be read such that its 'strangeness' is brought out. This requires that tradition be made 'more *difficult*' before its simplicities may be accurately grasped, and this making difficult is a fundamental task for the theologian.

Beyond the field of patristics, the significance of Williams's defence of innovation lies in the foundations it provides for his own constructive theology. Running through his doctrinal contributions, as well as his leadership of the Anglican Communion, has been a wish to disrupt simple oppositions. By understanding and interrogating their founding assumptions, details and likely mutual dependence, deeper comprehension may be gained and agreement may grow. This will sometimes require innovations in language and reasoning.

## An Evangelical Assessment

Evangelicalism is a more protean concept than the other denominations in this chapter, lacking unified institutions at the global or national level and including elements of some of these other denominations. Nevertheless, many twentieth-century churches and theologians have understood themselves as evangelical in their witness and theology. Typically, these have not self-identified with a tradition, often narrating their history back no further than recent founding or inspiring figures. The Baptist theologian Stanley Grenz (1950–2005) pioneered an alternative approach within modern evangelicalism by seeking to relate it to historic evangelicalism, which may be traced back to the 1730s religious revivals in Britain and New England, and even earlier to Pietism, which emerged in Germany in the late seventeenth century.[21] Among the important continuing traits of modern evangelicalism, Grenz identifies a Pietist concern with experience rather than with doctrine for its own sake, with the reformation of life, and with the integration of theology with spirituality.

Grenz's historical engagements were theoretically informed by the hermeneutics of Paul Ricoeur (1913–2005), for whom language, meaning and truth are generated by pushing at the boundaries of received understanding. Metaphor, Ricoeur writes, is a 'creation of language that comes to be at that moment, a *semantic innovation* without status in the language as something already established'.[22] Meaning is thereby emergent, awaiting adoption by the linguistic community. Furthermore, in Ricoeur's narrative theory a 'tradition is constituted by the interplay of innovation and sedimentation'.[23] Innovation produces new paradigms, but over time these become 'emplotted', establishing norms that change only slowly and may be resistant to change.

For Grenz, theology is a discipline at the service of the community of faith, reflecting on Christian faith and identity. The community rather than the Kingdom of God is, he therefore argues, theology's principal 'integrative motif'.[24] Nevertheless, this community cannot be straightforwardly identified with current churches. Grenz's theology and ecclesiology are oriented by an eschatological motif, with churches functioning as signs of a fullness that is, at present, only partly realised, rather than themselves possessing a completed fullness.

Grenz promotes tradition, understood as the Church's heritage, as a second source of theology alongside Scripture.[25] This could be viewed as endorsing an evangelical conservatism based on a closely defined set of doctrinal and moral stances. However, Grenz acknowledged culture as a third source of theology. This is because, if community is taken seriously, Christians must accept that their theology is embedded in both the ecclesial and the secular communities that they inhabit. Grenz delineates the progressive mutual estrangement of Scripture and tradition in later medieval theology and the increasing privileging of tradition over Scripture, against which the Protestant Reformers reacted with their principle of *sola scriptura*. The more and less direct results of this separation were tradition's devaluation in Protestant theology, its elimination in Anabaptist theology, its undercutting within the broadly secular Enlightenment, and its overthrow by Protestant Liberalism.[26] However, Grenz contends that tradition must, and in reality always does, function as theology's 'hermeneutical trajectory'. Scripture, he asserts, is never *sola*, but 'functions in an ongoing and dynamic relationship with the Christian tradition'. He pointedly continues:

> It is simply not possible to step back from the influence of tradition in the act of interpretation or in the ascription of meaning. Interpretive communities that deny the reality of this situation and seek an interpretation unencumbered by the 'distorting' influence of fallible 'human' traditions are in fact enslaved by interpretive patterns that are allowed to function uncritically precisely because they are unacknowledged.[27]

Grenz's critique shows that his object in his nonfoundational project is the theological deepening of evangelical theology. He insists that tradition be pneumatologically mediated, offering 'resources' that are put to theological use, rather than perceiving sources as possessing an objective authority to which theologians must passively respond.[28]

Doctrinally, a core element of Grenz's project is his promotion of the Trinity as theology's 'structural motif'. Engaging with Augustine, Richard of St Victor, Thomas Aquinas and other historical sources, Grenz argues that the Godhead has a social character. Moreover, when knowing God, humans partake in God's image through the power of the Spirit, which mediates to them the truths of Scripture.[29] This is no mere 'social Trinity' in the sense that the nature of God is inferred via the observable traces or signs of God in the world. Instead, Trinitarian explanation is bidirectional. Although the 'economic' Trinity has epistemic primacy, because human knowledge necessarily begins with observable realities, the 'immanent' Trinity, which transcends earthly realities, is ontologically prior. Grenz thereby founds a relational, reciprocal ontology in which God is neither purely transcendent nor completely knowable. With a view to re-sourcing their theological tradition, other Evangelical theologians such as Robert E. Webber have embraced this theological method of ecumenical engagement with tradition to address a variety of topics in doctrine, ecclesiology and liturgy.[30]

# Innovative Engagements with Tradition

Across all major denominations, twentieth-century theologians were resolved to rethink received understandings of specific doctrines. In so doing, they addressed their own varied theological inheritances. In all the instances to be discussed, these were a product of the Reformation and of Roman Catholic responses to it. This section of the chapter is the longest of the three and will discuss engagements with Christian doctrines including the Trinity, the Incarnation, the Resurrection, the soul, salvation, preservation and eschatology.

## Reformed Theology

From the early 1920s, the Swiss theologian Karl Barth (1886–1968) developed a dialectical theology that called into question two key elements of his Calvinist inheritance. The first was predestination. John Calvin (1509–64), and even more so his successor Theodore Beza (1519–1605), suggested that every individual human was, because of their election by Christ, either saved or damned, and that their status as either saved or damned was divinely foreknown. However, when presenting the second part of his doctrine of God, Barth states that he has 'had to leave the framework of theological tradition to a far greater extent than in the first part', which deals with God's knowledge, being and nature. Although he would have 'preferred to follow Calvin's doctrine of predestination much more closely, instead of departing from it so radically', his reading of Scripture and meditation upon it led him, he continues, 'irresistibly to reconstruction'.[31] For Barth, a key shortcoming of classic treatments of predestination is their individualism, according to which it is individual humans, rather than humanity collectively, who are designated as either saved or damned. In his own doctrine of election, Barth focuses not on foreknowledge or predetermination but on God's election of Christ, which indicates a relational basis to election that incorporates an element of equality. Human destiny may be considered only in the context of God's unambiguously positive election, or choice, of Christ. Moreover, God elects not individual humans, but the communities of Israel and the Church. For Barth, election is thus fundamentally collective.[32] This is reiterated in his interpretation of assurance, which could be viewed as the seeking of signs by a person by self-examination that, although others may be damned, he or she is among the elect. However, Barth regards assurance as possible only through giving to the 'rejected' neighbour to counter their supposed rejection. The elect thereby become bearers of witness, just as the elect Christ himself bears witness.[33]

Barth also challenges the received Calvinist understanding of the soul, regarding his position as even further from tradition than his doctrine of election. He writes: 'None of the older or more recent fathers known to me was ready to take the way to a theological knowledge of man which I regard as the only possible one.'[34] Barth thereby again justifies a methodology of direct scriptural reading, adding that biblical scholars are unreliable sources because they fail to recognise the link between exegesis and dogma. On this ground, he rejects classic soul–body dualism, and the notion of a mental soul that is separable from the physical body, regarding this as an illegitimate import from Greek metaphysics into Christian theology.[35] Although Reformed theology has not always emphasised this Platonic view of the soul, it is prominent in the theology of Calvin himself. In contrast to Calvin, Barth states that humans may be considered either as a soul or as a body. In addition, he writes, spirit 'arouses the soul as the life of man' but is not identical with it. Soul, he continues, 'owes its being and existence to the Spirit. It is spiritual soul. But it is not a kind of prolongation or continuation of that divine action. It is the creature grounded by this action, and the action of this creature.'[36] After advancing this view of finite humanity held in being by the spirit, Barth rules out at length the reduction of his anthropology to either a materialist or a spiritualist conception of the human person.[37] Nevertheless, his rejection of the categories classically used to conceive the soul in favour of the theological notion of spirit makes the conceptual understanding of his position difficult.

A third major topic on which Barth departs from orthodox tradition is the resurrection of human beings. Classically, theologians have seen humans as sharing in the resurrection of Christ by, as Paul says, being raised from the dead as a spiritual body.[38] However, in Barth's opinion this belief indicates an illegitimate conflation of temporal human life with the eternal divine life. The human experience of time is categorically different from God's relation to time. Human temporality comprises a finite, allotted span, beginning in the past, continuing through the present and terminating at a point in the future. For Barth, this allotment should not be regarded as a restriction or threat to temporal life imagined as a potentially infinite linear series of moments. When faced with the conviction that their craved duration and perfection will not be realised, humans should not, he insists, become anxious.[39] Rather, they are called to confidence, trust, praise and thanksgiving for the gift of life, which satisfies them precisely through determining and setting boundaries to their existence. Death is the necessary radical negation of life and existence, yet, because God is Lord of death, is subject to his control alone.[40] At death, humans are handed over to God rather than to any other force or power. God in his eternity relates to temporality by assuming it and thereby fulfilling it in the man Jesus, who existed before time in his Father's will and is now ascended and so contemporaneous with all times. Against this backdrop, Barth contends, it is the man Jesus, and not any other human, who is resurrected from the dead. Other humans enjoy eternalised life, by which they become eternally present to divine subjectivity. The upshot of Barth's understanding of death is that humans should value current fleshly life as redeemed, rather than forever postponing the right ordering of their life and relation with God for the sake of seeking meaning or ultimacy in some hoped-for future existence beyond fleshly life. However, Barth may be critiqued for domesticating death and, from a pastoral perspective, for giving insufficient weight to its horror, such as through the pain that may accompany it.[41]

Barth's theology made a major impact on twentieth-century theology both directly and through exponents such as Eberhard Jüngel (1934–2021). However, Barth honestly identified some of its shortcomings and hoped that these might be corrected by Jürgen Moltmann (b. 1926). Above all, though Barth rightly recognised the importance of his own Trinitarian Christology, he realised that his strong focus on the second person of the Trinity had impeded a proper account of the work of the Holy Spirit.[42] Moltmann recognised the importance of Barth's Trinitarianism for Reformed theology, but broke open the Hegelian absolute subjectivity that Barth had assigned to the Godhead. In so doing, he also contested Barth's depersonalising presentation of the Godhead as three 'modes' of being. For Moltmann, the divine life cannot be refracted through Christ but circulates between the three divine persons, who stand in real relations with each other. By implication, the Spirit's operation is the precondition for the history of Jesus, through its activity in the birth of John the Baptist to his older, barren mother, and in John's later baptism of Jesus, when it manifests in the form of a dove. In *The Spirit of Life*, Moltmann presents the Spirit as establishing Jesus in his special relation with God, through which he knows himself to be God's beloved Son. The Spirit indwells in Jesus, bringing the divine energies to 'rapturous and overflowing fullness' in him.[43] Moltmann urges that

> the eternal birth of the Son from the Father and the eternal issuing of the Spirit from the Father are . . . so much one that the Son and the Spirit must be seen, not as parallel or successive to one another, but *in* one another.[44]

On these grounds, Moltmann calls into question the phrase added to the Nicene–Constantinopolitan Creed known as the *filioque*, that the Spirit 'proceeds from the Father and the Son', rather than from the Father alone, arguing that the addition entails the subordination of the Spirit to the Son. Although the Spirit gives itself kenotically, it does so as Jesus' companion in his suffering, which is a corollary of Jesus' own kenosis.

Barth had thought that his Trinitarianism could be rebalanced while his supernaturalist doctrine of God remained intact. Indeed, in his later work he remained committed to a supernaturalising eschatology, convinced that God's only possible response to the world was judgement, and that his own early notion that positive political or social changes may be caused or willed by God amounted to a hubristic refusal of this fact.[45] However, Moltmann saw that Barth's notion of absolute divine subjectivity needed to be reunited with the Hegelian vision of divine activity in history from which Barth had severed it. In his *Theology of Hope*, Moltmann sought to combine the transcendent and the historical, seeing eschatology cosmically as in continuity with present life but equally as contradicting it in the appearance of Christ in glory, the resurrection of the dead, the perfecting of created beings and the renewal of the created order.[46] For Moltmann, the future is grounded in *promise*, which refers to a 'not yet existing reality' that will be a 'new creation out of nothing' according to its own unique process. He writes:

> Revelation, recognised as promise and embraced in hope, thus sets an open stage for history, and fills it with missionary enterprise and the responsible exercise of hope, accepting the suffering that is involved in the contradiction of reality, and setting out towards the promised future.[47]

The 'historical character of human existence' and the 'anticipatory illumination of contexts and prospects in terms of universal history' coordinate with revelation thus understood. Yet, in present history, no more may be gained than a foretaste of the glorified Christ, who remains hidden in a future that is unfinished.

In Scotland, Thomas F. Torrance (1913–2007) promoted Barth's project, above all by editing the English translation of his *Church Dogmatics*. However, Torrance was more concerned than Barth to understand the philosophical and methodological implications of dialectical theology, and did so in ways that cut across classic denominational theological divides. A notable instance is his discussion of space. Modern Protestant theologians had tended to disregard what they viewed as metaphysical categories, wishing to remain with Barth in the realm of dogmatics. They regarded Roman Catholic theologians, in contrast, as compromised by their captivity to the scholastic philosophical framework derived from Aristotle. Torrance and others cited the Eucharist as a primary example of this, protesting that Christ could not possibly be contained 'within' the appearances of bread and wine. So far as space was concerned, Torrance accepted the Reformed critique that modern theology had too readily accepted Aristotle's 'receptacle' notion of space as that within which Christ may be 'contained'. Rather, citing patristic and Anglican sources in his support,

Torrance understood space as the 'seat of relations or the place of meeting and activity in the interaction between God and the world'.[48]

Ever more through the course of his work, Torrance contended that theologians must take the categories of space and time seriously, and therefore must embrace the findings of other intellectual disciplines. This imperative derives from Christian theology itself. Torrance writes:

It is in and through the universe of space and time that God has revealed himself to us in modes of rationality that he has conferred upon the creation and upon us in the creation, and it is in and through the same universe of space and time that theology makes its disciplined response to God's self-revelation.[49]

Torrance recognised the increasingly unitary conception of space–time that science promotes, suggesting that this is more amenable to theological engagement than are classic Newtonian views of space as a grid and time as linear. 'This universe of space and time', he avers, 'far from being alien – is the universe in which God has planted us.'[50] Torrance continues that the 'pursuit of natural science is one of the ways in which man, the child of God, fulfils his distinctive function in the creation', and is therefore a 'religious duty'. Theology and science each have their own distinct objects. They nevertheless operate in partnership, through the 'same rational structures of space' and by each providing knowledge of things through their natures. Torrance envisions the theology–science divide being providentially overcome by a 'massive new synthesis' of the two disciplines.[51]

## Lutheran Theology

The theologian and pastor Dietrich Bonhoeffer (1906–45) was arrested for his involvement in a plot to assassinate Adolf Hitler and was executed a month before the end of the Second World War in Europe. He has been best known for the prison writings of his final two years. Bonhoeffer's main importance lies in his radical theology of the relation between Church and world. This required him to reappraise elements of Lutheranism, in which the Church had become subservient to the state, by returning to Luther himself and drawing resources for resistance out of the earlier Lutheran tradition.[52] Bonhoeffer broadly accepts Luther's position that orders exist within earthly life that promote justice and limit the spread of sin. He understands these orders as mandates, and identifies four: work, marriage and family, government and Church.[53] Importantly, the state depends on the mandate of government for its legitimacy. If the state disregards this mandate, and fails to perform its 'divine task of preserving the world, with its institutions which are given by God, for the purpose of Christ', it cannot legitimately command obedience.[54] Bonhoeffer's ecclesiology is frequently traditional, emphasising the importance of hierarchy and authority especially in times of turmoil. Nonetheless, the Church's order and power may never be derived from, nor maintained by, the state. Bonhoeffer insists that they can only be derived from the person and example of Christ.

This stance is summed up in the ambiguous and contested phrase 'religionless Christianity'. By this, Bonhoeffer primarily means that there is no 'religious a priori' of humankind.[55] Humans are not 'naturally' oriented to the Christian faith, nor to any other belief or religion, even though, Bonhoeffer claims, the entire history of Christian theology and preaching supposes this. Bonhoeffer acknowledges that Barth recognised this in his early writings, but argues that he failed to advance beyond a 'positivism of revelation' that, despite his stated aims, conserved two key features of religion, which are metaphysical and individualistic understandings of topics such as salvation, and failed to offer con-crete ethical guidance.[56] Bonhoeffer claims that the demythologising of Rudolf Bultmann (1884–1976) did not go far enough, because although it addressed obvious targets like miracles and the Ascension, it failed to rebut understandings of religion as metaphysical and individualistic. In this respect, Bonhoeffer is a radically liberal theologian, recognising that new times demand new theology, even though his big objection to liberal theology is that it 'conceded to the world the right to determine Christ's place in the world'.[57] From this perspective, Bonhoeffer wishes to *retain* mythological concepts, providing that these are ultimately grounded in faith in the incarnate Christ rather than in a notion of cultural religion.[58]

Bonhoeffer wrote when the authority of Jesus and his teaching were no longer taken for granted in society, nor in politics, nor even in churches. His compatriot Wolfhart Pannenberg (1928–2014) pursued the question of how belief in Jesus and his teaching is grounded. He conceded that Jesus' authority cannot rest on Christology alone. Rather, it lies in the endorsement of Jesus' claims about himself by God. Because this endorsement occurs only after Jesus' death, that death cannot determine his identity. Death cannot provide the contents of Jesus' life, even though it is the precondition for his resurrection.[59] Jesus' claim to authority through the Resurrection therefore exhibits a 'proleptic structure', meaning that statements he makes are endorsed only later.[60] Presented in the gospels both negatively, by means of the empty tomb, and positively, in the Easter appearances, the Resurrection performs several functions. It shows the beginning of the end of the world. It validates Jesus' pre-Easter activity to the Jews. It identifies Jesus as the Son of Man. It reveals God in Jesus. It inaugurates the transition to the Gentile mission. It is explained in the words of the risen Jesus in a unity of event and word. The delayed Parousia should not be regarded as disproving Jesus' claim to authority, but as enabling humans to 'hold on to the tension that binds this past event with the end of the world which has not yet arrived'.[61] Pannenberg's Resurrection theology was a significant departure in Lutheran theology from the classic theology of the cross, maintaining a clear focus on the person of Christ rather than on attendant theories about law, sin, works and free will.

## Roman Catholic Theology

Anticipating the rapprochement between theology and science that was advocated by Thomas F. Torrance, Pierre Teilhard de Chardin (1881–1955) worked at the intersection of the disciplines of theology and palaeontology. In the wake of Darwin's theory of bio-logical evolution and the opening of China to Western scientists after it became a repub-lic, fossil excavation was the early twentieth-century equivalent of mapping the human genome. Provoking a fundamental rethinking of received understandings of human ori-gins and human nature, it called into question some widely accepted dogmas that had been defined at the Council of Trent (1545–63).

For Teilhard, the key points of contention were the designation of Adam as the first parent of all humans, the existence of an earthly paradise, the Fall and original sin.[62] Regarding human origins, Teilhard viewed the scientific evidence obtained from field-work as pointing not to a single prototype of the species but to emergence through several evolutionary channels. Moreover, science also led him to doubt the possibility that there could have been any place in the created world from which sin was absent. The world is deeply interconnected, Teilhard argues, and throughout its history has been impregnated with evil. This suggests that the Fall should be understood not as a discrete, contingent event in distant history, but as an expression of the 'perennial and universal law of imperfection which operates in humankind *in virtue* of its being *in fieri* [in process of becoming]'.[63] Fault, Teilhard continues, is the shadow side of creation, and the created order requires redemption from the beginning. Teilhard was convinced that, in advancing this view of sin as originally all-pervasive, he was taking sin more seriously than those who traced it to a narrated historical event that might not have happened.

Teilhard's theological vision was grounded in a strongly linear and future-oriented view of history, which was in line with Paul's potent image of the 'whole creation groaning in travail together' awaiting its redemption.[64] Teilhard identifies Christ in his cosmic dimension with the 'Omega' point of harmony and unity, towards which our currently chaotic and disunified world is moving.[65] This is not to present Christ as a mere function of the universe: for Teilhard, although Omega indeed possesses an immanent aspect, it is equally characterised by externality, being the gifted consummation of the created order from outside. In common with other portions of the New Testament, he regards paradise as the salvation that is continually offered to all, and associates the supreme transgression with the point to come when humans will separate into two groups of apostates and believers.[66]

Edward Schillebeeckx (1914–2009) was also concerned with the relation between theology and history, and brought Roman Catholic dogma into interaction with hermeneutical and critical theory. For the Belgian Dominican, Christology, and thus the doctrine of God, have become too closely tied to the past, and to the supposition that this past is objectively accessible today. The Resurrection, Schillebeeckx argues, is not a dogma that has been historically verified by the empty tomb; rather, the Christian belief in the Resurrection is grounded in a present assurance of faith, which is from God.[67] Schillebeeckx's hermeneutics lead him to relocate other doctrinal *loci* from the past into the present. Regarding the atonement, he questions satisfaction theories, according to which Christ suffered his Father's just wrath for human sin and thereby made amends for it. Such theories have the effect, Schillebeeckx suggests, of interiorising suffering within the life of God and within human life. However, on his interpretation the cross is not an intra-divine transaction, but the 'index of the anti-divine forces in our human history, which have to be combated and which Jesus nonetheless inwardly overcame through his solidarity with God'.[68] By dissociating salvation from the historical context of Jesus' life, message and liberating praxis, Schillebeeckx argues, satisfaction theories of the atonement have subverted Christian resistance to the continuing suffering of the world due to sin's persistence in social structures. This is a theme that liberation theologians of many different persuasions have taken up.

Schillebeeckx also provocatively calls into question the relevance of classic Christology, arguing that Jesus was not overly concerned with his own identity, and that he was sent to his death precisely in the name of doctrinal orthodoxy. Jesus' identification with his Father was grounded, for Schillebeeckx, in the 'Abba' experience of discovering the ground of his own life in God. Endorsing an expansive view of religious consciousness, Schillebeeckx suggests that its potentialities, 'which cannot be circumscribed in advance, should make us wary of seeking the ground of Jesus' original *Abba* experience too quickly in anything other than his creaturely human status'.[69] His focus is on the message and manner of Jesus' life and on the change (*metanoia*) that these may bring in believers. The meaning of this message and life will therefore be fully known only eschatologically.[70] At present, Christians are continuing to discover what salvation is, and it will not be concretely realised in earthly life until long into the future.

*Orthodox Theology*

Only gradually has the work of Sergius Bulgakov (1871–1944), the Russian theologian who was exiled to Paris under Lenin, come to be significantly disseminated and discussed. Bulgakov's theological vision leads him, like de Lubac and the Greek Orthodox theologian John Zizioulas (b. 1931), to a critique of neo-scholasticism. This had been a feature of Orthodox theology since the seventeenth century, through Westernisation and to attempt to bolster Orthodoxy against Protestantism. However, Bulgakov insists, God does not create by an arbitrary fiat by which he posits a world that exists in a causal relation to himself. Rather, creation is due to the eternally creative activity by which God freely and necessarily directs love outside of himself and reveals that love.[71]

Bulgakov unfolds a 'kenotic sophiology' of the radical mediation of divine presence to the world through *Sophia* (divine wisdom), which is both the divine essence and God's love energetically realised in creation. Humiliation and descent are the ways through which God relates to the world, not only in the suffering of the cross but across several aspects of the divine life.[72] In presenting the different aspects of his kenoticism, Bulgakov takes care to consider both God's own immanent Trinitarian life and God's economic relating to the world. The immanent Trinitarian life is grounded in the self-emptying of the Son in submitting to birth from the Father and to obedience to him, but also in the self-emptying of the Spirit, who gives up its hypostatic self to be the binding love between the Father and the Son in their own kenoses. Sacrifice is thus present immanently in God, but more radically in the economic Trinity, by which God fully enters into the life of the world. Bulgakov writes:

> One must accept the kenosis of the Incarnation in all its terrifying seriousness: It is the *metaphysical* Golgotha of the self-crucifixion of the Logos in time. The *historical* Golgotha was only a *consequence* of the metaphysical one. One must accept in all its force this voluntary, so to speak, dying of the Second hypostasis and His burial in time, as a result of which His birth in time was possible.[73]

In the Incarnation, God curtails his power by the synergy of the divine and human wills, and surrenders foreknowledge of future events, voluntarily limiting his divine attributes. In Jesus Christ, God relinquishes his glory and really assumes the creaturely properties of temporality, development, limitation, emotion and physical suffering. Similarly, the Holy Spirit accommodates its power to the capacity of creaturely humans to receive only finite gifts. By so doing, Christ and the Spirit do not hand over any part of themselves to another power or realm. Rather, they descend in order to fully inhabit the creative life that they themselves produce and sustain by their own ongoing creativity.

## Conclusion

This chapter has shown that few serious twentieth-century theologians operated with an uninterrogated notion of 'tradition'. On the contrary, the century was characterised by constructive critical engagements with received concepts of tradition and with rereadings of tradition. By the mid-century, theologies based on handed-down propositional schemas and inherited doctrinal historiographies appeared far less tenable than at the century's opening. By the late century, a new desire to engage with tradition was stirring within what may be termed, broadly, evangelicalism. In both the West and the East, there was much innovative rethinking of individual doctrines, which required the interrogation of post-Reformation developments of tradition.

Many twentieth-century doctrinal innovations arose in two or more denominational traditions. Occasionally, they were separate from each other. For instance, Moltmann did not depend on Bulgakov for the kenotic element of his Trinitarian theology. However, cross-denominational reading and sharing were the norm, and contributed to five common developments: 1) A concern to take seriously the *radical intimacy of God's ongoing relation with the world*, whether in Barth's doctrines of election and eternalisation or in Bulgakov's sophiology, which, although sharply differentiated in style, were similarly motivated. 2) In Christology a greater interest in the *constructive potential of the doctrine of the Resurrection* that redressed an earlier privileging of the cross, including in Schillebeeckx's presentation of the Resurrection as structuring present faith, or, again very differently, in Pannenberg's view of Jesus' resurrection as endorsing the claims to authority that he made during his earthly life. 3) The *increased prominence, in Trinitarian perspective, of pneumatology*, whether in the Church, as with Lossky, or in the world, as with Bulgakov and Moltmann. 4) An *eschatological reframing of history* no longer in terms of an outworking from past origins but with reference to an anticipated future consummation, such as in Teilhard's theology of evolution towards Omega and in Moltmann's theology of promise. 5) A *renewed determination, grounded in a revived doctrine of the Incarnation, to engage with other intellectual disciplines and their real-world impacts*, such as Bonhoeffer's theology of the mandates and Torrance's hoped-for synthesis of theology with post-Newtonian science. None of the theologians presented in this chapter accepted all the elements of the theological tradition they inherited, and the full appraisal of some still requires more research. Nevertheless, the twentieth century was indisputably a time of tremendous theological innovation, in which Christian tradition was reimagined and rearticulated.[74]

## Notes

1. Vladimir Lossky, 'Tradition and Traditions' [1952], in *In the Image and Likeness of God*, Thomas E. Bird (trans.) (Crestwood, NY: St Vladimir's Seminary Press, 1974), pp. 141–68: 143–4, 157.
2. Lossky, 'Tradition and Traditions', p. 152.
3. Lossky, 'Tradition and Traditions', pp. 154–65.
4. Joseph Ratzinger, 'Revelation and Tradition' [1963], in Karl Rahner and Joseph Ratzinger, *Revelation and Tradition*, W. J. O'Hara (trans.) (New York: Herder & Herder, 1966), pp. 26–49: 27–8.
5. Ratzinger, 'Revelation and Tradition', pp. 45–6.
6. Yves Congar, *Tradition and Traditions: An Historical and a Theological Essay*, Michael Naseby and Thomas Rainborough (trans.) (London: Burns & Oates, [1960–3] 1966), p. 253. Themes are summarised in Yves Congar, *The Meaning of Tradition*, A. N. Woodrow (trans.) (San Francisco, CA: Ignatius, [1963] 2004), and Joseph Famerée and Gilles Routhier, *Yves Congar* (Paris: Cerf, 2008), pp. 117–47. On the active subject, see Andrew Meszaros, *The Prophetic Church: History and Doctrinal Development in John Henry Newman and Yves Congar* (Oxford: Oxford University Press, 2016), pp. 89–126, 214–18.
7. Congar, *Tradition and Traditions*, pp. 264–5.
8. Congar, *Tradition and Traditions*, p. 338.
9. Congar, *Tradition and Traditions*, pp. 287–8, 323–8, as well as the tables on pp. 307 and 426.
10. Henri de Lubac, *Augustinianism and Modern Theology*, Lancelot Sheppard (trans.) (New York: Crossroad, [1965] 2000), pp. 106, 115, 179, 182, 207, 215; Henri de Lubac, *The Mystery of the Supernatural*, Rosemary Sheed with John M. Pepino (trans.) (New York: Crossroad, [1965] 1998), pp. 37, 80, 207.

11. De Lubac, *Augustinianism and Modern Theology*, p. 179.

12. De Lubac, *The Mystery of the Supernatural*, p. 37.

13. De Lubac, *The Mystery of the Supernatural*, p. 37; de Lubac, *Augustinianism and Modern Theology*, p. 147; see David Grumett, 'De Lubac, Grace, and the Pure Nature Debate', *Modern Theology* 31 (2015), 123–46.

14. Karl Rahner, 'Current Problems in Christology' [1954], in *Theological Investigations*, vol. 1, Cornelius Ernst (trans.) (Baltimore, MD: Helicon, 1964), pp. 149–200: 149; discussed in Robert A. Krieg, 'A Fortieth-Anniversary Reappraisal of "Chalcedon: End or Beginning?"', *Philosophy and Theology* 9 (1995), 77–116. Rahner's essay was first titled 'Chalcedon: End or Beginning?'.

15. Rahner, 'Current Problems in Christology', p. 179.

16. Rahner, 'Current Problems in Christology', pp. 156–8, 162, 172.

17. Rahner, 'Current Problems in Christology', pp. 180–3.

18. Rowan Williams, *Arius: Heresy and Tradition*, 2nd ed. (London: SCM, [1987] 2001), pp. 177, 228–9.

19. Williams, *Arius*, pp. 238–9; also pp. 21–2.

20. Williams, *Arius*, pp. 234–8: 235.

21. Brian S. Harris, *The Theological Method of Stanley J. Grenz: Constructing Evangelical Theology from Scripture, Tradition, and Culture* (Lewiston, NY: Mellen, 2011), pp. 66–79.

22. Paul Ricoeur, *The Rule of Metaphor: The Creation of Meaning in Language*, Robert Czerny with Kathleen McLaughlin and John Costello (trans.) (London: Routledge, [1975] 2003), pp. 114–15, original emphasis. See Mabiala Justin-Robert Kenzo, *Dialectic of Sedimentation and Innovation: Paul Ricoeur on Creativity after the Subject* (New York: Lang, 2009), pp. 85–156.

23. Paul Ricoeur, *Time and Narrative*, vol. 1, Kathleen McLaughlin and David Pellauer (trans.) (Chicago: University of Chicago Press, [1983] 1984), pp. 68–9, 76–7: 68.

24. Stanley J. Grenz and John R. Franke, *Beyond Foundationalism: Shaping Theology in a Postmodern Context* (Louisville, KY: Westminster John Knox, 2001), pp. 203–73; Stanley J. Grenz, *Revisioning Evangelical Theology: A Fresh Agenda for the 21st Century* (Downers Grove, IL: InterVarsity, 1993), pp. 137–62.

25. Grenz and Franke, *Beyond Foundationalism*, pp. 93–166; Harris, *The Theological Method of Stanley J. Grenz*, pp. 147–61, 169–79.

26. Grenz and Franke, *Beyond Foundationalism*, pp. 102–8.

27. Grenz and Franke, *Beyond Foundationalism*, pp. 112–13.

28. Grenz and Franke, *Beyond Foundationalism*, pp. 120–9.

29. Grenz and Franke, *Beyond Foundationalism*, pp. 169–202. For other instances, see Jason S. Sexton, *The Trinitarian Theology of Stanley J. Grenz* (London: T&T Clark, 2013), pp. 76–120.

30. Robert E. Webber, *Ancient–Future Faith: Rethinking Evangelicalism for a Postmodern World* (Grand Rapids: Baker, 1999).

31. Karl Barth, *Church Dogmatics*, G. W. Bromiley and T. F. Torrance (eds), 14 vols (Edinburgh: T&T Clark, [1932–67] 1936–77), vol. 2, part 2, p. x. For critical assessment of how closely Scripture supports Barth's doctrine of election, see Matthias Grebe, *Election, Atonement and the Holy Spirit: Through and beyond Barth's Theological Interpretation of Scripture* (Eugene, OR: Pickwick, 2014), pp. 10–99.

32. Barth, *Church Dogmatics*, vol. 1, part 2, pp. 306–9, 325.

33. Barth, *Church Dogmatics*, vol. 1, part 2, pp. 339–40. See David Gibson, *Reading the Decree: Exegesis, Election and Christology in Calvin and Barth* (London: T&T Clark, 2009), pp. 73–5, 82–3, 170–7.

34. Barth, *Church Dogmatics*, vol. 3, part 2, p. ix.

35. Barth, *Church Dogmatics*, vol. 3, part 2, p. 380. See Yaroslav Viazovski, *Image and Hope: John Calvin and Karl Barth on Body, Soul, and Life Everlasting* (Eugene, OR: Pickwick, 2015), pp. 188–214, 254–7; Marc Cortez, *Embodied Souls, Ensouled Bodies: An Exercise in Christological Anthropology and Its Significance for the Mind/Body Debate* (London: T&T Clark, 2011), pp. 75–109.

36. Barth, *Church Dogmatics*, vol. 3, part 2, p. 372.
37. Barth, *Church Dogmatics*, vol. 3, part 2, pp. 382–94.
38. 1 Cor. 15:42–4.
39. Barth, *Church Dogmatics*, vol. 3, part 2, p. 563; see Viazovski, *Image and Hope*, pp. 215–49, 257–9.
40. Barth, *Church Dogmatics*, vol. 3, part 2, pp. 625–33, 609–16.
41. Nathan Hitchcock, *Karl Barth and the Resurrection of the Flesh: The Loss of the Body in Participatory Eschatology* (Cambridge: Clarke, 2013), pp. 94–108.
42. Laurence W. Wood, 'From Barth's Trinitarian Christology to Moltmann's Trinitarian Pneumatology', *The Asbury Theological Journal* 55:1 (2000), 51–67.
43. Jürgen Moltmann, *The Spirit of Life: A Universal Affirmation*, Margaret Kohl (trans.) (London: SCM, 1992), pp. 60–1. For synopsis, Wilson Varkey, *Role of the Holy Spirit in the Protestant Systematic Theology: A Comparative Study between Karl Barth, Jürgen Moltmann, and Wolfhart Pannenberg* (Carlisle: Langham, 2011), pp. 197–250.
44. Moltmann, *Spirit*, p. 72.
45. Barth, *Church Dogmatics*, vol. 2, part 1, pp. 634–8.
46. T. David Beck, *The Holy Spirit and the Renewal of All Things: Pneumatology in Paul and Jürgen Moltmann* (Eugene, OR: Pickwick, 2007), pp. 121–46; Ryan A. Neal, *Theology as Hope: On the Ground and the Implications of Jürgen Moltmann's Doctrine of Hope* (Eugene, OR: Pickwick, 2009), pp. 210–22.
47. Jürgen Moltmann, *Theology of Hope: On the Ground and the Implications for a Christian Eschatology*, James W. Leitch (trans.), new ed. (London: SCM, 2002), p. 73; also pp. 56–63, 89–93.
48. Thomas F. Torrance, *Space, Time and Incarnation* (London: Oxford University Press, 1969), pp. 22–51: 24.
49. Thomas F. Torrance, *The Ground and Grammar of Theology: Consonance between Theology and Science* (Edinburgh: T&T Clark, 2001), p. 1.
50. Torrance, *The Ground*, p. 5.
51. Torrance, *The Ground*, p. 14.
52. Michael P. DeJonge, *Bonhoeffer's Reception of Luther* (Oxford: Oxford University Press, 2017), pp. 183–206.
53. Dietrich Bonhoeffer, *Ethics*, Eberhard Bethge (ed.), Neville Horton Smith (trans.) (London: Collins, [1949] 1964), pp. 179–84.
54. Bonhoeffer, *Ethics*, p. 308; see DeJonge, *Bonhoeffer's Reception of Luther*, pp. 128–34, 210–13.
55. Dietrich Bonhoeffer, *Letters and Papers from Prison*, Reginald H. Fuller, Frank Clarke and John Bowden (trans.), enlarged ed. (New York: Touchstone, [1944] 1997), p. 280.
56. Bonhoeffer, *Letters and Papers*, pp. 285–6, 328. See Ralf K. Wüstenberg, *A Theology of Life: Dietrich Bonhoeffer's Religionless Christianity*, Doug Stott (trans.) (Grand Rapids: Eerdmans, 1998), pp. 21–6, 68–99.
57. Bonhoeffer, *Letters and Papers*, p. 327.
58. Bonhoeffer, *Letters and Papers*, p. 329.
59. Svein Rise, *The Christology of Wolfhart Pannenberg: Identity and Relevance*, Brian MacNeil (trans.) (Lewiston, NY: Mellen University Press, 1997), pp. 203–12.
60. Wolfhart Pannenberg, *Jesus: God and Man* (London: SCM, [1968] 2002), pp. 66–73.
61. Pannenberg, *Jesus*, pp. 106–8.
62. Pierre Teilhard de Chardin, 'Note on Some Possible Historical Representations of Original Sin' [1922], in *Christianity and Evolution: Reflections on Science and Religion*, René Hague (trans.) (San Diego: Harvest, 1974), pp. 45–55; see David Grumett and Paul Bentley, 'Teilhard, Original Sin, and the Six Propositions', *Zygon* 53:2 (2018), 303–30.
63. Teilhard de Chardin, *Christianity and Evolution*, p. 51; also pp. 187–98.
64. Rom. 8:22.
65. Teilhard de Chardin, *Christianity and Evolution*, pp. 143–4, 242–3.
66. Teilhard de Chardin, *Christianity and Evolution*, pp. 52–3; Luke 23:43, Matt. 25:31–3.

67. Edward Schillebeeckx, *Jesus: An Experiment in Christology*, Hubert Hoskins and Marcelle Manley (trans.), The Collected Works of Edward Schillebeeckx 6 (London: T&T Clark, [1974] 2014), p. 610.
68. Schillebeeckx, *Jesus*, p. 612; Daniel Minch, *Eschatological Hermeneutics: The Theological Core of Experience and Our Hope for Salvation*, Studies in Edward Schillebeeckx (New York: Bloomsbury, 2018), pp. 102–3.
69. Schillebeeckx, *Jesus*, p. 614, and generally pp. 120–240, 599–627.
70. Minch, *Eschatological Hermeneutics*, pp. 77–80, 117.
71. Sergius Bulgakov, *The Lamb of God*, Boris Jakim (trans.) (Grand Rapids: Eerdmans, [1933] 2008), pp. 119–24, 128–30; Robert F. Slesinski, *The Theology of Sergius Bulgakov* (Yonkers, NY: St Vladimir's Seminary Press, 2017), pp. 143–73.
72. Bulgakov, *The Lamb of God*, pp. 213–47, 314–15, 370–2; Paul L. Gavrilyuk, 'The Kenotic Theology of Sergius Bulgakov', *Scottish Journal of Theology* 58 (2005), 251–69; Slesinski, *The Theology of Sergius Bulgakov*, pp. 45–59.
73. Bulgakov, *The Lamb of God*, p. 232.
74. I am grateful for discussion of this chapter with University of Edinburgh PhD students including Cameron Clausing, B. J. Condrey, Andrew Johnson, John McLuckie and Craig Meek.

# Bibliography

Barth, Karl, *Church Dogmatics*, G. W. Bromiley and T. F. Torrance (eds), 14 vols (Edinburgh: T&T Clark, [1932–67] 1936–77).

Beck, T. David, *The Holy Spirit and the Renewal of All Things: Pneumatology in Paul and Jürgen Moltmann* (Eugene, OR: Pickwick, 2007).

Bonhoeffer, Dietrich, *Ethics*, Eberhard Bethge (ed.), Neville Horton Smith (trans.) (London: Collins, [1949] 1964).

Bonhoeffer, Dietrich, *Letters and Papers from Prison*, Reginald H. Fuller, Frank Clarke and John Bowden (trans.), enlarged ed. (New York: Touchstone, [1944] 1997).

Bulgakov, Sergius, *The Lamb of God*, Boris Jakim (trans.) (Grand Rapids: Eerdmans, [1933] 2008).

Congar, Yves, *The Meaning of Tradition*, A. N. Woodrow (trans.) (San Francisco: Ignatius, [1963] 2004).

Congar, Yves, *Tradition and Traditions: An Historical and a Theological Essay*, Michael Naseby and Thomas Rainborough (trans.) (London: Burns & Oates, [1960–3] 1966).

Cortez, Marc, *Embodied Souls, Ensouled Bodies: An Exercise in Christological Anthropology and Its Significance for the Mind/Body Debate* (London: T&T Clark, 2011).

DeJonge, Michael P., *Bonhoeffer's Reception of Luther* (Oxford: Oxford University Press, 2017).

Famerée, Joseph and Gilles Routhier, *Yves Congar* (Paris: Cerf, 2008).

Gavrilyuk, Paul L., 'The Kenotic Theology of Sergius Bulgakov', *Scottish Journal of Theology* 58 (2005), 251–69.

Gibson, David, *Reading the Decree: Exegesis, Election and Christology in Calvin and Barth* (London: T&T Clark, 2009).

Grebe, Matthias, *Election, Atonement and the Holy Spirit: Through and beyond Barth's Theological Interpretation of Scripture* (Eugene, OR: Pickwick, 2014).

Grenz, Stanley J., *Revisioning Evangelical Theology: A Fresh Agenda for the 21st Century* (Downers Grove, IL: InterVarsity, 1993).

Grenz, Stanley J. and John R. Franke, *Beyond Foundationalism: Shaping Theology in a Postmodern Context* (Louisville, KY: Westminster John Knox, 2001).

Grumett, David, 'De Lubac, Grace, and the Pure Nature Debate', *Modern Theology* 31 (2015), 123–46.

Grumett, David and Paul Bentley, 'Teilhard, Original Sin, and the Six Propositions', *Zygon* 53:2 (2018), 303–30.

Harris, Brian S., *The Theological Method of Stanley J. Grenz: Constructing Evangelical Theology from Scripture, Tradition, and Culture* (Lewiston, NY: Mellen, 2011).

Hitchcock, Nathan, *Karl Barth and the Resurrection of the Flesh: The Loss of the Body in Participatory Eschatology* (Cambridge: Clarke, 2013).

Kenzo, Mabiala Justin-Robert, *Dialectic of Sedimentation and Innovation: Paul Ricoeur on Creativity after the Subject* (New York: Lang, 2009).

Krieg, Robert A., 'A Fortieth-Anniversary Reappraisal of "Chalcedon: End or Beginning?"', *Philosophy and Theology* 9 (1995), 77–116.

Lossky, Vladimir, 'Tradition and Traditions' [1952], in *In the Image and Likeness of God*, Thomas E. Bird (trans.) (Crestwood, NY: St Vladimir's Seminary Press, 1974), pp. 141–68.

Lubac, Henri de, *Augustinianism and Modern Theology*, Lancelot Sheppard (trans.) (New York: Crossroad, [1965] 2000).

Lubac, Henri de, *The Mystery of the Supernatural*, Rosemary Sheed with John M. Pepino (trans.) (New York: Crossroad, [1965] 1998).

Meszaros, Andrew, *The Prophetic Church: History and Doctrinal Development in John Henry Newman and Yves Congar* (Oxford: Oxford University Press, 2016).

Minch, Daniel, *Eschatological Hermeneutics: The Theological Core of Experience and Our Hope for Salvation*, Studies in Edward Schillebeeckx (New York: Bloomsbury, 2018).

Moltmann, Jürgen, *The Spirit of Life: A Universal Affirmation*, Margaret Kohl (trans.) (London: SCM, 1992).

Moltmann, Jürgen, *Theology of Hope: On the Ground and the Implications for a Christian Eschatology*, James W. Leitch (trans.), new ed. (London: SCM, 2002).

Neal, Ryan A., *Theology as Hope: On the Ground and the Implications of Jürgen Moltmann's Doctrine of Hope* (Eugene, OR: Pickwick, 2009).

Pannenberg, Wolfhart, *Jesus: God and Man* (London: SCM, [1968] 2002).

Rahner, Karl, 'Current Problems in Christology' [1954], in *Theological Investigations*, vol. 1, Cornelius Ernst (trans.) (Baltimore, MD: Helicon, 1964), pp. 149–200.

Ratzinger, Joseph, 'Revelation and Tradition' [1963], in Karl Rahner and Joseph Ratzinger, *Revelation and Tradition*, W. J. O'Hara (trans.) (New York: Herder & Herder, 1966), pp. 26–49.

Ricoeur, Paul, *The Rule of Metaphor: The Creation of Meaning in Language*, Robert Czerny with Kathleen McLaughlin and John Costello (trans.) (London: Routledge, [1975] 2003).

Ricoeur, Paul, *Time and Narrative*, vol. 1, Kathleen McLaughlin and David Pellauer (trans.) (Chicago: University of Chicago Press, [1983] 1984).

Rise, Svein, *The Christology of Wolfhart Pannenberg: Identity and Relevance*, Brian MacNeil (trans.) (Lewiston, NY: Mellen University Press, 1997).

Schillebeeckx, Edward, *Jesus: An Experiment in Christology*, Hubert Hoskins and Marcelle Manley (trans.), The Collected Works of Edward Schillebeeckx 6 (London: T&T Clark, [1974] 2014).

Sexton, Jason S., *The Trinitarian Theology of Stanley J. Grenz* (London: T&T Clark, 2013).

Slesinski, Robert F., *The Theology of Sergius Bulgakov* (Yonkers, NY: St Vladimir's Seminary Press, 2017).

Teilhard de Chardin, Pierre, *Christianity and Evolution: Reflections on Science and Religion*, René Hague (trans.) (San Diego: Harvest, 1974).

Torrance, Thomas F., *The Ground and Grammar of Theology: Consonance between Theology and Science* (Edinburgh: T&T Clark, 2001).

Torrance, Thomas F., *Space, Time and Incarnation* (London: Oxford University Press, 1969).

Varkey, Wilson, *Role of the Holy Spirit in the Protestant Systematic Theology: A Comparative Study between Karl Barth, Jürgen Moltmann, and Wolfhart Pannenberg* (Carlisle: Langham, 2011).

Viazovski, Yaroslav, *Image and Hope: John Calvin and Karl Barth on Body, Soul, and Life Everlasting* (Eugene, OR: Pickwick, 2015).

Webber, Robert E., *Ancient–Future Faith: Rethinking Evangelicalism for a Postmodern World* (Grand Rapids: Baker, 1999).

Williams, Rowan, *Arius: Heresy and Tradition*, 2nd ed. (London: SCM, [1987] 2001).

Wood, Laurence W., 'From Barth's Trinitarian Christology to Moltmann's Trinitarian Pneumatology', *The Asbury Theological Journal* 55:1 (2000), 51–67.

Wüstenberg, Ralf K., *A Theology of Life: Dietrich Bonhoeffer's Religionless Christianity*, Doug Stott (trans.) (Grand Rapids: Eerdmans, 1998).

# 3

# Scripture and Criticism

*Angus Paddison*

## Introduction

In what follows I explore the nature and future direction both of biblical criticism and interpretation of Scripture. Two things need to be said by way of introduction. First, to attribute the status of 'Scripture' to the bundle of ancient texts otherwise termed 'the Bible' is to profess that this is a single text in which God is enduringly involved, and which accordingly is to be recognised as authoritative by the community which has determined to follow Jesus, the Church.[1] To refer to the biblical texts as Scripture is to indicate that these seemingly random texts have a superintended purpose.[2] Biblical scholars, as biblical critics, need not be professionally aligned with such a commitment, either because such a commitment is seen to frustrate the ends of biblical criticism or because such commitments are regarded to be outside the realm of what it is proper to biblical criticism. Second, all the terms we are unpacking – biblical criticism, historical criticism, ideological criticism, theological interpretation of Scripture – are each in their own way shorthand, referring to a family of approaches and specialisations. Within their family groupings, practitioners have a range of different motivations, and each of the groupings has their own sub-sub-disciplines. To give an example, historical criticism is a hugely diverse industry that no scholar could possibly master in a single professional career (most Pauline scholars find enough to do in their own terrain without presuming they can move into historical Jesus studies), but historical criticism is itself just one type of biblical criticism (literary criticism is another type). Any assessment of biblical criticism or theological interpretation must be alert to this sometimes wild diversity. As true as it is to say that the territories explored in this essay are made up of many parts, so it is also necessary to insist that the territories do not possess impermeable boundaries. Although some occupants of the different territories are keen to erect defined boundaries beyond which they have not wished to proceed, we will argue that when it comes to understanding the Bible as Scripture we need porous, not watertight, boundaries between different approaches and disciplines. A theological approach to Scripture should be polyphonic.

This essay has five parts. First, I outline some of the ways in which we can understand 'biblical criticism'. Second, I investigate ideological criticism and suggest its significance for those who approach the Bible as Scripture. Third, I unpack the nature of theological interpretation of Scripture as a movement that has to some significant measure been a negative reaction to forms of biblical criticism. Fourth, some critical questions are asked of theological interpretation, as it is invited to take on new conversation partners. Fifth, and finally, the political assumptions of biblical criticism are critiqued.

# What Is Biblical Criticism?

Armed with the reminder that biblical criticism is not a single entity, but rather an array of approaches, we need to say something about the family resemblances between these different approaches. A definition of biblical criticism offered by a prominent twentieth-century biblical scholar, J. W. Rogerson, is a good place to start:

> [Biblical criticism is] the use of every available branch of human knowledge to deter-mine the accuracy of manuscript and other written witnesses to the biblical texts, to enquire after the authorship and circumstances of their composition, and to assess their historical and scientific accuracy.[3]

Three aspects of this definition call for elaboration. First, as Rogerson is keen to estab-lish in his writings, we should not restrict biblical criticism to modernity as though only moderns possessed the instincts to be biblical critics. While biblical criticism came to prominence with the advances of historical criticism and its associated tools (archaeology, advanced knowledge of biblical languages, textual criticism, awareness of the significance of genre to understanding texts), under Rogerson's definition of biblical criticism Origen's (185–254 CE) *Hexapla* would surely fall, in which the Hebrew text was placed alongside Greek versions of the text.[4] It is a fallacy to suppose that only moderns can see the inher-ent tensions and difficulties presented by the biblical texts.[5] The ages attributed to the patriarchs in Genesis 5 or the sequencing of light's creation before the sun and the moon in Genesis 1 are two obvious examples with which Augustine wrestled.[6] Indeed, one can say with Benedict Viviano that the questions of biblical (historical) criticism are *directly* prompted by the Bible's deliberate inclusion of parallel versions of the same events.[7] A question such as, 'Why does Jesus' clearance of the Temple occur at the beginning of Jesus' ministry in John's Gospel, but at the end of the Synoptic Gospels?' is not itself a modern question but is directly prompted by the text, although as John Barton points out there are some responses to the question distinctive both to modern biblical criticism (which has an appreciation of the different interests of the authors) and to modern forms of biblical inerrancy (which in defensive mode has been keen to 'reconcile' the different chronol-ogies of Jesus' ministry).[8] In a related manner, Barton warns us against an overly linear understanding of biblical criticism's emergence, as if biblical criticism was purely a matter of time's ripening.[9]

While the link with reason is indispensable, biblical criticism is not to be exclusively imagined as the emergence of an enlightened mindset, the modern reader shrugging off ecclesial encumbrances and emerging into the light of reason. While biblical criticism certainly draws on a host of modern influences and is part of the story of modernity, so too does it draw on Reformation strains and its emphasis on reading the text apart from the Church's tradition. These Reformation strains build on Renaissance emphases on sources and original languages which themselves draw from ancient philological traditions. So, we are better seeing biblical criticism not so much as an upward trajectory but rather as an approach to the biblical texts that has been ever present in some form, waxing and waning.[10]

Second, Rogerson's use of the word 'accuracy' in his definition of biblical criticism is strikingly modern in its instincts. 'Accuracy' has a hint of foundationalism, as though the truth of the Christian gospel depended upon the facticity of every event in the Bible (which it does not). Moreover, historical critical work is related to but distinct from historical work. We must distinguish between the historian and the historical *critic*. The archaeologist on the search for evidence of Noah's Ark is undertaking historical work, but it would be hard to define their work as historical-*critical*. Practitioners of biblical criticism share a resolve not to predetermine their findings. Equally, the historical *critic* is open to the possibility that things spoken of in the text did not happen the way they are spoken of in the text.[11] The text cannot be assumed to be a transparent window into the past.

Third, and expanding on this second point, Rogerson's definition merges biblical criticism rather swiftly with historical criticism. Historical criticism's point of initiation is that the text is a *source* ahead of, or rather than, an agent of divine communication. Before we say more about historical criticism it is important to make reference to those (James Barr, John Barton) who remind us first that biblical criticism is not reducible to historical criticism, and then second that the questions raised by historical critics have a vital link to literary investigations of the texts. Historical criticism is part of what constitutes biblical criticism, but it is not the whole of it. With this reminder of the relationship but distinction between biblical and historical criticism in place, we can explore the nature of historical criticism in further detail. Walter Moberly, a practitioner of theologically orientated readings of Scripture, offers this account of historical criticism, proposing that it is

> characterised by studying the Bible as a collection of ancient documents that are to be understood precisely as ancient documents, whose sense is determined by philological and historical questions about likely meaning in antiquity, irrespective of how the material came to be read subsequently by Jews and Christians.[12]

The account of the historical critic reading the biblical text 'irrespective of how the material came to be read subsequently' draws us to three principles of historical criticism set out by John J. Collins.[13] First, the historical critic is autonomous. The historical critic is independent of the authority of received tradition. This means, in an important sense, historical critics see themselves as operating free from the tutelage of the Church. In some constructions of historical criticism there is a competitive relationship between the Church and the freedom of scholarship. The more one is bound to the Church, the less free, the more constricted, will be the scholarship. We will probe this set of assumptions in the final part of this essay. Second is the principle of analogy. One can make historical judgements about the provenance of a text because there is a fundamental degree of similarity between our time and the times that gave rise to the biblical texts. There is no need for the mediation of tradition. Third is the principle of criticism. The findings of historical criticism are provisional, and always open to revision and overturning. This makes the findings of historical criticism unstable ground on which to build foundations of faith. Looking at the variety of historical Jesus-es presented by scholars, it would be easy to sympathise with bewildered lay Christians drawn to ask which one they are to follow.

As we reach towards the end of this section, what might we say is ingredient to biblical criticism? A useful starting point is John Barton's insistence that a biblical critic brackets out the question of truth.[14] First, the text is understood. *Then*, any questions of truth that theology might raise are introduced. This is a central element of biblical criticism – the discrete vocation it has, separate from the office of systematic theology. The preservation of specific tasks for biblical critics vis-à-vis other theological vocations need not necessarily mean there is no interchange between biblical criticism and theology. Indeed, the appropriate distance at the right time between theology and biblical criticism can serve theology, with biblical criticism acting 'as the first stage in the development of a seriously critical theology'.[15] Robert Carroll's words imply that theology can cross the boundaries separating it from critical work *after* biblical criticism has carried out its decluttering work. James Barr, a strong influence on John Barton, likewise emphasised the independence of biblical criticism from the clutches of the Church. For Barr, biblical criticism is not antithetical to faith, but its instincts to avoid being swamped by the claims of faith have deep theological roots:

> The movement of critical scholarship grew out of the whole tradition of theological exegesis, with its questionings, its reliances, its antinomies. If it came to emphasize historicity, the importance of historical alignment and historical realities, that was not a novelty, imported from outside the theological world . . . it was because historicity had long been central to the older theological tradition.[16]

Therefore, biblical critics propose, we should not see the independence biblical criticism is keen to preserve as anti-theological, but rather as an instinct in tune with theology itself. Later, we will see how theological interpretation invites us to reimagine the boundaries between biblical study and systematic theological work, but first we must delve into the contribution of ideological criticism, a form of biblical criticism that came to prominence in the twentieth century. No account of biblical criticism can bypass the enduring contribution made by ideological criticism.

## The Entry of Ideological Criticism

Ideological criticism represents a vital turn in twentieth-century biblical criticism. Indeed, as it insists that the text's interests may not coincide with our interests, and that the biblical authors wrote 'to persuade people to see the world as *they* see it and not as it is in itself', we can see ideological criticism as the high point of biblical criticism's insistence that distance be placed between the text and the assumptions of the reader.[17] Text, readers and authors all fall under the gaze of the ideological critic. Ideological criticism is marked by the search for the covert deployment of power, in how the text was compiled, what was included (and not included) in the final text, in how power over people is and was a feature of the text and, crucially, in whose interests the text has been interpreted and whose interests have been advanced and marginalised by these interpretations. In this latter variation – ideological criticism as scrutiny of the interests at play in interpretation – any presumption that there is an objective truth capable of being neatly extracted from the text by interpreters devoid of context, interests or perspectives is destabilised. As F. W. Dobbs-Allsopp points out, ideological criticism unsettles the very ground on which historical critics had presumed to stand:

> Part of what motivates historical critics to historicize the biblical texts which they study is the belief that the authors of these texts would have been unavoidably marked by the historical epoch in which they were embedded. The contradiction arises in these critics' failure to realize that they too must be unavoidably marked by their own historical epochs.[18]

Examples of ideological criticism abound. Old Testament scholars unearth the ideology at work in the 'historical' accounts of the kings or in the prophetic writings.[19] Feminist scholars unearth the significance of women in Paul's ministry, a contribution silenced by male interpreters over the centuries.[20] Pauline scholars interrogate how Paul's texts are exercises in the 'discourse of power'.[21] Or, more recently, James Crossley has unearthed the varieties of historical Jesus-es on offer in recent decades and has mapped these versions to their cultural contexts. Crossley's interest is in the 'cultural Jesus' and in exposing how the scholarly quests for Jesus are bound up in the politics and ideology of their time.[22]

As ideological criticism critiques the interpretation of Bible in modernity (though not without showing interest in pre-modern interpretation), it is helpful to see it as a form of postmodern biblical interpretation. We do not tend to worry about the lack of a single definition of the 'modern' era, so it is surely forgivable that the term 'postmodern' is capacious too. The safest way to capture postmodernism is to see it not as the terminating point of modernity, but crucially as bound to its endurance.[23] Postmodernity needs modernity. Postmodern instincts invite us to loop back and interrogate the claims made for modernity. In a pacific vein of writing, Fred Burnett wills us to see postmodern biblical interpretation not as marking the end of historical criticism (as if we could now move on in a Whiggish sense of progression) but as allowing us to reconfigure the claims made for it.[24] The 'post' in postmodernism is thus to be treated cautiously. Modernity is not something we have sloughed off, like a snake shedding its skin.

Ideological criticism makes three signal contributions to approaches interested in the Bible as Scripture. First, all theological work is invested in securing what Rowan Williams calls 'theological integrity',[25] the correspondence between what we say we are talking about and what we are *really* talking about. Discourse that conceals – be that the text itself or the 'meaning' of the text advanced by an interpreter – is discourse that frustrates communication. Ideological criticism reminds us that biblical texts are part of the lineage of flawed communication that is ours because we are fallen and so drawn to frustrate the necessary link between communication and communion. The insights of ideological criticism can therefore contribute to a theological assessment and appropriation of the text as a very human text. Second, there is a crossover between ideological reading and theological interpretation which may seem surprising. Both are interested in destabilising the disinterested reader of biblical criticism, the ideal reader who is (apparently) capable of bracketing out the question of truth temporarily. With different motivations, an approach to the Bible as Scripture and ideological criticism both unsettle the value-free reader. Both are postmodern movements, in that they make sense of modernity and seek to query it. Third, an approach to the Bible as Scripture has much to learn from the culturally engaged, ethically alert impulses of ideological interpretation. We will argue for the polyphonic conversations that theological interpretation needs to be engaging in below, but contact with the political, extra-ecclesial interests of ideological interpretation are vital to interpretation keen to promote the common good. In her 1988 presidential address to the Society of Biblical Literature, as the first female president of the scholarly society, Elisabeth Schüssler Fiorenza called time on the 'rhetoric of disinterestedness and presupposition-free exegesis' in favour of an emphasis on 'the political context of biblical scholarship and its public responsibility'.[26] Many biblical scholars have picked up this baton, not least James Crossley, who, in a manifesto-like article, beckons biblical critics away from purely antiquarian interests and towards rich conversations with scholars across the humanities.[27] Crossley's impassioned plea is not, I submit, antithetical to impulses native to reading the Bible as Scripture. It is to such impulses I now turn.

## The Re-emergence of Theological Interpretation

The re-emergence of theological interpretation of Scripture (abbreviated hereafter to 'theological interpretation') can be understood, at least in part, as a reaction to biblical criticism.[28] Thus, the provocatively titled *Reclaiming the Bible for the Church*, edited by Carl Braaten and Robert Jenson, clearly implies that the Bible had been *lost* to critical scholarship. The use of the more irenic word 're-emergence' to head this section is intended to strike a different tone from Braaten and Jenson's volume title. Theological interpretation is not the initiation of something new (once, there was no reading of the Bible that was not theological). Nor is theological interpretation the resuscitation of an ancient theology, the mere repetition in our time of what was said in former times. Rather, theological interpretation is best seen as the rejoining of a conversation by academic theologians that the Church's worship and practice had always maintained: the vivifying connection between the biblical text and discipleship. The movement that is theological interpretation attempts to overcome the divide that separates biblical scholars from systematic theologians. Whether for reasons of ideology (theology distrusted as a source of contamination) or practicalities (biblical criticism and systematic theology draw on very different tools, and each in its own right is a discrete discipline, and the sheer amount published and researched calls for disciplinary boundaries), theology and biblical criticism drifted apart from one another. Theological interpretation rediscovers the co-dependence of biblical and theological work. Without each other, both are impoverished.[29]

Articulated dogmatically, rather than in terms of disciplinary boundaries, theological interpretation is the attempt to follow through the biblical text's relationship to the Christian life, the Church, its readers, and to the world – *all* of this in relation to the triune God. John Webster offers a capacious account of theological interpretation which helps us see its relationship to historical criticism:

> The much-canvassed term 'theological interpretation of scripture' embraces a range of attitudes and projects – a desire to go further than critical-historical investigation of text and context, an interest in readers and reading communities, an orientation of biblical and dogmatic theology to revelation. They converge to the extent that they treat the Bible as scripture, that is, as more than a set of clues to the history of antique religious culture, and so as a text which may legitimately direct theological reason because in some manner it affords access to God's self-communication.[30]

Theological interpretation both directs reading of the text to Christian ends *and* sketches what is going on when Christians read this text as an authority within (or over) their lives. Thus, theological interpretation incorporates a dual attention to the actual reading of the text – this is what we might call its exegetical aspect – and to lending theological order to understanding the nature and purpose of the text and its reading by Christians – this is what we might call its dogmatic aspect. Both the exegetical and the dogmatic tasks of theological interpretation are carried out in conversation with a historical tradition in which the theological interpreter is an active participant. Theological interpretation is not an exercise first of all in originality – it begins with a basic responsiveness to a reality that precedes the reader. 'The theologian', Rowan Williams writes, 'is always beginning in the middle of things. There is a practice of common life and language already there.'[31] Accordingly, both the exegetical and the dogmatic tasks of theological interpretation are dynamic, attentive to what has been said *already* about the text in the life of the Church but aware that no theology can ever just be repetition of what has been said before.

As a dogmatic/systematic exercise, theological interpretation speaks of what Kathryn Tanner calls 'the whole', offering 'a sense of how to bring together all the elements of Christian involvement into unity around an organizing center or centers'.[32] Precisely because theological interpretation as a dogmatic exercise offers an account of *the whole* of the task of Christian reading, it is necessarily resourced through a wide-ranging conversation: the text itself; the insights of biblical criticism; hermeneutics; historical and contemporary theology; the teaching of the Church; wisdom gathered from outside the Church; our current context; and the faith of Christian people as a source of theology, all of these in relation to God.[33] Precisely to offer a dogmatic theological account of Scripture and its readers, to think about 'the whole' it is necessary to keep all these different foci of attention in lively interaction.

Having sketched the nature of biblical criticism, the ideological turn in biblical criticism and the re-emergence of theological interpretation, it now remains to raise some critical questions, both in relation to theological interpretation and biblical criticism.

## Some Critical Questions for Theological Interpretation

Our point of departure for the critical analysis that follows is best taken from an instance of theological interpretation itself, and here I alight upon an essay of Richard Briggs. In an essay that originated as the Thiselton Lecture at St John's College, Nottingham, Briggs critiques the 'application' model of theological interpretation – evident in I. Howard Marshall's *Beyond the Bible* – where one seeks to move from 'there' to 'here' by applying biblical principles. Briggs exposes this 'application' approach to theological critique. In its place Briggs offers this model of how 'the biblical world' corresponds to 'the world' around us: 'The real world – the world that really matters – is the one found within Scripture, the one to which Scripture witnesses. The world in which we live turns out to be best understood from the scriptural world first.'[34]

There is conveyed here a common form of imagining the relationship between the text and the world that deserves unsettling. Bidding greater attention be paid to the two-testament canon, Briggs argues that the dialectic of the two testaments problematises any spatial quandary that we have to *somehow* move from 'there' to 'here'. Scripture *itself* offers us an account of time significantly at odds with the linear account we work with as standard. 'Christian readers of the two-testament Scripture are . . . invited to understand their own time within the providential purview of the one God of Scripture', Briggs writes.[35] Wander too far from the real world proposed by the Bible, Briggs warns, and we will suppose that it is down to our ingenuity to connect our world with the biblical world. Scripture rather calls us to live intensively in *its* world. *This* particular narrative is the story that shapes our life. The imaginary here is a territorial one: identity is bounded, by the one canon and by the Church. Briggs's proposal can be positioned alongside other contributors to theological interpretation.

For Robert Jenson, concerns about how to relate our world to the biblical world get things the wrong way around. 'We are socialized', Jenson writes, 'to suppose that the "real world" is a world outside faith's story of God with his people, outside the church doors, outside the covers of the Book, a world "out there".'[36] 'Do not', Jenson counsels in an earlier essay, 'when reading Scripture try to figure out how what you are reading fits into some larger story; there *is* no larger story.'[37] The real world, that is the biblical world, is the world that has been claimed by God in Christ. Jenson reverses the direction of traffic, bidding us to see the real world as the biblical world, in conscious debt to Karl Barth. This is reminiscent of Barth's famous charge: 'When we come to the Bible with our questions – How shall I think of God and the universe? . . . How present myself? – it answers us, as it were, "My dear sir, these are *your* problems: you must not ask *me*!"'[38] Scripture's world *is* our world in this theological register.

Such approaches to theological interpretation that promote a renarration of the world's story sit lightly to practical concerns either about *how* the Bible might relate to lives and contexts outside the doors of the church, or to the interwoven lives of those who read the text as an authority. Bypassed here are the tasks of thinking theologically about the everyday complexity of biblical reading, the ways in which ordinary believers 'bring together a fidelity to a *particular* text and still regard the whole world as a text which has been brought into being by God'.[39] In the strains of theological interpretation identified, the Church is presumed to be radically distinct from the culture in which it is embedded. Text and church are here closely related, with the church as a defined culture. Paul Fiddes promotes a somewhat different reading of the boundaried nature of the canon, and by extension the Church, in a cosmopolitan rather than defensive register. A canon, Fiddes reminds us, rightfully draws attention to *these* texts, imposing an obligation on those who subscribe to the canon to attend to the particularity of these texts. But this invitation is not to the exclusion of attention to other texts:

> The notion of canon obliges us, not only to explore the material so marked off, but to bring it into conjunction with other territories. It is as if *all* writings are near neighbours, all lie on the immediate side of the further boundary, and their proximity cannot be ignored.[40]

Fiddes's proposal is informed by his immersion within Wisdom literature. It is no coincidence that David Ford, another theologian attentive to the category of Wisdom, has beckoned us away from highly contrastive modes of theological thinking which 'tend to insulate from history and prescind from eschatology'.[41] Wisdom readings are on the lookout for the Spirit's work in the world, are aware that this work is not to be boxed into the culture of 'the Church',[42] and are alert to the possibility that what we think of as the Church may not be so.[43]

Theological interpretation, exemplified by Briggs, works with clearly defined boundaries. We can either live in time as the world imagines it, *or* we can live in time as the Bible imagines it. Evident here is an imagination that makes it difficult to see that the Church relates to its wider social location not competitively – more of the world means less of the Church – but in a co-determined manner, a mode in which 'belief and unbelief are . . . constantly interacting and changing'.[44] The Church, Scripture and our understanding of the scriptural text is not unshaped by our proximate, overlapping contexts. This is not fate, but a reality we have good theological reason for affirming. Theological interpretation must be careful not to dissolve the paradox of revelation: only God can reveal God's self, but God can only reveal God's self in 'our space and time'.[45] There can therefore be no bypassing *how* God reveals God's self in the time of this world. Theological interpretation should do all it can to avoid implying that the Church and the extra-ecclesial world are necessarily in tension with one another. Reacting against strains in postliberal theology that imagine a conflictual model of Church/culture or Church/world engagement, Paul Murray acerbically notes, '[a]s a glance around the congregation in any large urban parish church reveals, questions as to whether the Church should be open to the world, and if so how, are made somewhat irrelevant by the realisation that the world in all its diversity is already present within the Church'.[46] Theological attention, alert to a world that has been claimed in the Christ-event, needs to be paid to the manner of this Church/world interaction, and how it infuses biblical reading. Ideological criticism has much to teach us here.

A way forward for theological interpretation is to map the relation of 'the empirical and everyday existence of churches' to theological articulation of the Bible's role and life in the actual Church, the Church that in its concreteness is the object of God's enduring grace.[47] For all its attention to the Church, much of the discourse of theological interpretation remains curiously detached from 'the actual messy reality of ecclesial practice in all its diversity'.[48] The gap between normative theological accounts of Scripture's status, location, and its reading and the concrete reality of how the text is actually encountered by believers is problematic if, as we must assume, theological accounts of Scripture have their primary home within communities of faith, not apart from such communities. The Church is always the 'condition of the possibility' for theological interpretation.[49] The telling of how the Church actually reads Scripture and what theologians want to say about Scripture and its divinity 'must be informed by and fulfilled in the telling of the other'.[50]

If theological interpretation has an underdeveloped account of the life of Scripture in the concrete setting of churches, it also needs to be recognised that (academic) practical theology, the obvious ally here, is itself only just beginning to develop a sustained conversation with Scripture. That Scripture has not been a strong feature of practical theology may be, as Mark Cartledge proposes, explained by the theological predilections of many practical theologians, whose first instincts are not to appeal to the authority of the Word, but to the role of experience.[51] Cartledge argues that practical theology sits 'loose' with its engagement with Scripture, seeming either 'reluctant or under the spell of social science'.[52] If this is so, and if my argument can be accepted that theological interpretation has demonstrated its own reluctance to engage with the concrete experience of the Church's reading of the Bible, then the time is surely ripe for developing some new conversations.

To be sure, there are figures within practical theology who have begun to clear the way for a renewed conversation. Zoë Bennett's *Using the Bible in Practical Theology* makes a clear case for how text and life are to be understood together, mediating between what she calls 'the tyranny of experience' and 'the tyranny of the text'. In a demonstration that the Bible can be used to support a wide variety of theological schools and approaches, Bennett argues that the bringing together of text and context is itself a biblical way of working. What Paul in his letters was doing was placing alongside one another the experience of his communities and the voice of the Hebrew Scriptures, in an attempt to illuminate both. Intriguingly, Bennett, via John Ruskin, emphasises figural reading of the Bible. Bennett's figural reading is not, as in the manner of Lindbeck (and perhaps Briggs), a model where the text absorbs the world, but where text and the world are laid alongside one another, and through this laying alongside, new insights are allowed to emerge. It is not about making connections, but *seeing* connections, Bennett argues. Just as with the 'Old' and the 'New' Testament, so too with our experience and the gospel texts, '[t]o lay two things alongside one another is to invite a fresh viewing of each in the light of each other'.[53] Typology in the hands of Bennett does not enclose the reader within the biblical world – whatever that might be – but allows the Bible to spill over into the lives and contexts of readers, and indeed the lives and contexts of those same readers to spill over into the space of the text. This is a hospitable form of typology, fit for a public theology that prioritises the world's interests ahead of the Church's self-interest. What Bennett calls 'hermeneutic immediacy' overlays 'the biblical story onto the contemporary scene, to bring out features of this contemporary scene and evaluate them, and to illuminate the meaning in practice of the biblical text'.[54]

In order for Bennett's emphases to take flight in theological interpretation there would need to be a reorientation towards the importance and authority of experience. Theological interpretation's default setting has been to work with models of Scripture speaking *to* the Church. Intriguingly, this theological model is reinforced by John Barton's form of biblical criticism which is suspicious of ideological interpretation and its propensity, as he sees it, to violate the boundary between the text and the interests of the interpreter. Thus, Barton's two-stage model of interpretation. In a similar vein Barth worries that when the Church 'instead of expounding the Bible gives itself with deadly seriousness to the problem of hermeneutics' it risks becoming the 'distracted and therefore the chattering church'.[55] There is of course always the danger of 'the collapse of faith into ourselves'.[56] But such concerns surely need to be balanced alongside attention to a text that speaks *within* the life of a community not barricaded from the world, but immersed in the world, a world that is both the object of God's desire and to which God is non-negotiably related. A theological account of the reader of Scripture needs to embrace our location of reading 'in the world of shared space and time' as the *very* 'place of our encounter with a present or living Christ and which must, therefore, hold an unparalleled authority for Christian thought and reflection'.[57] In order to allow experience and practice a role, theological interpretation must not succumb to contrastive theologies, neither collapsing the world into the text, nor the text into the world.

To overcome contrastive ways of thinking is to resist the temptation that there is 'a gulf between theological reason and the complex, constantly renegotiated particularities of situational life'.[58] Theological interpretation in some of its settings has been keen to see Church and canon as boundaries of meaning – Bennett would take us to a place where the limits of Church and canon were not impassable borders but places of encounter and negotiation with other sources of authority, be they are our experience or neighbouring accounts of the common good. Boundaries are there to serve and enhance the dynamic, historical nature of the Christian life.

The invitation here is to imagine a theological interpretation which prioritises the world's interests ahead of the Church's and which looks to actual readings of Scripture in the life of churches as aids to this task. By looking to the Church's readings, theological interpretation may find that, paradoxically, it becomes less ecclesiocentric.

## Some Critical Questions for Biblical Criticism

This final part explores what a less boundaried, more hospitable biblical criticism might look like. Just as I have pushed at the boundaries of theological interpretation, so a similar set of questions need to be asked of biblical criticism.

Proponents of biblical/historical criticism claim that one of the strengths of the approach is its capacity to accommodate different interpreters, with no view as to what such interpreters might privately believe. 'It has created', John J. Collins advances, 'an arena where people with different faith commitments can work together and have meaningful conversations.'[59] Historical criticism allows people with different (or no) faith commitments to enter into a conversation about the meaning of texts through appeal to common criteria and in the knowledge that what will convince is the strength of the (rational) argument. The alternative, for Collins, is a series of reading communities, each pursuing their own interests and each with their own criteria. For Collins, this is an agonistic vision he wants to discourage.

This notion that biblical criticism is a project of social cohesion and is thus political is allied to biblical criticism's zeal not to be consumed by theological systems or ecclesial dogma.[60] Theology, so it is insisted, bears the legacy of being the 'queen of the sciences', ordering all other disciplines to its rationality. A biblical studies freed from the tutelage of theology can enter into dialogue with the other disciplines of the university. In James Crossley this extends to a manifesto where, of all the conversation partners he sets out for twentieth-century biblical studies, the Church is absent.[61] In a different, but related, vein, Joachim Schaper guards the independence of biblical criticism strongly when he writes that biblical criticism as historical criticism 'must never let itself be governed by *dogmatically inspired* hermeneutical axioms. If it does, it ceases to be historical and critical. In fact, a hermeneutics governed by dogmatic axioms makes fresh and surprising insights impossible.'[62]

Schaper's concern about dogma's capacity to norm biblical study resembles Barton's insistence that biblical critics set to one side, temporarily, questions of truth so that they can access the text as plainly as possible. The process of understanding 'any' (the use of this word emphasises that there is nothing special or distinctive about the biblical text) text is a 'two-stage operation. The first stage is a perception of the text's meaning; the second, an evaluation of that meaning in relation to what one already believes to be the case.'[63] Violation of this principle risks our religious convictions telling us what the biblical text meant.[64] The biblical reader who reads within (and not apart) from the mediation of tradition 'knows in advance what it is bound to turn out to mean – because the church or some other tradition of interpretation claims to know already'.[65] Likewise, Barr emphasises that one of the marks of biblical criticism is that you cannot say, 'this interpretation is right because I am a Presbyterian and I know what is right'.[66] Returning to Collins, biblical criticism trades in a common currency – rationally based arguments – and leaves dogma to one side. Herein lies both biblical criticism's capacity to be critical and its capacity to be hospitable to a range of scholars, regardless of what they privately believe.

Three things can be said by way of critical response to these positions. First, questions must be raised about the political project of biblical criticism as Collins imagines it. It is a certain definition of social cohesion that relies upon the exclusion of the knowledge and insights that come through faith. Evident in the imaginary here is a notion of faith as dispensable, something for the weekend, 'an optional cognitive attribute of an individual'[67] rather than a corporate way of knowing the biblical text capable of making a public contribution. To deem faith inadmissible as an entry point to generating knowledge is its own dogma, in the pejorative sense Schaper uses the term, namely inflexible and closed to alternative modes of reasoning. Any faith-centred ways of knowing which acted in the way that Barr, Schaper and Collins imagine are is amply mirrored by a secular imaginary which excludes all religious ways of knowing the world *tout court*. A host of recent writing on the role of theology in the modern university beckons us to a more hospitable and hopeful vision than that imagined by strains of biblical criticism.[68]

Second, we need to say something about biblical criticism's inescapable relationship to the Church. Theological interpretation calmly reminds biblical criticism that it can never imagine itself as entirely independent of the Church, the community which looks upon the biblical texts as sacred, authoritative and/or holy. Indeed, it is the very fact that billions of followers of Jesus continue to read the biblical text that keeps it culturally relevant. As Robert Jenson continually insists in his writings, without the Church, the formation of the random, often unspectacular texts we call Scripture would make little sense.[69] Like it or not (and some do not), biblical scholarship and the Church are mutually implicated.[70] Even those who are interested in the Bible's role in culture would have to concede that the Bible would soon wither were it not connected, in some way, with faith. Happily, it is possible to point to biblical scholars who see the Church as an important and quite legitimate arena for their work.[71]

Third, a biblical criticism open to theological reasoning will be of benefit to both ways of knowing. The imaginary interlocutor of Barr who says that the text means this because she is a Presbyterian and ends the engagement with the text there is not making a Presbyterian argument, but a bad argument. It is not hard to see Barton's or Barr's views of religious ways of handling the biblical text as a caricature. Equally, it is dismissive of pre-modern readings of the biblical text to propose that only a stance which puts to one side religious convictions can generate new knowledge of the text. Once there was no way of reading the biblical text other than theological ways, and one wonders what status the long history of such reading has in perspectives promoted by Barr et al. The text has been and continues to be, of course, mishandled by some religious readers, but this is not itself an argument for barricading serious biblical study from religious ways of knowing the text. To be fair, biblical criticism does not hold a monopoly on uncharitable views of their opponents. In common with many fledgling movements, early forms of (modern) theological interpretation had a tendency to revert to polemical caricatures of historical criticism. There is a view of historical criticism as the siren voice of reason in a fog of dogma which is the reverse of the view that historical criticism is an irritant, an enemy of faith-based ways of knowing the text. It is not hard to see how both perspectives only serve to entrench each other. Care must be taken, however, that theological interpretation is not defined by its opposition to historical criticism. Happily, some of the recent contributions to theological interpretation have been more pacific in their approach to historical criticism. In similar fashion, biblical criticism would be well advised to avoid caricaturing theological ways of knowing. In summary, both biblical criticism and theological interpretation need to be more hospitable to one another. One of the crucial homes for such hospitable interactions will be the university.

## Conclusion

The proposals I have presented for the futures of biblical criticism and theological interpretation intentionally mirror one another. Theological interpretation should chase the Bible's relationship to the world by looking to the actual reading of the Bible in Christian lives. Equally, theological interpretation has much to learn from ideological criticism. In turn, biblical criticism should be more open to the insights of faith and theological perspectives on the text. Both proposals, if they are to take flight, call for attention to the nature and ends of the two settings in which the Bible is read – churches and universities. Wise biblical reading is bound up with the quality of our life together in these two communities.

## Notes

1. Or, attributed authority by the Church. The distinction is theologically important (is authority bestowed on the text by the Church *or* recognised by the Church?), but probing of the distinction is not relevant here.

2. See Michael C. Legaspi, 'The End(s) of Historical Criticism', accessed at http://www.bible interp.com/articles/legaspi357930.shtml.

3. J. W. Rogerson, 'Historical Criticism and Biblical Authority', in *The Oxford Handbook of Biblical Studies*, edited by J. W. Rogerson and Judith M. Lieu (Oxford: Oxford University Press, 2006), pp. 841–59: 846–7.

4. Frances Young, *God's Presence: A Contemporary Re-capitulation of Christianity* (Cambridge: Cambridge University Press, 2013), p. 30, highlights the philological interests of the Fathers as a point of continuity between patristic interpretation and present-day historical critical interpretation.

5. Equally, it is erroneous to suppose that only trained biblical critics can spot difficulties in the text. Anyone who asserts this cannot have listened in to Christians pondering the biblical text and the questions it raises. On the day I wrote this I had led an Ordinary Theology discussion group where members were talking about the different infancy narratives and the questions these differences raised.

6. Rogerson, 'Historical Criticism and Biblical Authority', p. 847.

7. Benedict Thomas Viviano, 'The Historical-Critical Method in Modern Biblical Studies', in *Catholic Hermeneutics Today: Critical Essays* (Eugene, OR: Cascade, 2014), pp. 1–13: 10.

8. John Barton, *The Nature of Biblical Criticism* (Louisville, KY: Westminster John Knox Press, 2007), p. 19.

9. This is a constant emphasis of his *The Nature of Biblical Criticism*.

10. Barton, *Nature of Biblical Criticism*, p. 6.

11. James Barr, 'Historical Reading and the Theological Interpretation of Scripture', in *Bible and Interpretation: The Collected Essays of James Barr*, vol. 1, *Interpretation and Theology*, John Barton (ed.), 2 vols (Oxford: Oxford University Press, 2013), pp. 28–45: 28; Joachim Schaper, 'Historical Criticism, "Theological Exegesis", and Theology', in *Theology, University, Humanities: Initium Sapientiae Timor Domini*, edited by Christopher Craig Brittain and Francesca Aran Murphy (Eugene, OR: Cascade, 2011), pp. 75–90: 77.

12. R. W. I. Moberly, 'Theological Interpretation, Second Naiveté, and the Rediscovery of the Old Testament', *Anglican Theological Review* 99 (2017), 651–70: 658.

13. John J. Collins, *The Bible after Babel: Historical Criticism in a Postmodern Age* (Grand Rapids: Eerdmans, 2005), pp. 5–6.

14. Barton, *Nature of Biblical Criticism*, p. 58.

15. Robert P. Carroll, *Wolf in the Sheepfold: The Bible as Problematic for Theology* (London: SCM, 1991), p. 145.

16. James Barr, 'Biblical Scholarship and the Unity of the Church', in *Bible and Interpretation: The Collected Essays of James Barr*, vol. 1, *Interpretation and Theology*, John Barton (ed.), 2 vols (Oxford: Oxford University Press, 2013), pp. 17–27: 19.

17. Eryl W. Davies, *Biblical Criticism: A Guide for the Perplexed* (London: Bloomsbury T&T Clark, 2013), p. 74 (emphasis original).

18. F. W. Dobbs-Allsopp, 'Rethinking Historical Criticism', *Biblical Interpretation* 7 (1999), 235–71: 244.

19. David J. A. Clines, *Interested Parties: Ideology of Writers and Readers of the Hebrew Bible* (Sheffield: Sheffield Academic Press, 1995).

20. Elisabeth Schüssler Fiorenza, *In Memory of Her: A Feminist Theological Reconstruction of Christian Origins*, 2nd ed. (London: SCM, 1995).

21. Sandra Hack-Polaski, *Paul and the Discourse of Power* (Sheffield: Sheffield Academic Press, 1999).

22. James G. Crossley, *Jesus in an Age of Neoliberalism: Quests, Scholarship and Ideology* (Durham: Acumen, 2012).

23. See David J. A. Clines, 'The Postmodern Adventure in Biblical Studies', in *Auguries: The Jubilee Volume of the Sheffield Department of Biblical Studies*, edited by David J. A. Clines and Stephen D. Moore (Sheffield: Sheffield Academic Press, 1998), pp. 276–91.

24. Fred W. Burnett, 'Postmodern Biblical Exegesis: The Eve of Historical Criticism', *Semeia* 51 (1990), 51–80.
25. Rowan Williams, 'Theological Integrity', in *On Christian Theology* (Oxford: Blackwell, 2000), pp. 3–15.
26. Elisabeth Schüssler Fiorenza, 'The Ethics of Biblical Interpretation', *Journal of Biblical Literature* 107 (1988), 3–17: 11.
27. James G. Crossley, 'An Immodest Proposal for Biblical Studies', *Relegere: Studies in Religion and Reception* 1 (2012), 153–77.
28. Parts of what follow are revised from an earlier delivery as a Thiselton Lecture to St John's College, Nottingham, to whom I am grateful for the invitation and feedback.
29. Markus Bockmuehl, '"Bible versus Theology": Is "Theological Interpretation" the Answer?', *Nova et Vetera* 9 (2011), 27–47.
30. John Webster, 'Theologies of Retrieval', in *The Oxford Handbook of Systematic Theology*, edited by John Webster, Kathryn Tanner and Iain Torrance (Oxford: Oxford University Press, 2007), pp. 583–99: 591. Cited in Darren Sarisky, *Scriptural Interpretation: A Theological Exploration* (Chichester: Wiley-Blackwell, 2013), p. 135.
31. Rowan Williams, *On Christian Theology* (Oxford: Blackwell, 2000), p. xii (emphasis original).
32. Kathryn Tanner, *Jesus, Humanity and the Trinity: A Brief Systematic Theology* (Minneapolis, MN: Fortress Press, 2001), p. xiii. Cited in Nicholas M. Healy, 'What Is Systematic Theology?', *International Journal of Systematic Theology* 11 (2009), 24–39: 24.
33. See Healy, 'What Is Systematic Theology?', p. 26, and Orlando O. Espín, *The Faith of the People: Theological Reflections on Popular Catholicism* (Maryknoll, NY: Orbis, 1997), p. 2.
34. Richard S. Briggs, '"These Are the Days of Elijah": The Hermeneutical Move from "Applying the Text" to "Living in Its World"', *Journal of Theological Interpretation* 8 (2014), 157–74: 158.
35. Briggs, '"These Are the Days of Elijah"', p. 169.
36. Robert W. Jenson, 'The Strange New World of the Bible', in *Sharper Than a Two-Edged Sword: Preaching, Teaching and Living the Bible*, edited by Michael Root and James J. Buckley (Grand Rapids, MI: Eerdmans, 2008), pp. 22–31: 26.
37. Robert W. Jenson, 'Scripture's Authority in the Church', in *The Art of Reading Scripture*, edited by Ellen F. Davis and Richard B. Hays (Grand Rapids, MI: Eerdmans, 2003), pp. 27–37: 34.
38. Karl Barth, 'The Strange New World within the Bible', in *The Word of God and the Word of Man*, Douglas Horton (trans.) (New York: Harper and Row, 1957), pp. 28–50: 43.
39. Paul Fiddes, *Seeing the World and Knowing God: Hebrew Wisdom and Christian Doctrine in a Late-Modern Context* (Oxford: Oxford University Press, 2013), p. 324.
40. Paul Fiddes, 'Concept, Image and Story in Systematic Theology', *International Journal of Systematic Theology* 11 (2009), 3–23: 16–17.
41. David F. Ford, *Christian Wisdom: Desiring God and Learning in Love* (Cambridge: Cambridge University Press, 2007), p. 78.
42. Ford, *Christian Wisdom*, pp. 87–8.
43. Nicholas Adams and Charles Elliott, 'Ethnography is Dogmatics: Making Description Central to Systematic Theology', *Scottish Journal of Theology* 53 (2000), 339–64: 360.
44. Luke Bretherton, 'Coming to Judgment: Methodological Reflections on the Relationship between Ecclesiology, Ethnography and Political Theory', *Modern Theology* 28:2 (2012), 167–96: 184.
45. Oliver Davies, *Theology of Transformation: Faith, Freedom and the Christian Act* (Oxford: Oxford University Press, 2013), p. 99.
46. Paul D. Murray, 'A Liberal Helping of Postliberalism Please', in *The Future of Liberal Theology*, edited by Mark D. Chapman (Aldershot: Ashgate, 2002), pp. 208–18: 215.
47. Bretherton, 'Coming to Judgment', p. 168.
48. Paul D. Murray, 'Searching the Living Truth of the Church in Practice: On the Transformative Task of Systematic Ecclesiology', *Modern Theology* 30 (2014), 251–81: 253.
49. Healy, 'What Is Systematic Theology?', p. 36.

50. Murray, 'Searching the Living Truth of the Church in Practice', p. 258.
51. Mark J. Cartledge, 'The Use of Scripture in Practical Theology: A Study of Academic Practice', *Practical Theology* 6 (2013), 271–83: 279–80.
52. Cartledge, 'Use of Scripture in Practical Theology', p. 281.
53. Zoë Bennett, *Using the Bible in Practical Theology: Historical and Contemporary Perspectives* (Farnham: Ashgate, 2013), pp. 49–50.
54. Bennett, *Using the Bible in Practical Theology*, p. 73.
55. Karl Barth, *The Christian Life*, Church Dogmatics, vol. 4, part 4, *Lecture Fragments*, Geoffrey W. Bromiley (trans.) (Edinburgh: T&T Clark, 1981), p. 139.
56. Nicholas M. Healy, 'Practices and the New Ecclesiology: Misplaced Concreteness?', *International Journal of Systematic Theology* 5 (2003), 287–308: 302.
57. Davies, *Theology of Transformation*, p. 17.
58. Davies, *Theology of Transformation*, p. 72.
59. Collins, *Bible after Babel*, p. 10.
60. For a critical perspective on Collins's presentation of historical criticism as a social, rather than intellectual, project see Michael C. Legaspi, 'What Ever Happened to Historical Criticism?', *Journal of Religion and Society* 9 (2007), accessed at https://dspace2.creighton.edu/xmlui/bitstre am/handle/10504/64566/2007-22.pdf?sequence=1.
61. Crossley, 'Immodest Proposal for Biblical Studies'.
62. Schaper, 'Historical Criticism', p. 89, original emphasis.
63. Barton, *Nature of Biblical Criticism*, p. 159.
64. Barton, *Nature of Biblical Criticism*, p. 165.
65. Barton, *Nature of Biblical Criticism*, p. 124.
66. Barr, 'Biblical Scholarship and the Unity of the Church', p. 22.
67. R. W. L. Moberly, 'Biblical Hermeneutics and Ecclesial Responsibility', in *The Future of Biblical Interpretation: Responsible Plurality in Biblical Hermeneutics*, edited by Stanley E. Porter and Matthew R. Malcolm (Downers Grove, IL: InterVarsity, 2013), pp. 133–56: 138.
68. See Stephen Heap, *The Universities We Need: Theological Perspectives* (Abingdon: Routledge, 2017).
69. Robert W. Jenson, 'Hermeneutics and the Life of the Church', in *Reclaiming the Bible for the Church*, edited by Carl E. Braaten and Robert W. Jenson (Grand Rapids, MI: Eerdmans Publishing, 1995), pp. 89–106.
70. Burnett, 'Postmodern Biblical Exegesis', p. 67.
71. See, for example, Louise J. Lawrence, *The Word in Place: Reading the New Testament in Contemporary Contexts* (London: SPCK, 2009).

# Bibliography

Adams, Nicholas and Charles Elliott, 'Ethnography is Dogmatics: Making Description Central to Systematic Theology', *Scottish Journal of Theology* 53 (2000), 339–64.

Barr, James, *Bible and Interpretation: The Collected Essays of James Barr*, vol. 1, *Interpretation and Theology*, John Barton (ed.) (Oxford: Oxford University Press, 2013).

Barth, Karl, *The Christian Life*, Church Dogmatics, vol. 4, part 4, *Lecture Fragments*, Geoffrey W. Bromiley (trans.) (Edinburgh: T&T Clark, 1981).

Barth, Karl, 'The Strange New World within the Bible', in *The Word of God and the Word of Man*, Douglas Horton (trans.) (New York: Harper and Row, 1957), pp. 28–50.

Barton, John, *The Nature of Biblical Criticism* (Louisville, KY: Westminster John Knox Press, 2007).

Bennett, Zoë, *Using the Bible in Practical Theology: Historical and Contemporary Perspectives* (Farnham: Ashgate, 2013).

Bockmuehl, Markus, '"Bible versus Theology": Is "Theological Interpretation" the Answer?', *Nova et Vetera* 9 (2011), 27–47.

Braaten, Carl E. and Robert Jenson (eds), *Reclaiming the Bible for the Church* (Grand Rapids, MI: Eerdmans Publishing, 1995).

Bretherton, Luke, 'Coming to Judgment: Methodological Reflections on the Relationship between Ecclesiology, Ethnography and Political Theory', *Modern Theology* 28:2 (2012), 167–96.

Briggs, Richard S., '"These Are the Days of Elijah": The Hermeneutical Move from "Applying the Text" to "Living in Its World"', *Journal of Theological Interpretation* 8 (2014), 157–74.

Burnett, Fred W., 'Postmodern Biblical Exegesis: The Eve of Historical Criticism', *Semeia* 51 (1990), 51–80.

Carroll, Robert P., *Wolf in the Sheepfold: The Bible as Problematic for Theology* (London: SCM, 1991).

Cartledge, Mark J., 'The Use of Scripture in Practical Theology: A Study of Academic Practice', *Practical Theology* 6 (2013), 271–83.

Clines, David J. A., *Interested Parties: Ideology of Writers and Readers of the Hebrew Bible* (Sheffield: Sheffield Academic Press, 1995).

Clines, David J. A., 'The Postmodern Adventure in Biblical Studies', in *Auguries: The Jubilee Volume of the Sheffield Department of Biblical Studies*, edited by David J. A. Clines and Stephen D. Moore (Sheffield: Sheffield Academic Press, 1998), pp. 276–91.

Collins, John J., *The Bible after Babel: Historical Criticism in a Postmodern Age* (Grand Rapids, MI: Eerdmans, 2005).

Crossley, James G., 'An Immodest Proposal for Biblical Studies', *Relegere: Studies in Religion and Reception* 1 (2012), 153–77.

Crossley, James G., *Jesus in an Age of Neoliberalism: Quests, Scholarship and Ideology* (Durham: Acumen, 2012).

Davies, Eryl W., *Biblical Criticism: A Guide for the Perplexed* (London: Bloomsbury T&T Clark, 2013).

Davies, Oliver, *Theology of Transformation: Faith, Freedom and the Christian Act* (Oxford: Oxford University Press, 2013).

Dobbs-Allsopp, F. W., 'Rethinking Historical Criticism', *Biblical Interpretation* 7 (1999), 235–71.

Espín, Orlando O., *The Faith of the People: Theological Reflections on Popular Catholicism* (Maryknoll, NY: Orbis, 1997).

Fiddes, Paul, 'Concept, Image and Story in Systematic Theology', *International Journal of Systematic Theology* 11 (2009), 3–23.

Fiddes, Paul, *Seeing the World and Knowing God: Hebrew Wisdom and Christian Doctrine in a Late-Modern Context* (Oxford: Oxford University Press, 2013).

Fiorenza, Elisabeth Schüssler, *In Memory of Her: A Feminist Theological Reconstruction of Christian Origins*, 2nd ed. (London: SCM, 1995).

Ford, David F., *Christian Wisdom: Desiring God and Learning in Love* (Cambridge: Cambridge University Press, 2007).

Fowl, Stephen E., 'Theological Interpretation of Scripture and Its Future', *Anglican Theological Review* 99 (2017), 671–90.

Hack-Polaski, Sandra, *Paul and the Discourse of Power* (Sheffield: Sheffield Academic Press, 1999).

Healy, Nicholas M., 'Practices and the New Ecclesiology: Misplaced Concreteness?', *International Journal of Systematic Theology* 5 (2003), 287–308.

Healy, Nicholas M., 'What Is Systematic Theology?', *International Journal of Systematic Theology* 11 (2009), 24–39.

Heap, Stephen (ed.), *The Universities We Need: Theological Perspectives* (Abingdon: Routledge, 2017).

Jenson, Robert W., 'Hermeneutics and the Life of the Church', in *Reclaiming the Bible for the Church*, edited by Carl E. Braaten and Robert W. Jenson (Grand Rapids, MI: Eerdmans Publishing, 1995), pp. 89–106.

Jenson, Robert W., 'Scripture's Authority in the Church', in *The Art of Reading Scripture*, edited by Ellen F. Davis and Richard B. Hays (Grand Rapids, MI: Eerdmans, 2003), pp. 27–37.

Jenson, Robert W., 'The Strange New World of the Bible', in *Sharper Than a Two-Edged Sword:*

*Preaching, Teaching and Living the Bible*, edited by Michael Root and James J. Buckley (Grand Rapids, MI: Eerdmans, 2008), pp. 22–31.

Lawrence, Louise J., *The Word in Place: Reading the New Testament in Contemporary Contexts* (London: SPCK, 2009).

Legaspi, Michael C., 'The End(s) of Historical Criticism', accessed at http://www.bibleinterp.com/articles/legaspi357930.shtml.

Legaspi, Michael C., 'What Ever Happened to Historical Criticism?', *Journal of Religion and Society* 9 (2007), accessed at https://dspace2.creighton.edu/xmlui/bitstream/handle/10504/64566/2007-22 .pdf?sequence=1.

Marshall, I. Howard, *Beyond the Bible: Moving from Scripture to Theology* (Grand Rapids, MI: Baker Academic, 2004).

Moberly, R. W. L., 'Biblical Hermeneutics and Ecclesial Responsibility', in *The Future of Biblical Interpretation: Responsible Plurality in Biblical Hermeneutics*, edited by Stanley E. Porter and Matthew R. Malcolm (Downers Grove, IL: InterVarsity, 2013), pp. 133–56.

Moberly, R. W. L., 'Theological Interpretation, Second Naiveté, and the Rediscovery of the Old Testament', *Anglican Theological Review* 99 (2017), 651–70.

Murray, Paul D., 'A Liberal Helping of Postliberalism Please', in *The Future of Liberal Theology*, edited by Mark D. Chapman (Aldershot: Ashgate, 2002), pp. 208–18.

Murray, Paul D., 'Searching the Living Truth of the Church in Practice: On the Transformative Task of Systematic Ecclesiology', *Modern Theology* 30 (2014), 251–81.

Rogerson, J. W., 'Historical Criticism and Biblical Authority', in *The Oxford Handbook of Biblical Studies*, edited by J. W. Rogerson and Judith M. Lieu (Oxford: Oxford University Press, 2006), pp. 841–59.

Sarisky, Darren, *Scriptural Interpretation: A Theological Exploration* (Chichester: Wiley-Blackwell, 2013).

Schaper, Joachim, 'Historical Criticism, "Theological Exegesis", and Theology', in *Theology, University, Humanities: Initium Sapientiae Timor Domini*, edited by Christopher Craig Brittain and Francesca Aran Murphy (Eugene, OR: Cascade, 2011), pp. 75–90.

Schüssler Fiorenza, Elisabeth, 'The Ethics of Biblical Interpretation', *Journal of Biblical Literature* 107 (1988), 3–17.

Schüssler Fiorenza, Elisabeth, *In Memory of Her: A Feminist Reconstruction of Christian Origins* (New York: Crossroad, 1984).

Tanner, Kathryn, *Jesus, Humanity and the Trinity: A Brief Systematic Theology* (Minneapolis, MN: Fortress Press, 2001).

Viviano, Benedict Thomas, 'The Historical-Critical Method in Modern Biblical Studies', in *Catholic Hermeneutics Today: Critical Essays* (Eugene, OR: Cascade, 2014), pp. 1–13.

Webster, John, 'Theologies of Retrieval', in *The Oxford Handbook of Systematic Theology*, edited by John Webster, Kathryn Tanner and Iain Torrance (Oxford: Oxford University Press, 2007), pp. 583–99.

Williams, Rowan, *On Christian Theology* (Oxford: Blackwell, 2000).

Young, Frances, *God's Presence: A Contemporary Re-capitulation of Christianity* (Cambridge: Cambridge University Press, 2013).

# 4

## Reason, Method, System

*Christine Helmer*

### Introduction and Approach

How theology is defined as an academic discipline is a function of history. Medieval theologians, like Thomas Aquinas, understood theology to be a *scientia*, or a demonstrative mode of reasoning based on propositions revealed by God. Theologians in the modern period, specifically those of the seventeenth and eighteenth centuries in the West, continued this tradition. They organised theological knowledge as a system of revealed propositions, primarily drawing upon the articles from the Apostles' Creed, from which they derived other theological and ethical claims. When academic scholarship in the eighteenth and early nineteenth century turned to consider history as significant for knowledge claims, theologians took up the philological and historical study of language and texts into their discipline. From medieval *scientia* to modern *historia*, theology is a field of study that appropriates, uses and transforms ways of knowing respective to the wider academic culture to which it is related.

The question of 'reason, system and method' in the theology of the twentieth century must therefore be addressed, as is the aim of this essay, in view of broader cultural, historical and political movements. The question of how theology produces knowledge about the Christian religion is one that must be answered in relation to academic and ecclesial considerations concerning how theologians and Church leaders engaged, integrated or repudiated ideas and claims pertaining to ways of knowing deployed by their colleagues. I begin with some presuppositions before embarking on a survey of distinctive theological rationalities in the twentieth century.

That theology's own way of knowing is rightly understood to be coterminous with the respective intellectual and religious cultures in which it is practised is itself a historical claim. The claim that theology is a function of culture was advanced by early twentieth-century theologians, particularly in Germany, who sought to connect their discipline to new developments in the humanities and social sciences. In a talk delivered in 1906, *Protestantism and Progress* – as its English title runs – German systematic theologian Ernst Troeltsch developed a theory that understood modern culture to be characterised by a distinctive religious spirit that developed alongside and in complex relations to other aspects of human experience, such as politics, society, economics and the arts.[1] Troeltsch thought that modern religion, which he identified with Protestantism, expressed cultural values common to yet distinct from other fields of human experience. Religion was not immune to influences from other experiential domains. Conversely, the arts, politics, social organisation, economics and intellectual currents would also be affected by the religious developments of the modern era.

Troeltsch's account of religion in modern culture would be foundational to one significant way in which theology was studied in the twentieth century. Theologians taking up Troeltsch's perspective regarded theology as the articulation of the knowledge of modern religion, namely Protestantism, and so saw theological rationality to develop in close connection with developments in other sciences (*Wissenschaften*). Theologians like Troeltsch, Adolf von Harnack and Wilhelm Herrmann did not regard theology as a divine science to which only the privileged recipients of revelation had access, but an academic discipline that negotiated its claims in view of other sciences, particularly those new disciplines emerging at the time, such as ethnography, ethnomusicology, sociology and economics.

Can we rightly assume that this distinctive type of theology understood to emerge in coterminous relation with other sciences is properly representative of theology in the twentieth century? Theology is indeed a discipline characterised by diversity. Theologies differ from each other in their connections to distinct ecclesial bodies. The Roman Catholic Church demands that its theologians assent to, have knowledge of and promote its core dogmatic teachings. Liberal Protestant churches expect their theologians to render doctrinal limits more porous and to integrate sociological and critical theories into their constructive approaches. Evangelical churches expect their theologians to adhere to denominational tenets and to render biblical propositions into doctrinal formulations. Theological activity can thus differ in relation to particular allegiances to faith and tradition, to ecclesial polity and to the respective Church's understanding of its role in the world. Theology also represents a diversity of positions concerning its own intellectual mandate. The question of theology as an intellectual activity concerns how theologians understand reason in matters of faith or how Church bodies prescribe particular uses of reason to investigate Christian commitments. Theologians can appreciate (or not) Bible and revelation as significant for ways of theological knowing; they can regard as important (or not) the task of asking questions about received terms and inherited traditions; they can presuppose doctrine (or not) as foundational to all theological work; they can be creative (or not) in articulating their claims. A theologian's individual proclivities, institutional location and ecclesial allegiances inform his or her exercise of a discipline that has many different ways of proceeding.

If twentieth-century theology is characterised by its diversity, then I must ask how this diversity can be represented in this essay while adequately giving an account of the three terms listed in its title: reason, method, system. Different theologies offer differing accounts of these terms and their relations. Indeed, the very choice of these terms – reason, method, system – is itself already an insinuation that a distinct tradition has made constructive use of these terms as central to that particular theological self-understanding.

A particular strand of twentieth-century Protestant theology – with resonances in Roman Catholic theology – is indeed responsible for impressing these terms and their relations as central to the theological task. This is the theological tradition that emerged in early twentieth-century German intellectual culture and was developed by particular theologians in Europe and North America. It has, as I will argue, a trajectory that begins early in the century with historicist commitments and then later in the century takes a linguistic turn. This particular trajectory plays a key role in determining the predominance of the three terms—reason, method, system—in our thinking about the nature and practice of theology over this period. This move from history to language frames the survey I undertake. The final section addresses the contemporary alternatives to this tradition.

I acknowledge that my choice to track this particular tradition in order to analyse the three terms is related to the acknowledged power that this tradition has wielded in contemporary theology. The relation of power to knowledge is a significant insight that late twentieth- and early twentieth-first-century scholars have incorporated into their reflections. Knowledge is not universal. Reason is not 'pure', to allude to the Kantian term denoting human rationality stripped of historical, cultural and linguistic particulars. Knowledge is, rather, related to the persons and institutions who claim knowledge as their prerogative. Power determines knowledge, and not the other way around. Taking this insight into account requires admitting that there are reasons having to do with power which have underscored the dominance of this particular theological tradition.

And so, the tradition I centrally trace here has been critically ascertained in terms of power. The theologians identified with this tradition represent the attributes deemed to be markers of power in Western academic culture: white, male and sympathetic to European culture and education. Because of these privileges, they have occupied tenured positions in higher education and have controlled access to these institutions and the ways by which knowledge in these institutions is produced and circulated. They have occupied influential positions at elite institutions, at which a primary task is to socialise future generations of theologians in research methods and institutional power. The academic tradition of theology embodied by the European model and appropriated by North American institutions inevitably represents the particular interests that sustain this tradition.

Institutional power and epistemological power are reciprocal. The criticism directed against this tradition concerns its claims to truth that are articulated from a perspective of privilege. From the perspective of this theological tradition itself, its methods of academic enquiry and claims to knowledge are 'pure'. According to the critique, the theologians making claims to knowledge are unaware that their particularities – such as social class and gender – inevitably inflect their research and how they move with ease in the halls of power. Progressive theologians today stress the significance of critically dismantling the traditional particular that elevates itself unconsciously to the universal. The epistemological sticking point is that knowledge always and inevitably has a subjective dimension involving personal and cultural positioning and perspective. How academic methods ought best to negotiate the subjective in the quest for truth and knowledge is a matter of discussion and debate. That subjectivity plays a role in determining knowledge claims is an important insight to consider, particularly when addressing theological traditions that very often claim knowledge on the basis of power, even by appeal to divine power.

In deference to the contemporary consensus, I acknowledge that power – institutional and epistemological – is a significant explanation for the dominance of the particular theological tradition discussed here. The proponents of this tradition uphold reason, method and system as integral to the theological production of knowledge. The overarching question, then, is: is it possible to produce theology without reducing argument to power? Can we exit this circularity in order to make a case for the importance of thinking about reason, method, system in theology, even if that thinking is practised within a particular framework that privileges these terms, so that we can catch sight of what matters – namely the theological work of defining how God relates to the world and how humans relate to God?

As persons, we use language to articulate our thoughts. As academics, we aim to convince by argument. What thoughts count as arguments is, of course, a matter of discussion and revision. But what we have are tools to communicate and to understand, and through this reciprocal process – which of course presupposes a willingness to encounter the other as other – one attempts to make a case for a particular point of view. It might be that at the end of this essay my readers think about the insights I offer and finds reasons to integrate them into their way of thinking or to reject them.

I begin in Germany at the beginning of the twentieth century, a time at once of great promise and innovation and of rapid descent into fascism and war, and in response to the tension this doubleness provoked, theologians created a distinct kind of theological reason.

## History

Optimism was in the air at the turn of the twentieth century. The Chicago World's Fair of 1893 showcased it. Exhibits celebrated American achievements in science and technology, while others represented global peoples and their religions. Colonialism and imperialism represented the global reach of the modern ethos of progress of the human race towards a goal of dominion over nature and indigenous peoples. But critique too was in the air. Anthropologist Franz Boas was already working on his theory about the relativity of culture, and two decades into the new century, theologian Ernst Troeltsch articulated his discomfort with the familiar Christian determination of this path of historical progress.

The academic environment in Germany at this time was analogously marked with faith in human progress, albeit also with a dose of unease. The term 'modernity' was up for debate. How could Germany claim a status alongside the modern nation states of England and France? The military general Otto von Bismarck united Germany under the Prussian flag in 1871 and had created the world's first modern welfare state with universal health insurance. Germany's intellectuals built an academic foundation boasting the first modern research university in 1809. With Berlin as the flagship, Marburg, Göttingen and Heidelberg also became synonymous with academic innovations, such as neo-Kantian philosophy, the history of religions, specifically *Orientalistik* (Orientalism) and the *Wissenschaft des Judentums* (Jewish studies) as well as the methods of history and hermeneutics for the *Geisteswissenschaften* (humanities) as these became distinguished from the *Naturwissenschaften* (natural sciences) at this time.[2] The emergence of the social sciences solidified the German universities as the go-to place for the world's researchers. As part of his graduate work at Harvard University, W. E. B. DuBois studied sociology and economics at the University of Berlin from 1892 to 1894. American theologians regularly went to Germany to study with the theological luminaries from the later nineteenth through the twentieth century. *Bildung*, or culture and education, represented Germany's contribution to the modern world, even as idiosyncratic developments in Europe swiftly paved the way for the Great War.

The theologian who most embodied the turn-of-the-century optimism was Albrecht Ritschl (1822–89). His thought is significant for understanding a shift in theological method that has to do with the question of theological viability in the university. Ritschl introduced neo-Kantian philosophy into theology in order to underscore an empirical-historical direction that was becoming prevalent in research methods in the humanities. This innovation was accompanied by a polemic against a more speculative form of theology based on classical metaphysics as well as a decisive rejection of Pietism, as evidenced by his three-volume opus on the history of Pietism (1880–6). History was not only an academically legitimate tool to assess how the divine revelation in Christ was expressed and represented in the history of Christianity, but could also show how the consciousness of Christ that was foundational to the Bible was generative through various Christian formations. Ritschl thus introduced the two fundamental categories of history and revelation that would dialectically frame Protestant theology until Wolfhart Pannenberg united them in his *Revelation as History* from 1961. The question of access to revelation through historical scrutiny made theological rationality compatible with accepted academic methods while also making room for the idiosyncrasy of revelation that was theology's purview. Theology since Schleiermacher was a positive science, meaning that its academic investigation had the function of addressing the needs of the contemporary Church. The Church founded on the distinctive revelation of God in Christ was its particular content, and so was able to be integrated into theology's academic rationality without suspicion of fideism.

The philosophical shift to neo-Kantianism resulted in a new theological vocabulary. Ritschl was a Lutheran theologian. His analytical focus was on the doctrine of justification. Justification in the terms of Protestant Orthodoxy was explained as the Trinity's indwelling in the soul.[3] On Ritschl's account, 'essential righteousness' referred to an occult substance that could not be verified empirically or historically. Instead of 'substance metaphysics', Ritschl used the Kantian language of synthetic and analytic judgement to explain justification from both the divine and human sides – divinity's work was synthetic, acknowledging the reality that had already taken place in Christ, while humanity's reception was analytic, in which faith in justification is the result of divine agency. The sinner became a saint, and with this transformation, a participant in the Church. In the Church, the sinner's justification attains historical reality. Justification converts the self-enclosed sinner to living for the service of the other. Christian communities throughout history are united together in their individual orientations to a common goal, in Kant's terminology of the kingdom of ends, or in biblical terms, the Kingdom of God. Ethical action, which Ritschl identifies as the reality referred to by the doctrine of 'reconciliation', is the way by which individuals reverse the effects of evil by working on behalf of the good of humanity. Ritschl pictured the relation between justification and reconciliation as two foci of an ellipsis. Justification's reality anchored the believer in ethical work focused on realising the divine kingdom on earth, bit by bit.

Ritschl had an enormous influence on one decisive strand of Protestant theology, namely on theologians who were interested in moving beyond the confessional perspective set by Protestant Orthodoxy. These theologians, such as Wilhelm Herrmann – Karl Barth's teacher – and church historian Adolf von Harnack, saw Ritschl's connection between value judgements and historical thinking as conducive to arguing for theology's rationality as viable in the research university. Ritschl's work, they thought, was successful in integrating various academic resources, such as logical judgements, a neo-Kantian approach to value and final causality, ethics and historicism, in order to make academic sense of revelation in Christ. Because of the neo-Kantian appreciation of faith as an idiosyncratic source for knowledge in theology, theologians were able non-anxiously to bring their particular discipline into alignment with other academic disciplines. Historicism continued to be a dominant resource for assigning a 'natural' frame to the supernatural, as Schleiermacher had initiated at the beginning of the nineteenth century. By the end of that century, historicism's role in excising supernatural vestiges in theological content was complemented by the philosophical resources that neo-Kantianism offered in addition to the emerging social sciences, particularly sociology.[4]

To sum up – Ritschl's programme was taken up by his students, who perpetuated his insistence on carving out a particular understanding of theology to assert its academic viability. This position of course had polemical edges that also affected the direction that theology would take in the twentieth century. Ritschl polemicised against the Pietists and Lutheran confessionalists because he thought they smuggled outdated Platonist and mystical-philosophical categories into theological rationality. By insisting on the primacy of experience and doctrine, these groups abdicated intellectual commitments stipulated by the modern university and continued to posit supernatural realities that Protestant theology in the university could not afford to entertain. Academic legitimacy was central to Ritschl's theological innovations. Participation in the modern university required critical questioning of residues of the supernatural in theology that could not be explained in historical terms.

The polemic had a lasting effect on Protestant theology. An uncharitable reception of Friedrich Schleiermacher was the collateral damage. In 1924, Emil Brunner deployed a version of Ritschl's polemic against the theologian to whom the formation of modern theology is credited.[5] Schleiermacher, according to Brunner, conflated mystical experience with a philosophy of identity. The result was a conversion of God's objective revelation in Christ into a phenomenon of interiorised subjectivity. Schleiermacher took theology back into the unverifiable realm of mysticism and metaphysics. But the deployment of Ritschl's polemic in the early twentieth century had a different function than that intended by Ritschl three decades earlier. The context had shifted. A new challenge to theology had emerged. This was not the problem posed to theology's legitimacy by supernatural elements that did not bow to the criteria of modern historiography. This challenge was one that was developed by theologians critical of Ritschl's theological programme, and still interested in theology's viability in the research university. It was the spectre of irrationality posed by some theologians' newfound interest in religion.

## Religion

The excision of supernatural elements was part of the theological agenda among theologians who were anxious to secure theological legitimacy in the academy on historical grounds. Protestant theology had known a lengthy history of polemic against 'superstition', beginning with the Protestant reformation's iconoclasm and continuing with the Enlightenment critique against miracles functioning as evidence for Jesus' peculiar attributes. One factor in this polemic was the anti-Catholic association of the 'magical' with the doctrine of transubstantiation and the ontological elimination of supernatural beings, like saints. Another factor was the connection between critical philosophy and empiricism that relegated religion to the realm of practical reason. Historicism as an academic discipline developed along these ontologically deflationary lines.

The excision of the supernatural did not last. Ritschl's theological framing of the modern progress narrative was soon called into question. Theologians and scholars of religious history became fascinated with religious elements that eluded domestication by the processes of religious rationalisation. Jewish thinker Gershom Scholem sought to identify the non-rational foundations of Judaism in mysticism, and the Roman Catholic theologian Jacques Maritain secured mysticism as a significant way of knowing in epistemology. Luther scholars, like Holl and Harnack, were interested in identifying the mystical roots of Luther's religious experience, and scholars like Max Weber documented a fascination with the Hebrew prophets who defied religious authority.[6] These projects when undertaken by Protestants were not without antipathy towards both Catholicism and Judaism. The Lutherans sought to distinguish Luther's non-rational religion from any connection to the Catholic Middle Ages, and a leading historian of the development of the Septuagint, Paul de Lagarde, was a German nationalist who perpetuated anti-Semitic ideas in his writings, some of which were read by Hitler.

While scholars in Europe investigated the irrational in religious culture, European colonial powers were embarked in distant campaigns of horror and desecration. Between 1904 and 1908 Germany instigated the first brutal genocide of the century against the Herero and Nama people in their colonial territory of German Southwest Africa (now Namibia). Leopold II of Belgium forced millions to endure untold atrocities between 1884 and 1908 for the purpose of mercantile extraction of rubber from the Congo. The Boer War (1899–1902) involving Britain in South Africa exacerbated tensions between white British rule and the colonial population oppressed by it. Policies were legislated that deprived Black people of their vote and expropriated their land. Mohandas Ghandi endured violence as he modelled nonviolent resistance against colonial British rule on behalf of Indian sovereignty.

The First World War broke out in 1914, its cause as absurd as the irrational destruction it would unleash upon the world. Harnack, along with ninety-three German academics, quickly signed on to a Manifesto from 4 October that defended the Kaiser's decision to go to war. At its end, in 1918, the four empires of Austria-Hungary, Russia, the Ottomans and Germany no longer existed. The devastation continued as the Spanish flu ravaged a war-torn globe, killing more during 1918–19 than the total sum of war casualties. Germany's power to speak was crushed by the Treaty of Versailles in 1919, and the consequences would open the door to the rise of fascism, a second world war and the Holocaust of Europe's Jews.

The non-rational, mirrored in religion, colonialisation and global geopolitics, informed a new theological rationality taking shape during the first decades of the twentieth century. A first study in this vein concentrated on the inner logic of a historical idea that on the surface appears illogical. Max Weber wrote his *Protestant Ethic and the Spirit of Capitalism* in 1904–5 to make sense of the irrationality he observed in Calvinist confessional culture.[7] What drove Calvinists to an infinite cycle of wealth acquisition that irrationally precluded the enjoyment of its benefits? Weber reconstructed a trajectory that explained how Calvinism left behind a doctrine of double predestination that assigned all human works to the judgement of the eternal divine will. In its modern manifestation, Calvinism, he argued, embodied an anti-eudaemonistic ethic without reference to a transcendent God that aimed at wealth acquisition as its end. The rationalisation of religion spelt its instrumentalisation for economic gain.

Two books were published in Germany in 1917 that signalled a theological recognition of the irrational side of modern progress. Church historian Karl Holl published a talk he delivered for the four-hundredth anniversary of the Protestant Reformation in Berlin. The book, *What Did Luther Understand by Religion?*, is acknowledged to be at the origins of the Luther Renaissance, a movement of Lutheran theologians in Germany and the Nordic countries that re-examined Luther as a historical figure with a dramatic spiritual biography.[8] The title of Holl's work connotes this shift from regarding Luther as a systematic thinker to an important figure in the history of religion. Significant in Holl's portrait of Luther's religious experience is the confrontation with the divine wrath. This experience defied its rationalisation as the doctrine of justification. Holl's theological work was to reconstruct Luther's experience of justification as the encounter with the non-rational deity. God is unpredictable in the divine wrath; any certainty of justification is unavailable, even as the predicted outcome, in the midst of experiencing the divine wrath. Holl develops the idea of paradox: the human wills the personal annihilation that the divine wrath demands.

Another Lutheran theologian, also in 1917, addressed Luther's non-rational God. Rudolf Otto published *The Holy*, a book that would be both vilified and recognised as a foundational text in the modern study of religion.[9] Otto had written his doctoral dissertation on Luther's pneumatology and had edited the first edition of Schleiermacher's speeches *On Religion* for a one-hundredth anniversary publication in 1899. The influences of both predecessors were apparent in his phenomenology of religious affect that gave an account of different divine impositions on human experience. Like Holl's, Otto's God was Luther's – a God of dynamic unpredictable opposites. Unlike Holl, Otto identified Luther's experience in terms of its significance for the history of religion. Otto created a new Latin term to denote the referent of an experience reserved for only the most special mediators of the divine. God is the *mysterium tremendum et fascinans*, the Wholly Other in whose presence one experiences terror and awe.

Theologians and scholars of religion assigned the disruption of linear historical progress to a non-rational God. They secured the divine transcendence by invoking Luther's 'God above God', the divine majesty that is beyond human control, the God who remains hidden even in revelation, the abyss beyond good and evil. This God who defied form would prove theologically generative and politically significant for the next generation of theologians.

## Dialectic

In 1918 a young pastor in Safenwil, Switzerland, articulated Europe's shock and laid responsibility at the feet of his nineteenth-century theological predecessors. Karl Barth articulated a new type of theological thinking, one that captured the irrationality of war and the divine freedom from human history. The label assigned to Barth's early work is 'dialectical theology', but the term is not quite right. In fact, Barth's rhetoric underscores the failure of dialectic that his predecessors had deployed to work out God's intimate relation to world history. Hegel had used dialectic as the logical model to work out a meta-narrative of God's own becoming in positing and then sublating the world's historical development. A century later, Barth deployed dialectic precisely to highlight its *failure*. Theology required a new form to capture a content that defied comprehension. Affirmation and negation are posited, without any resolution. Barth comments on this dizzying mountaintop walk: 'Only on this narrow cliff ridge can we walk – and keep walking, for if we stand still, we will fall.'[10] Barth's iconoclastic creation of a failed dialectic captured the zeitgeist of living 'between the times', as the title of the journal Barth inspired denotes. In 1923, the same year in which the journal issued its first volume, the Frankfurt School of critical theory was founded. Two of its philosophers, Theodor Adorno and Max Horkheimer, took up Barth's 'negative dialectic' in their own work.

Barth, like the theologians of the Luther Renaissance, read Luther's *Lectures on Romans* (1515–16), which had been published in 1908. With his own commentary on Paul's Letter to the Romans – published in 1919, and more importantly the revised second edition in 1922[11] – Barth signalled a bold departure from any connection to Luther and the historical method characterising the Luther Renaissance. The new work's title, *Römerbrief*, evaded any historical attribution of authorship, even to its biblical author. As part of his approach to a theological exegesis, Barth situated himself in solidarity with the letter's author, the Apostle Paul, rather than regarding Paul's text as object of historical study. The theological positioning imbued the text with an existential function. The text staged a 'waiting for God' in a time of geopolitical crisis. Barth together with Paul took on this particular theological disposition that was appropriate given the theological determination of the biblical text's content, namely the divine revelation in Christ. Barth's theological hermeneutic thus consisted of interpreting the text for its witness to the Word of God and waiting for God's advent as something entirely dependent on the divine freedom to reveal the divine self in the Word. When revelation occurred, it was not the gospel of mercy in Christ, as Luther had insisted in 1515. Revelation in a time of crisis meant judgement on human sin. Yet Barth integrated both sides of the divine Word, judgement and grace, into the concept of revelation. Judgement was but the flip side of grace; the 'No' in the service of the 'Yes'.

The 'war to end all wars' was the beginning of the end of disastrous developments in Europe and around the globe. Between 1915 and 1922 two million Armenians were massacred by Turks, Stalin instigated the Great Purge between 1936 and 1939, with at least 700,000 executed. Fascism spread on the European continent, with Mussolini claiming total power over Italy in 1922 and Franco over Spain in 1939. In the midst of all this, the global economy collapsed in 1929. But no development would be as consequential for world history and European Jewry as the 1932 election in Germany of an Austrian house painter and former felon, Adolf Hitler. Hitler's rhetoric of German supremacy countered the deep humiliation at Versailles. Millions of Germans raised their right arms in the fascist salute as Hitler consolidated presidency and chancellorship in 1933 through a series of politically calculated thuggish moves. Totalitarianism was established as a regime of terror. Concentration camps were set up to torture and murder anyone considered a liability to the regime's Aryan laws imposed in 1934, including the disabled, queer and Jews, in addition to political resisters, communists, Roma and members of the Confessing Church. A second world war was inevitable.

In 1934 a group of Lutheran, Reformed and United theologians met in Barmen to craft a statement that decisively protested the takeover of the Protestant churches by the Nazis. The document, issued in May of that year, bore Barth's imprint both in terms of its genre and its content. The 'failed dialectic' structures the six articles. Each article begins with a citation from the Bible, then an affirmative proposition, followed by its negation. The first article sets the non-negotiable basis for the Barmen Declaration. It begins by citing three Johannine verses that insist on Jesus Christ as singular mediator of his Father.[12] The position affirms 'trust and obedience' 'in life and death' to 'Jesus Christ as he is attested for us in Holy Scripture'.[13] The source for this position is 'Holy Scripture', which in Barth's theology is the Word of God in one of its three forms – Bible, doctrine, proclamation. As such, it is a witness to the 'one Word of God', Jesus Christ. With this first article, Barth and his theological colleagues set the position in starkest contrast to its negation: any 'false doctrine' that is legitimated by an appeal to divine revelation occurring independently of and outside of this particular revelation of the Word of God in Jesus Christ.

The Barthian imprint is undeniable: Jesus Christ is the one divine Word, not the twofold word of law and gospel that the Lutherans, like Hans Asmussen, wanted to see reflected in Barmen. Of all six articles, only Article 5 gestures to the Lutheran collaboration. Lutheran theology of 'law' concedes the biblical point in 1 Peter 2:17, cited by Barmen, that the state is the divinely appointed institution by which the first use of the law is administered to secure peace and curb violence. Yet, while the Lutherans deployed this idea in the service of the 'two-kingdoms' doctrine, Barth rejected this move in the first negation (out of two) of Article 5: 'We reject the false doctrine, as though the State, over and beyond its special commission, should and could become the single and totalitarian order of human life, thus fulfilling the Church's vocation as well.' The single Lordship of Jesus Christ could not be divided into two words, law and gospel, whereby law is construed independently of the gospel and thus could serve as additional source of revelation. Furthermore, the Nazi dictatorship could not be legitimated with an appeal to divine appointment. Lutherans, like Paul Althaus and Werner Elert, were in support of the so-called 'Aryan paragraph' of 1933 civil service reforms which prohibited Christians of Jewish descent from occupying ecclesiastical offices. Another Lutheran theologian, Emanuel Hirsch, plotted to have his Göttingen colleague, Karl Barth, removed from his professorship for refusing to swear the oath of allegiance to the Führer that was imposed on civil servants, which included university professors and pastors, in 1934 and 1935.

While Barth posited divine transcendence to open up the conceptual space for the possibility of divine interruption, the Lutheran theologian Dietrich Bonhoeffer turned immanence into the site of resistance. His idea of Jesus as the 'man for others' was a lonely contribution to the dominant Lutheran theology that legitimated the Church's integration into the Nazi ideology. The two-kingdoms idea had been one way in which the Lutherans advocated for obedience to the state, as the ultimate authority over the state was God. Even a National Socialist dictatorship, according to this theory, was the way in which God ruled through one of the divine 'masks'. Bonhoeffer rejected the common law/gospel dialectic that underscored Lutheran theological subservience to the state. His theological rationality was based entirely on the living person of Jesus *pro me*, Christ as centre of human existence, history and nature, and as centre, radically immanent in the world.[14] The 'man for others' transformed subjectivity so that it would embody this new kind of personhood for others. Being a Christian meant not mere belief but rather the responsibility of acting faithfully in a fallen world. Bonhoeffer submitted his own person to the test of his theology. He realised his notion of Christian community by teaching in the prohibited seminaries of the Confessing Church. Together with military and intellectual elites from his Berlin circle, he was involved in the failed assassination of Hitler of 20 July 1944. For this political action, Bonhoeffer actualised his idea that when Christ calls, 'he bids you come and die'.

These two theologians represent different theological rationalities deployed for the purpose of resistance. But first they diagnosed the totalitarian regime of National Socialism as a system. The inheritance of systematic theological thinking enabled them to theologically grasp the political situation according to its systemic evil. The entire system was based on the evils of racism and anti-Semitism, designed to exterminate those who did not fit in, aimed at war and the subjugation of the conquered. Bonhoeffer learned about racism first-hand as an attendee of Abyssinian Baptist Church in Harlem while a student at Union Theological Seminary in New York from 1930 to 1931.[15] He returned to Germany and worked out an understanding of Christ's immanence in the system, immanently containing the mandate for ethical responsibility that ended on the cross. Yet even the cross represented the reality of resistance to the system that pronounced the death sentence. Barth too applied systematic reason to the political regime. The entire system was corrupted by human sin and evil. Judgement was issued from outside the system; the divine transcendence intersected the system as a vertical line from above and, as such, interrupted the system in judgement on the whole. For Bonhoeffer, divine immanence resisted co-option by the system to which it succumbed; for Barth, resistance gains its power from the divine interruption from outside the system.

These two models – one transcendent, the other immanent – represent two theological rationalities constructed for resisting National Socialism. These models became significant proposals for theological work after the Second World War. Barth based his multi-volume system of theology, the *Church Dogmatics*, on the transcendent positioning of the Trinity as epistemological key to the entire system. His commitment to the Trinity as organising principle of theology inspired Roman Catholic and Protestant theologians in the second half of the twentieth century to concentrate their historical, doctrinal, ethical studies on the Trinity. Bonhoeffer's writings became important to theologians struggling with the questions of how to live as a Christian when the system is post-Christian, secular or capitalist. Barth's system ended up resonating in particular with theologians in the Anglo-Saxon world who were interested in systematic construction. As a prisoner in Tegel, Bonhoeffer wrote prophetic words: 'we can be Christians today in only two ways, through prayer and in doing justice among human beings'.[16] His insistence on discipleship as resistance and communities dedicated to justice became important for theologians committed to political liberation, such as in the anti-apartheid movement in South Africa and in the contemporary global movements for justice for Black and brown people.

## System?

Crisis ruptured theology's ambitions for meta-narrative and logical system. A new theological rationality was created, characterised by a failed dialectic, the theological task in keeping rupture open for the possibility of the interruption of the Wholly Other, and the attributes of transcendence, wrath and justice. The only vehicle by which interruption occurred, while yet eluding any human control, was a divinity that retained freedom even in revelation. Such theological motifs led to the creation of new theological rationalities that would deeply impress themselves upon subsequent generations.

The historical method had long been deployed by biblical scholars and Church historians in order to connect sacred history to historical referents. Barth's *Römerbrief* broke this historiographical monopoly in academic biblical scholarship with its insistence on 'theological' exegesis. The biblical text was to be read according to its divine intention – as witness to the Word of God. Ernst Troeltsch had early on in the century advocated a historical method, rejecting metaphysical underpinnings to historical necessity and formulating his well-known three criteria for historical method:[17] criticism to highlight historical probability, analogy, correlation to document interrelatedness of events to antecedent and consequent happenings.[18] But between 1902 and 1923 he reconceptualised his historical understanding of Christianity. Rather than advocating for a contingent basis to a superior religion, Troeltsch applied his idea of historical relativism to Christianity itself. In 'The Place of Christianity among the World Religions', Troeltsch presupposes the new findings in the study of world religions that had transpired in order to explain that the value of absoluteness was contingent upon the culture in which that criterion was applied.[19] There could be no normative, objective standpoint from which all of world history could be evaluated. Historical study could only take place within particular perspectives, each perspective acknowledging its respective value-laden lens. Troeltsch internalised the collapse of a confident Europe's leadership in world-historical progress that had been so deeply intertwined with Christianity by exposing Christianity as merely one among other religions. From then on, the study of religion was freed from the nineteenth-century theological-philosophical hierarchies that had been mapped by Christian thinkers on to the historical progress of religion. The way was paved for one of the central questions occupying theologians in the second half of the twentieth century: namely, the theology of religious pluralism.

If the nineteenth-century meta-narrative was undone by historical relativism, then its systematic thinking was also open to intellectual undoing. Franz Rosenzweig's *Star of*

*Redemption* exemplifies the transition from Hegelian dialectic to what he calls 'new thinking', an exercise in deploying negative dialectic to work out an 'anti-system'.[20] Rosenzweig literally embodied the devastation of the First World War in the writing of *Star*. While stationed on the Balkan front in an anti-aircraft unit as a soldier for the German army, Rosenzweig jotted this work down on bits pieces of paper that he sent to his mother in Kassel. The architecture of *Star* on the surface concerns the 'All', a system interconnecting God, world and self. Yet the systematic deduction is betrayed by disparate avenues emphasising locality and finitude that afford access into the system. These disparate points inform the 'anti-system' in which theology and philosophy, Judaism and Christianity, are cross-cut with specific themes of revelation and finitude, creation and redemption. In fact, the motifs of fear and death subvert any attempt to interpret the system as an overarching apotheosis based on an Absolute's exit and return. In conversation with Eugen Rosenstock-Huessy and Hans Ehrenberg, Rosenzweig wove the theme of the dialogical construction of knowledge into his work. Language and dialogue are particular, even as they intend the universal. Love, as Stephanie Brenzel has pointed out in a recent study of *The Star of Redemption*, is what holds the system together, in the particularity of finite relationships and in the desire of system's unity.[21] Love, to allude to Plato's *Symposium*, is the only hope humans have in the midst of the nihilism of war.

Lutheran theologians after the war also took up an 'anti-system' rationality. In fact, they developed this perspective in order to underscore both a biblical hermeneutic and a theological world view that resisted any speculation into the divine eternity. Werner Elert was the Lutheran theologian whose iteration of the law/gospel dialectic inspired a generation of Lutheran theologians to structure their theological outlook by a binary. God's word of law spelt judgement on a sinful world, while God's word of gospel transformed evil into its opposite, beauty and goodness. This dialectic, originally conceived as a biblical hermeneutic in order to identify passages conveying Christ's forgiveness, was amplified into what David Yeago has analysed as an 'overarching worldview'.[22] The world exists according to the realm of law under the divine judgement, while the gospel interrupts the world in order to save. God's twofold word is mapped on to two realities: the fallen world and its divine interruption. When read back into the doctrine of God, divinity is also conceived according to this binary between law and gospel. A Lutheran doctrine of God conceived in this way cannot guarantee a metaphysical unity to God. When supplemented with the Lutheran motif of the hidden and revealed God (*deus absconditus* and *deus revelatus*), the resulting theology recapitulates Luther's unpredictable God above God who defies theological systematisation. Lutheran theology in the second half of the twentieth century is decisively anti-systematic, with a reliance on the word over metaphysics, *kerygma* over philosophy, and gospel without empirical concretion in the realm of the world of law. Of the last—a law that must humiliate before the gospel may do its work—Marit Trelstad says that it is abusive.[23]

# Language

The topography of the post-war world changed dramatically. The Allies divided Germany into four zones, with Berlin a divided city. The 'Iron Curtain' was spread across Eastern Europe from the Baltic states to Bulgaria and Albania. Colonial powers were expelled from Africa. The United States became a military world leader, with tendrils extending into Central and South America and battle fronts opened in Korea and eventually Vietnam. The Cold War between the capitalist West and the communist East saw the build-up of nuclear arms. Human self-annihilation and the destruction of the planet became a distinct historical possibility.

The 1960s was the decade in which protests and activism signalled the necessity for change. The Roman Catholic Church was one of the institutions that was challenged by the demands for change. In 1961 Pope John XXIII convened a council, called Vatican II, that charted an unprecedented direction for a Church that had resisted modern currents. The council took place from 1962 to 1965. Its aim was *aggiornamento* – coming to terms with the modern world with a spirit of openness. The groundwork for the council had been laid by the 'new theology' (*nouvelle théologie*) espoused by some French theologians who had adopted historical methods in their studies of Thomas Aquinas and the Bible. Other proponents of this theological movement, like the French Jesuit Henri de Lubac, recovered patristic sources and theology, particularly in biblical interpretation. Karl Rahner, a German Jesuit, constructed an innovative Catholic understanding of revelation by appealing to Martin Heidegger's notion of transcendental experience. These theologians were instrumental in canvassing support for the new articulations of doctrine and in writing up the conciliar documents that signalled change, in some cases, dramatic change. The Latin Mass was replaced by the vernacular; a new ecclesiological position emphasised the importance of the 'people of God'; an appreciation for intra-Christian and religious pluralism facilitated the promotion of ecumenical and interreligious dialogue. Theologians and the Catholic faithful spent the rest of the century and the start of the next wrestling with the question of the council's faithfulness to preceding tradition.

A Lutheran theologian and junior professor at Yale Divinity School, George Lindbeck, was invited, along with Edmund Schlink from the University of Heidelberg, to attend the Vatican II deliberations as Protestant observers. This invitation redirected Lindbeck to devote his theological work to ecumenism. The name 'evangelical catholics' identified an intra-Protestant movement that sought to repair, from the Protestant perspective, the mutual anathematisations with Rome that had transpired since the sixteenth century. This work aimed to actualise to some degree the third article of the Creed's proposition of faith in the 'one, holy, catholic, and apostolic Church'. Lindbeck contributed to this movement by envisaging a theological model of dialogue that bypassed the usual stalemate of doctrinal difference. His cultural-linguistic model, documented in *The Nature of Doctrine* from 1984, was used to frame the Lutheran–Catholic dialogues taking place in the second half of the twentieth century.[24] These dialogues culminated in the signing of the *Joint Declaration on the Doctrine of Justification* on 31 October 1999 in Augsburg, Germany. This was no coincidence – it was the traditional celebration of Luther's *Ninety-Five Theses* that in popular imagination signalled the break with Rome, and Augsburg, the site of the Augsburg Confession of 1530 in which Protestant Reformers presented their list of doctrinal beliefs to the Emperor Charles V. The *Joint Declaration* remains the only ecumenical statement signed by Rome, and one that the Methodists and Anglicans adopted in 2016, and with which Reformed churches 'associated' in 2017.

Work towards the *Joint Declaration* had been prepared by the 'Catholic Luther' which had been the object of historical enquiry on both sides of the Tiber. While the 'German Protestant Luther' had been propped up in the early part of the century by Church historians interested in relegating Catholics to a medieval past, historical theologians such as Heiko Oberman framed Luther's theological innovations as the end point of a medieval philosophical and theological trajectory. The implications of this new framing were significant for a revisionist historiography of continuity between the medieval and early modern periods, an appreciation for the role that philosophy has in Luther's own articulation of theological and doctrinal claims, and a takedown of the usual identity markers that had condemned Roman Catholicism to anti-scriptural works righteousness. Just as a theological rationality of historical reconstruction of Luther's religious experience had shaped the way in which Protestant theologians shifted from system to history as their method at the turn of the twentieth century, they now oriented their perspectives to a more ecumenically conceived theological method of comparison, which, while not producing compatibility, had decisive practical effects in the forms of shared worship, non-anxious 'mixed' marriages and common scholarship in Bible and theology.

Lindbeck's 'cultural-linguistic' theological model presupposed that religion functioned as a world view. Lindbeck derived this idea from his studies of both Ludwig Wittgenstein's philosophy of language and Clifford Geertz's cultural anthropology. While religion functioned as a culture, the 'linguistic' dimension recovered Luther's insight about the 'new language' of the Holy Spirit. In the first instance, a religious culture involved the learning of and practice in the discourse constituting the culture itself. Lindbeck recapitulated Luther's understanding of the Holy Spirit as providing Christians with a new grammar. Lindbeck then identified doctrine along the analogical lines of grammatical rules in language. Doctrine funds different kinds of Christian discourse: worship, education, preaching, hymns etc. The theologian's task is to identify the doctrinal rules operating in distinctive religious language games. To use an ecumenical example: Roman Catholics see the doctrine of justification as one among different doctrines, while Lutherans isolate justification as the chief doctrine regulating, as it were, the whole of Christian discourse and practice.

Lindbeck's model proved attractive to some theological constituencies interested in deepening Barth's commitment to theological exegesis of the Bible. Theologians favouring this model insisted on retrieving pre-critical hermeneutical methods because they had been developed to secure the Bible's subject matter in doctrinal articulation. The Bible and early Church doctrines are inseparable according to this approach. Doctrine has its origins in the *regula fidei* (rule of faith) that guided the earliest interpretations of the Bible. In historical Church debates, theologians and Church leaders explicated this rule in various doctrines that identified the object of Christian faith. The connection between Bible, doctrine and pre-critical hermeneutics is meant to counteract a modern historical-critical interpretation of Scripture that supposedly opens the scriptural material to be verified by historical criteria, thereby detracting from its true doctrinal meaning. This synthesis also privileges linguistic articulations of the *regula fidei*. The actual content of what is retrieved is understood to be articulated in the creeds of the early Church. Retrieval thus means recovering the *regula fidei* in these specific linguistic formulations as the original deposit of revealed truth.

Retrieval also means showing how this original deposit is faithfully represented in subsequent Christian generations. History is the milieu in which retrieval occurs. Yet history must be constructed in order to guarantee that the original deposit has been faithfully rendered for the purpose of retrieval. Like medieval scribes who faithfully copied biblical manuscripts, contemporary theologians working broadly according to Lindbeck's model must determine which protagonists have documented the deposit correctly. The early and medieval Church is privileged for such faithfulness. Augustine, Anselm and Aquinas are preferred over figures like Luther and Schleiermacher. From the modern period only Karl Barth and Hans Urs von Balthasar are welcomed; Bultmann and Rahner, less clearly so. The 'Great Tradition', as it is usually capitalised, is a reconstruction of a timeline on which particular male *doctores ecclesiae* are situated. These theologians and their doctrines have become the subject of numerous handbooks in theology and doctoral dissertations.

The theological rationality deployed by proponents of this model purports to be invested in doctrine and the 'Great Tradition'. Yet the very aim of retrieval itself demonstrates that the method is indebted more to postmodern construction than to historical reconstruction. The theologians of the 'Great Tradition' are selected according to the criterion of their faithfulness to normative doctrine; their inclusion and placement along a chronology of doctrinal succession conveys the impression that the Holy Spirit is working exclusively in this direction of reception and also in precisely those contemporary theologians who have inherited this tradition and are preserving it for the next generation. The resulting position is both anti-realist and coherentist. I have recently renamed this the 'epistemic advantage model of theology' to highlight its distinctive Christ–culture divide.[25] Access to the 'Christ' side of the divide is guaranteed by the converting agency of the Holy Spirit. Once converted, the 'Christ' side demands antipathy to what is deemed to be 'cultural', namely, features of culture that allegedly threaten the biblical and doctrinal premises set up. A recent example in the United States concerns whether critical race theory is a feature of culture that is antithetical to the gospel, and thereby to be rejected, or whether the struggle for racial equality is actually mandated by the gospel. Political power is very much bound up with this kind of theological positioning along an antithetical Christ–culture axis.

## Experience

The 'epistemic advantage model of theology' gave systematic theological thinking a boost at a time in which the endeavour of systematic theology was being called into question by another group of theologians. These theologians, beginning with Roman Catholic priests and nuns in South America, identified liberative praxis, not the systematic elaboration of doctrine, as *the* theological task. Pursuit of economic justice, civil rights, women's rights, and not the business of the retrieval and reception of doctrine, characterised the work of such liberation theologians. Their participation in struggling communities and their work to resist dominant forces of oppression gave rise to theologies that were local and contextual, and oriented to the gospel's transformative power in the concrete political world.

Some Latin American countries in the 1970s and 1980s were the original sites of liberation theology. Various military and paramilitary groups were fighting for control of El Salvador in the 1980s. Economic volatility and insurgents threatened Peru's stability. Guerilla warriors on the political right, aided by the Americans, and fighters on the left perpetrated violence in Colombia through the early 1990s. Brazil's military rule exacerbated extremes in income equality, and Honduras continues to suffer from high rates of murder and sexual violence. Some theologians in these predominantly Roman Catholic countries saw the plight of these peoples and chose to protest the Church's collusion with government powers that had left millions in poverty and victims of ongoing violence. These theologians took seriously the motto that God had a 'preferential option for the poor'. Gustavo Gutiérrez, a Peruvian theologian and Roman Catholic priest, took up this identification of God in solidarity with the marginalised and defenceless. In 1971, he published the book A *Theology of Liberation* that gave the name 'liberation theology' to the movement.[26] Liberation theologians, priests and nuns chose to live together with the poor in their communities and work with them to promote economic and social justice. They developed a new method for doing theology, one that would begin with praxis, the practice of working for justice together with the victims of inequality and violence. Such praxis would drive theological reflection, ensuring that theology would be written by those living and working in the real world for the sake of transforming that same real world.

Those who spoke out against injustices quickly made enemies; those who challenged the victimisation of the powerful were threatened and killed. Óscar Romero, Archbishop of San Salvador, was gunned down in 1980 as he celebrated Mass at his church in El Salvador. Later that year, four American Catholic church women were raped and killed by the El Salvador National Guard. Like civil rights activists in the US, leaders of resistance in Latin America were attacked by those whose interests preserved the status quo.

An attack also came from within the Church itself. In 1984, Joseph Cardinal Ratzinger, who later became Pope Benedict XVI, issued a formal 'warning' to liberation theologians. Ratzinger launched his criticism from his office as Head for the Doctrine of the Congregation of the Faith, the department in the Vatican responsible for maintaining theological orthodoxy in the Church. His statement thus carried the weight of Catholic authority that demanded obeisance. Ratzinger took issue with what he saw to be the theoretical basis for liberation theology. He thought that liberation theology conceived 'liberation' in the terms of the class struggle that Marxism advocated. Marxism, Ratzinger chided, was an atheist philosophy and thereby opposed to the truth of the Christian gospel. By using an atheistic philosophy, liberation theologians furthermore conflated the gospel message of liberation from sin and the historical liberation from economic injustice. Ratzinger explained that true doctrine requires a clear distinction between human work and divine work, between the human effort to create social and political justice in the world and the divine effort to justify the sinner through the Church's sacraments. World and Church, liberation and salvation, history and eternity – these were opposites that theologians needed to keep distinct from each other. Their work was to illuminate salvation, not to confuse it with politics.

A dividing line was thus drawn between two kinds of theologians. On the one side, liberation theologians sought to reflect theologically on their solidarity with the poor and their work to embody God's justice in community with them. On the other hand, theologians representing the Church's teaching authority sought to identify doctrinal orthodoxy by making and sustaining theological distinctions. From their vantage point, liberation theologians exposed the Church's alliance with the political and economic oppression of society's vulnerable. From his vantage point, Cardinal Ratzinger identified the doctrinal truth that God is the only one who saves. While the liberation theologians discerned God to be working justice in the world while also justifying the sinner, the representatives of orthodoxy clearly distinguished between God's prerogative of mediating grace in the Church and the political work of liberating the poor from interests of the rich. Theology was the prerogative of the ecclesial elite, not produced on the stinking garbage heap of poverty.

Two kinds of theological rationalities characterise contemporary Christian theology. On the one hand, the epistemic advantage model is allied with the orthodox tradition that it faithfully receives and hands to the next generation. On the basis of its own theoretical assumptions regarding religion as a world view, this model establishes a strong Christ–culture dichotomy. Culture, or world, is perceived as an enemy admixture which is to be resisted. Hence, proponents of this rationality can often polemicise against Marxism, the confusion of justification with justice, or critical race theory as alien to the gospel truth.

On the other hand, a contextual theology draws its concepts from local experiences, particularly from practices of working for justice. These local theologies do not aspire to systematicity. For contextual rationalities, the type of theological thinking that assumes

comprehensiveness can be attained is in fact merely substituting the local for the universal. The danger of the false universal is its alliance with power. Contextual theologies
also do not prohibit borrowing methods from the social sciences in order to give richer
descriptions of systemic sin in sociological terms.[27] In fact, critical theory and ethnography
are significant to its methodology and understanding of God as a liberative force who is in
solidarity with the suffering and frees them from oppression.

## Conclusion

The story of theology in the twentieth century is one of trauma and judgement, system and
interruption, dialectic and resistance. Theological reflection in this century has come to a
greater recognition that theological reason is embedded in the conditions of the modern
world, struggling to accommodate new developments, reacting to them, while also contributing to the production of modernity. Theological rationality is part of the culture of
knowledge deployed in institutions dedicated to learning and education; it is intertwined
with the social, cultural and political movements of the modern world. Theology bears
witness to the signs of the times – sometimes in prophetic resistance to the world as it is,
sometimes according to the vision of the world as it ought to be.

## Notes

1. Ernst Troeltsch, *Protestantism and Progress: A Historical Study of the Relation of Protestantism to
   the Modern World*, W. Montgomery (trans.) (reprint, Eugene, OR: Wipf and Stock, 1999). The
   original German title from 1906 is translated literally as 'The Significance of the Reformation
   for the Rise of the Modern World'.
2. See Suzanne Marchand's excellent work, *German Orientalism in the Age of Empire: Religion,
   Race, and Scholarship* (Cambridge: Cambridge University Press, 2010).
3. For detailed argument, see ch. 2 of Christine Helmer, *Theology and the End of Doctrine* (Louisville,
   KY: Westminster John Knox Press, 2014). See Albrecht Ritschl, *The Christian Doctrine of
   Justification and Reconciliation*, vol. 3, *The Positive Development of the Doctrine*, H. R. Mackintosh
   and A. B. Macauley (ed. and trans.) (Edinburgh: T&T Clark, 1900).
4. For an excellent anthology, see Christophe Chalamet (ed.), *The Challenge of History: Readings
   in Modern Theology* (Minneapolis: Fortress, 2020).
5. Emil Brunner, *Die Mystik und das Wort*, 2nd ed. (Tübingen: J. C. B. Mohr [Paul Siebeck], 1928).
6. Max Weber, *Das antike Judentum*; published in English as: *Ancient Judaism*, Hans H. Gerth
   and Don Martindale (trans.) (New York: Free Press, 1952). This work was first published in
   1917–19 in the *Archiv für Sozialwissenschaft*.
7. Max Weber, *The Protestant Ethic and the Spirit of Capitalism*, 3rd Oxford ed./expanded 1920 version, Stephen Kalberg (intro. and trans.) (New York/Oxford: Oxford University Press, 2002).
8. Karl Holl, *What Did Luther Understand by Religion?*, James Luther Adams and Walter F. Bense
   (ed.), Fred W. Meuser and Walter R. Wietzke (trans.) (Philadelphia, PA: Fortress, 1977).
9. It is important to note that the original German title, *Das Heilige: Über das Irrationale in der
   Idee des Göttlichen und sein Verhältnis zum Rationalen*, is mistranslated in the English as *The Idea
   of the Holy: An Inquiry into the Non-rational Factor in the Idea of the Divine and its Relation to the
   Rational*. I would translate Otto's title as 'The Holy: On the Irrational in the Idea of Divinity
   and Its Relation to the Rational'.
10. Karl Barth, 'The Word of God as the Task of Theology' (1922), in *The Word of God and
    Theology*, Amy Marga (trans.) (London/New York: T&T Clark, 2011), pp. 171–98: 191.
11. Karl Barth, *The Epistle to the Romans*, Edwyn C. Hoskyns (trans.) (Oxford: Oxford University
    Press, 1968).

12. 'I am the way, and the truth, and the life; no one comes to the Father, but by me' (John 14:6). 'Truly, truly, I say to you, he who does not enter the sheepfold by the door, but climbs in by another way, that man is a thief and a robber . . . I am the door; if anyone enters by me, he will be saved' (John 10:1, 9). Confessional Synod of the German Evangelical Church, 'Theological Declaration of Barmen' (Barmen, 1934), accessed at https://sacred-texts.com/chr/barmen.htm.

13. 'Theological Declaration of Barmen'.

14. Cf. Dietrich Bonhoeffer, 'Lectures on Christology', in *Berlin: 1932–1933*, Larry L. Rasmussen (ed.), Isabel Best and David Higgins (trans.), Dietrich Bonhoeffer Works 12 (Minneapolis, MN: Augsburg Fortress, 2009), pp. 324–7.

15. See Reggie L. Williams, *Bonhoeffer's Black Jesus: Harlem Renaissance Theology and an Ethic of Resistance* (Waco, TX: Baylor University Press, 2014).

16. Dietrich Bonhoeffer, *Letters and Papers from Prison*, John W. de Gruchy (ed.), Isabel Best, Lisa E. Dahill, Reinhard Krauss and Nancy Lukens (trans.), Dietrich Bonhoeffer Works 8 (Minneapolis: Augsburg Fortress, 2009), p. 389.

17. On Troeltsch, see Christopher Adair-Toteff, *The Anthem Companion to Ernst Troeltsch*, Anthem Companions to Sociology (London: Anthem Press, 2017).

18. Ernst Troeltsch, 'On the Historical and Dogmatic Methods in Theology', Jack Forstman (trans.), *Gesammelte Schriften*, vol. 2 (Tubingen: J. C. B. Mohr [Paul Siebeck], [1898] 1913), pp. 728–53.

19. Ernst Troeltsch, 'The Place of Christianity among the World Religions', in *Christian Thought: Its History and Application*, Friedrich von Hügel (ed.) (London: University of London Press, 1923).

20. Franz Rosenzweig, *The Star of Redemption*, Barbara E. Galli (trans.), Modern Jewish Philosophy and Religion: Translations and Critical Studies (Madison, WI: University of Wisconsin Press, 2005).

21. Stephanie Brenzel, 'As Strong as Death: Franz Rosenzweig's Philosophy of Love in "The Star of Redemption"' (PhD Dissertation, Northwestern University, Evanston, IL, 2019).

22. David S. Yeago, 'Gnosticism, Antinomianism, and Reformation Theology: Reflections on the Costs of a Construal', *Pro Ecclesia* 2:1 (1993), 37–49.

23. Marit Trelstad, 'C̶h̶a̶r̶i̶t̶y̶ Terror Begins at Home: Luther and the "Terrifying and Killing" Law', in *Lutherrenaissance: Past and Present*, edited by Christine Helmer and Bo Kristian Holm, Forschungen zur Kirchen- und Dogmengeschichte 106 (Göttingen: Vandenhoeck & Ruprecht, 2015), pp. 209–23.

24. George A. Lindbeck, *The Nature of Doctrine: Religion and Theology in a Postliberal Age* (Philadelphia, PA: Westminster Press, 1984).

25. Helmer, *Theology and the End of Doctrine*.

26. Gustavo Gutiérrez, *A Theology of Liberation*, Sister Caridad Inda (trans.) and John Eagleson (ed.) (Maryknoll, NY: Orbis, 1973).

27. See Lilian Calles Barger, *The World Come of Age: An Intellectual History of Liberation Theology* (Oxford: Oxford University Press, 2018).

# Bibliography

Adair-Toteff, Christopher, *The Anthem Companion to Ernst Troeltsch*, Anthem Companions to Sociology (London: Anthem Press, 2017).

Barger, Lilian Calles, *The World Come of Age: An Intellectual History of Liberation Theology* (Oxford: Oxford University Press, 2018).

Barth, Karl, *The Epistle to the Romans*, Edwyn C. Hoskyns (trans.) (Oxford: Oxford University Press, 1968).

Barth, Karl, 'The Word of God as the Task of Theology (1922)', in *The Word of God and Theology*, Amy Marga (trans.) (London/New York: T&T Clark, 2011), pp. 171–98.

Bonhoeffer, Dietrich, 'Lectures on Christology', in *Berlin: 1932–1933*, Larry L. Rasmussen (ed.),

Isabel Best and David Higgins (trans.), Dietrich Bonhoeffer Works 12 (Minneapolis, MN: Augsburg Fortress, 2009), pp. 324–7.

Bonhoeffer, Dietrich, *Letters and Papers from Prison*, John W. de Gruchy (ed.), Isabel Best, Lisa E. Dahill, Reinhard Krauss and Nancy Lukens (trans.), Dietrich Bonhoeffer Works 8 (Minneapolis, MN: Augsburg Fortress, 2009).

Brenzel, Stephanie, 'As Strong as Death: Franz Rosenzweig's Philosophy of Love in "The Star of Redemption"' (PhD Dissertation, Northwestern University, Evanston, IL, 2019).

Brunner, Emil, *Die Mystik und das Wort*, 2nd ed. (Tübingen: J. C. B. Mohr [Paul Siebeck], 1928).

Chalamet, Christophe (ed.), *The Challenge of History: Readings in Modern Theology* (Minneapolis, MN: Fortress, 2020).

Confessional Synod of the German Evangelical Church, 'Theological Declaration of Barmen' (Barmen, 1934), accessed at https://sacred-texts.com/chr/barmen.htm.

Gutiérrez, Gustavo, *A Theology of Liberation*, Sister Caridad Inda and John Eagleson (trans.) (Maryknoll, NY: Orbis, 1973).

Helmer, Christine, *Theology and the End of Doctrine* (Louisville, KY: Westminster John Knox Press, 2014).

Holl, Karl, *What Did Luther Understand by Religion?*, James Luther Adams and Walter F. Bense (eds), Fred W. Meuser and Walter R. Wietzke (trans.) (Philadelphia, PA: Fortress, 1977).

Lindbeck, George A., *The Nature of Doctrine: Religion and Theology in a Postliberal Age* (Philadelphia: Westminster Press, 1984).

Marchand, Suzanne, *German Orientalism in the Age of Empire: Religion, Race, and Scholarship* (Cambridge: Cambridge University Press, 2010).

Otto, Rudolf, *Das Heilige: Über das Irrationale in der Idee des Göttlichen und sein Verhältnis zum Rationalen*; published in English as *The Idea of the Holy: An Inquiry into the Non-rational Factor in the Idea of the Divine and Its Relation to the Rational*, John W. Harvey (trans.) (Oxford: Oxford University Press, 1958 [1923]).

Ritschl, Albrecht, *The Christian Doctrine of Justification and Reconciliation*, vol. 3, *The Positive Development of the Doctrine*, H. R. Mackintosh and A. B. Macauley (ed. and trans.) (Edinburgh: T&T Clark, 1900).

Rosenzweig, Franz, *The Star of Redemption*, Barbara E. Galli (trans.), Modern Jewish Philosophy and Religion: Translations and Critical Studies (Madison, WI: University of Wisconsin Press, 2005).

Trelstad, Marit, ~~Charity~~ Terror Begins at Home: Luther and the "Terrifying and Killing" Law', in *Lutherrenaissance: Past and Present*, edited by Christine Helmer and Bo Kristian Holm, Forschungen zur Kirchen- und Dogmengeschichte 106 (Göttingen: Vandenhoeck & Ruprecht, 2015), pp. 209–23.

Troeltsch, Ernst, 'On the Historical and Dogmatic Methods in Theology', Jack Forstman (trans.), *Gesammelte Schriften*, vol. 2 (Tubingen: J. C. B. Mohr [Paul Siebeck], [1898] 1913), pp. 728–53.

Troeltsch, Ernst, 'The Place of Christianity among the World Religions', in *Christian Thought: Its History and Application*, Friedrich von Hügel (ed.) (London: University of London Press, 1923).

Troeltsch, Ernst, *Protestantism and Progress: A Historical Study of the Relation of Protestantism to the Modern World*, W. Montgomery (trans.) (reprint, Eugene, OR: Wipf and Stock, 1999).

Weber, Max, *Das antike Judentum*; published in English as *Ancient Judaism*, Hans H. Gerth and Don Martindale (trans.) (New York: Free Press, [1917–19] 1952).

Weber, Max, *The Protestant Ethic and the Spirit of Capitalism*, 3rd Oxford ed./expanded 1920 version, Stephen Kalberg (intro. and trans.) (New York/Oxford: Oxford University Press, 2002).

Williams, Reggie L., *Bonhoeffer's Black Jesus: Harlem Renaissance Theology and an Ethic of Resistance* (Waco: Baylor University Press, 2014).

Yeago, David S., 'Gnosticism, Antinomianism, and Reformation Theology: Reflections on the Costs of a Construal', *Pro Ecclesia* 2:1 (1993), 37–49.

# 5

# Catholicism and Ecumenism

*Tracey Rowland*

To do justice to the history of Catholic ecumenism in a single essay is a daunting task. There are so many intertwining threads worthy of attention. Many of these revolve around friendships between Christians from different traditions. The stand-out examples are the pairs: Halifax and Portal, Halifax and Mercier, Barth and Balthasar, Hanselmann and Ratzinger, but there are numerous others stretching back into the nineteenth century, including the relationship between two of the most famous Victorians to convert to Catholicism, Ambrose Phillips de Lisle (1808–78) and George (Fr Ignatius) Spencer (1799–1864). If intellectual friendship was the most significant mode of ecumenical engagement, the most significant developments were the intellectual convergences on three fronts. First, Catholic scholars in the neo-patristic or *ressourcement* movement concluded that the causes of the Reformation lay in late Catholic scholasticism, and thus, in order to heal the schisms of the sixteenth century, it was necessary to revisit the late medieval debates, and to acknowledge the mistakes of that time. Second, there arose neo-patristic movements in both Catholicism and Eastern Orthodoxy with shared interests in Trinitarian anthropology and *communio* ecclesiology. Thirdly, Protestant theology took a decidedly anti-liberal turn after the First World War with the result that scholars from Catholic, Protestant and Orthodox traditions began to agree about the need for theology in all of its dimensions to be Trinitarian, Christocentric and biblical. Each of these three developments had an impact upon the drafting of documents at the Second Vatican Council (1961–5) and upon the ecumenical policies of the post-conciliar papacies, especially the papacy of Benedict XVI.

At the turn of the twentieth century the reigning pontiff was Leo XIII. He had a special interest in relations with the churches of Eastern orthodoxy and with the Catholic Uniate churches. In 1894 he produced two encyclicals on these topics. The first, *Praeclara gratulationis publicae* ('On the Reunion of Christendom') was primarily addressed to the representatives of Eastern Orthodoxy. This encyclical was criticised for its tone, perceived by some as patronising, but it did at least offer 'an invitation to peace and reconciliation'. In Pope Leo's assessment, the papacy, not the understanding of the processions within the Trinity, was the major issue dividing the Eastern and Western branches of Christianity. He therefore exhorted those in the East to recognise the primacy of the Petrine office. He did not, however, suggest how the office might be exercised so as not to offend Orthodox sensibilities. In the second of the 1894 encyclicals – *Orientalium dignitas* – Pope Leo argued against the Latinisation of the Uniate churches, implicitly affirming the principle that providing there is unity on matters of doctrine, linguistic and other cultural differences are not a barrier to full communion. These two encyclicals were followed by *Provida Matris*, in which Pope Leo called for prayers 'to hasten the work of reconciliation with our separated brethren'. In 1896 a further encyclical – *Satis cognitum* – offered a theological reflection on church unity and appealed to non-Catholics for reunion with the See of Rome.

The Leonine era can be seen to mark the modern beginnings of a papal plea for a 'spiritual ecumenism', an expression coined by l'Abbé Paul Couturier from Lyon (1881–1953). Spiritual ecumenism is a 'priority of prayer' approach to Christian unity. Couturier worked with Russian refugees in France following the Bolshevik revolution of 1917. During this time around one million Russians were forced into exile, including many leading intellectuals. Paris became a centre of Russian Orthodox life, and opportunities arose for friendships to develop between Russian and French theologians. The Institut de théologie orthodoxe Saint-Serge, established in Paris in 1925, became a hub for the development of such friendships. It was here that Yves Congar OP (1904–95), who was arguably the greatest Catholic ecumenist of the twentieth century, met Nicolas Berdyaev (1874–1948) and Fr Sergius Bulgakov (1871–1944), among others. In a work of tribute to W. A. Visser't Hooft of the World Council of Churches, Congar wrote: 'I know how much my understanding and love of the Orthodox Church owe to personal friendships . . . For all of us, the Orthodox celebration of the liturgy has opened the door to a certain understanding of the scriptural texts, and to that world of tradition and saintliness of which the Orthodox Church is the hallowed sanctuary.'[1] In a later work entitled *Dialogue between Christians: Catholic Contributions to Ecumenism*, Congar described the interpenetrating Saint-Serge and Institut Catholique de Paris circles in greater detail:

> Nicolas Berdyaev was its outstanding personality, together with Jacques Maritain, who without doubt owes his awakening to an historical understanding of things and his sense of historical typology to his contact with Berdyaev. Emmanuel Mounier, who was associated with the launching of *Esprit*, also frequented this circle where I also made the acquaintance of Père Lev Gillet and other Orthodox friends. For some time the Abbé Pierre Baron had been talking to me about Khomiakov on whom he wished to write a thesis and he took me to a course of lectures which the Abbé A. Gratieux was delivering on Khomiakov and the Slavophil movement at the Institut Catholique. The Abbé welcomed me with the lively and unreserved sympathy from which I was to benefit still more later on when we met again, either at his home at Châlons-su-Marne or that of a wonderful mutual friend at Vitry-le-François. The Abbé Gratieux was not only my first Russian teacher but also 'the last of the slavophiles', as his nephews maliciously dubbed him. Since he had known the son of Alexis Stepanovich Khomiakov personally and had had numerous conversations with him, he constituted a link in the living tradition of slavophile thought.[2]

During the same period (the 1920s and 30s) the experience of the First World War (1914–18) had the effect of highlighting the importance of a united Christendom. It is a poignant fact that both Pope Benedict XV, whose reign fell across that of the war (1914–22), and Emperor (now Blessed) Karl of Austria-Hungary, tried to intervene to stop the carnage, but both men were beaten down by politicians and Masonic intrigues to destroy the Catholic House of Hapsburg and its empire.[3] The only 'peace' before 1918 occurred on Christmas Eve 1914 when the combatants spontaneously exchanged gifts and attended religious services together. The Christmas truce events of 1914 demonstrated that a common belief in the Incarnation could transcend nationalism. Similarly, in the post-Second World War period, the common experience of neo-pagan fascism had the effect of drawing Christians of all denominations together in the awareness that their own internal differences were nothing compared to the difference between Christians of all denominations on the one side, and fascists and also communists on the other.

The First World War also had quite a dramatic effect upon Protestant theology. In his work on the life of Max Josef Metzger (1887–1944), a German priest who served as an army chaplain during the First World War and who later became the founder of the Una Sancta ecumenical movement in 1938 before his execution by Nazis in 1944, Leonard Swidler described the effect of the 1914–18 war on Protestant theology in the following terms:

> Protestant theology underwent a radical change at the time of the First World War. During the nineteenth century the strongest school in Protestant theology was 'liberal theology', in which the Scriptures were treated as just another set of human documents, and the Christian religion was analyzed as merely the latest and highest evolutionary expression of humanity's religious drive. But in the pessimism following the First World War Protestant theologians turned away from its former presuppositions and methods, and, particularly under the leadership of Karl Barth, again saw the Bible primarily as the word of God spoken to humanity. Theology became much more God-centered than humanity-centered; the various critical methods were made strictly ancillary to the search for God's message to humanity.[4]

Swidler went on to note that such changes made Protestant theology 'a more apt partner for a dialogue with Catholic theology, which had been a stubborn opponent of the "liberal theology"'.[5]

Towards the end of the First World War, in 1917, Pope Benedict XV established a Congregation for the Oriental Churches and a Pontifical Oriental Institute, and in 1920 he declared St Ephrem, the Syrian monk, to be a Doctor of the Church. These initiatives were followed by Pope Pius XI in 1924, who encouraged the Benedictines to work for the reunion of the Catholic and Eastern Churches. As a consequence, in 1925 Dom Lambert Beauduin (1873–1960) established a community of monks dedicated to Christian unity. Initially the community lived at Amay-sur-Meuse in the diocese of Liège, but in 1939 the community moved to Chevetogne in the diocese of Namur. Dom Beauduin also launched the ecumenical journal *Irénikon*. In 1927 Pius XI then supported the Dominican establishment of the Istina Centre (now Institute) for ecumenical studies in Paris, which flourished under the leadership of Fr Christophe-Jean Dumont (1898–1991) OP, who was renowned as a relationship-builder among leaders of different ecclesial communities. Having thus mobilised the Benedictine and Dominican orders in the cause of ecumenism, in 1929 Pius XI founded the Pontifical Collegium Russicum for studies in Russian culture and spirituality in Rome. In 1935 Maria Sagheddu (1914–39) joined the Trappist monastery at Grottaferrata and offered her life as a spiritual sacrifice for Christian unity. She was beatified by John Paul II in 1983 and is venerated within the Catholic Church as the patron saint of ecumenism.

Returning to the intellectual convergences, the decade of the 1930s saw the rise of the *ressourcement* (back to the patristic sources) movement in France. This movement challenged the hegemony of neo-scholasticism, especially the 'baroque' appropriations of Thomism, and the narrowly juridical accounts of ecclesiology that were ascendant in the Counter-Reformation era. One of the leaders of the movement, Henri de Lubac SJ (1896–1991), had been wounded during the First World War, and because of his ongoing health

problems he was excused from attending lectures and advised to read his way through the
works of the Church Fathers at his own pace. As a consequence, unlike so many others of
his generation, he approached the publications of St Thomas Aquinas from the perspective of the patristics, not through the lens of the sixteenth-century commentators who
were reacting, sometimes in an extreme way, to Protestant claims and sensibilities. At the
same time Etienne Gilson (1884–1978), a philosopher and historian of medieval thought
and academic supervisor of the Russian Orthodox theologian Vladimir Lossky (1903–58),
was drawing attention to themes in late medieval scholasticism central to the backstory of
the rise of Protestantism. Gilson concurred with de Lubac's assessment that baroque scholasticism represented a break with classical Thomism and that it was part of the problem
of 'modernism', not a solution to it.

Hans Boersma, a contemporary theologian from the Reformed tradition, has used the
metaphor of a 'frayed tapestry' to describe what happened to Western Christianity from
the late medieval period forward.[6] In agreement with the *ressourcement* scholars, he traces
the traumas of the Reformation and the rise of secularism to various wrong moves made
in Catholic intellectual life in the late medieval period. In the following passage he summarises and affirms the *ressourcement* or *nouvelle théologie* contributions to the genealogy of
Protestantism and secularism:

> According to *nouvelle théologie*, the desacramentalizing of Western society had resulted
> from a number of factors: (1) the juridicizing of ecclesial authority through the 11th
> century Gregorian Reform (Congar); (2) the increasing opposition between Scripture
> and Church as distinct authorities between 1100 and 1300 (Congar); (3) the loss of
> the sacramental unity between the Eucharistic and ecclesial bodies of Christ through
> the 12th century Berengarian controversy (de Lubac); (4) the 'discovery of nature' in
> the 12th century and the growing autonomy of the natural realm among the mendicant
> orders in the 13th century (Chenu); and (5) the separation of nature and the supernat-
> ural in the sixteenth- and seventeenth-century reactions to Baianism and Protestantism
> (de Lubac).[7]

Boersma also noted that *ressourcement* or *nouvelle théologie* or what are now more commonly called *Communio*-style Catholic scholars share with Protestants an interest in the
theology of the laity, an interest in biblical theology, a common rejection of the idea that
Scripture and tradition offer two completely separate sources of authority and a common
opposition to neo-scholastic constructions of the nature and grace relationship. In coming
to an awareness of the problems inherent in both late medieval and baroque theology,
the *ressourcement* theologians, some of whom who were later to found the *Communio:
International Catholic Review* in 1972, found themselves in a very empathetic position vis-
à-vis Protestant theologians of non-liberal varieties.

Following the above inventory, Boersma concludes that 'the tragic split of the
Reformation was the result of theological developments that had been in the making for
centuries', and thus to undo the damage the intellectual tapestry needs to be rewoven.[8] In
particular, he recommends an approach to biblical hermeneutics that is spiritual, the continued reintegration of Scripture and tradition, the continued development of *communio*
ecclesiology and, most fundamentally of all, a reappropriation of a sacramental ontology.[9]
All of these projects have been fostered in *ressourcement/communio* theology circles since
at least the early 1960s. For example, Henri de Lubac and Joseph Ratzinger have been
champions of spiritual biblical hermeneutics, the reintegration of Scripture and tradition

was affirmed in the Vatican II document *Dei verbum* upon which Ratzinger, de Lubac and also Karl Rahner (1904–84), among other lesser names, had worked, *communio* ecclesiology was developed by Hans Urs von Balthasar (1905–88) and taken up by John Paul II and Ratzinger/Benedict, and sacramental ontology has been a recurring theme in the publications of Angelo Scola, Marc Ouellet, David L. Schindler and Nicholas J. Healy Jr.

Some *ressourcement* scholars were also influenced by the Protestant treatment of salvation history. Here the prime example is Oscar Cullmann's (1902–99) influence on Jean Daniélou (1905–74). In 1960 Daniélou wrote that 'if Protestantism [once] went further in the direction of the laicization of Christianity, it is now leading the way towards the renewal of its eschatological significance'.[10] Daniélou favourably compared Karl Barth (1886–1968) to Dom Odo Casel (1886–1948), seeing in both a common reaction against a 'rationalism that is unmindful of the mystery of God' and which 'seeks to penetrate the divine darkness by stealth'. In a broadside against liberal-correlationist theologies, Daniélou concluded:

> We have seen the collapse of all the systems that claim that they are maintaining Christian values while cutting them off from their doctrinal and sacramental roots, or that try to conserve the fragrance of Christianity without keeping its substance. We know the impotence of moralism, even if it be evangelical, in the face of the amoralism of Nietzsche, if the brotherhood that is preached is not based upon the dogmatic reality of the divine sonship and the union of Christians within the mystical Body of Christ.[11]

Such statements were music to evangelical Protestant ears and represent the mid-twentieth-century convergence of agreement among Catholic scholars and non-liberal Protestant scholars about the need for theology, including moral theology, to be both biblical and Christocentric. Douglas Farrow has drawn attention to this element of the Catholic–Protestant *rapprochement* with his observation that a Christocentric moral theology unites Martin Luther not only with Sts Paul and Augustine but also with Karl Barth and John Paul II. Or, to put this another way, John Paul II, Barth and Martin Luther all agree with Sts Paul and Augustine that moral theology needs to be related to Christ. While Catholics were often accused by Protestants of basing their moral theology on Greek philosophy, the Second Vatican Council affirmed the project of setting moral theology on strong Christocentric foundations. This call was taken up by John Paul II in his encyclical *Veritatis splendor* (1993) and in the works of moral theologians such as Servais Pinckaers OP (1925–2008) and Livio Melina. Farrow also observes that what the Catholic Church objected to was not Luther's *solo Christo* or *sola gratia*, but his *sola fide*. Farrow suggests that Luther made the mistake of 'freeze-framing' one moment of evangelical truth – that of the act of faith – while neglecting the theological virtues of hope and love. He agrees with Luther that love is formed by faith (*caritas fidei formata*) but insists that faith is also shaped and nurtured by love (*fides caritate formata*). Farrow concludes that Catholics can allow 'Luther's experiment in Freedom, but only if we are prepared to repeat the exercise twice over, integrating the results according to the traditional ascending order of the theological virtues'.[12]

Louis Bouyer (1913–2004), who was for a time a Lutheran minister before converting to Catholicism, also employed a tapestry metaphor to describe what happened in the intellectual life of the Church from the fourteenth century onwards. He spoke of a 'worm-eaten framework of a decadent medievalism'.[13] Specifically, Bouyer argued that the negative aspect of the Reformation 'neither follows from its positive principles, nor is it a necessary consequence of their development or vindication, but appears simply as a survival, within Protestantism, of what was most vitiated and corrupt in Catholic thought at the close of the Middle Ages'.[14] According to Bouyer, 'all the "heresies" Protestantism may have fostered, far from being its creations, even creations warped in their nature by the dead weight of a routine, unreformed system, appear already to be taking shape in the nominalist thinkers before the Reformation'.[15]

Nonetheless, Bouyer believed that one of the hallmarks of Protestantism was its tendency to exaggerate the remedies in an anti-Catholic direction. For example, Luther's interest in the subjective side of faith was accompanied by the denial of the objective value of sacraments and of all the other means of grace, and his affirmation of the sovereignty of God was accompanied by the belief that there was absolutely nothing that the human person could do in response to God that could claim to be of any religious value or 'merit'. Bouyer's point here was really the inverse side of Barth's famous statement that the problem with Catholic theology is the little word 'and'. When Protestants say grace, Catholics want to add 'and nature'; when Protestants say faith, Catholics want to add 'and reason', and so on. For Bouyer and other Catholic ecumenists of the middle years of the twentieth century, the various forms of Protestantism were the result of extreme reactions to defective elements within late scholasticism, poetically described as a worm-eaten or frayed tapestry. Speaking of the state of theology at the time of the Reformation, Yves Congar wrote:

> The theology which had come to be taught nearly everywhere, that at any rate known to the Reformers, was the driest and most complicated form of scholastic nominalism. Luther learnt his theology from Gabriel Biel, among the nominalists, and it was against them that he reacted, though to some extent with their help. Nominalism prepared for the Reformation in that it began to undermine faith in human reason and to develop a voluntarist and actualist theological outlook, that of the *Potentia absoluta* or dominion of the divine will over the essential laws implanted in the nature of things.[16]

Congar also observed that at the time of the Reformation there were those within the Catholic Church, such as Pope Adrian VI (1459–1523) and Reginald Cardinal Pole (1500–58), who blamed a corrupt Roman Curia for much of the strife. Curial corruption was another factor in the destruction of Christian unity the mid-century Catholic ecumenists were prepared to acknowledge. As Joseph Ratzinger remarked:

> [Prior to the Lutheran explosion] for nearly half a century, the Church was split into two or three obediences that excommunicated one another, so that every Catholic lived under excommunication by one pope or another, and, in the last analysis, no one could say with certainty which of the contenders had right on his side. The Church no longer offered certainty of salvation; she had become questionable in her whole objective form – the true Church, the true pledge of salvation, had to be sought outside the institution. It is against this background of a profoundly shaken ecclesial consciousness that we are to understand that Luther, in the conflict between his search for salvation and the tradition of the Church, ultimately came to experience the Church, not as the guarantor, but as the adversary of salvation.[17]

In accord with Congar, Louis Bouyer was also interested in Pole's judgements and regarded Pole, along with a number of Christian humanist scholars scattered throughout Europe, as the most clear-sighted cleric on the Catholic side as the tapestry began to tear. Those in Bouyer's roll call of scholars who were positively trying to address the defects in late scholastic thought included: Ambrogio Traversari (1386–1439) and Giannozzo Manetti (1396–1459) in Italy, Johann Reuchlin (1455–1522) from Germany, Desiderius Erasmus Roterodamus (1466–1536) from Holland, John Colet and Thomas More in England, Ximenez Cardinal de Cisneros (1436–1517) in Spain, Josse van Clichtove (1472–1543) from Flanders, and Jacques Lefèvre d'Étaples (1455–1536) in France. Bouyer praised Pole for understanding that

> the only form of Catholic Counter-Reformation that could possibly be of any effect would be one which took over into the Church the great religious insights, the great reforming efforts the Protestants had at heart . . . while at the same time ridding them of their deviations, which in any case were only accidental.[18]

Bouyer's description of Pole's remedy for the theological crises of the sixteenth century is essentially the same as the stance adopted by Hans Urs von Balthasar. Balthasar stood opposed to ecumenical strategies which took the form of whittling down the substance of the opposing traditions to a lowest common denominator of agreement. Instead he wanted a Catholic theology which affirmed the positive elements in Protestantism, and he praised Karl Barth's *Church Dogmatics* (the work of the more mature Barth), for attaining 'a breadth of subject matter and historical range that is coextensive with the Catholic understanding'.[19] He also observed that Barth's work has two crucial features: 'the most thorough and penetrating display of the Protestant view and the closest *rapprochement* with the Catholic'.[20]

The relationship between Barth and Balthasar began when Balthasar became a student chaplain at the University of Basel in 1940. Their friendship was fostered by a mutual appreciation of the music of Mozart. They were also both reacting against the dominant stream of theology within their traditions. In Barth's case this was liberal Protestantism, in Balthasar's it was what he called sawdust scholasticism, which he thought encouraged secularism. In 1941 Barth invited Balthasar to attend his seminar on the Council of Trent, and in the academic year 1948–9 Balthasar delivered a series of lectures on the subject of Karl Barth and Catholicism which developed into his 1951 book, published in English under the title *The Theology of Karl Barth*. In it, Balthasar praised Barth for laying the foundations for Christocentrism, for an understanding of the historicity of nature, and for an understanding of the created character of worldly truth. Moreover, Balthasar observed that Barth formalised the Protestant–Catholic contrasts in such a way that 'occasionally the form almost dissolves in the content, so that the Protestant aspect seems reducible to a "corrective" or a "dash of spice" lending piquancy to the Catholic dough'.[21] D. Stephen Long describes Balthasar's *Karl Barth* book as 'one of the most important "overtures" to "ecumenical dialogue" in the twentieth century'.[22] Long also draws attention to the fact that Balthasar gives epistemic priority to Barth's *Church Dogmatics* over his commentary *The Epistle to the Romans*, reading the earlier document through the lens of the later, while Barth, implicitly acknowledging this, joked that Balthasar towed around the *Church Dogmatics* in his briefcase, especially volume 2, part 1 on the divine perfections, 'like a cat her youth'.[23]

It is now a matter of history that Balthasar never succeeded in converting Barth, since Barth argued that the Catholic *analogia entis* concept, or more specifically Erich Przywara SJ's (1889–1972) version of the concept which Balthasar sought to defend, was 'the

invention of the anti-Christ'. Nonetheless, the friendship between the two Swiss theologians showcased the kind of ecumenical dialogue which would later be described as a form of
'receptive ecumenism' where both parties are open to receiving gifts from other traditions.

Thomas Joseph White OP has observed that the controversy between Barth and
Przywara over the *analogia entis* reverberated into three interrelated topics in twentieth-
century theology: the relationship between Christianity and the metaphysics of being;
the relationship between Christological grace and the understanding of the meaning and
purpose of human nature; and the relationship between Christian faith and human reason.
In relation to the first of these – Christianity and metaphysics – White notes that 'at stake
in this dispute is the basic question of whether or in what way a *ressourcement* of classical
metaphysics is required *within modern theology*, as a dimension of one's response to secular
modernity'.[24] In relation to the second topic – Christology and anthropology – White suggests that while both thinkers were profoundly Christological, the 'balance and relation of
these two poles (Christology/anthropology) is diverse in the thought of each'.[25] In relation
to the third topic – faith and reason – White concludes that

> only by understanding all things in the light of the uncreated Logos who is love – the
> Logos who became flesh – is the rationality of the creation and of the human person
> fully manifest, such that this same rationality is opened up from within to its plenary
> fulfilment in God.[26]

Martin Bieler adds that for Balthasar the metaphysics of being is an integral part of God's
revelation in the world:

> For Balthasar, Christ himself is the concrete *analogia entis*, because he measures all
> dimensions between God and human beings through his own person in the unity of
> his divine and human nature. The philosophical *analogia entis* has the same relation to
> Christ as world history has to the history of Christ: It is like promise to fulfilment, and
> like provisional to final.[27]

As Boersma and others have noted, it is precisely this territory of the nature and grace
relationship and associated ways of understanding sacramentality that requires ecumenical
attention, picking up the discussion from where Barth and Balthasar ended. The territory
of sacramental theology remains an area in which there have been fewer convergences, in
part because of the Protestant aversion to the word 'and'. Congar described the issue with
Barth as 'the tendency to consider exclusively the sovereign causality of God in God himself without realizing that this causality injects something real *into us* and ultimately con-
fers on us the capacity for con-causality with God!'[28] The convergences that have taken
place tend to be more in the territories of ecclesiology and the revelation–Scripture–
tradition triad than in the field of theological anthropology.

In *The Primacy of Peter*, Charles Journet (1891–1975) described a Catholic–Protestant
fault line as a difference over the way in which the presence of Christ constitutes
Christianity. The Protestant position he described as a mnemic concept, the Catholic
position he described as an ontological concept. According to the typically Protestant
account, Christ is only present in time by way of signs, tokens and promises, whereas,
according to the Catholic account, Christ is really and truly present *in time* under the guise
of signs, tokens and promises.[29] Navigating a path of unity through this particular fault line
remains an ecumenical challenge bequeathed to the theologians of the twenty-first cen-

tury. Nonetheless, just as the theology of the *ressourcement* scholars 'opened up avenues of dialogue that previously had been unthinkable',[30] new convergences may well arise in the coming decades from Protestants such as Boersma who appreciate the need to tackle the ontological questions.

Significantly, the ontological issues are no longer confined to constructions of the relationship between nature and grace and between history and ontology but now include the pair masculinity and femininity. Today the giant woolly mammoth in the room is the issue of what to make of sexual difference, theologically speaking. Early hopes for a reunion between the Church of England and its affiliates and the Catholic Church have reached a deadlock due to lack of agreement about this particular theological building block. The Church of England's moral theology, especially in the subfield of sexual ethics, is also running along a different trajectory from that of the magisterial teaching of the Catholic Church. Arguably both of these issues go back to the difference, flagged by Journet, of how God relates to the human person in history.

John Paul II's *Catechesis on Human Love*, which is the flagship for Catholic magisterial teaching in the field of sexual ethics, was based on his exegesis of the first three chapters of the book of *Genesis* as well as his theological anthropology, which placed sexual intimacy within the context of a couple's participation in the generative love of the Trinity. This approach to sexual difference and the theology of marriage has been developed by Cardinals Angelo Scola, Marc Ouellet and the late Carlo Caffarra (1938–2017) and also by Bishop Jean Laffitte, Livio Melina, José Granados, José Noriega and Margaret McCarthy, among others. Fundamentally, the Catholic Church's opposition to contraception, cohabitation, homosexual practices and women priests comes down to an interpretation of the book of *Genesis*, along with an understanding of how the three Persons of the Holy Trinity relate to individual human persons through the sacraments in time. These are all ultimately foundational issues about the economy of salvation and sacramentality.

While any hope of a major corporate reunion of the Catholic and Anglican churches was lost once Anglicans decided to ordain women, a smaller-scale reunion occurred between 2011 and 2012 with the establishment of three ordinariates for former Anglicans (canonical structures juridically equivalent to a diocese) in accordance with the apostolic constitution *Anglicanorum coetibus* of 2009. The three ordinariates are: the Ordinariate of Our Lady of Walsingham (covering England, Wales and Scotland), the Ordinariate of the Chair of St Peter (covering the United States and Canada) and the Ordinariate of Our Lady of the Southern Cross (covering Australia and Japan). At the time of the promulgation of *Anglicanorum coetibus* Cardinal Levada stated:

> It is the hope of the Holy Father, Pope Benedict XVI, that the Anglican clergy and faithful who desire union with the Catholic Church will find in this ecumenical structure the opportunity to preserve those Anglican traditions precious to them and consistent with the Catholic faith. Insofar as these traditions express in a distinctive way the faith that is held in common, they are a gift to be shared in the wider Church. The unity of the Church does not require a uniformity that ignores cultural diversity, as the history of Christianity shows.[31]

This creation of Ordinariates was in part the fruit of efforts undertaken early in the twentieth century by Lord Halifax (representing the Anglican side) and Fr Etienne Portal and Cardinal Mercier (representing the Catholic side). Halifax (1839–1934) had developed a friendship with Etienne Fernand Portal (1855–1926), a French Vincentian priest, during the winter of 1889–90 when both were living on the island of Madeira. They were then to work together on ecumenical projects for the next thirty-six years. Portal founded the *Anglo-Roman Review* and wrote a pamphlet titled *The Anglican Ordinations*. Leo XIII responded by establishing a commission to examine the issue of Anglican Orders and appointed Cardinal Merry del Val y Zulueta (1865–1930) to the Commission. Merry del Val and the Archbishop of Westminster, Herbert Cardinal Vaughan (1832–1903), were not sympathetic to the claims of the Church of England. The outcome was the papal bull *Apostolicae curae* (1896). This document declared Anglican Orders to be 'utterly null and void'. In 1903 Merry del Val became the Vatican's Secretary of State, and he retained this post until 1914. During this period he accused Portal of modernism and prohibited him from publishing and speaking in public. As a consequence, the ecumenical work of Portal and Halifax entered a doldrums period until the 'Lambeth Appeal' of 1920.

The 'Lambeth Appeal' was a statement from the Anglican bishops of the United Kingdom and countries of the British Commonwealth, along with US Episcopalians, to the effect that they would welcome discussions with Rome on reunion. Following this appeal, Lord Halifax approached the Belgian First World War hero, Joseph-Desiré Cardinal Mercier (1851–1926), to open up a line of communication. A series of meetings were then chaired by the cardinal until his death in 1926. These became known as the Malines Conversations. Halifax and Portal approached Mercier because it was thought that the members of the English hierarchy were not enthusiastic about any institutional reunion. By the time of the fourth conversation, the pro- and anti-reunion battle was being fought out within the Curia between Cardinal Gasparri, the Secretary of State under Pius XI, who supported the idea of a corporate reunion, and Cardinal Merry del Val, who remained opposed. The English Jesuit Francis Woodluck (1871–1940) was also an opponent of the Conversations, while, typically, the English Dominicans did not toe the Jesuit line. Both Bede Jarrett OP (1871–1933) and Vincent McNabb OP (1868–1943) sent letters of support to the participants in the Conversations.

At the fourth meeting, Mercier produced a paper titled 'L'Eglise Anglicane unie non absorbée', which had been written by Dom Lambert Bauduin. This document drew upon themes in an earlier proposal of Ambrose Phillips de Lisle which would give the Archbishop of Canterbury patriarchal status, in communion with Rome, allowing for a continuation of the Anglican liturgy and elements of Anglican canon law.

The Conversations came to an end after the fourth meeting as a result of a confluence of factors: the deaths of both Cardinal Mercier and Fr Portal in 1926, the opposition from the English hierarchy and Cardinal Merry del Val, and also, finally, opposition from King George V. In his *The Malines Conversations Revisited*, J. A. Dick concluded that the strongest concern among the opponents of the Conversations was related to the concept of a corporate reunion rather than a process of individual conversions; because a corporate reunion would suggest that Anglican Orders are valid, it could possibly lead to the abolition of the Catholic hierarchy established after 1850, and there were fears of 'Anglican modernists' gaining entry into the Catholic Church under the cover of institutional reunion.[32] A psychological factor not mentioned is that for recusant Catholics whose families had suffered for their refusal to abandon the 'old faith', the idea of corporate reunion often seemed like an injustice to the suffering of the English martyrs.

In their report on the Malines Conversations, the Catholics stated that it was clear that the Protestant Thirty-Nine Articles of Religion were not the 'insurmountable obstacle' they had feared, because many Anglicans consider the Articles as practically obsolete.

They further predicted that 'in proportion as mutual understanding and doctrinal agreement advance, it will become possible to arrange a satisfactory adjustment of disciplinary rules, however delicate a matter that may seem at present'. With regard to such disciplinary matters, the Anglicans at the Second Malines meeting said they desired to keep the use of the vernacular, including their English Rite, for all liturgical purposes, communion under both kinds, and married clergy. In their report on the Conversations, the Anglicans were effusive in their praise of Cardinal Mercier, stating:

> The Cardinal's gracious presidency secured an atmosphere in which the plainest speaking on either side was compatible with unbroken friendliness and an ever-increasing desire for a sympathetic understanding of the several positions entertained by those who had met for conference under his roof . . . They are convinced that it is on the lines of such friendly conversations that true progress is to be made in achieving the reunion of Christendom, which must be so near to all Christian hearts; and they would express the earnest hope that similar conferences may be continued in the future, in order that the work begun with Cardinal Mercier's blessing and under his auspices may be still further carried on, and by God's blessing and in God's time fulfil words so constantly on the Cardinal's lips 'Ut unum sint'.[33]

'God's time' finally arrived with the pontificate of Joseph Ratzinger/Benedict XVI, an intellectual heavily influenced by the theology of John Henry Newman, whom he beatified, and a man who appreciates solemn liturgy and choral music. Ratzinger/Benedict could easily understand why Anglicans might prefer their King James English to what some have called the 'oikish translations' of the contemporary Roman missal, or why, in other words, Anglicans who are doctrinally in agreement with Catholics might not want to abandon the beauty of their own liturgies to endure the banality of suburban parish folk Masses. The Ordinariate was a scaled-down version of the proposals of de Lisle, Bauduin and Mercier, but the most that could be achieved in an era of female clergy. Similarly, the Anglican–Roman Catholic International Commission (ARCIC) established by the Archbishop of Canterbury Michael Ramsey and Pope Paul VI in 1967 has produced several documents presenting agreements on doctrinal issues, including Eucharistic theology, but the decision to ordain women has meant that there are limits to what it can achieve. As Cardinal Levada explained the problem:

> For Catholics, the issue of the reservation of priestly ordination to men is not merely a matter of praxis, or discipline, but is, rather, doctrinal in nature and touches the heart of the doctrine of the Eucharist itself and the sacramental nature, or constitution, of the Church. It is therefore a question which cannot be relegated to the periphery of ecumenical conversations, but needs to be engaged directly in honesty and charity by dialogue partners who desire Christian unity, which, by its very nature, is Eucharistic.[34]

Conversely, while the divisions between the Catholic Church and the Anglican Church have widened due to their different responses to the issue of the theological significance of sexual difference, members of the Catholic Church and the churches of Eastern Orthodoxy have found they occupy common ground around many of the issues thrown up by the sexual revolution of the 1960s and the contemporary theological debates about masculinity and femininity. It is also the case that the scholars of Eastern Orthodoxy never abandoned the sacramental ontology of the Church Fathers and thus find themselves on common ground with Catholics about such central topics as the meaning of the Eucharist and Eucharistic ecclesiology.

By the eve of the Second Vatican Council, Yves Congar had concluded that 'dogmatically and canonically, the main factor in the Oriental schism is the refusal to submit to the primacy of the Roman See; [while] actually and historically, the schism is the result of a gradual and general estrangement'.[35] Assuming this to be the case, ecumenical work with the representatives of Eastern Orthodoxy has tended to proceed on a two-track strategy – the path of diplomacy to heal centuries-old wounds – and the path of intellectual engagement around the understanding of the power of the Petrine office and different approaches to Trinitarian theology. The period between 1963 and 1979 is sometimes described as the 'dialogue of charity', while the period after 1979, the year of the establishment of the Joint International Commission for Theological Dialogue between the Roman Catholic Church and the Orthodox, is described as the 'dialogue of doctrine', but both kinds of dialogue continue in tandem. Key documents produced by the Commission include: 'The Mystery of the Church and of the Eucharist in the Light of the Mystery of the Holy Trinity', 'The Sacrament of Order in the Sacramental Structure of the Church, with Particular Reference to the Importance of the Apostolic Succession for the Sanctification and Unity of the People of God', 'The Ecclesiological and Canonical Consequences of the Sacramental Nature of the Church – Ecclesial Communion, Conciliarity and Authority', 'The Role of the Bishop of Rome in the Communion of the Church in the First Millennium' and 'Primacy and Synodality in the Church'. These documents drew on ideas from Nikolai Nikolayevich Afanas'ev (1893–1966) and John Zizioulas, Henri de Lubac, Joseph Ratzinger and Paul McPartlan, among others. In this context what is significant is the common endorsement of *communio* ecclesiology, also called Eucharistic ecclesiology, which links ecclesiology to both sacramental theology and Trinitarian theology. In both cases, Orthodox and Catholic, the ecclesiology of the nineteenth-century Tübingen theologian Johann Adam Möhler (1796–1838) is a source of inspiration, particularly his work *Die Einheit der Kirche*, which Congar published as the first volume in his *Unam Sanctam* series.

Underlying all this work is a common Catholic–Orthodox convergence on the significance of the patristic theological heritage. This element was well summarised in the following two paragraphs extracted from the paper of Archbishop Hilarion (Grigory Alfeyev) delivered at the 9th International Conference on Russian monasticism and spirituality at the Bose monastery in Italy:

> Russian 20th-century theology has given much attention to the patristic heritage. The systematic study of the works of the holy Fathers, which began in Russia in the first half of the 19th century and reached its climax in the early 20th century, was continued after the 1917 revolution by the theologians of the Russian emigration. At the St Sergius Theological Institute in Paris, the works of such teachers as Archimandrite Cyprian (Kern) and the fathers Sergi Bulgakov, Georges Florovsky, John Meyendorff and of Nicholas Lossky paved the way for the further study of the holy Fathers. Florovsky was to be the chief impetus behind the 'patristic renaissance' in Russian 20th-century theology: his were the key concepts for the interpretation of the patristic heritage, in particular the idea of the 'neo-patristic synthesis' . . . The idea expressed by Florovsky – which had been 'hanging in the air' throughout the 20th century – has inspired many outstanding patristic scholars not only among the Russian diaspora but also among Western scholars. I would like here to pay tribute to those theologians who, though

themselves not belonging to the Eastern theological traditions, have succeeded in uncovering the heritage of the great Fathers of the Eastern church, both for themselves and for the Western world. First should be mentioned Irenee Hausherr, Hans Urs von Balthasar, Henri de Lubac, Jean Daniélou, Walther Volker, Werner Jaeger, Johannes Quasten, John Kelly and Gilles Prestige, as well as, among those still with us, such scholars as Jaroslav Pelikan, Cardinal Christoph Schönborn, Hieromonk Gabriel Bunge (whose books have begun to appear in Russian) and Sebastian Brock. The 'patristic renaissance' of the 20th century would have been impossible without these persons, true zealots of theological scholarship, who in their works were able (in the literal or figurative sense) to reach across the confessional barriers separating them from the Orthodox tradition.[36]

With regard to the Petrine office, the contemporary work is focused on how to understand the notion of primacy. Among Catholic theologians there is almost universal agreement that the occupant of the Chair of Peter is not an absolute monarch. As Joseph Ratzinger expressed the principle, 'the Pope is not an absolute monarch whose will is law, but the guardian of the authentic tradition'.[37] Similarly, Louis Bouyer wrote:

> St. Thomas Aquinas explains that the title 'vicar of Christ', given to those who rule the Church in succession to the apostles, does not mean that they can modify in the least its essential structure or its basis, but that their power is so dependent on what God has done, once and for all, on Christ, and entrusted to his apostles, that it is restricted to preserving this legacy, without altering or adding to it. The Church they govern is 'constituted by the faith and the sacraments of the faith. Consequently, just as they are not allowed to set up another Church, neither may they hand down another faith or institute other sacraments.[38]

Balthasar's 1974 work published in English as *The Office of Peter and the Structure of the Church* set out an account of the Petrine office as an ecclesial mission circumscribed by the deposit of the faith and subject to the influence of other ecclesial missions such as the Pauline prophetic mission and the Johannine mission of prayer at the foot of the cross.[39] Paul McPartlan, a Catholic representative on the Joint International Commission, in his 2013 work *A Service of Love: Papal Primacy, the Eucharist and Church Unity*, further explored the patristic concepts of 'first in honour' and 'president in love' with reference to the Petrine mission. While it is often observed that the papacy of Jorge Bergoglio/ Francis follows the Ignatian military model of governance, with the pope acting as a chief commander of all the cardinal generals and episcopal colonels, there has as yet been no attempt to offer a theology associated with this model.

As a macro-level assessment of the current state of play in Catholic–Orthodox ecumenism, Aidan Nichols has offered the following conclusion:

> The possibility of overcoming the Eastern schism lies in the ability of the Catholic Church to extract the positive teaching of those mediaeval and modern councils that follow on the patristic age of the seven councils and to re-express this teaching in a new context, with complementary supplementation from the Eastern tradition, presenting the whole in the forum of a fresh ecumenical council to which the Orthodox bishops would be invited (as they were, qua equal participants, to Florence). The grounds for such a possibility in terms of fundamental ecclesiology and, more specifically, in terms

of a theology of the councils, have been identified in an admirable way by the French historical and dogmatic theologian Père Bertrand de Margerie of the Society of Jesus.[40]

Joseph Ratzinger has also offered as a general principle the idea that Rome must not require more from the East with respect to the doctrine of papal primacy than had been formulated and was lived during the first millennium, while the churches of the East should cease to oppose as heretical developments that took place in the Western branch of Christianity during the second millennium.

Once the issue of the understanding of papal primacy is settled, there remains the issues of the understanding of the *filioque* in Trinitarian theology and the indissolubility of marriage in sacramental theology. Of these two issues, the *filioque* problem appears to be close to a resolution, relying on a mutual acceptance of the Trinitarian theology of St Maximus the Confessor. A study published by the Pontifical Council for Promoting Christian Unity on *The Greek and the Latin Traditions Regarding the Procession of the Holy Spirit* distinguishes between what the Greeks mean by 'procession', in the sense of taking origin from, applicable only to the Holy Spirit relative to God the Father, and what the Latins mean by 'procession', as the more common term applicable to both God the Son and God the Holy Spirit. Metropolitan John Zizioulas has suggested that this approach shows a way forward towards reconciliation.[41]

The issue of the theology of marriage operative in the Orthodox churches is obviously a more complex problem. One possibility is that John Paul II's Christocentric Trinitarianism and especially his attempt to develop a catechesis on human love which situates the whole phenomenon of human love and sexuality within a Trinitarian context may well start to resonate with Orthodox theologians, since a hallmark of Orthodox theology for centuries has been precisely its focus upon the Trinity. Young Catholic and Reformed evangelical scholars who are contending with the implosion of Western Christianity may well find that they have much to learn from the anti-rationalism of Eastern Orthodoxy's intellectual traditions while young Greeks and Russians and others from the Orthodox churches might find the sacramental theology of a Polish pope with a strong interest in Trinitarian anthropology to be a much needed supplement to their own already rich understanding of the significance of the Trinity in human life. Alternatively, Walter Kasper has been trying to move the Catholic theology of marriage in an Orthodox direction, though with little support outside the countries of Germany, Austria and Belgium, and with deep opposition from Poland and the countries of Africa and from younger clergy around the world whose intellectual formation took place under the influence of John Paul II's catechesis on human love and the moral theology of *Veritatis splendor*.

John Paul II's most significant contributions to the ecumenical movement flow from his two 1995 ecumenical encyclicals. The first – *Orientale lumen* – was issued to mark the centenary of the publication of *Orientalium dignitas* of Leo XIII. In this document, John Paul II observed that Christians of the East and West are united in the martyrdoms of the twentieth century. The concentration camps claimed the lives of Orthodox and Catholic without distinction. He also stated that in some cases Christian truths were better explained in one tradition than in another, and he praised the Orthodox churches for their reflections on Trinitarian theology, especially the role of the Holy Spirit in the economy of salvation, and the concept of the divinisation of the human person through participation in the life of the Trinity. John Paul II also endorsed projects designed to give Catholics a deeper knowledge of Eastern liturgy and the spiritual traditions of the Fathers and Doctors of the Christian East, and of Eastern approaches to evangelisation.

In the same month of 1995 John Paul II issued the encyclical *Ut unum sint*, which was directed more broadly to all those Christians outside of the Catholic Church, not exclusively those of Eastern Orthodoxy. Again he referred to an ecumenical witness of martyrs in the twentieth century. He recalled that in the closing days of the Second Vatican Council the mutual ex-communications of 1054 were jointly renounced in ceremonies in Rome and Constantinople, and he praised Pope Paul VI for his work in bringing this about. John Paul II also made mention of the importance of Sts Cyril (826–69) and Methodius (815–85), who were the subject of an earlier encyclical – *Slavorum Apostoli* (1985) – and of the baptism of St Vladimir, Grand Prince of Kiev, in 988. In his Apostolic Letter *Euntes in mundum* of 1988, which was issued to celebrate the millennium of St Vladimir's baptism, there is paragraph after paragraph of praise for the achievements of St Vladimir and his grandmother St Olga as well as Sts Cyril and Methodius, who John Paul II decreed to be patron saints of Europe, along with St Benedict. When reading this particular document, one gets the impression that John Paul II is happily speaking 'Slav to Slav' and showing off his knowledge of the history of Christianity in Russia, Belarus and Ukraine. Throughout all these publications it is clear that John Paul II regarded the monastic life of Eastern Orthodoxy to be one of its greatest treasures, and he declared that 'communion is made fruitful by the exchange of gifts between the Churches insofar as they complement each other'.

Arguably, however, the greatest ecumenical achievement during the papacy of John Paul II (1978–2005) was the agreement reached with representatives of the Lutheran Church known as the *Joint Declaration on the Doctrine of Justification*. Bishop George Anderson, head of the Evangelical Lutheran Church of America, said it was 'Ratzinger who untied the knots' when it looked as though the document would be shipwrecked by officials from the Pontifical Council for the Promotion of Christian Unity.[42] Michael Root, a member of the Declaration's drafting team, described Ratzinger's role in the ratification of the Declaration as 'indispensable'. He stated that 'by his participation in the Regensburg initiative of Lutheran Bishop Hanselmann, Ratzinger went beyond the call of duty and contributed to a far more satisfying outcome than a signing ceremony without an adequate theological explanation'.[43]

The idea of an informal meeting including Ratzinger, the Lutheran theologian Joachim Track and the Catholic theologian Heinz Schütte, who was a former student of Ratzinger's, along with Hanselmann, came from Hanselmann, who became a friend of Ratzinger's when they were both Bavarian bishops, though of different communions. Like Barth and Balthasar, the two shared a love of music. The key sentence in the Declaration reads:

> By grace alone, in faith in Christ's saving work and not because of any merit on our part, we are accepted by God and receive the Holy Spirit, who renews our hearts while equipping us and calling us to do good works.

Ratzinger's work on the *Joint Declaration* not only showcased his commitment to ecumenism but also his Mercier-style approach. This might be described as relaxed fireside chats among well-educated friends with deep knowledge of the history of how a particular part of the tapestry was initially frayed.

This stance of not downplaying the importance of doctrinal differences has been emphasised in many magisterial documents going all the way back to *Mortalium animos*, a publication of Pius XI in 1928. It also appears in *Unitatis redintegratio* (1964), the *Decree on Ecumenism* issued at the Second Vatican Council. *Unitatis redintegratio* declared that

'Nothing is so foreign to the spirit of ecumenism as a false irenicism, in which the purity of Catholic doctrine suffers loss and its genuine and certain meaning is clouded.' The importance of ecumenists having a strong knowledge of dogmatic theology as well as the history of this branch of theology was emphasised in 1993 in the *Directory for the Application of Principles and Norms of Ecumenism* approved by John Paul II.

Nonetheless, Heinrich Fries (1911–98) and Karl Rahner argued in favour of a different approach in their joint work *Unity of the Churches: An Actual Possibility*. Fries and Rahner acknowledged that there needed to be agreement on 'the fundamental truths of Christianity, as they are expressed in Holy Scripture, in the Apostles' Creed, and in that of Nicaea and Constantinople'.[44] Beyond that, they suggested that doctrinal differences should be tolerated, including differences in the field of moral theology. Ratzinger, however, found this pragmatic approach unsatisfactory.[45] As Matthew Levering explains his objection:

> The unified Church might be a marvel of pragmatic skill, but it would completely lack the ability to account for its structures in terms of God's instituting Word . . . at present, each side of the Reformation-era divisions has a way of accounting for the origin of its Church structure in Christ's will. But the unified Church would have no plausible account of its divine justification. This would prove deadly, since what people want from the Church is God's salvific Word.[46]

D. Stephen Long has used the expression 'unity through subtraction' to describe the approach of reducing everything to ethics/praxis and ignoring dogma, while Congar called this kind of approach 'liberal ecumenism'. This muting of the significance of dogma is, however, different from the situation described in Paragraph 17 of *Unitatis redintegratio* that in the study of revelation theologians from the Western and Eastern branches of Christianity have followed different methods and expressed theological ideas in different idioms, and that, as a consequence, 'from time to time one tradition has come nearer to a full appreciation of some aspects of a mystery of revelation than the other, or has expressed it to better advantage'. The Fathers of the Second Vatican Council were of the view that in such cases 'these various theological expressions are to be considered often as mutually complementary rather than conflicting'.

While there may be different theological expressions and methodologies, an idea that has been rejected in Catholic magisterial teaching is that each ecclesial community might have its own piece of truth to bring to the table to create a much larger theological jigsaw. Or, to apply the metaphor differently, the idea that Catholics might hold some pieces of the Christian jigsaw, Lutherans others, Calvinists yet another part of the puzzle and so on. This kind of mentality was criticised in the year 2000 document of the Congregation for the Doctrine of the Faith (CDF) published as the *Declaration on the Unity and Salvific Universality of Jesus Christ and the Church*, and otherwise known as *Dominus Iesus*. This declaration of the CDF, under Ratzinger's leadership, reiterated the teaching of the Second Vatican Council that the single Church of Christ 'subsists in the Catholic Church, governed by the successor of Peter and by the bishops in Communion with him'.

As pope, Ratzinger continued to work on ecumenical fronts, bringing to the Petrine office his own personal gift of a capacity to sort out intellectual knots with reference to historical sensitivities. In his first pastoral visit outside of Rome, in the city of Bari, in which the remains of St Nicholas of Myra are venerated by Orthodox pilgrims, he described ecumenical work with the Orthodox Church as a fundamental commitment of his papacy. To this end he cultivated a very strong relationship with the Ecumenical Patriarch Bartholomew I. He made a visit to Fanar in November 2006 and invited the Ecumenical Patriarch to address the Synod on the Word held in 2008.

Ratzinger also sought to improve relations with the Russian Orthodox Church. In 2009 he met with Archbishop Hilarion (Grigory Alfeyev), who had publicly praised Ratzinger's intellectual critiques of secularism. Archbishop Hilarion spoke of his desire to bridge the gap between Catholicism and Orthodoxy by means of cultural collaboration, in the hope of hastening the time of closer doctrinal and ecclesial relations between Catholics and the Orthodox worldwide. To this end Hilarion established the St Gregory Nazianzus Foundation to support Christianity in the West.

In the 1960s at the University of Bonn, Ratzinger had directed a thesis by Vinzenz Pfnür on the doctrine of justification in Luther, and in the circle of his doctoral students there were two Orthodox students, Damaskinos Papandréou and Stylianos Harkianakis, who later became metropolitans of the Patriarchy of Constantinople. These early intellectual engagements with scholars from other Christian traditions served him well later in his life. There is also something fitting or 'convenient' – to use the medieval concept – about the first German pope since the Reformation being the person to make substantial progress towards a Catholic–Lutheran *rapprochement*.

In 2017 the Joint Commemoration of the 500th Anniversary of the Reformation by both Catholics and Lutherans was noted for its tone of mutual respect. It was the first time in the history of these centenary anniversaries that it was not celebrated with German nationalistic pomp and unadulterated Lutheran bravado, and certainly the first time that there has been Catholic participation. The crucial document was 'From Conflict to Communion' – a Report of the Lutheran–Roman Catholic Joint Commission for Unity, co-published by the Lutheran World Federation and the Pontifical Council for the Promotion of Christian Unity. The document offers a meticulous analysis of points of current agreement and areas where differences persist. Paragraph 90 observes that 'while the Council of Trent largely defined Catholic relations with Lutherans for several centuries, its legacy must now be viewed through the lens of the actions of the Second Vatican Council (1962–1965)' and further, that the Council's Dogmatic Constitution on the Church (*Lumen gentium*), the Decree on Ecumenism (*Unitatis redintegratio*), the Declaration on Religious Freedom (*Dignitatis humanae*), and the Dogmatic Constitution on Divine Revelation (*Dei verbum*) are foundational documents for Catholic ecumenism.

As a consequence, following a century of Catholic ecumenism, both spiritual and doctrinal, Douglas A. Sweeney, the Director of the Jonathan Edwards Centre at Trinity Evangelical Divinity School, can write:

Signs of hope for a better way forward abound. In my own neck of the woods, evangelicals are sinking deeper roots in Church history, growing more catholic in their handling of the Bible, and working much harder on the doctrine of the Church than they ever have before. Roman Catholics are paying more attention to the Scriptures, rethinking old answers to dogmatic questions via *ressourcement*, and working more fervently on dialogue with others. Most importantly, Benedict XVI weighed in on Scripture, Tradition and the Church's teaching office. With impressive erudition – greater learning, many have argued, than any other pontiff since the Reformation era – he has treated this triad with sympathy for Protestants and readiness to further Catholic teaching through development, setting an agenda for the rest of us to follow.[47]

While it is difficult to predict future developments, one possibility is that the current divisions over the meaning of sexual difference may well force Protestants to tackle the ontological issues at the heart of Catholic theological anthropology and sacramental theology, leading to further convergences, at least among the non-liberal theologians, while a Russophone pope may well be on the Holy Spirit's wish list.

# Notes

1. Yves Congar, 'Ecumenical Experience and Conversion: A Personal Testimony', in *The Sufficiency of God: Essays on the Ecumenical Hope in Honour of W. A. Visser't Hooft*, edited by Robert C. Mackie and Charles C. West (London: SCM Press, 1963), pp. 71–87: 72.
2. Yves Congar, *Dialogue between Christians: Catholic Contributions to Ecumenism*, Philip Loretz SJ (trans.) (London: Geoffrey Chapman, 1966), pp. 7–8.
3. See James and Joanna Bogle, *A Heart for Europe: The Lives of Charles and Empress Zita of Austria-Hungary* (London: Gracewing, 2000).
4. Leonard Swidler, *Blood Witness for Peace and Unity: The Life of Max Joseph Metzger* (New Jersey: Dimension Books, 1986), p. 50.
5. Swidler, *Blood Witness*, p. 50.
6. Cf. Hans Boersma, *Heavenly Participation: The Weaving of a Sacramental Tapestry* (Grand Rapids: Eerdmans, 2011).
7. Boersma, *Nouvelle Théologie and Sacramental Ontology: A Return to Mystery* (Oxford: Oxford University Press, 2009), p. 293.
8. Boersma, *Nouvelle Théologie*, p. 293.
9. Boersma, *Nouvelle Théologie*, p. 293.
10. Jean Daniélou, *Approches du Christ* (Paris: Bernard Grasset, 1960), p. 104.
11. Daniélou, *Approches du Christ*, p. 104.
12. Douglas Farrow, *Theological Negotiations: Proposals in Soteriology and Anthropology* (Ada, MI: Baker Academic, 2018), p. 87.
13. Louis Bouyer, *The Spirit and Forms of Protestantism*, A. V. Littledale (trans.) (London: Harvill Press, 1956), p. 194.
14. Bouyer, *Spirit and Forms of Protestantism*, p. 164.
15. Bouyer, *Spirit and Forms of Protestantism*, pp. 161–2.
16. Yves Congar, *Divided Christendom: A Catholic Study of the Problem of Reunion* (London: Geoffrey Bles, 1939), p. 17.
17. Joseph Ratzinger, *Principles of Catholic Theology* (San Francisco: Ignatius, 1987), p. 196.
18. Louis Bouyer, *The Word, Church and Sacraments in Protestantism and Catholicism* (New York: Desclee, 1961), p. 24.
19. Hans Urs von Balthasar, *The Theology of Karl Barth: Exposition and Interpretation* (San Francisco: Ignatius, 1992), p. 23.
20. Balthasar, *The Theology of Karl Barth*, p. 23.
21. Balthasar, *The Theology of Karl Barth*, p. 23.
22. Stephen D. Long, *Saving Karl Barth: Hans Urs von Balthasar's Preoccupation*, (Minneapolis: Fortress, 2014), p. 88.
23. Manfred Lochbrunner, *Hans Urs von Balthasar und seine Theologen-kollegen* (Würzburg: Echter Verlag, 2009), p. 279.
24. Thomas Joseph White (ed.), *The Analogy of Being: Invention of the Antichrist or the Wisdom of God?* (Grand Rapids: Eerdmans, 2011), p. 10.
25. White, *The Analogy of Being*, p. 11.
26. White, *The Analogy of Being*, p. 26.
27. Martin Bieler, 'Analogia entis as an Expression of Love According to Ferdinand Ulrich', in *The Analogy of Being: Invention of the Antichrist of Wisdom of God*, edited by Thomas Joseph White (Grand Rapids: Eerdmans, 2011), p. 316.

28. Congar, *Dialogue between Christians*, p. 12.

29. Charles Journet, *The Primacy of Peter*, John Chapin (trans.) (Baltimore: Newman Press, 1954), p. 9.

30. Boersma, *Nouvelle Théologie*, p. 14.

31. William Levada, 'Note of the Congregation for the Doctrine of the Faith about Personal Ordinariates for Anglicans Entering the Catholic Church' (Vatican City, 2009).

32. John A. Dick, *The Malines Conversations Revisited* (Leuven: Leuven University Press, 1989), p. 191.

33. Lord Halifax et al., *The Conversations at Malines 1921–1925* (Oxford: Oxford University Press, 1927), p. 44.

34. William Levada, 'Five Hundred Years after St. John Fisher: Benedict's Ecumenical Initiatives to Anglicans' (Kingston, ON, 2010).

35. Yves Congar, *After Nine Hundred Years: The Background of the Schism between the Eastern and Western Churches* (New York: Fordham University Press, 1959), p. 89.

36. Grigory Alfeyev, 'The Patristic Heritage and Modernity', Paper delivered at the 9th International Conference on Russian monasticism and spirituality, Bose Monastery, Italy, 2001.

37. Alcuin Reid, *The Organic Development of the Liturgy* (Farnborough: St Michael's Abbey Press, 2005), p. 10.

38. Bouyer, *The Spirit and Forms of Protestantism*, p. 201.

39. Hans Urs von Balthasar, *The Office of Peter and the Structure of the Church* (San Francisco: Ignatius Press).

40. Aidan Nichols, *Theology in the Russian Diaspora: Church, Fathers, Eucharist in Nikolai Afanas'ev, 1893–1966* (Cambridge: Cambridge University Press, 2008), p. 371.

41. John Zizioulas, *One Single Source: An Orthodox Response to the Clarification on the Filioque*, Orthodox Research Institute, accessed at www.orthodoxresearchinstitute.org/articles/dogmatics/john_zizioulas_single_source.htm.

42. John Allen Jr, 'Ratzinger Credited with Saving Lutheran Pact', *National Catholic Reporter*, 10 September 1999.

43. Michael Root, 'Ratzinger and the Doctrine of Justification', in *Joseph Ratzinger and the Healing of the Reformation Divisions*, edited by Emery de Gaál and Matthew Levering (Steubenville: Emmaus Academic, 2019), p. 432.

44. Heinrich Fries and Karl Rahner, *Unity of the Churches: An Actual Possibility*, Ruth C. L. Gritsch and Eric W. Gritsch (trans.) (Philadelphia: Fortress, 1985), p. 7.

45. Joseph Ratzinger, *Church, Ecumenism and Politics: New Essays in Ecclesiology*, Robert Nowell (trans.) (New York: Crossroad, 1988).

46. Matthew Levering, 'Doctrine and Ecumenism', in *Joseph Ratzinger and the Healing of the Reformation Divisions*, edited by Emery de Gaál and Matthew Levering (Steubenville: Emmaus Academic, 2019), p. 25.

47. Douglas A. Sweeney, 'Ratzinger on Scripture, Tradition and Church: An Evangelical Assessment', in *Joseph Ratzinger and the Healing of the Reformation Divisions*, edited by Emery de Gaál and Matthew Levering (Steubenville: Emmaus Academic, 2019), p. 458.

# Bibliography

Alfeyev, Grigory, 'The Patristic Heritage and Modernity', Paper delivered at the 9th International Conference on Russian monasticism and spirituality, Bose Monastery, Italy, 2001.

Allen, John, Jr, 'Ratzinger Credited with Saving Lutheran Pact', *National Catholic Reporter*, 10 September 1999.

Balthasar, Hans Urs von, *The Office of Peter and the Structure of the Church* (San Francisco: Ignatius Press, 1986).

Balthasar, Hans Urs von, *The Theology of Karl Barth: Exposition and Interpretation* (San Francisco: Ignatius, 1992).

Bieler, Martin, 'Analogia entis as an Expression of Love According to Ferdinand Ulrich', in The Analogy of Being: Invention of the Antichrist of Wisdom of God, edited by Thomas Joseph White (Grand Rapids: Eerdmans, 2011).

Boersma, Hans, Heavenly Participation: The Weaving of a Sacramental Tapestry (Grand Rapids: Eerdmans, 2011).

Boersma, Hans, Nouvelle Théologie and Sacramental Ontology: A Return to Mystery (Oxford: Oxford University Press, 2009).

Bogle, James and Joanna, A Heart for Europe: The Lives of Charles and Empress Zita of Austria-Hungary (London: Gracewing, 2000).

Bouyer, Louis, Orthodox Spirituality and Protestant and Anglican Spirituality (London: Burns & Oates, 1969).

Bouyer, Louis, The Spirit and Forms of Protestantism, A. V. Littledale (trans.) (London: Harvill Press, 1956).

Bouyer, Louis, The Word, Church and Sacraments in Protestantism and Catholicism (New York: Desclee, 1961).

Congar, Yves, After Nine Hundred Years: The Background of the Schism between the Eastern and Western Churches (New York: Fordham University Press, 1959).

Congar, Yves, Dialogue between Christians: Catholic Contributions to Ecumenism, Philip Loretz SJ (trans.) (London: Geoffrey Chapman, 1966).

Congar, Yves, Divided Christendom: A Catholic Study of the Problem of Reunion (London: Geoffrey Bles, 1939).

Congar, Yves, 'Ecumenical Experience and Conversion: A Personal Testimony', in The Sufficiency of God: Essays on the Ecumenical Hope in Honour of W. A. Visser't Hooft, edited by Robert C. Mackie and Charles C. West (London: SCM Press, 1963), pp. 71–87.

Daniélou, Jean, Approches du Christ (Paris: Bernard Grasset, 1960).

Dick, John A., The Malines Conversations Revisited (Leuven: Leuven University Press, 1989).

Doyle, Dennis M., 'Journet, Congar, and the Roots of Communion Ecclesiology', Theological Studies 58 (1997): 461–79.

Farrow, Douglas, Theological Negotiations: Proposals in Soteriology and Anthropology (Ada, MI: Baker Academic, 2018).

Fries, Heinrich and Karl Rahner, Unity of the Churches: An Actual Possibility, Ruth C. L. Gritsch and Eric W. Gritsch (trans.) (Philadelphia: Fortress, 1985).

Howsare, Rodney, Hans Urs von Balthasar and Protestantism: The Ecumenical Implications of His Theological Style (London: T&T Clark, 2005).

Journet, Charles, The Primacy of Peter, John Chapin (trans.) (Baltimore: Newman Press, 1954).

Levada, William, 'Five Hundred Years after St. John Fisher: Benedict's Ecumenical Initiatives to Anglicans' (Kingston, ON, 2010).

Levada, William, 'Note of the Congregation for the Doctrine of the Faith about Personal Ordinariates for Anglicans Entering the Catholic Church' (Vatican City, 2009).

Levering, Matthew, 'Doctrine and Ecumenism', in Joseph Ratzinger and the Healing of the Reformation Divisions, edited by Emery de Gaál and Matthew Levering (Steubenville: Emmaus Academic, 2019).

Lochbrunner, Manfred, Hans Urs von Balthasar und seine Theologen-kollegen (Würzburg: Echter Verlag, 2009).

Long, D. Stephen, Saving Karl Barth: Hans Urs von Balthasar's Preoccupation, (Minneapolis: Fortress, 2014).

Lord Halifax et al., The Conversations at Malines 1921–1925 (Oxford: Oxford University Press, 1927).

McPartlan, Paul, A Service of Love: Papal Primacy, the Eucharist and Church Unity (Washington, DC: Catholic University of America Press, 2013).

Murray, Paul D., Receptive Ecumenism and the Call to Catholic Learning: Exploring a Way for Contemporary Ecumenism (Oxford: Oxford University Press, 2008).

Nichols, Aidan, *Theology in the Russian Diaspora: Church, Fathers, Eucharist in Nikolai Afanas'ev, 1893–1966* (Cambridge: Cambridge University Press, 2008).

Ratzinger, Joseph, *Church, Ecumenism and Politics: New Essays in Ecclesiology*, Robert Nowell (trans.) (New York: Crossroad, 1988).

Ratzinger, Joseph, *Principles of Catholic Theology* (San Francisco: Ignatius, 1987).

Reid, Alcuin, *The Organic Development of the Liturgy* (Farnborough: St Michael's Abbey Press, 2005).

Root, Michael, 'Ratzinger and the Doctrine of Justification', in *Joseph Ratzinger and the Healing of the Reformation Divisions*, edited by Emery de Gaál and Matthew Levering (Steubenville: Emmaus Academic, 2019).

Sweeney, Douglas A., 'Ratzinger on Scripture, Tradition and Church: An Evangelical Assessment', in *Joseph Ratzinger and the Healing of the Reformation Divisions*, edited by Emery de Gaál and Matthew Levering (Steubenville: Emmaus Academic, 2019).

Swidler, Leonard, *Blood Witness for Peace and Unity: The Life of Max Joseph Metzger* (New Jersey: Dimension Books, 1986).

Vickers, Mark, *Reunion Revisited: 1930s Ecumenism Exposed* (London: Gracewing, 2017).

White, Thomas Joseph (ed.), *The Analogy of Being: Invention of the Antichrist or the Wisdom of God?* (Grand Rapids: Eerdmans, 2011).

Wigley, Stephen. D., *Karl Barth and Hans Urs von Balthasar* (London: T&T Clark, 2007).

Zizioulas, John, One Single Source: An Orthodox Response to the Clarification on the Filioque, Orthodox Research Institute, accessed at www.orthodoxresearchinstitute.org/articles/dogmatics/john_zizioulas_single_source.htm.

# Fundamentalism and Evangelicalism

*Andrew Atherstone*

## Introduction

'Evangelicalism' and 'fundamentalism' – terms coined in the 1820s and 1920s respectively – are both highly contested global movements.[1] Their theological and ecclesial identities have been argued over extensively, as has the nature of the relationship between them.[2] Fundamentalism was named initially for *The Fundamentals* (1910–15), a collection of conservative theological essays distributed with the help of Californian oil money to Protestant ministers worldwide.[3] Counted among the contributors were a remarkably diverse range of evangelical theologians from both sides of the Atlantic, who could not all be easily dismissed as 'wilfully purblind obscurantists' or 'bigoted ecclesiastics'.[4] Yet fundamentalism's connection with the evangelical movement which brought it to birth has long been disputed. This chapter examines the theological rhetoric surrounding their relationship through a detailed case study of one particular outbreak of fundamentalist debate – in Britain in the 1950s – which is illustrative of the wider global phenomenon. It demonstrates how fundamentalism is a highly malleable but potent theological category, with strong emotive associations. This case study, from a mid-century English and predominantly Anglican context, reveals that the contested language surrounding fundamentalism and evangelicalism has as much to do with public image, and the struggle for ecclesial or cultural superiority, as with doctrinal distinctives. The British debate was paralleled in multiple other twentieth-century contexts.

## The Billy Graham Factor

Fundamentalism is often associated with evangelical Nonconformity, vibrant among conservative American Baptists and Presbyterians, for example. Yet even the Church of England, noted for its comprehension of diverse doctrines, encompassed a lively network of conservative evangelicals in the 1920s and 1930s who displayed fundamentalist characteristics.[5] Their influence soon dwindled, and the intense fundamentalist/modernist disputes of the interwar period seemed forever consigned to the past. By 1951, *The Times* could reasonably claim that the theological controversy over fundamentalism was now 'almost stilled'.[6] Two years later, at the Evangelical Fellowship of Theological Literature in Cambridge, Douglas Harrison (Archdeacon of Sheffield) observed that the traditional Protestant emphasis on the supreme authority of Scripture had proven 'most vulnerable to the acids of historical criticism'. Much of older evangelicalism, and indeed of classical Anglicanism, was 'near-fundamentalism', he suggested, but he was glad that those tendencies had now passed away.[7] British readers picked up Norman Furniss's *The Fundamentalist Controversy, 1918–1931* (1954), a critical account published in the United States, but its limited chronological scope confirmed the widespread assumption that fundamentalism was a suitable topic for historical study, not a contemporary concern. In Furniss's judgement, the fundamentalist movement, though once potent, was no longer able 'to capture the headlines'.[8] These assumptions about evangelicalism's trajectory as it entered the second half of the twentieth century proved misguided. In the words of Hugh Montefiore (Dean of Gonville and Caius College, Cambridge, and later Bishop of Birmingham), if the fundamentalism controversy had lain buried amidst forgotten battles, in the mid-1950s it 'burst from the grave with new power'.[9]

The catalyst for reignition of the controversy in Britain was the arrival of American preacher Billy Graham for major evangelistic campaigns. The complaint of Bryan Reed (general secretary of the Methodist Youth Department) was typical, at the start of the three-month Greater London Crusade in March 1954. He warned that Graham's attitude to the Bible was 'a crude literalism and rigid fundamentalism which lingers on in the Southern States of America but which was abandoned by every scholar of repute half a century ago.' Reed was particularly anxious lest young people be drawn into the 'narrow fundamentalist groups' who were Graham's main supporters.[10] From an Anglican perspective, *Crockford's Clerical Directory* began to worry about the rise of biblical fundamentalists within English universities and theological colleges, or those so close to being fundamentalists 'that no ordinary magnifying glass can detect any significant difference'. These young men held views of the Bible long discarded by every theology professor and diocesan bishop, and their 'erroneous dogmatism' was a threat to the Church of England's ministry.[11] In March 1955 the annual Founders' Day of the Society for Promoting Christian Knowledge was warned of 'the recrudescence of fundamentalism' which made the Bible the 'be-all and end-all of the Christian religion' and thus 'deformed the truth'.[12] Methodist scholar Gordon Rupp joined the chorus of disapproval, lamenting that Graham's crusades had given 'fundamentalist pietism' its 'biggest boost' for fifty years. Fundamentalism, he suggested, was 'a symptom of something sick in the mind of Christendom', which would only drive 'the estranged millions' further away from the Church.[13] The *Bible League Quarterly*, however, queried Rupp's logic. If Graham's fundamentalism really did estrange non-Christians, why had crowds flocked to hear him preach in such unprecedented multitudes?[14]

Preaching in Latin at St Paul's Cathedral in July 1955 before the Canterbury Convocation, Eric Kemp (Chaplain of Exeter College, Oxford, and later Bishop of Chichester) highlighted a number of dangers facing the Church of England, including the rebirth of a 'factious attitude of mind', reminiscent of the Puritans, among evangelical young men at school and university. They interpreted the Bible contrary to both reason and Church tradition, and laid exclusive claim to the title Christian. 'Thoughtful Anglicans of every colour fear that a great danger has now arisen from this source', Kemp added darkly, 'and that a greater still is on the way.'[15] He had first-hand experience of a difficult relationship with the Oxford Inter-Collegiate Christian Union (OICCU), who refused to cooperate with non-evangelicals and opposed the work of his college chapel. More than once, young men who Kemp led to the Christian faith were 'captured by the OICCU and told that my teaching was not true Christianity'.[16] The *Church Times* expanded on these themes, offering an exposé of the conservative evangelical network:

It is a closed, tight, unyielding and intransigent body, chiefly masculine, which holds itself aloof from any historic Christian tradition. It is a fellowship of the converted. All who belong have had an experience in which they have 'found Christ'. For them, the Bible is an infallible authority . . . Reason is at a discount. It is experience that counts. You either believe or you do not.

These young evangelicals, according to the analysis, were 'profoundly defective' in theology, exclusivist in their attitudes (even referring to their churchgoing parents as 'unsaved'), and arrested in their intellectual development. They engaged in sport, but only because it provided evangelistic opportunities, while their academic studies suffered due to perpetual prayer meetings and tea parties. They were nurtured as schoolboys in evangelical camps organised by 'fervent undergraduates', and at university were handed on to the same network, 'already indoctrinated'.[17] Probably the Church Times had in mind the Scripture Union 'Bash Camps', founded in the 1930s for boys from England's elite public schools. One Cambridge undergraduate, John Creasey, sounded the alarm over the Cambridge Inter-Collegiate Christian Union (CICCU), which he believed was doing 'incalculable' damage to the Christian faith. The CICCU had recently refused to take part in a university mission led by Michael Ramsey (Bishop of Durham), considering him doctrinally 'unsound', and instead were planning their own mission with Billy Graham in November 1955. Creasey implored all Anglican clergy to warn students going up to university from their parishes against the 'all-out menace' of the Inter-Varsity Fellowship of Evangelical Unions (IVF), of which the CICCU and the OICCU were a part.[18]

Shortly before Graham's Cambridge crusade, these concerns hit the national press in a flurry of correspondence in The Times, initiated by Canon Harry Luce (headmaster of Durham School). He argued that since universities exist to advance learning, fundamentalism should not be allowed a hearing there – a mid-century attempt to 'no-platform' the speaker. Those who paid no heed to 'modern scholarship' should be 'laughed out of court' by the universities, Luce continued, and fundamentalism would result only in 'disillusionment and disaster for educated men and women in this twentieth-century world'.[19] Other prominent Anglicans chimed in. Bishop Ramsey, perhaps stung by the CICCU's cold shoulder, denounced the 'crudity' of fundamentalist doctrine which involved 'stifling' the mind. Fundamentalist converts were won in the universities, he warned, 'at a cost both of moral casualties and of an alienation of thoughtful men and women from the Christian faith'.[20] Russell Barry (Bishop of Southwell) acknowledged that fundamentalism

> meets an obvious psychological need, but by a very dangerous prescription which may cure the symptom only to kill the patient. It may temporarily offer peace of mind, but frequently leads to acute conflict later and eventually to 'giving up religion'. England is strewn with such religious casualties . . .

In Bishop Barry's opinion, the Church of England stood for 'the tradition of intellectual freedom. If we betray that, we shall have sold our birthright.'[21] John Collins (Precentor of St Paul's Cathedral and later chairman of the Campaign for Nuclear Disarmament) dismissed biblical fundamentalism as 'an evil doctrine' which led, like all movements claiming an infallible authority, to 'intolerance, bigotry, and violence'.[22] In the view of another correspondent, 'the Christian mind is essentially the liberal mind'. Therefore, the rise of fundamentalism among candidates for ordination in the Church of England was especially disquieting:

For while it is always true that an honours degree is no passport into the kingdom of God, it is also true that in a critical age a religion that cannot hold the allegiance of trained thinkers must defeat its ends.[23]

However, Garfield Williams (former Dean of Manchester) advised that instead of criticising Billy Graham, other schools of thought should ask themselves why they failed to produce evangelists of his ability.[24]

Faced by this barrage of denunciation, evangelicals in the Church of England rushed to Graham's defence. The octogenarian Herbert Gresford Jones (former Bishop of Kampala, Uganda) suggested that this flare-up over fundamentalism was simply the latest skirmish in the 'age-long battle' between reason and revelation.[25] One of Graham's key Anglican supporters, John Stott (Rector of All Souls, Langham Place, London), concurred that God's revelation was

> often in conflict with the unenlightened reason of sinful men ... The proud human intellect still needs to be abased – in England as in Corinth – and the only way to enter the Kingdom of God is still to become like a little child.[26]

These were risky sentiments to publish on the eve of a mission to Cambridge, where human intellect was especially prized. One of the CICCU's senior advisors, Basil Atkinson, proclaimed that Graham's gospel was 'in accord with true scholarship illumined by revelation', originating in the New Testament, and would still be preached long after the 'transient' gospel of modernism had been 'superseded and discarded'.[27] When Mervyn Stockwood (Vicar of the University Church, Cambridge) accused the CICCU of 'spiritual arrogance',[28] Atkinson wrote privately to Stott of 'that serpent Stockwood' who 'stank of brimstone'. Evangelicals like Atkinson anticipated 'a terrific continuous fight' in the University, but prayed that the Graham mission would bring 'real revival' among senior members and much-needed reform of college chapels.[29]

The *Life of Faith*, an evangelical newspaper, suggested that these concerns over resurgent fundamentalism were in fact 'a tacit acknowledgement of the virility of Evangelical life and scholarship'.[30] Luce had called for CICCU fundamentalists to be laughed out of court, so the *Life of Faith* itself resorted to humour, with a satirical poem by hymn-writer Timothy Dudley-Smith (editorial secretary of the Evangelical Alliance, and later Bishop of Thetford), one of the supporters of the CICCU mission. It opened with the lines:

> Oh, hang your head for Cambridge
> Where, deluded in their youth,
> There are students who would still regard
> The Word of God as truth;
> Who, in spite of current catchwords
> And the modern churchman's creed,
> Hold a fundamental Gospel
> For a fundamental need.

Turning Luce's appeal to 'modern scholarship' on its head, Dudley-Smith concluded in mocking tones:

> You cannot preach to men in gowns
> What passed with men in skins;

You must have modern scholarship
To save from modern sins.[31]

The *Life of Faith*'s report of Graham's Cambridge crusade was accompanied by a cartoon of a young man in suit and tie with a Bible under his arm (perhaps representing Graham himself or a Cambridge undergraduate), standing at a signpost pointing in opposite directions to 'Fundamentalism' and 'Modernism'. The upward fundamentalist path of 'faith', via 'The Bible says' (one of Graham's best-known catchphrases) led to 'The Truth'. The downward modernist path via 'modern scholarship', 'reason', 'outworn theories', 'human opinions', 'higher criticism', 'philosophy' and 'evolution' led to 'darkness', 'confusion', 'materialism' and 'doubt'. The accompanying Bible text from 2 Peter spoke of the 'sure word of prophecy', from the Holy Spirit, shining in a dark place.[32] These tropes were familiar, but some of the *Life of Faith*'s evangelical readers took exception to the association of 'modern scholarship' as the doorway to darkness. The editor apologised, acknowledging that the conservative evangelical embrace of scholarship was in fact one of the most heartening developments of the post-war generation. The cartoonist also agreed that he should have written 'destructive criticism' not 'modern scholarship', but this slip of the pen betrayed lingering evangelical assumptions.[33]

In a defence of the evangelical position, Stott acknowledged that fundamentalism had been brought into disrepute by its association, especially in America, with 'extremes and extravagances', so that it was now often 'almost synonymous with obscurantism'. He argued that every evangelical should be both a 'fundamentalist' and a 'higher critic', welcoming the historical and literary scholarship of the critics, though not all their philosophical presuppositions. Stott warned against 'excessively literalist' interpretations which mangled metaphor and poetry, explaining that the Bible was given as 'a handbook for sinners not a textbook for scientists'.[34] Frederic Cockin (Bishop of Bristol) had rebuked evangelicals for believing the Bible to be 'dictated by the Holy Spirit using human writers as His pen',[35] but Stott rejected such accusations as simply 'absurd':

> We do indeed believe that the Holy Spirit spoke through the human authors so directly that their words were His words, but we do not imagine that the process was a mechanical one. Pens and dictaphones are lifeless instruments; the Biblical authors were living agents.[36]

Nevertheless, to John Burnaby (Regius Professor of Divinity at Cambridge) this rationale seemed far too ambiguous.[37] In private he wrote to Stott, 'I find it difficult to distinguish what you say, if I have understood it rightly, from "fundamentalism" as commonly understood.'[38] Decades later, Stott claimed that he had consistently repudiated the label 'fundamentalism' since the mid-1950s,[39] but in fact he originally welcomed it, if understood to mean 'strict adherence' to the Christian fundamentals: 'Now if this is fundamentalism, one hopes that every reader of *Crusade* is a fundamentalist!'[40]

Some evangelicals took pride in a 'fundamentalist' identity. For example, Methodist minister Frank Ockenden welcomed the fundamentalist badge as meaning belief in the verbal inspiration of Scripture with a rejection of both evolutionary theory and rationalistic higher criticism.[41] He was happy to be known as a biblical 'literalist'.[42] Likewise, Charles Moore (Vicar of St Augustine's, Highbury) announced:

> To be a member of Christ's Church in the true Bible sense a man must of necessity be a 'fundamentalist'. He must earnestly believe in the foundation truths of Holy Scripture

as the 'inspired word of God'. He must not be ashamed nor afraid to be called an 'extremist', 'a bigot', nor 'narrowminded' for Christ's sake . . .

Christians, Moore continued, should count it 'an honour' to be classed as fundamentalist.[43] Thomas Hewitt (secretary of the Church Society) also asserted that every conservative evangelical 'is, of course, a fundamentalist, if that word receives its true meaning'.[44] Stella Aldwinckle (Oxford Pastorate chaplain) defended Billy Graham against accusations of 'emotionalism' and 'fundamentalism'. Nevertheless, she argued that if fundamentalism meant accepting the authority of Scripture as decisive in matters of doctrine, 'then in this sense the Church has always been, and must remain, "fundamentalist"'. Biblical criticism had 'no power to destroy the fundamental facts on which the Church's Faith is built'.[45] Stott announced that Graham had repudiated the title, and *The Times* agreed that Graham was not a fundamentalist 'in the older sense of the word' and that fundamentalism could now be 'pronounced dead'.[46] However, this concerned those like Kenneth de Courcy, one of Graham's erstwhile backers, who provocatively declared:

A great many very sincere fundamentalists have prayed, worked and given money in support of Dr Graham thinking him to be an exponent of their faith . . . To be quite frank I want to know whether I have parted with money under a deception or not.[47]

Others distanced themselves from this terminology. For example, A. T. Houghton (general secretary of the Bible Churchmen's Missionary Society) affirmed an 'infallible' Bible but repudiated the term 'fundamentalist' because of its American associations.[48] Douglas Johnson (general secretary of the IVF) honoured the early fundamentalists for 'battling for the biblical theism of the apostles . . . against a series of insidious Deisms and Pantheisms which have come very near to destroying the true faith'. He claimed that every great revival in English religion had begun among those who believed that 'the supernatural interventions of God are of *the very essence* of the Christianity of the Bible'. Nonetheless, because the title 'fundamentalist' was widely misunderstood, Johnson recommended that IVF members stick with 'the name "Evangelical" or, better still, simply "Christian"'.[49] This was not an ecumenical rejection of party labels but rather a presumption that evangelicals were the true Christians and therefore should claim that broader title. Another evangelical minister worried that 'fundamentalist' denoted 'sub-normal and unintelligent', and pleaded for a return to the name 'evangelical' as of greater dignity. '"Fundamentalism" is a bogey!', he proclaimed; 'Let that word die the death! Judgment rests with modern scholarship. Let it assume the black cap and speak the words of doom. Who cares for that neck!'[50]

## Episcopal Assaults

The Anglican episcopate led the assault upon English fundamentalism, concerned at the inroads it was making within the national church. Strong criticism was heard even among evangelicals, like the Islington Conference in January 1956, the largest annual gathering of evangelicals in the Church of England. In the closing conference sermon, Christopher Chavasse (Bishop of Rochester) announced that fundamentalism should be a 'truly Catholic word' but through American associations had come to represent 'the narrow obscurantism of an exclusive cult'. In his diagnosis, fundamentalism's chief error was 'Bibliolatry', especially belief in the 'verbal inerrancy' of Scripture. He lambasted a crude literalism which received the Genesis hymn of creation with 'scientific exactitude', which insisted on the historicity of Adam and Eve, and Jonah's great fish, and which taught that dashing out the brains of Babylonian babies really was 'happy' (Psalm 137).[51] Such an approach, Chavasse suggested, was idolatrous:

> Literalism is the last ditch of Fundamentalism; and it is so obviously, and even profanely, untenable that it impels the question why are good people prepared to go to such fantastic lengths, and even to degrade God's Holy Word into the mechanically inspired dictation of automatic writing, in order to retain this impossible shibboleth of the 'verbal inerrancy of Holy Scripture'? The answer is as old as the Golden Calf in the history of Israel.[52]

Chavasse maintained that the Jewish scribes and Pharisees who rejected the Messiah were first-century fundamentalists, as were the apartheid promoters of the Dutch Reformed Church in modern South Africa. Their mistake was to exalt the Scriptures as an infallible authority alongside the Son of God himself. Continuing his attack upon the dictation theory, the bishop insisted that the Bible never claimed to be 'the actual *words* of God'. Its authors were 'the pen-men, not the pens, of God', producing multiple genres stamped with human personality: 'It is merely stupid to make them what they are not, or to force them into one pattern of Literalism, as if God had purposed to dictate text-books for scientists or anthropologists.'[53] This attack on the doctrine of verbal inerrancy, from one of the leading evangelical bishops at the key evangelical conference, was met with an outcry from some of his co-religionists. Correspondents in the *English Churchman* thought Chavasse's teaching was 'provocative and dangerous' and had shrouded Islington with 'darkness'.[54] Others worried that it might indicate a new liberal policy on the Islington platform.[55]

Chavasse's assault was followed by Michael Ramsey, who identified four 'closely knit features' of modern English fundamentalism, as represented by the IVF: a view of Scripture which overlooked its human composition; a single focus on penal substitutionary atonement which was 'a very distorted version of the apostolic gospel'; a call to immediate decision at the end of sermons or missions, which played to the emotions not the mind; and a 'highly individualistic' doctrine of the Holy Spirit which neglected Church and sacraments.[56] Ramsey noticed that this fundamentalist 'phenomenon' was on the rise and saw an explanation in the psychology of young people:

> It sweeps schoolboys into its camps, and undergraduates into its revival missions. It produces an ardent discipleship often marked by zeal and self sacrifice. And why? It offers authority and security, quick and sure, to a generation restless and insecure. Other and more wholesome versions of Christianity offer security indeed – but rather more slowly: the security of growing gradually into the spiritual life of the Church, or the security of bringing a thoughtful and honest mind to rest upon the verities of the Christian faith. But here is security – in a single night. Hither, young man: drown your worries in the rapture of conversion: stifle your doubts by abdicating the use of your mind. A rousing sermon, a hurricane of emotion, a will to leap in the dark – and peace at once and for ever.[57]

The bishop predicted that these sudden evangelical 'conversions' would lead to 'a backwash of moral casualties and disillusioned sceptics'. He called upon his fellow Anglicans to return to the historic threefold method of Scripture, tradition and reason in order to 'withstand the bibliolatrists as stoutly as Hooker withstood the Puritans of his day'. The movement was both heretical and sectarian, Ramsey averred.[58] Leslie Hunter (Bishop of Sheffield) imitated Ramsey's analysis, deriding fundamentalism as 'heresy' and 'a perversion of the truth'. He deplored the recent revival of 'a crude and almost idolatrous attitude to the Bible', especially the old doctrine of verbal inspiration which had been 'out-argued and discarded a hundred years ago', held by no Anglican bishop or respectable scholar 'within living memory'. Hunter believed that fundamentalism was attractive to fearful people who wanted the comfort of religion while escaping the 'duty of thinking' and the 'pains of doubt'. Anglicanism, by contrast, asserted the bishop, offered 'the whole truth' not 'short cuts to Zion'.[59]

The *Church Times* welcomed Ramsey's intervention and warned that 'crude fundamentalism' in universities and theological colleges was threatening 'the future character of the priesthood' and the very foundations of the Church of England.[60] The *Life of Faith*, however, criticised him for launching 'a full-scale attack . . . unrestrained almost to violence . . . a travesty of the facts'.[61] At the annual meeting of the Fellowship of Evangelical Churchmen in April 1956, Philip Edgcumbe Hughes (secretary of the Church Society) answered Ramsey point by point. To the charge of bibliolatry, for example, he retorted that the Church should be more concerned with the 'gross doctrine' of Anglo-Catholics like Ramsey who 'worship a piece of bread' at the Eucharist. Hughes mocked: 'Let him search England from end to end and he will not find a single "fundamentalist" prostrated before a Bible and worshipping his God as locally present under the forms of paper and ink.'[62] Among other evangelical reactions was that of A. G. Pouncy (Rector of Bebington, Cheshire) who wrote in his parish magazine of his anger, amazement and sorrow at Ramsey's attack. He defended the academic credentials of the IVF, which numbered no less than eleven university professors among its vice presidents, and pointed to the IVF's *New Bible Commentary* (1953) as testimony to the 'breadth and depth, quality and virility' of contemporary evangelical scholarship. Pouncy acknowledged that some styles of evangelism were 'more zealous than wise', but for Ramsey 'to castigate . . . almost all fundamentalist evangelism as froth and bubble is a grave perversion of the truth'.[63] Pouncy himself had been converted at an evangelical house party for school boys in the 1930s, and his curate Peter Barratt had likewise experienced sudden conversion during his first weeks as a Cambridge undergraduate in 1950. In these matters Ramsey was 'tragically misinformed and misled', Pouncy told his parishioners, publicly reaffirming his belief

> in the fundamentalism which, as Wesley did, 'offers Christ' to needy men and women, as Sin-bearer, Saviour and Sovereign for ever. So long as God allows me the privilege of living and working with you in Bebington, so long shall I, if God help me, press you all thus to come to Christ and be saved, whether it be popular or not.[64]

Perhaps regretting his unguarded language, Ramsey claimed that he was not trying to stir up a 'heresy hunt' against conservative evangelicals as a body, and indeed knew of no evangelical parochial clergyman to whom his charges applied. His concern was rather with the 'extravagances' of undenominational missions like the CICCU.[65] Nevertheless, many Anglican evangelicals embraced the IVF's doctrine and methods, and rightly believed that they too were under attack. Part of Ramsey's concern was that evangelicals were at root un-Anglican. As Archbishop of Canterbury in 1962, he confessed in conversation with the poet John Betjeman that the 'chief trouble' with the Church of England was 'the alarming increase of bigoted fundamentalists in it, who ought really to become Strict Baptists or some such extreme nonconformist sect'.[66] These trends worried many.

The *Church of England Newspaper* acknowledged that an increasing number of conservative evangelicals, or 'youthful fundamentalists', were seeking Anglican ordination.[67] L. W. Barnard (a clergyman in Wiltshire) complained that fundamentalism was 'rife' in evangelical circles, and that a 'childish' approach to the Bible was prevalent among ordinands and clergy trained in the evangelical colleges. The antidote was a university honours degree in theology: 'For no man who had been through the theological mill could possibly support Fundamentalism unless he was suffering from schizophrenia.'[68] Biblical fundamentalism, Barnard reiterated, was 'rampant' within the Church of England, which was being 'held to ransom by obscurantists'.[69]

Educationists joined the assault. Former headmaster Sir John Wolfenden (Vice Chancellor of the University of Reading) told a conference of schoolteachers in Oxford in January 1956 that there was a growing antithesis between 'the free and fearless ranging of the intellect' and the rise of a 'neo-obscurantism' or 'literal-minded fundamentalism'. He was frightened at the large number of young people arriving at university 'with their minds firmly closed, locked, bolted and barred'.[70] More pungently, the *Journal of Education*, edited by literary critic Boris Ford, derided the 'curiously popular primitive sort of fundamentalism' for its 'abdication of reason and responsibility', a 'crass' approach to biblical interpretation and a 'shockingly uncontrolled and atavistic emotionalism'. This naïve form of religion was particularly attractive to children, the journal asserted, because it behaved like a 'secret society' with 'priggish intolerance' of outsiders, 'fervid support of half-understood rites and slogans' and 'cloistered seclusion from the ordinary affairs of life'. But converts who developed critical faculties were likely to turn away from their youthful excesses 'with contempt, even with a sense of shame' at a 'childish phase outgrown'. Fundamentalism was deeply 'contra-educational', Ford insisted, and schools bore a responsibility to counteract it.[71] Kathleen Bliss likewise lamented the growth of 'American-style fundamentalism' within British schools, which bred 'insufferable arrogance' and 'anti-intellectualism'. Echoing George Orwell's dystopian world, she observed:

> Reason as an element in religious discourse is not only abandoned but despised; an attitude of double-think keeps the criteria applied to other fields of knowledge rigorously out of anything deemed religious. The effect is to thrust many of the more intelligent into more extreme scepticism and to insure (*sic*) that those who come through this phase often do so by repudiating religion altogether.[72]

However, a group of headteachers from grammar and independent schools came to the defence of school Christian Unions as the fruit of the evangelical revival within Anglicanism, not as an American derivative. Such discussion groups were of 'considerable educational value', they argued, even if the members were immature. If educationists encouraged the growth of school societies in every other sphere, such as politics and current affairs, why not in religion also?[73]

Further concern was expressed at the York Convocation, representing the northern dioceses in the Church of England. Canon Edwin T. Kerby (Vicar of Pendlebury, near Manchester), aged 78, worried about the 'amazing influence' of fundamentalism in English schools and universities in the 1950s.[74] The education committee noted that many young people arrived at university 'already indoctrinated' by their school Christian Unions, but that the IVF was especially responsible for propagating 'uncritical fundamentalism'. The characteristics of these evangelical undergraduates included an emphasis on penal substitutionary atonement, rejection of baptismal regeneration, boycotting of college chapel and an 'intolerant individualism', though combined with a 'real zeal' for prayer, Bible study and personal discipleship. University chaplains confessed fear at the movement's growing influence, since many young fundamentalists went on to teach Religious Knowledge in schools, thus perpetuating the cycle.[75] Russell Barry (Bishop of Southwell) agreed that the dominance of fundamentalists in schools and universities was a matter of 'grave concern'. Despite their laudable 'devotion and self-discipline', they were 'uncooperative, self-contained, censorious towards their fellow Christians and, in general, sectarian through and through'. In the bishop's diagnosis, fundamentalism ministered to 'the same psychological need' as Communism and Roman Catholicism, answering to the widespread 'hunger for spiritual security in an insecure and bewildering world'. Such a phenomenon was to be expected in the turbulent Cold War period, offering an 'authoritative religion', but he lamented the rise of 'intolerant and inhospitable dogmatism'. Especially concerning to the bishop was that a large proportion of Church of England ordination candidates came from fundamentalist networks, a threat to the future ministry of the Church and incompatible with 'the Anglican ethos' which prized 'openness and liberality of mind'. It was bad enough to encounter closed minds among his fellow sexagenarians, Barry concluded, but among teenage undergraduates it was 'absolutely awful'.[76] According to the *Church Gazette* (magazine of the Church Society) this was nothing less than a fundamentalist 'witch hunt'. If the bishops really had no desire to drive conservative evangelicals out of the Church of England, then why were they constantly attacking them? The episcopal assaults seemed to the *Church Gazette* particularly obtuse since the conservative evangelicals were successfully filling churches, producing ordinands and 'winning men for Christ all over the country'.[77]

The octogenarian Bernard Heywood (former Bishop of Ely) added his lament at the spread of 'the cult of Fundamentalism' within English universities.[78] From a younger but equally hostile perspective, Kenneth Leech, an 18-year-old Anglo-Catholic in Manchester, called it the 'cult of unreason', which turned the Bible into 'an infallible text-book' as if the heart of Christianity was 'a Word who became not flesh but paper'.[79] Geoffrey Lampe (Edward Cadbury Professor of Theology at Birmingham, and later Regius Professor of Divinity at Cambridge) accused the IVF of leading fundamentalist recruits astray on a foolish 'quest for unassailable certainty'. They approached the Bible not 'in a spirit of humble enquiry', but 'with their minds made up'; not glorifying God through critical reasoning but dishonouring God with 'intellectually dishonest apologetics'.[80] The *Church Times* agreed that 'unassailable certainty' seemed very attractive to 'a generation which feels lost in the vastness of an expanding universe', but observed that infallibility (whether fundamentalist or Roman) did 'violence to the integrity of the human personality and to the real nature of the gospel'.[81] Not all readers found this analysis convincing, however. On the simple test of knowing a tree by its fruit, one layman thought Professor Lampe should instead be asking why fundamentalism produced 'virile and devotional' Christians but other traditions did not see similar results.[82]

The fullest critical assessment was *Fundamentalism and the Church of God* (1957), by Anglo-Catholic monk Gabriel Hebert, member of the Society of the Sacred Mission. Written in a gentler tone, avoiding the heightened rhetoric which characterised the wider controversy, Hebert nonetheless criticised the IVF and conservative evangelicals in the Church of England for their doctrine of scriptural inerrancy. He accused the IVF's *New Bible Commentary* of treating its readers like children, and warned of the 'peril of Bibliolatry', which identified the Word of God with the written words of Scripture.[83] Advocating an end to theological partisanship, Hebert appealed for the IVF to come together with the rival Student Christian Movement (SCM), harnessing their complementary strengths in an ecumenical spirit.[84] His analysis was welcomed by Archbishop Ramsey, and reviewed by the *Church Times* under the provocative title 'A Heresy Explored'.[85] However, the *Church Gazette* retorted that Hebert, like Don Quixote, was merely tilting at windmills in his accusations against conservative evangelicals. He was propounding 'a new form of liberalism', guilty of 'milk-and-water mediocrity' in his thinking and a 'middle-of-the-road' approach to the Christian faith which 'cuts very little ice with the world, which is not too uncomfortable for the flesh, and which on the whole does not unduly worry the Devil'.[86] Similarly, reviewing Hebert for the IVF's Graduates' Fellowship, evangelical clergyman Herbert Carson asserted that without the inerrancy of Scripture, 'the gospel degenerates into the pious platitudes and pitiful homilies of liberal religious speculation'.[87]

The necessity of evangelical separation from the liberalism of the SCM was part of the heroic founding narrative of the IVF, reiterated in John Pollock's *A Cambridge Movement* (1953), the authorised history of the CICCU. These tensions between competing approaches to student Christianity showed no signs of abating, as the theological arguments were repeatedly replayed.[88] In his 1957 analysis of the fundamentalism prevalent within 'pietistic conservative evangelicalism', Philip Lee-Woolf (general secretary of the SCM) argued that the controversy was not at core doctrinal. Fundamentalism, he suggested, met a deep psychological need for friendship and security. He noticed that these evangelical networks were predominantly young, male and professional – recruiting especially from grammar schools and universities, and among medics, accountants, civil servants and city businessmen. They were bound together in 'tightly-knit groups with a wonderful sense of fellowship, at once sweeping forward and held together in comradeship under the pressure of a ruined and condemned world'. They lived a lonely suburban life and were 'strongly reactionary' on sociopolitical questions, with no interest in challenging unjust institutions and structures. These young evangelicals, according to Lee-Woolf, feared 'Laodicean liberalism' and wanted a faith which offered 'authority and assurance, in place of unsolved questions and a world too bewildering to understand', and therefore they ran to an infallible book and a fixed dogmatic position even at the cost of 'stifling the free exercise of the mind'. They displayed 'intense loyalty' to their evangelical fellowships, which were escapist 'ghettoes' and fundamentalist 'factories' turning out Christians after a fixed pattern. Their isolationist mentality, Lee-Woolf concluded, was damaging and 'dangerous' for both the mission and unity of the Church.[89] These sentiments were not likely to foster the IVF/SCM rapprochement for which Hebert called.

Cyril Bowles (Principal of Ridley Hall, Cambridge, and later Bishop of Derby) struck a more conciliatory note. Preaching before the University of Cambridge in March 1958 he warned against an 'anti-fundamentalist witch-hunt' and observed that some of those attempting 'to pursue Biblical fundamentalism to the kill' were themselves 'fundamentalists of some other kind'. In particular, the 'ecclesiastical fundamentalists', or Anglo-Catholics, had simply substituted 'The Bible says' with 'The Church teaches'.[90] They had more in common with evangelical fundamentalists than they wished to acknowledge. 'The distinguishing marks of fundamentalism of every kind are the same', Bowles declared:

> an alleged, absolute certainty, an exclusive claim, and a sectarian policy. The basic assertion is identical in form: We have the truth of God, you have not; we are the Church of God, you are not; we have the grace of God, you have not; I have the guidance of God, you have not.[91]

## Evangelical Apologias

The 'fundamentalist' label was cast about so widely in the assaults upon the IVF that some non-evangelicals were caught in the crossfire. Even C. S. Lewis, an Anglo-Catholic, found himself suspected of being a fundamentalist because of his belief in miracles.[92] Anti-fundamentalism, as much as fundamentalism, was an identifiable phenomenon. Evangelical physicist Donald MacKay (later a professor of neuroscience at Keele University) complained at the deep-seated prejudice and 'sectarian name-calling' prevalent in anti-fundamentalist circles.[93] Alan Stibbs (Vice Principal of Oak Hill theological college) reassured the 1958 Islington Conference that the epithets 'obscurantist' and 'fundamentalist' were merely a 'smoke-screen of abuse' by which non-evangelicals in the Church of England tried to dodge the central issue of the authority of Scripture.[94]

One of the most articulate defenders of the conservative evangelical position was J. I. Packer (tutor at Tyndale Hall, Bristol), an emerging young scholar.[95] Writing in 1958, he complained at 'the fusillade of sniping comment – sometimes patronizing, sometimes pompous, sometimes hysterical', which had rained down on 'fundamentalism' over the previous two years.[96] Fundamentalism, he observed, had become 'the whipping-boy of English Protestantism':

> It has been damned, like Socrates, for corrupting the youth; it has been pictured as a sworn foe of scholarship; its spirit has been likened to that of political totalitarianism, and its published utterances to political propaganda; it has been described as the great barrier to ecumenical progress and, indeed, as holding within itself a threat of fresh schism. A sequence of public utterance by leaders in the Churches and in education have rung the changes on these themes in tones varying from cool patronage to mild hysteria. Today anti-fundamentalism has become a fashion, almost a craze.[97]

The labels 'fundamentalism' and 'fundamentalist', Packer noted, were similar to 'Puritan' and 'Methodist' in previous eras, 'little more than ecclesiastical Billingsgate, "odious names" used to express and evoke emotional attitudes towards those one dislikes rather than to convey any exact information about them'.[98] But he viewed the controversy as proof of British evangelicalism's resurgent strength in the post-war period, especially among young people. It was precisely this evangelical resurgence, Packer argued, which brought forth such violent and alarmist denunciations which were merely 'the bluster of nervousness, in face of the spectacle of a supposedly dying evangelicalism becoming once more a force to be reckoned with'.[99]

Part of Packer's strategy was to welcome the anti-fundamentalist critiques, but to insist that evangelicalism should not be judged by its most immature exponents. In particular, it was wrong to measure the movement by its undergraduates. Packer acknowledged that among young evangelicals there was much 'rootless, churchless, shallow, arrogant, froth-and-bubble piety'. He himself, as a young convert at Oxford in the 1940s, had told his college chaplain that theological study was 'a waste of time' and had held 'many other stupid notions which it is now no pleasure to think of'.[100] More broadly, he admitted that evangelicals in the 1950s were still suffering from 'a bad hangover of Victorian pietism'.[101] For several decades they had 'skimped their theological homework', neglecting intellectual endeavour, and been guilty of 'more than a dash of obscurantism' in the recent past. If by the fundamentalist furore they were reaping the fruit of their former neglect, Packer welcomed the controversy for provoking evangelicals to more rigorous scholarly and cultural engagement.[102] He saw the post-war resurgence of Puritan theology as especially hopeful in restoring 'spiritual depth and moral fibre' to the British movement.[103]

In an article for the American magazine *Christianity Today*, closely associated with Billy Graham, Packer drew an explicit parallel between the British controversy and the efforts of neo-evangelicals in the United States to drop the 'fundamentalist' label.[104] This branding exercise was held in common by post-war evangelicals on both sides of the Atlantic. In his fullest apologia, *'Fundamentalism' and the Word of God* (1958), Packer counselled British evangelicals to reject the 'fundamentalist' nomenclature for three reasons. First, as demonstrated, it was 'a theological swear-word', a stigma and reproach, vaguely defined but expressed with contempt and therefore prejudicial to constructive engagement.[105] Second, it was too closely identified with the interwar American fundamentalists, who Packer criticised as 'intellectually barren', guilty of 'distrust of reason, shoddy apologetics, cultural barrenness, eccentric individualism, indifference to churchmanship', and generally shallow and unstable.[106] He praised them for their desire in the 1920s and 1930s 'to defend the evangelical faith against a militant and aggressive Liberalism' because it was 'better to fight clumsily than not to fight at all'.[107] However, Packer continued,

> there is no doubt that their Evangelicalism was narrowed and impoverished by their controversial entanglements. Their Fundamentalism was Evangelicalism of a kind, but a somewhat starved and stunted kind – shrivelled, coarsened and in part deformed under the strain of battle . . . Evangelicalism at its best has shown itself to be a much richer thing than this Fundamentalism which we have been describing: intellectually virile, church-centred in its outlook, vigorous in social and political enterprise and a cultural force of great power. The careers and achievements of such men as John Calvin, John Owen, John Wesley, Jonathan Edwards and Abraham Kuyper reflect something of the breadth of Evangelicalism when it is true to itself.[108]

Packer especially emphasised that obscurantism had no place within 'true Evangelicalism', which should be known instead for its 'confident intellectualism expressive of robust faith in God, whose Word is truth'.[109] Third, he argued that British evangelicals should reject the 'fundamentalist' label because it was a new name, giving the illusion of novelty, whereas the historic title 'evangelical' was a better way to demonstrate their spiritual ancestry.[110] Anglican clergyman John C. King (later editor of the *Church of England Newspaper*) agreed that 'fundamentalist' was a title that evangelicals should eschew. He observed:

> 'Fundamentalist' suggests an ostrich with its head in the sand, a preacher who never reads an up-to-date book, an enthusiast for old-time religion. The term conveys a flavour of absurdity and inadequacy in the light of modern knowledge. It is a label that would be disowned by many to whom it is applied. Just as many a man would rather claim to belong to the Labour Party than the Socialist Party, or would rather be known as a Conservative than a Tory, so many Evangelicals would decline to accept the grubby label 'Fundamentalist'.[111]

Speaking in 1960 at the Oxford Conference of Evangelical Churchmen, Packer reiterated that fundamentalism had begun as 'a fight for noble cause' but had developed an 'ignoble ethos'. Its identity had been disfigured and 'tainted' by the 'sad mistakes' of American fundamentalists.[112] Sir Edwyn Hoskyns (Dean of Corpus Christi College,

Cambridge) – in a sermon against biblical fundamentalism preached in the 1930s but posthumously published in 1960 when it had a new resonance – denounced the movement as proud, unteachable and having no place 'either for Biblical criticism, or for theology, or for philosophy, or for the possibility that other fields of study can throw any light upon the Biblical material'.[113] 'If this is fundamentalism', replied Packer, 'God save us from it!' But he argued that obscurantism had no place within the historic conservative evangelical tradition, and if anyone did oppose biblical scholarship that would simply make them 'a bad Evangelical and a bad Christian'.[114] Because of these negative associations, 'fundamentalism' was a 'most unsuitable title' for evangelicals.[115] Nevertheless, despite these cautions, the formal 'findings' of the Oxford Conference of Evangelical Churchmen did not reject the fundamentalist label outright. Instead, they appealed again for careful theological discrimination:

> We affirm that in so far as Fundamentalism means upholding the inspiration and trust-worthiness of Scripture, and the Deity, Virgin Birth, Atoning Work, Bodily Resurrection, and Personal Return of Christ it is to be approved as authentic Evangelical testimony to the fundamentals of the Christian creed.
> We affirm that in so far as Fundamentalism means an obscurantist attitude to Biblical scholarship, a mechanical doctrine of inspiration, and an arbitrary literalism in Biblical interpretation it is false to the principles of historic Evangelicalism.[116]

These 'findings' were endorsed by the Evangelical Alliance and other evangelical societies in Britain as part of their 'Bible Year' celebrations in 1961, marking the three hundred and fiftieth anniversary of the Authorised Version, which culminated in a National Bible Rally at the Royal Albert Hall.[117]

During the 1960s Anglican evangelicals continued to wrestle over their theological and ecclesial identity, seeking to shed their ghettoised and fundamentalist reputation. The first National Evangelical Anglican Congress at Keele University in 1967, chaired by Stott, marked a watershed moment in which they decisively renounced separatism and instead embraced ecumenical dialogue.[118] The gathered delegates, numbering almost a thousand, expressed their desire to 'shake free' from the 'negative and impoverishing "anti"-attitudes' which had dogged the movement, like anti-intellectualism.[119] In an official pre-Congress essay, Packer suggested that a 'fundamentalist' approach to Scripture need not be obscurantist or unscholarly, but none tried to rehabilitate the fundamentalist brand.[120] Symbolic of these new broader attitudes, Archbishop Ramsey was an honoured keynote speaker at Keele, which shocked Nonconformist evangelicals that 'an avowed enemy of fundamentalism' was invited on to the platform.[121] Relationships subsequently deteriorated between former evangelical friends inside and outside the Church of England, but on both sides of the ecclesial divide they agreed in resisting a fundamentalist identity. When Martyn Lloyd-Jones (minister of Westminster Chapel, London) was asked directly in a 1970 television interview, 'Are you a fundamentalist?', he replied that he preferred to call himself a 'conservative evangelical'. He suggested that the attitude of British evangelicals compared with American fundamentalists was 'a little more intelligent. I mean, I have very little sympathy with the man who just holds up a Bible and says, "I believe this from cover to cover, every comma and full stop", and all the rest of it.'[122] Nevertheless, like Packer and Stott, Lloyd-Jones held this rejection of an overly simplistic fundamentalist literalism hand in hand with belief in the plenary verbal inspiration of Scripture, which he saw as a classic evangelical doctrine.

## Conclusion

This detailed case study of one particular fundamentalist controversy in Britain in the 1950s reveals a number of interwoven themes, which were paralleled in other twentieth-century contexts on both sides of the Atlantic in the dynamic and contested relationship between evangelicalism and fundamentalism. It is illustrative of the wider discourse.

First, it shows the recurring power of 'fundamentalist' epithets to stir up theological passions. The rhetoric was strident; the reactions were fierce. For many, 'fundamentalism' signified the worst excesses of evangelical theology, a bête noire to be chased from the Church, with no quarter given. Ecclesiastics, notably the Church of England's episcopate, were especially alarmed that fundamentalism was corrosive of a traditional Anglican ethos. As large numbers of conservative evangelicals entered ordained ministry in the 1950s, many converted through Billy Graham's crusades, bishops feared for the future. 'Fundamentalism' functioned as a convenient battle cry, summoning non-evangelicals to the ramparts, to defend the Church from these American-influenced intruders. Its potency lay in its emotive associations, even if these were phantoms.

Second, as many commentators identified, fundamentalism was not merely an expression of theology. Some looked to psychological or sociological explanations, especially as the prospect of nuclear holocaust loomed large for the post-war generation. Preaching before the University of Oxford in October 1955, Christopher Evans (Chaplain of Corpus Christi College, Oxford) suggested that fundamentalism was partly 'a search for security in a world terrifyingly insecure'.[123] Observers noticed that fundamentalism seemed to appeal especially to adolescents in school and university, providing camaraderie, clarity of purpose and direct lines of authority. It bore some hallmarks of a restive counter-cultural movement. 'Above all', suggested the *Church Times* of the young fundamentalists, 'there is the urge to be different from one's parents'.[124] Evangelical networks such as school Christian Unions, 'Bash Camps' and the Inter-Varsity Fellowship not only drilled recruits in conservative evangelical doctrine but strengthened the bonds of affection and corporate identity.

Third, 'fundamentalism' was a highly malleable category, serviceable in dispute precisely because undefined. It could be synonymous, for example, with the so-called 'dictation theory', which Packer dismissed as 'a complete hoax', never held by any Protestant theologian.[125] Slippery terminology and theological sleight of hand hindered careful engagement but aided polemic. In the British controversy in the 1950s, 'fundamentalism' was most strongly associated with the verbal inspiration of Scripture, perhaps combined with penal substitutionary atonement and a conversionist impulse. Creationism, pre-millennialism, apocalyptic prophecy and right-wing politics – prominent characteristics in the United States – barely featured in the British arguments. Nonetheless, Anglican evangelicals like Stott and Packer shared in common with their American 'neo-evangelical' collaborators like Billy Graham and Carl Henry a strong desire to shed their fundamentalism reputations. 'This debate is not about words', Packer claimed; 'A rose by any other name would smell as sweet; and the conservative evangelical viewpoint remains the same, whatever it may be called.'[126] Nevertheless, as this chapter has shown, the debate was very much about words. The relationship between evangelicalism and fundamentalism could not be reduced to doctrinal distinctives, but concerned the power of rhetoric, branding and public relations. When James Barr's *Fundamentalism* (1977) revived the attempt to tar IVF evangelicals with the fundamentalist brush, it provoked a hostile response partly because Stott and Packer had been labouring for over twenty years to kill off those lingering associations.[127] The relationship between fundamentalism and evangelicalism, placed under the spotlight in British discourse in the 1950s, and in multiple other global contexts before and since, remains highly contested. The plasticity of 'fundamentalist' categories ensures that these controversies will continually recur.

# Notes

1. For the coinage of 'evangelicalism', see Andrew Atherstone and David Ceri Jones, 'Evangelicals and Evangelicalisms: Contested Identities', in *The Routledge Research Companion to the History of Evangelicalism*, edited by Andrew Atherstone and David Ceri Jones (Abingdon: Routledge, 2019), pp. 1–21: 2.

2. Standard introductions, in a vast literature, include George Marsden, *Understanding Fundamentalism and Evangelicalism* (Grand Rapids: Eerdmans, 1996); Joel A. Carpenter, *Revive Us Again: The Reawakening of American Fundamentalism* (New York: Oxford University Press, 1997); George Marsden, *Fundamentalism and American Culture*, 2nd ed. (New York: Oxford University Press, 2006).

3. Timothy E. W. Gloege, *Guaranteed Pure: The Moody Bible Institute, Business, and the Making of Modern Evangelicalism* (Chapel Hill:, NC University of North Carolina Press, 2015), pp. 162–92.

4. Douglas Johnson, 'The Word "Fundamentalist"', *Christian Graduate* 8 (March 1955), p. 25.

5. Andrew Atherstone, 'Evangelicalism and Fundamentalism in the Inter-War Church of England', in *Evangelicalism and Fundamentalism in the United Kingdom during the Twentieth Century*, edited by David W. Bebbington and David Ceri Jones (Oxford: Oxford University Press, 2013), pp. 55–75.

6. 'Mrs Humphrey Ward Centenary: "Robert Elsmere" and Anglican Thought', *The Times*, 11 June 1951, p. 6.

7. D. E. W. Harrison, 'Scripture and Tradition: The Situation Today', in *Scripture and Tradition*, edited by F. W. Dillistone (London: Lutterworth, 1955), pp. 133–50: 135–6.

8. Norman F. Furniss, *The Fundamentalist Controversy, 1918–1931* (New Haven, CT: Yale University Press, 1954), p. 181.

9. Hugh Montefiore, 'Fundamentalism Today', *Church of England Newspaper*, 16 August 1957, p. 11.

10. Bryan H. Reed, 'Youth and the Billy Graham Campaign', *Methodist Recorder*, 11 March 1954, p. 12.

11. 'Preface', in *Crockford's Clerical Directory* (1953–4), p. xxi.

12. 'Face the End of the World without Fear!', *Church Times*, 11 March 1955, p. 1.

13. E. G. Rupp, 'The Bible Says . . .?', *Manchester Guardian*, 30 May 1955, p. 3.

14. E. J. Poole-Connor, 'Editor's Notes', *Bible League Quarterly* 224 (January–March 1956), p. 207.

15. 'Our Glorious Heritage: The Latin Sermon at St Paul's', *Church Times*, 8 July 1955, p. 3.

16. Eric Kemp, *Shy but Not Retiring* (London: Continuum, 2006), p. 87.

17. 'Misplaced Enthusiasm', *Church Times*, 22 July 1955, p. 10.

18. Letter from John Creasey, *Church Times*, 5 August 1955, p. 10.

19. Letter from H. K. Luce, *The Times*, 15 August 1955, p. 7.

20. Letter from Michael Ramsey, *The Times*, 20 August 1955, p. 7.

21. Letter from Russell Barry, *The Times*, 23 August 1955, p. 9.

22. Letter from L. John Collins, *The Times*, 27 August 1955, p. 3.

23. '"With Authority": Faith and the Open Mind', *The Times*, 3 September 1955, p. 8.

24. Letter from Garfield Williams, *The Times*, 22 August 1955, p. 7.

25. Letter from H. Gresford Jones, *The Times*, 18 August 1955, p. 9.

26. Letter from John Stott, *The Times*, 25 August 1955, p. 14.

27. Letter from B. F. C. Atkinson, *The Times*, 17 August 1955, p. 9.

28. Letter from Mervyn Stockwood, *The Times*, 26 August 1955, p. 9.

29. Basil Atkinson to John Stott, 26 August 1955, Lambeth Palace Library (LPL), John Stott Papers 5/15, fo. 317.

30. 'Assault on "Fundamentalism"', *Life of Faith*, 18 August 1955, p. 568.

31. Timothy Dudley-Smith, 'Reproof', *Life of Faith*, 25 August 1955, p. 584.

32. Cartoon with Geoffrey Golden, 'Billy Graham at Cambridge: Mission in the University', *Life of Faith*, 10 November 1955, p. 763.

33. Herbert F. Stevenson, 'Modernism v. Fundamentalism', *Life of Faith*, 24 November 1955, p. 812.

34. John Stott, 'Fundamentalism', *Crusade* 1 (November 1955), pp. 10–11; republished in John Stott, *Fundamentalism and Evangelism* (London: Crusade, 1956).

35. F. A. Cockin, 'Introduction', in *The London Syllabus of Religious Education* (London: London County Council, 1947), p. 15.

36. Stott, 'Fundamentalism', p. 11.

37. John Burnaby to John Stott, 25 August 1955, LPL, John Stott Papers 5/15, fos 320–1.

38. John Burnaby to John Stott, 8 October 1955, LPL, John Stott Papers 5/15, fo. 311.

39. David L. Edwards and John Stott, *Essentials: A Liberal–Evangelical Dialogue* (London: Hodder and Stoughton, 1988), p. 89.

40. Stott, 'Fundamentalism', p. 10. See further Alister Chapman, 'Evangelical or Fundamentalist? The Case of John Stott', in *Evangelicalism and Fundamentalism in the United Kingdom during the Twentieth Century* (Oxford: Oxford University Press, 2013), edited by David W. Bebbington and David Ceri Jones, pp. 192–208.

41. Frank Ockenden, 'Why I Am a Fundamentalist', *Bible League Quarterly* 222 (July–September 1955), pp. 162–5.

42. Frank Ockenden, 'The Bogey of "Literalism"', *Bible League Quarterly* 225 (April–June 1956), pp. 209–11.

43. Charles Moore, 'Dwelling Together in Unity', *English Churchman*, 29 July 1955, p. 360.

44. Letter from Thomas Hewitt, *Church of England Newspaper*, 16 March 1956, p. 10.

45. Stella Aldwinckle, 'After-Thoughts on Billy Graham', *Christian Witness: A Quarterly Magazine on Evangelism* 9 (June 1956), p. 6.

46. Letter from John Stott, *The Times*, 25 August 1955, p. 14; 'Evangelizing', *The Times*, 14 September 1955, p. 9.

47. Letter from Kenneth de Courcy, *English Churchman*, 30 September 1955, p. 465.

48. Letter from A. T. Houghton, *Church of England Newspaper*, 2 September 1955, p. 10.

49. Johnson, 'The Word "Fundamentalist"', p. 26.

50. Walter H. Denbow, 'Fundamentalist or Evangelical?', *English Churchman*, 26 August 1955, p. 403.

51. Christopher Chavasse, 'Fundamentalism', *Theology* 59 (March 1956), pp. 93–5.

52. Chavasse, 'Fundamentalism', p. 95.

53. Chavasse, 'Fundamentalism', pp. 95–6.

54. Letters from P. Crichton Hanwell and John S. Benson, *English Churchman*, 17 February and 2 March 1956, pp. 69, 93.

55. Letter from Colin C. Kerr, *Church of England Newspaper*, 27 January 1956, p. 10.

56. Michael Ramsey, 'The Menace of Fundamentalism', *The Bishoprick* 31 (February 1956), p. 24.

57. Ramsey, 'The Menace of Fundamentalism', pp. 24–5.

58. Ramsey, 'The Menace of Fundamentalism', pp. 25–6.

59. Leslie Hunter, 'The Error of Fundamentalism', *Sheffield Diocesan Review* 9 (April 1956), pp. 5–7.

60. 'Fundamentalism', *Church Times*, 10 February 1956, p. 3.

61. Herbert F. Stevenson, 'Archbishop-Elect Criticizes "Fundamentalism"', *Life of Faith*, 9 February 1956, p. 84.

62. Philip E. Hughes, 'The Archbishop of York's Charge of Heresy Considered' (typescript, April 1956), LPL, John Stott Papers 5/15, fo. 296.

63. A. G. Pouncy, 'The Rector's Letter', *The Lychgate: The Magazine of Saint Andrew the Parish Church of Bebington* (March 1956), pp. 3–5, copy at Bebington Central Library.

64. Pouncy, 'The Rector's Letter', p. 5.

65. Michael Ramsey to Philip E. Hughes, 7 and 19 May 1956, LPL, John Stott Papers 5/15, fos 302–3.

66. John Betjeman to Cecil Roberts, 21 December 1962, in *John Betjeman: Letters*, vol. 2, *1951 to 1984*, edited by Candida Lycett Green (London: Methuen, 1995), p. 240.

67. 'Fundamentalism', *Church of England Newspaper*, 26 August 1955, p. 6.

68. Letter from L. W. Barnard, *Church Times*, 16 October 1959, p. 11.

69. Letter from L. W. Barnard, *Church Times*, 30 October 1959, pp. 11–12.

70. Quoted in Gabriel Hebert, *Fundamentalism and the Church of God* (London: SCM Press, 1957), p. 140.

71. 'Religion Made Easy?', *Journal of Education* 88 (September 1956), p. 377.

72. Kathleen Bliss, 'The Bible as Counterpoise', *Journal of Education* 88 (September 1956), p. 406.

73. 'Evangelical Movements in Schools', *Journal of Education* 88 (December 1956), p. 521.

74. *York Journal of Convocation* (May 1956), p. 49.

75. 'Report of the Joint Committee on Education', in *York Journal of Convocation* (May 1957), appendix, p. xxiv.

76. *York Journal of Convocation* (May 1957), pp. 92–5.

77. 'Fundamentalism', *Church Gazette and Intelligencer* 56 (July–August 1957), pp. 2–3.

78. Bernard Heywood, 'Fallacies of Fundamentalism: Reason and Reverence in the Use of Holy Scripture', *Church Times*, 3 January 1958, p. 9.

79. Letter from Kenneth Leech, *Church Times*, 17 January 1958, p. 12.

80. G. W. H. Lampe, 'Bible and Its Authority: The Strength and Weakness of Fundamentalism', *Church Times*, 9 May 1958, p. 11.

81. 'Fundamentalism', *Church Times*, 9 May 1958, p. 3.

82. Letter from E. E. Button, *Church Times*, 16 May 1958, p. 11.

83. Hebert, *Fundamentalism and the Church of God*, pp. 95, 138.

84. Hebert, *Fundamentalism and the Church of God*, p. 27.

85. Michael Ramsey, 'Fundamentalism: A New Approach', *York Quarterly: The Organ of the Archbishop* 4 (August 1957), pp. 6–8; 'A Heresy Explored', *Church Times*, 23 August 1957, p. 4.

86. J. F. Wallace, 'Fundamentalism and the Church of God', *Church Gazette and Intelligencer* 57 (March–April 1958), pp. 14–16.

87. H. M. Carson, 'Fundamentalism and the Church of God', *Christian Graduate* 10 (September 1957), p. 146.

88. Douglas Johnson, *Contending for the Faith: A History of the Evangelical Movement in the Universities and Colleges* (Leicester: Inter-Varsity Press, 1979); Steve Bruce, 'The Student Christian Movement and the Inter-Varsity Fellowship: A Sociological Study of Two Student Movements' (PhD thesis, University of Stirling, 1980).

89. Philip Lee-Woolf, 'Fundamentalism', *Christian News-Letter* 5 (July 1957), pp. 31–6.

90. C. W. J. Bowles, *The Many Fundamentalisms* (London: SPCK, 1958), pp. 5–6, 13.

91. Bowles, *The Many Fundamentalisms*, p. 12.

92. C. S. Lewis, *Reflections on the Psalms* (London: Geoffrey Bles, 1958), p. 109. For Lewis's surprising reputation as an honorary evangelical, see Stephanie L. Derrick, *The Fame of C. S. Lewis: A Controversialist's Reception in Britain and America* (Oxford: Oxford University Press, 2018).

93. Letter from D. M. MacKay, *Christian News-Letter* 5 (July 1957), pp. 40–1.

94. Alan M. Stibbs, 'The Authority of the Holy Scriptures' (1958), p. 12, copy at LPL, John Stott Papers 5/15, fos 274–6.

95. Alister McGrath, *To Know and Serve God: A Biography of James I. Packer* (London: Hodder and Stoughton, 1997), pp. 80–9.

96. J. I. Packer, 'Fundamentalism: The British Scene', *Christianity Today* 2 (29 September 1958), p. 3.
97. J. I. Packer, 'The Fundamentalism Controversy: Retrospect and Prospect', *Faith and Thought: Journal of the Victoria Institute* 90 (Spring 1958), p. 35.
98. Packer, 'The Fundamentalism Controversy', p. 35.
99. Packer, 'The Fundamentalism Controversy', p. 37.
100. J. I. Packer, 'Biblical Christianity', *Christian News-Letter* 5 (July 1957), p. 38.
101. Packer, 'Biblical Christianity', p. 39.
102. Packer, 'The Fundamentalism Controversy', p. 38.
103. Packer, 'Fundamentalism: The British Scene', p. 6.
104. Packer, 'Fundamentalism: The British Scene', p. 3.
105. J. I. Packer, *'Fundamentalism' and the Word of God: Some Evangelical Principles* (London: Inter-Varsity Fellowship, 1958), p. 30.
106. Packer, *'Fundamentalism' and the Word of God*, pp. 32, 36.
107. Packer, *'Fundamentalism' and the Word of God*, p. 33.
108. Packer, *'Fundamentalism' and the Word of God*, pp. 33–4.
109. Packer, *'Fundamentalism' and the Word of God*, p. 34.
110. Packer, *'Fundamentalism' and the Word of God*, p. 40.
111. John C. King, '"Fundamentalism": Some Observations', *English Churchman*, 30 May 1958, p. 255.
112. J. I. Packer, 'The Origin and History of Fundamentalism', in *The Word of God and Fundamentalism: The Addresses Given at the Oxford Conference of Evangelical Churchmen, 19th to 21st September, 1960*, edited by Thomas Hewitt (London: Church Book Room Press, 1961), pp. 104, 106.
113. E. C. Hoskyns, 'Fundamentalism', in *We Are the Pharisees* (London: SPCK, 1960), p. 67.
114. Packer, 'The Origin and History of Fundamentalism', p. 108.
115. Packer, 'The Origin and History of Fundamentalism', p. 111.
116. 'Findings of the Conference', in *The Word of God and Fundamentalism: The Addresses Given at the Oxford Conference of Evangelical Churchmen, 19th to 21st September, 1960*, edited by Thomas Hewitt (London: Church Book Room Press, 1961), p. 25.
117. *National Bible Rally, Royal Albert Hall: Souvenir Programme* (October 1961), LPL, John Stott Papers 5/15, fo. 277. For criticism, see 'Bible Year Affirmation', *Bible League Quarterly* 245 (April–June 1961), pp. 222–3.
118. Andrew Atherstone, 'The Keele Congress of 1967: A Paradigm Shift in Anglican Evangelical Attitudes', *Journal of Anglican Studies* 9 (November 2011), pp. 175–97.
119. Philip Crowe (ed.), *Keele '67: The National Evangelical Anglican Congress Statement* (London: Falcon, 1967), para. 84.
120. J. I. Packer, 'The Good Confession', in *Guidelines: Anglican Evangelicals Face the Future*, edited by J. I. Packer (London: Falcon, 1967), pp. 11–38: 25.
121. 'What Sort of History Is This?', *Evangelical Times* (May 1967), p. 2.
122. Quoted in Robert Pope, 'Lloyd-Jones and Fundamentalism', in *Engaging with Martyn Lloyd-Jones: The Life and Legacy of 'the Doctor'*, edited by Andrew Atherstone and David Ceri Jones (Nottingham: Apollos, 2011), pp. 197–219: 217–18.
123. C. F. Evans, 'The Inspiration of the Bible', *Theology* 59 (January 1956), p. 12.
124. 'Misplaced Enthusiasm', *Church Times*, 22 July 1955, p. 10.
125. Packer, 'Biblical Christianity', p. 37.
126. Packer, 'The Fundamentalism Controversy', p. 36.
127. For analysis of the Barr controversy, see Harriet A. Harris, *Fundamentalism and Evangelicals* (Oxford: Clarendon Press, 1998).

# Select Bibliography

Aldwinckle, Stella, 'After-Thoughts on Billy Graham', *Christian Witness: A Quarterly Magazine on Evangelism* 9 (June 1956), pp. 4–7.

Atherstone, Andrew, 'Evangelicalism and Fundamentalism in the Inter-War Church of England', in *Evangelicalism and Fundamentalism in the United Kingdom during the Twentieth Century*, edited by David W. Bebbington and David Ceri Jones (Oxford: Oxford University Press, 2013), pp. 55–75.

Atherstone, Andrew, 'The Keele Congress of 1967: A Paradigm Shift in Anglican Evangelical Attitudes', *Journal of Anglican Studies* 9 (November 2011), 175–97.

Atherstone, Andrew and David Ceri Jones, 'Evangelicals and Evangelicalisms: Contested Identities', in *The Routledge Research Companion to the History of Evangelicalism*, edited by Andrew Atherstone and David Ceri Jones (Abingdon: Routledge, 2019), pp. 1–21.

Bowles, C. W. J., *The Many Fundamentalisms* (London: SPCK, 1958).

Bruce, Steve, 'The Student Christian Movement and the Inter-Varsity Fellowship: A Sociological Study of Two Student Movements' (PhD thesis, University of Stirling, 1980)

Carpenter, Joel A., *Revive Us Again: The Reawakening of American Fundamentalism* (New York: Oxford University Press, 1997).

Chapman, Alister, 'Evangelical or Fundamentalist? The Case of John Stott', in *Evangelicalism and Fundamentalism in the United Kingdom during the Twentieth Century*, edited by David W. Bebbington and David Ceri Jones (Oxford: Oxford University Press, 2013), pp. 192–208.

Chavasse, Christopher, 'Fundamentalism', *Theology* 59 (March 1956), pp. 92–7.

Crowe, Philip (ed.), *Keele '67: The National Evangelical Anglican Congress Statement* (London: Falcon, 1967).

Derrick, Stephanie L., *The Fame of C. S. Lewis: A Controversialist's Reception in Britain and America* (Oxford: Oxford University Press, 2018).

Edwards, David L. and John Stott, *Essentials: A Liberal–Evangelical Dialogue* (London: Hodder and Stoughton, 1988).

Evans, C. F., 'The Inspiration of the Bible', *Theology* 59 (January 1956), pp. 11–17.

Furniss, Norman F., *The Fundamentalist Controversy, 1918–1931* (New Haven, CT: Yale University Press, 1954).

Gloege, Timothy E. W., *Guaranteed Pure: The Moody Bible Institute, Business, and the Making of Modern Evangelicalism* (Chapel Hill, NC: University of North Carolina Press, 2015).

Harris, Harriet A., *Fundamentalism and Evangelicals* (Oxford: Clarendon Press, 1998).

Harrison, D. E. W., 'Scripture and Tradition: The Situation Today', in *Scripture and Tradition*, edited by F. W. Dillistone (London: Lutterworth, 1955), pp. 133–50.

Hebert, Gabriel, *Fundamentalism and the Church of God* (London: SCM Press, 1957).

Hewitt, Thomas (ed.), *The Word of God and Fundamentalism: The Addresses Given at the Oxford Conference of Evangelical Churchmen, 19th to 21st September, 1960* (London: Church Book Room Press, 1961).

Hoskyns, E. C., *We Are the Pharisees* (London: SPCK, 1960).

Hunter, Leslie, 'The Error of Fundamentalism', *Sheffield Diocesan Review* 9 (April 1956), pp. 5–7.

Johnson, Douglas, *Contending for the Faith: A History of the Evangelical Movement in the Universities and Colleges* (Leicester: Inter-Varsity Press, 1979).

Johnson, Douglas, 'The Word "Fundamentalist"', *Christian Graduate* 8 (March 1955), pp. 22–6.

Kemp, Eric, *Shy but Not Retiring* (London: Continuum, 2006).

Lee-Woolf, Philip, 'Fundamentalism', *Christian News-Letter* 5 (July 1957), pp. 31–6.

Lewis, C. S., *Reflections on the Psalms* (London: Geoffrey Bles, 1958).

McGrath, Alister, *To Know and Serve God: A Biography of James I. Packer* (London: Hodder and Stoughton, 1997).

Marsden, George, *Fundamentalism and American Culture*, 2nd ed. (New York: Oxford University Press, 2006).

Marsden, George, *Understanding Fundamentalism and Evangelicalism* (Grand Rapids: Eerdmans, 1996).

Ockenden, Frank, 'Why I Am a Fundamentalist', *Bible League Quarterly* 222 (July – September 1955), pp. 162–5.

Packer, J. I., 'Biblical Christianity', *Christian News-Letter* 5 (July 1957), pp. 37–40.

Packer, J. I., *'Fundamentalism' and the Word of God: Some Evangelical Principles* (London: Inter-Varsity Fellowship, 1958).

Packer, J. I., 'The Fundamentalism Controversy: Retrospect and Prospect', *Faith and Thought: Journal of the Victoria Institute* 90 (Spring 1958), pp. 35–45.

Packer, J. I., 'Fundamentalism: The British Scene', *Christianity Today* 2 (29 September 1958), pp. 3–6.

Packer, J. I., 'The Good Confession', in *Guidelines: Anglican Evangelicals Face the Future*, edited by J. I. Packer (London: Falcon, 1967), pp. 11–38.

Pollock, John, *A Cambridge Movement* (London: John Murray, 1953).

Pope, Robert, 'Lloyd-Jones and Fundamentalism', in *Engaging with Martyn Lloyd-Jones: The Life and Legacy of 'the Doctor'*, edited by Andrew Atherstone and David Ceri Jones (Nottingham: Apollos, 2011), pp. 197–219.

Ramsey, Michael, 'The Menace of Fundamentalism', *The Bishoprick* 31 (February 1956), pp. 24–6.

Stott, John, *Fundamentalism and Evangelism* (London: Crusade, 1956).

# 7

# Synagogue, *Sho'ah* and State

*Mark Lindsay*

## Introduction

The Christian Church, as well as its various theologies, have been both influenced and challenged by their existence alongside and within the Synagogue and the State, from the middle of the first century until the present day. Indeed, these two institutional realities have been, for the Church, far more than conversation partners, or even competitors for the allegiance of souls. They have been ever-present hermeneutical motifs, by which and against which Christianity has sought to understand itself. The *Sho'ah* of the twentieth century – more commonly known as the Holocaust of the Jews under Nazism – not only introduced a third interpretive paradigm, but has also caused the Church to fundamentally rethink its relationship to the other two. It is this quadrilateral conversation – between the Church, on the one hand, and the Synagogue, the State and the *Sho'ah* on the other – with which this chapter is concerned.

Let me begin, though, with a caveat around language and terminology. To speak of 'the State' in the history of Christian thought is problematic enough: one is at immediate risk of being wedged between a Calvinistic coextensivity of Church and State at one end, and what we might call a Yoderian repudiation of positive statehood at the other.[1] A much more nuanced reading of the Church's relationship with and understanding of the State is needed, particularly if the Church is to find its way in a pluralistic, post-Christendom world, that does not entail a retreat into the catacombs.

To speak of 'the Synagogue' is even more vexed. For centuries, both formal and colloquial Christian discourse employed the term 'synagogue' as a shorthand for unbelieving, and thus disobedient, Jews – a disparagement of Jews who, despite knowing the truth of the gospel of Christ, nevertheless refused to accept him.[2] Just as the *Judensau* of Cologne Cathedral, or the blind and dishevelled *Sinagoga* on the flying buttresses of Paris's Notre Dame, reified in stone the Church's 'teaching of contempt',[3] the very word 'synagogue' has likewise carried undisguised connotations of moribund infidelity into the very soul of Christianity. Again, while recognising the need for the Church to confess its mischievous rendering of this word, a reclaiming of the term is also necessary, if Christian belief and practice is not to slip back into the antisemitic caricatures of centuries past.

Finally, a word needs to be said about the word *Sho'ah*. Precisely how to speak of the unspeakable has been a source of considerable debate for the past fifty or so years. Etymologically, 'holocaust' at first seemed appropriate, if needlessly macabre: literally a 'whole burnt offering', with referents in the Septuagint, this term has more recently fallen out of favour, not merely because it foregrounds a particular manner of death, but more so because of the implication that, in some way, the sacrificial victims were offered to, and accepted by, God.[4] *Churban* speaks appropriately of destruction, and has been favoured by some scholars, such as Ignaz Maybaum.[5] Its limitation, though, is that it is also used to refer to the razing of the First and Second Temples, in 586 BCE and 70 CE respectively, and thus connotes no singularity of the Jewish suffering under Nazism.[6] The word *Sho'ah*, therefore, has come to stand as the 'best' term for the Nazis' war against the Jews – though even this word is fraught with complications. As Elie Wiesel once said, 'No word is adequate [but] at least [*Sho'ah*] is a Hebrew word.'[7] All of this is simply to say that the very words with which this chapter has to deal – Synagogue, *Sho'ah* and State – are each, in their own way, semantically charged. Space precludes a further discussion of this difficulty but, at the very least, we are helped if we acknowledge that this linguistic terrain is something of a minefield.

## Synagogue

In Acts 24:5, we read of St Paul's trial before Governor Felix in Caesarea, at the start of which he is accused of being 'an agitator among all the Jews throughout the world, and a ringleader of the sect (αἱρέσεως) of the Nazarenes'. The employment of the term 'heresy' to describe the embryonic Christian Church is instructive for our purposes here, for the simple reason that it denotes not so much a group that broke away from Jewish communities of the first century, but rather a faction, or sect, within Judaism.[8] As Elaine Pagels notes, despite the historical record suggesting that Jesus' main enemies were the representatives of Roman imperialism, 'the gospel writers chose . . . to focus instead upon intra-Jewish conflict – specifically upon their own quarrel with those who resisted their claims that Jesus was the Messiah'. She continues: 'it is probably fair to say that in every case the decision to place the story of Jesus within the context of God's struggle against Satan tends to minimise the role of the Romans, and to place increasing blame instead upon Jesus' *Jewish* enemies'.[9] It is simply rhetorical consistency, then, to find in Revelation a reference to 'fake Jews' – those who say they are Jews, but are not – as the 'synagogue of Satan' (Rev. 2:9). With apparent scriptural justification, therefore, unbelief, and satanic allegiance, cohere within the symbol of the 'synagogue', as the diabolical antithesis to the ἐκκλησία of the 'true Israel'.

Anti-Jewish polemic through the centuries repeated this usage of 'synagogue' as a symbol of Jewish corruption. In 388 CE, Ambrose of Milan protested an order of Theodosius I for the rebuilding of the synagogue in Callinicum, which had been destroyed by the town's monks, on the grounds that it was 'a home of unbelief, a house of impiety, a receptacle of folly, which God himself has condemned'.[10] Similar ideas of moribund infidelity lay behind Abbot Suger's description of a deputation of rabbis to Innocent II in 1131 as 'the blind synagogue'.[11] Even John Duns Scotus, who in many ways was far more respectful of Hebrew religion than many of his contemporaries, thought that 'the synagogue ought to have been buried' – with honour, yes, but buried nonetheless.[12] Martin Luther's now infamously vitriolic rejection of Judaism may therefore have been rhetorically more strident, but was not thereby inconsistent with his theological predecessors. God, said Luther, has the misfortune of having 'to endure that in their synagogues . . . [the Jews] come and stand before him and plague him grievously'.[13] Such synagogues are 'nests of devils', and so ought to be burnt down, for the protection of Christian society.[14]

It should not be surprising, then, that ecclesial and theological discourse well into the twentieth century reiterated the same antipathy in similar terms. Immediately prior to the

Russian Revolution of 1917, for example, synagogues were regarded not merely as sites of religious oddity, but as possible hubs of political subversion. What gave rise to such concern? Usually nothing, other than the coils of *eruv* wire, that were stored in the local synagogue for use by villagers on the Sabbath, and which were believed – at least by those who were prone to thinking the worst of Jews – to be telephone cables for disseminating treason.[15] In Germany, the situation was similar. For Adolf von Harnack, the synagogue worship of Hebrew religion in Jesus' day was best represented by the 'priests and Pharisees [who] held the nation in bondage and murdered its soul'.[16] In Harnack's portrayal of early Christianity, Judaism was 'on all hands' understood to be 'a sect judged and rejected by God, a society of hypocrites, a synagogue of Satan'.[17] No wonder that he rejoiced, then, that through Paul, Christianity's 'breach with the synagogue' had released the new religion from the 'husk [that was] the whole of the Jewish limitations attaching to Jesus' message'.[18]

Harnack's celebrated pupil, Karl Barth, was even less restrained in his use of synagogue imagery. It was a powerful linguistic device with which he repudiated the dead letter of religion generally. While Judaism as such was not in his sights – Barth was equally if not more critical of Christian religiosity – 'the synagogue' nonetheless served representative rhetorical force. Katherine Sonderegger has shown just how dependent Barth's theology of Israel is on a typology of history in which 'the synagogue' is identified with the passing form of humanity (*der vergehende Mensch*)[19] – with that mode of humanity's being that is characterised by 'the frailty of the flesh, suffering, dying, death . . .'[20] Debate continues as to whether or not Barth's theology of the Jewish people, and Judaism per se, is inherently pejorative. His resistance to all forms of 'Paulinism'[21] – that is, to every religious system that would proclaim itself rather than God – suggests that Barth's objection was to the hubris of human religiosity in general, rather than to Judaism in particular. Nevertheless, Sonderegger is regrettably correct: 'the term "Synagogue" is derogatory throughout *Dogmatics* without exception'.[22]

Barth's employment of synagogue rhetoric can be profitably contrasted with the interpretive work of his contemporary, Rudolf Bultmann. For Bultmann, far from being merely a figurative device through which anonymised religion could be critiqued, the Synagogue was synonymous with the dead letter of Jewish law. As an ossification of God's presence amongst the Jews, synagogue-religion handcuffed Israel to its past, immobilised its leaders into social and political impotence, and eliminated even the possibility 'of science and art', and every other form of 'cultural intercourse with other nations'.[23] In Bultmann's vision, the synagogue represented not just religious death, but cultural death as well.

One remarkable albeit inconsistent exception to this pattern is Dietrich Bonhoeffer, whose report from Union Theological Seminary – where he was one of three Sloane Fellows between 1930 and 1931 – mentioned synagogues in positive, rather than negative, ways. Rather than employing the term 'synagogue' as merely a referent for unbelieving Judaism, Bonhoeffer instead noted, with conspicuous appreciation, that topical sermons in which the pressing issues of the day were expounded could be heard not only in Methodist, Baptist and 'community' churches, but indeed also in the synagogues of New York. Of course, Bonhoeffer was not endorsing this type of sermon – it was, he said, 'an ethical and social idealism' that stood 'in place of' the gospel. Nevertheless, the synagogue was not, for him, an archaic relic of a faithless religion but, on the contrary, a place in which – in Judaism's own terms – contemporary matters of social urgency were addressed with lively relevance.[24]

As I have suggested, Bonhoeffer was only an inconsistent exception to a longer tradition in which the term 'synagogue' was used in fundamentally negative terms. In the early

1930s, Bonhoeffer was unable completely to distance himself from a tendency towards caricature. Writing in late 1932 to Helmut Rößler on the nature of divine command, Bonhoeffer argued that, whatever 'love your neighbour' means, it must have a different meaning in the Church than it does in the synagogue. Why? Because 'law in the church . . . does not mean that God is distant from me as a matter of principle (as it does in the synagogue!)'.[25] His experience of inspiring sermons aside, it would appear that, at least at this point in his life, Bonhoeffer's perception of Judaism – as represented by the 'synagogue' – was of a religion that kept God at arm's length.

By the end of the decade, however, the question of Jewish–Christian relations had changed decisively, with the violent advent of Nazism, and the cannibalistic *Kirchenkampf* by which the German churches tore themselves asunder. And Bonhoeffer's attitude changed with it. In a lecture delivered to the Council of the Confessing Church in Pomerania, in October 1938, Bonhoeffer chastised the Council for its introspective attention to matters of governance and polity, instead of to the *Sachfragen* – the 'crucial theological questions' – of 'gospel and law, proclamation and youth, church and synagogue . . .'[26] As Dirk Schulz has recognised, that the relationship of church and synagogue was now one of the urgent *Sachfragen* demonstrates that, for Bonhoeffer, old stereotypes were no longer applicable. The ever-present reality of Jewish persecution 'demanded basic theological reflection capable of overcoming the traditional reservation and prejudice against Judaism'.[27]

Like far too much of Christianity's historic contempt towards Judaism, however, anti-Jewish antipathy intentionally connoted by synagogue imagery did not stay safely contained within the pages of dogmatic textbooks or even in the words of sermons. On the night of 9–10 November 1938, more than 1,400 synagogues were systematically destroyed across Germany and Austria during the infamous *Kristallnacht* ('Night of Broken Glass'). To be sure, the pogrom was instigated by leading Nazis – in particular, Josef Goebbels and Reinhard Heydrich – and encouraged as an example of 'popular' resistance against Jewish influence. Nonetheless, this burning of synagogues was not without religious significance or even precedence. Indeed, it could even be claimed that *Kristallnacht* was the logical, if perhaps not inevitable, *telos* of the teachings of Harnack, Luther and Scotus. Had they not wanted, and even called for, the burning and burying of the synagogues, in order that both Christianity and Christian culture be kept safe?

Of course, theological rhetoric is not the same as mob violence. It would be both anachronistic and unreasonable to sheet home the blame for the 1938 pogrom to people like Harnack, whose intent – however poorly worded – was strictly theological. Moreover, given that there were no large-scale persecutions of Jews in Martin Luther's time – and certainly none that was state-sanctioned in the way that *Kristallnacht* was – it is far from clear that Luther actually intended his own diatribes against the Jews and their synagogues to be taken literally. Nevertheless, it is impossible to conclude anything other than that the history of Christian doctrine and polemic has employed the word 'synagogue' in almost exclusively derogatory terms, as a cipher of unbelief at best, and devilish depravity at worst. That the middle of the twentieth century saw this rhetoric reified in a frenzy of state-inspired destruction should be, therefore, neither unsurprising to the Church, nor a matter of indifference to it.

# State

In 1911, Ernst Troeltsch noted that the churches were seeking to make their voices heard 'amid all the social confusion [and conflicts] of the present day'. Going on to say that such conflicts were due 'in part to the growth of large modern unified States', Troeltsch intentionally connected the daily complexities of Christian living with the reality of contemporary politics.[28] At the end of his survey, and notwithstanding his conclusion that 'nowhere does there exist an absolute Christian ethic', Troeltsch nevertheless claimed that 'all that [Christians] can do is to learn to control the world-situation in its successive phases'.[29] In hindsight – and knowing now that the soon-to-erupt First World War would shatter Christianity's moral edifice – Troeltsch's claim seems oddly bold. Yet, with the Edinburgh World Missionary Conference barely a year in the past, Troeltsch was articulating a widespread sense of Christian optimism: that the gospel was on the march across the globe, and that the Christian ethic, if not the Churches themselves, was the panacea for precisely those social ills occasioned – and thus not fixable – by modern politics.

That Troeltsch understood Christian engagement with social, and therefore political, issues to be a self-evident duty should not, however, cause us to think that his was the only, or even the majority, view. The twentieth-century history of ecclesial interaction with State power is a varied and contentious set of narratives. At one level, this is as it should be. As Jens Zimmermann rightly notes,

> orthodox theology has always recognized the dual citizenship of Christian existence: the Christian lives in the future age with its beginning kingdom of God embodied by the church on the one hand, and in the waning, present age with its demands by the secular state for allegiance and societal duties on the other.[30]

With that tension always inevitably in view, it is hardly surprising that theologies of Church–State relations during the twentieth century represented a multiplicity of perspectives. At one end of the spectrum, liberationist and feminist theologians took it for granted that sin is systemic and social, as much as it is personal, and thus requires corporate as well as individual redress, typically *against* institutions of State power. At the opposite end were those Church agencies, and individual theologians, who preferred to moderate Christian activism to within socially acceptable boundaries, which usually meant limiting such activism to specifically Christian or churchly affairs. Yet, right in the middle, we can also find examples of Churches and their theologies that sought neither to oppose the State nor to eschew political engagement, but on the contrary to cooperate *with* State machinery in the implementation of legislative agendas.

Clodovis Boff has summarised the first of these options brilliantly by noting that liberationist theologies presuppose 'an energetic protest' against historically and socially embedded inequalities.[31] Thus, under the influence of people like Gustavo Guttiérez, Leonardo Boff and Juan Luis Segundo, South American theologians in the 1960s–70s became 'militant agents of inspiration for the life of the church at its grass roots and those of society'. '[P]opular movements and Christian groups came together in the struggle for social and political liberation, with the ultimate aim of complete and integral liberation.'[32]

Rosemary Radford Ruether insisted upon something similar, with her vision of feminist theology being equally political. 'Sexism', she said, is 'a serious expression of human sinfulness, of alienation from authentic existence'.[33] But the quest for liberation was not thereby to be limited to the pursuit of gender equality. It was, on the contrary, a wholesale seeking after

> a society that affirms the values of democratic participation, of equal value of all persons as the basis for their civil equality . . .; a democratic socialist society that dismantles [both] sexist and class hierarchies, that restores ownership and management of work to the base communities of workers themselves . . .[34]

For Radford Ruether, theological feminism was a holistic, rather than particular, subversion of the sinfulness of entrenched enslavement. In both intent and consequence, therefore, liberationist theologians of all stripes took their stand against the State, precisely because it was the manifestation of embedded inequality, as well as the perpetuator of it.

The US witnessed its own form of liberationism at a similar period, notably through the civil rights movement. As James Cone so starkly realised, 'any theology in America that did not engage the religious meaning of the African American struggle for justice' was – and is – bankrupt.[35] Cone was not the only Christian leader who held this view. While the struggle for racial equality and desegregation could in principle have remained an entirely political affair, the highly visible presence of clergy amongst the movement's leadership – Ralph Abernathy, James Bevel, Jesse Jackson and Martin Luther King Jr – rendered it a fight against State authority in which the Christian churches, as well as their operative theologies, were deeply implicated.

But Cone's point, of course, is that far too much of American Christianity *was* bankrupt; 'the public meaning of Christianity was *white*'.[36] Perhaps it was not intrinsically so, but it was at least presumptively so. And it is here that we see exemplified the opposite end of the engagement spectrum, in which political activism as a Christian necessity was deliberately repudiated. That is, while not every Church was intentionally racist, a very many were opposed to racial activism on the grounds that it was seen to be a social and not a spiritual issue. No doubt, argues Cone, there were significant (white) theologians – Cone singles out Reinhold Niebuhr – who were theologically committed to the pursuit of justice and equality. But Niebuhrian justice was only ever 'proximate' – a 'balance of power between powerful collectives', that thus had nothing to say to those from whom all power but the power of resistance had been stripped.[37]

Twenty-five years earlier, Dietrich Bonhoeffer had been the victim of similar ecclesial conservatism. Following his arrest and subsequent imprisonment by the Gestapo, Bonhoeffer knew that not even the Confessing Church would or could include him on its official intercessory prayer lists (*Fürbittenliste*).[38] In part, to do so would have been a 'red rag' to the Nazi regime. In larger part, however, it was because the Confessing Church did not consider political activity of any kind, let alone sedition, to be theologically legitimate or ecclesially appropriate. It had signalled this as early as 1934 when, in its Barmen Declaration, it had failed to make any mention of the Nazi State 'except insofar as State policies impinged upon ecclesiastical matters'.[39] As Helmut Gollwitzer later acknowledged, 'we totally deferred our political opposition to Nazism . . . [It] was not our task to build a small anti-Nazi sect within the Church, but . . . to bring the Church to Christian consciousness.'[40] Thus, when Karl Barth protested in 1935 that the Confessing Church 'still has no heart for the millions who suffer unjustly . . . When it speaks, it speaks only about its own affairs', he was voicing a lament that was shared by only a few.[41]

Between these contrasting extremes – of intentional praxis *against* the State, and an equally intentional resistance to such praxis – was a third option, by which Christian theologies in the twentieth century were (again intentionally) coordinated into the service of State policy. The utterly Nazified *Deutsche Christen Bewegung* is arguably the most obvious and egregious example, but this sort of *gleichgeschaltet* Christianity was always a contested form of the faith, both within the Churches themselves, and within the National Socialist government. A more insidious instance, perhaps, is the support given by the Dutch Reformed Church (*Nederduitse Gereformeerde Kerk*) to the apartheid policies of successive South African governments between 1948 and 1994.

The gradual domination of the DRC by a neo-Kuyperian Calvinism, which included an Afrikaner version of Kuyper's 'sphere sovereignty' principle,[42] eventually led to a situation in which 'there was very little that separated Afrikaner nationalism and the DRC'.[43] And so, according to its landmark 1974 report *Ras, Volk en Nasie*,[44] the Church owed the governing National Party its unequivocal support for the government's policy of 'separate development', because such a concept was embedded within the pages of Scripture. In its exegesis of the Babel story, for example, the report concluded that 'the diversity of races and peoples to which the confusion of tongues contributed is an aspect of reality which God obviously intended for this dispensation'.[45] What was striking about the DRC's position was not that racial politics received endorsement from a particular theology, but that the Church from which this theology emerged was both keen to grant its endorsement, and in a strong enough position socially that its support made a palpable difference. According to Susan Rennie Ritner, as the 'dominant church of the Afrikaner people', the DRC *could* have tempered the political ambitions of the National Party. Instead, however, it was the Church that pressed towards a 'more precise refinement . . . of apartheid', and the Church that 'insisted upon progressively sterner definitions of "separateness"'.[46]

John de Gruchy has demonstrated that the downfall of apartheid policies was due, in significant part, to the rediscovery within the DRC of a very different form of Calvinism from that which had been learned through Kuyper. Nonetheless, it remains the case that State-enforced racial segregation received its legitimation in post-war South Africa through the operative theology of the DRC. For at least three generations, the Church had marched in time to the State's drum; tellingly, and in contrast to the German experience of 1934, when a *status confessionis* was declared in 1977, it had to be declared by outsiders, not from within.[47]

## Sho'ah

The Jewish Holocaust under Nazism is the site where, in the middle years of the twentieth century, theological interpretations of Synagogue and State coalesced. Without denying that antisemitism has a much longer and more complicated history, the *Sho'ah* would not have happened without: 1) an entrenched dehumanisation of Jews within Christian doctrine, for which the image of the demonically faithless synagogue was a primary symbol; and 2) an ambiguous doctrine of the State within German ecclesiology that was never sure whether to join forces with it or ignore it, and was sure only that the Church was not called to *resist* it.

It has been frequently noted that, of all European nations at the start of the twentieth century, Germany was by no means the most obvious one in which genocidal antisemitism might have been expected to occur. Russia had a far more recent history of pogroms, beginning with the Odessa riot in 1821, and then a sweeping series of anti-Jewish violence in Ukraine and southern Russia between 1881 and 1884, and again in Odessa, Kishinev and Kiev between 1903 and 1907. In the three years following the 1917 revolution, tens of thousands of Russian Jews were killed by Bolshevik soldiers and their sympathisers, in Belorussia and Galicia.[48] France, too, was rife with anti-Jewish sentiment, much of it expressed violently. The notorious Dreyfus Affair so exacerbated existing hostility against French Jewry that Theodor Herzl was forced to conclude that antisemitism as such was so deeply entrenched as to be ineradicable. The only possible solution was the creation of a new homeland, a sovereign Jewish state. Thus, the birth of the modern Zionist movement at the dawning of the twentieth century was a direct consequence of the strength of French antisemitism.[49] In other words, while Germany was hardly free of such prejudice, neither was it the most obvious contender for the site of history's most comprehensive genocide.

The Sho'ah itself can be only briefly described here. While much remains historiographically contested, the main features are easy enough to identify. Neither Adolf Hitler nor the National Socialist Party more broadly had ever disguised their visceral hatred of Jews, and so, once the Nazis had seized power in January 1933, the question was simply how, not whether, Germany's Jews would be eliminated, and what 'elimination' would in fact mean. The policy path to Auschwitz was, nevertheless, 'twisted', rather than straightforward.[50] Initial legislative repression and imprisonment in concentration camps gave way, from 1937, to forced migration, including a bizarre plan to relocate Europe's Jews to Madagascar. Then, once the Second World War had started, ghettoisation, forced labour and eventual transportation to 'the East' were the publicly acceptable euphemisms for mass incarceration and murder in the death camps of Bełżec, Sobibor, Chełmno, Treblinka and Auschwitz-Birkenau. Notwithstanding older debates between the 'functionalists' and 'intentionalists',[51] and between those who see in the Holocaust an event sui generis and those who regard it as simply another example of genocide, the brutally inescapable fact is that, by the time of Germany's capitulation to the Allies in April 1945, at least six million Jews had been murdered as a direct result of Nazi policy.

But the question remains: why did the Sho'ah occur in Germany, and not elsewhere?[52] There is no single answer to this, but the confluence of our two previous themes – demonic synagogue imagery and a particularly uncertain theology of the State – ensured that the German Churches were woefully unprepared, and even unwilling, to stand in the way of its enactment. There is no better evidence for this than the myriad examples throughout the Kirchenkampf of Church leaders determining ecclesial responses to Nazi antisemitism on the basis of a self-serving distinction between Jews and Jewish Christians. In the wake of the boycott of Jewish business on 1 April 1933, for example, the German Evangelical Church Federation issued a memorandum in which it affirmed the government's anti-Jewish measures as a sign of 'German discipline', and said that the Church had an obligation to defend only those Jews who had converted to Christianity. The real issue was not 'the persecution of the Jews . . . but a protective measure for the safeguarding of the German Volk'.[53] Even within the Confessing Church, opposition to the State's antisemitic measures was voiced only on behalf of baptised Jews. Similarly, from the Catholic side, and in response to the same boycott, Archbishop Gröber of Freiburg noted in a letter that he had 'immediately intervened on behalf of the converted Jews'.[54] But what really was the difference between baptised and non-baptised Jews? Not their race, but only their religion. In other words, baptism was understood to be sufficiently efficacious to address religious infidelity, but it could do nothing to cleanse racial impurity. Jews who did not convert remained racially defiled (about this, baptism could do nothing) but also – and for the Churches, this was far more critical – wilfully disobedient to God. That is to say, it was the Jews' adherence to their Judaism – to the Synagogue – that removed the Churches' obligation to defend them.

This abrogation of responsibility was compounded by an ambivalence towards the Nazi State that was embedded within German ecclesiology. For at least four hundred years, ever since Martin Luther had first proposed his 'two kingdoms' doctrine, German Christianity had presumed *both* the Churches' right to determine their own doctrine free of secular interference, *and* the State's right to expect ecclesial adherence to secular order. The Peace of Augsburg of 1555, in which the principle of *cuius regio, eius religio* ('whose realm, his religion') had been enshrined, further cemented the assumption that – while being theoretically equal in status (Luther's intended point) – the being of the Church *in* the world, and not vice versa, rendered the Church effectively subordinate to the State's social ordering. That the Churches' leading decision-makers were typically members of the conservative elite, and that Nazism promised protection from the evils of Communism and liberal democracy – both of which were associated with international Jewry – almost guaranteed the Hitler State a compliant Christian ally. As Baranowski has noted, the first priority of the ecumenical Confessing Church was not to protest against the regime as such, but to come to a tolerable arrangement with the regime, in order that the sociocultural position of the Protestant Church could be preserved intact.[55] Or, as Victoria Barnett has said even more starkly, 'The only thing all Confessing Christians had in common was their opposition to the absolute demands of Nazi ideology on their religious faith.'[56] In sum, a visceral fear of the unconverted Jew – at once a religious and racial threat – and an equally deep-seated reluctance to regard the Church as anything other than the State's partner in God's providential ruling of the social order, rendered the Churches themselves impotent in face of Nazism's persecution of Europe's Jewish population.

## Conclusion

In the decades since the end of the Second World War, there has been, thankfully, a reckoning by the Churches with themselves, particularly with regard to Christian understandings of both (biblical and post-biblical) Judaism and State power. Slow in some places, more rapidly in others, there has emerged out of this reckoning a growing recognition that, insofar as the *Sho'ah* happened within the bosom of Western Christendom, it was allowed to do so, at least in part, because of the Churches' long-held antipathy to the 'synagogue' of 'faithless Jews', and a similarly longstanding uncertainty about the limits of State authority. The result of this ecclesial-doctrinal awakening has been threefold: 1) a widespread acknowledgement of the Churches' need – not just in Europe, but throughout the world – to repent of institutionalised antisemitism;[57] 2) to seek reconciliation with the people from whom Jesus came; and 3) to be more prepared to speak prophetically against institutionalised power, whether that power be wielded by States, global corporates or even the rhetorical muscle of popular discourse. While it has been the European Churches in which much of the energy for this reckoning has been generated, in fact the global Church has been impacted.

It would be false to claim that it was the *Sho'ah* alone that occasioned this ecclesial metanoia. It would be equally false to claim that all Churches, and all Christian theologies, have now been purged of those theological presuppositions about Synagogue and State by which the horrors of the twentieth century were made possible. The influence of the so-called 'court evangelicals' in the wake of the 2016 US Presidential elections demonstrates the persistence, at least in some quarters, of an unhealthy collusion between Christian and political interests; and the recent emergence of 'fulfillment theology' is nothing other than supersessionism under a new name. That is to say, neither the prophetically cruciform life of the Church nor the integrity of Christian doctrine can be taken for granted in the twenty-first century. As Zimmermann has said, the Church 'must always be vigilant in examining its own presuppositions and motivations'.[58] Nevertheless, the Sho'ah has imposed a new hermeneutical frame through which Christian attitudes towards both the Jewish people and the representatives of institutionalised power must now be viewed. Naturally, this new hermeneutic does not stand alone, and nor does it guarantee any particular outcome. But, the Church's reflections on 'the Synagogue' and 'the State' cannot now be done without at least reference to 'the fundamental wound' that was and is the Sho'ah.[59]

# Notes

1. See, for example, John H. Yoder, 'Karl Barth and the Problem of War', in *Karl Barth and the Problem of War and Other Essays on Barth*, edited by Mark Thiessen Nation (Eugene, OR: Cascade Books, 2003), pp. 1–106: 72; George Hunsinger, 'Karl Barth and the Politics of Sectarian Protestantism: A Dialogue with John Howard Yoder (1980)', in *Disruptive Grace: Studies in the Theology of Karl Barth*, edited by George Hunsinger (Grand Rapids: Eerdmans, 2000), pp. 114–28: 124. Stanley Hauerwas argues that even Reinhold Niebuhr, while sharply critical of 'social gospelers' such as Walther Rauschenbusch, nonetheless never questioned the assumption that Christianity and democratic statehood were, and *ought to be*, hand in glove. Stanley Hauerwas, 'A Christian Critique of Christian America (1986)', in *The Hauerwas Reader*, edited by John Berkman and Michael Cartwright (Durham: Duke University Press, 2001), pp. 459–80: 466–7.
2. See Katherine Sonderegger, *That Jesus Christ Was Born a Jew: Karl Barth's 'Doctrine of Israel'* (University Park: Penn State University Press, 1992), p. 73 n. 62.
3. The term comes from Jules Isaac's *L'Enseignement de Mépris* (1962), which was translated as *The Teaching of Contempt Contempt: The Christian Roots of Antisemitism*, H. Weaver (trans.) (New York: Holt, Rhinehart and Winston, 1964).
4. Moreover, as non-Jewish groups have also sought to find their place within the history of Nazi genocide – for example, the Roma, Jehovah's Witnesses, and gays and lesbians – Jewish survivors have sought a more particular word for their own unique form of victimisation.
5. Ignaz Maybaum, *The Face of God after Auschwitz* (Amsterdam: Polak & Van Gennep, 1965).
6. It has not helped that Maybaum's own use of this word rests upon an ultimately hopeful doctrine of providence, in which *even* those events that are *churban* are both redemptive and creative in the overarching sovereignty of God. See my *Reading Auschwitz with Barth: The Holocaust as Problem and Promise for Barthian Theology* (Eugene, OR: Pickwick Publications, 2014), pp. 31–4.
7. Elie Wiesel, 'Twentieth Anniversary Keynote', in *What Have We Learned? Telling the Story and Teaching the Lessons of the Holocaust: Papers of the 20th Anniversary Scholars' Conference*, edited by Franklin H. Littell, Alan L. Berger and Hubert G. Locke (Lewiston, NY: Mellen, 1993), p. 8. Wiesel's colleague Richard Rubenstein agrees, saying that 'it is by no means certain that we have even been successful in giving the event an appropriate name'. Richard L. Rubenstein, *After Auschwitz: History, Theology, and Contemporary Judaism* (Baltimore: John Hopkins University Press, 1992), p. 83.
8. The same word is to refer to the Sadducees (Acts 5:17), and also by St Paul himself to refer to the various factions that were causing chaos within the Christian community in Corinth (1 Cor. 11:19).
9. Elaine Pagels, *The Origin of Satan: How Christians Demonized Jews, Pagans, and Heretics* (New York: Vintage Book, 1996), p. 15. Italics original.
10. Ambrose, *Epistle* 40.14. Seventy years later, the Theodosian Code forbade the construction of new synagogues, and ordered that those that already existed be kept in their current condition. *Codex Theodosianus* 16.8.25.

11. Constant J. Mews, 'Abelard and Heloise on Jews and *Hebraica Veritas*', in *Christian Attitudes towards the Jews in the Middle Ages: A Casebook*, edited by Michael Frassetto (New York & London: Routledge, 2013), pp. 83–108: 85.

12. *In Sententias* 4, d.3, q.4.

13. Martin Luther, 'Von den Juden und ihren Lügen', *Weimarer Ausgabe* 53, pp. 417–552: 419. Luther here uses the term *Schulen*; however, it should be recognised that, from at least as early as the thirteenth century, *Schul* and *Synagogue* were used interchangeably by German Jews.

14. Luther, 'Von den Juden und ihren Lügen', pp. 523, 536.

15. According to rabbinic tradition, an *eruv* is an enclosure, formed by wire or rope, around a designated area – sometimes a whole suburb, or even an entire village – that symbolically turns a public space into a private space. By this quite literal loophole, Jews can carry out certain tasks on the Sabbath that would normally be permitted only within the home. See Dan Cohn-Sherbok, *The Crucified Jew: Twenty Centuries of Christian Anti-Semitism* (London: Fount Books, 1992), p. 182.

16. Adolf von Harnack, *What Is Christianity?*, Thomas Bailey Saunders (trans.) (London: Williams & Norgate, 1912), p. 106.

17. Adolf von Harnack, *History of Dogma*, vol. 1, Neil Buchanan (trans.) (London: Williams & Norgate, 1894), p. 177.

18. Harnack, *What Is Christianity?*, p. 183.

19. Karl Barth, *Kirchliche Dogmatik*, vol. 2, part 2 (Zürich: Evangelischer Verlag, 1948), p. 286; Sonderegger, *That Jesus Christ Was Born a Jew*, p. 72.

20. Karl Barth, *Church Dogmatics*, vol. 2, part 2, Geoffrey W. Bromiley and Thomas F. Torrance (eds) (Edinburgh: T&T Clark, 1957), p. 261.

21. Karl Barth, *The Epistle to the Romans*, Edwyn C. Hoskyns (trans.) (Oxford: Oxford University Press, [1933] 1968), p. 527.

22. Sonderegger, *That Jesus Christ Was Born a Jew*, p. 82.

23. Rudolf Bultmann, *Primitive Christianity in Its Contemporary Setting*, R. H. Fuller (trans.) (New York: Meridian, 1956), pp. 59–61.

24. Dietrich Bonhoeffer, 'Report on My Year of Study at Union Theological Seminary in New York, 1930/31', in *Barcelona, Berlin, New York: 1928–1931*, Douglas W. Stott (trans.), Clifford J. Green (ed.), Dietrich Bonhoeffer Works 10 (Minneapolis: Fortress, 2008), pp. 305–20: 313.

25. Dietrich Bonhoeffer, 'Letter to H. Rößler, 25 December 1932', in *Berlin: 1932–1933*, Isabel Best and David Higgins (trans.), Larry L. Rasmussen (ed.), Dietrich Bonhoeffer Works 12 (Minneapolis: Fortress, 2009), p. 84.

26. Dietrich Bonhoeffer, 'Lecture on the Path of the Young Illegal Theologians of the Confessing Church', 26 October 1938, in *Theological Education Underground: 1937–1940*, Victoria Barnett, Claudia D. Bergmann, Peter Frick and Scott A. Moore (trans.), Victoria Barnett (ed.), Dietrich Bonhoeffer Works 15 (Minneapolis: Fortress, 2012), p. 436.

27. Dirk Schulz, 'Editor's Afterword to the German Edition', in *Theological Education Underground: 1937–1940*, Victoria Barnett, Claudia D. Bergmann, Peter Frick and Scott A. Moore (trans), Victoria Barnett (ed.), Dietrich Bonhoeffer Works 15 (Minneapolis: Fortress, 2012), pp. 574–5.

28. Ernst Troeltsch, *The Social Teachings of the Christian Churches*, Olive Wyon (trans.) (New York: Harper Torchbooks, 1960), vol. 1, p. 23.

29. Troeltsch, *The Social Teachings of the Christian Churches*, vol. 2, p. 1013.

30. Jens Zimmermann, 'Between the Times: The Church's Political Vocation in Eschatological Perspective', *Canadian Theological Review* 1:1 (2012), 65–80: 65.

31. Leonardo Boff and Clodovis Boff, *Introducing Liberation Theology* (Tunbridge Wells: Burns & Oates, 1987), p. 3.

32. Boff and Boff, *Introducing Liberation Theology*, pp. 68, 72.

33. Rosemary Radford Ruether, *Sexism and God-Talk* (Boston: Beacon Press, 1983), p. 193.

34. Ruether, *Sexism and God-Talk*, p. 232.

35. James Cone, *The Cross and the Lynching Tree* (Maryknoll, NY: Orbis, 2011), p. xvi.

36. Cone, *The Cross and the Lynching Tree*, p. xvii.
37. Cone, *The Cross and the Lynching Tree*, p. 71.
38. Eberhard Bethge, *Dietrich Bonhoeffer: Eine Biographie* (Gütersloh: Christian Kaiser, [1967] 1994), p. 894.
39. Mark Lindsay, *Covenanted Solidarity: The Theological Basis of Karl Barth's Opposition to Nazi Antisemitism and the Holocaust* (New York: Peter Lang, 2001), p. 182.
40. Victoria Barnett, *For the Soul of the People: Protestant Protest against Hitler* (New York: Oxford University Press, 1992), p. 55.
41. Eberhard Busch, *Karl Barth: His Life from Letters and Autobiographical Texts*, John Bowden (trans.) (Grand Rapids: Eerdmans, 1994), p. 261.
42. The notion that God rules the world directly in relation to each area of life, and which was thus employed to justify both the givenness and the separateness of ethnic groups as distinct entities.
43. John de Gruchy, 'Calvin(ism) and Apartheid in South Africa in the Twentieth Century', in Irena Backus and Philip Benedict (eds), *Calvin and His Influence, 1509–2009* (Oxford: Oxford University Press, 2011), p. 310.
44. *Ras, Volk en Nasie en Volkereverhoudinge in die lig van der skrif*; published in English as *Human Relations and the South African Scene in the Light of Scripture* (Cape Town: Dutch Reformed Church Publishers, 1976).
45. *Ras, Volk en Nasie en Volkereverhoudinge in die lig van der skrif*, p. 18.
46. Susan R. Ritner, 'The Dutch Reformed Church and Apartheid', *Journal of Contemporary History* 2:4 (1967), 17–37: 17.
47. That the South African Church was *in status confessionis* was declared in Dar es Salaam by the Sixth Assembly of the Lutheran World Federation. This can be contrasted with the declaration by Bonhoeffer and Barth in September 1933 – from *within* the German Church – that a similar situation was operative in Germany.
48. Oleg Budnitskii, *Russian Jews between the Reds and the Whites, 1917–1920*, Timothy J. Portice (trans.) (Philadelphia: University of Pennsylvania Press, 2012), p. 1.
49. Cohn-Sherbok, *The Crucified Jew*, pp. 170–2.
50. Karl Albert Schleunes, *The Twisted Road to Auschwitz: Nazi Policy toward German Jews, 1933–1939* (Urbana: University of Illinois Press, 1970).
51. 'Functionalism' refers to the interpretive school led by historians such as Hans Mommsen and Martin Broszat, who argued that the Holocaust was an evolving bureaucratic response on the part of government officials (including in the military) to actualise what they understood to be Hitler's ultimate agenda, but without there being any specific plan or order. The 'intentionalist' school, by contrast, represented chiefly by Lucy Dawidowicz, Karl Dietrich Bracher and Andreas Hillgrüber, argued that the Holocaust as it was eventually enacted had always been Hitler's explicit plan and that, moreover, the Second World War itself was merely a cover under which the real goal – the extermination of the Jews – could be achieved.
52. Of course, much of the killing of Jews was done in occupied territories outside Germany, principally in Poland, Ukraine and western Russia. It was, however, conceived and duly authorised in Germany, by members of Germany's Nazi government, and its supporting bureaucracy.
53. Wolfgang Gerlach, *And the Witnesses Were Silent: The Confessing Church and the Persecution of the Jews*, Victoria Barnett (trans.) (Lincoln: University of Nebraska Press, 2000), p. 56.
54. Ludwig Volk (ed.), *Kirchliche Akten über die Reichskonkordatsverhandlungen, 1933* (Mainz: Matthias-Grünewald, 1969), p. 11.
55. Shelley Baranowski, *The Confessing Church, Conservative Elites, and the Nazi State*, Texts and Studies in Religion 28 (London: Edwin Mellen Press, 1986), p. 3.
56. Barnett, *For the Soul of the People*, p. 5.
57. See, for example, Synod of the Evangelical Church of the Rhineland, 'Towards a Renewal of the Relationship between Christians and Jews' (1980), accessed at https://www.bc.edu/content

/dam/files/research_sites/cjl/texts/cjrelations/resources/documents/protestant/EvChFRG1980
.htm; Second Vatican Council, 'Declaration on the Relation of the Church to Non-Christian
Religions, *Nostra aetate* 28 October 1965', accessed at https://www.vatican.va/archive/hist_co
uncils/ii_vatican_council/documents/vat-ii_decl_19651028_nostra-aetate_en.html.
58. Zimmermann, 'Between the Times', p. 79.
59. Dietrich Ritschl, *The Logic of Theology* (London: SCM Press, 1986), p. 128.

# Bibliography

Ambrose, 'Epistle 40', in *Nicene and Post-Nicene Fathers*, Second Series, vol. 10, H. De Romestin
(trans), P. Schaff and H. Wace (eds) (Edinburgh: T&T Clark, 1980).

Baranowski, Shelley, *The Confessing Church, Conservative Elites, and the Nazi State*, Texts and
Studies in Religion 28 (London: Edwin Mellen Press, 1986).

Barnett, Victoria, *For the Soul of the People: Protestant Protest against Hitler* (New York: Oxford
University Press, 1992).

Barth, Karl, *Church Dogmatics*, vol. 2, part 2, Geoffrey W. Bromiley and Thomas F. Torrance (eds)
(Edinburgh: T&T Clark, 1957).

Barth, Karl, *The Epistle to the Romans*, Edwyn C. Hoskyns (trans.) (Oxford: Oxford University Press,
[1933] 1968).

Barth, Karl, *Kirchliche Dogmatik*, vol. 2, part 2 (Zürich: Evangelischer Verlag, 1948).

Bethge, Eberhard, *Dietrich Bonhoeffer: Eine Biographie* (Gütersloh: Christian Kaiser, [1967] 1994).

Boff, Leonardo and Clodovis Boff, *Introducing Liberation Theology* (Tunbridge Wells: Burns & Oates,
1987).

Bonhoeffer, Dietrich, 'Lecture on the Path of the Young Illegal Theologians of the Confessing
Church', 26 October 1938, in *Theological Education Underground: 1937–1940*, Victoria Barnett,
Claudia D. Bergmann, Peter Frick and Scott A. Moore (trans.), Victoria Barnett (ed.), Dietrich
Bonhoeffer Works 15 (Minneapolis: Fortress, 2012).

Bonhoeffer, Dietrich, 'Letter to H. Rößler, 25 December 1932', in *Berlin: 1932–1933*, Isabel Best and
David Higgins (trans.), Larry L. Rasmussen (ed.), Dietrich Bonhoeffer Works 12 (Minneapolis:
Fortress, 2009).

Bonhoeffer, Dietrich, 'Report on My Year of Study at Union Theological Seminary in New York,
1930/31', in *Barcelona, Berlin, New York: 1928–1931*, Douglas W. Stott (trans.), Clifford J. Green
(ed.), Dietrich Bonhoeffer Works 10 (Minneapolis: Fortress, 2008) pp. 305–20.

Budnitskii, Oleg, *Russian Jews between the Reds and the Whites, 1917–1920*, Timothy J. Portice
(trans.) (Philadelphia: University of Pennsylvania Press, 2012).

Bultmann, Rudolf, *Primitive Christianity in Its Contemporary Setting*, R. H. Fuller (trans.) (New York:
Meridian, 1956).

Busch, Eberhard, *Karl Barth: His Life from Letters and Autobiographical Texts*, John Bowden (trans.)
(Grand Rapids: Eerdmans, 1994).

*Codex Theodosianus*, in *Theodosiani libri XVI cum constitutionibus Sirmondianis et Leges novellae ad
Theodosianum pertinentes*, vol. 1, part 2, T. Mommsen and P. M. Meyer (eds) (Berlin: Weidmann,
1905).

Cohn-Sherbok, Dan, *The Crucified Jew: Twenty Centuries of Christian Anti-Semitism* (London: Fount
Books, 1992).

Cone, James, *The Cross and the Lynching Tree* (Maryknoll, NY: Orbis, 2011)

Gerlach, Wolfgang, *And the Witnesses Were Silent: The Confessing Church and the Persecution of the
Jews*, Victoria Barnett (trans.) (Lincoln: University of Nebraska Press, 2000).

Gruchy, John de, 'Calvin(ism) and Apartheid in South Africa in the Twentieth Century', in *Calvin
and His Influence, 1509–2009*, edited by Irena Backus and Philip Benedict (Oxford: Oxford
University Press, 2011).

Harnack, Adolf von, *History of Dogma*, vol. 1, Neil Buchanan (trans.) (London: Williams &
Norgate, 1894).

Harnack, Adolf von, *What Is Christianity?*, Thomas Bailey Saunders (trans.) (London: Williams & Norgate, 1912).

Hauerwas, Stanley, 'A Christian Critique of Christian America (1986)', in *The Hauerwas Reader*, edited by John Berkman and Michael Cartwright (Durham: Duke University Press, 2001), pp. 459–80.

Hunsinger, George, 'Karl Barth and the Politics of Sectarian Protestantism: A Dialogue with John Howard Yoder (1980)', in *Disruptive Grace: Studies in the Theology of Karl Barth*, edited by George Hunsinger (Grand Rapids: Eerdmans, 2000), pp. 114–28.

Isaac, Jules, *L'Enseignement de Mépris*; published in English as *The Teaching of Contempt: The Christian Roots of Antisemitism*, H. Weaver (trans.) (New York: Holt, Rhinehart and Winston, [1962] 1964).

John Duns Scotus, *In Sententias*, in *Joannis Duns Scoti: Doctoris Subtilis, Ordinis Minorum. Opera Omnia*, Luke Wadding (ed), vol. 16 (Paris: Vives, 1894).

Lindsay, Mark, *Covenanted Solidarity: The Theological Basis of Karl Barth's Opposition to Nazi Antisemitism and the Holocaust* (New York: Peter Lang, 2001).

Lindsay, Mark, *Reading Auschwitz with Barth: The Holocaust as Problem and Promise for Barthian Theology* (Eugene, OR: Pickwick Publications, 2014).

Luther, Martin, 'Von den Juden und ihren Lügen', *Weimarer Ausgabe* 53, pp. 417–552.

Maybaum, Ignaz, *The Face of God after Auschwitz* (Amsterdam: Polak & Van Gennep, 1965).

Mews, Constant J., 'Abelard and Heloise on Jews and *Hebraica Veritas*', in *Christian Attitudes towards the Jews in the Middle Ages: A Casebook*, edited by Michael Frassetto (New York and London: Routledge, 2013), pp. 83–108.

Pagels, Elaine, *The Origin of Satan: How Christians Demonized Jews, Pagans, and Heretics* (New York: Vintage Book, 1996).

*Ras, Volk en Nasie en Volkereverhoudinge in die lig van der skrif* (Capetown: Nasionale Pers, 1974); published in English as *Human Relations and the South African Scene in the Light of Scripture* (Cape Town: Dutch Reformed Church Publishers, 1976).

Ritner, Susan R, 'The Dutch Reformed Church and Apartheid', *Journal of Contemporary History* 2:4 (1967), 17–37.

Ritschl, Dietrich, *The Logic of Theology* (London: SCM Press, 1986).

Rubenstein, Richard L., *After Auschwitz: History, Theology, and Contemporary Judaism* (Baltimore: John Hopkins University Press, 1992).

Ruether, Rosemary Radford, *Sexism and God-Talk* (Boston: Beacon Press, 1983).

Schleunes, Karl Albert, *The Twisted Road to Auschwitz: Nazi Policy toward German Jews, 1933–1939* (Urbana: University of Illinois Press, 1970).

Schulz, Dirk, 'Editor's Afterword to the German Edition', in *Theological Education Underground: 1937–1940*, Victoria Barnett, Claudia D. Bergmann, Peter Frick and Scott A. Moore (trans.), Victoria Barnett (ed.), Dietrich Bonhoeffer Works 15 (Minneapolis: Fortress, 2012).

Second Vatican Council, 'Declaration on the Relation of the Church to Non-Christian Religions, *Nostre aetate* 28 October 1965'.

Sonderegger, Katherine, *That Jesus Christ Was Born a Jew: Karl Barth's 'Doctrine of Israel'* (University Park: Penn State University Press, 1992).

Synod of the Evangelical Church of the Rhineland, 'Towards a Renewal of the Relationship between Christians and Jews' (1980).

Troeltsch, Ernst, *The Social Teachings of the Christian Churches*, Olive Wyon (trans.), 2 vols (New York: Harper Torchbooks, 1960).

Volk, Ludwig (ed.), *Kirchliche Akten über die Reichskonkordatsverhandlungen, 1933* (Mainz: Matthias-Grünewald, 1969).

Wiesel, Elie, 'Twentieth Anniversary Keynote', in *What Have We Learned? Telling the Story and Teaching the Lessons of the Holocaust: Papers of the 20th Anniversary Scholars' Conference*, edited by Franklin H. Littell, Alan L. Berger and Hubert G. Locke (Lewiston, NY: Mellen, 1993).

Yoder, John H., 'Karl Barth and the Problem of War', in *Karl Barth and the Problem of War and Other Essays on Barth*, edited by Mark Thiessen Nation (Eugene, OR: Cascade Books, 2003), pp. 1–106.

Zimmermann, Jens, 'Between the Times: The Church's Political Vocation in Eschatological Perspective', *Canadian Theological Review* 1:1 (2012), 65–80.

# 8

# Religion(s)

*Paul Hedges*

## Introduction

To discuss the concept of 'religion(s)' in relation to twentieth-century theology is to discuss the awareness of Christianity as a religion amongst other religions.[1] This entails an understanding of what the term religion is taken to signify, and will necessitate an exploration into the context of at least the previous century and beyond, as that is where the modern English usage of the term religion is inherited from. Nevertheless, specific trajectories exist within twentieth-century theology, and some key figures and traditions for exploring the term, concept and ideological formation of religion will be explored.

    I begin by discussing the history of the term religion, including how it was constructed especially in nineteenth-century theological constructions of the concept of 'world religions'. The chapter proceeds through the twentieth century by looking at some key figures alongside discussions of some general trends, especially in wider ecclesiastical contexts, with a particular focus on Ernst Troeltsch, Karl Barth and Paul Tillich. The focus is therefore upon the Protestant world, but Catholic thinkers are engaged along the way. The final part does not so much focus on individuals as on four significant movements or trends: towards dialogue; developing the theology of religions; the discipline of comparative theology; and feminist and post-colonial concerns. I conclude by looking at some current trends, suggesting how religion may be considered theologically today, calling upon a reading of Barth beyond Barth.

## The Genealogy of Religion

Wilfred Cantwell Smith (1916–2000) made a landmark contribution to the history of intellectual thought in 1962 with his book *The Meaning and End of Religion*. He argued, cogently and persuasively, that the modern English usage of the term 'religion' was essentially the creation of a particular lineage of thought that came from a modern, Western and primarily Protestant context.[2] In addition, Smith argued that no other language has traditionally had any term which equates to this modern Western usage. For instance, the Sanskrit term *dharma*, often translated as 'religion', is best understood as something closer to 'duty'; the Arabic *deen* more closely relates to terms such as 'culture', 'custom' or 'law' than religion; and the Chinese *zongjiao* is actually a modern coinage (first employed in Japan) to provide an equivalent to the English term religion because no native term was deemed adequate.[3] This information is not simply an interesting linguistic anomaly. It is deeply conceptually significant. To be able to think of there being a range of religions, and so to imagine the relationship between them as distinct 'religious traditions', and to discuss how the 'Christian religion' relates to any perceived 'non-Christian religion', is only possible within a certain modern European context, underlaid by notions of the secular (again a modern Western notion). It is also embedded within the heritage of colonialism.[4]

Smith argued that the matter was readily resolved by employing two concepts: 'cumulative tradition' to speak about the historical trajectory of specific traditions; and 'faith' to refer to the internal aspects of spirituality and belief. Others have argued that such attempts to reinstate 'religion' miss the entirely constructed nature of the concept (something that applies equally to 'faith'): it is argued by some to be entirely meaningless and employed only for political and apologetic purposes.[5] Such critics argue we should completely abandon anything that looks like the concept 'religion' as it is embroiled in a Western, Protestant, colonial legacy. Critical dismissals of the term religion have, though, often been overstated.

Accepting many serious problems with how religion is often employed does not mean abandoning it, and other scholars argue it can still be employed.[6] I will briefly summarise a few key points of substantial arguments. First, to argue that the origins of a term limit what it potentially means commits the etymological fallacy. The current author has argued that we can employ religion as an 'essentially contested concept', meaning that, while problematic and not capable of precise definition, it nevertheless serves a useful role.[7] This does not mean that we can simply employ it as before, a matter discussed further in the next section. Second, historically those traditions typically termed religions today have interacted as related realms of human culture in their own terms; 'religion(s)' is not simply the imagination of modern Western Protestant scholars.[8] Third, even if we accept the argument that the concept of religion, and even the religions as we know them (Hinduism, Buddhism etc.) are the creation of modern Western academic category construction,[9] it can be argued that they do actually exist now. People claim and follow traditions which they understand as religions and which go by these markers. Fourth, in the period we are looking at here, religion was primarily understood, discussed and described in the lineage that Smith uncovers. Discussing the concept in modern theology makes a discussion of its genealogy something of a moot point. Nevertheless, reflecting on this legacy today requires a critical reflection on the term, as will be discussed.

This discussion has been brief. Much detail around how a term for Christian piety (*religio*) morphed from a singular concept to, with the Reformation, a plural concept (Catholic and Protestant religions), then, with a growing awareness of the world beyond Europe, a term to describe many 'religions' has not been covered. However, here it is simply important to be aware that 'religion' is not simply a descriptor of facts out there in the world, but a modern and colonial imposition that shapes the data.

## The Science of Religion, Mission, and Comparative Studies

This survey of twentieth-century theology must begin, at least, around the mid-nineteenth century, because the trajectories and thought forms that shape it do not begin out of nowhere. Importantly, it should be noted that what are seen as the origins of the academic study of religion, including in figures such as Friedrich Max Müller (1823–1900), the 'father of religious studies', were imbricated in theological and missionary apologetical concerns.[10] While there is often a perceived distinction between figures leading into either the study of religion or those streams we may broadly term the theology of religions and comparative theology, there was no clear and simple divide. The Sanskritists Müller and

Monier Monier-Williams (1819–99) both had missionary agendas, while James Legge (1815–97), the famous scholar of Chinese traditions, and John Nichol Farquhar (1861–1929), who was the first Professor of Comparative Religion at Manchester University, UK, were both themselves missionaries.[11] Further, important and scholarly studies of non-Christian religions were undertaken by theologians, such as Frederick Denison Maurice (1805–72) and Rowland Williams (1817–70), the latter's *Christianity and Hinduism* being probably the single most sophisticated study of Hinduism in English in the nineteenth century.[12] Indeed, many important twentieth-century scholars of religion were also Christian theologians, such as Smith[13] and Rudolf Otto (1869–1937).[14] Even scholars who vehemently objected to confessional theologians in the study of religion have been argued to be entrapped within theological conceptions of religions, with Ninian Smart (1927–2001) being an example.[15] This is not to suggest that one person cannot be both a theologian and a scholar of religion, nor that the former compromises the latter. However, a distinct division of two camps is problematic. Indeed, from the nineteenth century and into the twentieth century, much that was termed as part of the new 'science of the study of religion' (or became later the 'history of religion', 'religious studies' etc.) was directly apologetic or implicitly (if not explicitly) founded on Christian theological principles. The latter, it is argued, is an issue that still permeates the contemporary study of religion.[16]

Returning to the question of religion, one way in which explicit Christian – especially Protestant – norms become embedded in conceptions of the academic study of religion, and so mutually informs theology, is in the World Religions Paradigm (WRP).[17] As historian Tomoko Masuzawa has shown in relation to the nineteenth century, this categorisation, which often distinguished between categories such as 'primitive religions', 'ethnic religions', 'universal religions' or 'world religions', was not based on a scientific and comparative study of the evidence, but in the ideological agendas of the classifiers.[18] As the twentieth century developed, scholars increasingly recognised what were often termed the 'great' or 'living' religions as a set of around six to eight generally recognised 'world religions' (which shrinks or expands depending on the context), typically including: Buddhism, Christianity, Hinduism, Judaism, Islam, Sikhism and Zoroastrianism.[19] Moreover, the WRP gives a basis for understanding these as essentially similar and discrete units which can be readily compared. So, for instance, in university courses, textbooks and in popular representations we find that each of these can be studied around common categories such as: founders, scriptures, rituals, doctrines etc.[20] This analytical framework, it is argued, does intellectual violence to the traditions so described, for a variety of reasons: many traditions do not have set or fixed doctrines or beliefs, or these may not be primary for identification in a tradition; certain texts are not universally accepted or seen as foundational, while whatever terms such as 'Scripture' may mean are very different from tradition to tradition. The boundaries of traditions may be much more fluid and permeable in many contexts than the WRP framework allows.[21]

The distinctly Protestant foundations of the concept religion in the WRP is shown in the way that, typically, belief and creedal statements are stressed over ritual and communal action, in such a way that even Catholicism can be construed as outside the primary framework of religion.[22] Approaching the question of 'religion(s)' in theology today must begin with this understanding that the very term is, in many ways, a Protestant theological term.

## Key Markers: Ernst Troeltsch and Karl Barth

The creation of the conception of 'world religions' was a concern of Ernst Troeltsch (1865–1923). A German liberal Protestant theologian, Troeltsch's work was marked by the concern with the history of religions. Masuzawa notes of him that

> [t]he career of Ernst Troeltsch roughly coincided with the period of change in the meaning of the term 'world religions', from the highly selective and frankly evaluative sense (universal or universalistic religions as opposed to national or ethnic religions) to the avowedly neutral and inclusive sense (any major living religions of the world).[23]

As Troeltsch elucidates his aims, he sees it as impossible to undertake theology without reference to the history of religions and the placement of Christianity in relation to other traditions, stating: 'the rise of the comparative history of religion has shaken the Christian more deeply than anything else'.[24] However, in at least his earlier work, an explicit Lutheran theological agenda drove his interpretation of the data.[25] This can be seen directly in his 1902 book *The Absoluteness of Christianity and the History of Religions*. While Christians were, Troeltsch believed, 'shaken', the shaking had not been sufficient to knock Christianity off its pedestal as the pinnacle of the religious hierarchy. In *The Absoluteness of Christianity*, Troeltsch argued that the superior religion could be identified, within the supposedly objective study of the history of religion (or *religionsgeschichte Schule*), based upon an analytical study of the sense of a 'higher, spiritual and eternal world' centred around a set 'of absolutely transcendent religious values'.[26] Here, a clear ranking of types of religions is found, with certain traditions pejoratively categorised as 'natural religions', which for Troeltsch included those he saw as 'polytheisms and polydemonisms of the lower stages',[27] his terminology of 'lower' and hence 'higher' clearly defining the hierarchy of religious worth amongst the traditions defined. Echoing well-established apologetics, often based on readings of the Pauline corpus,[28] Troeltsch's next level was 'religions of law', a category which included both Judaism and Islam. The highest category for Troeltsch was 'religions of redemption'. In it, Brahmanism (Hinduism) and Buddhism were placed alongside Christianity.[29] Nevertheless, as Troeltsch's title suggests, his interest was in affirming Christianity as the 'absolute' religion. Hence, despite recognising that Hinduism and Buddhism, like Christianity, sought redemption, Troeltsch's Lutheran presuppositions shaped his conception of what religion should be. Hinduism and Buddhism, he believed, relied upon the human's own striving for redemption and so lacked 'grace'. Further, he critiqued them both for a stress on the 'mystical' as well as failing to have a personal deity, which he saw as imperative.[30] For Troeltsch, therefore, the 'strongest and most concentrated revelation of personalistic religious apprehension' was found only in Christianity.[31]

To be fair to Troeltsch, his later work was marked by a less direct apologetic imperative. In *The Place of Christianity among the World Religions*, published over twenty years later, he argued that history pointed towards recognising the individual or distinctive characteristics of each religion:

> Thus the universal law of history consists precisely in this, that the Divine Reason, or the Divine Life, within history, constantly manifests itself in always-new and always-peculiar individualisations – and hence its tendency is not towards unity or universality

at all, but always towards the fulfillment of the highest potentialities of each separate department of life.[32]

Nevertheless, Troeltsch again concluded that Christianity 'possesses the highest degree of validity attained among all the historical religions which we are able to examine'.[33] However, his thought was no longer marked by the clear certainty that he could rank every religion by Christian criteria, arguing that every 'comprehensive religion' could 'find contact with each other'.[34] For Masuzawa, this places him in a universalising trend in Christian theology,[35] and Alan Race sees him in the lineage of Christian pluralist theology.[36] It is this later trajectory that, perhaps, marks him most clearly from Karl Barth (1886–1968), to whose work I now turn.

A Swiss Reformed theologian, Barth was foundational for dialectical, or neo-orthodox, theology.[37] Barth reacted against the kind of liberalism found in Troeltsch, especially what many may have seen as the relativism of Christianity's position through the history of religion.[38] Troeltsch himself, though, was at pains to stress that he was not a relativist. Arguably, Barth's position was more radical than simply attempting to resist the tide of the history of religion, or comparative religion. Barth sought to define revelation against religion as two diametrically opposing principles.

It is possible to analyse Barth's categorisation of religion from at least two angles. From one, it is a fairly conservative Protestant, even distinctly Augustinian-Lutheran, reading of human sinfulness. Religions, institutions and traditions are inherently depraved because of the concept of original sin. As Barth states: 'religion is unbelief . . . [I]t is the one great concern, of godless man.'[39] In this, it stands in contrast to, but not particularly challenging, the WRP of Protestant liberal thought. It is worth unpacking this somewhat. For many nineteenth-century liberal Protestants, religion was a universal human category. Often inspired by a logos theology which saw sparks of the *logos spermatikos* present in all human beings, religious traditions were essentially humanity's striving for, or in response to, the divine creator and their own inherent recognition of religiosity.[40] Barth believed that humans made their own systems of belief, but these spring from sinful nature and are not objects of revelation, as a liberal logos-theology-inspired view of religions could state.[41] However, in this sense, Barth simply gives a less liberal WRP categorisation: he recognises many traditions (religions) of a similar type existing alongside each other. Indeed, for Barth, this includes Christianity as another religion. Because revelation only consists in the historical instantiation of Jesus of Nazareth, Christianity as a tradition stemming from this is simply religion, meaning that it too is fallible and may be equally corrupt as any non-Christian religion.[42] This standard reading of Barth, as noted, parades religions as representatives of the WRP, though now not understood as relating to a 'Divine Life' as in Troeltsch, but simply as representations of human sinfulness.

It is notable, here, that while generally read in line with exclusivist trends in the theology of religion,[43] in the Dutch tradition Barth has, at times, been read in a liberal light. That is to say, if all religions are examples of human failing, then Christianity cannot be held up as an exemplar of religion *par excellence*.[44]

I offer here, though, a more radical reading of Barth, possibly extending outside the author's own intentions,[45] for a more fundamental critique of 'religion(s)'. One key part of Barth's thought, especially against liberal accounts of non-Christian religions as lower stages of an 'evolutionary' progression towards Christianity,[46] is that religion and revelation stand as opposites, not as part of one natural progression of thought.[47] For Barth, humans might seek God, but could not find deity on their own terms. God, as Jesus, could only come in an act of absolute grace to the human. Barth states:

> From the standpoint of revelation religion is clearly seen to be a human attempt to anticipate what God in His revelation wills to do and does do. It is the attempted replacement of the divine work by human manufacture. The divine reality offered and manifested to us in revelation is replaced by a concept of God arbitrarily and wilfully evolved by man.[48]

If we, however, step beyond Barth, we could take him as providing a radical, even liberal, critique of colonial and Western conceptions of religion. As read through figures such as Hendrik Kraemer (1888–1965), who became the primary interpreter and transmitter of Barth's work in missionary and theology of religions circles as an essentially exclusivist denial of other religions,[49] the principle thrust and reception of Barth is as discussed above. Indeed, Kraemer's reading of Barth is towards an exclusivist theology that posits a radical discontinuity between Christianity and other traditions.[50] However, if we read Barth's notion of manufacture alongside critiques of the conception of 'religion(s)' as manufactured,[51] then his call is not to an exclusivist theology, but away from specific human constructions of 'religion(s)' in which the integrity of each is upheld. Here, 'revelation' may stand as a proxy for that which exceeds our typical ways of knowing. In Levinasian terms, revelation is the 'Face of the Other'.[52] This is contrasted with the human anticipation and manufacture of traditions according to our own expectations, which may be said to be an arbitrary construction based upon parochial and regional expectations.

## Denominations, Ecumenism, Missions and Councils

If the twentieth century began with the liberal trajectory in theology predominant, marked by events such as the Edinburgh Missionary Conference of 1910, which gave its blessing to fulfilment theology,[53] Barth's objections would prove decisive. By the time of the Tambaran Missionary Conference in 1938, Kraemer's exclusivist interpretation of Barth predominated.[54]

This is not to say that other theological stances on the subject of religion(s) did not exist. In a study of *The Buddha and the Christ*, Burnett Hillman Streeter (1874–1937) was amongst theologians who advocated an essentially liberal stance towards other religions.[55] However, perhaps most work in such a direction was undertaken by a range of Catholic theologians. These included Jean Daniélou (1905–74) and Henri de Lubac (1896–1991),[56] both Jesuits who had long been engaged with the encounter of Christianity and the global religious landscape.[57] Jacques Dupuis (1923–2004), another Jesuit contributor to such debates, credits Daniélou as 'the first Western exponent of the "fulfilment theory"'.[58] However, this has been a motif in Christian theology for a long time, certainly from the mid-nineteenth century in English Protestant thought, and can also be traced back to the Jesuits of the sixteenth and seventeenth centuries, if not back to Justin Martyr or even biblical precedents.[59] The discourse in this period on religion(s) was often a recapitulation of previous themes, and so the next significant marker in the debate who needs to be discussed is Paul Tillich (1886–1965).

## A Key Marker: Paul Tillich

If Protestant theology in the twentieth century is marked by theological giants, then Tillich takes a place alongside Barth as the other defining figure of the century. A German-American Lutheran, he was also an existentialist philosopher and added a landmark contribution to thinking about religion. The thrust of Tillich's definition can actually be encapsulated in a very short phrase, which is one of his most famous quotations, as 'ultimate concern', but to quote more extensively:

> Religion, in the largest and most basic sense of the word, is ultimate concern . . . Manifest in the moral sphere as the unconditional seriousness of moral demand[,] . . . [i]n the realm of knowledge as the passionate longing for ultimate reality[,] . . . in the aesthetic of the human spirit as the infinite desire to express ultimate meaning.[60]

Tillich's thought harks back through a liberal lineage to Friedrich Schleiermacher (1768–1834), for whom religion was a 'feeling of absolute dependence'.[61] Religion is perceived as an innate human instinct underlying the human striving after God. As suggested, this is not antithetical to Barth's conception of religion. However, whereas for Barth this human striving led us astray, for Tillich it was witness to a finding as well. In Tillich, the conception of religion must be tied to his concept of a theology of correlation. Tillich believed that while giving it a new name, he had simply voiced a tendency which had always occurred in theology, of relating it to the prevailing cultural and intellectual milieu.[62] In Tillich's case, the principal contemporary cultural form to relate to was existentialism.[63] Tillich understands existentialism as both an attitude and a philosophy. As the former, it is 'the most radical form of the courage to be as oneself'.[64] As the latter, it points to a 'content' as the school of 'Existentialism' which asserts 'that man (sic) is able to transcend, in knowledge and life, the finitude, the estrangement, and the ambiguities of human experience'.[65] He sees existentialism starting with Søren Kierkegaard (1813–65) breaking away from the 'essentialism' of Georg W. F. Hegel (1770–1831).[66] In developing his methodology of correlation, Tillich equates Christian teachings on the Fall and sin to existential concerns about estrangement,[67] and so equates the teachings of Christianity, or religion, to wider human philosophy and psychological concerns. These points will allow a deeper appreciation of the issues raised in Tillich's definition of religion as 'ultimate concern'.

In giving content to his definition of religion as ultimate concern, Tillich highlighted three manifestations of this in various areas: in terms of morality; in terms of knowledge; and in terms of aesthetics. This, we may note, is quite distinct from classical nineteenth-century liberal theological conceptions of religion where religion is seen as the manifestation of humanity's longing for God. The latter is, arguably, exemplified in fulfilment theology, whether in logos theology forms as found in Williams, or Karl Rahner's (1904–84) concept of the 'anonymous Christian'.[68] Tillich sees the longing in wider terms, about how we act, how we know and how we sense. Tillich's wider and less dogmatic conception of religion is not simply focused on the WRP, i.e. traditions with texts and doctrines, but offers a more radical critique of religion than Barth, raising moral, intellectual, and aesthetic aspects. Moreover, Tillich does not close down the discussion by positing a strictly Christian answer: that the creature responds to its creator, and that we have a longing for God.[69]

Tillich represents trends within the mid to late twentieth century which moved away from the exclusivist trends associated with Barth and Kraemer. In ecclesiastical terms this was reflected in moves from mission towards dialogue.

## Towards Dialogue: World Council of Churches and Vatican Initiatives

The 1960s was a new period of openness in life and thought in the Western world, exemplified in the hippy movement and challenges to tradition. Theologically too, doors were opened. It is beyond the scope of this chapter to assess the significance of the Second Vatican Council (1962–5). Nevertheless, in terms of thinking about 'religion(s)' conceptually, its influence was minimal. It asserted religion as a common heritage of humanity, and saw all humans as responding to the 'light' of God. Its importance is in the permissions it granted. Before and after the council, a stance characterised by the dictum *extra ecclesiam nulla salus* ('outside the church there is no salvation') changed to seeing other religions as partners in dialogue. The religious Other, rather than being the demonic perversion of Satan, in more exclusivist views,[70] or simply a stepping stone to Christianity, became a partner to be engaged, in some ways, as an equal. Though interpretations of Vatican II, and subsequent pronouncements, are debated, especially the balance of mission and dialogue.[71] Moreover, the permissions of Vatican II emboldened the World Council of Churches, leading to a series of councils and statements which also placed dialogue central in their framework.[72] Since these events, specific theologians such as Stanley Samartha (1920–2001),[73] Wesley Ariarajah[74] and others have helped lead Protestant Christian reflection on its situation in the context of religious diversity, and hence how to think about the question of religion(s). Notably, specific local dynamics and contextual situations affect debates.[75]

This brief survey has not attempted to be exhaustive, but one issue must be addressed: the significance of the *Sho'ah*. It calls for not simply a recognition of the social exclusion of Jews, but a recognition of theological guilt. The central teachings and texts of the Christian tradition have been key drivers in antisemitism and contributed to the hatred of Jews and the deaths of the Holocaust. This is not simply overblown rhetoric, as we see direct links from the Johannine portrayal of Jews as the Devil's children to Luther's desire to see synagogues burn, to Hitler's atrocities.[76] This recognition of Christianity's implication in the Holocaust played a large part in the rethinking first of Judaism at Vatican II, and then the next logical step of the relationship to the other Abrahamic cousin, Islam.[77] That *Nostra Aetate* decreed that Allah is the Christian God is not without major significance.[78]

## Founding the Theology of Religions: Theological and Intellectual Currents

The theology of religions has a longer gestation stemming from at least the mid-nineteenth century, but is most visible as a distinct discipline in the late twentieth century.[79] A landmark work is Alan Race's 1983 book *Christian and Religious Pluralism*, which defined the standard vocabulary of the theology of religions typology. Before addressing the typology, it is worth spending a bit of time thinking about what the theology of religions means.

The theology of religions names an academic field, or area of theological speculation within the wider realm of systematic theology, that is distinct from missiology or apologetics. It marks, in theological terms, the 'shaking' that Troeltsch spoke of.[80] For the best part of two thousand years, the traditions which we term as Christianity have generally responded to the religious Other as an object of mission. The theology of religions, while not incompatible with understanding other religions as objects of mission,

asks a new question: what exactly is the relationship of Christianity to these other traditions, analysable through the history of religions and other non-theological disciplines?
Mission, conversion or antagonism, while possible answers, are not an a priori given. This
has been a question from the time of Troeltsch and before. Certainly, a radical thinking of related questions occurred with European colonial missions to India and China
in particular, where cultures, philosophical systems and textual traditions that were in
many ways in advance of European Christendom were found.[81] Moreover, if we follow
the insights of Smith and subsequent scholarship in the study of religions, the answer has
somewhat been tamed. That is to say, in framing the questions around religions, these
other traditions have been fitted to some extent to Western and Protestant categories.
However, an issue that may be made explicit here, and has been implicit in this paper so
far, is that the category of religion ought not to be used simply to frame other traditions
within Christian terms. The WRP has to some extent done this. However, opening the
question from religions meaning Catholicism and Protestantism (primarily) to the possibility of there being many religions has forced a new narrative into the Western and
Christian standpoint.[82] It is a challenge, or shaking, to traditional Christian notions of
identity and self-perception.

The theology of religions typology, while challenged, remains the predominant terminology.[83] At base, the original threefold terminology is quite simple. Exclusivisms are
theological stances which stress the radical discontinuity between Christian religion (var-
iously understood) and non-Christian religions; the Christian narrative provides salvation
and is Truth, therefore other religions do not save and are false. A debate within exclusivist stances concerns universalism: can those from other religions be saved, despite their
religion, through the gracious love of God?[84] Inclusivisms are what Race terms a 'dialectical yes and no', in that the absolute truth of my religion is asserted, but the partial truth
of other religions also affirmed. This affirmation can be more or less positive.[85] This raises
a point that the typology, it is argued, is best understood as a heuristic system of markers
rather than a logically compelling set of terms into which everybody neatly falls.[86] Finally,
pluralisms names the stance that many religions may offer forms of 'salvation'. As a
Christian stance, it sees the Christian narrative as a path to Truth, but not the only one.[87]

Beyond the classical threefold typology, a fourth paradigm is now often included: par-
ticularisms.[88] This can be expressed in a sixfold systematisation:

1) each faith is unique; alterity is stressed over similarity, therefore seeming common
   elements in religious experience or doctrine are regarded as superficial;
2) it is only possible to speak from a specific tradition; there can be no pluralistic
   interpretation;
3) the Holy Spirit may be at work in other faiths, requiring them to be regarded with
   respect and dignity;
4) no salvific potency resides in other faiths; they are somehow involved in God's plans
   for humanity, but in ways we cannot know;
5) particularity is based in a postmodern and postliberal world view;
6) the Trinity and Christ are grounding points from which to do theology and approach
   other faiths.[89]

Particularist stances take seriously the critical insight of 'religion(s)'. However, they
polemically utilise this to assert Christian supremacy. The possibility of religions, which is
both theoretically possible and a historical actuality, is denied.[90] Also, its claim of respect

of the religious Other has been coherently argued to be based in a very suspect narrative that is actually a ploy to maintain Christian dominance and degrade other traditions.[91]

## Comparative Theology

In this section, I refer to what has been termed the new comparative theology, a primarily late twentieth-century movement that continues into the twenty-first. This is in contrast to the old comparative theology, which is used to name the apologetic approaches of the nineteenth and early twentieth centuries. [92] The new comparative theology, here simply comparative theology, names an endeavour that seeks to engage in constructive theological learning from other religious traditions. It is most associated with Francis X. Clooney, but includes many others, such as James Fredericks and Michelle Voss Roberts.[93] As theology, it is defined as 'faith seeking understanding', and a meeting of theology with comparative religion.[94] While relating Christianity with other religions, it does not seek to compare in any competitive sense, nor make judgements on truth, which for Clooney is an act to be indefinitely deferred.[95] Rather, comparative theologians seek to cross the border into a deep engagement and understanding of the Other's world in order to return and enrich their own.[96] The basic assumption is not that religions share much in common, for it is very much in differences that new insights will be learnt. But it sees religious worlds as areas where some equivalence exists, making the border crossing legitimate and viable, because certain similar types of questions or ventures may be undertaken.

As a discipline, comparative theology has been particularly undertaken by Catholic theologians in the post-Vatican II context, though such border crossing has typified inter-religious learning for centuries.[97] Comparative theology resists stereotyped or simplistic attempts to draw common frameworks that typify the WRP. Recent studies have asked how comparative theology may operate after religion.[98]

## Silenced Voices: Feminist and Post-colonial Trends

This chapter has so far narrated a story almost entirely populated by white Western males. In as far as the discussion has been what passes for 'mainstream' theological discussion, this may be said to be an accurate reflection of twentieth-century theology. However, it is a problematic and unsatisfactory narrative. As studies of global Christianity have increasingly demonstrated, the shift through the twentieth century has been from a Christianity centred on the Global North to the Global South. Moreover, dynamics of hegemonic colonial and neo-colonial power complexes have privileged a primarily North-Western European theological discourse, with Germanic and anglophone theological worlds predominant.[99] Again, the rise of feminist theology has been a feature of the twentieth century, especially pronounced – at least in academic theology – from around the 1960s.[100] Discussion of the significance of either post-colonial, broadly speaking, or feminist theology remain, however, marginal in most theological contexts, and certainly so around conceptions of 'religion(s)'. Attention to these contexts is, arguably, imperative. The insights can be noted through five key points.

First, global religious environments highlight the way that the WRP is very much a fixture of a particular parochial and regional conceptualisation.[101] Second, feminist theologies of liberation have been a pathway into pluralist theologies, as women across religious traditions recognise they may share more in common with each other than with male counterparts in their own respective traditions.[102] Third, women's religiosity in global contexts has highlighted the porous, syncretic and unstable nature of religious boundaries, exemplified in Chung Hyun Kyung's celebration of her identity:

> When people ask what I am religiously, I say, 'My bowel is Shamanist. My heart is Buddhist. My right brain, which defines my mood, is Confucian and Taoist. My left brain, which defines my public language, is Protestant Christian, and, overall, my aura is eco-feminist' . . . So, my body is like a religious pantheon. I am living with communities of Gods, a continuum of divinity, and a family of religions.[103]

Fourth, observing the history of Christianity beyond the Western world highlights different ways of envisaging the tradition: for instance, the way so-called Nestorian Christians enculturated into China, in what has been termed 'Taoist Christianity', around the seventh and eight centuries.[104] Fifth, an issue raised in global contexts, and related to our first and third points here, is what is termed multiple religious identities. This is directly raised in the quote by Chung. While it is no longer simply an issue outside the West, it is becoming more common there too. That it can be very natural in many places needs to be addressed as part of how we understand religion and its borders.[105]

The significance of these issues could be further elaborated. However, they have arguably been marginal in what normally gets to pass as mainstream theological discussion. They certainly, though, cannot be ignored and will be an aspect of our final discussion.

## Theology after Religion: Moving Forward

In lieu of a conclusion, I wish to end this chapter by returning to a discussion that has been highlighted through this chapter: if religion is a created and problematic term, how does theology think about religious diversity, and the idea of the 'Christian religion', after 'religion(s)' is abandoned? This, primarily, has been a debate of the twenty-first century, though drawing strong streams from twentieth-century debates. While the argument of this chapter is that the term 'religion(s)' can be retained, this is provisional on the abandonment of the WRP. To use 'religion(s)' in theology it must first be emptied of theology. Here I may return to the discussion on Barth, where I suggested we need to embrace Barth beyond Barth by recognising the human and 'sinful' construction of religion as a false construction. Such a move is not a comfortable one in many ways. Do religions share, for instance, a common framework of such things as scripture? The answer to this is no. Certainly many traditions have significant books. But for Buddhism and Confucianism, for instance, these books are not divine 'revelation', but the result of human insights. Meanwhile, the Bible, it can be argued, is not a natural analogue to the Qur'an in Islam because, understood as the eternal Word of God, the Qur'an has closer analogues to traditional Christian conceptions of Jesus than to the biblical text itself.[106] The encounter with the religious Other, it may be argued, should not be naturalised as some easy encounter with our brethren across borders, but an uncomfortable and even unsettling exchange with the Other.[107] The Otherness of the Other is known, it may be argued, more in where we find difference and that which we do not understand than in what seems familiar and equates to what we already know. Can a Christian dialogue meaningfully with a Muslim without engaging why it is that the Muslim cannot see Jesus in the same way as the Christian? To see from the place of the Other, to see what they see, is the engagement with religious difference.[108]

The challenge, in the terms of comparative theology, is to cross the border and return. But in that crossing we may never return as we were before, for we see what we saw before differently. In Clooney's description, to be a comparative theologian is to be a 'marginal' person because she moves outside the centre of her tradition with such vision.[109] Arguably, to engage 'religion(s)' theologically today is to be 'shaken' from our understanding of what Christianity is and how it may relate to any other 'religion'. If Christianity is a 'religion' for us we must recognise that we see it in a particular way. We must leave religion to embrace it again, stripped from a vision that is Western, male, colonial, Protestant and modern. Can any of us today leave this vision of 'religion' behind? If not, almost certainly, we do not know what Christianity is, nor can we say how it relates to any other 'religion'.

# Notes

1. The author wishes to thank his research assistant Nursheila Muez for invaluable help in preparing this chapter. It may be useful to employ inverted commas each time religion(s) is mentioned, however, it may then be ignored by the reader. Therefore, I will employ them only where it seems useful to highlight the constructed and problematic nature of the term. Again, using religion(s) highlights the construction of the term as potentially plural as discussed below, but will be reserved for cases where it may usefully be highlighted.
2. Wilfred Cantwell Smith, *The Meaning and End of Religion* (London: SPCK, [1962] 1978), pp. 15–79.
3. For an overview of these debates and relevant references, see Paul Hedges, *Understanding Religion: Theories and Methods for Studying Religiously Diverse Societies* (Berkeley, CA: University of California Press, 2021), ch. 1.
4. On the co-creation of religion and the secular in modern thought, see Timothy Fitzgerald, *Discourse on Civility and Barbarity* (Oxford: Oxford University Press, 2007), and the overview in Hedges, *Understanding Religion*, ch. 16, and on colonialism and its impact, Hedges, *Understanding Religion*, ch. 7.
5. The term 'empty signifier' is associated with Willi Braun, 'Religion', in *Guide to the Study of Religion*, edited by Willi Braun and Russell T. McCutcheon (London: Continuum, 2000), pp. 3–18, but see also Russell T. McCutcheon, *Manufacturing Religion: The Discourse on Sui Generis Religion and the Politics of Nostalgia* (Oxford: Oxford University Press, 1997), and Timothy Fitzgerald, *The Ideology of Religious Studies* (Oxford: Oxford University Press, 2000), as two foundational statements, but more recently see also Brent Nongbri, *Before Religion: A History of a Modern Concept* (New Haven, CT: Yale University Press, 2013).
6. On what may be shared by those on different sides of this debate, see Paul Hedges, 'The Deconstruction of Religion: So What?', *Religious Studies Project* (2016), accessed at http://www.religiousstudiesproject.com/response/the-deconstruction-of-religion-so-what/.
7. See Hedges, *Understanding Religion*, ch. 1, and Paul Hedges, 'Multiple Religious Belonging after Religion: Theorising Strategic Religious Participation in a Shared Religious Landscape as a Chinese Model', *Open Theology* 3 (2017), 48–72.
8. See the arguments on this in, for instance, Hedges, *Understanding Religion*, ch. 1, and Hedges, 'Multiple Religious Belonging after Religion'. The idea that complex structures such as 'religions' must be, inherently, Western creations can be critiqued in terms of post-colonial scholarship as non-Western agency is denied; see Hedges, *Understanding Religion*, ch. 7.
9. A further extension of Smith's argument was that most religions are named by Western scholars, which some have extended to argue that any sense of these being unified traditions is part of a Western creation of these traditions. Such arguments, however, are distinctly Orientalist, *pace* Said, in that they deny any indigenous agency and assume that complex structures of thought and institutional organisation, especially across regional/national boundaries, can only be created by Western systems. For a survey of these debates related to Hinduism, see Hedges, *Understanding Religion*, ch. 7, especially case study 7A.
10. This is explicit in Friedrich Max Müller, *On Missions: A Lecture Delivered in Westminster Abbey*

on December 3, 1873, with an Introductory Sermon by Arthur Penrhyn Stanley, D.D. (London: Longmans, Green Co., 1873). For a discussion around such issues, see Paul Hedges, 'The Science of Religion, Comparative Religion, Mission, and the Birth of Comparative Theology', in Brill Handbook on Comparative Theology, edited by Wilhelmus Pim Valkenberg (Leiden: Brill, 2019), and Paul Hedges, 'Post-colonialism, Orientalism, and Understanding: Religious Studies and the Christian Missionary Imperative', The Journal of Religious History 32:1 (2008), 55–75.

11. Eric J. Sharpe, Comparative Religion: A History (LaSalle, IL: Open Court, [1975] 1991).

12. Christianity and Hinduism is a shorthand often used for Rowland Williams, Paraméswara-jnyána-góshthí: A Dialogue on the Knowledge of the Supreme Lord, in Which Are Compared the Claims of Christianity and Hinduism, and Various Questions of Indian Religion and Literature Fairly Discussed (Cambridge: Deighton, Bell and Co, 1856). On the significance of Williams's work, as well as on Maurice, see Paul Hedges, Preparation and Fulfilment: A History and Study of Fulfilment Theology in Modern British Thought in the Indian Context (Bern: Peter Lang, 2001), pp. 51–87, Paul Hedges, 'Rowland Williams and Missions to the Hindu', in Religious Dynamics under the Impact of Imperialism and Colonialism: A Sourcebook, edited by Marion Eggert, HansMartin Krämer, Björn Bentlage and Stefan Reichmuth (Leiden: Brill, 2016), pp. 197–211, and Hedges, 'The Science of Religion'.

13. In addition to works such as Smith, The Meaning and End, he wrote such theological works as Towards a World Theology: Faith and the Comparative History of Religion (London: Macmillan, 1981). This theological stance was also found in another Smith whose textbook on 'world religions' remains popular: see Huston Smith, The World's Religions (New York: HarperCollins, [1958] 2009, first published as The Religions of Man).

14. His best-known work, foundational for the study of religious experience, The Idea of the Holy: An Inquiry into the Non-rational Factor in the Idea of the Divine and Its Relation to the Rational (Oxford: Oxford University Press, 1923), was essentially a theological treatise. On debates around confessional approaches and the academic study of religious experience, see Paul Hedges, 'Encounters with Ultimacy? Autobiographical and Critical Perspectives in the Academic Study of Religion', Open Theology 4 (2018), 355–72, and Craig Martin, 'Experience', in The Oxford Handbook of the Study of Religion, edited by Michael Stausberg and Steven Engler (Oxford: Oxford University Press, 2016), pp. 525–40.

15. On Smart's objection to theologians, see his obituary, Paul Morris, 'Ninian Smart: Comparative Theologian, Poet, Philosopher, and Global Citizen', Religion 31:4 (2001), 353–4. A critique of him as invested in theological conceptions of religion is found in Fitzgerald, The Ideology of Religious Studies, pp. 54–71.

16. See especially Fitzgerald, The Ideology of Religious Studies.

17. See Christopher R. Cotter and David G. Robertson, After World Religions: Reconstructing Religious Studies (London: Routledge, 2016).

18. Tomoko Masuzawa, The Invention of World Religions (Chicago: University of Chicago Press, 2005); see especially pp. 107–20.

19. 'Great' often signified numerical size, global reach or influence, while 'living' religions indicated systems still seen as powerful forces on the global stage. In the latter part of the twentieth century, this was often extended to include traditions often previously dismissed which are typically identified as 'indigenous religions'.

20. On the creation and narratives around this, see Cotter and Robertson, After World Religions, Masuzawa, The Invention of World Religions, and Hedges, Understanding Religion, ch. 1.

21. For discussions and debates on this, an overview can be found in Hedges, Understanding Religion, ch. 1, 3 and 7.

22. See Marianne Moyaert, 'Christianity as the Measure of Religion? Materializing Theories of Religion', in Twenty-First Century Theologies of Religions: Retrospection and Future Prospects, edited by Elizabeth J. Harris, Paul Hedges and Shanthikumar Hettiarachchi (Leiden: Brill-Rodopi, 2016), pp. 239–60, and Marianne Moyaert, 'Inappropriate Behavior? On the Ritual

Core of Religion and Its Challenges to Interreligious Hospitality', *Journal for the Academic Study of Religion* 27:2 (2014), 222–42; see also Hedges, *Understanding Religion*.

23. Masuzawa, *The Invention of World Religions*, p. 310.

24. Ernst Troeltsch, 'Christianity and the History of Religion', in *Religion in History*, James Adams and Walter Bense (trans.) (Minneapolis, MN: Fortress, [1897] 1991), pp. 77–86: 77.

25. See Reinhold Bernhardt, *Christianity without Absolutes* (London: SCM Press, 1994), p. 75.

26. Ernst Troeltsch, *The Absoluteness of Christianity and the History of Religions* (London: SCM Press, [1902] 1971), p. 109.

27. Troeltsch, *The Absoluteness of Christianity*, p. 108.

28. Specifically on this in relation to Judaism and the trope of 'law', see Gareth Lloyd Jones, 'Law', in *A Dictionary of Jewish–Christian Relations*, edited by Edward Kessler and Neil Wenborn (Cambridge: Cambridge University Press, 2005), pp. 257–8, and Amy-Jill Levine, *The Misunderstood Jew: The Church and the Scandal of the Jewish Jesus* (New York: HarperCollins, 2006), pp. 126–7. On the wider context of Christian antisemitism, see Paul Hedges, *Religious Hatred: Prejudice, Islamophobia and Antisemitism in Global Context* (London: Bloomsbury, 2021), especially ch. 3, pp. 90–4 and pp. 109–10.

29. Troeltsch, *The Absoluteness of Christianity*, p. 108.

30. Troeltsch, *The Absoluteness of Christianity*, pp. 110–12.

31. Troeltsch, *The Absoluteness of Christianity*, p. 112. On the way that a very Lutheran, rather than simply Christian, lens lay behind Troeltsch's thought here, see Bernhardt, *Christianity without Absolutes*, p. 75.

32. Ernst Troeltsch, 'The Place of Christianity among the World Religions', in *Attitudes toward Other Religions*, Owen C. Thomas (ed.) (London: SCM Press, 1969), pp. 73–92: 79.

33. Troeltsch, 'The Place of Christianity among the World Religions', p. 83.

34. Troeltsch, 'The Place of Christianity among the World Religions', pp. 89, 90.

35. Masuzawa, *Invention*, pp. 309–24.

36. Alan Race, *Christians and Religious Pluralism: Patterns in the Christian Theology of Religions* (London: SCM Press, 1983), p. 37.

37. For a standard survey of Barth, see Daniel W. Hardy, 'Karl Barth', in *The Modern Theologians: An Introduction to Christian Theology since 1918*, edited by David F. Ford and Rachel Muers (Oxford: Blackwell, 2005), pp. 21–42.

38. See Owen C. Thomas, 'Exclusivism: Karl Barth', in *Attitudes toward Other Religions*, edited by Owen C. Thomas (London: SCM Press, 1969), pp. 93–6: 93.

39. Karl Barth, *Church Dogmatics*, vol. 1, part 2, in *Church Dogmatics: A Selection*, G. W. Bromiley (ed. and trans.) (New York: Harper Torchbooks, 1962), p. 51.

40. For a study of this in nineteenth-century theology, centred around fulfilment theology, see Hedges, *Preparation and Fulfilment*, especially pp. 36–7. The concept of the *logos spermatikos* is often referenced to Justin Martyr in these discussions; see David Cheetham, 'Inclusivisms: Honouring Faithfulness and Openness', in *Christian Approaches to Other Faiths*, edited by Paul Hedges and Alan Race (London: SCM Press, 2008), pp. 63–84: 66.

41. On such ideas, see Hedges, *Preparation and Fulfilment*.

42. Barth, *Church Dogmatics*, vol. 1, part 2, p. 297.

43. The theology of religion typology terms are discussed below, but I assume the terms 'exclusivism', 'inclusivism' and 'pluralism' are well enough known to be employed as placeholders here.

44. My thanks to Hendrik Vroom for this insight in a personal correspondence with the author.

45. On such a reading, the arguments of Hans-Georg Gadamer on the possibilities of hermeneutics to read beyond an author's own intentions are important; see *Truth and Method* (London: Continuum, [1960] 1975).

46. See Hedges, *Preparation and Fulfilment*.

47. See Thomas F. Torrance, *Karl Barth: An Introduction to His Early Theology 1910–1931* (Edinburgh: T&T Clark, 2000), pp. 57ff.

48. Barth, *Church Dogmatics*, vol. 1, part 2, p. 299.

49. See, for instance, Daniel Strange, 'Exclusivisms: Indeed Their Rock Is Not Like Our Rock', in *Christian Approaches to Other Faiths*, edited by Paul Hedges and Alan Race (London: SCM Press, 2008), pp. 36–62: 42–4, Hedges, *Preparation and Fulfilment*, pp. 369–74, and Hendrik Kraemer, *The Christian Message in a Non-Christian World* (Grand Rapids, MI: Kregel, [1938] 1947).

50. On reading exclusivisms as radical discontinuity, see Paul Hedges, *Controversies in Interreligious Dialogue* (London: SCM Press, 2010), pp. 22, 30.

51. See, for example, McCutcheon, *Manufacturing Religion*, Lionel M. Jensen, *Manufacturing Confucianism: Chinese Traditions and Universal Civilization* (Durham, NC: Duke University Press, [1997] 2003).

52. See Emmanuel Levinas, *Ethics and Infinity* (Pittsburgh, PA: Duquesne University Press, 1985), and for a discussion in an interreligious context, see Oddbjørn Leirvik, *Interreligious Studies: A Relational Approach to Religious Activism and the Study of Religion* (London: Bloomsbury, 2014), pp. 18–25.

53. On the conference's theological stance, see Hedges, *Preparation and Fulfiment*, pp. 231–75.

54. See Hedges, *Preparation and Fulfilment*.

55. See Burnett Hillman Streeter, *The Buddha and the Christ* (London: Macmillan, 1932), and Hedges, 'The Science of Religion'.

56. See Jacques Dupuis, *Christianity and the Religions: From Confrontation to Dialogue* (Maryknoll, NY: Orbis, 2001), pp. 47–52.

57. Figures such as Francis Xavier (1506–52) and Matteo Ricci (1552–1610) are both notable figures from a previous period.

58. Dupuis, *Christianity and the Religions*, p. 47.

59. The definitive study of modern British fulfilment theology is Hedges, *Preparation and Fulfilment*; on a wider overview of the concept, see Cheetham, 'Inclusivisms', pp. 66–9.

60. Paul Tillich, *Theology of Culture*, R. C. Kimball (ed.) (New York: Oxford University Press, 1959), pp. 7–8.

61. See Friedrich Schleiermacher, *The Christian Faith*, H. R. Mackintosh and J. S. Stewart (trans.) (Philadelphia: Fortress, [1820–1] 1976), p. 132; also Anna S. King and Paul Hedges, 'What Is Religion? Or, What Is It We Are Talking About?', in *Controversies in Contemporary Religion: Education, Law, Politics, Society and Spirituality*, edited by Paul Hedges, vol. 1 (Oxford: Praeger, 2014), pp. 1–30: 5.

62. See Paul Tillich, *Systematic Theology*, vol. 1 (Welwyn, Hertfordshire: James Nisbet & Co., 1968), pp. 67–74.

63. See David H. Kelsey, 'Paul Tillich', in *The Modern Theologians: An Introduction to Christian Theology since 1918*, edited by David F. Ford and Rachel Muers (Oxford: Blackwell, 2005), pp. 62–75.

64. Paul Tillich, *The Courage to Be* (Fontana, CA: Fontana Library, [1952] 1962), p. 123.

65. Tillich, *The Courage to Be*, p. 125.

66. Tillich, *The Courage to Be*, p. 125.

67. Tillich, *The Courage to Be*, p. 127, and Tillich, *Systematic Theology*, vol. 1, pp. 43–4.

68. Some may object to a pairing of these two figures, given, in certain ways, quite different theological trajectories, the former from a logos theological source inspired by figures such as Samuel Taylor Coleridge (1772–1834), and the latter through a distinctive Jesuit training. Nevertheless, it is possible that strands stemming from seventeenth-century Jesuit thought influenced both (the Jesuit narratives of India and China and theories of 'natural theology' influencing Hindu and Confucian traditions were well-known intellectual ideas), while appeals to similar theological rationales in the Fathers and biblical texts can also be found. On British sources for fulfilment theology, see Hedges, *Preparation and Fulfilment*, pp. 17–21 and *passim*; on common tropes of 'logos' and 'fulfilment', see Cheetham, 'Inclusivisms', pp. 66–9, and more specifically on Rahner, see Karen Kilby, *A Brief Introduction to Karl Rahner* (New York: Crossroad, 2007), pp. 30–7 and Cheetham, 'Inclusivisms', pp. 69–74. On a reading of

Farquhar and Rahner as differing trends in fulfilment style thinking, see Hedges, *Controversies in Interreligious Dialogue*, pp. 24–5.

69. This dynamic, typical of the fulfilment model of someone like Farquhar, met each aspect of Hindu teaching with what he saw as its 'crown' or 'fufilment' in Christian teachings; see John Nicol Farquhar, *The Crown of Hinduism* (London: Oxford University Press, 1913). For a study of Farquhar's dynamics, see Hedges, *Preparation and Fulfilment*, pp. 277–341.

70. This, for instance, had been posited of Pure Land Buddhism by some Catholic theologians upon their encounter with it in Japan; see Fritz Buri, 'The Concept of Grace in Paul, Shinran, and Luther', *Eastern Buddhist* 9:2 (2004), 21–42, and Streeter, *The Buddha and the Christ*, pp. 89–92, 103–10. Interestingly, this accusation was based not so much upon an encounter with the philosophical stance and practice of Buddhism per se, but with what were perceived as the similarities with Lutheranism, with it being asserted that the 'Lutheran heresy' had been placed there by the Devil to hinder their mission.

71. For a variety of stances on this, and debates on various themes, see Edmund Kee-Fook Chia, *World Christianity Encounters World Religions: A Summa of Interfaith Dialogue* (Pennsylvania: Liturgical Press, 2018), especially pp. 111–29, and Gavin D'Costa, 'Catholicism and the World Religions: A Theological and Phenomenological Account', in *The Catholic Church and the World Religions: A Theological and Phenomenological Account*, edited by Gavin D'Costa (London: T&T Clark, 2011), pp. 1–33.

72. On the connections, see Clare Amos, 'Vatican and World Council of Church Initiatives: Weaving Interreligious Threads on Ecumenical Looms', in *Contemporary Muslim–Christian Encounters: Developments, Diversity and Dialogue*, edited by Paul Hedges (London: Bloomsbury, 2015), pp. 185–200.

73. See Stanley Samartha, *One Christ – Many Religions* (Maryknoll, NY: Orbis, 1991).

74. See S. Wesley Ariarajah, 'Power, Politics, and Plurality: The Struggles of the World Council of Churches to Deal with Religious Plurality', in *The Myth of Religious Superiority*, edited by Paul Knitter (Maryknoll, NY: Orbis, 2002), pp. 176–93.

75. On this question in relation to the Anglican tradition a number of recent surveys have offered perspectives; see Paul Hedges, 'Anglican Interfaith Relations from 1910 to the Twenty-First Century', in *The Oxford History of Anglicanism*, vol. 5, *Global Anglicanism c. 1910–2000*, edited by William L. Sachs (Oxford: Oxford University Press, 2018), pp. 76–97, Clare Amos and Michael Ipgrave, 'An Untidy Generosity: Anglicans and the Challenge of Other Religions', in *The Oxford Handbook of Anglican Studies*, edited by Mark Chapman, Sathianathan Clarke and Martyn Percy (Oxford: Oxford University Press, 2015), pp. 427–48, and Ian Markham, 'Interreligious Relations in the Anglican Communion', in *The Wiley-Blackwell Companion to the Anglican Communion*, edited by Ian Markham, J. Barney Hawkins IV, Justyn Terry and Leslie Nuñez Steffensen (Chichester: Wiley-Blackwell, 2013), pp. 657–65. Specifically on Buddhism, see Paul Hedges, 'Towards an Anglican Theology of Buddhism', *Studies in Interreligious Dialogue* 26:1 (2016), 37–56.

76. The classic work is Rosemary Radford Ruether, *Faith and Fratricide: The Theological Roots of Anti-Semitism* (New York: Seabury Press, 1974); for overviews, see Ronald H. Miller, 'Judaism: Siblings in Strife', in *Christian Approaches to Other Faiths*, edited by Paul Hedges and Alan Race (London: SCM Press, 2008), pp. 176–90, or Hedges, *Religious Hatred*, pp. 51–65, 99–104, and on the specific Lutheran trajectory, see Dan Cohn-Sherbok, *The Crucified Jew: Twenty Centuries of Christian Anti-Semitism* (Grand Rapids, MI: William B. Eerdmans, 1992), pp. 71–4.

77. On the issue with Judaism, see Marc Saperstein, *Moments of Crisis in Jewish–Christian Relations* (London: SCM Press, 1989), pp. 38–50, and on Catholicism's relation to Islam, see Christian W. Troll, 'Catholicism and Islam', in *The Catholic Church and the World Religions: A Theological and Phenomenological Account*, edited by Gavin D'Costa (London: T&T Clark, 2011), pp. 71–105. Notably, though, the rethinking on Judaism, which has made its relationship to the Catholic Church part of ecumenical relations rather than interreligious relations, is not accepted by all; see Roy H. Schoeman, 'Catholicism and Judaism', in *The Catholic Church*

*and the World Religions: A Theological and Phenomenological Account*, edited by Gavin D'Costa (London: T&T Clark, 2011), pp. 34–70, especially pp. 62–3.

78. See Paul Hedges, 'The Contemporary Context of Muslim–Christian Dialogue', in *Contemporary Christian–Muslim Encounters: Developments, Diversity and Dialogues*, edited by Paul Hedges (London: Bloomsbury Academic, 2015), pp. 17–32: 24.

79. Christian reflection on the traditions we term 'religions', of course, stretches back to the beginnings of the tradition (however that is dated), but as a distinct discipline the theology of religions is new. For some reflection and references on the origins of Christian reflections in comparative terms and in relation to religious difference, see Paul Hedges, *Comparative Theology: A Critical and Methodological Perspective* (Leiden: Brill, 2017), p. 6.

80. In a different frame, but employing Andrew Shanks's concept of Jesus as 'the Shaken One', the theology of religions can be considered under the motif of being 'shaken'; see Graham Adams, 'The Theology of Religions: Through the Lens of "Truth-as-Openness"', *Brill Research Perspectives in Theology* 3:1 (2019), 1–107.

81. That the advances of 'European' science and modernity came in relation to learning from the wider world, which helped what had been a 'backward' Europe advance, see John Hobson, *The Eastern Origins of Western Civilisation* (Cambridge: Cambridge University Press, 2004), and Jonathan Lyons, *The House of Wisdom: How the Arabs Transformed Western Civilization* (London: Bloomsbury, 2010).

82. This is argued in Paul Hedges, 'The Old and the New Comparative Theologies: Discourses on Religion, the Theology of Religions, Orientalism and the Boundaries of Traditions', *Religions*, special edition, 'European Responses to the New Comparative Theology', 3:4 (2012), 1120–37.

83. A survey of debates is in Paul Hedges, 'A Reflection on Typologies', in *Christian Approaches to Other Faiths*, edited by Paul Hedges and Alan Race (London: SCM Press, 2008), pp. 17–33, and for a critical update, see Elizabeth J. Harris, Paul Hedges and Shanthikumar Hettiarachchi (eds), *Twenty-First Century Theologies of Religions: Retrospection and Future Prospects* (Leiden: Brill-Rodopi, 2016), especially Hedges, 'The Theology of Religions Typology Redefined', pp. 76–81.

84. This chapter is not intended as a discussion on the terms and debates within the theology of religions; therefore, for fuller accounts of exclusivisms, see Hedges, *Controversies in Interreligious Dialogue*, pp. 20–3, Strange, 'Exclusivisms', and Race, *Christians and Religious Pluralism*, pp. 10–37.

85. For fuller accounts of inclusivisms, see Hedges, *Controversies in Interreligious Dialogue*, pp. 23–6, Cheetham, 'Inclusivisms', and Race, *Christians and Religious Pluralism*, pp. 38–69.

86. The debate on this is primarily found between the interpretations of Perry Schmidt-Leukel, 'Exclusivism, Inclusivism, Pluralism: The Tripolar Typology – Clarified and Reaffirmed', in *The Myth of Religious Superiority: A Multifaith Exploration*, edited by Paul Knitter (Maryknoll, NY: Orbis, 2005), pp. 13–27, and Hedges, 'A Reflection on Typologies'. For a discussion, see Hedges, *Controversies in Interreligious Relations*, pp. 19–20, which explains why the author favours the heuristic approach.

87. For fuller accounts of pluralisms, see Hedges, *Controversies in Interreligious Dialogue*, pp. 26–7, 109–45, Perry Schmidt-Leukel, 'Pluralisms', in *Christian Approaches to Other Faiths*, edited by Paul Hedges and Alan Race (London: SCM Press, 2008), pp. 85–110, and Race, *Christians and Religious Pluralism*, pp. 70–105. It is worth noting that while Hick's work is often taken as defining of pluralism – see John Hick, *An Interpretation of Religion* (London: Macmillan, 1989), and *The Rainbow of Faiths* (London: SCM Press, 1995), for responses to his critics – it is certainly not the only form; see Hedges, *Controversies in Interreligious Dialogue*, pp. 115–18, for a discussion on Hick and other forms of pluralist theologies. Further, arguably, the current most comprehensive and compelling statements of a pluralist approach are found in the work of Perry Schmidt-Leukel; see *God beyond Boundaries: A Christian and Pluralist Theology of Religions* (Munster: Waxmann, 2017) and *Religious Pluralism and Interreligious Theology* (Maryknoll, NY: Orbis, 2017).

88. The fourfold typology was most fully advanced in Hedges, *Controversies in Interreligious Dialogue*, and is distinct from Knitter's fourfold typology; see Paul F. Knitter, *Introducing Theologies of Religion* (Maryknoll, NY: Orbis, 2002). In recent writings Knitter has used the terms of, and cited, the Hedges typology (e.g. Paul F. Knitter, 'Inter-Religious Dialogue and Social Activism, in *The Wiley-Blackwell Companion to Inter-Religious Dialogue*, edited by Catherine Cornille (Oxford: Wiley-Blackwell, 2013), pp. 133–48: 136). The most definitive survey of current debates is Harris et al. (eds), *Twenty-First Century Theologies of Religions*.

89. Hedges, 'Particularities: Tradition-Specific Post-modern Perspectives', in *Christian Approaches to Other Faiths*, edited by Paul Hedges and Alan Race (London: SCM Press, 2008) pp. 112–35: 112–13.

90. See Hedges, *Controversies in Interreligious Dialogue*, pp. 75–7, and Hedges, *Understanding Religion*, ch. 1.

91. See Hedges, *Controversies in Interreligious Dialogue*, pp. 194–6.

92. On this distinction, see Hugh Nicholson, *Comparative Theology and the Problem of Religious Rivalry* (Oxford: Oxford University Press, 2011). Notably, though, the stark contrast between these two can be questioned, with certain continuity rather than contrast being seen, though recognising that they are different endeavours; see Hedges, 'Old and the New', and Hedges, 'The Science of Religion'.

93. For a survey, see Francis Clooney, *Comparative Theology: Deep Learning across Religious Borders* (Oxford: Wiley-Blackwell, 2010), pp. 41–52, and Hedges, *Comparative Theology*, pp. 10–15, 47.

94. Clooney, *Comparative Theology*, p. 10.

95. For debate around this, see Hedges, *Comparative Theology*, pp. 7, 50.

96. Hedges, *Comparative Theology*, pp. 20–1, 27–8, 41–2.

97. See Clooney, *Comparative Theology*, pp. 24–35.

98. For discussions of this in comparative theology, see Hedges, *Comparative Theology*, pp. 27–39, John J. Thatamanil, 'Comparative Theology after Religion', in *Planetary Loves: Spivak, Postcoloniality and Theology*, edited by Stephen D. Moore and Mayra Rivera (New York: Fordham University Press, 2010), pp. 238–57, and see Judith Gruber, '(Un)Silencing Hybridity: A Postcolonial Critique of Comparative Theology', in *Comparative Theology in the Millennial Classroom: Hybrid Identities, Negotiated Boundaries*, edited by Mara Brecht and Reid B. Locklin (London: Routledge, 2016), pp. 21–35. On the Gruber–Clooney debate, see Hedges, *Comparative Theology*, pp. 41–2.

99. Widely on the rise of global theologies, see Philip Jenkins, *The Next Christendom: The Coming of Global Christianity*, 3rd ed. (Oxford: Oxford University Press, 2011), and on their relegated status in these debates, see Hedges, *Controversies in Interreligious Dialogue*, pp. 44–52.

100. In relation to debates around theologies of religions and other areas, see Jeanine Hill Fletcher, 'Feminisms: Syncretism, Symbiosis, Synergetic Dance', in *Christian Approaches to Other Religions*, edited by Paul Hedges and Alan Race (London: SCM, 2008), pp. 136–54, Hedges, *Controversies in Interreligious Dialogue*, pp. 197–227, and Ursula King, 'Feminism: The Missing Dimension in the Dialogue of Religions', in *Pluralism and the Religions: The Theological and Political Dimensions*, edited by John D'Arcy May (London: Cassell, 1998), pp. 40–55.

101. See Hedges, *Understanding Religion*, ch. 10.

102. See Fletcher, 'Feminisms'.

103. Hyun Kyung Chung, 'Seeking the Religious Roots of Pluralism', in *Christian Approaches to Other Faiths*, edited by Paul Hedges and Alan Race (London: SCM Press, [1997] 2009), pp. 72–5: 72, 73–4.

104. See Michael Palmer, *The Jesus Sutras: Rediscovering the Lost Religion of Taoist Christianity* (London: Piatkus, 2001), and for a more sober reflection, see Daniel H. Bays, *A New History of Christianity in China* (Oxford: Wiley-Blackwell, 2012), pp. 7–11.

105. On the naturalness of border crossing, termed strategic religious participation rather than multiple religious identities, in the Chinese context, which disrupts the WRP, see Hedges, 'Multiple

Religious Belonging after Religion'; also on this see Hedges, *Understanding Religion*, ch. 1, 2, 3. On theological debates around Christian–Buddhist identities, see Rose Drew, *Buddhist and Christian? An Exploration of Dual Belonging* (London: Routledge, 2011). For accounts setting this within wider narratives, see Duane R. Bidwell, *When One Religion Isn't Enough: The Lives of Spiritually Fluid People* (Boston: Beacon Press, 2018), and Hedges, 'Theology in a Shared Religious Landscape: The Implications of Strategic Religious Participation for Thinking about God(desse)s and Beyond God(desse)s', in *Theology without Walls: The Transreligious Imperative*, edited by Jerry L. Martin (London: Routledge, 2019).

106. See Hedges, *Understanding Religion*, p. 261, box 11.4.
107. As an example, I have argued that we cannot resort to such notions as a 'global ethic', as it reads the Other as too easily like us, and means we are not disturbed; see Hedges, *Controversies in Interreligious Dialogue*, pp. 254–70.
108. See Rowan Williams, 'Christian Identity and Religious Plural', cited in Hedges, *Controversies in Interreligious Dialogue*, p. 112.
109. See Clooney, *Comparative Theology*, pp. 157–60.

# Bibliography

Adams, Graham, 'The Theology of Religions: Through the Lens of "Truth-as-Openness"', *Brill Research Perspectives in Theology* 3:1 (2019), 1–107.

Amos, Clare, 'Vatican and World Council of Church Initiatives: Weaving Interreligious Threads on Ecumenical Looms', in *Contemporary Muslim–Christian Encounters: Developments, Diversity and Dialogue*, edited by Paul Hedges (London: Bloomsbury, 2015), pp. 185–200.

Amos, Clare and Michael Ipgrave, 'An Untidy Generosity: Anglicans and the Challenge of Other Religions', in *The Oxford Handbook of Anglican Studies*, edited by Mark Chapman, Sathianathan Clarke and Martyn Percy (Oxford: Oxford University Press, 2015), pp. 427–48.

Ariarajah, S. Wesley, 'Power, Politics, and Plurality: The Struggles of the World Council of Churches to Deal with Religious Plurality', in *The Myth of Religious Superiority*, edited by Paul Knitter (Maryknoll, NY: Orbis, 2002), pp. 176–93.

Barth, Karl, *Church Dogmatics*, vol. 1, part 2, in *Church Dogmatics: A Selection*, G. W. Bromiley (ed. and trans.) (New York: Harper Torchbooks, 1962).

Bays, Daniel H., *A New History of Christianity in China* (Oxford: Wiley-Blackwell, 2012).

Bernhardt, Reinhold, *Christianity without Absolutes* (London: SCM Press, 1994).

Bidwell, Duane R., *When One Religion Isn't Enough: The Lives of Spiritually Fluid People* (Boston: Beacon Press, 2018).

Braun, Willi, 'Religion', in *Guide to the Study of Religion*, edited by Willi Braun and Russell T. McCutcheon (London: Continuum, 2000), pp. 3–18.

Buri, Fritz, 'The Concept of Grace in Paul, Shinran, and Luther', *Eastern Buddhist* 9:2 (2004), 21–42.

Cheetham, David, 'Inclusivisms: Honouring Faithfulness and Openness', in *Christian Approaches to Other Faiths*, edited by Paul Hedges and Alan Race (London: SCM Press, 2008), pp. 63–84.

Chia, Edmund Kee-Fook, *World Christianity Encounters World Religions: A Summa of Interfaith Dialogue* (Pennsylvania: Liturgical Press, 2018).

Chung, Hyun Kyung, 'Seeking the Religious Roots of Pluralism', in *Christian Approaches to Other Faiths*, edited by Paul Hedges and Alan Race (London: SCM Press, [1997] 2009), pp. 72–5.

Clooney, Francis, *Comparative Theology: Deep Learning across Religious Borders* (Oxford: Wiley-Blackwell, 2010).

Cohn-Sherbok, Dan, *The Crucified Jew: Twenty Centuries of Christian Anti-Semitism* (Grand Rapids, MI: William B. Eerdmans, 1992).

Cotter, Christopher R. and David G. Robertson, *After World Religions: Reconstructing Religious Studies* (London: Routledge, 2016).

D'Costa, Gavin, 'Catholicism and the World Religions: A Theological and Phenomenological Account', in *The Catholic Church and the World Religions: A Theological and Phenomenological*

*Account*, edited by Gavin D'Costa (London: T&T Clark, 2011), pp. 1–33.

Drew, Rose, *Buddhist and Christian? An Exploration of Dual Belonging* (London: Routledge, 2011).

Dupuis, Jacques, *Christianity and the Religions: From Confrontation to Dialogue* (Maryknoll, NY: Orbis, 2001).

Farquhar, John Nicol, *The Crown of Hinduism* (London: Oxford University Press, 1913).

Fitzgerald, Timothy, *Discourse on Civility and Barbarity* (Oxford: Oxford University Press, 2007).

Fitzgerald, Timothy, *The Ideology of Religious Studies* (Oxford: Oxford University Press, 2000).

Fletcher, Jeanine Hill, 'Feminisms: Syncretism, Symbiosis, Synergetic Dance', in *Christian Approaches to Other Faiths*, edited by Paul Hedges and Alan Race (London: SCM, 2008), pp. 136–54.

Gadamer, Hans-Georg, *Truth and Method* (London: Continuum, [1960] 1975).

Gruber, Judith, '(Un)Silencing Hybridity: A Postcolonial Critique of Comparative Theology', in *Comparative Theology in the Millennial Classroom: Hybrid Identities, Negotiated Boundaries*, edited by Mara Brecht and Reid B. Locklin (London: Routledge, 2016), pp. 21–35.

Hardy, Daniel W., 'Karl Barth', in *The Modern Theologians: An Introduction to Christian Theology since 1918*, edited by David F. Ford and Rachel Muers (Oxford: Blackwell, 2005), pp. 21–42.

Harris, Elizabeth J., Paul Hedges and Shanthikumar Hettiarachchi (eds), *Twenty-First Century Theologies of Religions: Retrospection and Future Prospects* (Leiden: Brill-Rodopi, 2016).

Hedges, Paul, 'Anglican Interfaith Relations from 1910 to the Twenty-First Century', in *The Oxford History of Anglicanism*, vol. 5, *Global Anglicanism c. 1910–2000*, edited by William L. Sachs (Oxford: Oxford University Press, 2018), pp. 76–97.

Hedges, Paul, *Comparative Theology: A Critical and Methodological Perspective* (Leiden: Brill, 2017).

Hedges, Paul, 'The Contemporary Context of Muslim–Christian Dialogue', in *Contemporary Christian–Muslim Encounters: Developments, Diversity and Dialogues*, edited by Paul Hedges (London: Bloomsbury Academic, 2015), pp. 17–32.

Hedges, Paul, *Controversies in Interreligious Dialogue and the Theology of Religions* (London: SCM Press, 2010).

Hedges, Paul, 'The Deconstruction of Religion: So What?', *Religious Studies Project* (2016), accessed at http://www.religiousstudiesproject.com/response/the-deconstruction-of-religion-so-what/.

Hedges, Paul, 'Encounters with Ultimacy? Autobiographical and Critical Perspectives in the Academic Study of Religion', *Open Theology* 4 (2018), 355–72.

Hedges, Paul, 'Multiple Religious Belonging after Religion: Theorising Strategic Religious Participation in a Shared Religious Landscape as a Chinese Model', *Open Theology* 3 (2017), 48–72.

Hedges, Paul, 'The Old and the New Comparative Theologies: Discourses on Religion, the Theology of Religions, Orientalism and the Boundaries of Traditions', *Religions*, special edition, 'European Responses to the New Comparative Theology', 3:4 (2012), 1120–37.

Hedges, Paul, 'Particularities: Tradition-Specific Post-modern Perspectives', in *Christian Approaches to Other Faiths*, edited by Paul Hedges and Alan Race (London: SCM Press, 2008), pp. 112–35.

Hedges, Paul, 'Post-colonialism, Orientalism, and Understanding: Religious Studies and the Christian Missionary Imperative', *The Journal of Religious History* 32:1 (2008), 55–75.

Hedges, Paul, *Preparation and Fulfilment: A History and Study of Fulfilment Theology in Modern British Thought in the Indian Context* (Bern: Peter Lang, 2001).

Hedges, Paul, 'A Reflection on Typologies', in *Christian Approaches to Other Faiths*, edited by Paul Hedges and Alan Race (London: SCM Press, 2008), pp. 17–33.

Hedges, Paul, *Religious Hatred: Prejudice, Islamophobia and Antisemitism in Global Context* (London: Bloomsbury, 2021).

Hedges, Paul, 'Rowland Williams and Missions to the Hindu', in *Religious Dynamics under the Impact of Imperialism and Colonialism: A Sourcebook*, edited by Marion Eggert, Hans Martin Krämer, Björn Bentlage and Stefan Reichmuth (Leiden: Brill, 2016), pp. 197–211.

Hedges, Paul, 'The Science of Religion, Comparative Religion, Mission, and the Birth of Comparative Theology', in *Brill Handbook on Comparative Theology*, edited by Wilhelmus Pim Valkenberg (Leiden: Brill, forthcoming).

Hedges, Paul, 'Theology in a Shared Religious Landscape: The Implications of Strategic Religious Participation for Thinking about God(desse)s and Beyond God(desse)s', in *Theology without Walls: The Transreligious Imperative*, edited by Jerry L. Martin (London: Routledge, 2019).

Hedges, Paul, 'The Theology of Religions Typology Redefined', in *Twenty-First Century Theologies of Religions: Retrospection and Future Prospects*, edited by Elizabeth J. Harris, Paul Hedges, and Shanthikumar Hettiarachchi (Leiden: Brill-Rodopi, 2016), pp. 76–92.

Hedges, Paul, 'Towards an Anglican Theology of Buddhism', *Studies in Interreligious Dialogue* 26:1 (2016), 37–56.

Hedges, Paul, *Understanding Religion: Theories and Methods for Studying Religiously Diverse Societies* (Berkeley, CA: University of California Press, 2021).

Hick, John, *An Interpretation of Religion* (London: Macmillan, 1989).

Hick, John, *The Rainbow of Faiths* (London: SCM Press, 1995).

Hobson, John, *The Eastern Origins of Western Civilisation* (Cambridge: Cambridge University Press, 2004).

Jenkins, Philip, *The Next Christendom: The Coming of Global Christianity*, 3rd ed. (Oxford: Oxford University Press, 2011).

Jensen, Lionel M., *Manufacturing Confucianism: Chinese Traditions and Universal Civilization* (Durham, NC: Duke University Press, [1997] 2003).

Jones, Gareth Lloyd, 'Law', in *A Dictionary of Jewish–Christian Relations*, edited by Edward Kessler and Neil Wenborn (Cambridge: Cambridge University Press, 2005), pp. 257–8.

Kelsey, David H., 'Paul Tillich', in *The Modern Theologians: An Introduction to Christian Theology since 1918*, edited by David F. Ford and Rachel Muers (Oxford: Blackwell, 2005), pp. 62–75.

Kilby, Karen, *A Brief Introduction to Karl Rahner* (New York: Crossroad, 2007).

King, Anna S. and Paul Hedges, 'What Is Religion? Or, What Is It We Are Talking About?', in *Controversies in Contemporary Religion: Education, Law, Politics, Society and Spirituality*, vol. 1, edited by Paul Hedges (Oxford: Praeger, 2014), pp. 1–30.

King, Ursula, 'Feminism: The Missing Dimension in the Dialogue of Religions', in *Pluralism and the Religions: The Theological and Political Dimensions*, edited by John D'Arcy May (London: Cassell, 1998), pp. 40–55.

Knitter, Paul F., 'Inter-Religious Dialogue and Social Activism', in *The Wiley-Blackwell Companion to Inter-Religious Dialogue*, edited by Catherine Cornille (Oxford: Wiley-Blackwell, 2013), pp. 133–48.

Knitter, Paul F., *Introducing Theologies of Religion* (Maryknoll, NY: Orbis, 2002).

Kraemer, Hendrik, *The Christian Message in a Non-Christian World* (London: Edinburgh House Press, [1938] 1947).

Leirvik, Oddbjørn, *Interreligious Studies: A Relational Approach to Religious Activism and the Study of Religion* (London: Bloomsbury, 2014).

Levinas, Emmanuel, *Ethics and Infinity* (Pittsburgh, PA: Duquesne University Press, 1985).

Levine, Amy-Jill, *The Misunderstood Jew: The Church and the Scandal of the Jewish Jesus* (New York: HarperCollins, 2006).

Lyons, Jonathan, *The House of Wisdom: How the Arabs Transformed Western Civilization* (London: Bloomsbury, 2010).

McCutcheon, Russell T., *Manufacturing Religion: The Discourse on Sui Generis Religion and the Politics of Nostalgia* (Oxford: Oxford University Press, 1997).

Markham, Ian, 'Interreligious Relations in the Anglican Communion', in *The Wiley-Blackwell Companion to the Anglican Communion*, edited by Ian Markham, J. Barney Hawkins IV, Justyn Terry and Leslie Nuñez Steffensen (Chichester: Wiley-Blackwell, 2013), pp. 657–65.

Martin, Craig, 'Experience', in *The Oxford Handbook of the Study of Religion*, edited by Michael Stausberg and Steven Engler (Oxford: Oxford University Press, 2016), pp. 525–40.

Masuzawa, Tomoko, *The Invention of World Religions* (Chicago: University of Chicago Press, 2005).

Miller, Ronald H., 'Judaism: Siblings in Strife', in *Christian Approaches to Other Faiths*, edited by Paul Hedges and Alan Race (London: SCM Press, 2008), pp. 176–90.

Morris, Paul, 'Ninian Smart: Comparative Theologian, Poet, Philosopher, and Global Citizen', *Religion* 31:4 (2001), 353–4.

Moyaert, Marianne, 'Christianity as the Measure of Religion? Materializing Theories of Religion', in *Twenty-First Century Theologies of Religions: Retrospection and Future Prospects*, edited by Elizabeth J. Harris, Paul Hedges and Shanthikumar Hettiarachchi (Leiden: Brill-Rodopi, 2016), pp. 239–60.

Moyaert, Marianne, 'Inappropriate Behavior? On the Ritual Core of Religion and Its Challenges to Interreligious Hospitality', *Journal for the Academic Study of Religion* 27:2 (2014), 222–42.

Müller, Friedrich Max, *On Missions: A Lecture Delivered in Westminster Abbey on December 3, 1873, with an Introductory Sermon by Arthur Penrhyn Stanley, D.D.* (London: Longmans, Green Co., 1873).

Nicholson, Hugh, *Comparative Theology and the Problem of Religious Rivalry* (Oxford: Oxford University Press, 2011).

Nongbri, Brent, *Before Religion: A History of a Modern Concept* (New Haven, CT: Yale University Press, 2013).

Otto, Rudolf, *The Idea of the Holy: An Inquiry into the Non-rational Factor in the Idea of the Divine and Its Relation to the Rational* (Oxford: Oxford University Press, 1923).

Palmer, Michael, *The Jesus Sutras: Rediscovering the Lost Religion of Taoist Christianity* (London: Piatkus, 2001).

Race, Alan, *Christians and Religious Pluralism: Patterns in the Christian Theology of Religions* (London: SCM Press, 1983).

Ruether, Rosemary Radford, *Faith and Fratricide: The Theological Roots of Anti-Semitism* (New York: Seabury Press, 1974).

Said, Edward, *Orientalism: Western Conceptions of the Orient* (London: Penguin, 1985).

Samartha, Stanley, *One Christ – Many Religions* (Maryknoll, NY: Orbis, 1991).

Saperstein, Marc, *Moments of Crisis in Jewish–Christian Relations* (London: SCM Press, 1989).

Schleiermacher, Friedrich, *The Christian Faith*, H. R. Mackintosh and J. S. Stewart (trans.) (Philadelphia: Fortress, [1820–1] 1976).

Schmidt-Leukel, Perry, 'Exclusivism, Inclusivism, Pluralism: The Tripolar Typology – Clarified and Reaffirmed', in *The Myth of Religious Superiority: A Multifaith Exploration*, edited by Paul Knitter (Maryknoll, NY: Orbis, 2005), pp. 13–27.

Schmidt-Leukel, Perry, *God beyond Boundaries: A Christian and Pluralist Theology of Religions* (Munster: Waxmann, 2017).

Schmidt-Leukel, Perry, 'Pluralisms', in *Christian Approaches to Other Faiths*, edited by Paul Hedges and Alan Race (London: SCM Press, 2008), pp. 85–110.

Schmidt-Leukel, Perry, *Religious Pluralism and Interreligious Theology* (Maryknoll, NY: Orbis, 2017).

Schoeman, Roy H., 'Catholicism and Judaism', in *The Catholic Church and the World Religions: A Theological and Phenomenological Account*, edited by Gavin D'Costa (London: T&T Clark, 2011), pp. 34–70.

Sharpe, Eric J., *Comparative Religion: A History* (LaSalle, IL: Open Court, [1975] 1991).

Smith, Huston, *The World's Religions* (New York: HarperCollins, [1958] 2009).

Smith, Wilfred Cantwell, *The Meaning and End of Religion* (London: SPCK, [1962] 1978).

Smith, Wilfred Cantwell, *Towards a World Theology: Faith and the Comparative History of Religion* (London: Macmillan, 1981).

Strange, Daniel, 'Exclusivisms: Indeed Their Rock Is Not Like Our Rock', in *Christian Approaches to Other Faiths*, edited by Paul Hedges and Alan Race (London: SCM Press, 2008), pp. 36–62.

Streeter, Burnett Hillman, *The Buddha and the Christ* (London: Macmillan, 1932).

Thatamanil, John J., 'Comparative Theology after Religion', in *Planetary Loves: Spivak, Postcoloniality and Theology*, edited by Stephen D. Moore and Mayra Rivera (New York: Fordham University Press, 2010), pp. 238–57.

Thomas, Owen C., 'Exclusivism: Karl Barth', in *Attitudes toward Other Religions*, edited by Owen C. Thomas (London: SCM Press, 1969), pp. 93–6.

Tillich, Paul, *The Courage to Be* (Fontana, CA: Fontana Library, [1952] 1962).

Tillich, Paul, *The Shaking of the Foundations* (West Drayton, Middlesex: Penguin, [1949] 1962).

Tillich, Paul, *Systematic Theology*, vol. 1 (Welwyn, Hertfordshire: James Nisbet & Co., 1968).

Tillich, Paul, *Theology of Culture*, R. C. Kimball (ed.) (New York: Oxford University Press, 1959).

Torrance, Thomas F., *Karl Barth: An Introduction to His Early Theology 1910–1931* (Edinburgh: T&T Clark, 2000).

Troeltsch, Ernst, *The Absoluteness of Christianity and the History of Religions* (London: SCM Press, [1902] 1971).

Troeltsch, Ernst, 'Christianity and the History of Religion', in *Religion in History*, James Adams and Walter Bense (trans.) (Minneapolis, MN: Fortress, [1897] 1991), pp. 77–86.

Troeltsch, Ernst, 'The Place of Christianity among the World Religions', in *Attitudes Toward Other Religions*, edited by Owen C. Thomas (London: SCM Press, 1969), pp. 73–92.

Troll, Christian W. 'Catholicism and Islam', in *The Catholic Church and the World Religions: A Theological and Phenomenological Account*, edited by Gavin D'Costa (London: T&T Clark, 2011), pp. 71–105.

Williams, Rowan, 'Christian Identity and Religious Plurality', Plenary Session Paper from the World Council of Churches Assembly, Porto Alegre (2006), accessed at https://www.oikoumene.org /resources/documents/rowan-williams-presentation.

Williams, Rowland, *Paraméswara-jnyána-góshthí: A Dialogue on the Knowledge of the Supreme Lord, in Which Are Compared the Claims of Christianity and Hinduism, and Various Questions of Indian Religion and Literature Fairly Discussed* (Cambridge: Deighton, Bell and Co., 1856).

# 9

# God

## Daniel Castelo

Speaking of 'God' in the twentieth century draws on patterns inherited from antecedent frameworks and faces new challenges of its own in an increasingly interconnected world. In the former category, one continues to see the difficulty in English that the word 'God' – reminiscent of its Greek forebear, *theos* – can be a common noun, a particular name or an implicit title tied to specific functions, such as creation and providence. That issue of indeterminacy alone creates possibilities for misunderstanding, conflation and nonsensicality (and in turn justifies the use of quotes for most instances of the word throughout the present article). As a result, it is typically not clear what the referent of 'God' is from case to case in casual conversation, mass polling and even some cases of formal theological literature. Naturally, this issue is not native to the twentieth century, but it was exacerbated with an increased diversity in voices, options and perspectives during this era.

As for new challenges, one must recognise that the twentieth century was uniquely plagued with violence, terrorism, the rise and fall of autocratic regimes, wealth disparity and ecological disasters, all of which were quickly televised or shared through electronic means of communication to an onlooking world. These happenings altered people's sensibilities and outlooks, including their religious and theistic beliefs. People repeatedly and openly have asked the 'God question' during this century in the light of many, mass-publicised developments: is it possible to believe in 'God' (whoever or whatever the referent) this side of two world wars? Auschwitz? The rise and fall of the USSR? Global warming? The list could go on. Given the circumstances involved and the manner in which the questions were raised in the first place, no clear resolution related to these queries emerged during the century. As a result, by the end of the twentieth century and the dawning of the twenty-first, plenty of unease surrounding 'God'-related matters continued in Western, North Atlantic contexts. The terror attacks of September 11, 2001 – undertaken in the name of theistic devotion – and the rise since that time of what has become known as the 'new atheism' are just two indicators of this theologically unsettled mood.

The situation in the West may paint a dismal picture regarding the future for 'God', but developments in what is termed the 'Global South' would offer a different outlook. In many locations across the globe, especially on the continent of Africa, Christian religious devotion has been on the rise in unforeseen ways. Over the last few decades of the twentieth century in particular, one can document a Christian revival of an unprecedented kind on this continent as well as in Asia and Latin America. Based on these considerable demographic changes, one could say that the centre of gravity for Christianity has shifted southward, something that northern Christians generally have yet to appreciate fully.

Treating of 'God' in the twentieth century, then, is an expansive and multifaceted endeavour. What follows will develop the above themes, all the while recognising that the depiction is selective and so by no means representative of all that could be considered, given the vastness of both the topic and the time frame.

## 'God' as a (Continual) Problem in the Modern West

A popularly known fact from Christian antiquity is that the first Christians were sometimes deemed 'atheists' by the Roman Empire for their refusal to pay tribute to the traditional gods. Justin Martyr notes in his *First Apology*:

> Hence are we called atheists. And we confess that we are atheists, so far as gods of this sort are concerned, but not with respect to the most true God, the Father of righteousness and temperance and the other virtues, who is free from all impurity. Both Him, and the Son . . . and the prophetic Spirit, we worship and adore, knowing them in reason and truth.[1]

Today, many atheists in North Atlantic culture are such because of their refusal to pay tribute to a different divinity, the 'God' of Christendom – that ever-shifting deity who was made possible by mutations inherent to a Constantinian arrangement in which the Christian Church (in its many forms) and the Western state (in its many forms) have been tied for centuries for mutually benefiting purposes. This Constantinian relationship has been of such a kind that acts of resistance are inevitable given the intellectual developments of the last few centuries. One such resistance has been the rise of modern atheism. This variety of atheism, however, is certainly different from the kind highlighted and represented by Justin.

And yet, for all the contrasts that exist between these two scenarios – the Western civic religion of the early Church period and the emergence of Christendom – interesting parallels are observable. One such parallel is the often-unquestioned assumption – lodged at the very heart of what it means to be a Westerner – that belief in divinity (of whatever kind) is crucial for the state's success and well-being. A lingering feature of Western religion, then, is that it is typically associated with Western empire. This was the case during Western Christianity's minority, pre-Constantine, persecuted status when the gods of the Roman Empire were prominent as state-supporting divinities, as well as during Christianity's flourishing and predominance as the religion *par excellence* of the West. Of course, the differences are also significant: the gods of the Roman pantheon and the God of Jesus Christ have different character profiles, qualities and demands. The point being stressed here, however, is that Western citizenship and Western religiosity have gone hand in hand for millennia, a situation that was bound to be questioned over time.

Given such questioning, one might think that a summary statement of the twentieth century would be the decline of religiosity in the West, and in a certain sense, that reading would be true – revivals and movements of Christian vitality notwithstanding. It appears to us looking back on the Middle Ages that it was impossible not to believe in 'God' during that era. On the contemporary scene, however, it feels like we have made an about-turn culturally in that it is now difficult and unintuitive to believe in 'God' at all.[2] And yet, the situation is more complex than a simple narrative of radical and blatant decline would have us believe.

An overarching claim for the moment would be this: our current situation in the North Atlantic is one of existential–theological contradiction, with an entrenched longing for 'God' on the one hand and intellectual and cultural pressure to abandon such a notion on the other. That the question 'Is belief in "God" possible after X?' continues to persist (with 'X' referring to any mass tragedy or challenge, whether created by nature or humanity) suggests that our age is still tempted towards faith generally and belief in 'God' particularly. As evidence of this point, surveys of North America and Europe repeatedly show that a significant majority of the population in these regions continues to believe in 'God' or 'some higher power'. These surveys do not suggest much on the surface in terms of how this belief impacts on people's lives, but at least at a preliminary level, the various closures and finalities associated with Nietzsche's remark that 'God is dead' (including a North American movement called the 'death of God theology') are at day's end premature – something which Nietzsche himself was keen to observe: 'God is dead; but given the way of men, there may still be caves for thousands of years in which his shadow will be shown.'[3]

The twentieth century, then, can be characterised as 'shadowed' or 'haunted' by 'God'.[4] This language of 'shadowed' or 'haunted' is apropos in that it seems that 'God' is both desirable in some broad sense and yet impossible to accommodate in another. The desirability stems at least partially from the Western heritage of civic religion alluded to above – belief in divinity is simply inherent to the longstanding Western way of life. But the impossibility is due to the plausibility structures of the dominant 'social imaginary' (to use the language of Charles Taylor)[5] of the contemporary West that make transcendence increasingly inadmissible. This imaginary continues to perpetuate the modernist heritage that the world is 'disenchanted' (that is, rid of various 'supernatural' presences), that the political and the 'natural' are independent orders, and that the point of reference for meaning and fulfillment is anthropologically immanent. Again, to use the language of Taylor, this 'flattening' process that directs questions of significance back to the self creates a buffering of the self from all else that is.[6] In its wake, this process creates an existential void of transcendence that the immanent approach cannot adequately fill. As a result, 'God' is difficult to imagine and so a 'problem' in the West, but it is a notion that nevertheless is obstinately present – it will simply not go away.

Some have thought that this process will ultimately right itself, that this 'problem' will dissipate over time by becoming outdated or unfashionable. Prognosticators of various kinds, especially during the 1960s, thought this would be the case relatively soon. What they failed to realise in their assessments is that the predicament of 'God' being a 'problem' is itself a product of various *theological* judgements made prior to the twentieth century. The factors mentioned above (disenchantment, flattening, the autonomising of the political and natural orders, the location of meaning within immanence and so on) were theological moves whose confluence led to this state of affairs. And so, the North Atlantic world is not so much on thoroughly new terrain as it is on a trajectory that has experienced a number of developments and mutations.[7] The situation of the twentieth century is but one phase within this long process. For this reason, even in increasingly secularised contexts in which agnosticism and atheism of various sorts seem more intellectually possible and respectable, the 'absence of God' continues to be, in a variety of ways and circumstances, 'felt'. One such proof of this sentiment is precisely that people continue to ask if belief in 'God' is possible. Whatever answers are proffered, the question itself is indicative of this unique, theistic 'shadowing' or 'haunting'.

Within this 'haunted' setting, theists and atheists pursue the 'God question' in varying degrees of continuity with bequeathed tendencies – that is, in the light of the theological judgements alluded to above that were made in prior eras. The polyvalences associated with the term 'God' and their attendant conflationary tendencies add further dynamics to consider.

For instance, some theists may hold to a kind of deism and still feel part of a Christian orbit.[8] This connection, however, is only partially justifiable. Certainly, Christians since their origins have cast the 'God' of their confession as, say, a providential creator, and deism itself represents one of those theological judgements made in the light of increased intellectual pressures within modernity. Faced with sweeping changes in the Western worldview, the formulators of modern deism could be cast as attempting to 'save' or 'redeem' the faith from irrelevance. However, deism excludes such pivotal Christian beliefs as the presence and work of the Son and Spirit within the economy of history; in other words, deism is not Trinitarian and so counter to orthodox Christian claims made for centuries. Others could hear reference to 'God' in public, state-related settings and go on to assume, in conformity with aspects of their particular identity, that they live in a 'Christian nation', which can result in an assumed, imperialistic view that one's ways are 'God's' ways and the public realm in turn must reflect these – despite the civic presence of those from many different backgrounds and beliefs. This approach reflects a kind of Constantinianism that bears resemblance to the colonial project, one that has long been associated with a number of problematic theological assumptions. Still others could argue for the existence of 'God' and 'God's truth' in the Bible and do so on modern epistemological and rational grounds. Whereas this approach may pitch Christian faith as a 'reasonable option', such reasonableness may compromise the ability to account for Christian claims that do not fit this paradigm, including mystery, paradox, Christ's resurrection and so on. These cases and many more are easily detectable in broadly theological conversations from the twentieth century. Unfortunately, throughout these varying accounts, the question of this divinity's particular identity is usually left unattended or underdeveloped.

Resistances to this 'shadowing' in the form of varying contemporary atheisms also show an intricate dependence on past theological judgements. As a result, theisms and atheisms of various kinds are often mirror images of one another in the modern period. Put another way, there are as many kinds of atheisms as there are theisms, for plausibility structures contributing to one usually are doing so for the other. As Michael Buckley notes of the modern condition, 'Atheism does not stand alone. The term and the persuasions which cluster around it take their meaning from the divine nature which has been asserted by the religions and the philosophies, by the superstitious practices and the mystical experiences of those who adhere to the divine existence.'[9] He continues: 'the central meaning of atheism is not to be sought immediately in atheism; it is to be sought in those gods or that god affirmed, which atheism has either engaged or chosen to ignore as beneath serious challenge.'[10] As a result, both theism and atheism may reflect fundamentalist tendencies in their inability or refusal to account for alternatives beyond themselves; instead, they may rely on shared assumptions that align them into a kind of kinship, placing them into a 'sibling rivalry' of sorts. Given the running theme of this piece in terms of the indeterminacy associated with the term 'God', different outcomes could result from this parasitic relationship of atheism upon theism, some of which could be blatantly contradictory. For instance, Buckley raises the interesting case of Baruch Spinoza, who was seen as a spiritual resource – a prompt for theistic faith – by Vladimir Solovyov, yet deemed by Nietzsche as a precursor to his own atheist programme.[11]

Such a connection helps elucidate the logic behind what Jürgen Moltmann has called 'protest atheism',[12] a theme symptomatic of many theological discussions in the twentieth century. At work here is a kind of 'metaphysical rebellion' (to use the language of Albert Camus)[13] that operates out of the disconnect felt between theistic claims and lived, witnessed reality. This disquietude leading to metaphysical rebellion is detectable within the nineteenth century, but it was significantly intensified in the twentieth, especially after two world wars and the Holocaust (the latter having direct theological significance given its connection to the religio-ethnic identity of Judaism). An often-cited exemplar of this spirit from the late nineteenth century is Fyodor Dostoyevsky's *The Brothers Karamazov*, in which there is a scene where one of the brothers, Ivan, refuses a divinely offered ticket that represents the logic and warrants for why children suffer. His refusal is based on the judgement that the ticket is not worth the sacrifice – no justification or eventual resolution can exist for a child's tears. A popular twentieth-century exemplar of this mood would be Elie Wiesel's *Night*, with its account of 'God' hanging in the gallows of concentration camp life, a scene which has been referenced by Christian theologians dozens of times so as to illustrate the difficulty of believing in 'God' after something like Auschwitz.[14] In both cases, 'God' is seen as untenable in the light of experienced reality. A child's tears or the gallows at Buna raise the point that a good and/or all-powerful 'God' would not/ should not/could not let these events take place. Inherent to this reaction are assumptions of what this 'God' is or must be (including the prioritised attributes of goodness and power – and these cast in a particular, modern way) and how this 'God' ought to engage, respond or account for lived human experience, which is itself 'given' in a certain, unvarnished sense. To simply expand on this last point, *humans* commit violence against children, and *humans* execute other humans in concentration camps, yet the moral outrage on display when these two (and other) cases are raised is not anthropologically directed but theologically so. It is as if when the structures of common morality are severely transgressed, a notion of transcendence becomes increasingly relevant only for the sake of problematising it. When left to their own worst impulses, humans may find it appealing to blame 'God' in their 'shadowed' or 'haunted' situation so as to avoid a reckoning with their 'buffered' – and ultimately monstrous – selves.

This spirit of protest destabilises two theological frameworks. The first would be theodicy. Usually associated with the work of Gottfried Wilhelm Leibniz, theodical projects emerged in earnest in the modern period as a way of 'mathematising' the natural and theological realms in a way consistent with the increasingly dominant intellectual frameworks of the time.[15] The 'God' associated with theodicy was in many ways a deistic divinity, with the themes of creation, goodness, providence and power all front and centre. Leibniz's famous 'best of all possible worlds' alternative – in which 'God', who is perfect, good and the like could not help but create the best world possible, that is, this world as we know it – led to a kind of philosophical-theological fatalism that was deemed so rigid and ruthless by some that it was soon problematised by those who took a long look at the Lisbon earthquake a few decades later (1755).[16] The popular deist theological construct, a form of theism to be sure but questionably a thoroughgoing Christian alternative, set up intelligibility and plausibility expectations that would necessarily be unsustainable with increased pressure. And so, the rise and fall of theodical projects is just one phenomenon of this existential–theological contradiction. Many assume that a theodical 'God' is the proper (or only) framework for casting a divinity, but that framework can only fail over time given the pressures of lived reality. Therefore, the parasitic nature of atheism comes to light in this case when one sees reactions to the theodical 'God'. 'Protest atheism' or 'atheism for God's sake' is a reaction to a very specific God-construct, one that is often grounded within theodical, and so deistic, claims. And, as we have noted, such a reaction is funded by those very same claims as well. As we have stated, this is a sibling dispute of a theological kind. 'Protest atheists' are typically decrying the possibility of a theodical 'God'. That this 'God' is not altogether the Christian God is typically lost on those making the protest, resulting for some in the rejection of all forms of theism.

The heightened spirit of protest associated with the twentieth-century theological world also challenges a second, related, and yet vaster domain – that which some have called 'classical theism', a form of theism that relies on ancient metaphysical categories. Theistic sympathisers to protest atheism as well as other theologians seeking new paths claim the need to renounce this past conceptual construct for the sake of offering a more palatable alternative.[17] Support for this resistance is buoyed via a 'fall narrative' (espoused influentially by Adolf von Harnack) in which the early Christians who were inclined to metaphysical speculation are cast as abandoning the riches of the biblical tradition for the intellectual wares of their day.[18] This 'corruption' of Christian God-talk is said to include the uncritical adoption of Aristotle's 'Unmoved Mover' and a host of attributes that on the surface sound strange to the biblical meta-narrative (including aseity, simplicity, immutability and so on).[19] One of the most reviled features of this framework has been divine impassibility, the notion that 'God' does not suffer or is not affected by outside forces. Critics contend that this God-construct was perpetuated unquestioningly for centuries and thereby makes appearances in some notable theological figures, including Augustine and Aquinas.[20] Such sweeping narratives typically function as 'straw men' for what are cast as more appealing alternatives, ones that either adopt a different, explicit metaphysical scheme or aim to be (in their words) more 'biblical' in their orientation. In the case of reactions to divine impassibility, the option is clear: a depiction of a suffering or passible 'God' is more faithful to a crucified Christ than many historical metaphysical alternatives from Christian antiquity. As famously articulated in one of his letters from prison, Dietrich Bonhoeffer remarks that 'only the suffering God can help'.[21]

Criticisms of 'classical theism' typically fall short on a number of points. First, they often fail to demarcate how complex and intricate God-talk has been over the many centuries of Christian history. To raise a simple but sometimes neglected point: figures such as Origen, Augustine and Aquinas live in different contexts, so that their theistic constructs are significantly varied; cross-identifying their theologies into a single project loses sight of these differences. A second shortcoming is also conflationary in nature: these critics often identify the 'God' of 'classical theism' with what amounts to be an 'immovable God', One who is incapable of a 'real' relation with the world because of the logical consequences of holding certain divine attributes such as simplicity, immutability and impassibility. This particular reading of past figures essentially stresses that what is said at the register of the doctrine of God must determine everything else that follows, thereby openly inviting a tension between what is deemed to be biblical revelation and Greek metaphysical reasoning.[22] Again, these are sweeping narratives that fail to account for the complexity and nuance of past theological voices. Collectively, they constitute a gesture of rejecting a past theistic view (however artificial of a construct it may be) for the sake of offering a more contemporary one that is meant to be more appealing and viable. That these readings persisted is but one further manifestation of the 'shadowed' or 'haunted' theological milieu in which the twentieth century found itself: Theists felt the need to offer alternatives because they sensed that theism on the whole is on tenuous ground culturally and intellectually.

Are there ways forward in this morass of sentiment that 'God' is ultimately a 'problem'? Yes, one does find strategies from the twentieth century worth highlighting. Three in particular will be mentioned.

Given some of the common themes mentioned above, a first point of order for a remediation of this situation is the claiming of the particularity of the Christian God, which on traditional grounds would include the dogma of the Trinity. One of the most significant developments in twentieth-century Western Christianity has been the revitalisation of Trinitarianism. A number of prominent figures have been associated with this development, including the Roman Catholic theologians Karl Rahner, Yves Congar, and Catherine LaCugna. Often associated with this revival of Trinitarian thought has been social Trinitarianism, the theological endeavour of actively connecting the dogma of the Trinity with human social and political arrangements, especially as these highlight mutuality, interdependence, and the like. But in terms of this essay, this revival is significant for the purposes of claiming the specificity of Christian God-talk in the light of the pressures towards indeterminacy regnant within the modern Western milieu. Karl Barth, the most significant Protestant theologian of the twentieth century, was aware of the problem and sought to respond to it in his *Church Dogmatics* through a Trinitarian intervention:

> What we are trying to bring to practical recognition by putting [the doctrine of the Trinity] first is something which has not been concealed in the history of dogmatics and which has often enough been stated very strongly, namely that this is the point where the basic decision is made whether what is in every respect the very important term 'God' is used in Church proclamation in a manner appropriate to the object which is also its norm.[23]

Barth continues: 'The doctrine of the Trinity is what basically distinguishes the Christian doctrine of God as Christian, and therefore what already distinguishes the Christian concept of revelation as Christian, in contrast to all other possible doctrines of God or concepts of revelation.'[24] Barth keeps at the forefront of his project the question 'Who is God?', which he finds basic to any other theistic exploration. In pressing this question, Barth makes reference to a kind of construct of the divine name, 'Yahweh-Kyrios', which is based on the two-testament biblical witness. For Barth, 'the doctrine of the Trinity is not and does not seek to be anything but an explanatory confirmation of this name'.[25] Although ultimately critical of Barth's inconsistency in following through with the implications of this move, Kendall Soulen believes Barth's insight is critical not only for addressing the problem of supersessionism but also for stressing the identity of the Christian God in a post-Constantinian age.[26] This act of naming and identifying accomplishes many things, but for the present task, it specifies the God of Christian confession as One who has a particular character, One who has acted in particular ways within history and One who has revealed specific purposes and ends for the creation. In summary, this kind of specificity reorients God-talk by placing a premium on identifying who is 'God' before going on to do any other kind of theological work. Such work accentuates the critical acumen required of those seeking to pursue God-talk this side of Constantinianism, Christendom and modernity.

A second point for remediation within this situation is a reclaiming of the enchanted nature of reality. Within Christian circles, this has demonstrated itself in a renewed interest by some in the West in classical Christian traditions such as Roman Catholicism and Eastern Orthodoxy; it also shows itself in the rise of revivalist Christian movements such as Pentecostal and charismatic fellowships. A common thread among these alternatives is that the 'closed', naturalistic paradigms of modernity, ones that often are seen as problematising theism, are themselves worth problematising on grounds that they are too reductive. Developments in the faith–science dialogue have been helpful here, as has been the above-noted revival within Christian thought in Trinitarian thinking, which by its very nature underscores the way the Christian God is active within history via its emphasis on the incarnate Son and the life-giving and sanctifying Spirit. A focus on the Spirit in particular highlights mediation, which would emphasise how the Christian God is active in and through the created realm. Such strategies would resist naturalistic reductions on the one hand and open up possibilities for new kinds of frameworks on the other that would welcome and work out synergistic and noncompetitive dynamics between the Creator and the creation that would place the Christian God once again at the centre rather than at the margins of experienced and embodied life.

A third point for remediation has to do with claiming the Christian doctrine of God in the midst of embodied, lived reality. In this way, the 'problem of God' is integrated with the 'problems of humanity' surrounding us. What is indicated by 'embodied, lived reality' is the manner in which people's lives, including their identities and physical bodies, traffic in a world replete with oppression and injustice – circumstances that oftentimes in the West have resonances with the speech, attitudes and practices of Christendom. How can the Christian doctrine of God speak to conditions in which people are marginalised on account of who they are in their very selves? Questions like this one concretise what is often abandoned to abstraction by theodical endeavouring. Although these trends have received more and more attention in twenty-first-century theology, their genesis has roots in various twentieth-century proposals, including feminist,[27] Black[28] and disability[29] liberation movements. Such efforts inspire a critical awareness of how theology can be used by dominant structures to perpetuate unjust arrangements, and that critical awareness in turn can be a prompt for reintegrating an account of the Christian gospel as 'good news' that is truly freeing and humanising for both those who are pushed to the margins and those who are entrenched in the powerful centre.

## 'God' in the Global South

Whereas much of the present article has focused on Western, North Atlantic settings, developments within Christianity in what is sometimes referred to as the 'Global South' have been surprising of late, especially since the turn of the twentieth century. During this century, 'the center of gravity in the Christian world . . . shifted inexorably away from Europe, southward, to Africa and Latin America, and eastward, toward Asia'.[30] To illustrate the significance of this century's shifts in Christian demographics, Philip Jenkins observed in 2011 that 'in 1900 Europe was home to two-thirds of the world's Christian population; today, the figure is about 25 percent, and by 2025 it will fall below 20 percent.'[31] For those of us in the North Atlantic world, it may be difficult to appreciate these changes, in part because they feel so removed from our immediate experience. In particular, it may be challenging to appreciate how the Global South operates out of different social imaginaries, ones that by and large share resonances with an 'enchanted' perspective of the world:

> [These newer churches in the Global South] preach messages that, to a Westerner, appear simplistically charismatic, visionary, and apocalyptic. In this thought-world, prophecy is an everyday reality, while faith-healing, exorcism, and dream-visions are all fundamental parts of religious sensibility. For better or worse, the dominant churches of the future could have much in common with those of medieval or early modern European times.[32]

Despite this difficulty, northerners should be mindful not to evaluate these contexts disparagingly in ways similar to how they sometimes do with their own past – that is, by excessively valorising an eventual 'enlightenment' that calls into question an 'enchanted' view. Such a bias could very well get in the way of fruitful and respectful dialogue.

One of the differences between the Christianity of medieval Europe and that of twentieth-century Africa or Asia is that the former had the 'God' of Christendom available in a way the latter has not. In fact, the latter may very well be on similar terrain to what Paul encountered at the Areopagus (as narrated in Acts 17), in which Paul first notes all the many gods throughout Athens and then goes on to make a connection between a marker to an 'unknown god' and the God of Christian confession. In quite a startling way, Paul says, 'What therefore you worship as unknown, this I proclaim to you.'[33] Paul continues that the god who made all things does not live in shrines or temples, nor need anything from humans. This god 'allotted the times of [mortals'] existence and the boundaries of the places where they would live, so that they would search for God, and perhaps grope for him and find him – though indeed he is not far from each one of us'.[34] At this point, Paul quotes what is an apparently common phrase known to his hearers, 'In him we live and move and have our being.'[35] In other words, Paul lived and stepped into 'enchanted' contexts – ones in which divinities were everywhere to be identified and recalled – and was unafraid to make connections between the Christian faith and what was 'already there'. The narrative certainly ends on particular claims related to the God of Jesus Christ and the Resurrection, but not before engaging in a unique way with the theological diversity at work in the context in which Paul found himself. This last point is important to highlight because those who have a 'God' of Christendom in their theological imaginary might be inclined to proclaim these public divinities as superstitions or evil spirits, thereby denouncing what is publicly available as inconsequential or wrongheaded. In contrast, the 'indigenous discovery of Christianity'[36] requires a kind of flexibility that Christianity has demonstrated before but that northerners may find difficult to accommodate. Given Christianity's change in its epicentre, however, northerners have choices: they can ignore these new realities, they can condescendingly assume that they have already 'arrived' at a posture that will inevitably work itself out in these southern contexts as well, or they can dialogically engage with these new fellow Christians with the hope of understanding them and the work of the Christian God in their midst. Should the latter option be chosen, it could very well lead to a northern 're-enchantment' and 'reawakening' of its own.

As these Christians in the Global South gain and exercise their voice in the theological realm, one should expect a number of proposals that vary considerably from a methodological perspective.

Take the African experience as one such case. As Okechukwu Ogbonnaya highlights early on in his text devoted to an African understanding of the Trinity,

> Many oppressed peoples . . . seem to criticise the conception of the Divine imposed on them by the West, but fail to make an alternative proposal that is truly liberating . . . In order for theological discourse or God-talk to change, Africans must begin using their own experience and traditional philosophical 'categories'. It will not do to discuss 'African concepts' and then to turn around and present more of the same Eurocentric perspective unchanged by the discussion.[37]

Ogbonnaya and others face the challenge of rendering an African Christian theology that stems from the African context that can nevertheless connect with traditionally Christian understandings while at the same time resisting potential conceptual reductions native to Western thought-forms. Obviously, this challenge is not easy to navigate. Some may find the scales of this process tipping in one direction or another, as is the case with some readers of John Mbiti's approach, which catalogues names and attributes for the 'One Supreme God' among more than 270 peoples on the continent in terms that Westerners can understand.[38] Like their counterparts in the North, the theologians of the Global South will vary in their proposals and disagree with one another, given the kind of discipline theology is. Such debate should be welcomed and deemed fitting.

One of the great benefits of having theologians from different contexts involved in theological reflection is the way genuine alternatives to regnant paradigms can emerge. An example of this type of contribution is the work of Jung Young Lee that casts the Trinity in a way East Asians can appreciate. Lee is very well aware of how all theology is contextual in the sense that it operates within domains related to particular human understandings and experiences. This admission, one that northerners often have difficulty admitting for themselves and their own theology, is registered concretely by Lee: 'Through my personal journey, I have discovered that yin-yang symbolic thinking is not only a part of my thought orientation but also one of the most important ways, if not the most important, for East Asian people to understand their thought and life.'[39] What Lee is after is the way people in a most basic sense construct knowledge (including theological knowledge). He is willing to admit for himself and other East Asian people what simply 'makes sense' to them at this fundamental level and, in turn, what must be operative in order for them to appreciate something like the doctrine of the Trinity. For Lee, the contribution of yin-yang symbolism for the doctrine of the Trinity includes a greater awareness and integration of such themes as open-endedness, inclusivity, codependence and complementarity, which are distinct from conflictual and binary approaches characteristic of the West. The result from this alternative approach is a marked and fruitful way for thinking of the triune God's unity and diversity, a vision that can open up vistas for Westerners long entrenched within their own paradigms surrounding God-talk. Those possibilities should continue to present themselves as Christianity continues to emerge as a predominantly non-Western religion.

## Notes

1. Justin Martyr, *First Apology*, ch. 6.
2. Charles Taylor is often credited with this economy of expression; see *A Secular Age* (Cambridge: Belknap, 2007), p. 25.
3. Friedrich Nietzsche, *The Gay Science*, Walter Kaufmann (trans.) (New York: Vintage, [1887] 1974), p. 167.
4. Relying on Taylor's analysis, James K. A. Smith highlights this point in *How (Not) to Be Secular* (Grand Rapids: Eerdmans, 2014).
5. Taylor, *A Secular Age*, pp. 171–6.
6. Taylor, *A Secular Age*, pp. 31–41.
7. Taylor, *A Secular Age*, p. 95.
8. See Christian Smith, *Soul Searching* (Oxford: Oxford University Press, 2005).
9. Michael J. Buckley, *At the Origins of Modern Atheism* (New Haven, CT: Yale University Press, 1987), p. 14.
10. Buckley, *At the Origins of Modern Atheism*, p. 15.
11. Buckley, *At the Origins of Modern Atheism*, p. 12.
12. Jürgen Moltmann, *The Crucified God: The Cross of Christ as the Foundation and Criticism of*

*Christian Theology*, R. A. Wilson and John Bowden (trans.) (Minneapolis: Fortress, [1973] 1993), p. 221.

13. Albert Camus, *The Rebel*, Anthony Bower (trans.) (London: Penguin Classics, 2000), ch. 2, 'Metaphysical Rebellion', pp. 29–75.

14. Marcel Sarot, 'Auschwitz, Morality and the Suffering of God', *Modern Theology* 7:2 (1991), 135–52.

15. See Gottfried Wilhelm Leibniz, *Theodicy: Essays on the Goodness of God, the Freedom of Man, and the Origin of Evil* (London: Routledge and Kegan Paul, [1710] 1951), p. 128.

16. An example of this resistance would be Voltaire, 'Author's Preface to the Lisbon Earthquake' [1755–6], in *The Works of Voltaire*, William F. Fleming (trans.), vol. 36 (Chicago: DuMont, 1901), pp. 5–7.

17. The person most often associated with this tendency is Jürgen Moltmann, both in *The Crucified God* and *The Trinity and the Kingdom*, Margaret Kohl (trans.) (Minneapolis: Fortress, [1980] 1993).

18. On this fall narrative, see Paul L. Gavrilyuk, *The Suffering of the Impassible God* (Oxford: Oxford University Press, 2004), pp. 1–14 and 'Appendix'.

19. An important expression of this view is Clark H. Pinnock, *Most Moved Mover* (Grand Rapids: Baker Academic, 2001).

20. An example of this reading is John Sanders, 'Historical Considerations', in *The Openness of God*, edited by Clark Pinnock et al. (Downers Grove, IL: InterVarsity, 1994), pp. 59–100.

21. Dietrich Bonhoeffer, *Letters and Papers from Prison* (New York: Touchstone Simon and Schuster, [1970] 1997), p. 361.

22. As we have already noted, these readings sometimes emerge in the context of emphasising a more robustly 'biblical' option (Clark Pinnock and his colleagues), but they also are expressed along Trinitarian (Moltmann in *The Trinity and the Kingdom*) and Christological (again Moltmann in *The Crucified God*) lines of enquiry. As for Christology, the specific themes of kenosis and the atonement play a crucial role in justifying the need to reject past 'classical' approaches. See, for instance, Lucien Richard, *A Kenotic Christology* (Washington, DC: University Press of America, 1982) and Hastings Rashdall, *The Idea of Atonement in Christian Theology* (London: Macmillan, 1920).

23. Karl Barth, *Church Dogmatics*, vol. 1, part 1, G. W. Bromiley (trans.) (Edinburgh: T&T Clark, 1936), p. 301.

24. Barth, *Church Dogmatics*, vol. 1, part 1, p. 301.

25. Barth, *Church Dogmatics*, vol. 1, part 1, p. 348.

26. R. Kendall Soulen, 'YHWH the Triune God', *Modern Theology* 15:1 (1999), 25–54: 26.

27. Elizabeth A. Johnson, *She Who Is: The Mystery of God in Feminist Theological Discourse* (New York: Crossroad, 1992); Rosemary Radford Ruether, *Sexism and God-Talk* (Boston: Beacon, 1983).

28. James H. Cone, *God of the Oppressed* (Maryknoll, NY: Orbis, 1997).

29. Nancy L. Eiesland, *The Disabled God* (Nashville: Abingdon, 1994).

30. Philip Jenkins, *The Next Christendom*, 3rd ed. (Oxford: Oxford University Press, 2011), p. 1.

31. Jenkins, *The Next Christendom*, p. 2.

32. Jenkins, *The Next Christendom*, p. 10.

33. Acts 17:23, NRSV.

34. Acts 17:26–7, NRSV.

35. Acts 17:28, NRSV.

36. Lamin Sanneh, *Whose Religion Is Christianity?* (Grand Rapids: Eerdmans, 2003), p. 10.

37. A. Okechukwu Ogbonnaya, *On Communitarian Divinity* (St. Paul, MN: Paragon, 1994), p. x.

38. John S. Mbiti, *Concepts of God in Africa* (London: SPCK, 1970), p. xiii.

39. Jung Young Lee, *The Trinity in Asian Perspective* (Nashville: Abingdon, 1996), p. 21.

# Bibliography

Barth, Karl, *Church Dogmatics*, vol. 1, part 1, G. W. Bromiley (trans.) (Edinburgh: T&T Clark, 1936).

Bonhoeffer, Dietrich, *Letters and Papers from Prison* (New York: Touchstone Simon and Schuster, [1970] 1997).

Buckley, Michael J., *At the Origins of Modern Atheism* (New Haven, CT: Yale University Press, 1987).

Camus, Albert, *The Rebel*, Anthony Bower (trans.) (London: Penguin Classics, 2000).

Cone, James H., *God of the Oppressed* (Maryknoll, NY: Orbis, 1997).

Eiesland, Nancy L., *The Disabled God* (Nashville: Abingdon, 1994).

Gavrilyuk, Paul L., *The Suffering of the Impassible God* (Oxford: Oxford University Press, 2004).

Jenkins, Philip, *The Next Christendom*, 3rd ed. (Oxford: Oxford University Press, 2011).

Johnson, Elizabeth A., *She Who Is: The Mystery of God in Feminist Theological Discourse* (New York: Crossroad, 1992).

Justin Martyr, *First Apology*, M. Dods et al. (trans.), Ante-Nicene Fathers 2 (Edinburgh: T&T Clark, 1870).

Lee, Jung Young, *The Trinity in Asian Perspective* (Nashville: Abingdon, 1996).

Leibniz, Gottfried Wilhelm, *Theodicy: Essays on the Goodness of God, the Freedom of Man, and the Origin of Evil* (London: Routledge and Kegan Paul, [1710] 1951).

Mbiti, John S., *Concepts of God in Africa* (London: SPCK, 1970).

Moltmann, Jürgen, *The Crucified God: The Cross of Christ as the Foundation and Criticism of Christian Theology*, R. A. Wilson and John Bowden (trans.) (Minneapolis: Fortress, [1973] 1993).

Moltmann, Jürgen, *The Trinity and the Kingdom*, Margaret Kohl (trans.) (Minneapolis: Fortress, [1980] 1993).

Nietzsche, Friedrich, *The Gay Science*, Walter Kaufmann (trans.) (New York: Vintage, [1887] 1974).

Ogbonnaya, A. Okechukwu, *On Communitarian Divinity* (St. Paul, MN: Paragon, 1994).

Pinnock, Clark H., *Most Moved Mover* (Grand Rapids: Baker Academic, 2001).

Pinnock, Clark H., Richard Rice, John Sanders, William Hasker and David Basinger (eds), *The Openness of God* (Downers Grove, IL: InterVarsity, 1994).

Rashdall, Hastings, *The Idea of Atonement in Christian Theology* (London: Macmillan, 1920).

Richard, Lucien, *A Kenotic Christology* (Washington, DC: University Press of America, 1982).

Ruether, Rosemary Radford, *Sexism and God-Talk* (Boston: Beacon, 1983).

Sanneh, Lamin, *Whose Religion Is Christianity?* (Grand Rapids: Eerdmans, 2003).

Sarot, Marcel, 'Auschwitz, Morality and the Suffering of God', *Modern Theology* 7:2 (1991), 135–52.

Smith, Christian, *Soul Searching* (Oxford: Oxford University Press, 2005).

Smith, James K. A., *How (Not) to Be Secular* (Grand Rapids: Eerdmans, 2014).

Soulen, R. Kendall, 'YHWH the Triune God', *Modern Theology* 15:1 (1999), 25–54.

Taylor, Charles, *A Secular Age* (Cambridge: Belknap, 2007).

Voltaire, 'Author's Preface to the Lisbon Earthquake'[1755–6], in *The Works of Voltaire*, William F. Fleming (trans.), vol. 36 (Chicago: DuMont, 1901).

# 10

# Spirit

*Veli-Matti Kärkkäinen*

## Introduction: A Pneumatological Renaissance

In recent years, one of the most exciting developments in theology has been an unprece-dented interest in the Holy Spirit.[1] The reverberations of this Spirit renaissance can be felt everywhere from new theological studies in the academy to publications of popular books to the emergence of new spiritual orientations and movements such as green or libera-tion pneumatology. The Roman Catholic Elizabeth Dryer vividly describes this renewed enthusiasm over pneumatology:

> Renewed interest in the Holy Spirit is visible in at least three contexts: individual Christians who hunger for a deeper connection with God that is inclusive of all of life as well as the needs of the world; the church that seeks to renew itself through life-giving disciplines and a return to sources; and the formal inquiry of academic philosophy and theology. In effect, one can hear the petition, 'Come Creator Spirit' on many lips these days . . .[2]

While there may be several reasons for the resurgence of pneumatology in our cultural and religious environment in postmodern, pluralistic societies, four somewhat interrelated reasons in theology and spirituality seem to be of decisive importance. First, the entrance of the Eastern Orthodox churches into the official ecumenical organisation, the World Council of Churches (WCC), has made the rich pneumatological and spiritual tradition of this ancient Church family more easily available to other churches. The doctrine of the Spirit has always played a more prominent role in Eastern Orthodox theology, with roots in the classical works of Athanasius, Cyril of Alexandria and the three Cappadocians (Basil the Great, his brother Gregory of Nazianzus and their friend, another Gregory, from Nyssa). The Eastern Church gives a balanced priority to pneumatology, whereas in the Christian West (Roman Catholicism, Anglicanism and Protestantism) the focus is at times placed so much on Christology that the Spirit's role appears to be somewhat marginal. The Eastern Church's cultivated pneumatological sensitivity comes to the fore in doctrine, liturgy and spirituality.

Second, the dramatic spread of the Pentecostal and charismatic movements throughout the world has made other Christians wake up to the significance of the Holy Spirit in the everyday lives of all Christians. The rise of the charismatic movement within virtually every mainstream church has ensured that the Holy Spirit figures prominently on the theological agenda. A 'new experience of the reality and power of the Spirit has had a major impact upon the theological discussion of the person and work of the Holy Spirit', remarks the Anglican Alister McGrath.[3]

Third, there is the massive and dramatic shift of the Christian Church from the Global North (Europe and North America) to Global South (Africa, Asia and Latin America). That has meant – particularly in Africa, already the most 'Christianised' continent – a new and fresh rediscovery of the charismatic element in church and personal Christian life.

Finally – and greatly surprisingly to many – increasing and more sustained contacts with other living faith traditions, whether Abrahamic (Judaism, Islam) or great Asiatic ones, has opened up Christian theology to the possibility of the spirituality/Spirit/spirits being conceived from a different perspective. Just think of Sufi Islam, a vibrant grassroots movement whose influence, similarly to the Christian charismatic phenomenon, extends widely beyond its own contours. It has helped revitalise and reinvigorate the lives of millions and millions who submit to Allah and his Spirit.

These and related developments, including the rise to the centre of theological attention the investigation into the doctrine of the Trinity and a fresh appreciation of spirituality in liturgy, have further contributed to the pneumatological renaissance. In the Christian world at large, the issuing of publications, celebration of special services and organising of lectures and research programmes related to the pneumatology witness to the continuing heightened import of the doctrine of the Spirit. An illustrative example from the world's largest Christian family, the Roman Catholic Church: In preparation for the commencement of the third millennium, it paid special attention to the spirituality of the Holy Spirit.[4] Significantly, the General Assembly of the WCC, under the overall theme 'Come Holy Spirit – Renew the Creation', already in its 1991 World Assembly focused theological reflection on various aspects of the doctrine of the Holy Spirit in relation to the Church, ecumenism and creation. Two years later, the WCC-related Faith and Order meeting was held at Santiago de Compostela, Spain, and offered a groundbreaking theological understanding between the Spirit and koinonia (communion) of the Church. Similarly, the following WCC General Assembly at Harare, Zimbabwe (1997) gave attention to pneumatological topics and founded a joint working group between Pentecostal-charismatic Christians and the WCC. One of the purposes of this team is to assess the meaning of the pneumatological renaissance for the Christian Church worldwide. And so forth.

These 'signs of the Spirit' and many others are reverberations from a renewed theological reflection on the Spirit that had already begun during previous generations of contemporary theology. It was the 'Church Father' of the twentieth century, Karl Barth, who wrote these often-quoted programmatic words towards the end of his life as he reflected on the starting point of Christian theology:

> Everything that one believes, reflects and says about God the Father and God the Son . . . would be demonstrated and clarified basically through God the Holy Spirit, the *vinculum pacis* between Father and Son. The work of God in behalf of creatures for, in, and with humanity would be made clear in a teleology which excludes all chance.[5]

Not without reason, Barth considered pneumatology a major focus of the theology of the future. And the great Russian Orthodox theologian Nikolai Berdyaev, in his fierce opposition to materialism, argued for 'The Reality of Spirit' and the search for 'The New Spirituality [for] The Realization of Spirit'.[6]

While the rise of interest in the Spirit among academicians and other theological pro-
fessionals is noteworthy, as already implied above, we should not ignore the great significance of the Spirit-experience among the ordinary Christians. The Catholic theologian
John R. Sachs asks pointedly: 'What is it that invites us, perhaps compels us, to think and
to speak about the Spirit today?' He responds himself by mentioning several reasons, such
as:

> an incredible interest today in the Spirit and spirituality. People are paying attention
> to the spiritual dimension of their lives and often seem to be experiencing the Spirit
> in ways and places that often challenge traditional theologies and Church structures
> and sometimes have little connection with traditional religious practice. The Spirit is
> present and active beyond the official structures and ordained ministries of the Church.[7]

It has been the task of the rapidly growing Pentecostal and charismatic movements to
remind the Church catholic that in the devotion to God's Spirit, it is not theology that is
primary but rather a revitalisation of the experience of the Spirit. Even though the experience of the Spirit always leads to theological reflection about its meaning, spirituality is
the first contact point.[8]

Alongside renewed and varied interest in the Spirit, a number of significant theological
'turns' have emerged beginning from the mid-twentieth century and even earlier; these
have helped reorient and re-source pneumatology, the doctrine of the Holy Spirit. Before
that, a careful look at the foundational question of the complex relation of the Spirit of
God to human (and immanent) spirit(uality), including also the divine Spirit's relation to
the 'natural' order, will be attempted. Around just these questions, there has been and, in
some quarters, still continues to be a fierce debate and a pronounced disagreement.

## On Pneumatological 'Method': The Divine, the Human, and the 'Natural'

### The Divine Spirit and the Human Experience

In his 1929 essay 'The Holy Spirit and Christian Life', Karl Barth vehemently subjected to
criticism any liberal equation between the divine Spirit and human spirit. The target of his
criticism was of course the nineteenth-century (and earlier) liberal and idealist equation
of the spirit of God with the human spirit, as exemplified in the giant of New Testament
research F. C. Baur's conception of the spirit as 'Christian consciousness'.[9] Other liberal
luminaries such as Albrecht Ritschl and Friedrich Schleiermacher represented the same
view,[10] and it continued all the way to the mid-twentieth century. Just think of the British
G. W. H. Lampe's *God as Spirit*,[11] with its deeply modalistic theology, and others.[12] As
often, Barth went to the other extreme, radically separating the two, namely the Divine
Spirit and human experience. This separation is accentuated by the fact that not only is
the human 'spirit' different from the divine Spirit because of creatureliness, but it is also
at variance with God. In other words, there is an alleged antithesis between the divine
(revelation) and human (experience).[13]

Interestingly enough, before Barth, albeit for other reasons, the nineteenth-century
biblical critic Hermann Gunkel's *The Influence of the Holy Spirit* rejected the liberal view
as not being consonant with the biblical testimonies. Ironically, while himself staying
in the liberal camp,[14] Gunkel argued that in both testaments, particularly in the first,

charismatic and other 'supernatural' effects of the Spirit are present.[15] Notwithstanding many problems in his own proposal – the details of which we need not go into here – let us acknowledge Gunkel's challenging of the immanentist liberal paradigm. That said, its liability is the resulting radical divide between the immanentist, 'natural' workings of the divine Spirit and its nature-transcending effects. This is where the contemporary leading biblical scholar on the Spirit, John Levison, joins the conversation by taking Gunkel as the main protagonist in his monumental *Filled with the Spirit*. Levison defines succinctly the main question brought about by the German scholar: 'If the spirit is to be associated exclusively with the supernatural and mysterious, what then is to be made of the spirit of life, the spirit that gives breath?'[16] This is *the* crucial question for the purposes of trying to understand the formative 'turns' in the doctrine of the Spirit in twentieth- and twenty-first-century theology. Again, Levison's own constructive proposal aside (which suffers from a total identification of the divine and human spirit in the Old Testament to the point that he chooses to put 'spirit' in lower case and, related, a failure to see that in the New Testament both the 'supernatural' and immanent works of the Spirit are present), this pointed question reflects the desire among contemporary theologians to envision the work of the Spirit both in transcendent and immanent terms. This has become a major defining trend among a variety of leading pneumatologists across the ecumenical spectrum: just think of the Eastern Orthodox John Zizioulas, the Roman Catholic Karl Rahner, the Lutheran Wolfhart Pannenberg, the Reformed Jürgen Moltmann, the Baptist/evangelical Clark Pinnock, the Pentecostal Amos Yong, among others. With distinctive nuancing and varying emphases, they all call for a mutual dynamic relationship between the divine Spirit and human experience, as well as the divine Spirit's work in the natural order. In other words, in the work of the one and the same divine Spirit there are various facets.

In sum: proposals briefly engaged in this section, namely, classical liberalism's immanentist conflation of the divine and human spirit, Barth's total separation between the human spirit and the divine Spirit, as well as Levison's incapacity to see the mutual dynamic in both testaments' view of the Spirit are being corrected in current theology. While not devoid of his own problems, particularly modalism, Paul Tillich rightly rejected Barth's separation between the divine Spirit and human experience and worked out a profound multilayered account of the Spirit, to be engaged below. Even more promisingly, Moltmann's panentheistically oriented dynamic mutual conditioning of the divine Spirit and the human spirit helps further clarify and deepen the relationship between the two.[17] He rightly insists on a mutual correlation. A dynamic balance

> is to be found in God's *immanence* in human experience, and in the *transcendence* of human beings in God. Because God's Spirit is present in human beings, the human spirit is self-transcendently aligned towards God. Anyone who stylizes revelation and experience into alternatives ends up with revelations that cannot be experienced, and experiences without revelation.[18]

The Spirit of God is not so external to human experience that it cannot be experienced (*contra* Barth), nor is the Spirit of God so much identified with the human spirit that its otherness is denied (*contra* liberalism). This dynamic correlation of the divine and human points in the same direction as Tillich's profound idea of 'ecstasy', that is, the human spirit's 'going out' (*ek-stasis*) of itself 'in' to the divine Spirit, without ceasing to be the human spirit.[19]

In other words: earlier approaches' incapacity to hold together the deep and complex continuity between the Spirit of God as she is at work in creation, providence, historical occurrences and ordinary human experiences on the one hand, and on the other, as a special gift of salvation, in celebration of sacraments, Pentecostal experiences of charismatic endowment and spiritual discernment, has been defeated by the above-mentioned scholars. The late Wolfhart Pannenberg's programmatic statement says it all:

> God's Spirit is not only active in human redemption as he teaches us to know the eternal Son of the Father in Jesus of Nazareth and moves our hearts to praise of God by faith, love, and hope. The Spirit is at work already in creation as God's breath, the origin of all movement and all life, and only against this background of his activity as the Creator of all life can we rightly understand on the one hand his work in the ecstatics of human conscious life, and on the other hand his role in the bringing forth of the new life in the resurrection of the dead.[20]

Another decisive issue for contemporary theology has to do with the relationship between two kinds of world view, as it were: one in which God's Divine Spirit's creative, sustaining and perfecting work in the world, both human and natural, is being acknowledged and celebrated, and the other, in which no such divine agency is allowed or recognised.

## The Divine Spirit and Naturalism

What the Asian-American (Malaysian-Chinese) Pentecostal theologian Amos Yong names the 'cosmology of personal agency' has a long and lasting legacy in human history and is by no means a matter only of a bygone era. In such cosmology, beyond the physical causes are spirits, even divine spirits. In contrast to this spirit-sensitivity, most people in the post-Enlightenment West live under 'natural cosmologies'[21] that are essentially monist (materialist). Notwithstanding the complexity of the issue, a safe way to define naturalism is the view 'that everything that exists is a part of nature and that there is no reality beyond or outside of nature'.[22] It is the default position of much of secular culture.[23] There are of course variations to this dual theme, such as the continuing attempts towards 'reenchantment without supernaturalism', to cite the title of a book by process philosopher David Ray Griffin.[24] Yet a 'foundational' difference exists between these two kinds of experience of the Spirit's presence or absence. Whereas for many people the Spirit-experience is the most intimate and familiar part of life, for others it is virtually unknown and abstract.

The acknowledgement of this divide is the starting point for the constructive pneumatological proposal of the Reformed German Michael Welker and his *God the Spirit*. The problem of 'the modern consciousness of the distance of God'[25] has to do with the total alienation from God of most modern (Western) people. In contrast, Welker observes, among Pentecostals/charismatics and many other Christians there is a vivid, almost child-like enthusiasm about God's presence here and now. Whereas for Pentecostals and charismatics God seems to be near, for many Christians the talk about the Spirit of God makes no sense. The secular common sense intuits God's Spirit as 'ghost'.[26] Welker blames theology for modernity's captivity to three forms of Western thought, none of which allows for the 'reality of the Spirit'. The first is 'old European metaphysics', which assumes one universal system of reference established by religion. In this scheme, the Spirit is conceived as ubiquitous, a totalising universal force or structure. Second is 'dialogical personalism', which builds on an I–Thou encounter (of Martin Buber and his followers, including Barth). In this the Spirit is that which creates and sustains divine–human (and human–human) relationship. In the third form, 'social moralism', the Kantian dream of religion as the source of progress is in the forefront; in it the human participates in God's work in the world. The first version does not allow for specific, 'charismatic' or otherwise extraordinary works of the Spirit. Although the second form is not without biblical support, in that the Spirit is the 'Go-Between', it also limits the Spirit's role to the personal, social and pious spheres. While the last form is not without its merits, it also may at its worst reduce the Spirit to a principle of moral and common human good.[27]

As a corrective to these reductionist and limited pneumatological gateways, Welker 'seeks first to articulate the broad spectrum of experiences of God's Spirit, searches and quests for the Spirit, and skepticism toward the Spirit that define the contemporary world'.[28] Instead of abstract and numinous accounts of the Spirit, 'pneumatologies of the beyond', which associate the Spirit with strange and obscure actions and experiences removed from real life, Welker seeks to speak of the Spirit and experiences of the Spirit in specific, concrete, earthly terms; this is 'realistic' pneumatology.[29] Instead of highlighting the few biblical passages that depict the Spirit as an incomprehensible, numinous power, he advises us to pay attention to the majority of references that speak about the Spirit in concrete, understandable terms.[30] That paradigm funds a 'pluralistic'[31] approach that is in keeping with the diversity and complexity of the contemporary world and the celebration of plurality in various postmodern visions.[32]

To sum up: in much of contemporary pneumatology, artificial and theologically fatal juxtapositions between the Divine Spirit and human experience, between the 'natural' and 'supernatural' workings and occurrences, as well as the immanentist and transcendent work of the Spirit, are being transcended. Related, artificial dualities between the personal and communal, between nature and person and so forth are also being defeated.

As a result, important thematic 'turns' have emerged in contemporary pneumatology. Along with these turns – and perhaps in some way also preparing them – some important theological and ecumenical steps have been taken in the painful and divisive debate about the place and status of the Spirit in the Trinity, the so-called *filioque* question. We will first briefly outline these turns and then attempt a more detailed survey and assessment of leading themes, movements and theologians of contemporary pneumatologies.

## Pneumatological 'Turns' and Their Theological Promise

### Doctrine of the Spirit Then and Now: A Brief Comparison

Even at the expense of oversimplification, by way of introduction to many details in mapping out leading themes and emphases in contemporary pneumatology, it might be useful to make a brief comparison between the past and the present. Often in the past, the doctrine of the Spirit was mainly – even though of course not exclusively – connected with certain kinds of topics and themes, particularly the doctrine of salvation in which (especially in the Christian West) the Spirit represented the 'subjective' side of the reception of salvation, whereas Christology formed the 'objective' basis. Alongside salvation, the inspiration and illumination of Scripture has been routinely linked with the Spirit. Similarly, some issues of ecclesiology and sacramentology were framed pneumatologically to complement the Christological discussion. A particularly important role for the Spirit was given in individual and communal spirituality. In various Christian traditions, from mysticism to Pietism to classical liberalism and beyond, the Spirit's work was appreciated in animating and refreshing inner spiritual life. The point made here is that although the Spirit was regularly invoked and her work highlighted, often the Spirit's role in tradition was in some sense limited to the sphere of the Church and Christian life (notwithstanding wonderful testimonies to the Spirit's role also in nature, society and the world at large among the medieval mystics, the Reformed Calvin and some others).

Without in any way leaving behind these central spheres of the Spirit, beginning from the mid-twentieth century, a more comprehensive and holistic way of doing pneumatology has also emerged. Today the Spirit is also connected with other theological topics, such as creation, environment, society, work, Christology (the so-called Spirit-Christologies) and eschatology. There is an attempt to give the Spirit a more integral and central role. Political, social, environmental, liberationist and other 'public' issues are being invoked by the theologians of the Spirit in the beginning of the third millennium. Just consider the importance of the Old Testament idea of the Spirit of God as the Spirit of Life, which has also been related to the conceptions of life in biology and natural sciences.

While, of course, there is no equating the Spirit of God with the human spirit or 'public spirit' in society, in many ways contemporary pneumatologies display a more robust continuity between the divine Spirit and human spirit. That is of course not to undermine the work of the Spirit of God as special gift of salvation, but rather to expand, so to speak, the sphere of the Spirit of God. As a result, contemporary pneumatology also expresses a desire to connect the Spirit with ethics and life, which is, after all, a thoroughly biblical idea. Furthermore, contemporary theology seeks to relate pneumatology to particular contexts, for example, allowing women to express their experience of the Spirit in a unique way. Pneumatologies of our days give voices to the poor and oppressed and to testimonies from Africa, Asia and Latin America in a way never before done in the history of reflection on the Spirit. Last but not least, contemporary theologies show an enthusiastic desire to connect the Spirit of God with the spirits of religions – in other words, to do theology of religions from a pneumatological perspective.[33]

Alongside these marked turns, as mentioned, a long-standing debate about the role and place of the Spirit in the Trinity has been revived with a view towards a more coherent and constructive understanding.

## The Place of the Spirit in Trinity: On the filioque Question

The term *filioque* – Latin for 'and from the Son' – refers to the addition by Latin Christianity to the Niceno-Constantinopolitan Creed of 381 concerning the dual procession of the Spirit both from the Son and from the Father. The original form of the Creed said that the Holy Spirit 'proceeds from the Father'. While some of the historical details are debated,[34] it is clear that in the first major breach of the Christian Church in 1054 the *filioque* clause played a major role along with political, ecclesiastical and cultural issues. The reasons for the insertion of the dual procession into the Creed are both biblical and historical – the details of which do not have to occupy us here; suffice it to say that the New Testament itself hardly gives a unanimous account of the Spirit's derivation (John 14:16, 26; 15:26; 16:7, among others).[35]

From the beginning, the Christian East has objected vigorously to this addition, claiming that it was a one-sided addition without ecumenical consultation,[36] that it compromises the monarchy of the Father as the source of divinity,[37] and that it subordinates the

Spirit to Jesus with theological corollaries in ecclesiology, the doctrine of salvation and so on.[38] Even with its exaggerations, the Eastern critique of the *filioque* is important both ecumenically and theologically and should not be dismissed.[39] The West did not have the right to unilaterally add *filioque*. At the same time, it can be argued that *filioque* is not heretical, even though ecumenically and theologically it is unacceptable and therefore should be removed. This is the growing consensus of both Protestant and Roman Catholic theologians.[40] An alternative to *filioque* that reads 'from the Father through the Son' would be acceptable also to the Christian East.[41] At the same time, it would be important for the East to be able to acknowledge the nonheretical nature of the addition.

The cash value for our discussion is this: helping rehabilitate, so to speak, the place and role of the Spirit in Trinity, in relation to the Father and Son, funds a more integral and solid pneumatological imagination and constructive theological work.

Now, the rest of the essay will delve into mapping out and assessment of the implications for the third millennium's pneumatology of these important turns and solutions. Since there is of course no way in the space of this contribution to try to give a comprehensive, detailed account of themes, issues and leading pneumatologists, suffice it to focus on key defining moves and trends by beginning from the importance of the grassroots-level experience of the Spirit manifested in the rapidly growing Pentecostal-charismatic phenomenon. Recall that the importance of the grassroots Spirit-experience among the faithful should not be dismissed; rather, its theological value and force should be duly noted.

## Towards a More Holistic, Dynamic and Comprehensive Account of the Spirit

### Pentecostal and Charismatic Experiences and Testimonies

When speaking of this rapidly growing and proliferating myriad of movements, it is useful to follow the typology suggested by *The New International Dictionary of Pentecostal and Charismatic Movements*.[42] That typology lists, first, (classical) Pentecostal denominations such as Assemblies of God or Foursquare Gospel, owing their existence to the famous Azusa Revival; second, charismatic movements, Pentecostal-type spiritual movements within the established churches (the largest of which is the Roman Catholic Charismatic Renewal); and third, neo-charismatic movements, some of the most notable of which are the Vineyard Fellowship in the US, African Initiated Churches and the China House Church movement, as well as an innumerable number of independent churches and groups all over the world. In terms of numbers, the charismatic movements (about 200 million) and neo-charismatics (200–300 million) well outnumber classical Pentecostals (75–125 million).

If there is a common denominator to this highly diverse phenomenon, it has to do with a unique spirituality. 'In Pentecostalism, as in most conservative, traditionalist, and evangelical Christian traditions, the orthodox doctrine of the Holy Spirit as divine person continues to prevail', explains Amos Yong. He adds something important:

> Yet Pentecostals go beyond many of their orthodox Christian kindred to say that the Holy Spirit continues to act in the world and interact personally with human beings and communities. In this tradition, then, there is the ongoing expectation of the Holy Spirit's answer to intercessory prayer, of the Spirit's continual and personal intervention in the affairs of the world and in the lives of believers even when not specifically prayed

for, and of the Spirit's manifestation in the charismatic or spiritual gifts (as enumerated by St. Paul in 1 Corinthians 12:4–7).[43]

Here there is a textbook example of what Welker above mentioned of the intimacy of the Spirit-experience among some Christians.

Another way of speaking of the Pentecostal view of the Spirit is to refer to the category of 'empowerment', which Harvard theologian and observer of the movement Harvey Cox names 'primal spirituality'. For Cox, this movement represents a spiritual restoration of significance and purpose to lift the people from despair and hopelessness.[44]

Whereas for most other Christians the presence of the Spirit is just that, *presence*, for Pentecostals the presence of the Spirit in their midst implies *empowerment*. While this empowerment often manifests itself in spiritual gifts such as speaking in tongues, prophesy or healings, it is still felt and sought for by Pentecostals even when those manifestations are absent. Pentecostalism has thus offered a grassroots challenge to established churches and theologies, especially those endorsing the so-called cessationist principle, which holds that miracles or extraordinary charismata ceased at or near the end of the apostolic age.[45] Often ridiculed for emotionalism, Pentecostals introduced a dynamic, enthusiastic type of spirituality and worship life to the contemporary Church, emphasising the possibility of experiencing God mystically. Pentecostals call this initial empowerment experience Spirit baptism,[46] and it is normally (but not exclusively) expected to be accompanied with speaking in tongues. Other gifts of the Spirit such as prophesying, prayer for healing, and works of miracles are enthusiastically embraced and sought for by Pentecostals. A related belief is the capacity to fight 'spiritual warfare' and exorcise demonic spirits, if necessary. This is a significant part of Pentecostal spirituality especially outside the Global North.[47]

## In Search of a Holistic Pneumatology in 'Mainstream' Theologies

For the lack of a better word, to distinguish from Pentecostal-charismatics (the previous subsection) and 'contextual'/'global' interpretations of the Spirit (the following subsection), the elusive and ambiguous term 'mainstream' is used. It refers to Catholic, Protestant and Anglican theologies of the Spirit which do not identify themselves with a particular agenda such as liberationist or feminist.[48] As mentioned above, a stated desire and tendency is to envision the work of the Holy Spirit in holistic, comprehensive and 'world-embracing' terms without subordinating the Divine to the human or natural forces.

Standing on the honourable shoulders of Karl Rahner, Yves Congar, Hans Urs von Balthasar and others,[49] among the living Roman Catholic pneumatologists few have published more widely on various aspects of the doctrine of the Spirit than the American Benedictine Fr Kilian McDonnell. He laments the limited, secondary role given to the Holy Spirit in both Catholic and Protestant theology:

In both Protestantism and Catholicism, the doctrine of the Holy Spirit, or pneumatology, has to do mostly with private, not public experience. In Protestantism, the interest in pneumatology has been largely in pietism where it is a function of interiority and inwardness. In Roman Catholicism, its dominant expression has been in books on spirituality or on the charismatic renewal, or when speaking of the structural elements of the church. In the West, we think essentially in Christological categories, with the Holy Spirit as an extra, an addendum, a 'false' window to give symmetry and balance to theological design. We build up our large theological constructs in constitutive

Christological categories, and then, in a second, nonconstitutive moment, we decorate the already constructed system with pneumatological baubles, a little Spirit tinsel.[50]

With many contemporaries, the Benedictine theologian is searching for a more inclusive, life-affirming approach to the Spirit because '[c]ontemporary theology has turned from a theology of the Word to a theology of the World'.[51] While suffering from serious modalistic tendencies, the Dutch theologian Hendrikus Berkhof's programmatic *The Doctrine of the Holy Spirit* (1964) had already issued a similar call. The Spirit, the 'vitality' of God, 'God's inspiring breath by which he grants life in creation and re-creation'[52] works in the world but also in salvation (or regeneration, as Berkhof wishes to name it).[53] Berkhof's view of the Spirit was inclusive and universalistic, building on the long Reformed tradition from John Calvin all the way to Abraham Kuyper. Echoing the latter, Berkhof concludes that

> the Spirit of God also inspires man's culture. The Old Testament connects him with agriculture, architecture, jurisdiction, and politics (Cyrus as God's anointed one!). In general all human wisdom is the gift of God's Spirit. This relation between the Spirit and creation is much neglected in Christian thinking.[54]

In other words, 'The Spirit is not locked up in the church.'[55]

At about the same time as Berkhof, a powerful push towards an even more comprehensive and multilayered account of the Spirit came from the Lutheran liberal theologian Paul Tillich. Importantly to him, as in tradition, pneumatology was not part of the doctrine of grace or ecclesiology but occupied an important, separate place in dogmatics, in volume 3 of his *Systematic Theology*. Its title, 'Life and the Spirit',[56] gives a clue about the underlying vision. Tillich's main goal is not only to connect theology and culture – the main motif of this theology – but also to attempt to transcend the dividing line between the Spirit and spirit. For Tillich, the Spirit of God is the life-giving principle that makes human life and the life of the whole creation meaningful and specific. Thus, Tillich was

> concerned with binding together God and the world, or more precisely, God as Spirit and the human person as spirit. Ecstasy occurs when the human being as spirit is grasped by the divine Spirit. For Tillich, 'human spirit' means more than human nature and embraces the whole human reality: morality, culture and religion. The role of the Spirit in Tillich's theology is neither the churchy Spirit of ecclesiastical piety, nor the experiential Spirit of pietism, but the universalist Spirit who bridges all the gaps.[57]

Widely regarded as the most significant and undoubtedly most widely debated contemporary pneumatological proposal is that of Moltmann, *The Spirit of Life* (1992). Having already made important contributions to the doctrine of the Holy Spirit in a number of theological works, including the Church, Trinity, creation and Christology, this monograph argues for a new kind of paradigm. The (original German) subtitle, 'A Holistic Pneumatology', communicates well the main goal. Moltmann sees the Spirit of God at work everywhere there is promotion of life, growth, inclusivity and reaching for one's potential; conversely, whatever destroys, eliminates, frustrates and violates life is not from the Spirit of God. Moltmann laments the approach to the Spirit in mainline theology which tends, on the one hand, to regulate the Spirit's movements within the confines of the Church structures and, on the other hand, to limit the Spirit's sphere of operation to the work of redemption alone. In this outlook, the Spirit is 'cut off both from bodily life and from the life of nature'.[58] He reminds us that in the biblical understanding the word *spirit* does not denote something antithetical to matter and body; rather, 'spirit' in the Bible refers to life-giving force and energy.[59] The expression that Moltmann uses to describe his panentheistic orientation to pneumatology is 'immanent transcendence'.[60]

Though more traditional in his approach, the Reformed Moltmann's late Lutheran colleague Pannenberg, in his search for a world-embracing pneumatology, laboured distinctively in the science-theology field. While not without its critics, Pannenberg's linking of the Spirit with the 'force field' concept borrowed from contemporary physics (Michael Faraday and others) is an interesting theological experiment: '[T]he presence of God's Spirit in his creation can be described as a field of creative presence, a comprehensive field of force that releases event after event into finite existence.'[61] Pannenberg sees in this parallel great potential for faith and science dialogue. While the biblical view of life as the function of the Spirit of life and the modern scientific view of life as the function of the living cell as a self-sustaining and reproducing system are not identical, the move in contemporary science towards understanding explanations built on movement and energy has provided theology new prospects. From a theological perspective he surmises that the Spirit as life-principle corresponds to the scientific idea of force field.[62] Joining science-religion experiments with great expertise, the Anglican clergyman and particle physicist from England John Polkinghorne speaks of the hidden presence of the Spirit of God in the world created by God. In this understanding, 'the sanctifying work of the Spirit is a continuing activity that awaits its final completion in the creation of the community of the redeemed, a consummation that will be manifested fully only at the eschaton'. On this basis, Polkinghorne is convinced that some kind of congruence between the insights of science and theology can be on the horizon.[63]

Alongside these various yet in many ways interrelated attempts to widen, make more comprehensive and reconceive for the sake of the contemporary world the account of the Spirit, a large number of various kinds of 'contextual' or 'global' theologians have laboured on seeking to connect Spirit with agendas such as gender, liberation, environment, sociopolitical equality and the religio-cultural context of Africa, Asia and Latin America.

# In Search of Contextual and Global Accounts of the Spirit

*Emerging Interpretations of the Spirit from the Margins: Liberationist Pneumatologies*

While Christian theology, including pneumatology, up until the last decades of the second millennium has been predominantly the business of white male theologians from Europe and North America, that limitation is undergoing energetic challenging, balancing and enriching as female theologians of diverse backgrounds – the feminist (white women), womanist (African-American women), *mujerista* (Hispanic/Latina women) and others – have joined forces with other liberationists such as sociopolitically oriented Black theology as well as theologians with agendas such as care for the environment in producing a more inclusive account of the Spirit. Calling these theologies interpretations from the margins is only half-truth: women alone outnumber men in churches and often are the main religious educators at home.

A form of liberation theology, feminist theology, in keeping with the biblical prophetic tradition, reminds us that 'the Spirit's presence is consistently linked with the power to denounce social wrongdoing, announce comfort for those who are suffering, and bring about justice for the poor'.[64] The Day of Pentecost is rightly hailed as the day when the liberating work of the Holy Spirit was manifest and visible. Both men and women, the free and the slaves, were recipients of God's empowering spiritual power.[65] Feminist theologians' focus on the feminine or maternal characteristics of the Holy Spirit helps counterbalance masculine pronouns for Father and Son. This is of course nothing totally foreign to Christian tradition, nor has it been properly appreciated. Applying feminine images to the Spirit is biblically legitimate since in the Bible the role of the Spirit involves activities more usually associated with maternity and femininity in general: inspiring, helping, supporting, enveloping, bringing to birth and similar. Of all the Trinitarian persons, the Holy Spirit is more often related to intimacy. Rosemary Radford Ruether reminds us that the 'identification of the roles of Wisdom with a masculine Logos-Christ' 'largely repressed any development of a female personification of the divine, based on the figure of Wisdom, in the writings of church fathers'.[66] Consequently, balancing and diverse metaphors of the Spirit are needed.

An essential aspect of the world-embracing, holistic and inclusive account of the Spirit's work in life is the Spirit's role in the environment and nature. 'Of all the activities that theology attributes to the Spirit, the most significant is this: the Spirit is the creative origin of all life . . . [T]he Spirit is the unceasing, dynamic flow of divine power that sustains the universe, bringing forth life.'[67] The Catholic feminist Elizabeth Johnson appeals to Christians to see the ministry of the Spirit – the same Spirit that raised Jesus Christ to new incorruptible life – also in the natural sphere, particularly in midst of the 'damaged earth, violent and unjust social structures, the lonely and broken heart', all of whom 'cry out for a fresh start'. The Creator Spirit comes to this suffering, abyss and devastation 'to wash what is unclean; to pour water upon what is drought-stricken; to heal what is hurt; to loosen up what is rigid; to warm what is freezing; to straighten out what is crooked and bent'.[68] Other 'green' pneumatologists have joined in the common reflection on the role of the Spirit in renewing and preserving nature. Mark I. Wallace's *Fragments of the Spirit: Nature, Violence, and the Renewal of Creation*[69] seeks to rediscover in the theological tradition resources for a green pneumatology based on the idea of a biocentric role of the Spirit as the Giver of Life. The Spirit is best understood not as a metaphysical entity but as a healing life-force. He argues that if the Spirit and the earth condition each other, then God as Spirit is vulnerable to the dramatic effects of ecocide. In his book *Finding God in the Singing River*, Wallace uses a striking metaphor when he wants to 'retrieve a central but neglected Christian theme – the idea of God as carnal Spirit who imbues all things – as the linchpin for forging a green spirituality responsive to the environmental needs of our time'. This is in keeping with the observation that the biblical texts do not 'divorce the spiritual from the earthly, but, moreover, they figure the Spirit as a creaturely life-form interpenetrated by the material world'.[70]

Other alternative and complementary approaches to pneumatology can be found in contemporary theology such as the politically oriented *God's Spirit: Transforming a World in Crisis* by Geiko Müller-Fahrenholz[71] and *Work in the Spirit* by Miroslav Volf,[72] which relate pneumatological discussion to political realities and to work.

## Spirit Testimonies from the Global South

Christian theology can no longer be done only from the perspective of Euro-American cultures. The majority of all Christians can be found in the Global South, in the continents of Asia, Africa and Latin America. While academic theology is still dominated by views of (mostly) white (male) theologians with strong European flavour, a burgeoning theological creativity is happening all over the world as theologians from Asia, Africa and Latin America join the conversation and help the global Church to come to a more adequate and inclusive understanding of theology.

The Latin American context is deeply shaped by not only folk religiosity but also the influence of Catholic piety and the rapidly growing Pentecostal and charismatic movements, including their importance to the Roman Catholic Church. While generalisations are just that, namely *generalisations*, there is much truth in the saying that whereas in Africa theology begins with a shout of joy, in Latin America theological reflection starts from a cry of despair.[73] The Roman Catholic Belgian-born Brazilian José Comblin reminds us in his important work *The Holy Spirit and Liberation* that whereas too often Western theology and liturgy have lost interest in the Holy Spirit, now 'the new experience Christians are finding in those communities that aspire to the integral liberation of the peoples of the continent of Latin America is precisely an experience of the Holy Spirit'.[74] While socially and politically oriented, Liberation theology is essentially spiritual theology, as is illustrated in the book title of another Brazilian, Jon Sobrino, *Spirituality of Liberation: Toward Political Holiness*. 'Spirituality is no less a prime dimension of the theology of liberation than is liberation itself. Spirituality and liberation call for one another.'[75]

No wonder several Latin American theologians have called on the Church for a renewed concern for the poor and underprivileged:

> Those who conform to the movement of the Spirit by forming communities made up of friends meeting in people's houses are the poor . . . The ruling classes want a church organized from the top down; the poor want a church built from the bottom up: they are the ones in conformity with the will of the Spirit. The Spirit works by founding new base communities, from which springs new life . . . The Spirit is the one who gathers the poor together so as to make them a new people who will challenge all the powers of the earth. The Spirit is the strength of the people of the poor, the strength of those who are weak. Without the Spirit, the poor would not raise their voices and conflict would not raise its head.[76]

Differently from Europe and North America, in the African context religion permeates all aspects of life (very similarly to the Asian and Latin American contexts). In the words of the premier Kenyan theologian John Mbiti, 'there is no formal distinction between the sacred and the secular' or between 'the spiritual and material areas of life'.[77] For Africans, the world of the spirits is as real as the visible world, perhaps even more real. The visible world is 'enveloped in the invisible spirit world'.[78] Consequently, rather than the 'distance of the Spirit' (Welker), there is the 'cosmology of personal agency' at work everywhere. In many African cultures, living in a close relation to God are the spirits, including ancestors. Called by various names, these are real powers, created by God to mediate his power. Among the spirits, ancestors, living closer to the living community, are a central feature of all African religiosity.

Ironically, though, African theologians lament that much of theologising in Africa, created and mentored by Christians from outside, lacks the vitality of pneumatology. A main reason is the secular and thus less spiritual mindset of people, including many missionaries from the Global North.[79] This is also the reason for the 'irresistible attraction of the modern pentecostal movement as represented in the Independent Churches in Africa' with its appeal to spiritual power here and now.[80]

In the words of the Sri Lankan Roman Catholic liberationist Aloysius Pieris, '[t]he Asian context can be described as a blend of a profound religiosity (which is perhaps Asia's greatest wealth) and an overwhelming poverty'.[81] Asian religiosity is rich and variegated and, as mentioned, touches all aspects of life. In contrast to the Western modernist dualism between the sacred and secular, for most Asians not only is religion an irreducible part of all life but also undergirds beliefs, decisions and behaviour of everyday life. Even with rapid developments in technology and education, Hinduism, Buddhism, Confucianism and a host of other religions, most of them manifested in forms that used to be called 'animistic' (having to do with spirits), permeate all of life. Much as in Africa, religion is visible and part of everyday life. Thus, talk about God/gods can be carried on everywhere, from the street markets to luxurious hotels to desperate slums to exotic restaurants. 'The spirit-world is alive and is doing well in Asia.'[82]

Similarly to their African counterparts, theologians from Asia have employed a number of pregnant metaphors and symbols drawn from their own soil to illustrate the nature and ministry of the Holy Spirit, such as the Taoist tao, 'which is characterized by the receptiveness of change. Like the Holy Spirit, tao is patient and yielding. It changes, without intent, like buds opening. It accomplishes everything by inaction.'[83] Another famous Asian set of concepts, yin and yang, has likewise been utilised in various ways. Yin, which usually denotes femininity – in a mutually conditioning relation to yang masculinity – is an appropriate way of speaking of the Spirit as 'she', in female and maternal images. 'The abstruseness of the Spirit in the Trinity has to do with her pervasiveness. She is present everywhere and at all times, and is known in both personal and impersonal categories.'[84]

In the multireligious environment of Asian lands, the question of the relation of the Spirit of God to other spirits has become a burning issue. According to the Indian theologian and ecumenist and one-time director of the World Council of Churches' Interfaith Department, Stanley J. Samartha, this question has 'somewhat aggressively thrust itself on the theological consciousness of the church' in recent years.[85] Ironically, however, Samartha notes:

> In many theology textbooks, even those devoted particularly to the work of the Holy Spirit, one looks in vain for a careful, sympathetic, and extended treatment of the work of the Spirit in relation to the life and thought of people of other faiths, cultures, and ideologies.[86]

It is to be expected that in the beginning of the third millennium Asian theologians will take leadership in helping the Christian Church grasp in a more adequate way the complexities of the 'spiritual discernment'.

## Concluding Words: Whither Pneumatology of the Third Millennium?

The rapid and wide interest in the Holy Spirit in contemporary ecumenical and international theology, both in academia and among the faithful in Christian communities, has energised new discoveries and insights. Whereas in much of traditional theology, particularly in pre-modern traditions, there was a marked difference between the divine Spirit and human experience, in the post-Enlightenment liberal interpretations, those two got virtually equated, thus allotting any surplus to the Spirit of God. While Barth's attempt to separate again the divine and human does not serve as a constructive proposal, he helped contemporary theology to continue pondering upon a more dynamic and mutual relationship. Guided by Tillich, Berkhof and a number of Catholic theologians, most recent pneumatological work has been successful in imagining the work and presence of the Spirit of God in the world in diverse, dynamic and multilayered terms.

If the Spirit of God, as the Bible testifies, is present everywhere (Psalms 104:29–30; 139:7–12), it does not do to relate pneumatology only to the inner spirituality of the Christian and the sphere of the Church, as important as they may be. Rather, the Spirit's work, as is evident in much of the most recent literature consulted above, is related to all aspects of the world God has created, is sustaining and will be consummating. A telling example of this kind of daring and bold experimentation in 'loosing the Spirit(s)' is a recent collection of essays titled *Interdisciplinary and Religio-Cultural Discourses on a Spirit-Filled World: Loosing the Spirits* (2013). As the contents of this volume make plain, there is an immense breadth to this contemporary pneumatological search, with chapters from international authors treating the theme in relation to history, art, politics, economics, biological evolution, interreligious and intercultural dialogue and more besides.[87] Even this partial list of the topics engaged provides a fairly reliable forecast of the directions to be taken in the continuing probing into the mysteries and works of the Spirit of God. It is going to be interdisciplinary, it will engage all kinds of issues in history, society and cosmos, and it will also include a definite interreligious component. At the same time, classical topics related to Trinity and the Spirit's role therein, soteriology (doctrine of salvation), particularly as it relates to the needs and issues of the secular and religiously pluralistic contexts of our times, Church and sacraments and, say, the inspiration and interpretation of Scripture will in no way be ignored.

An inviting feast of the Spirit it will be, indeed! And for sure, it comes to us, to cite the telling title of the late British missionary bishop's autobiography, with *Unfinished Agenda*.[88]

# Notes

1. This chapter is based on and repeats materials (often merely with minor changes and revisions) from the following writings of mine: *Pneumatology: The Holy Spirit in Ecumenical, International, and Contextual Perspectives*, 2nd rev. ed. (Grand Rapids: Baker Academic Books, 2018), chh. 1, 5, 6, 7 and Epilogue; *Spirit and Salvation: A Constructive Christian Theology for the Pluralistic World*, vol. 4 (Grand Rapids: Eerdmans, 2016), part 1; *Holy Spirit: A Guide to Christian Theology* (Louisville, KY: Westminster John Knox Press, 2012), chh. 1, 7 and 8. I have also consulted widely *Holy Spirit and Salvation: The Sources of Christian Theology* (Louisville, KY: Westminster John Knox Press, 2010).

2. Elizabeth A. Dreyer, 'An Advent of the Spirit: Medieval Mystics and Saints', in *Advents of the Spirit: An Introduction to the Current Study of Pneumatology*, edited by Bradford E. Hinze and D. Lyle Dabney (Milwaukee: Marquette University Press, 2001), p. 123.

3. Alister McGrath, *Christian Theology: An Introduction*, 5th ed. (Oxford: John Wiley & Sons, 2011), p. 227.

4. John Paul II, *Celebrate 2000!: Reflections on the Holy Spirit: Weekly Readings for 1998*, selected and arranged by Paul Thigpen (Ann Arbor: Servant Publications, 1997).

5. *Schleiermacher-Auswahl mit einem Nachwort von Karl Barth*, p. 311, as cited in McDonnell, 'A Trinitarian Theology of the Holy Spirit?', *Theological Studies* 46:2 (1985), 191–227: 193.

6. Chapter titles (1 and 7, respectively) in Nikolai Berdyaev, *Spirit and Reality* (London: G. Bles, [1939] 1946).

7. John R. Sachs, '"Do Not Stifle the Spirit": Karl Rahner, the Legacy of Vatican II, and Its Urgency for Theology Today', in *Catholic Theological Society Proceedings* 51 (1996), edited by E. Dreyer, p. 15.

8. See further Kilian McDonnell, 'Theological Presuppositions in Our Preaching about the Spirit', *Theological Studies* 59:2 (1998), 219–35.

9. F. C. Baur, *Paul the Apostle of Jesus Christ, His Life and Work, His Epistles and His Doctrine*, A. Menzies (trans.), vol. 2 (London: William and Norgate, 1875), part 3, p. 123.

10. For Schleiermacher's view of the Spirit, see Veli-Matti Kärkkäinen (ed.), *Holy Spirit and Salvation*, pp. 241–6.

11. G. W. H. Lampe, *God as Spirit* (Oxford: Clarendon, 1977).

12. For a detailed discussion of G. W. H. Lampe, G. Gerlemann, Alfred Bertholet and others, see John R. Levison, *Filled with the Spirit* (Grand Rapids: Eerdmans, 2009), pp. 8–11.

13. Karl Barth, 'The Holy Spirit and Christian Life', Michael Raburn (trans.) (2002), accessed at http://www.academia.edu/11930438/Karl_Barth_The_Holy_Spirit_and_the_Christian_Life.

14. An ironic indication of the deep influence of modernism and liberalism on Gunkel's own view of the Spirit, though, is that he adopted the secessionist downplaying of the miraculous view of his own times. See Hermann Gunkel, *The Influence of the Holy Spirit: The Popular View of the Apostolic Age and the Teaching of the Apostle Paul*, R. A. Harrisville and P. A. Quanbeck II (trans.) (Philadelphia: Fortress, [1888] 1979), pp. 1–5 ('Author's Preface to the Second and Third German Editions').

15. See particularly his comparative statement (between the two testaments) in Gunkel, *Influence of the Holy Spirit*, pp. 48–9.

16. Levison, *Filled with the Spirit*, p. 7.

17. In Veli-Matti Kärkkäinen, *Trinity and Revelation: A Constructive Christian Theology for the Pluralistic World*, vol. 4 (Grand Rapids: Eerdmans, 2014), ch. 10, a novel proposal of 'classical panentheism' is presented and defended. While not to be identified with Moltmann's panentheism, it shares important common features with it as well as with a number of other, similar kinds of moderate panentheism in various strands of current theology.

18. Jürgen Moltmann, *The Spirit of Life: A Universal Affirmation*, Margaret Kohl (trans.) (Minneapolis: Fortress, 2001), p. 7, emphasis in original. Similarly, Barth's dichotomist view is rejected by George S. Hendry, *The Holy Spirit in Christian Theology* (London: SCM Press, 1965), pp. 96–117.

19. Paul Tillich, *Systematic Theology*, vol. 3 (Chicago: University Press of Chicago, 1963), pp. 111–12.

20. Wolfhart Pannenberg, *Systematic Theology*, vol. 3, Geoffrey W. Bromiley (trans.) (Grand Rapids: Eerdmans, 1998), p. 1.

21. Amos Yong, 'On Binding, and Loosing, the Spirits: Navigating and Engaging a Spirit-Filled World', in *Interdisciplinary and Religo-Cultural Discourses on a Spirit-Filled World: Loosing the Spirits*, edited by Veli-Matti Kärkkäinen, Kirsteen Kim and Amos Yong (New York: Palgrave Macmillan, 2013), pp. 1–13: 4–5.

22. Stewart Goetz and Charles Taliaferro, *Naturalism* (Grand Rapids: Eerdmans, 2008), p. 6.

23. For a typology of naturalisms and its theological implications, see Veli-Matti Kärkkäinen, *Creation and Humanity: A Constructive Christian Theology for the Pluralistic World*, vol. 3 (Grand Rapids: Eerdmans, 2015), pp. 31–9.

24. David Ray Griffin, *Reenchantment without Supernaturalism: A Process Philosophy of Religion* (Ithaca, NY: Cornell University Press, 2001).

25. The title for ch. 1 in Michael Welker, *God the Spirit: A Problem of Experience in Today's World*, John F. Hoffmeyer (trans.) (Minneapolis: Fortress, 1994).

26. Welker, *God the Spirit*, pp. 1–13.

27. Welker, *God the Spirit*, pp. 40–9.

28. Welker, *God the Spirit*, p. ix.

29. Welker, *God the Spirit*, pp. 46–9; see also pp. 338–9.

30. Welker, *God the Spirit*, pp. 50–1.
31. Welker, *God the Spirit*, pp. 21–7.
32. Welker, *God the Spirit*, pp. xii, 28–40.
33. See further Veli-Matti Kärkkäinen, 'Spirit(s) in Contemporary Christian Theology: An Interim Report of the Unbinding of Pneumatology', in *Interdisciplinary and Religio-Cultural Discourses on a Spirit-Filled World: Loosing the Spirits*, edited by Veli-Matti Kärkkäinen, Kirsteen Kim and Amos Yong (New York: Palgrave Macmillan, 2013), pp. 29–40; Veli-Matti Kärkkäinen, 'Holy Spirit and Other Spirits: An Interim Report of the State of the Theology of the Holy Spirit in a Contemporary Pluralistic World', *Catalyst: Contemporary Evangelical Resources for United Methodist Seminarians*, online journal (26 March 2014), accessed at http://www.catalystresour ces.org/holy-spirit-and-other-spirits/.
34. The standard view is that this addition was first accepted by the Council of Toledo in 589 and ratified by the 809 Aachen Synod. It was incorporated in later creeds such as that of the Fourth Lateran Council in 1215 and the Council of Lyons in 1274.
35. Against the standard view, Richard Haugh surmises that the addition happened just by way of transposition without any conscious theological reason. Richard Haugh, *Photius and the Carolingians: The Trinitarian Controversy* (Belmont, MA: Norland, 1975), pp. 160–1.
36. 'Can a clause deriving from one theological tradition simply be inserted in a creed deriving from another theological tradition without council?', in *Spirit of Truth*, p. 32.
37. It is an established view in the East that the Father is the 'source' (*arche*) of the divinity. In defence, see e.g. Kallistos Ware, *The Orthodox Church* (New York: Penguin Books, 1993), pp. 210–14.
38. Vladimir Lossky has most dramatically articulated the charge of 'Christomonism' against Western theology. According to him, Christianity in the West is seen as unilaterally referring to Christ, the Spirit being an addition to the Church, to its ministries and sacraments. Vladimir Lossky, 'The Procession of the Holy Spirit in Orthodox Trinitarian Doctrine', in John H. Erickson and Thomas E. Bird (eds), *In the Image and Likeness of God* (Crestwood, NY: St. Vladimir's Seminary Press, 1974), pp. 71–96. See also Nikos A. Nissiotis, 'The Main Ecclesiological Problem of the Second Vatican Council and Position of the Non-Roman Churches Facing It', *Journal of Ecumenical Studies* 2:1 (1965), 31–62. All of these three objections – that it was a unilateral act, that it subordinates the Son to the Spirit and that it compromises the Father's monarchy – were already presented by the most vocal critic in history, the ninth-century patriarch of Constantinople, Photius, in his *On the Mystagogy of the Holy Spirit* (Astoria, NY: Studion Publications, 1983), pp. 51–2, 71–2 especially.
39. For an important Orthodox statement, see Nick Needham, 'The Filioque Clause: East or West?', *Scottish Bulletin of Evangelical Theology* 15 (1997), 142–62.
40. So e.g. Wolfhart Pannenberg, *Systematic Theology*, vol. 1, Geoffrey W. Bromiley (trans.) (Grand Rapids: Eerdmans, 1991), p. 319. For a helpful discussion, see Lukas Vischer (ed.), *Spirit of God, Spirit of Christ: Ecumenical Reflections on the Filioque Controversy* (London: SPCK/Geneva: WCC Publications, 1981). Only a tiny majority of contemporary Western theologians support the addition. The best-known advocate of *filioque* was Karl Barth, who feared that dismissing it would mean ignoring the biblical insistence on the Spirit being the Spirit of the Son. See Barth, *Church Dogmatics*, vol. 1, part 1, p. 480.
41. Boris Bobrinskoy, *The Mystery of the Trinity: Trinitarian Experience and Vision in the Biblical and Patristic Tradition*, Anthony P. Gythiel (trans.) (Crestwood, NY: St. Vladimir's Seminary Press, 1999), pp. 302–3.
42. Stanley M. Burgess and Eduard M. van der Maas (eds), *The New International Dictionary of Pentecostal and Charismatic Movements*, rev. and expanded ed. (Grand Rapids: Zondervan, 2002).
43. Yong, '"The Spirit Hovers over the World": Toward a Typology of "Spirit" in the Religion and Science Dialogue', online essay, *Metanexus* (16 October 2004), accessed at http://www.metane xus.net/spirit-hovers-over-world/.

44. Harvey Cox, *Fire from Heaven: The Rise of Pentecostal Spirituality and the Reshaping of Religion in the Twenty-First Century* (Reading, MA: Addison-Wesley, 1995), pp. 81–2.

45. See further Cox, *Fire from Heaven*, pp. 299–301.

46. See Frank Macchia, 'Baptized in the Spirit: Towards a Global Theology of Spirit Baptism', in *The Spirit in the World: Emerging Pentecostal Theologies in Global Context*, edited by Veli-Matti Kärkkäinen (Grand Rapids: Eerdmans, 2009), pp. 3–20.

47. See further Yong, 'The Demonic in Pentecostal-Charismatic Christianity and in the Religious Consciousness of Asia', in *Asian and Pentecostal: The Charismatic Face of Christianity in Asia*, edited by Allan Anderson and Edmond Tang, 2nd rev. ed. (Eugene, OR: Wipf and Stock, 2011), pp. 73–102.

48. That I am not focusing here on Orthodox pneumatologies whose emphasis is on the mystical, spiritual and sacramental domains without in any way undermining cosmic and natural dimensions is just because of the brevity of space. The interested reader may consult Kärkkäinen, *Pneumatology*, pp. 106–10.

49. For a survey, see Kärkkäinen, *Pneumatology*, pp. 111–19.

50. Kilian McDonnell, 'The Determinative Doctrine of the Holy Spirit', *Theology Today* 39:2 (1982), 142–61: 142.

51. McDonnell, 'The Determinative Doctrine', p. 142. See also his magnum opus *The Other Hand of God: The Holy Spirit as the Universal Touch and Goal* (Collegeville, MN: Michael Glazier Books, 2003).

52. Hendrikus Berkhof, *The Doctrine of the Holy Spirit* (Atlanta: John Knox Press, 1964), p. 14.

53. Berkhof, *The Doctrine of the Holy Spirit*, pp. 69–70.

54. Berkhof, *The Doctrine of the Holy Spirit*, pp. 95–6.

55. Berkhof, *The Doctrine of the Holy Spirit*, p. 104.

56. Tillich, *Systematic Theology*, vol. 3, pp. 11–294.

57. As explained by the Catholic commentator McDonnell in 'The Determinative Doctrine of the Holy Spirit', p. 155.

58. Moltmann, *The Spirit of Life*, p. 8; also p. 2.

59. Moltmann, *The Spirit of Life*, p. 40.

60. Moltmann, *The Spirit of Life*, p. 35.

61. Wolfhart Pannenberg, *An Introduction to Systematic Theology* (Grand Rapids: Eerdmans, 1991), pp. 383–4.

62. Wolfhart Pannenberg, *Systematic Theology*, vol. 2, Geoffrey W. Bromiley (trans.) (Grand Rapids: Eerdmans 1994), pp. 76–84.

63. John Polkinghorne, 'The Hidden Spirit and the Cosmos', in *The Work of the Spirit: Pneumatology and Pentecostalism*, edited by Michael Welker (Grand Rapids, Eerdmans: 2006), pp. 169–82: 171.

64. Johnson, *She Who Is*, p. 136.

65. Victoria B. Demarest, *Sex and Spirit: God, Woman and Ministry* (St Petersburg: Sacred Arts International, 1977), pp. 38–9.

66. Rosemary Radford Ruether, *Goddesses and the Divine Feminine: A Wisdom Religious History* (Berkeley: University of California Press, 2005), p. 132.

67. Elizabeth A. Johnson, *Women, Earth and Creator Spirit* (Mahwah, NJ: Paulist Press, 1993), p. 42.

68. Johnson, *Women, Earth and Creator Spirit*, p. 43.

69. Mark I. Wallace, *Fragments of the Spirit: Nature, Violence, and the Renewal of Creation* (New York: Continuum, 1996).

70. Mark I. Wallace, *Finding God in the Singing River* (Minneapolis: Augsburg Fortress, 2005), pp. 6, 8 respectively.

71. Geiko Müller-Fahrenholz, *God's Spirit: Transforming a World in Crisis*, John Cumming (trans.) (New York: Continuum, 1995).

72. Miroslav Volf, *Work in the Spirit: Toward a Theology of Work* (Eugene, OR: Wipf and Stock, 2001).

73. See further William Dyrness, *Learning about Theology from the Third World* (Grand Rapids: Zondervan, 1990), pp. 71–2.

74. José Comblin, *The Holy Spirit and Liberation*, Paul Burns (trans.) (Maryknoll, NY: Orbis, 1989), p. xi.

75. Jon Sobrino, *Spirituality of Liberation: Toward Political Holiness*, Robert R. Barr (trans.) (Maryknoll, NY: Orbis, 1988), p. 49.

76. Comblin, *The Holy Spirit and Liberation*, pp. 94–5, 99.

77. John S. Mbiti, *African Religions and Philosophy* (London: Heinemann, 1969), p. 2.

78. Tokunboh Adeyemo, 'Unapproachable God: The High God of African Traditional Religion', in *The Global God: Multicultural Evangelical Views of God*, edited by Aída Besançon Spencer and William David Spencer (Grand Rapids: Baker, 1998), pp. 127–45: 130–1.

79. Osadolor Imasogie, *Guidelines for Christian Theology in Africa* (Achimota, Ghana: Africa Christian Press, 1993), p. 81.

80. Imasogie, *Guidelines for Christian Theology in Africa*, p. 81.

81. Aloysius Pieris, 'Western Christianity and Asian Buddhism: A Theological Reading of Historical Encounters', *Dialogue* 7 (May–August 1980), 49–85: 61–2.

82. Yeow Choo Lak, 'Preface', in *Doing Theology with the Spirit's Movement in Asia*, in *Doing Theology with the Spirit's Movement in Asia*, edited by John C. England and Alan J. Torrance (Singapore: ATESEA, 1991), p. vi.

83. Jung Young Lee, *The Theology of Change: A Christian Concept of God in an Eastern Perspective* (Maryknoll, NY: Orbis, 1979), p. 110.

84. Jung Young Lee, *The Trinity in Asian Perspective* (Nashville: Abingdon, 1996), p. 95.

85. Stanley J. Samartha, *Between Two Cultures: Ecumenical Ministry in a Pluralist World* (Geneva: WCC Publications, 1996), p. 187.

86. Stanley J. Samartha, *Courage for Dialogue: Ecumenical Issues in Inter-Religious Relationships* (Geneva: WCC Publications, 1981), p. 76.

87. All essays in Veli-Matti Kärkkäinen, Kirsteen Kim and Amos Yong (eds), *Interdisciplinary and Religio-Cultural Discourses on a Spirit-Filled World: Loosing the Spirits* (New York: Palgrave Macmillan, 2013).

88. Lesslie Newbigin, *Unfinished Agenda: An Autobiography* (Grand Rapids: Eerdmans, 1985).

# Bibliography

Adeyemo, Tokunboh, 'Unapproachable God: The High God of African Traditional Religion', in *The Global God: Multicultural Evangelical Views of God*, edited by Aída Besançon Spencer and William David Spencer (Grand Rapids: Baker, 1998), pp. 127–45.

Barth, Karl, *Church Dogmatics*, vol. 1, part 1, G. W. Bromiley and T. F. Torrance (eds) (Edinburgh: T&T Clark, 1956).

Barth, Karl, 'The Holy Spirit and Christian Life', Michael Raburn (trans.) (2002), accessed at http://www.academia.edu/11930438/Karl_Barth_The_Holy_Spirit_and_the_Christian_Life.

Baur, F. C., *Paul the Apostle of Jesus Christ, His Life and Work, His Epistles and His Doctrine*, A. Menzies (trans.), vol. 2 (London: William and Norgate, 1875).

Berdyaev, Nikolai, *Spirit and Reality* (London: G. Bles, [1939] 1946).

Berkhof, Hendrikus, *The Doctrine of the Holy Spirit* (Atlanta: John Knox Press, 1964).

Bobrinskoy, Boris, *The Mystery of the Trinity: Trinitarian Experience and Vision in the Biblical and Patristic Tradition*, Anthony P. Gythiel (trans.) (Crestwood, NY: St. Vladimir's Seminary Press, 1999).

Bolli, Heinz (ed.), *Schleiermacher-Auswahl mit einem Nachwort von Karl Barth*, (Munich: Siebenstern-Taschenbuch, 1968).

Burgess, Stanley M. and Eduard M. van der Maas (eds), *The New International Dictionary of Pentecostal and Charismatic Movements*, rev. and expanded ed. (Grand Rapids: Zondervan, 2002).

Comblin, José, *The Holy Spirit and Liberation*, Paul Burns (trans.) (Maryknoll, NY: Orbis, 1989).

Cox, Harvey, *Fire from Heaven: The Rise of Pentecostal Spirituality and the Reshaping of Religion in the Twenty-First Century* (Reading, MA: Addison-Wesley, 1995).

Demarest, Victoria B., *Sex and Spirit: God, Woman and Ministry* (St Petersburg: Sacred Arts International, 1977).

Dreyer, Elizabeth A., 'An Advent of the Spirit: Medieval Mystics and Saints', in Bradford E. Hinze and D. Lyle Dabney (eds), *Advents of the Spirit: An Introduction to the Current Study of Pneumatology* (Milwaukee: Marquette University Press, 2001).

Dyrness, William, *Learning about Theology from the Third World* (Grand Rapids: Zondervan, 1990).

Haugh, Richard, *Photius and the Carolingians: The Trinitarian Controversy* (Belmont, MA: Norland, 1975).

Hendry, George S., *The Holy Spirit in Christian Theology* (London: SCM Press, 1965).

Goetz, Stewart and Charles Taliaferro, *Naturalism* (Grand Rapids: Eerdmans, 2008).

Griffin, David Ray, *Reenchantment without Supernaturalism: A Process Philosophy of Religion* (Ithaca, NY: Cornell University Press, 2001).

Gunkel, Hermann, *The Influence of the Holy Spirit: The Popular View of the Apostolic Age and the Teaching of the Apostle Paul*, R. A. Harrisville and P. A. Quanbeck II (trans.) (Philadelphia: Fortress, [1888] 1979).

Imasogie, Osadolor, *Guidelines for Christian Theology in Africa* (Achimota, Ghana: Africa Christian Press, 1993).

John Paul II, *Celebrate 2000!: Reflections on the Holy Spirit: Weekly Readings for 1998*, selected and arranged by Paul Thigpen (Ann Arbor: Servant Publications, 1997).

Johnson, Elizabeth A., *She Who Is: The Mystery of God in Feminist Theological Discourse* (New York: Crossroad, 1992).

Johnson, Elizabeth A., *Women, Earth and Creator Spirit* (Mahwah, NJ: Paulist Press, 1993).

Kärkkäinen, Veli-Matti, *Creation and Humanity: A Constructive Christian Theology for the Pluralistic World*, vol. 3 (Grand Rapids: Eerdmans, 2015).

Kärkkäinen, Veli-Matti, *Holy Spirit: A Guide to Christian Theology* (Louisville, KY: Westminster John Knox Press, 2012).

Kärkkäinen, Veli-Matti, 'Holy Spirit and Other Spirits: An Interim Report of the State of the Theology of the Holy Spirit in a Contemporary Pluralistic World', *Catalyst: Contemporary Evangelical Resources for United Methodist Seminarians*, online journal (26 March 2014), accessed at http://www.catalystresources.org/holy-spirit-and-other-spirits/.

Kärkkäinen, Veli-Matti (ed.), *Holy Spirit and Salvation: The Sources of Christian Theology* (Louisville, KY: Westminster John Knox Press, 2010).

Kärkkäinen, Veli-Matti, *Pneumatology: The Holy Spirit in Ecumenical, International, and Contextual Perspectives*, 2nd rev. ed. (Grand Rapids: Baker Academic Books, 2018).

Kärkkäinen, Veli-Matti, *Spirit and Salvation: A Constructive Christian Theology for the Pluralistic World*, vol. 4 (Grand Rapids: Eerdmans, 2016).

Kärkkäinen, Veli-Matti, 'Spirit(s) in Contemporary Christian Theology: An Interim Report of the Unbinding of Pneumatology', in *Interdisciplinary and Religio-Cultural Discourses on a Spirit-Filled World: Loosing the Spirits*, edited by Veli-Matti Kärkkäinen, Kirsteen Kim and Amos Yong (New York: Palgrave Macmillan, 2013), pp. 29–40.

Kärkkäinen, Veli-Matti, *Trinity and Revelation: A Constructive Christian Theology for the Pluralistic World*, vol. 4 (Grand Rapids: Eerdmans, 2014).

Lak, Yeow Choo, 'Preface', in *Doing Theology with the Spirit's Movement in Asia*, edited by John C. England and Alan J. Torrance (Singapore: ATESEA, 1991).

Lampe, G. W. H., *God as Spirit* (Oxford: Clarendon, 1977).

Lee, Jung Young, *The Theology of Change: A Christian Concept of God in an Eastern Perspective* (Maryknoll, NY: Orbis, 1979).

Lee, Jung Young, *The Trinity in Asian Perspective* (Nashville: Abingdon, 1996).

Levison, John R., *Filled with the Spirit* (Grand Rapids: Eerdmans, 2009).

Lossky, Vladimir, 'The Procession of the Holy Spirit in Orthodox Trinitarian Doctrine', in *In the*

*Image and Likeness of God*, edited by John H. Erickson and Thomas E. Bird (Crestwood, NY: St. Vladimir's Seminary Press, 1974), pp. 71–96.

Macchia, Frank, 'Baptized in the Spirit: Towards a Global Theology of Spirit Baptism', in *The Spirit in the World: Emerging Pentecostal Theologies in Global Context*, edited by Veli-Matti Kärkkäinen (Grand Rapids: Eerdmans, 2009), pp. 3–20.

McDonnell, Kilian, 'The Determinative Doctrine of the Holy Spirit', *Theology Today* 39:2 (1982), 142–61.

McDonnell, Kilian, *The Other Hand of God: The Holy Spirit as the Universal Touch and Goal* (Collegeville, MN: Michael Glazier Books, 2003).

McDonnell, Kilian, 'Theological Presuppositions in Our Preaching about the Spirit', *Theological Studies* 59:2 (1998), 219–35.

McDonnell, Kilian, 'A Trinitarian Theology of the Holy Spirit?', *Theological Studies* 46:2 (1985), 191–227.

McGrath, Alister, *Christian Theology: An Introduction*, 5th ed. (Oxford: John Wiley & Sons, 2011).

Mbiti, John S., *African Religions and Philosophy* (London: Heinemann, 1969).

Moltmann, Jürgen, *The Spirit of Life: A Universal Affirmation*, Margaret Kohl (trans.) (Minneapolis: Fortress, 2001).

Müller-Fahrenholz, Geiko, *God's Spirit: Transforming a World in Crisis*, John Cumming (trans.) (New York: Continuum, 1995).

Needham, Nick, 'The Filioque Clause: East or West?', *Scottish Bulletin of Evangelical Theology* 15 (1997), 142–62.

Newbigin, Lesslie, *Unfinished Agenda: An Autobiography* (Grand Rapids: Eerdmans, 1985).

Nissiotis, Nikos A., 'The Main Ecclesiological Problem of the Second Vatican Council and Position of the Non-Roman Churches Facing It', *Journal of Ecumenical Studies* 2:1 (1965), 31–62.

Pannenberg, Wolfhart, *An Introduction to Systematic Theology* (Grand Rapids: Eerdmans, 1991).

Pannenberg, Wolfhart, *Systematic Theology*, vol. 1, Geoffrey W. Bromiley (trans.) (Grand Rapids: Eerdmans, 1991).

Pannenberg, Wolfhart, *Systematic Theology*, vol. 2, Geoffrey W. Bromiley (trans.) (Grand Rapids: Eerdmans 1994).

Pannenberg, Wolfhart, *Systematic Theology*, vol. 3, Geoffrey W. Bromiley (trans.) (Grand Rapids: Eerdmans, 1998).

Photius, *On the Mystagogy of the Holy Spirit* (Astoria, NY: Studion Publications, 1983).

Pieris, Aloysius, 'Western Christianity and Asian Buddhism: A Theological Reading of Historical Encounters', *Dialogue* 7 (May–August 1980), 49–85.

Polkinghorne, John, 'The Hidden Spirit and the Cosmos', in *The Work of the Spirit: Pneumatology and Pentecostalism*, edited by Michael Welker (Grand Rapids, Eerdmans: 2006), pp. 169–82.

Ruether, Rosemary Radford, *Goddesses and the Divine Feminine: A Wisdom Religious History* (Berkeley: University of California Press, 2005).

Sachs, John R., '"Do Not Stifle the Spirit": Karl Rahner, the Legacy of Vatican II, and Its Urgency for Theology Today', in *Catholic Theological Society Proceedings* 51, edited by E. Dreyer (1996), p. 15.

Samartha, Stanley J., *Between Two Cultures: Ecumenical Ministry in a Pluralist World* (Geneva: WCC Publications, 1996).

Samartha, Stanley J., *Courage for Dialogue: Ecumenical Issues in Inter-Religious Relationships* (Geneva: WCC Publications, 1981).

Sobrino, Jon, *Spirituality of Liberation: Toward Political Holiness*, Robert R. Barr (trans.) (Maryknoll, NY: Orbis, 1988).

Stylianopoulos, Theodore G. and S. Mark Heim (eds), *Spirit of Truth: Ecumenical Perspectives on the Holy Spirit* (Brookline, MA: Holy Cross Orthodox Press, 1986).

Tillich, Paul, *Systematic Theology*, vol. 3 (Chicago: University Press of Chicago, 1963).

Vischer, Lukas (ed.), *Spirit of God, Spirit of Christ: Ecumenical Reflections on the Filioque Controversy* (London: SPCK/Geneva: WCC Publications, 1981).

Volf, Miroslav, *Work in the Spirit: Toward a Theology of Work* (Eugene, OR: Wipf and Stock, 2001).

Wallace, Mark I., *Finding God in the Singing River* (Minneapolis: Augsburg Fortress, 2005).

Wallace, Mark I., *Fragments of the Spirit: Nature, Violence, and the Renewal of Creation* (New York: Continuum, 1996).

Ware, Kallistos, *The Orthodox Church* (New York: Penguin Books, 1993).

Welker, Michael, *God the Spirit: A Problem of Experience in Today's World*, John F. Hoffmeyer (trans.) (Minneapolis: Fortress, 1994).

Yong, Amos, 'On Binding, and Loosing, the Spirits: Navigating and Engaging a Spirit-Filled World', in *Interdisciplinary and Religo-Cultural Discourses on a Spirit-Filled World: Loosing the Spirits*, edited by Veli-Matti Kärkkäinen, Kirsteen Kim and Amos Yong (New York: Palgrave Macmillan, 2013), pp. 1–13.

Yong, Amos, 'The Demonic in Pentecostal-Charismatic Christianity and in the Religious Consciousness of Asia', in *Asian and Pentecostal: The Charismatic Face of Christianity in Asia*, edited by Allan Anderson and Edmond Tang, 2nd rev. ed. (Eugene, OR: Wipf and Stock, 2011), pp. 73–102.

Yong, Amos, '"The Spirit Hovers over the World": Toward a Typology of "Spirit" in the Religion and Science Dialogue', online essay, *Metanexus* (16 October 2004), accessed at http://www.meta nexus.net/spirit-hovers-over-world/.

# 11

# Christ

## Christophe Chalamet

It should come as no surprise that how we consider Christ, what we say of him, says much about how we view Christianity and envisage and practise Christian theology. The twentieth century offers rich reflections on this topic, a good deal of which rightly seeks to remind us that, before being a topic, what is in view is a historical *person* who lived a long time ago, or, more precisely, a theological *title*, namely *Christos* (Χριστός), the Greek translation of *messiah* (מָשִׁיחַ, *māšîaḥ*), meaning 'the anointed one'. This title was conferred upon a person, Jesus of Nazareth, who may not have claimed it for himself, but who, according to the Synoptic Gospels, does not appear to have denied it either.[1]

The history of twentieth-century reflections on Christ presents a dizzying array of proposals and revisions.[2] Whether Christian theology made much progress on this theme in the course of the previous century is not as clear as we may first imagine. If it did not, this should not be disheartening: Christian theology ever circles around the same old mountains, contemplating them always anew though many outstanding thinkers have previously considered these topics. In many ways, twentieth-century 'Christology' continued to wrestle with problems inherited from the nineteenth century as well as from much older pronouncements (e.g. those made at the Council of Chalcedon in 451). Still, the astounding diversification and richness of Christological constructs in recent decades testifies to the vitality of Christian theology globally and signals how the Christian faith and theology are still very much 'on the move'. For Christians, Christ – before being a theological topic, a theme calling for rigorous investigation and thought – is the *living Jesus*, the Son of God who, having been crucified, was 'made' Lord and Messiah by God (Acts 2:36). For Christian faith, Christology concerns not a remote or even dead subject, but asks about the one from Galilee who, having been put to death in infamous circumstances, was raised anew by God to new life: he is 'Emmanuel', 'God-with-us'.

Twentieth-century Christology began, at least among modern Protestant thinkers, with a strong focus on Jesus' 'personality'. In fact, this term – *Persönlichkeit* – was a keyword of the early twentieth century, used to designate not just Jesus, but also God's being, and the human being's calling. Why a predilection for this concept? In Christology it simultaneously allowed for historical consideration of Jesus' life and for theological elaboration at a time when religious psychology was gaining traction. Before the First World War, modern Protestant theologians were very attuned to the Synoptic presentation of Jesus, although some presupposed key insights found in Paul's epistles, notably the Apostle's key statement 'God was in Christ' (Θεὸς ἦν ἐν Χριστῷ, 2 Cor. 5:19).

# Early Twentieth Century

## Against Supranaturalism: Ernst Troeltsch (1865–1923)

Not everyone began with the claim that 'God was in Christ'. Some contested such statements, at least when formulated in an a priori, supranaturalist fashion. Ernst Troeltsch rejected such dogmatic assumptions and called for a different starting point in concrete *history* and in history *as a whole*. '"Christology" is a science', he wrote, 'only for a strict supranaturalistic perspective. To any other perspective, it is an object of faith and imagination (*Phantasie*).'[3] This of course did not mean Troeltsch had no interest in the person of Christ; indeed, as he said, 'any Christianity without Christ drifts away, experience tells us; it is like the afterglow which follows sundown'.[4] The 'person of Jesus' remains crucial. But instead of immediately presupposing that God reveals Godself definitively and absolutely in him, we should begin by studying the historical phenomenon of religion *as a whole* – and especially of 'positive' religions, i.e. those which claim to rest upon a particular revelation – in order eventually to undertake a modern, scientific consideration of Christianity and thus also of Jesus' personality.[5] This, in a nutshell, was Troeltsch's 'anti-dogmatic' challenge to Protestant theology at the turn of the twentieth century.[6]

## Wilhelm Herrmann (1846–1922)

Two giants of twentieth-century theology were trained during the first decade of the new century just as Troeltsch's programme was being debated and often resisted. In their earliest works, Rudolf Bultmann (1884–1976) and Karl Barth (1886–1968) made clear they were to pursue another path than Troeltsch's. They combined insights from Albrecht Ritschl, Friedrich Schleiermacher, Immanuel Kant and Martin Luther to propose a highly existential Christology. Their common teacher in this school was Wilhelm Herrmann. Here, the scientific standing of theology did not depend upon general considerations concerning the history of religions, comparative analysis of these traditions or even, more broadly, on historical scholarship at all. Rather, it arose from analysis of the Christian experience (*Erlebnis*) of God as mediated by the 'power' of Christ's 'inner life'. As with Troeltsch, Jesus' 'personality' was of the highest importance here, and the ancient doctrine of the two natures was not directly thematised. Yet, the point of Christology was to talk about 'salvation', i.e. the event of God's salutary manifestation in history in the figure of Jesus. The link with reformational theology was much more vital here than in Troeltsch, who called for a 'new' Protestantism, since the Enlightenment rendered 'old' Protestantism of the sixteenth-century reformers irretrievable.

## Adolf von Harnack (1851–1930)

In this pre-war period there was a third major Christological option alongside Troeltsch and Herrmann, though it too centred on the notion of 'personality'. In his very successful book *What Is Christianity?* (*Das Wesen des Christentums*, 1900), Adolf von Harnack offered a presentation of Jesus (and Christianity) which sought to separate the 'husk' from the 'kernel', i.e. what is 'of alien growth' from what is 'original'.[7] As he saw it – rather shockingly to many today – 'the whole of the Jewish limitations attaching to Jesus' message' was part of the husk, which Jesus' disciples eventually discarded 'in the strength of Christ's spirit'.[8]

One of Harnack's major theses was that Jesus as such does not belong in the gospel. It is possible to summarise the gospel without mentioning Jesus, or the Christian confession of Jesus as Christ: 'In the combination of these ideas – God the Father, Providence, the position of human beings as God's children, the infinite value of the human soul – the whole Gospel is expressed.'[9] Jesus thus only has a strictly external relation to the gospel, which, importantly, Harnack understands to mean the message Jesus himself preached: throughout the book Harnack stresses that Jesus announced rather than embodied the gospel. When, later, Harnack does connect Jesus and the gospel – now not just as the message proclaimed by Jesus, but also the message concerning Jesus – he sees him as 'its personal realization and its strength'.[10]

In common with much modern liberal theology, Harnack is suspicious of Church doctrine, and this finds expression in his contrast between the gospel message and doctrine (or ceremony). Genuine spiritual religion stands over against its intellectual elaboration. Towards the end of his lecture cycle, Harnack said to the many students who gathered to hear him week after week, from all the faculties at the University of Berlin: 'Gentlemen (sic), it is religion, the love of God and neighbour, which gives life a meaning; knowledge cannot do it.'[11]

Liberal theology denies that people must first accept doctrinal pronouncements concerning Christ, e.g. his two natures. Rather, personal encounter with Jesus must be primary; only then may doctrine follow (or not). As Harnack himself put it:

How great a departure from what he thought and enjoined is involved in putting a 'Christological' creed in the forefront of the Gospel, and in teaching that, before one can approach it, one must learn to think rightly about Christ. That is putting the cart before the horse. One can think and teach rightly about Christ only if, and in so far as, one has already begun to live according to Christ's Gospel.[12]

And so, 'it is a perverse proceeding to make Christology the fundamental substance of the Gospel', and the way the Apostle Paul 'ordered his religious conceptions, as the outcome of his speculative ideas', Harnack concludes, 'unmistakeably exercised an influence in a wrong direction'.[13] Rather than limit the plurality of views concerning Jesus, the Church should encourage limitless Christological creativity. Protestantism may be fragmented, divided – also in its views about Jesus Christ – 'but we do not wish it otherwise; on the contrary, we want still more freedom, still greater individuality in utterance and doctrine'![14]

Harnack was a historian who was convinced that history, as a science, can access what lies behind time: the timeless, or the absolute. Having presented Jesus' teachings in rather romantic terms – they 'breathe peace, joy, and certainty', as he put it – he wrote: 'Words effect nothing; it is the power of the personality that stands behind them.'[15] Analysing Jesus' teaching, the great historian focused on the 'kingdom of God', interpreting it as an inward – and thus also personal, even individual – reality.[16] While, were he to live in 1900, Jesus would certainly side with the poor, as there is a 'profoundly socialistic' dimension to his message, at bottom 'the Gospel makes its appeal to the inner man . . .'[17] Harnack urged:

let us fight, let us struggle, let us get justice for the oppressed, let us order the circumstances of the world as we with a clear conscience can, and as we may think best for our neighbour; but do not let us expect the Gospel to afford us any direct help [. . .]; it is concerned not with material things but with the souls of human beings.[18]

Harnack's views would not remain unchallenged.

## Albert Schweitzer (1875–1965) and Eschatology

Later world-famous as a medical doctor in Lambarene (Gabon), Albert Schweitzer was also a liberal theologian who contended that much in the modern presentations of the 'life of Jesus' belonged to the realm of imagination rather than genuine scholarship. In his critically acclaimed book *The Quest of the Historical Jesus*, Schweitzer interpreted Jesus' message and person to be entirely pervaded by an eschatological outlook. Everything about Jesus was eschatologically determined: both his message and his acts become intelligible only in the light of his conviction concerning the imminent coming of God's kingdom. Schweitzer concluded that Jesus 'will be to our time a stranger and an enigma', for he cannot be as easily be transferred into our own times as the authors of lives of Jesus imagined. They hoped we could bring him 'straight into our time as a teacher and saviour', but 'he did not stay; he passed by our time and returned to his own'.[19]

What has theology to do with the rediscovery, by Schweitzer – and before him by Hermann Samuel Reimarus and Johannes Weiss – of the eschatological nature of Jesus' message? Schweitzer placed this question squarely at the centre of the theological – and Christological – agenda. Soon a new generation of theologians took it up, though addressing it very differently than Schweitzer, who himself remained an advocate of neo-Protestant, Enlightenment liberalism, despite his piques against nineteenth-century theology.[20]

## Walter Rauschenbusch (1861–1918)

Walter Rauschenbusch is a final pre-war Christological thinker who deserves our attention here. Rauschenbusch, later a Baptist pastor, was born in the United States to German Lutheran immigrant missionaries. Sent back to Germany to be schooled, he became well acquainted with German theology, studying at various universities before pursuing seminary training at Rochester Baptist Seminary. He pastored in the Hell's Kitchen neighbourhood of Manhattan, where he encountered the slum poverty and became committed to the movement known as Social Christianity, or the Social Gospel. Later, as a professor at Rochester Baptist Seminary, he penned *Christianity and the Social Crisis*, published in 1907, a work that brought him national acclaim in the United States.

Social Christianity aimed not to replace but to complement the 'individualistic Gospel' with a 'social Gospel': the former concerned individual sin and salvation – 'God and the soul, the soul and its God', as Harnack summarised 'the whole of the Gospel' in his lectures[21] – while the latter concerned 'social evil', 'the sinfulness of the social order' and the redemption of that order.[22]

Without always realising the extent of their debt, many contextual and liberation theologies today owe much to Rauschenbusch and other Social Gospel Christians. Social Christianity was significantly ahead of its time with its forceful attempt to overcome any dualist split between the material and the spiritual, the profane and the sacred, the worldly and the religious. Arguing that the gospel 'is concerned not with material things but with the souls of human beings', as Harnack put it (see above), was, it was charged, a major error in the interpretation of Jesus' message and of the Christian faith as a whole. Rauschenbusch spoke for many Social Christians when he wrote: 'Theology has not been a faithful steward of the truth entrusted to it. The social gospel is its accusing conscience.'[23] This sentence is found in his most famous book, *A Theology for the Social Gospel*, first published in 1917, the year before his untimely death at the age of fifty-six.[24]

The truth once entrusted to theology but lost along the way was the truth of the reality of the Kingdom of God, which Christian theology, already in the first centuries of its existence, 'carefully wrapped in several napkins and forgot'.[25] Rauchenbusch took literally Alfred Loisy's well-known claim about Jesus, who foretold the kingdom, and yet it was the Church that came.[26] The Kingdom of God was the heartbeat of the Social Gospel.[27] The kingdom was not a purely eschatological or ethical reality, i.e. as a futurist reality or as a reality which humans can build. Rather, it was both the horizon of the world and the blueprint for a transformation of this world: 'on earth as it is in heaven' aptly summarises the Social Gospel's programme, if we place the emphasis on the first two words ('on earth'). For the kingdom is 'the organized fellowship of humanity acting under the impulse of love'.[28]

If, as Rauschenbusch sees it, the theology of the Social Gospel centres on the kingdom as the reality of redemption from sin, what then of Christ? In ways reminiscent of Schleiermacher's treatment in The Christian Faith, sin and salvation are the twin categories (and realities), understood socially and not merely individually. Theology concerns itself with these realities, with little or no interest in 'the more speculative doctrines', as '[i]ts interests lie on earth, within the social relations of the life that now is'.[29] For 'the social gospel is above all things practical'.[30]

What does this mean for Christology? Rauschenbusch answers in A Theology for the Social Gospel, in two chapters entitled 'The Initiator of the Kingdom of God' and 'The Social Gospel and the Atonement'.[31] Jesus, in all his ministry, was 'the initiator of the Kingdom': he 'set in motion the historical forces of redemption', in order 'to overthrow the Kingdom of Evil'.[32] What matters is Jesus' message, his actions, rather than his being (the concern of the classical doctrine of the two natures) or what he underwent (his incarnation, death and resurrection).[33] Rauschenbusch creatively transfers key Christological themes from the Bible and tradition to society: the righteousness of the kingdom must be incarnated in our world, in society, for our world is called to a resurrection, a redemption from its enslavement to sin.[34] Displaced in this way, Rauschenbusch thinks it might be possible to retrieve 'a Christ who is truly personal', a Jesus who is 'a real personality' – that important term from these years – out from under Hellenising dogma and 'alien importations'.[35]

Jesus personally achieved 'a new type of humanity', becoming 'the primal cell of a new social organism'.[36] His 'personality' is 'a call to the emancipation of our own personalities', and his disciples were, and still are, called to convey this 'powerful current' in human history and throughout the world.[37] Unfortunately, Christian theology has not been conducive to this experience of Jesus as 'a Liberator'.[38] Especially in the West, it has preferred to reflect on the ways in which Christ atoned for the world's sin. Rauschenbusch suggests theologians have erred in talking so much about 'substitution', 'satisfaction', 'imputation' and the like.[39] Yes, Jesus bore sin, but in a different sense: what killed him was religious bigotry, the ruling class's power, corrupt justice, mob spirit, militarism and class contempt.[40] His death was 'an integral part of his life', his life was no 'mere staging for his death' or something 'almost negligible in the work of salvation'.[41]

These are the main contours of Rauschenbusch's Christology. It focuses narrowly once again on Jesus' own life, rather than on his birth, death and resurrection. Such focus on Jesus' work of liberation still resonates today in many regions of the world. And Rauschenbusch made a signal contribution by connecting Christ and his work to sin understood not just as 'private sin', but as 'organized sin', which manifests itself in multiple ways, including the 'exploitation of the poor', 'war and militarism', the rule of 'despotic government' and the reduction of 'the patrimony of a nation into the private property of a small class'.[42] Remarkably, Rauschenbusch denounced racial oppression in the United States and its roots in slavery:

> When negroes are hunted from a Northern city like beasts, or when a Southern city degrades the whole nation by turning the savage inhumanity of a mob into a public festivity, we are continuing to sin because our fathers created the conditions of sin by the African slave trade and by the unearned wealth they gathered from slave labour for generations.[43]

Even a superficial acquaintance with recent and contemporary contextual theologies which have sprung up in many parts of the world alerts us that they share key insights – Christological and otherwise – with this American son of a German immigrant and the Social Gospel movement which inspired him and to which he significantly contributed.

## Mid-Twentieth Century

### The 'Dialectical Revolution'

Troeltsch, Herrmann, Harnack, Schweitzer, Rauschenbusch: these figures of early twentieth-century Protestant theology were challenged by a new generation of theologians immediately after the end of the First World War, including Karl Barth, Eduard Thurneysen and Friedrich Gogarten, Emil Brunner and Rudolf Bultmann, Paul Tillich and others who simply could not continue in the direction in which their teachers had pointed.

Karl Barth was among the first to express a radical dissatisfaction with the theology he had absorbed as a student.[44] The signal that something was deeply amiss – an event often recounted in theological scholarship – was his German teachers' efforts to legitimise their nation's war effort theologically by invoking God and religious symbols. This compelled Barth to seek a new way of grounding theology. This search led him to Paul's Epistle to the Romans and, after long months of study, to his famous commentary, *The Epistle to the Romans* (1st ed. 1919; 2nd ed. 1922), which remains a classic of twentieth-century theology. Barth's Christology, in this book, is burgeoning and somewhat sketchy. In opposition to much of modern theology, he insists that what matters, in the Christian faith, is neither our own 'experience' (*Erlebnis*) – *contra* his teacher Wilhelm Herrmann – nor 'religion' as such, nor our own contribution to the coming of the kingdom – *contra* Rauschenbusch and Social Christianity. What matters is Jesus Christ as the very Word of God who both judges us – killing our self-confidence and self-reliance – *and* vivifies us. Certainly, God enters into relation with the world, with his human creature, but this in no way reduces the abyss which exists between creatures and their creating, reconciling and redeeming God.

By 1924, Barth was giving his first lectures on dogmatic theology as a professor at the University of Göttingen and discovering unsuspected riches in the tradition of seventeenth-century Protestant orthodoxy he had previously been taught to despise. Here he found a particular key in the ancient teaching concerning Jesus' essential participation in the divine Word according to which his humanity can at no moment be considered independently or in abstraction from the Word (*an-hypostasis*). His humanity, his person (*hypostasis*) is entirely rooted in (*en-hypostasis*) his 'personal' identity as the Son of God. As Barth says, 'in the humanity of Christ the *content* of revelation as well as the subject is God *alone* . . . [T]he historical phenomenon of Jesus as such is a creature of the triune God.'[45] Christ's humanity 'did not exist *prior* to its union with the Logos. It has no independent existence alongside or apart from him.'[46] This doctrinal element fit perfectly with the kind of asymmetry Barth had been defending since the end of the First World War, namely that we do not 'have' God (in our experience, in our conscience, even in our faith), but that God 'has' us: we are God's creatures. It also served as a bulwark against 'low' Christologies with their focus 'on the man Jesus of Nazareth, on the hero, the religious personality, his inner life so far as we may know it, his view of God, of the world and of life'.[47]

## Emil Brunner

In 1927 Emil Brunner published the first monograph on Christology by a member of the dialectical school: *The Mediator: A Study of the Central Doctrine of the Christian Faith*.[48] It is a highly readable, half-scholarly book regularly reprinted in subsequent decades. After a long survey of the flaws of modern Christologies, especially those of Schleiermacher and Ritschl, and the limits of historical research in relation to faith, Brunner turns to the two traditional subfields of Christology, namely the 'person' and the 'work' of the Mediator. His main guide throughout is Martin Luther, for 'interest in the divine nature of Christ has never been more clearly expressed by anyone than by Luther'.[49] Brunner is interested in showing the qualitative uniqueness of Christ, not merely his standing as *primus inter pares*. Without the scholarly apparatus of Barth's Göttingen lectures, Brunner seeks to say similar things, namely that understanding who the Mediator is, and his incarnation, means tracing 'the "impulse" of this movement, that which gives it power, direction, decisiveness . . . in eternity'.[50] We see here the dynamic motif of *senkrecht von oben* ('straight from above') which was so important to the dialectical theologians, especially Barth and Brunner. In Christology, this meant a rejection of all forms of adoptianism, i.e. any notion that the human Jesus eventually 'became' the Son of God. No: 'the self-movement of God towards humanity is the theme of the Bible'.[51] Brunner's book is a dogmatic exercise in Christology aimed to restate the ancient doctrine of Chalcedon. Despite his assertion that 'the significance of Christmas and of Good Friday is only perceived in the light of Easter',[52] much emphasis is placed on the Incarnation as such. One is struck by the absence of commentary on the Scriptures, in many sections of the book, including in the chapter on 'The Person and Teaching of Christ'.[53] Brunner's dogmatic study is rather disconnected from the gospel narratives. Even if some of its basic insights – e.g. on God's 'self-movement' in Christ – remain important, the book has not aged well.

## Barth's Doctrine of Reconciliation (*Church Dogmatics*, vol. 4)

The works of the 'dialectical school' are perhaps best called 'theologies of the Word', and the major achievement of this school, with regard to Christology, is undoubtedly the massive fourth volume of Karl Barth's *Church Dogmatics*, on the doctrine of reconciliation, published in three parts between 1953 and 1959. Within six years, Barth thus published three thousand pages on Christ's person and work.[54] It is not easy to master such an overwhelming amount of material, and the students of Barth's *oeuvre* are still in the process of receiving it. Not just the sheer quantity, but the quality of these volumes, the level of precision with which Barth deals with the Bible and the history of Christian thought, is astounding. The structure of these volumes, based on the hymn of Philippians 2 – i.e. kenosis and exaltation – as well as on the entire movement of the fourth gospel – John's telling of the Son coming from and returning to the Father – but also on a new interpretation of the three offices of Christ as priest, king and prophet (*munus triplex*), is equally impressive and has rightly been compared to a cathedral.[55]

What did Barth achieve in this massive construal of 'reconciliation'? A restatement of God's journey 'into the far country' of fallen humanity, of God's 'self-movement' (to use Brunner's expression) into our rebellious world, a movement of humiliation in which God precisely demonstrates God's power and glory as well as God's faithfulness to God's covenant, which God fulfils in his Son, Jesus Christ. One of Barth's decisive insights consists in saying that who God is, as the holy, powerful and wise one, must be learned by paying attention, from beginning to end, to the historical figure Jesus of Nazareth, the Christ of God. God assumes human flesh in this particular human person, and so Christology cannot at any moment float above this man. This means that any attention to the Logos, detached from the concrete man Jesus, becomes problematic. We should not loosen what God has bound! But God has not bound 'something' to the world: God, in freedom, has bound *Godself* to the world. Jesus Christ is the authentic witness to this free binding of God to God's creation.

Compared to his Göttingen lectures from the mid-1920s – and Brunner's *Mediator* from 1927 – Barth is now much more attentive to the concrete historicity, rootedness and particularity of Jesus of Nazareth:

> The Word did not simply become any 'flesh', any man humbled and suffering. It became Jewish flesh. The Church's whole doctrine of the incarnation and the atonement becomes abstract and valueless and meaningless to the extent that this comes to be regarded as something accidental and incidental.[56]

True universalism, in Christian theology, utterly depends on how we account for this kind of particularity. This does not mean, however, that Barth has now switched to a Christology 'from below': the man Jesus does not at some point become the Son. Rather, the Son comes to be known by human beings as this man Jesus of Nazareth. Barth's mature theology never severs Christology from its Trinitarian matrix. Chalcedonian doctrine remained the overall framework for him, even as he was committed to rearticulating the ancient formulas.[57] Barth's decisive intention was to 'actualize' the 'old doctrine of the incarnation',[58] i.e. to interpret the union of the two 'natures' as an event and a process (*Vorgang*)[59] so that '*nothing* of the *static* dimension at the broad center of the traditional doctrine of the person of Christ is left'.[60] This is the 'transposition' Barth thought was necessary for theology in our time.[61] Recent proposals, such as Bruce L. McCormack's kenotic Christology, pursue very fruitfully this same direction.[62]

Barth refuses any Christology which focuses so much on love that it loses sight of judgement upon sin, understood as rebellion, enmity against God. The sending of God's Son into the far country is costly above all to God, who takes upon Godself the verdict which should have been rendered upon sinners. Christ, as the eternal Son of God, is the 'judge', but in obedience to the Father he consents to be judged in our place, to endure the judgement of the Father, not out of masochistic tendencies, but in order to reconcile the world with God. At Easter, in his passion and resurrection, Jesus Christ does not achieve the *possibility* of salvation – to be concretised or actualised by us, for instance through faith – but its reality (John 19:30: 'it is accomplished'; Τετέλεσται), by representing all of humanity in the Godforsakenness of the cross. Faith is the acknowledgement of the reconciliation Christ has accomplished in his life, death, and in his being-raised by the Father. In all this,

Barth steers clear from a *theologia crucis* which centres on Good Friday to the detriment of the Resurrection, and from a *theologia gloriae* which circumvents the radical humiliation of God in the event of the cross.[63]

## Rudolf Bultmann and Paul Tillich

At the same time Barth was writing his lectures on 'reconciliation', Rudolf Bultmann and Paul Tillich, too, were at the peak of their theological existence. Bultmann was following a rather different path than Barth, emphasising that, with Christ, action precedes identity or essence: it is not the person or nature of Christ that makes the cross into a saving event, but rather the cross as the *event* of salvation that identifies Jesus as the Christ.[64]

Here, Bultmann, following his teacher Wilhelm Herrmann, focuses Christology upon what God or Christ effects for me (*pro me*) in the event of the justification of the sinner. This amounts to a stark reduction of Christology to Christ's saving event, which should not be located in a 'there and then' (*illic et tunc*), i.e. a place and time in a distant place and time, as if Christ saved the world on the cross of Golgotha. Rather, it should be interpreted as God's action in the 'here and now' (*hic et nunc*) of proclamation and the human answer to it in faith. Where Barth was seeking to unfold Christology in all its breadth, with a Trinitarian backdrop, giving priority to the facticity and identity of Jesus Christ as the one God sent *pro nobis*, Bultmann was concentrating Christology on the event of justification in order to ponder its existential efficacy in the present moment.

Paul Tillich was pursuing yet another line – one which often found Bultmann's agreement, at least in their later years[65] – and, like Bultmann, much more succinctly than Barth: the second volume of Tillich's *Systematic Theology*, entitled 'Existence and the Christ', published in 1957, amounts to only 180 pages. For Tillich, 'the Christ' is one of the symbols – alongside 'Son of Man', 'Son of God', 'Logos' and others – used to interpret 'the fact "Jesus"'.[66] The Christological problem derives from the 'existential predicament' of human beings who wonder whether this predicament can be overcome.[67] This is in line with Tillich's method of 'correlation', in which human beings pose questions – and *are* in fact the question – before revelation 'answers' this question. This means that Christology 'is a function of soteriology' – a claim Bultmann would have supported.[68]

Tillich strives for a certain balance that avoids two mistakes: the 'denial of the Christ-character of Jesus as the Christ', and the 'denial of the Jesus-character of Jesus as the Christ'.[69] Nicaea risked losing the Jesus-character of Jesus as the Christ, but it managed, despite its 'very inadequate conceptual tools', to avoid this error.[70] Harnack was wrong to disparage the influence of Hellenistic thought on the 'pure' gospel message and to elim-inate the 'Christ-character of the event Jesus' when he stated that Jesus does not belong within the gospel proclaimed by Jesus.[71] This process was unavoidable, as Christianity spread through the Greek world. Tillich wishes to steer clear from both modern liberal views and traditional or orthodox claims, with a particular distrust of terms such as 'incar-nation', which, when taken literally, have 'pagan connotations' and imply 'a mythology of metamorphosis'; incarnation has nothing to with 'a literalism which takes pre-existence and post-existence as stages in a transcendent story of a divine being which descends from and ascends to a heavenly place'; it points, rather, in the direction of the Logos' 'total manifestation in a personal life'.[72] Tillich is certainly right to be searching for a way beyond liberalism and traditional orthodoxy, but his insightful construal is somewhat vague, and his presentation of 'the Christ' is rather abstract and disembodied. To take one example, his comments on Jesus' passion and resurrection amount to twelve pages only, with a good dose of 'demythologising' – or 'deliteralising', as Tillich prefers to put it – with regard to the Resurrection.[73]

## Eastern Orthodoxy and Roman Catholicism

### Eastern Orthodoxy

As a century of deep political, social and cultural upheavals, as well as the emergence of the ecumenical movement, the twentieth century was a time of heightened contact and dialogue across confessional boundaries. Key Eastern Orthodox thinkers like Sergius Bulgakov and Vladimir Lossky went into exile, finding their way to Paris (among other places), where the Institut Saint-Serge became a central place for Orthodox theology. Another Russian exilé in Paris, Nicolas Berdyaev, writing in 1911, suggests that, whereas Western Christianity sees God as 'external' to human beings so that they must 'tend to' God, in Eastern Orthodoxy God is the 'deifying subject, the Holy Spirit interior to human beings. Here, God descends toward human beings, the human accepts Christ within himself. In Orthodoxy the human person does not soar towards God but bows down before him, in him.'[74] This vision is interesting, even if not entirely true to certain developments, as the dialectical school emphasised God's 'self-movement' towards creation (though rejecting, especially in the 1920s and 1930s, the notion of God 'within us'). Sergius Bulgakov's theandric Christology, moreover, articulates both the theme of kenosis (not just of the Son, but also of the Father in the begetting of the Son) and the human person's exaltation toward God.

Christian theology owes a deep debt to Orthodox theology for its way of articulating the relation of Christ and the Spirit, even if this was not entirely lacking in the West.[75] Orthodox theologians reminded twentieth-century Western theologians of the importance of speaking of Spirit and Christ together. Nikos Nissiotis (1924–86), a significant actor in ecumenical dialogues in the 1960s and 70s, is among the Orthodox scholars for whom Christ should never be separated from the Spirit of God, not just as the one who 'transmits' the Spirit, but also as the one whose entire ministry, from beginning to end, is exercised in the power of the Spirit.[76] French Dominican theologian Yves Congar similarly treated pneumatology and Christology in close relation, noting how they are constantly entangled in the New Testament writings.[77]

### Roman Catholicism

Roman Catholic theology made a significant contribution to Christology in the twentieth century. Only two prominent figures can be briefly mentioned here: Karl Rahner and Hans Urs von Balthasar. Rahner first articulated a Christology centred on the 'heart of Jesus' and on the Incarnation as the condition of possibility of faith and salvation – what he styled a 'transcendental Christology' – in an attempt to overcome neo-scholasticism and to buttress the humanity of Christ. Yet he failed to pay sufficiently close attention to Jesus' concrete history, including his crucifixion, resulting in a neglect of Good Friday (and of sin) that funds recurring critiques of Rahner's Christology. Typically, Rahner sees Christology as an anthropology which, being open to the Word, transcends itself, and anthropology as a deficient form of Christology. This close connection between Christology and anthropology is a hallmark of Rahner's theology. In his later years, with a clear option for a Christology from below, and so for an 'ascending Christology', Rahner placed a greater emphasis on the Resurrection, but his use of the Scriptures faded significantly, as can be seen in his 1976 *Foundations of Christian Faith* (*Grundkurs des Glaubens*). Today, Rahner is best known for his suggestion, articulated in 1954, that Chalcedon must become 'not only our end, but also our beginning': Christology, as he saw it, cannot simply mean deducing everything concerning Christ from such dogmatic formulas. They are not the 'final say' in Christian theology.[78]

Hans Urs von Balthasar, for his part, took up the theme of kenosis of the eternal Son of God and developed a Trinitarian theology of the cross which is a searching – but, to some, overly speculative – reflection on the depths of God's triunity. Christ's *missio* – his sending and thus the living of his entire life – is rooted in and perfectly mirrors his filial relation to the Father, i.e. his proceeding, or *processio*, from the Father. As in Barth, Balthasar is not primarily interested in essences, but in what Christ did and does as an agent in history: *this* is the locus of salvation, as *all* of Jesus' activity manifests God to the world.[79] And this activity is in no way arbitrary, but rather exemplifies the kenotic movement of self-giving which characterises God's triune communion. This theology of God's own inner drama and its unfolding in history has been sharply criticised in some quarters, and, indeed, it is in serious need of being reconnected to our concrete, broken world.[80]

# New Movements (1960–1980)

The 1960s saw the end of the dominance of dialectical theology. Some movements, such as the theology of the 'death of God', came and went, while others emerged and continue to make a significant contribution to Christological thinking: feminist theology, political theology, Black theology, liberation theology. In German-speaking theology, three major figures emerged, who can only be briefly presented here: Wolfhart Pannenberg (1928–2014), Jürgen Moltmann (b. 1926) and Eberhard Jüngel (1934–2021).

## *Wolhart Pannenberg, Jürgen Moltmann and Eberhard Jüngel*

### Wolfhart Pannenberg

Wolfhart Pannenberg is among those who signalled the emergence of a new generation of theologians in the late 1950s, with his programme of 'Revelation as History' and later with his monograph on Christology *Jesus: God and Man* (*Grundzüge der Christologie*, 1964). Here was an attempt to ground Christology not 'from above', but 'from below' in the man Jesus and his message – even as Pannenberg immediately considered Jesus' relation to God. A Christology 'from above' presupposes what it is supposed to show. Needed instead is an enquiry into Jesus' 'appearance in history', and how this appearance 'led to the recognition of his divinity'.[81] Unable to see things from God's standpoint, we have to admit that our thinking is always located in a particular context.[82] Suddenly, with Pannenberg – though echoing Ernst Käsemann's earlier call not to dissociate Christ's reconciling work from the particular earthly Jesus from Nazareth – history as such was making a comeback.[83] Whereas the dialectical school was fond of differentiating, in Martin Kähler's footsteps, between history as the past which scholars study (*Historie*) and history as a living reality which impacts upon us today (*Geschichte*), Pannenberg rejects this distinction and argues that history as such matters for theology: the history of Jesus itself is rich in soteriological meaning.[84] Thus, study of the Jesus who lived during the time of Tiberius must come first, before all the soteriological questions, and must serve as a criterion for them. To put it differently, the question concerning soteriology must derive from an enquiry about Jesus himself, otherwise faith loses its historical basis.[85]

Faith does not 'see' certain things in history which non-believers cannot see. There is no 'salvation history' only perceivable by faith: revelation can be read off history directly, as it were. Hence the importance, for Pannenberg, of the empty tomb as pointing to the historicity of the Resurrection. The New Testament is not just a witness to God's action in history: it is a historical source, and theologians need to begin with the historical Jesus it presents.[86] Needless to say, this approach to Christology was a stark departure from the basic options of the dialectical school, not least on the relation between faith and history. With Pannenberg, history was given much credit, too much according to some. Yet questions remain: is Pannenberg's supposed Christology 'from below' really from below? Does he pay sufficient attention to Jesus' Galilean background, to his Jewish roots? It seems not so. His Christology begins from one particular verse from the Synoptic Gospels: 'And I tell you, everyone who acknowledges me before others, the Son of Man also will acknowledge before the angels of God' (Luke 12:8 and parallels).[87] This verse plays a crucial role in Pannenberg's thought, as he sees in it the 'anticipation' (*prolepsis*) in the time of Jesus' ministry of the final judgement. Such a saying announces that the 'end' becomes a present historical 'event', even as we await final confirmation only to come with the end of history.

Among the lasting insights of Pannenberg's Christology is its refusal to identify Christ with God, stressing his self-distinction from the Father and his 'being-from-God' as attested in Phil. 2:6.[88] Pannenberg elaborates this distinctive theme in his *Systematic Theology*.[89]

## Jürgen Moltmann

In the 1960s and 1970s, Jürgen Moltmann published three works which were among the most discussed and influential books in those decades: *Theology of Hope* (1964), *The Crucified God* (1972) and *The Church in the Power of the Spirit* (1975).[90] Each of these three books would deserve a close analysis in relation to Christology, but it is arguably the second, *The Crucified God*, which had the most important implications. As the title indicates, Moltmann argues here that God is not at a remove from the crucified Jesus but shares in his suffering. The claim is at once a reply to the 'death of God' theology and to the abrupt end of the high hopes of the 1960s.[91] If his *Theology of Hope* placed major emphasis on God's promise and the 'raising up' of Jesus on Easter, he now felt compelled to consider hope in close relation with the *memoria passionis*, the dereliction of Good Friday. Distinctly Lutheran tones now came to the fore in this Reformed theologian's reflection.[92] To this introduction of Jesus' suffering and death into God's very being, Karl Rahner replied that the suffering and crucified God may be too close to our own predicament to help or to save us.[93] Moltmann remained unconvinced by this defence of the *deus impassibilis* and *immutabilis*.

## Eberhard Jüngel

Jüngel also emerged in the 1960s as a leading Christological thinker. Here the continuities with Karl Barth and Rudolf Bultmann were more obvious.[94] His articulation of ideas was more sophisticated than Moltmann's – hampering any broad reception of his writings – but in several cases he was the first to articulate insights they would eventually share.[95] In his most important book, *God as the Mystery of the World* (1977), Jüngel, who is as interested in discerning a genuine 'death of God' theology as Moltmann was in *The Crucified God*, offers some interesting insights into the figure of Christ, the Easter event, and his parables.[96] Jüngel presents the man Jesus, and him alone, as *the* 'trace' of God in the world, the trace of God's triunity (*vestigia trinitatis*).[97] He considers the risen Christ as the *crucified* One, and 'the telling of the christological story' as a kerygmatic and sacramental event, i.e. a language-event (*Sprachereignis*) that actually – and not merely potentially – 'frees' those who hear it and respond to it in faith.[98] Jesus is 'the parable of God'; his utter dereliction or abandonment on the cross is *the* decisive saving event, insofar as he bears our godlessness, but it cannot be severed from his 'unique certainty' in relation to his Father, who 'identifies' with him in resurrecting him.[99] This leads Jüngel to a reflection on God's being as 'love', a statement which 'must accompany all talk about God', even the talk of divine 'anger' or 'judgement'.[100] Avoiding the apologetic tendencies of Pannenberg's proposal and maintaining a theological rigour and sophistication unequalled among his peers, Jüngel's insights remain deeply profitable to this day.[101]

## Feminist Theologies

Feminist theology was bound to raise certain specifically Christological questions concerning the 'person' and 'work' of Jesus of Nazareth. First, concerning the person, many feminist thinkers wrestle with the fact that Jesus was male. If God assumed not just human flesh, but male human flesh, what does this say about God? Does it imply God has a closer rapport with men than with women? Does that mean God is in some way gendered? Rejecting superficial dismissal of such questions, feminist theology has sought to enquire deeper into the implications of the confession that God became human as a male figure. Certain feminist authors built upon Paul Ricoeur's fecund definition of a 'symbol' as something that 'gives rise to thought'.[102] What does the symbol of the Incarnation occasion, what does it trigger among Christians and, more broadly, in a culture deeply shaped by Christianity? Historically speaking, it has led to a massive imbalance between women and men. Men alone have been seen as 'worthy' of representing God, of acting in the place of Christ. Mary Daly, one of the pioneers of feminist theology, famously quipped that, 'if God is male, then the male is God'.[103] If we are tempted to think this is too quick, attending to the historical consequences of the Incarnation on gender relations and on the role of women in the Church should make us patient upon such pronouncements. There is more than a grain of truth in the claim that, 'of all the doctrines of the church[,] Christology is the one most used to suppress and exclude women', since Jesus' maleness has at times been considered 'essential to his redeeming christic function and identity'.[104]

But feminist theology's questions do not simply concern Jesus as a 'person'. They also focus on his reconciliatory work, and especially his suffering. The gospels appear to say that his suffering was divinely ordained, that it was 'necessary' for Jesus to suffer – consider Mark 8:31, where the Greek verb δεῖ ('must') is used – in order for him to become the saviour. The rejection of 'redemptive suffering', and its historical abuse as a tool for legitimising mistreatment and oppression of women, is one of feminist theology's key concerns. And so, the gospel narratives have been scrutinised to criticise the interpretation of Jesus' cross as a form of 'salvific suffering'.[105] Feminist theology thus calls for a renewed interpretation of some of Christianity's central tenets, including the Incarnation and Christ's passion. As examples, two particularing promising avenues might be lifted up. Elizabeth A. Johnson, a Roman Catholic feminist scholar, has sought to retrieve the Apostle Paul's interpretation of Jesus as God's 'wisdom' (*sophia*), thereby shifting and expanding Christological imagery which traditionally centres on 'word' (*logos*).[106] Ivone Gebara, a Brazilian ecofeminist Roman Catholic theologian, is articulating a theology of the 'Christ power' of believers – including the unnamed people in the gospels – as they resist against the oppression of women and, more broadly, of fellow human beings, but also of our natural environment as a whole.[107]

## Black Theologies

Towards the end of the 1960s, an American 'Black theology' appeared, spearheaded by the work of James H. Cone but with roots in the spirituals and other expressions of the faith of African-American slaves in the nineteenth century. With this movement, Jesus ceased to be the blond and blue-eyed European of many traditional Western images and was named 'the Black Messiah', whose central message is found in Luke 4:18: 'liberation' from oppression, and Jesus Christ as liberator.[108] Not just Jesus is Black, but *God* too is Black, and '[w]e must become black with God!'[109] African Americans may thus identify with God, and also realise that God identifies with them.[110] The point here is not simply to denote one's skin-pigmentation, but rather to issue a political and theological statement in relation to oppression and marginalisation.[111] For, if Jesus is Black and if God is Black, this means that white people are *not* God.[112] Black theology was, and still is, an important attempt to retrieve the radical implications of Jesus' message, in stark opposition to a number of deficient portrayals of his prophetic message. It has been deepened over the years, as certain voices, such as Kelly Brown Douglas, have urged Black theology not to omit certain forms of oppression which also occur *within* the African-American community.[113]

Black theology, liberation theology and feminist theology have begun to intersect in interesting ways, and together contribute to an indispensible, indeed crucial Christology 'from the margins' and *for* the margins.[114]

## Liberation Theology

Liberation theology is, in many ways, an heir of the Social Gospel from the turn of the twentieth century, even as it goes further than that older movement. Here Christ is God 'made poor'. Jesus was

> born into a social milieu characterized by poverty. He chose to live with the poor. He addressed his gospel by preference to the poor. He lashed out with invective against the rich who oppressed the poor and despised them. And before the Father, he was poor in spirit.[115]

Jesus embodies God's 'preferential option for the poor' – liberation theology's central axiom – as well as God's liberation. His own resurrection is 'the realization' of his announcement (e.g. in Luke 4:18) of total liberation, especially from the 'reign of death'.[116] Jesus Christ liberator enjoins his people to follow in his footsteps and to struggle, as he himself did, for justice and freedom in the concrete economic, political and social situations of all who experience injustice and oppression. As with the Social Gospel, but with a stronger sense of sin as a 'systemic' reality in human societies, liberation theology centres on Jesus' acts, his life and passion, and on the kingdom he proclaimed and embodied, and for which he gave his life. Both theological movements are deeply distrustful of any dualism between the 'profane' and the 'sacred', or the 'material' and the 'spiritual'. Liberation theology, especially in its Roman Catholic versions, ponders the martyrdom of significant figures such as Óscar Romero (1917–80) and Ignacio Ellacuría (1930–89), associating these tragic deaths with Jesus' own crucifixion.

## A Global Christ

Much of twentieth-century Christology was European, and even German-speaking. This era is now fast receding, as theological reflection is finding new roots throughout the world. Many contextual Christologies are emerging, on all continents, including of course in countries which have known steep increases in Christian presence, e.g. in South Korea, China, and in several African countries.[117] The call for 'inculturation', in the aftermath of the Second Vatican Council, has been heard. There were only roughly 9 million Christians in Africa in 1900; they are now over 450 million, with numbers projected to reach 600 million by 2025.[118] It is not simply Christianity which is spreading, but particular modern expressions of Protestantism, especially Pentecostalism and evangelicalism. The consequences of these massive changes, also for Christology, cannot be overestimated.

Western Christians should not expect their sisters and brothers on other continents to adopt the European-born Christologies, even if these Christologies might enrich Christians in many different contexts. Western Christians need to be attentive to the new Christologies which are being articulated all around the world and to foster ongoing dialogue across geographical, and theological, borders. Undoubtedly, developments in Christology in the West this past century can be of value for Christians in Asia, Africa, the Americas and Oceania. Will Western theologians listen to the Christology emerging from these regions and discover new 'faces' of Jesus-Christ? Of course, it would not be the first time that, for example, African theologians make highly significant contributions to Christian theology – think only of Tertullian, Origen, Cyprian and Augustine! But what is new is the stronger presence, especially in recent years, of women's voices, and of liberationist perspectives.

Just as it is not certain that Western Christologies will 'speak' in other contexts, there is no guarantee that the contextual Christologies which are emerging in, say, various African countries will impact Western Christians, who may not be sensitive to the new 'offices' (*munera*) or metaphors which are being explored there, such as 'chief', '(proto-) ancestor', 'elder brother', 'healer' or 'master of initiation'.[119] But the sheer creativity of such Christologies should encourage Western theologians and Christians to renew traditional themes and create new themes which may 'revive' and expand ancient doctrines. 'We do not know what we believe if we do not say it in our own language', writes Jean-Marc Éla (1936–2008), a Roman Catholic theologian from Southern Cameroon who has significantly contributed to the effort of interpreting the Christian faith as an African.[120] What he says of theology as a whole applies also to Christology: it must 'begin theology anew, starting with the struggles of the black peoples as they resist a return to the chaos which preceded creation'. And this means 'returning to the tree of the Cross'.[121] With a clear liberationist perspective, Jean-Marc Éla envisages a theology 'under the tree', intimately related to history, since this is where God encounters the world; a theology done by Christians who are 'life companions and road companions' of their people.[122]

## Concluding Remarks

We will never be at the end of our consideration of Jesus of Nazareth, the Christ of God – not simply because his identity, his life and work stand at the very centre of the Christian faith and of Christianity, but because he himself, as the crucified and risen One, asks us to answer the question he poses to us always anew: who do you say that I am? That very question indicates that Christologies which focus mostly on what Christ effected and effects – i.e. on soteriology – without simultaneously considering his very identity as the Son of God and as Lord, deserve to be questioned. Albert Schweitzer was right: Jesus is both the one who comes close to us, and a stranger to us. More pointedly, we may discover, again and again, that it is as this man calls his disciples his 'friends' (John 15:15) and as he announces to them what he is about to endure for their sake and for the sake of the world (Mark 8:31, 9:31, 10:33), that both his alterity as the anointed one, and his intimate solidarity with humanity and creation (especially with 'the least of these' (Matt. 25:40,45), shine with the greatest clarity.

# Notes

1. Matt. 26:64; see also Matt. 27:11; Mark 15:2; Luke 22:70 and 23:3.
2. For a rich overview of Christology, not just in the twentieth century but in the entire Christian tradition (and beyond), see Francesca Aran Murphy and Troy A. Stefano (eds), *The Oxford Handbook of Christology* (Oxford: Oxford University Press, 2015).
3. Ernst Troeltsch, 'Geschichte und Metaphysik', *Zeitschrift für Theologie und Kirche* 8 (1898), 1–69: 63–4 (unless otherwise noted, all translations are my own).
4. Troeltsch, 'Geschichte und Metaphysik', pp. 61–2.
5. Troeltsch, 'Geschichte und Metaphysik', p. 53.
6. For a detailed analysis, see Sarah Coakley, *Christ without Absolutes: A Study of the Christology of Ernst Troeltsch* (Oxford: Clarendon Press, 1988). See also, more recently, Paul J. DeHart, *Unspeakable Cults: An Essay in Christology* (Waco: Baylor, 2021).
7. Adolf von Harnack, *What Is Christianity?*, Thomas Bailey Saunders (trans.) (Philadelphia: Fortress Press, [1900] 1986). This distinction is ubiquitous in Harnack's lectures; see esp. pp. 2, 12, 15, 55, 127, 130, 179–80, 217, 290, 292 and 299.
8. Harnack, *What Is Christianity?*, pp. 179–80.
9. Harnack, *What Is Christianity?*, p. 68 (revised).
10. Harnack, *What Is Christianity?*, p. 145. On the preceding page (144), Harnack restates his main thesis: 'The Gospel, as Jesus proclaimed it, has to do with the Father only and not with the Son.'
11. Harnack, *What Is Christianity?*, p. 300.
12. Harnack, *What Is Christianity?*, p. 147 (revised).
13. Harnack, *What Is Christianity?*, p. 184.
14. Harnack, *What Is Christianity?*, p. 276.
15. Harnack, *What Is Christianity?*, p. 48; 'peace, joy and certainty', p. 38.
16. Harnack, *What Is Christianity?*, p. 57.
17. Harnack, *What Is Christianity?*, p. 115; on the 'socialistic' dimension, Harnack writes: 'There can be no doubt . . . that if Jesus were with us today he would side with those who are making great efforts to relieve the hard lot of the poor and procure them better conditions of life.' Harnack, *What Is Christianity?*, p. 99.
18. Harnack, *What Is Christianity?*, p. 116 (revised).
19. Albert Schweitzer, *The Quest of the Historical Jesus*, John Bowden (ed.), W. Montgomery, J. R. Coates, Susan Cupitt and John Bowden (trans.) (London: SCM Press, 2000), p. 478.
20. For a similar assessment of Schweitzer, see Robert Morgan, 'Albert Schweitzer's Challenge and the Response from New Testament Theology', in James Carleton Paget and Michael J. Thate, *Albert Schweitzer in Thought and Action* (Syracuse, NY: Syracuse University Press, 2016), pp. 71–104: 93.
21. Harnack, *What Is Christianity?*, p. 142; see also pp. 34, 56 and 263.
22. Walter Rauschenbusch, *A Theology for the Social Gospel* (Nashville: Abingdon, [1917] 1978), pp. 22 and 5.
23. Rauschenbusch, *A Theology for the Social Gospel*, p. 53.

24. Rauschenbusch may have been at odds with Harnack concerning the intrinsic social dimension of the Gospel, but the similarity of their aim, namely the 'revival of the most ancient and authentic Gospel', is obvious. Rauschenbusch, A *Theology for the Social Gospel*, p. 26.

25. Rauschenbusch, A *Theology for the Social Gospel*, p. 21.

26. Alfred Loisy, *L'Évangile et l'Église* (Paris: Alphonse Picard, 1902), p. 111; *The Gospel and the Church*, Christopher Home (trans.) (Eugene: Wipf and Stock, 2001), p. 166. Rauschenbusch writes that, in the early Church, 'the name and idea of "the Kingdom" began to be displaced by the name and idea of "the Church" in the preaching, literature and theological thought of the Church'. Rauschenbusch, A *Theology for the Social Gospel*, p. 132.

27. Among the Swiss-German Social Christians, Rauschenbusch mentions (A *Theology for the Social Gospel*, p. 28) the following people who, except for the first two, are now almost entirely forgotten: Leonhard Ragaz (1868–1945), Hermann Kutter (1863–1931), Jean Matthieu (1874–1921), who was an editor of the Swiss-German Social Christian journal *Neue Wege*, Basel pastor Gustav Benz (1866–1937) and the Basel publisher and printer Friedrich Reinhardt (1866–1949).

28. Rauschenbusch, A *Theology for the Social Gospel*, p. 155. There are distinct Ritschlian overtones in this definition of the kingdom. Ritschl had made the kingdom the centrepiece of his own theology.

29. Rauschenbusch, A *Theology for the Social Gospel*, p. 31.

30. Rauschenbusch, A *Theology for the Social Gospel*, p. 42.

31. Rauschenbusch, A *Theology for the Social Gospel*, pp. 146–66, 240–79.

32. Rauschenbusch, A *Theology for the Social Gospel*, p. 147.

33. Rauschenbusch, A *Theology for the Social Gospel*, pp. 144, 147–8. 'Theology has been on a false trail in seeking the key to his life in the difficult doctrine of the two natures.' Rauschenbusch, A *Theology for the Social Gospel*, p. 150.

34. Rauschenbusch, A *Theology for the Social Gospel*, p. 148.

35. Rauschenbusch, A *Theology for the Social Gospel*, pp. 147–8 and 151. This is of course another debt to Harnack.

36. Rauschenbusch, A *Theology for the Social Gospel*, p. 152.

37. Rauschenbusch, A *Theology for the Social Gospel*, pp. 162 and 164.

38. Rauschenbusch, A *Theology for the Social Gospel*, p. 163.

39. Rauschenbusch, A *Theology for the Social Gospel*, p. 243.

40. Rauschenbusch, A *Theology for the Social Gospel*, pp. 248–58.

41. Rauschenbusch, A *Theology for the Social Gospel*, p. 260.

42. Rauschenbusch, A *Theology for the Social Gospel*, pp. 34–5 and 53. On militarism, see also pp. 255–6.

43. Rauschenbusch, A *Theology for the Social Gospel*, p. 79.

44. Another, older theologian, Erich Schäder (1861–1936), expressed a similar dissatisfaction, albeit in less rigorous or radical terms than Barth, in his *Theozentrische Theologie: Eine Untersuchung zur dogmatischen Prinzipienlehre* (Leipzig: A. Deichert, 2 vols, 1909–14).

45. Karl Barth, *The Göttingen Dogmatics: Instruction in the Christian Religion*, Hannelotte Reiffen (ed.), Geoffrey W. Bromiley (trans.) (Grand Rapids: Eerdmans, 1990), vol. 1, p. 90 (revised); *Unterricht in der christlichen Religion*, vol. 1, *Prolegomena* [1924], Hannelotte Reiffen (ed.) (Zurich: TVZ, 1985), p. 108.

46. Barth, *The Göttingen Dogmatics*, vol. 1, p. 157 (revised); *Unterricht*, p. 193. For a contemporary restating of this ancient doctrine, without any explicit mention of it (at least on these particular pages), with the intention to show that this doctrine steers clear of the monophysite tendencies many critics ascribe to it, see Rowan Williams, *Christ the Heart of Creation* (London: Bloomsbury, 2018), pp. 30–1 (see also, here with an explicit mention of the doctrine: p. 193, n. 57).

47. Barth, *The Göttingen Dogmatics*, vol. 1, p. 157 (revised); '*Unterricht*', p. 109.

48. Emil Brunner, *The Mediator: A Study of the Central Doctrine of the Christian Faith*, Olive Wyon

(trans.) (London: Lutterworth Press, 1934). For Karl Barth's appraisal of Brunner's book, see his letter to Brunner from 14 January 1929, in Karl Barth and Brunner, *Briefwechsel 1916–1996*, Eberhard Busch (ed.) (Zurich: TVZ, 2000), pp. 169–70, where Barth rejoices over the 'broad agreement' (*breite Übereinstimmung*) between them.

49. Brunner, *The Mediator*, p. 239, n. 1. Brunner, however, is convinced his book is in tune with the Reformed tradition, especially with regard to the doctrine of the *communicatio idiomatum*, 'the blending of the two natures', or rather the mutual communication of their respective properties (p. 343, n. 1).

50. Brunner, *The Mediator*, pp. 309–10.

51. Brunner, *The Mediator*, p. 488 (revised).

52. Brunner, *The Mediator*, p. 547.

53. Brunner, *The Mediator*, pp. 416–34.

54. As a theologian who sought to relate every single locus or theme of Christian theology to Jesus Christ, Barth had already significant things to say on Christ in his doctrine of creation (*Church Dogmatics*, vol. 3, parts 1–4, published between 1945 and 1951), which amounts to 2,700 pages, as well as in earlier volumes too. For a concise overview of these volumes, see Eberhard Bush, *The Great Passion*, Geoffrey W. Bromiley (trans.), Darrell L. Guder and Judith L. Guder (eds) (Grand Rapids and Cambridge: Eerdmans, 2004).

55. For a helpful, one-page overview of the structure of *Church Dogmatics*, vol. 4, parts 1–3, see Jüngel, *Karl Barth*, pp. 48–9.

56. Barth, *Church Dogmatics*, vol. 4, part 1, p. 166.

57. Barth, *Church Dogmatics*, vol. 4, part 1, p. 200; part 2, pp. 25–6, 60–3.

58. Barth, *Church Dogmatics*, vol. 4, part 2, pp. 105; *Kirchliche Dogmatik* (Zollikon and Zürich: Evangelische Verlag, 1932–67) (henceforth *KD*), vol. 4, part 2, p. 116.

59. This 'process' is expressed in the theme of the 'way' of the Son into the far country. See Georg Plasger, 'Jesus Christus', in *Barth Handbuch*, edited by Michael Beintker (Tübingen: Mohr Siebeck, 2016), pp. 307–13: 311. For a similar strategy, see Williams, *Christ the Heart of Creation*, p. 25.

60. Barth, *KD*, vol. 4, part 2, p. 117. See Bruce L. McCormack, 'Karl Barth's Historicized Christology: Just How "Chalcedonian" Is It?', in *Orthodox and Modern: Studies in the Theology of Karl Barth* (Grand Rapids: Baker Academic, 2008), pp. 201–33. Cf. George Hunsinger, 'Karl Barth's Christology: Its Basic Chalcedonian Character', in *Disruptive Grace: Studies in the Theology of Karl Barth* (Grand Rapids: Eerdmans, 2000), pp. 131–47.

61. Barth, *Church Dogmatics*, vol. 4, part 2, p. 108; *KD*, vol. 4, part 2, p. 119.

62. Bruce L. McCormack, *The Humility of the Eternal Son: Reformed Kenoticism and the Repair of Chalcedon* (Cambridge: Cambridge University Press, 2021).

63. Barth, *Church Dogmatics*, vol. 4, part 1, pp. 557–8.

64. Rudolf Bultmann, 'New Testament and Mythology', in *Kerygma and Myth: A Theological Debate*, edited by Hans-Werner Bartsch, vol. 1 (London: SPCK, 1962), p. 38. See also Rudolf Bultmann, 'The Christological Confession of the World Council of Churches', in *Essays Philosophical and Theological*, James C. G. Greig (trans.) (London: SCM Press, 1955), p. 280.

65. See Rudolf Bultmann and Friedrich Gogarten, *Briefwechsel 1921–1967*, Hermann Götz Göckeritz (ed.) (Tübingen: Mohr Siebeck, 2002), pp. 292–3.

66. See Paul Tillich, *Systematic Theology*, vol. 2 (Chicago: The University of Chicago Press, 1957), pp. 88 and 138. For other symbolic formulas, see p. 108.

67. Tillich, *Systematic Theology*, vol. 2, pp. 138–9.

68. Tillich, *Systematic Theology*, vol. 2, p. 150.

69. Tillich, *Systematic Theology*, vol. 2, p. 142.

70. Tillich, *Systematic Theology*, vol. 2, pp. 144–5.

71. Tillich, *Systematic Theology*, vol. 2, p. 46.

72. Tillich, *Systematic Theology*, vol. 2, p. 160. See also Williams, *Christ the Heart of Creation*,

pp. 12, 14; see also p. 149. Tillich suggests that his views on Christ are, as a whole, similar to those of Schleiermacher. Tillich, *Systematic Theology*, vol. 2, p. 150.

73. Tillich, *Systematic Theology*, vol. 2, pp. 152 and 164. See esp. 157 on the Resurrection: 'in an ecstatic experience the concrete picture of Jesus of Nazareth became indissolubly united with the reality of the New Being'.

74. See Nicolas Berdyaev, 'Christ de l'Orient, Christ de l'Occident: Le problème de l'Orient et de l'Occident chrétiens dans la conscience religieuse de Vladimir Soloviev', in *Chemins de la christologie orthodoxe*, edited by Astérios Argyriou (Paris: Desclée, 2005), pp. 335–47: 342. For an English translation (but with significant differences), see http://www.berdyaev.com/berdia ev/berd_lib/1911_053.html.

75. See John Calvin's theology, for starters, but also Tillich's *Systematic Theology*, vol. 3 (Chicago: University of Chicago Press, 1963), section II.B.3, on 'Spirit Christology'.

76. See Nikos A. Nissiotis, 'Pneumatological Christology as a Presupposition of Ecclesiology', in *Œcumenica: An Annual Symposium of Ecumenical Research*, vol. 2 (Minneapolis: Augsburg Press, 1967), pp. 235–52, esp. 236, 240. See also Nikos A. Nissiotis, *Die Theologie der Ostkirche im ökumenischen Dialog* (Stuttgart: Evangelisches Verlagswerk, 1968), esp. ch. 2 ('Die pneumatologische Christologie als Voraussetzung der Ekklesiologie'), pp. 64–85.

77. Yves Congar, *I Believe in the Holy Spirit*, David Smith (trans.) (New York: Crossroad, 2004).

78. See Rahner, 'Current Problems in Christology' [1954], in *Theological Investigations*, vol. 1, Cornelius Ernst (trans.) (Baltimore: Helicon, 1961), pp. 149–200: 151. On Rahner's Christology, see e.g. Evelyne Maurice, *La christologie de Karl Rahner* (Paris: Desclée, 1995), or Declan Marmion and Mary E. Hines (eds), *The Cambridge Companion to Karl Rahner* (Cambridge: Cambridge University Press, 2006).

79. See Mark A. McIntosh, *Christology from Within: Spirituality and Incarnation in Hans Urs von Balthasar* (Notre Dame: University of Notre Dame Press, 2000), pp. 5, 12, 32 and *passim*. Balthasar's key contribution to Christology is arguably found in *Theodramatik*, vol. 2: *Die Personen des Spiels*, part 2: *Die Personen in Christus* (Einsiedeln: Johannes Verlag, 1978); published in English as *Theo-Drama: Theological Dramatic Theory*, vol. 3: *The Dramatis Personae: Persons in Christ*, Graham Harrison (trans.) (San Francisco: Ignatius Press, 1992).

80. As McIntosh puts it, Balthasar's works have 'an undeniable scent of the sanctuary, a tendency to view everything in heavenly terms'. *Christology from Within*, p. 72. Balthasar was aware of this danger and tried to avoid it (see p. 73). Still: did he succeed?

81. Wolfhart Pannenberg, *Jesus: God and Man*, Lewis L. Wilkins and Duane A. Priebe (trans.) (London: SCM Press, 1968), p. 34.

82. Pannenberg, *Jesus: God and Man*, p. 35.

83. See Käsemann's article on 'The Problem of the Historical Jesus', in *Essays on New Testament Themes*, W. J. Montague (trans.) (London: SCM Press, [1954] 1964), pp. 15–47. Käsemann rightly stressed that 'the function of recalling the historical Jesus is, within the framework of the Gospel, a permanent necessity'. Ernst Käsemann, 'Blind Alleys in the "Jesus of History" Controversy', in *New Testament Questions of Today*, W. J. Montague (trans.) (London, SCM Press, 1969), pp. 23–65: 64.

84. Pannenberg, *Jesus: God and Man*, p. 49; *Grundzüge der Christologie*, p. 43.

85. Pannenberg, *Jesus: God and Man*, p. 43.

86. Pannenberg, *Jesus: God and Man*, p. 25.

87. Pannenberg, *Jesus: God and Man*, p. 59; *Grundzüge der Christologie*, p. 53. See also Wolfhart Pannenberg, *Systematic Theology*, vol. 2, Geoffrey W. Bromiley (trans.) (Grand Rapids: Eerdmans, 1994), pp. 334–7.

88. See Friedrich Gogarten, *Die Verkündigung Jesu Christi: Grundlagen und Aufgabe* (Heidelberg: Schneider, 1948), p. 500; see also Pannenberg, *Jesus: God and Man*, p. 286.

89. Pannenberg, *Systematic Theology*, vol 2, pp. 372–9 (a section titled 'The Self-Distinction of Jesus from the Father as the Inner Basis of His Divine Sonship'); see also pp. 325 and 385–8.

90. Jürgen Moltmann, *Theology of Hope: On the Ground and the Implications of a Christian Eschatology*,

James W. Leitch (trans.) (London: SCM Press, 2002); *The Crucified God: The Cross of Christ as the Foundation and Criticism of Christian Theology*, R. A. Wilson and John Bowden (trans.) (London: SCM Press, 1973); *The Church in the Power of the Spirit: A Contribution to Messianic Ecclesiology*, Margaret Kohl (trans.) (New York: Harper and Row, 1977). See also *The Way of Jesus Christ: Christology in Messianic Dimensions*, Margaret Kohl (trans.) (London: SCM Press, 1990).

91. Jürgen Moltmann, *A Broad Place: An Autobiography*, Margaret Kohl (trans.) (London: SCM Press, 2007), p. 103. In Moltmann's case, this realisation occured in the wake of the assassination of Martin Luther King Jr, on 4 April 1968 in Memphis, while Moltmann was taking part with five hundred other theologians in a conference on hope at Duke University.

92. Moltmann had been deeply influenced by a significant mid-twentieth-century Lutheran theologian, Hans-Joachim Iwand, especially by Iwand's lectures on Luther's 1518 Heidelberg Disputation; see Moltmann, *A Broad Place*, pp. 41 and 43. Cf. Jürgen Moltmann, *The Living God and the Fullness of Life*, Margaret Kohl (trans.) (Geneva, WCC Publications, 2016), p. 66.

93. Moltmann, *The Living God and the Fullness of Life*, p. 197.

94. See Eberhard Jüngel's dense little book *The Doctrine of the Trinity: God's Being Is in Becoming*, Horton Harris (trans.) (Edinburgh and London: Scottish Academic Press, 1976).

95. See, for instance, Jüngel's short study *Death: The Riddle and the Mystery*, Iain and Ute Nicol (trans.) (Edinburgh: Saint Andrew Press, 1975).

96. These come mainly in the final section of the book, 'On the Humanity of God'; see Eberhard Jüngel, *God as the Mystery of the World: On the Foundation of the Theology of the Crucified One in the Dispute between Theism and Atheism*, Darrell L. Guder (trans.) (Grand Rapids: Eerdmans, [1977] 1983), pp. 299–396.

97. Jüngel, *God as the Mystery of the World*, pp. 348–51.

98. Jüngel, *God as the Mystery of the World*, pp. 307 and 309.

99. Jüngel, *God as the Mystery of the World*, pp. 350, 361 and 367.

100. Jüngel, *God as the Mystery of the World*, p. 314.

101. For a recent, massive proposal which articulates a Christology of the 'name' Jesus Christ in close connection with the Christian *praxis* of reconciliation, in conversation with Karl Barth, Emmanuel Levinas, Eberhard Jüngel and Ingolf Dalferth (among others), see Heinrich Assel, *Elementare Christologie*, 3 vols (Gütersloh: Gütersloher Verlagshaus, 2020).

102. Paul Ricoeur, *The Symbolism of Evil*, Emerson Buchanan (trans.) (Boston: Beacon Press, 1969), p. 348.

103. Mary Daly, *Beyond God the Father: Toward a Philosophy of Women's Liberation* (Boston: Beacon Press, [1973] 1985), p. 19.

104. Elizabeth A. Johnson, *She Who Is: The Mystery of God in Feminist Theological Discourse* (New York: Crossroad, 1997), p. 151; see also p. 35.

105. Not only female theologians have been sensitive to this, of course. See Leonardo Boff, *Passion of Christ, Passion of the World: The Facts, Their Interpretation, and Their Meaning Yesterday and Today* (Maryknoll, NY: Orbis, [1977] 1988), pp. 111–15.

106. Johnson, *She Who Is*, ch. 8 (pp. 150–69, esp. 166–7).

107. Ivone Gebara, *Longing for Running Water: Ecofeminism and Liberation*, David Molineaux (trans.) (Minneapolis: Fortress, 1999).

108. See National Conference of the Black Theology Project, 'Message to the Black Church and Community' [1977], in *Black Theology: A Documentary History (1966–1979)*, edited by Gayraud S. Wilmore and James H. Cone (Maryknoll, NY: Orbis, 1979), pp. 345–6; see also p. 480.

109. James H. Cone, *A Black Theology of Liberation* (Maryknoll, NY: Orbis, [1970] 2000), p. 69.

110. Jacquelyn Grant, *White Women's Christ and Black Women's Jesus: Feminist Christology and Womanist Response* (Atlanta: Scholars Press, 1989), p. 212. See also Chigor Chike, 'Black Christology for the Twenty-First Century', *Black Theology: An International Journal* 8:3 (2010), 357–78: 373–4.

111. See Chike, 'Black Christology for the Twenty-First Century', p. 376, with reference to Michael N. Jagessar and Anthony G. Reddie (eds), *Black Theology in Britain: A Reader* (London: Equinox Publishers, 2007), p. 6.

112. Grant, *White Women's Christ and Black Women's Jesus*, p. 213.

113. Kelly Brown Douglas, *The Black Christ* (Maryknoll, NY: Orbis, 1994), pp. 85–7.

114. Thomas Bohache, *Christology from the Margins* (London: SCM Press, 2008). There is, however, a risk of producing ever smaller 'niches' or specialised subfields within theology in which scholars mostly read what others are writing within these subfields, instead of aiming to contribute to Christian theology as such or as a whole.

115. Gustavo Gutiérrez, *The Power of the Poor in History* (Maryknoll, NY: Orbis, 1983), p. 13.

116. Leonardo Boff, *Jesus Christ Liberator: A Critical Christology for Our Time* (Maryknoll, NY: Orbis, 1978), p. 122.

117. For brief surveys, see Murphy and Stefano (eds), *The Oxford Handbook of Christology*, ch. 25 ('Chinese Christologies') and ch. 27 ('Jesus Christ, Living Water in Africa Today'). For more details, see Muriel Orevillo-Montenegro, *The Jesus of Asian Women* (Maryknoll, NY: Orbis, 2006). See also John Parratt, *The Other Jesus: Christology in Asian Perspective* (Frankfurt: Peter Lang, 2012), pp. 17–61 and 131–2.

118. See Pew Forum, 'Global Christianity: A Report on the Size and Distribution of the World's Christian Population' (2011), accessed at http://www.pewforum.org.

119. See Anne Nasimiyu-Wasike, 'Christology and an African Woman's Experience', in *Faces of Jesus in Africa*, edited by Robert J. Schreiter (Maryknoll, NY: Orbis, 1991; London: SCM Press, 1992), pp. 70–81, as well as François Kabasele Lumbala's contributions, 'Christ as Chief', 'Christ as Ancestor and Elder Brother', pp. 103–15 and 116–27. See François Kabasele Lumbala, *Alliances avec le Christ en Afrique: Inculturation des rites religieux au Zaïre*, 2nd ed. (Paris: Karthala, [1987] 1994).

120. 'Nous ne savons pas ce que nous croyons si nous ne le disons pas dans notre propre langage.' Jean-Marc Éla, *Ma foi d'africain* (Paris: Karthala, 1985), p. 200.

121. Éla, *Ma foi d'africain*, pp. 215–16. On the cross, see pp. 140–4.

122. Éla, *Ma foi d'africain*, pp. 216 and 218.

# Bibliography

Assel, Heinrich, *Elementare Christologie*, 3 vols (Gütersloh: Gütersloher Verlagshaus, 2020).

Balthasar, Hans Urs von, *Theo-Drama: Theological Dramatic Theory*, vol. 3: *The Dramatis Personae: Persons in Christ*, Graham Harrison (trans.) (San Francisco: Ignatius Press, 1992).

Balthasar, Hans Urs von, *Theodramatik*, vol. 2: *Die Personen des Spiels*, part 2: *Die Personen in Christus* (Einsiedeln: Johannes Verlag, 1978).

Barth, Karl, *Church Dogmatics*, Geoffrey W. Bromiley, T. F. Torrance et al. (trans.) (Edinburgh: T&T Clark, 1936–75).

Barth, Karl, *The Epistle to the Romans*, Edwyn C. Hoskyns (trans.) (London-Oxford-New York: Oxford University Press, 1933).

Barth, Karl, *The Göttingen Dogmatics: Instruction in the Christian Religion*, Hannelotte Reiffen (ed.), Geoffrey W. Bromiley (trans.) (Grand Rapids: Eerdmans, 1990).

Barth, Karl, *Kirchliche Dogmatik* (Zollikon and Zürich: Evangelische Verlag, 1932–67).

Barth, Karl, *Unterricht in der christlichen Religion*, vol. 1, *Prolegomena* [1924], Hannelotte Reiffen (ed.) (Zurich: TVZ, 1985).

Barth, Karl and Emil Brunner, *Briefwechsel 1916–1996*, Eberhard Busch (ed.) (Zurich: TVZ, 2000).

Bartsch, Hans-Werner (ed.), *Kerygma and Myth: A Theological Debate*, vol. 1 (London: SPCK, 1962).

Berdyaev, Nicolas, 'Christ de l'Orient, Christ de l'Occident: Le problème de l'Orient et de l'Occident chrétiens dans la conscience religieuse de Vladimir Soloviev', in *Chemins de la christologie orthodoxe*, edited by Astérios Argyriou (Paris: Desclée, 2005), pp. 335–47.

Boff, Leonardo, *Jesus Christ Liberator: A Critical Christology for Our Time* (Maryknoll, NY: Orbis, 1978).

Boff, Leonardo, *Passion of Christ, Passion of the World: The Facts, Their Interpretation, and Their Meaning Yesterday and Today* (Maryknoll, NY: Orbis, [1977] 1988).

Bohache, Thomas, *Christology from the Margins* (London: SCM Press, 2008).

Brunner, Emil, *Der Mittler: Zur Besinnung über den Christusglauben* (Tübingen: Mohr, 1927).

Brunner, Emil, *The Mediator: A Study of the Central Doctrine of the Christian Faith*, Olive Wyon (trans.) (London: Lutterworth Press, 1934).

Bulgakov, Sergius, *The Lamb of God*, Boris Jakim (trans.) (Grand Rapids, MI: Eerdmans, 2008).

Bultmann, Rudolf, 'The Christological Confession of the World Council of Churches', in *Essays Philosophical and Theological*, James C. G. Greig (trans.) (London: SCM Press, 1955).

Bultmann, Rudolf and Friedrich Gogarten, *Briefwechsel 1921–1967*, Hermann Götz Göckeritz (ed.) (Tübingen: Mohr Siebeck, 2002).

Bush, Eberhard, *The Great Passion: An Introduction to Karl Barth's Theology*, Geoffrey W. Bromiley (trans.), Darrell L. Guder and Judith L. Guder (eds) (Grand Rapids and Cambridge: Eerdmans, 2004).

Chike, Chigor, 'Black Christology for the Twenty-First Century', *Black Theology: An International Journal* 8:3 (2010), 357–78.

Coakley, Sarah, *Christ Without Absolutes: A Study of the Christology of Ernst Troeltsch* (Oxford: Clarendon Press, 1988).

Cone, James H., *A Black Theology of Liberation* (Maryknoll, NY: Orbis, [1970] 2000).

Congar, Yves, *I Believe in the Holy Spirit*, David Smith (trans.) (New York: Crossroad, 2004).

Daly, Mary, *Beyond God the Father: Toward a Philosophy of Women's Liberation* (Boston: Beacon Press, [1973] 1985).

DeHart, Paul J., *Unspeakable Cults: An Essay in Christology* (Waco: Baylor, 2021).

Douglas, Kelly Brown, *The Black Christ* (Maryknoll, NY: Orbis, 1994).

Éla, Jean-Marc, *Ma foi d'africain* (Paris: Karthala, 1985).

Evans, Christopher H., *The Kingdom Is Always but Coming: A Life of Walter Rauschenbusch* (Grand Rapids: Eerdmans, 2004).

Gebara, Ivone, *Longing for Running Water: Ecofeminism and Liberation*, David Molineaux (trans.) (Minneapolis: Fortress, 1999).

Gogarten, Friedrich, *Die Verkündigung Jesu Christi: Grundlagen und Aufgabe* (Heidelberg: Schneider, 1948).

Grant, Jacquelyn, *White Women's Christ and Black Women's Jesus* (Atlanta: Scholars Press, 1989).

Gutiérrez, Gustavo, *The Power of the Poor in History* (Maryknoll, NY: Orbis, 1983).

Harnack, Adolf von, *What Is Christianity?*, Thomas Bailey Saunders (trans.) (Philadelphia: Fortress, [1900] 1986).

Hunsinger, George, 'Karl Barth's Christology: Its Basic Chalcedonian Character', in *Disruptive Grace: Studies in the Theology of Karl Barth* (Grand Rapids: Eerdmans, 2000), pp. 131–47.

Jagessar, Michael N. and Anthony G. Reddie (eds), *Black Theology in Britain: A Reader* (London: Equinox Publishers, 2007).

Johnson, Elizabeth A., *She Who Is: The Mystery of God in Feminist Theological Discourse* (New York: Crossroard, 1997).

Jüngel, Eberhard, *Death: The Riddle and the Mystery*, Iain and Ute Nicol (trans.) (Edinburgh: Saint Andrew Press, 1975).

Jüngel, Eberhard, *The Doctrine of the Trinity: God's Being Is in Becoming*, Horton Harris (trans.) (Edinburgh and London: Scottish Academic Press, 1976).

Jüngel, Eberhard, *God as the Mystery of the World: On the Foundation of the Theology of the Crucified*

*One in the Dispute between Theism and Atheism*, Darrell L. Guder (trans.) (Grand Rapids: Eerdmans, [1977] 1983).

Jüngel, Eberhard, *Karl Barth: A Theological Legacy*, Garrett E. Paul (trans.) (Philadelphia: Westminster Press, 1986).

Kabasele Lumbala, François, *Alliances avec le Christ en Afrique: Inculturation des rites religieux au Zaïre*, 2nd ed. (Paris: Karthala, [1987] 1994).

Kabasele Lumbala, François, 'Christ as Ancestor and Elder Brother', in *Faces of Jesus in Africa*, edited by Robert J. Schreiter (Maryknoll, NY: Orbis, 1991; London: SCM Press, 1992), pp. 116–27.

Kabasele Lumbala, François, 'Christ as Chief', in *Faces of Jesus in Africa*, edited by Robert J. Schreiter (Maryknoll, NY: Orbis, 1991; London: SCM Press, 1992), pp. 103–15.

Käsemann Ernst, 'Blind Alleys in the "Jesus of History" Controversy', in *New Testament Questions of Today*, W. J. Montague (trans.) (London, SCM Press, 1969), pp. 23–65.

Käsemann Ernst, 'The Problem of the Historical Jesus', in *Essays on New Testament Themes*, W. J. Montague (trans.) (London: SCM Press, [1954] 1964), pp. 15–47.

Loisy, Alfred, *The Gospel and the Church*, Christopher Home (trans.) (Eugene: Wipf and Stock, 2001).

Loisy, Alfred, *L'Évangile et l'Église* (Paris: Alphonse Picard, 1902).

McCormack, Bruce L., *The Humility of the Eternal Son: Reformed Kenoticism and the Repair of Chalcedon* (Cambridge: Cambridge University Press, 2021).

McCormack, Bruce L., 'Karl Barth's Historicized Christology: Just How "Chalcedonian" Is It?', in *Orthodox and Modern: Studies in the Theology of Karl Barth* (Grand Rapids: Baker Academic, 2008), pp. 201–33.

McIntosh, Mark A., *Christology from Within: Spirituality and Incarnation in Hans Urs von Balthasar* (Notre Dame, IN: University of Notre Dame Press, 2000).

Marmion, Declan and Mary E. Hines (eds), *The Cambridge Companion to Karl Rahner* (Cambridge: Cambridge University Press, 2006).

Maurice, Evelyne, *La christologie de Karl Rahner* (Paris: Desclée, 1995).

Moltmann, Jürgen, *A Broad Place: An Autobiography*, Margaret Kohl (trans.) (London: SCM Press, 2007).

Moltmann, Jürgen, *The Church in the Power of the Spirit: A Contribution to Messianic Ecclesiology*, Margaret Kohl (trans.) (New York: Harper and Row, 1977).

Moltmann, Jürgen, *The Crucified God: The Cross of Christ as the Foundation and Criticism of Christian Theology*, R. A. Wilson and John Bowden (trans.) (London: SCM Press, 1973).

Moltmann, Jürgen, *The Living God and the Fullness of Life*, Margaret Kohl (trans.) (Geneva, WCC Publications, 2016).

Moltmann, Jürgen, *Theology of Hope: On the Ground and the Implications of a Christian Eschatology*, James W. Leitch (trans.) (London: SCM Press, 2002).

Moltmann, Jürgen, *The Way of Jesus Christ: Christology in Messianic Dimensions*, Margaret Kohl (trans.) (London: SCM Press, 1990).

Morgan, Robert, 'Albert Schweitzer's Challenge and the Response from New Testament Theology', in *Albert Schweitzer in Thought and Action: A Life in Parts*, edited by James Carleton Paget and Michael J. Thate (Syracuse, NY: Syracuse University Press, 2016), pp. 71–104.

Murphy, Francesca Aran and Troy A. Stefano (eds), *The Oxford Handbook of Christology* (Oxford: Oxford University Press, 2015).

Nasimiyu-Wasike, Anne, 'Christology and an African Woman's Experience', in *Faces of Jesus in Africa*, edited by Robert J. Schreiter (Maryknoll, NY: Orbis, 1991; London: SCM Press, 1992), pp. 70–81.

National Conference of the Black Theology Project, 'Message to the Black Church and Community' [1977], in *Black Theology: A Documentary History (1966–1979)*, edited by Gayraud S. Wilmore and James H. Cone (Maryknoll, NY: Orbis, 1979), pp. 345–6.

Nissiotis, Nikos A., *Die Theologie der Ostkirche im ökumenischen Dialog: Kirche und Welt in orthodoxer Sicht* (Stuttgart: Evangelisches Verlagswerk, 1968).

Nissiotis, Nikos A., 'Pneumatological Christology as a Presupposition of Ecclesiology', in *Œcumenica: An Annual Symposium of Ecumenical Research*, vol. 2 (Minneapolis: Augsburg Press, 1967), pp. 235–52.

Orevillo-Montenegro, Muriel, *The Jesus of Asian Women* (Maryknoll, NY: Orbis, 2006).

Pannenberg, Wolfhart, *Grundzüge der Christologie* (Gütersloh: Gütersloher Verlagshaus Gerd Mohn, 1964).

Pannenberg, Wolfhart, *Jesus: God and Man*, Lewis L. Wilkins and Duane A. Priebe (trans.) (London: SCM Press, 1968).

Pannenberg, Wolfhart, *Systematic Theology*, vol. 2, Geoffrey W. Bromiley (trans.) (Grand Rapids: Eerdmans, 1994).

Parratt, John, *The Other Jesus: Christology in Asian Perspective* (Frankfurt: Peter Lang, 2012).

Pew Forum, 'Global Christianity: A Report on the Size and Distribution of the World's Christian Population' (2011), accessed at http://www.pewforum.org.

Plasger, Georg, 'Jesus Christus', in *Barth Handbuch*, edited by Michael Beintker (Tübingen: Mohr Siebeck, 2016), pp. 307–13.

Rahner, Karl, 'Current Problems in Christology', in *Theological Investigations*, vol. 1, Cornelius Ernst (trans.) (Baltimore: Helicon, 1961), pp. 149–200.

Rahner, Karl, *Foundations of Christian Faith: An Introduction to the Idea of Christianity*, William V. Dych (trans.) (New York: Seabury, 1978).

Rauschenbusch, Walter, *Christianity and the Social Crisis* (New York: Macmillan, 1907; Eugene, OR: Wipf and Stock, 2003).

Rauschenbusch, Walter, *A Theology for the Social Gospel* (Nashville: Abingdon, [1917] 1978).

Ricoeur, Paul, *The Symbolism of Evil*, Emerson Buchanan (trans.) (Boston: Beacon Press, 1969).

Schäder, Erich, *Theozentrische Theologie: Eine Untersuchung zur dogmatischen Prinzipienlehre* (Leipzig: A. Deichert, 2 vols, 1909–14).

Schleiermacher, Friedrich, *The Christian Faith* H. R. Mackintosh et al. (trans.) (London: Bloomsbury, 2016).

Schweitzer, Albert, *The Quest of the Historical Jesus*, John Bowden (ed.), W. Montgomery, J. R. Coates, Susan Cupitt and John Bowden (trans.) (London: SCM Press, 2000).

Tillich, Paul, *Systematic Theology*, vols 2 and 3 (Chicago: University of Chicago Press, 1957, 1963).

Troeltsch, Ernst, 'Geschichte und Metaphysik', *Zeitschrift für Theologie und Kirche* 8 (1898), 1–69.

Williams, Rowan, *Christ the Heart of Creation* (London: Bloomsbury, 2018).

# 12

## Liberation and Freedom

### Elina Vuola

The question of freedom has occupied Western philosophy and theology since their beginning. It has been approached from different angles, several epistemological and disciplinary perspectives, and with a variety of broader social and political contexts and underpinnings. My interest in this article is not to go through that extensive history but rather concentrate on how the concepts of freedom and liberation have been re-examined and reinterpreted in contemporary theology since the late twentieth century.

Especially the issue of liberation has been at the heart of various liberation theologies and their underlying political struggles. I will concentrate of liberation theology in the broad sense – or liberation theologies in the plural – especially on liberation and contextual theologies of the Global South (Latin America, Asia and Africa), Black theology and feminist theology. The last – which is not always called 'feminist' theology – is a cross-cutting way of thinking from a critical gender perspective within other liberation theologies. This has led to womanist and *mujerista* theologies, of African-American and Latina women's perspectives in the United States, and feminist liberation theologies elsewhere. The gender perspective has provided a critical perspective on how freedom and liberation have (not) been adequately elaborated even within these new theologies, which claim to have these two concepts at the heart of their work.

Since issues of freedom and liberation are central also in secular, non-theological, political movements and ways of thought (against racism, sexism, homophobia etc.), I will also examine how and why an adequate understanding of religion and theology is central to take into account in any enterprise which aims at human freedom and liberation. Much of gender studies and feminism, and not just in the Global North, have an attitude towards religion in general and theology in particular which leads to an overtly one-sided treatment of religion.

## Nothing between Fideism and Fundamentalism?

When browsing some theological dictionaries and encyclopedia for this article I noticed that surprisingly few of them have 'freedom' as a separate entry. For example, in the *Dictionary of Fundamental Theology* (Catholic), there is no 'freedom' between the entries on fideism and fundamentalism. Neither is there an entry on liberation.[1] In this dictionary, as in most others, liberation is most often dealt with in the context of liberation theology – understandably, and as I will do here – and not as a separate entry. Feminist and liberation theology-oriented dictionaries tend to deal with both. For example, in two guidebooks of feminist theology, there are entries for both 'liberation' and 'freedom'.[2] Also in the *Dictionary of Third World Theologies*, there is a separate entry for 'liberation', besides an extensive presentation of the various forms of liberation theologies.[3] Even though I am not drawing any huge conclusions of this short survey, the absence of these words in dictionaries of theology and religious studies is reflective of the way in which the two concepts have been framed in the context of Christian theology and also religious studies.

Freedom, and not only liberation, is central for especially Black theologies and feminist theologies. It reflects aspects of subjugation, marginalisation and oppression, which do not always relate easily to the political and social struggles against colonialism, imperialism and poverty in the Global South. Overcoming racism and sexism includes aspects of individual oppression and healing of it, which standard liberation theology – whether in Latin America or elsewhere – did not include in its early stages, and did so only after critical dialogue with theologies which placed sexism and racism at the centre of any understanding of liberation theology. It is possible to trace this process historically, for example through the documents of the meetings of the Ecumenical Association of Third World Theologians (EATWOT), published as books. Black theologians criticised Latin American liberation theologians for their avoidance of issues of race and racism. Feminist theologians from all parts of the world criticised their colleagues for their lack of understanding of how sexism is tied to all aspects of political struggles and is at the heart of Christian theology and its sacred texts. It is clear how it was the issues of gender that were the last to enter in definitions of liberation theology.

To have an entry on 'freedom, free will' – where the two concepts are paralleled – is a telling example of a somewhat narrow, albeit classical, understanding of freedom in Christian theology.[4] At the same time, the difficulty to include issues of racism and sexism in much of liberation theology is telling of a narrow understanding of liberation.

## Freedom *and* Liberation

According to a womanist understanding (critical of both Black theology and feminist theology), freedom means wholeness. It refers to the elimination of the interlocking systems of oppression such as sexism, racism, classism and heterosexism. Freedom also means that individual men and women have confronted the ways in which complex societal oppression has left them less than whole persons, spiritually, psychologically and emotionally. While freedom and wholeness point to this particular vision of reality, they also imply a liberation process of struggle towards that vision.[5] This kind of an understanding of the interstructuring of different forms of subjugation is a product of feminist and womanist theologies, impossible to find in any early presentation of either liberation or Black theology. At the same time, the womanist emphasis offers a critical view of such feminist theology, which understands women's oppression only or even primarily in terms of gender.

In 'secular' gender studies, this development has been named as intersectionality: gender is still a central analytical category, but it cannot be adequately understood without other forms of difference and social location, such as class, race etc. As I argue elsewhere, the idea of intersectionality – even when it was not named as such, but rather as interlocking[6] or interstructuring[7] – was present in feminist theology earlier than in any other field of gender studies.[8]

In the abovementioned *Dictionary of Feminist Theologies*, liberation is defined as the struggle for freedom from oppression as subjugated people become conscious of their situation and work to transform the conditions of their existence. Such transformation includes personal and social change. Liberation is here linked to the Reformation emphasis on

Christian freedom, historically conceived as freedom from the law and sin. Traditionally, liberation has been primarily understood in terms of interior consciousness as the freedom from personal guilt and sin. This individualistic view is expanded in feminist theology to include its expressions in historically constituted structures of oppression, including the family.[9]

According to another feminist theological dictionary,[10] liberation implies that people become aware of their oppression and can imagine another reality beyond that. Theologically, this is based on the assumption that God also wants freedom and liberation, which should become a reality in this life and history, not after it. Liberation means fundamentally the same thing for most people, but it is usually those who lack rights and freedoms or are suffering from a structural evil (sexism, racism, poverty etc.) who point out that these evils are socially constructed and therefore liable to deconstruction. They also define what freedom and liberation mean for them: sense of worth, dignity and equality acquire distinctive meanings on the basis of race, ethnicity and gender, or their combination. Thus, for example, there are both enormous differences between women's possibilities globally and similarities which they share on the basis of being women in patriarchal societies and religious communities.[11]

Interestingly, the critique of individualism in traditional theology gets a different meaning in the context of liberation theologies and their mutual dialogue. Feminist critique of the lack of the personal and individual aspects of oppression in liberation theologies, which have tended to focus on structures and the macro level of society, shows how the individual can be understood quite differently depending on the context in which theology is done. Where traditional theology lacked structures and societal hierarchies of power, liberation theology lacked the gendered, racialised individual and her experiences of racism and sexism, including in the churches and their theological-ethical teachings.

According to Virginia Fabella, Third World liberation theologies generally see liberation in a comprehensive way – as both personal and structural – though they may accentuate one or other aspect of it. Women doing theology understand liberation as freedom from all bondage: from androcentric practices in society, economic inequalities, racial and ethnic discrimination, and other forms of domination and exploitation. Thus, liberation is not a mere theme in liberation theology; it is its goal.[12] Similarly, Elsa Tamez states that liberation theology is not a reflection on the theme of liberation but 'a new manner' of doing theology. The contribution of liberation theology is its new method, not the theme.[13]

Thus, it seems there is a stronger conceptual link between freedom and liberation in those liberation theologies, which include a fundamental embodied, historical and both individually and communally experienced oppression, which is written on one's body, lived through it, suffered in it. For women, freedom means the basic freedom to be embodied subjects to make decisions over their bodies, including everything related to sexuality and reproduction. According to Tamez, Black theology includes two important theological affirmations: first, the knowledge of God that reveals God's self as liberator, and second, the blackness of God and of Christ as theological symbols in the struggles for freedom and liberation. The question of *imago Dei* is thus central for those liberation theologies, which deconstruct the traditional constructions of inequality in such theologies of creation which equate difference with inequality (such as most Christian theology on women and the relationship between women and men; orders of creation theology in South Africa during apartheid). Theologies of the body – or body theology – could thus be yet another way to understand different liberation theologies from the perspective of the inevitability of human bodily existence, one the one hand, and as critical reflection on the historical legacy of legitimating oppression on the basis of bodily differences, on the other. These come together in the simultaneous affirmation of the goodness of human embodiment in all its diversity (theologically, this very diversity as *imago Dei*) and the bodily experienced suffering and oppression (theologically, structural sin violating the *imago Dei*).

## What Is Liberation Theology?

Liberation theology can be defined either narrowly or broadly. In the former sense, it is limited to the Latin American liberation theology (*teología de la liberación, teologia da liber-tação*), born out of a specifically Latin American context in the late 1960s. In the broader sense, liberation theology also includes Black theology, feminist theology and variations of Asian and African liberation and contextual theologies. The broad definition stresses the interrelatedness of different structures of oppression and domination, as was presented above.

Liberation necessarily involves political, economic, social, racial, ethnic and sexual aspects – and all of them both at the individual, social and global level. The mutual dia-logue and critique between these different liberation theologies has had the effect that later Latin American liberation theology has become more encompassing. It includes all the above-mentioned variants, such as Latin American Black, feminist, ecological and indigenous theologies. It is possible to see all of them as the latest form of liberation the-ology, even though most of them take critical distance from earlier liberation theology. However, methodologically and epistemologically they can be understood as parts of the legacy of liberation theology which share the basic starting point of the need for liberation – in Christian contexts, this includes a critical evaluation of earlier theology and practices of the churches.

I will first deal with liberation theology in the narrower sense, which does not mean, as is often presented, that Latin American liberation theology 'came first'. In fact, most of the first works on Black, feminist and liberation theology were written at about the same time. Still, Latin American liberation theology has globally been so influential – and possibly better known than the other liberation theologies – that it is important to understand what early Latin American liberation theologians actually meant by liberation.

## Latin American Liberation Theology

In his classical work *A Theology of Liberation* (*Teologiá de la liberación: Perspectivas*) from 1971, the Peruvian Catholic theologian Gustavo Gutiérrez places liberation theologi-cally on a par with salvation, thus moving to a more theological direction from a mere political understanding of liberation from oppression and poverty. The book is funda-mentally a theological analysis of how salvation and liberation relate to each other in Christian theology. He presents the question 'What relation exists between salvation and the historical process of liberation of the human being?' as *the* problem of his theology. Since his thoughts in this book are largely shared by other liberation theologians of his generation, I will here present the relationship between liberation and salvation as he first presented it.[14]

According to Gutiérrez's well-known formulation, theology is the critical reflection on the praxis in the light of the Word of God accepted in faith. In this sense, theology is a second step, a reflection of a reality, which comes first also in theology: for him and other early liberation theologians, this reality was mainly the massive poverty and the realities of the poor of Latin America. What came to be called the preferential option for the poor (*la opción preferencial por los pobres*) is the commitment of the Church to the liberation of the poor. Thus, it refers primarily to the practices of the Church, its commitments, its preferences and its identity.

Interestingly, then, for Gutiérrez, liberation is paralleled and juxtaposed with salvation and not (only) societal oppression. This is where liberation theology is theological – according to Gutiérrez's own words, acting as a second step of analysis, after there is enough knowledge and understanding of different forms of oppression in different contexts. That information is best produced by social scientific methods, as a factual basis for any subsequent philosophical or theological analysis. Thus, even though academic theologians and churches should start with the praxis (of oppression and liberation from it), that first act is nevertheless non-theological. The ethical demand to do so is of course at the heart of liberation theology.

The critique of liberation theology, expressed for example by the Vatican in the 1980s, as reducing theology or faith to mere sociology or politics, stems from a common misunderstanding of liberation theology's central intent: to be not only interpretive but also profoundly transformative. This, in the case of theology and practices of the Church, is based on ethics, but also a new image of God, the Church, the human being – and the three in relation to each other. In a way, it is rather this strong spiritual and ethical (normative) aspect of liberation theology that could be critically seen as theological reductionism – not the 'political' as the Church hierarchy understood it.

Gustavo Gutiérrez delineates three different aspects or dimensions of liberation, which, according to my understanding, are central to take into account if one wants to understand liberation theology. Let us take a closer look at Gutiérrez's own understanding of liberation, which other liberation theologians largely share.

Gutiérrez emphasises the unity of history as his starting point. He says: 'concretely, there are not two histories, one profane, the other sacred, "juxtaposed" or "closely related", but only one human happening assumed irreversibly by Christ, Lord of history'.[15] Thus, this affirmation of the one and only human history (*una sola historia*) has a Christological foundation in incarnation. Human history and salvation history are united in Jesus' person. God's auto-revelation happens in human history. Here liberation theologians lean mostly on the Exodus story (Old Testament) and Jesus' incarnation (New Testament). In the history of theology, 'salvation' has almost exclusively had transcendental, spiritual connotations. Thus, liberation theologians prefer the concept liberation – not only in opposition to economic and political dependency but also as a more accurate term than salvation that bears the weight of other-worldly and exclusively spiritual connotations.

The historicisation of salvation is the theological backbone of Latin American liberation theology. Central to the biblical roots of this claim is the concept of the Kingdom of God. According to the Brazilian theologians Leonardo and Clodovis Boff, no other theological or biblical concept is as close to the ideal of integral liberation as this. Seeing the kingdom as God's absolute and universal project helps us to understand the link joining creation and redemption, time and eternity. The Kingdom of God is something more than historical liberations, which are always limited and open to further perfecting, but it is anticipated and incarnated in them in time.[16]

The dialectic of salvation and liberation is present in Gutiérrez's definition of the three dimensions of liberation. First, there is the dimension of economic, social and political liberation of the oppressed, the historical praxis (political order). Second, there is the personal and cultural transformation, the construction of the 'new human being' in a qualitatively different society (ethical order). Finally, there is the dimension of liberation from sin, which is the ultimate root of all injustice and reconciliation with God and other human beings (theological order). This last dimension is the 'orientating pole' – at least for a Christian – of the global process of liberation. The Kingdom of God is the eschatological finality of human existence.[17] These three dimensions are not parallel or chronological processes. They are 'three levels of signification of one complicated process that finds its profound meaning and full realization in the salvific work of Christ'.[18] They imply each other mutually. The first dimension is the realm of scientific rationality (social sciences), the second that of utopia of human self-liberation (ethics and philosophy), and the third that of faith (theology).

The third dimension gives ultimate meaning and transcendent motivation to the first. The ultimate motive for participating in the struggle for liberation is the conviction of the radical incompatibility of evangelical demands with an alienating and unjust society. Faith also provides a self-critical principle to the praxis of liberation. It keeps us from any confusion of the Kingdom of God with any historical event and from any absolutising of revolution. Faith simultaneously demands and judges our political praxis. The theological dimension of salvation and faith mediates the historical dimension of the utopian struggles for political and cultural liberation as the unifying or totalising principle of the latter, while the latter mediates the former as its concretising principle.[19]

Thus, because of its eschatological dimension, salvation is always something more than historical liberation. But if the relation between final, full salvation is denied and concrete historical liberation are denied, the historicity of God's action is also denied, as is the ultimate sense of human life. Creation and redemption are united. In liberation theology, the creation of the human being as the image of God (spirit, body) is taken seriously, but the ultimate meaning of life and historical liberation are never fully realised. Between the two is human history, in which God acts, even though not against the free will of human beings. To exempt history from God's salvific activity would be in fact to deny God's sovereignty.

The Kingdom of God is eschatological and cannot be reduced to history, but the only realm where it can manifest itself is human history. Participation in processes of human liberation is not only ethically justifiable, but is also an essential part of our incomplete knowledge of God and the Kingdom of God. History has its autonomy, and human beings are its subjects. Christian faith means, on the one hand, waiting and hoping for the Kingdom of God, and on the other hand, concrete commitment to the promotion of love and justice in history. This tension between utopia and reality is what marks liberation theology as a spiritual-theological movement among all the other liberation movements. There is a concrete, living hope in an eschatological utopia that gives meaning both to present-day struggles (so that they are not without sense) and to a larger horizon for human insufficiency.

The subjects of this new way of doing and understanding theology, according to liberation theologians, are the poor and the marginalised. However, much of the work of second-generation liberation theologians, in Latin American and beyond, has focused on the de- and reconstruction of the narrow understanding of this new subject of theology. Women, indigenous people, Afro-Latin Americans and sexual minorities, to name the most important groups, have questioned the exclusion of their specific experiences of oppression, freedom and liberation in liberation theology. Thus, issues of sexuality and sexual ethics, gender, racism and ecological concerns have both challenged some of the central claims of liberation theology and, at the same time, deepened and broadened them.

## Liberation Theologies in the Plural

In the broader meaning, liberation theology could – or should – be spoken of in the plural. As was said above, this does not mean that Latin American liberation theology is the original one and the rest are its variants. Rather, the cultural, geographical and thematic contexts of other liberation theologies broadened the Latin American focus on class, economical inequalities and the rather generalised 'poor' from the beginning.[20]

The broad definition of liberation theology stresses the interrelatedness of different structures of oppression and domination. Liberation from oppressive structures necessarily involves political, economic, social, racial, ethnic and sexual aspects. Liberation theology today has an explicit emphasis on seeing different forms of human oppression and suffering and liberation from them as layers in one complicated process. Liberation theologians have learned from each other through a critical dialogue: for example, the critique of the meagreness of analysis of racism and sexism and the emphasis on economic and class issues at the cost of cultural elements in Latin American liberation theology; or of a feminist theology from industrialised countries, which has been slow to admit that white, educated and affluent women are a small minority.

Black theology in the United States rose out of the civil rights and Black Power movements of the 1950s and 60s. However, its historical roots go back to the beginning of African slavery in the US and the founding of Black independent Baptist and Methodist churches in the late eighteenth and early nineteenth centuries. 'Blackness' is a similar category in Black theology as is 'poverty' in Latin American liberation theology. To be Black or poor is to be conscious both of one's oppression and of one's authentic humanity.

As in other liberation theologies, women's voices and critique have been central for the later development of Black theology. In the United States, African-American feminist theologians prefer to call their work womanist theology, according to a term borrowed from the African-American writer Alice Walker. Most Black and womanist theologians are Protestant. In a racist and sexist society, Black women cannot prefer one identity at the cost of the other: they are marginalised both as women and as members of a racialised minority.

As in the United States, the struggle against institutionalised racism, often legitimised by religious beliefs, has been the source of Black theology in Africa, especially in South Africa. Reformed Christianity in South Africa has been one of the ideological pillars of apartheid, the legal–religious–political system of the country for decades, which is why Black theology in the South African context has been different from that of the US. Important South African Black theologians have often also been leaders in the churches and different movements against apartheid. Because of the history of slavery and institutionalised racism, liberation and freedom for Black theologies have had a somewhat different meaning than for other liberation theologians. Especially freedom has been emphasised, in negro spirituals, struggles against slavery and Bible interpretation. Exodus has deep meaning for Latin American liberation theologians, too, as a biblical narrative of a God who acts in history, but for Black theology it is about a God who frees slaves from oppression to freedom.

Nowadays, a Black theology of liberation is also being developed in the Latin American and Caribbean context (*la teología negra de la liberación*), including a feminist version of it. Racism, the struggle against it, and its historical roots are different in the American subcontinent from those of North America and Africa. Afro-Latin American religions are well established in different regions: for example, *candomblé* in Brazil and *santería* in Cuba. These religions, which are a fusion of African, European and American religious traditions, have also helped to preserve Black culture in Latin America. They played no role in early liberation theology. There have been warnings about replacing the critiqued Eurocentrism with 'indiocentrism' in liberation theology. Brazilian scholars Josué A. Sathler and Amós Nascimento take a critical look at the generalised view of the 'Indio' in liberation theology,[21] in many ways analogous to a feminist critique of 'women'. They also analyse how syncretism is understood in the traditional terms of mission and conversion in liberation theology, which justifies an asymmetric position between African-based religions and Christianity. According to Sathler and Nascimento,

> there is a systematic rejection of the African and African-American element as constitutive of Brazilian multiculturalism, ethnic diversity and religious plurality. The great problem . . . is the inability to conceive simultaneously Native, European, and African cultures, without reducing them to something else that is, at the end, white, European, Catholic (Christian).[22]

Even inside formal Catholicism, popular religiosity or lived religion differs from 'official' doctrine and practice, for example in the centrality of the body (in ritual, healing, dance and so on), the sacredness or sacrality of (all spheres of) life, relationship to nature (land, water, earth, sacred places), everyday life at the centre of religious activity (prayers, healing, miracles, human relationships), concreteness and visuality (things such as ex-votos, votive offerings) and often, but not always, greater ritual space for women. The latter is especially true in African-based religions.

All feminist theologies share the importance of the analysis of sexism in different religious traditions, women's exclusion from both theology and positions of authority in religious institutions as well as the often explicit religious legitimisation of women's subordination. Many burning ethical issues, such as abortion and violence against women, cannot be adequately assessed without a critical feminist theological analysis of the religious underpinnings of ethical thinking.

Feminist theology today is global, ecumenical and interreligious. There is a variety of feminist theologies from different ethnic, racial and cultural contexts. In much of feminist thinking, the term 'woman' has been deconstructed and revealed to be a much too vague and homogeneous concept to include the multiple forms of oppression that women experience. This has happened mainly because of a simultaneous influence of postmodern theories on feminist theory and the critique from Third World and post-colonial feminists of the impossibility of a hegemonic feminist theory to include the experiences of women outside the Western academic world. In gender studies, this overlapping and mutual constitution of differences and different sources of oppression, transversing with gender, is called intersectionality.

A similar profound deconstruction of 'the poor' has not happened in most of mainstream Latin American liberation theology, in spite of the now common claim that the poor do not suffer only because of their material poverty but also – and even more – as women, indigenous or Black, and so on. This recognition of the multiple forms of poverty and the heterogeneous experiences of the poor happened mostly at the level of inclusion of new subjects within the more general and homogeneous 'poor'.[23] It is only after specific feminist, queer, Black and indigenous theologies of liberation established themselves also in Latin America that 'the poor' were no longer so narrowly presented as the locus of liberation theology. This does not mean that economic and material issues related to poverty have no importance. Quite to the contrary, the forms of liberation theology that took some critical distance of the first-generation liberation theology in fact clarified, concretised and pluralised 'the poor' – not only conceptually but also making clear that there is no one homogeneous way of being poor. In reality, the intersection of different forms of marginalisation and subjugation enforce each other. From quite early, there have been feminist theologians from both the Global South and the Global North – to name just a few, Rosemary Ruether and Elisabeth Schüssler Fiorenza from the United States and Ivone Gebara and María Pilar Aquino from Latin America – who have named their theology as feminist liberation theology.

From the very beginning, feminist theology has been interreligious, ecumenical and global. This has meant that the voices and critiques of women from the Global South were very early included in feminist theology. The ecumenical and interfaith organisations offered a concrete network of collaboration and mutual critique between feminist theologians from different parts of the world already in the 1960s and 70s. This narrative of global, ecumenical and interfaith feminist theology is largely untold.[24]

One concrete example of this somewhat different history and development of feminist theology is the early inclusion of what is today called intersectionality in 'secular' gender studies. For example, the Catholic feminist theologian Rosemary Ruether wrote already in 1975:

any women's movement which is *only* concerned about sexism and no other form of oppression, must remain a women's movement of the white upper class, for it is *only* this group of women whose *only* problem is the problem of being women, since, in every other way, they belong to the ruling class . . . Thus it seems to me essential that the women's movement reach out and include in its struggle the interstructuring of sexism with all other kinds of oppression, and recognise a pluralism of women's movements . . .[25]

Ruether and other first-generation feminist theologians stated already in the 1970s how gender should always be analysed in relation to class and race. Ruether used the term 'interstructuring', not 'intersectionality'. She is an example of a feminist theologian, who was practically and conceptually linked to liberation theology, which was both a theoretical and practical – even political – movement mainly in the Global South. The emphasis on the 'interstructuring of oppression' in feminist theology, since its very beginning, was an outcome of its connections to the global movement of liberation theologies, especially as they were practised and theorised in the context of EATWOT. It was a forum of liberation-theologically minded Christian theologians from all over the world, focusing on changes not only in theology but also in the Church(es) and society. Besides EATWOT, the ecumenical movement in general – especially the World Council of Churches – has been a key factor in the early development of both feminist theology and liberation theology globally, including Black theology in the US, Africa and Latin America. In the case of feminist theology, this meant an earlier inclusion of intersectionality and the perspective of the Global South in feminist theorising than possibly in any other field of gender studies, as was mentioned earlier.

# Reception

In August 1984, the Vatican Congregation for the Doctrine of the Faith, led by the German Cardinal Joseph Ratzinger, later Pope Benedict XVI, issued a document on 'certain aspects of liberation theology' that many groups and individuals interpreted as a virtual condemnation of Latin American liberation theology.[26] The critical reactions all over the Catholic world to these measures led to another Vatican document where both the theme of liberation and liberation theology were seen in a more nuanced light.[27] Even though the documents speak of liberation theologies in the plural, they nevertheless are aimed at the Latin American version of it. There is no mention of other liberation theologies in spite of the plural.

According to Anselm K. Min, the differences between the two documents are minor or accidental and should not be praised as a radical change in the Vatican evaluation of liberation theology.[28] What is noteworthy regarding the theme of this article is that the second document deals explicitly with both freedom and liberation, aiming at giving a correcting answer to liberation theology from the Magisterium. When reading the documents now, after many years of reading them, what struck me most was the harsh, tendentious and misconceived treatment of 'liberation theology' (always written in quotation marks) in the first, and the use of claims and original ideas taken from liberation theologians without ever mentioning it – or liberation theology at all – in the second. The first had a clear aim: to warn about liberation theology, listing all its deviations and errors. The second brings forward many liberation-theological issues at the core of the text, presenting them as the invention of the Vatican and finally, in a way, presenting a better liberation theology from Europe. The latter can be interpreted either as greater acceptance of some of liberation theology's central insights two years later after the first document, on the one hand, or as an appropriation of some undeniably Christian and biblical insights of liberation theology and presenting them in the context of the social doctrine of the Catholic Church, on the other. I thus depart to some extent from Min's evaluation.

Without referring to any liberation theologians by name, in hindsight the two documents form an intriguing whole, which tells about the challenge that liberation theology posed to the Magisterium of the Catholic Church. It is only with Pope Francis, of Argentina, that liberation theology has received some legitimacy and even recognition at the highest level of the Church. In the 1980s, the situation both in the Church and in Latin American societies was quite different.

*Libertatis nuntius* (1984) criticises liberation theology for several issues, such as the use of Marxist thought, for ideological deviations that betray the poor they want to defend, the reduction of salvation and liberation to politics, the politicisation of faith and the Scriptures and, last but not least, for an understanding of the Church which challenges the 'sacramental and hierarchical structure'. Some of the claims are simply not accurate, such as the predominance and importance of Marxism among liberation theologians, the identification of the Kingdom of God with human liberation movements and, most importantly, denial of salvation at the cost of earthly liberation. As explained above, Gutiérrez's classic book has an intent to explain the relationship between these two from the perspective of faith and Latin American reality.

*Libertatis conscientia* (1986) does not say anything about liberation theology explicitly. The tone and aim of the document are different from the first one. The section on the 'salvific and ethical dimension of liberation' is clearly influenced by Gutiérrez. In sum, the Magisterium not only discredited liberation theology when it most needed support and

understanding from the universal Church, but it also silenced individual liberation theologians (the most commonly known case is Leonardo Boff) and misinterpreted the reality
and circumstances of Latin America during the dictatorships.

It had been imagined that a change in the Vatican's assessment of liberation theology
would have occurred under Pope Francis. Certainly, as a Latin American himself, there
has been more understanding for liberation theology and its original context from Francis.
His deep commitment for the sake of the poor and marginalised as well as his personal
closeness to liberation theologians such as Gutiérrez makes his tone very different from his
predecessors. However, since the entire context of Latin American liberation theology has
changed as time has passed, it is easier to re-evaluate it, also taking into account its global
influence especially in academic theology worldwide. Poverty remains a major problem
even though the Cold War context has disappeared. The original emphasis of liberation
theology on the scandal of poverty thus continues to challenge Christian churches and
theology, and the biased – and unjust – interpretation of liberation theology as Marxist
does not have the same relevance as earlier.

Pope Francis does not address feminist theology, even as part of liberation theology,
in spite of his insistence that hope in Latin America has a woman's face (*Address of His
Holiness Pope Francis*, 2017). In the encyclical letter *Laudato si'* (2015), his emphasis
on the interconnectedness of ecological destruction and poverty is certainly something
new for a pope, but in none of these contexts does he make the link between poverty,
gender and the Church's traditional sexual-ethical teaching. This is a major problem for
poor women and (Catholic) feminist liberation theologians. There is a widespread global
consensus on addressing women's sexual and reproductive rights as an essential part of
reducing poverty.

Liberation theology was never only a Catholic phenomenon. Especially when we look
at it in its broad version, some liberation theologies such as Black theology have in fact
been predominantly Protestant. Both Latin American liberation theology and feminist
theologies from both the Global South and North have had prominent Protestant representatives. Globally, the overall influence of liberation theology, its method and its
challenge to Christian churches, have influenced the Protestant world probably more than
the Catholic Church. This can be seen in its reception in Protestant churches and various
ecumenical bodies, most notably the World Council of Churches. Academically, liberation theologies have changed theology and theological education in Catholic, Protestant
and secular institutions.

The Orthodox tradition is an intriguing exception in that there is practically no equivalent or explicit response to liberation theology. The Eastern understanding of the
human being, who is able to reach deification (*theosis*), likeness to or union with God,
could form an interesting reflection point for the discussion of *imago Dei* as the spiritual
core of all liberation theologies. *Theosis* is a process of transformation and the purpose of
human life, of which the Mother of God is the primary example.

However, the *Encyclopedia of Eastern Orthodoxy* does not even have entries on freedom
or liberation, not to speak of liberation theology.[29] I have come across only one book
which explicitly discusses Orthodoxy and political theology, and even asks why Orthodoxy
has not developed any liberation theology.[30] Most responses to contextual or liberation
theologies from the Orthodox perspective are reserved or even rejecting. According to
Kalaitzidis, referring to a handful of Orthodox theologians who have touched upon the
issue at all, the rejection is often based on a misunderstanding of liberation theology and
political theology.[31] It seems that one of the reasons is the supposed predominance of

Marxism in liberation theology, very much like in the Vatican responses. In both cases, the presupposition is unfounded and too generalising: a close reading of major liberation theologians would in fact make clear that the 'use of Marxism' in liberation theology, as common as this claim is, is in fact very problematic. There is no space here to deconstruct this claim in detail, but even a superficial glance at most liberation theologians' writings makes clear that even those who engage with Marxism do not do it in the narrow ideological way that the critique supposes.

Kalaitzidis offers several reasons for the Orthodox rejection of liberation theology. Overall, the effort to 'de-westernise' Orthodox theology, based on a polarisation of East and West, has overshadowed other theological questions and the challenges of the modern world for which the Orthodox theological response has been weak.[32] In spite of Orthodox female theologians' intent to develop an Orthodox theology of gender (not necessarily called feminist theology), which could be seen as the most developed form of liberation theology within Orthodoxy, it is usually not even mentioned by those Orthodox writers who criticise liberation and contextual theologies; Kalaitzidis is also here an exception. The gender issue is difficult to define as 'Western' – even though it is often done for political reasons, e.g. in Russia – since it is Orthodox women within the Church who question some of the gender constructions and their theological foundations from within the Church.

## Conclusions

Freedom and liberation are the red thread and backbone of all liberation theologies, even when they understand these somewhat differently or with a variety of emphases. Obviously, the option for the poor and its theological, epistemological, spiritual and political consequences are certainly a major innovation of Latin American liberation theology. However, a radical and critical question about the subject of theology goes further. As was said earlier, the differentiation and extension of the concept 'poor' is – at least formally – accepted nowadays by practically all liberation theologians. Liberation theologians have consciously taken 'the dominated and dependent Latin America' as their starting point, but they have not been as critical of other *loci* that define their theologising, such as race and gender. It is the level of inclusion of these, and the theological, epistemological and practical consequences of them, which has remained superficial.

It is, thus, important to present any form of liberation theology in this larger context of 'interstructuring of oppression', to quote Ruether, whether our audience is theological or secular – as in the case of understanding global feminist theology as an important part of gender theorising. At the same time, the later developments of liberation theology from the perspective of culturally, sexually and racially disadvantaged groups should be presented as the core of liberation theology, not just some derivation or version of true liberation theology. As Latin American liberation theology is, after decades, becoming more accepted in the hierarchy of the Catholic Church because of Pope Francis, it is important to remember that it is not this broad and multifaceted version of liberation theology that he is endorsing. Just to take an example, (poor) women's concerns are as far from any serious reconsideration as they were forty years ago.

Liberation theology was an important interlocutor in grassroots social movements in Latin America in the 1970s. Later social movements, such as the feminist movement, the LGBTQ movement, the ecological and indigenous movements, have not had the same impact on and closeness with liberation theology. Liberation theologians have frequently mentioned these new social movements, but as frequently without any critical analysis of the role of religion, theology and the Church in the formation of repressive sexualities and the issues of life and death tied to that.

Lack of dialogue and cooperation between liberation theology and new social movements has resulted in liberation theologians' lack of credibility in major contemporary social issues, such as sexual ethics, racism, religious syncretism, environmental issues and popular religion: all relevant for women, indigenous and African-American people. The overall result may be that liberation theology today is seen by many as white, Western, patriarchal and anti-sexual. In other words, that not even liberation theology can break away from the long legacy of Christian theology in legitimising sexism and racism.[33]

What is easily seen as mere 'adding' of new concerns and subjects to liberation theology reflects – and is possibly a result of – the lack of political engagement with contemporary social movements. This lack of dialogue and engagement has epistemological consequences for Latin American liberation theology today. It is my understanding that the often presumed crisis of liberation theology is not derived from the most often presented assumption of a causal relationship between the fall of socialism and liberation theology, as much as it is a result of the lack of engagement with the political demands, and the ways of theorising them, of contemporary social movements. These include the ecological movements whose demands and concerns have been somewhat easier to include in later liberation theology.[34]

Different liberation theologies, in their mutual critical dialogue, have changed the global theological – and philosophical and political – map forever. Their central demands have probably not changed religious institutions and churches as much as it was hoped. There are major differences between Christian churches, for example in issues concerning women and sexual ethics, which need to be attended if ecological and economic issues are considered important. Liberation theologies as some kinds of paradigm shifts have possibly had their greatest influence in academic theology and related fields. The immediate political contexts of liberation theologies have dramatically changed in some cases (such as democratisation in Latin America and the end of apartheid in South Africa), but most of the central issues have not. In some cases, it would even be possible to argue that they have been aggravated. If there is a future for a deepened theological understanding of liberation and freedom after liberation theologies, the only starting point is a substantial intertwining of all of them, including feminist theology and eco-theology. Especially in the case of these two, theologians should work in close cooperation with scholars from other fields who provide theologians with the most adequate knowledge of the situation, whether it is causes and outcomes of maternal mortality or climate change. The spaces where this is most difficult to achieve are the churches, and their teachings and practices. In that sense, in spite of many changes, basic theological questions about freedom and liberation, as they were addressed in the context of liberation theologies, are still not only incipient but deeply relevant.

# Notes

1. René Latourelle (ed.), *Dictionary of Fundamental Theology* (New York: Crossroad, 2000).
2. Letty M. Russell and J. Shannon Clarkson (eds), *Dictionary of Feminist Theologies* (Louisville, KY: Westminster John Knox Press, 1996); Lisa Isherwood and Dorothea McEwan (eds), *An A to Z of Feminist Theology* (Sheffield: Sheffield Academic Press, 1996).

3. Virginia Fabella and R. S. Sugirtharajah (eds), *Dictionary of Third World Theologies* (New York: Orbis, 2000).

4. Eugene TeSelle, 'Freedom, Free Will', in *The Cambridge Dictionary of Christianity*, edited by Daniel Patte (Cambridge: Cambridge University Press, 2010), p. 437.

5. Kelly Brown Douglas, 'Freedom', in *Dictionary of Feminist Theologies*, edited by Letty M. Russell and J. Shannon Clarkson (Louisville, KY: Westminster John Knox Press, 1996), pp. 121–2: 122.

6. See Douglas, 'Freedom'.

7. See, for example, Rosemary Radford Ruether, *New Woman, New Earth: Sexist Ideologies and Human Liberation* (San Francisco: Harper and Row, 1975).

8. Elina Vuola, 'Religion, Intersectionality, and Epistemic Habits of Academic Feminism: Perspectives from Global Feminist Theology', *Feminist Encounters: A Journal of Critical Studies in Culture and Politics*, 1:1 (2017), accessed at http://www.lectitopublishing.nl/feminist-encoun ters.

9. Joyce Ann Mercer, 'Liberation', in *Dictionary of Feminist Theologies*, edited by Letty M. Russell and J. Shannon Clarkson (Louisville, KY: Westminster John Knox Press, 1996), p. 168.

10. Isherwood and McEwan (eds), *An A to Z of Feminist Theology*.

11. Lisa Isherwood, 'Liberation', in *An A to Z of Feminist Theology*, edited by Lisa Isherwood and Dorothea McEwan (Sheffield: Sheffield Academic Press, 1996), pp. 121–2.

12. Virginia Fabella, 'Liberation', in *Dictionary of Third World Theologies*, edited by Virginia Fabella and R. S. Sugirtharajah (New York: Orbis, 2000), pp. 123–4.

13. Elsa Tamez, 'Liberation Theology', in *Encyclopedia of Religion*, edited by L. Jones, 2nd ed., vol. 8 (Detroit: Thomson Gale, 2005), pp. 5438–42: 5438–9.

14. See also Elina Vuola, *Limits of Liberation: Feminist Theology and the Ethics of Poverty and Reproduction* (Sheffield: Sheffield Academic Press, 2002) for a more profoundly critical discussion on the epistemological foundations of liberation theology.

15. Gustavo Gutiérrez, *A Theology of Liberation: History, Politics, and Salvation*, Caridad Inda (trans.) and John Eagleson (ed.) (New York: Orbis, 1988), p. 194.

16. Leonardo Boff and Clodovis Boff, *Introducing Liberation Theology*, Paul Burns (trans.) (New York: Orbis, 1987), pp. 64–5; Gutiérrez, *A Theology of Liberation*, pp. 203–14.

17. Gutiérrez, *A Theology of Liberation*, pp. 43–4, 91–2.

18. Gutiérrez, *A Theology of Liberation*, p. 92.

19. Anselm Kyongsuk Min, *Dialectic of Salvation: Issues in Theology of Liberation* (Albany: State University of New York Press, 1989), pp. 101–2.

20. See Elina Vuola, 'The Option for the Poor and the Exclusion of Women: The Challenges of Postmodernism and Feminism to Liberation Theology', in *Opting for the Margins: Postmodernity and Liberation in Christian Theology*, edited by Joerg Rieger (Oxford: Oxford University Press, 2003), pp. 105–26; Elina Vuola, 'Liberation Theology', in *New Dictionary of the History of Ideas*, edited by Maryanne C. Horowitz, vol. 3 (New York: Charles Scribner's Sons Reference Books, 2005), pp. 1269–72.

21. Josué A. Sathler and Amós Nascimento, 'Black Masks on White Faces: Liberation Theology and the Quest for Syncretism in the Brazilian Context', in *Liberation Theology, Postmodernity, and the Americas*, edited by David Batstone, Eduardo Mendieta, Lois Ann Lorentzen and Dwight N. Hopkins (London: Routledge, 1997), pp. 95–122.

22. Sathler and Nascimento, 'Black Masks on White Faces', p. 115.

23. See Vuola, *Limits of Liberation*; Vuola, 'The Option for the Poor and the Exclusion of Women'.

24. However, see my attempt to tell this narrative in Vuola, 'Religion, Intersectionality, and Epistemic Habits of Academic Feminism'.

25. Ruether, *New Woman, New Earth*, p. 125, emphasis in original.

26. Congregation for the Doctrine of the Faith, *Libertatis nuntius. Instruction on Freedom and Liberation* (Vatican, 1986), accessed at http://www.vatican.va/roman_curia/congregations/cfai th/documents/rc_con_cfaith_doc_19860322_freedom-liberation_en.html.

27. Congregation for the Doctrine of the Faith, *Libertatis conscientia. Instruction on Freedom and Liberation* (Vatican, 1986), accessed at http://www.vatican.va/roman_curia/congregations/cfai th/documents/rc_con_cfaith_doc_19860322_freedom-liberation_en.html.
28. Min, *Dialectic of Salvation*, pp. 117–22.
29. John Anthony McGuckin, *The Encyclopedia of Eastern Orthodox Christianity*, vols 1–2 (Chichester: Wiley-Blackwell, 2011). See also John Anthony McGuckin, *The Orthodox Church: An Introduction to Its History, Doctrine, and Spiritual Culture* (Malden, MA: Blackwell, 2008).
30. Pantelis Kalaitzidis, *Orthodoxy and Political Theology* (Geneva: WCC Publications, 2012).
31. Kalaitzidis, *Orthodoxy and Political Theology*, p. 53.
32. Kalaitzidis, *Orthodoxy and Political Theology*, pp. 75–6.
33. See this critique in more detail in Vuola, 'Latin American Liberation Theologians' Turn to Eco(theo)logy: Critical Remarks', in *Religion and Ecology in the Public Sphere*, edited by Celia Deane-Drummond and Heinrich Bedford-Strohm (London: T&T Clark/Continuum, 2011), pp. 91–110.
34. See, however, my critical evaluation of the epistemological base of that inclusion, which includes ecofeminism, in Vuola, 'Latin American Liberation Theologians' Turn to Eco(theo) logy'.

# Bibliography

Boff, Leonardo and Clodovis Boff, *Cómo hacer teología de la liberación*, M. A. Villegas (trans.) (Bogotá: Ediciones Paulinas, 1989); published in English as *Introducing Liberation Theology*, Paul Burns (trans.) (New York: Orbis, 1987).

Congregation for the Doctrine of the Faith, *Libertatis conscientia. Instruction on Freedom and Liberation* (Vatican, 1986), accessed at http://www.vatican.va/roman_curia/congregations/cfaith/documents /rc_con_cfaith_doc_19860322_freedom-liberation_en.html.

Congregation for the Doctrine of the Faith, *Libertatis nuntius. Instruction on Certain Aspects of the 'Theology of Liberation'* (Vatican, 1984), accessed at http://www.vatican.va/roman_curia/congre gations/cfaith/documents/rc_con_cfaith_doc_19840806_theology-liberation_en.html.

Douglas, Kelly Brown, 'Freedom', in Letty M. Russell and J. Shannon Clarkson (eds), *Dictionary of Feminist Theologies* (Louisville, KY: Westminster John Knox Press, 1996), pp. 121–2.

Fabella, Virginia, 'Liberation', in *Dictionary of Third World Theologies*, edited by Virginia Fabella and R. S. Sugirtharajah (New York: Orbis, 2000), pp. 122–4.

Fabella, Virginia and R. S. Sugirtharajah (eds), *Dictionary of Third World Theologies* (New York: Orbis, 2000).

Gutiérrez, Gustavo, *Teología de la liberación: Perspectivas*, 14th revised ed. (Salamanca: Ediciones Sígueme, [1971] 1990); published in English as *A Theology of Liberation: History, Politics, and Salvation*, Caridad Inda (trans.) and John Eagleson (ed.) (New York: Orbis, 1988).

Isherwood, Lisa, 'Liberation', in Lisa Isherwood and Dorothea McEwan (eds), *An A to Z of Feminist Theology* (Sheffield: Sheffield Academic Press, 1996), pp. 121–2.

Isherwood, Lisa and Dorothea McEwan (eds), *An A to Z of Feminist Theology* (Sheffield: Sheffield Academic Press, 1996).

Kalaitzidis, Pantelis, *Orthodoxy and Political Theology* (Geneva: WCC Publications, 2012).

Latourelle, René (ed.), *Dictionary of Fundamental Theology* (New York: Crossroad, 2000).

McGuckin, John Anthony (ed.), *The Encyclopedia of Eastern Orthodox Christianity*, vols 1–2 (Chichester: Wiley-Blackwell, 2011).

McGuckin, John Anthony, *The Orthodox Church: An Introduction to Its History, Doctrine, and Spiritual Culture* (Malden, MA: Blackwell, 2008).

Mercer, Joyce Ann, 'Liberation', in Letty M. Russell and J. Shannon Clarkson (eds), *Dictionary of Feminist Theologies* (Louisville, KY: Westminster John Knox Press, 1996), p. 168.

Min, Anselm Kyongsuk, *Dialectic of Salvation: Issues in Theology of Liberation* (Albany: State University of New York Press, 1989).

Pope Francis, *Address of His Holiness Pope Francis*, Meeting with the Executive Committee of CELAM, Apostolic Journey of His Holiness Pope Francis to Colombia (Bogotá, 2017).

Pope Francis, *Laudato si'*, Encyclical Letter of the Holy Father Francis on Care for Our Common Home (Vatican, 2015), accessed at http://w2.vatican.va/content/francesco/en/encyclicals/docu ments/papa-francesco_20150524_enciclica-laudato-si.html.

Ruether, Rosemary Radford, *New Woman, New Earth: Sexist Ideologies and Human Liberation* (San Francisco: Harper and Row, 1975).

Russell, Letty M. and J. Shannon Clarkson (eds), *Dictionary of Feminist Theologies* (Louisville, KY: Westminster John Knox Press, 1996).

Sathler, Josué A. and Amós Nascimento, 'Black Masks on White Faces: Liberation Theology and the Quest for Syncretism in the Brazilian Context', in *Liberation Theology, Postmodernity, and the Americas*, edited by David Batstone, Eduardo Mendieta, Lois Ann Lorentzen and Dwight N. Hopkins (London: Routledge, 1997), pp. 95–122.

Tamez, Elsa, 'Liberation Theology', in *Encyclopedia of Religion*, edited by L. Jones, 2nd ed., vol. 8 (Detroit: Thomson Gale, 2005), pp. 5438–42.

TeSelle, Eugene, 'Freedom, Free Will', in *The Cambridge Dictionary of Christianity*, edited by Daniel Patte (Cambridge: Cambridge University Press, 2010), p. 437.

Vuola, Elina, 'Latin American Liberation Theologians' Turn to Eco(theo)logy: Critical Remarks', in *Religion and Ecology in the Public Sphere*, edited by Celia Deane-Drummond and Heinrich Bedford-Strohm (London: T&T Clark/Continuum, 2011), pp. 91–110.

Vuola, Elina, 'Liberation Theology', in *New Dictionary of the History of Ideas*, edited by Maryanne C. Horowitz, vol. 3 (New York: Charles Scribner's Sons Reference Books, 2005), pp. 1269–72.

Vuola, Elina, *Limits of Liberation: Feminist Theology and the Ethics of Poverty and Reproduction* (Sheffield: Sheffield Academic Press, 2002).

Vuola, Elina, 'The Option for the Poor and the Exclusion of Women: The Challenges of Postmodernism and Feminism to Liberation Theology', in *Opting for the Margins: Postmodernity and Liberation in Christian Theology*, edited by Joerg Rieger (Oxford: Oxford University Press, 2003), pp. 105–26.

Vuola, Elina, 'Religion, Intersectionality, and Epistemic Habits of Academic Feminism: Perspectives from Global Feminist Theology', *Feminist Encounters: A Journal of Critical Studies in Culture and Politics*, 1:1 (2017), accessed at http://www.lectitopublishing.nl/feminist-encounters.

# 13

# The Secular – The Political

## Augustine and Political Augustinianism in Twentieth-Century Political Theology

### P. Travis Kroeker

The premise of this essay is that rereadings of Augustine and Augustinianisms are crucial for interpreting twentieth- (and twenty-first-)century Christian political theology. I begin with the debate between Carl Schmitt and Erik Peterson, contextualising it not only in relation to their differing ecclesial responses to modern secularism but also in response to Henri de Lubac's important account of ecclesiology in *Corpus Mysticum*, which also influenced in various ways the political-theological narratives of Ernst Kantorowicz, Sheldon Wolin, John Milbank and Charles Taylor. My constructive proposal – offered over against not only earlier forms of Christian realist Augustinianism such as Reinhold Niebuhr[1] and Robert A. Markus, but also more recent forms of liberal political Augustinianism such as Oliver O'Donovan, Robert Dodaro and Eric Gregory – will be to argue that a more 'apocalyptic' or figural reading of Augustine's two cities and their relation to ecclesiology and politics of the *saeculum* (in conversation with the work of Ivan Illich) facilitates another trajectory of interpretation that I identify as 'messianic' political theology.[2] Such a position is less dualistic with regard to Church and state and more amenable to an expansion of the sphere of 'the political' to include economy, technology and household in ways that illuminate the lived complexity of theological claims in a secular age.

Augustine and Augustinianism is crucial for our topic, and not only because Augustine bequeathed to the West and its entire history of theological politics and political theology the centrality of the *saeculum* (spawning a vast range of interpretations of its meaning).[3] In the twentieth century there has been a veritable explosion of interest in 'political Augustinianism'[4] that often quite directly engages the fraught relations in contemporary politics between the secular pluralism of religions and theologically committed critiques of political regimes, policies and institutions in both theoretical and practical terms. What is often overlooked, however, is the Augustinian debate at the heart of 'political theology' – a discourse made current in the twentieth century by the juridical theorist Carl Schmitt that has also become increasingly contested in recent times around the meaning of secularisation and secularism in liberal modernity. This is a discourse that has far exceeded earlier 'critics of modernity' such as Schmitt and less controversial philosophers such as Hannah Arendt and Eric Voegelin, to include the counter-Enlightenment critiques of a range of thinkers who identify as postmodern and postsecular. Many of those thinkers, from Schmitt, Arendt and Voegelin to Derrida, Foucault and Agamben, have also taken up the problematics of Augustine (and other early Christian thinkers) – not least in relation to languages of worship (not only 'worth-ship' in a religious sense, but also the cultic liturgies of public order), the philosophical-theological dramas of human being and becoming enacted historically, and governmentality or sovereignty in its various

interrelated forms. Of course, an essay such as this cannot engage such a wide range. I
begin with Schmitt because of his ongoing importance for political theologies, showing
the deeply Augustinian issues present in his and his interlocutors' work. I then turn to the
more recent Christian political Augustinians to mount a constructive argument for a more
'messianic' and apocalyptic account of Augustine's political theology that offers underap-
preciated (and often misunderstood) resources for the current debates on the secular and
the political.

## Political Theology: Schmitt, Peterson, de Lubac

The rubric 'political theology' as it came to be known in the twentieth century is
bequeathed by the notorious Carl Schmitt, whose first book by that title (1922) provides
us with two of its best-known claims. The first is the classic formulation of the political-
theological concept that lies at the heart of political theory, including that of modern
secular politics: 'Souverän ist, wer über den Ausnahmezustand entscheidet' ('Sovereign is
the one who decides on the [state of] exception [or emergency]').[5] For Schmitt, political
sovereignty cannot simply be established juridically by the rule of law or even the state;
it requires more than a procedure of decision-making or political judgement. It requires
a personal agency, which is why he remains fascinated by Thomas Hobbes – who is not
only the founder of modern political theory but also a political theologian of great power
precisely because of his capacity to employ great mythical and demonical images in his
political thinking. Despite the rationalistic technicisation and mechanisation of political
economy in the modern age through its secular 'disenchantment' (as Max Weber called it)
of the world, Hobbes recognised that the political remains radically related to the chaotic
passions that must be rightly ordered in speech through moral-political-juridical conformity to the needs of a security state.[6] It is not surprising perhaps that Hobbes's image
of sovereignty, the Leviathan, who will provide in his 'person' the power as of a 'mortal
god' to decide upon the interpretation of the law in a manner that neutralises warring
religious passions, is taken from the Book of Job – that great contestation regarding the
meaning of divine justice, not only between Job and the conventional opinions regarding
the 'problem of evil' of his friends, but also between Job and God and, beyond that, God
and Satan. In *Political Theology* Schmitt makes reference to a 'Protestant theologian' who
demonstrated that 'a philosophy of concrete life must not withdraw from the exception
and the extreme case, but must be interested in it to the highest degree'. He goes on: 'In
the exception the power of real life breaks through the crust of a mechanism that has
become torpid by repetition.'[7] The theologian is Søren Kierkegaard and the demonstration – 'the exception . . . thinks the general [or the universal] with extreme passion' – is
taken from *Repetition*, a meditation on the 'ordeal' (*Prøvelse*) of Job concerning the boundaries of justice, divine power and human suffering in an impassioned *agon* over against the
divine sovereign himself. These theological and religious collisions remain at the heart of
the political even (and perhaps especially) in secular settings of supposed 'neutrality' that
assume such extremes have been contained if not entirely tamed through exclusion or
juridical mechanisms.

This brings us to the second famous claim, at the beginning of the third essay:

> All significant concepts of the modern theory of the state are secularized theological
> concepts not only because of their historical development – in which they were trans-
> ferred from theology to the theory of the state, whereby, for example, the omnipotent

God became the omnipotent lawgiver – but also because of their systematic structure, the recognition of which is necessary for a sociological consideration of these concepts. The exception in jurisprudence is analogous to the miracle in theology.[8]

Of course, despite the banishment of the miraculous in Enlightenment rationality (and the deism of the modern constitutional state), exceptions and emergencies that require the suspension of the law continue to arise. Schmitt's founding exposition of sovereignty must here be read in conjunction with his founding concept of the political, namely, the distinction between friend (*Freund*) and enemy (*Feind*).[9] For Schmitt the ultimate challenge to this basic political principle is to be found in the words of Jesus: 'Love your enemies' (Matt. 5:44) – which Schmitt, in keeping with both conventional Christendom ethics and most liberal political ethics, regards as a private, spiritual and individual ethic, not a public, political ethic. Here too Schmitt remains in agreement with Hobbes's privatising interpretation of the 'singular mark' of New Testament prophecy, namely, that the teaching that '*Jesus is the Christ*, that is, the king of the Jews, promised in the Old Testament' (*Leviathan* 36.20; cf. 48.11ff.) can have no immediate political import, only a chiliastic historicist one. In other words, Christian messianism pertains to individual spiritual salvation whose political significance can only gain purchase with the embodied sovereignty of Christ at the end of time. In the meanwhile it may (and for Schmitt must) inform the virtues of political agency and citizenship that are, however, institutionally tied to the nation state as *katechon*, a spiritual and moral agency that Hobbes and other social contract theorists also emphasised.

Among the most interesting recent interventions in political theology are those that identify the importance of Henri de Lubac's Augustinian *Corpus Mysticum* for critically revisiting significant visions of the Western political tradition, including Schmitt. Jennifer Rust argues that both Carl Schmitt and Ernst Kantorowicz flatten out theoretically (and non-theologically) what de Lubac presents as an originally dynamic and performative, doxological and ethical, relation between *ekklesia* and Eucharist so as to further their own genealogical projects of secular political order.[10] Schmitt in particular seeks to recover a role for the secular power of Christendom as imperial 'restrainer' (*katechon*, 2 Thess. 2:6–7) of antinomian evil through the exercise of state sovereignty modelled on Romans 13. Erik Peterson criticised this on Augustinian grounds, arguing that a Trinitarian theology resists all attempts to ground a human politics.[11] I believe de Lubac's sacramental ecclesiocentrism, rooted in the Pauline and Augustinian vision of the messianic body as fully divine and fully human, both mystically hidden and fully public, offers a more compelling critique of Carl Schmitt's secularised Christendom political theology than that offered by Erik Peterson – not least because it is finally more Augustinian. Jacob Taubes, in keeping with Peterson's position, suggests that Augustinian Christianity rejects the 'problem' of political theology by 'eschatologising' the apocalypse – i.e. 'domesticating' messianic sovereignty by restricting it to the Church.[12] As I hope will become clear below, I do not consider this to be an accurate portrayal of Augustine.

Now it is true that Peterson's critique could be read another way; that is, he wants to subvert any and every compromise of the public witness of the messianic community entailed in shoring up a secular polis that does not liturgically participate in the messianic sovereignty of the heavenly Jerusalem. As neither Jewish nor pagan, at home in no earthly city, the Christian's citizenship is in heaven, the public cult of which on earth is the *ekklesia*. On Peterson's reading of the Book of Revelation, Hebrews and Paul, the liturgical political worship of the Church is a participation in the cosmic sovereignty of its heavenly imperator, Christ, whose eschatological *imperium* is 'opposed to all *imperia* of this world', and whose *militia* on earth is made up only of martyrs.[13] This mirrors Oliver O'Donovan's Church as 'eschatological society'; it is, by definition, otherworldly or 'afterworldly' and represents in its cultic worship the hidden kingdom of the ascended Christ. O'Donovan's reading of Colossians 2:15, Paul's claim that the principalities and powers that govern the world have been publicly subjected to divine sovereignty through the messianic rule of Jesus, qualifies this Pauline claim. While Paul claims that the messianic 'disarming' (*apekdusamenos*: 'stripping off the clothing') of these authorities has been accomplished by the cross 'in full public openness' (*en parresia*), thus founding a new cosmic sovereignty over against the pretentious judgements of human precepts, doctrines and traditions, O'Donovan claims rather the public hiddenness of this messianic apocalypse.[14] Until the final *parousia* of Christ, Paul's messianic political theology must be content to authorise a 'stripped-down' version of secular authority (Rom. 13) whose judicial task is to protect the social space for Christian mission. In this way does O'Donovan also agree with Schmitt regarding the *katechonic* (2 Thess. 2) role of the state as restraining evil through judicial authority.[15]

Giorgio Agamben provides yet another reading of Peterson that may help bring us back to why de Lubac is so important.[16] In contrast to the political theology of Carl Schmitt that emphasises the transcendent sovereignty of the one God, Peterson's emphasis on the public liturgical participation in the Trinitarian divine economy opens the door for an 'economic' political theology and an exploration of the doxological role of divine glory in the messianic *oikos* that may help break down the classical distinction between the private *oikos* and the public *polis*, between governmentality or pastoral household management and public juridical sovereignty. Such a broadening of the political and economic, Agamben argues, may be traced back to early Christianity – and especially to Paul, who calls himself an 'economist of the mysteries of God' (1 Cor. 4:1; cf. 9:17; Col. 1:25). That is, Paul understands his messianic mission (and that of the body of Christ) as one of serv-anthood or stewardship of the economy of divine mystery, an ongoing apocalypse of the recapitulation of 'all things' in Christ (Eph. 1:10).

Agamben, like Peterson, suggests that this Pauline language is not really political but rather more accurately an economic theology – Paul is interested in 'building up' (*oikod-omei*, 1 Cor. 8:1; 10:23) the messianic body, which is a liturgical community but not a *polis*.[17] Here Agamben radically divides what Paul unites, and it is because he remains unattuned to Paul's *theological* claims. When Agamben claims that the overtly political language of Philippians 1:27, 3:20 and Ephesians 2:19 is 'exceptional' and 'decidedly impolitical', he misses the apocalyptic mood and substance of Paul's messianic political theology. The building Paul refers to in 1 Corinthians 3:10f. has a messianic foundation, the mystery disclosed in the crucified 'Lord of glory' (1 Cor. 2:7) that the 'rulers of the world' failed to see but that is pneumatically disclosed to all who share in the 'mind (*nous*) of Christ' (2:16). The more intimate sphere of *oikos* is also public and political, which is why the 'household relations' addressed in Paul's letters are politically constituted in the same messianic mystery, which is also a 'mind'. When Paul says 'be citizens (*politeuesthe*) worthy of the constitution, the gospel'[18] (Phil. 1:27), he makes references to the *politeuma* founded in heaven (Phil. 3:20) where the messianic power governs. Hence the appropriateness of Paul's conjunction of political and economic language in Ephesians 2:19: 'you are fellow citizens (*sympolitai*) with the saints and members of the household (*oikeioi*) of God' as a building being built for divine dwelling. The point is that for Paul, as for all the New Testament authors, heaven is not a 'place' or 'other world' (as Nietzsche's *Hinterwelt* implies) but an invisible presence in continuity with the visible world ('on earth as it is in heaven') in a shared messianic political economy. I completely agree with Agamben's thesis that Pauline and early Christian theology is itself 'economic' and did not simply become so later through 'secularisation', but the 'eternal life' by which power is related to 'glory' (and not simply juridical governance) in the mystery of divine economy is for Paul as for Augustine fully political and economic.

The point of continuity, however, is consistently the cross. If one is to speak of an economy of glory, therefore, it must be related to the ignominious death of the Messiah crucified by all forms of worldly authority – religious, political, economic, cultural. The scandal of this claim about messianic sovereignty and glorification by way of the cross is clearly depicted in John 12, and it remains very hard to see even though it is fully public and present in all dimensions of created reality. As Paul states, however, the only access to the *theologia* is the *oikonomia* of its visible human and earthly representative,[19] the messianic *ekklesia* that corporately shares the 'mind (*phroneite*)' (Phil. 2:2,5ff.; cf. the *nous* of Rom. 12:1–2) of Christ characterised by humility and obedience to death on a cross. In the crucial book 10 of *City of God*, Augustine cites Romans 12 to formulate the embodiment of the 'living sacrifice' in the world in conformity with the 'form of a servant' offered in the crucified Messiah.[20] There is no radical division between 'being' and 'acting', between 'theology' and 'ethics' in this messianic enactment of the mysterious divine reconciliation of 'all things' in Christ. For de Lubac this is the sacramental heart of the mystical body of Christ, where 'mystical' means more than 'moral', but may not, because embodied and enacted in the everyday life of the world, 'be in any way taken as synonymous with "invisible"'.[21]

This allows de Lubac, following Augustine,[22] to call all members of the messianic body both 'Christs' and 'priests', and it allows me to dare place Mennonites and the Radical Reformation (which I interpret as a version of 'vernacular mysticism'), with their emphasis on the visible priesthood of all believers, into the Augustinian tradition of political theology understood as *corpus mysticum*. Eucharistic realism and ecclesial realism are united in the sacramental realism of the messianic body,[23] which has implications for political theology. It should be noted that in Augustine's biblical-exegetical formulation of messianic political theology in books 15–18 of *City of God*, which establishes the context for interpreting book 19 (itself placed into Augustine's apocalyptic conclusion, books 19–22),[24] the priest-king of Salem, Melchizedek, plays a more prominent prophetic and figural role than does Israel's king David.[25] This is significant for Augustine's claim that the messianic body must take the form of its priest-king, namely the form of the servant – a form prefigured in Melchizedek's offering of bread and wine to Abraham (Gen. 14:17–18), taken up in the royal messianic Psalm 110:4, and applied to Christ in Hebrews 5–7. The righteousness of this royal figure, also attached to 'Salem', or the city of peace that David renames Jerusalem (the possession of no tribe), is one that rules through the sacrifice of humility displayed above all in Christ and the martyrs. Augustine crucially and consistently relates the political question of peace to the apocalyptic question of worship, a liturgical worship that is also always represented as an incarnational ethic that takes the servant form of diaspora or pilgrimage in the secular world.[26]

The diaspora ethics of political economy that I am here relating to messianic political theology is nicely characterised by Augustine as one of proper use and enjoyment: a secular life in which we 'make use of earthly goods like pilgrims, without grasping after them'.[27] But this use is sacrificially offered up with reference to God so that 'inflamed by the fire of divine love', the form of worldly desire may be messianically reformed to reflect divine desire.[28] This is what it means to be economists of the divine mystery, and one of the great Christian witnesses to this ethic of political economy in our time is Wendell Berry, who resurrects the term 'usufruct' as the measure of good stewardship.[29] He suggests that the biblical passage most valuable in displaying this relationship is Revelation 4:11, in a suitably archaic translation: 'Thou art worthy, O Lord, to receive glory and honor and power: for thou hast created all things, and for thy pleasure they are and were created.'[30] The term *thelema*, here translated 'pleasure', is often translated 'will', but the ambiguity is nicely Augustinian – where will and love, and indeed pleasure, are closely related to represent motive power, and Berry calls it 'affection in action'.[31] The same word is used in Romans 12:2 in terms of proving the *thelema* of God as the measure of the completion of 'all things', and Jesus himself prays: 'thy *thelema* be done on earth as it is in heaven' (Matt. 6:10). The liturgical agency of worship entails attending in our use ('as if not' possessing) of worldly goods to God's pleasure in all things so as to bring about a divinely informed affection in action called 'peace' or 'well-being' or *shalom*. Such messianic passion, far from ruining the world (as Mark Lilla thinks it does),[32] will attend to the exhortation of the seer: 'Awake, and strengthen what remains and is on the point of death' (Rev. 3:2).

Mennonites as a people came into being by the desire, even unto martyrdom, of taking this messianic posture and practice seriously in all aspects of everyday human life, the *oikia*. I have called this stance 'Radical Reformation' in recognition of George Hunston Williams's nice historiographical observation, picked up by Mennonite historians, that this movement may be just as well if not better understood as a worldly or 'secular' vocational continuation of medieval monasticism, a monasticism in the world.[33] This is not simply a matter of a voluntary ecclesial identity or commitment to 'pacifism', but of a coherent and interrelated pattern (a *nomos*) of communal discipleship that includes economic simplicity and the renunciation of possessive desire. This is also in keeping with a Pauline economy (*oikonomia*, sometimes translated 'commission', 1 Cor. 9:17) that inhabits the mysterious freedom of messianic slavery in order to build up (*oikodome*,[34] 1 Cor. 8:1; 10:23) the common world that is nevertheless passing away (1 Cor. 7:31). The *nomos* of economic language here helps break down the sharp distinction between *oikos/oikia* (household) and *polis* (politics) that has long prevented the exploration of a more radical biblical political theology in which so-called 'domestic' (or indeed 'private') relations and institutional orders may not be separated from or opposed to 'public' or 'political' forms of organisation and authority. That is, our everyday, intimate decisions are also very much tied to public, political judgements. This 'love-knowledge' also opens up the entire Bible to a more figural political-ethical interpretation. It would require the Church, as an institutional ordering – the particular embodiment of the 'messianic body' – to relate itself actively and critically to all aspects of the economy of divine government which presides providentially over 'all things'.

My reading here may be compared and contrasted with Eric Gregory's recent influential articulation of a political Augustinianism that emphasises civic virtue consistent with secular liberal democracy without compromising Augustine's theological context of the *ordo amoris* rooted in a Trinitarian theology and the *totus Christus* ecclesiology of the central book 10 of the *City of God*. States Gregory:

> To put it bluntly, Book 10 of the *City of God* is the basic text for Augustinian politics: the heart of Augustine's account of the true worship of the crucified God and the charitable service of neighbor in collective *caritas* . . . A thicker vision of politics and citi-

zenship that is Augustinian is necessarily tied to the kind of God and the kind of desire disclosed in Jesus Christ. Christology should be *political* for Augustinians . . .[35]

I am certainly in full agreement with this, and yet Gregory, in keeping with other political Augustinians, hesitates to interpret this in the apocalyptic registers employed by Paul, Augustine and the traditions of 'vernacular mysticism' that includes Catholic women such as Julian of Norwich[36] as well as more apocalyptic 'radical reformation' critiques of Constantinian Christendom.[37] Such terms are too agonistic to help build up the secular body politic in an ethos of democratic citizenship, too 'hostile' to the necessities of imperial power or the modern security state. While he rejects R. A. Markus's account of the *saeculum* as religiously 'neutral', Gregory, like Markus, prefers language of 'ambivalence' that 'delivers Augustine from both apocalyptic hostility to Rome as an apostate demonic order and sacral identification of Rome as a sacramental vehicle of grace'.[38] In what follows, however, I shall argue that the agonistic language of Pauline and Augustinian citizenship is fully attuned to the religious and theological dimensions of sovereignty in a manner that may be called 'apocalyptic'. An apocalyptic perspective is characterised neither by hostility nor triumphalist opposition. Indeed, in the apocalyptic 2 Thessalonians 2 these are traits of apostasy and anomia in the 'mystery of lawlessness' that will be unveiled as 'satanic'. The messianic mind, by contrast, is 'not to be quickly shaken in mind or excited' but rather patiently waiting, not passively but actively working 'like hesychasts' (2 Thess. 3:12; 1 Thess. 4:11) in the political-ethical activity of building up the relations of love. While not hostile or triumphalistic, such a life of virtue is certainly 'agonistic' – as Augustine insists even in the heart of his apocalyptic account of peace in *City of God*, book 19, 25–8. The referral of the virtues of love and justice to the 'final peace' of the 'most glorious' city is a matter of ultimate citizenship enacted 'like a pilgrim' in the everyday political, economic and social life of this passing age.

## An Apocalyptic Reading of Augustine's Messianic Political Theology

The thesis of Charles Taylor's influential tome *A Secular Age*[39] might be summarised as follows: modern secularisation, a sociopolitical creation of the West, has given rise to an antireligious 'exclusive humanism' in reaction to a Latin Christendom obsessed with 'reform' – that is, to an externalised juridical-penal institutionalisation of Christianity that has lost the personal and incarnational essence of the original 'gospel' of the Messiah Jesus. Taylor identifies the source of this perversion of Latin Christianity as 'hyper-Augustinianism', which takes both Catholic and Protestant forms but is particularly reified and hardened in Calvinist Protestantism.[40] Like Augustine, hyper-Augustinians believe that only a small number of the human *massa damnata* will be saved from sin in order to dwell eternally with God; the majoritarian remainder will be condemned to eternal hell.[41] Theologically, this position is rooted in a juridical-penal understanding of the atonement in which divine wrath against human sin must be appeased, and Christ's sacrifice pays the debt of original sin. There is present here, argues Taylor, a tension between a juridical metaphor (payment of debt) and a redemption metaphor (freeing the captive), a tension between divine anger/wrath and divine love/mercy, between hell and heaven, that gets resolved in a rigid doctrinal logic in which ecclesial authorities display the all-too-human tendency to colonise divine violence in the service of their own. This logic is tied to a pernicious interpretation of suffering and punishment as a part of a providentially governed 'divine pedagogy', in a narrative of total human depravity and limited atonement. Politically, this view entails the belief that the godly minority should exercise political control so as to restrain evil and promote civil order.

Hyper-Augustinians emphasise divine punishment, foster a seamless and puritanical connection between piety and social order, and emphasise the transformation of the will in which virtue requires the disciplined, institutional imposition of the ordering of the good. But for hyper-Augustinians there are also real limits to such institutional, sociopolitical (re)ordering and reform due to the pervasive, incorrigible fact of human sinfulness, which must simply be coercively restrained in the earthly city. Think of Nietzsche's harshest articulation of Christian *ressentiment* against the sinful strong that gives birth to the juridical-penal conscience, which creates the 'responsible, sovereign moral self' through the internalisation of the transcendent 'evil eye', institutionally mediated through various disciplines of religio-moral self-surveillance.[42] Here you have a precis of Taylor's 'hyper-Augustinianism', and while he shares elements of the Nietzschean critique, Taylor also seeks to articulate a Christian vision that is able to address the critique from within a more faithful liberal Catholic political theology, one heavily indebted (Taylor claims)[43] to the work of Ivan Illich – particularly on the radical implications of a Christian understanding of incarnation that entails new motivation (divine compassion rather than penal pedagogy) and a new community ('Communion of Saints' rather than institutional Church) based on voluntary neighbour love that goes beyond external religious identitarian markers and institutional codes.

It is hard to know how Taylor himself would distinguish or reconcile his account of hyper-Augustinianism from or with his account of Augustine in *Sources of the Self* and the Augustinian turn to the inner, intimate self in which God is nearer to me than I am to myself.[44] One thing seems clear: neither account is articulated in highly theological or existential terms. In *Sources* the conceptual Augustinian doctrine of the soul is related to Plato on the one hand and Descartes on the other. In *A Secular Age* Taylor conceptually distinguishes hyper-Augustinian reform and political Augustinianism but nowhere clearly spells out the theological terms and existential consequences of the distinction. Hence it is difficult to agree with John Milbank that Taylor speaks in a theological voice. In fact, Milbank goes much further to suggest that Taylor is 'almost a modern equivalent of Augustine' in providing 'a kind of . . . theologized ecclesiastical history'.[45] Indeed, says Milbank, 'Taylor has, with *A Secular Age*, consummated his invention of a new intellectual genre – a kind of historicized existentialism.'[46] That Taylor is an intellectual historian of the highest order no one could contest; that he is theological and existential in an Augustine-like way, however, is questionable. I shall argue that Illich comes much closer to Augustine's existential historically informed political theology, and he does so because he shares Augustine's apocalyptic biblically formed theological perspective. Neither Milbank nor Taylor does so, and this has important political-theological consequences. Missing from Taylor's appropriation of Illich and critique of hyper-Augustinianism is the centrality of apocalyptic messianism in both Illich and Augustine, which mediates the spiritual causality of divine providence within the personal and political terms of created embodied reality, in a manner that resists the abuses of hyper-Augustinianism.

One of the central critiques Milbank makes of Taylor is that Taylor favours the 'disenchantment' of reality by Enlightenment cosmology, a cosmology that calls into question 1) the popular religious experience of natural reality as 'acts of God', 2) the assumption that the political and the religious orders are inseparable and 3) the belief that the world is full of invisible spiritual forces.[47] At stake here, among other things, is the question of what constitutes Christian 'sacramental mediation'. Milbank favours a 're-enchantment' of the world to go along with Taylor's affirmation of Illich's call for a 'festive conviviality', corresponding (for Taylor) to a 'Communion of Saints' in which there is no exclusionary hell or 'double predestination' but only an inclusive universalism rooted in incarnational love. Milbank's 're-enchantment' (as a kind of intellectual cultural romanticism) appears to accept Taylor's worry about Christian apocalypticism as somehow tied to hyper-Augustinianism, and yet Milbank seeks to find a place for the 'practical bent' of Latin Christianity[48] in which sacramental mediation also takes procedural and institutional forms. He settles upon 'medieval corporatism', and it seems that he considers this form of Christendom culture to model a more promising kind of Augustinianism.

It is not my brief to analyse Milbank's critical and constructive interpretation of Taylor as variants of a new kind of political Augustinianism, though I will return to this general question below. My point here is that Augustine's and Illich's thoroughgoing Christian apocalypticism are neither modes of '(re-)enchantment' nor, as apocalyptic stances are often represented, averse to a disciplined, critical consideration of the institutional and procedural contexts of embodied sociopolitical human existence. Taylor and Milbank, unlike Illich and Augustine, fail to plumb the depths of biblical apocalypticism, preferring instead to develop grand philosophico-historical narratives. Illich, by contrast, performs his messianic apocalyptic critique of modern Western culture with reference to

> the old Latin phrase: *Corruptio optimi quae est pessima* – the historical progression in which God's Incarnation is turned topsy-turvy, inside out. I want to speak of the mysterious darkness that envelops our world, the demonic night paradoxically resulting from the world's equally mysterious vocation to glory. My subject is a mystery of faith, a mystery whose depth of evil could not have come to be without the greatness of the truth revealed to us.[49]

The demonic perversion of truth is not simply a violation of the laws of reality but a personal turning away from an intimate revelation of divine reality in whose image human beings are created. Its correlative is a turning in worship towards a false substitute, the apostatic *mysterium iniquitatis* Paul speaks about in 2 Thessalonians 2,[50] revealed as anti-Messiah in the apocalypse of Messiah and as characterised by mendacious power and wicked deception. This is the personal, intimate character of sin that also has pervasive social and political consequences – the substitution of other-regarding personal love by self-securing institutional power. It may also be described as a turn away from the divine Spirit of love enfleshed in the person of Jesus towards a trust once again in the juridical, institutional constraints of external rules and codes of behaviour – a shift from a community rooted in *con-spiratio* (personal faith, love, sin, forgiveness inspired by the divine Spirit) to one rooted in *con-juratio* (the juridical state structure).[51] The impersonal, instrumental and juridical character of modern social and political ethics, related to risk assessment and technical requirements of security systems (be they legal, educational or medical), are the shared consequences of this shift in spiritual vision. While I cannot attend here to the rich detail of Illich's account, it is clearly an apocalyptic account derived from the New Testament, and it bears many political-theological similarities to Augustine's apocalyptic account of the contrast between the Roman Empire of his day and the biblical revelation of messianic authority, peace and justice that governs citizens of the heavenly city.

For Augustine as for Illich, political justice is a matter of the mimetic objects of love and worship, whether that is the earthly mediation of true justice in the servant form of the messianic king of the heavenly city, or the perverse mediation of false images of justice by demons led by the 'father of lies', *diabolus*. The spiritual and political tension between the two cities represents an apocalyptic conflict between the heavenly Jerusalem and the earthly Babylon, presided over by conflicting authorities.[52] I shall argue, in keeping with Illich's account and using some of his central topoi, that Augustine shares the (especially Pauline) apocalyptic urgency of the New Testament in which the conflict between the flesh and the spirit, first Adam and second Adam, messianic sovereignty and anti-messianic rebellion, may not be reduced to institutional authorities (such as 'Church and state'). Rather, they belong to very different orientations of life that extend from the inner conscience of each human being (the *con-spiratio* of the messianic *con-scientia*, we might say) to household relations, to cities and peoples, to the cosmic ordering of all things in keeping with the spiritual causality of divine causality apocalypsed in Christ – an apocalyptic sovereignty that may not be institutionalised in any authoritative human cultural form but that lives by faith, oriented towards the invisible Sovereign it worships not only in its ritual forms but in all acts of loving service in the world. The political-ethical corruption of the best by the worst is characterised by a reversal in 'use and enjoyment' displayed in the messianic *ordo amoris* in which earthly things are to be used with reference to the peace found in the heavenly city,[53] in which the true nature of things is ultimately revealed:

> For this peace is a perfectly ordered and perfectly harmonious fellowship in the enjoyment of God, and of one another in God. When we have reached that peace, our life will no longer be a mortal one; rather, we shall then be fully and certainly alive . . . a spiritual body standing in need of nothing; a body subject in every part to the will. This peace the heavenly city possesses in faith while on its pilgrimage, and by this faith it lives righteously (*iuste*), directing towards the attainment of that peace every good act which it performs either for God, or – since the city's life is inevitably a social one – for neighbour. (*City of God* 19.17)[54]

## Providence/Contingency

One of the most important features of Christian apocalypticism, argues Illich, following Hans Blumenberg, is the idea of contingency.[55] Briefly put, 'Contingency expresses the state of being of a world which has been created from nothing, is destined to disappear and is upheld in its existence by one thing, and one thing only: divine will.'[56] This idea of apocalyptic contingency owes its conceptual existence to Augustine's providential understanding that creation is at every moment the sovereign act of the completely gratuitous will of God, who brings reality into being *ex nihilo*.[57] This places a lot of weight on will, not only in terms of the divine will but also of the human will made in God's image. Gratuity or gift, 'a realm that comes into being in response to a call, rather than a determinative cause', is in fact the primary form of causation in the Bible – the causation of divine Word that constantly speaks the world into being.[58] The willed human response to this call is also highly consequential, both in terms of freely obeying the creative divine will or falling away from it in disobedience, or sin. Sin is on this view less the violation of a law than an intimate and relational infidelity that has natural and political consequences. The apocalyptic claim of the New Testament is, to put it in Pauline terms, that the whole of this creation is pregnant with the Messiah and is now (with the coming of Christ) groaning in labour (Rom. 8). The groaning consists in the messianic revelation of a new possibility, a neighbour love that crosses all social, political and cultural-religious boundaries as a 'free creation' in response to a divine call.[59] This call entails not only a disruption of conventional moral categories (male/female, Jew/Greek, slave/master, friend/enemy), and hence a social disruption of role and behaviour definitions, but also an account of virtue as suffering love that comes always only as a divine gift in response to a divine call that may be refused. And, of course, part of the messianic groaning and suffering of creation is that this call is resisted and refused (sin), resulting in both internal existential conflicts in the human will (Rom. 7) and sociopolitical and religious conflicts. This means that the 'mood, or ground-tone' of this new messianic way of being is contrition, 'a deep sorrow about my capacity to betray . . . relationships . . . and, at the same time, a deep confidence in the forgiveness and mercy of the other'.[60] Needless to say, this raises the stakes for social and political ethics considerably in the messianic community that seeks to live according to this newly revealed form of life, and it will find itself confronting not only internal collisions but also collisions with forms of life that are constituted quite otherwise, in power relations under human juridical and institutional control in the earthly city. Illich's argument is that the messianic apocalypse requires a radical, contingent faith that is constantly itself in danger of being perverted by sin, that is, 'the decision to make faith into something that is subject to the power of this world',[61] namely the 'anti-messianic'. This is the constant temptation within Christendom, and it has led to significant perversions in the modern West. I will return to this below, but wish now to turn to Augustine's important formulation of this providential contingency in what I call his vision of spiritual causality.

I begin with Augustine's discussion of causality in book 5 of City of God, which is crucial to Augustine's case for divine providence rather than fate as the principle of interpretation for political order, peace and justice. Roman historiography and political theory lacks insight into the spiritual causes of human action – the quest for happiness (felicitas) and the conditions of peace and justice that make it possible – because it lacks this theological principle. Augustine understands divine providence as the ordering of all reality according to the rational power of divine will – God's perfect free agency – over against the impersonal, external causality of fatum and fortuna. Only a providential account will overcome the problematic either–or distinction between the external mechanisms of nature (inanimate causality) and human free agency (moral causality) that seeks to establish a rational relation between them, a relation that cannot be accounted for via various earthly measures. Only a messianic measure will offer insight into the true ground of human liberation (freedom of the will) from bondage to perverse demonic affective and social orderings.

In City of God 5.9, Augustine develops his account by denying any contradiction between divine praescientia of all things that God has made and libera hominis voluntas. But this requires the recognition that the ordo causarum in which all motion (and motive) finds its intelligible principles is established by the divine word of creation, rooted in God's eternal will. The efficient causality of all that happens is tied to will, and ultimately to the divine will that gives life to everything; that is, there are 'no efficient causes which are not voluntary causes: belonging, that is, to that nature which is the "breath of life" (spiritus vitae)'. All bodies, inanimate as well as rational, are subject to God, the uncreated, uncaused breath of life who alone gives the power to move and the power to act freely: 'Thus the real cause which causes and is not caused, is God.' God freely establishes the spiritual terms of movement and agency (power), including free human agency (will), and this means that all motion and power must be understood in relation to God and the causal order established by divine Word and Spirit.

Augustine spells this out in *City of God* 5.11, which I shall quote at length:

Thus the supreme and true God, with his Word and the Holy Spirit, which three are one, is the one omnipotent God, creator and maker of every soul and every body; participation in whom brings happiness to all who are happy in the truth and not in illusion (*vanitas*). He has made man a rational animal; and when man sins he does not let him go unpunished, nor does he abandon him without mercy. He has given, to good and bad alike, the existence (*essentia*) they share with the stones, reproductive life (*vita seminalis*) they share with the plants, sentient life they share with the animals, and intellectual life they share only with the angels. From him comes every mode of being, every species, every order, all measure, number, and weight. From him comes all that exists in nature, whatever its kind (*genus*), whatever its value (*aestimatio*), and the seeds of forms (*semina formarum*), and the forms of seeds, and the motions of seeds and forms. He has given to flesh its origin, beauty, health, fertility in propagation, the arrangement and healthful concord of its members. He has also given the irrational soul memory, sense, and appetite; and in addition has given the rational soul mind, intelligence and will. Neither heaven nor earth, neither angel nor man, not even the inner parts of the smallest and lowliest creatures, nor the feather of a bird, nor a tiny flower of a plant, nor the leaf on a tree, has God left without a harmony and, as it were, a peace among their parts. In no manner can it be believed, then, that he should have willed the kingdoms of men, their dominations and their servitudes, to be outside the laws of his providence.[62]

Clearly for Augustine nature is not a closed system, but rather a dynamic, dramatic ordering animated by the living Spirit of the triune God. This principle is fully coherent with the further implication that human rational will images the divine will insofar as it moves freely towards the happiness it desires, and that it understands its motion and the entire order of causality only in relation to the God that created and continues to sustain them. The principles of political order and moral judgement concerning politics are therefore fundamentally tied to divine providence. Access to this moral order is to be found in the internal witness of conscience, says Augustine (5.12), by which he means a fully public and testable witness, not private consent to doctrine. Any conception of political power or measure of political order that does not attend to the love of justice therein attested (5.14) misses the mark, the true path of virtue.

While conscience is an inner spiritual measure, it is not autonomous – it finds its measure, however, not in an earthly city but in the heavenly one, the eternal City of God where true happiness is realised as a divine gift (5.16). This city is not directly present, nor does its sovereign rule in any directly visible way on earth (which is why 'the just shall live by faith', one of Augustine's, and Paul's, favourite biblical lines). It is accessible only in the worship and imitation of the true God, whose rule is mediated on the earth only in the form of the servant, a form whose authority is revealed not in the 'power-game' but in the 'justice-game'.[63] It is only in the inner spiritual and outer corporeal imitation of this form that one can make proper political judgements. Thus, when Augustine begins his critique of the Roman Empire in earnest in book 4 of *City of God*, he too (like Plato before him and Hobbes after him) will ground the act of political judgement in the 'human writ large' (4.3). At issue is the standard of true happiness, a life lived in harmony with the highest eternal good, in which worship of the true, immortal God will overcome the false measure of 'fear of death' rooted in excessive love of (or orientation towards) the temporal.

In contrast to those 'gangs of criminals on a large scale' who cannot rule themselves except by 'dividing the plunder' according to conventions of human justice, and arrogate to themselves political legitimacy by means of mortal power, the community of the just is displayed in another model – the martyrs who follow in the steps of the Apostles, who imitate the crucified Christ. Ultimately Augustine, as the title of his famous work signifies, will develop this political contrast between types of human being with reference to the two cities of the apocalypse: one ruled by the slain Lamb, the other by its lying mortal parodies who imitate the Devil. Is it not precisely here, in Augustine's apocalyptic interpretation of political judgement, that his account of spiritual causality will run afoul of political theorists who will reject it as too mythological and otherworldly to be of real practical or theoretical value? The burden of my argument will be to show that this is not the case, that it is precisely Augustine's apocalypticism that offers critical and constructive resources for political theology and ethics in our own *saeculum* no less than in his, and further, that it is crucial to understand his influential language of conscience and 'will' (also a central modern political category in the contractarian tradition) in the context of apocalyptic causality and not (as yet another recent interpreter has defined it)[64] as a disembodied inner selfhood.

## The Messianic Mediation of Virtue and Sin

In keeping with this apocalyptic cosmology, for Augustine, the Messiah, as both 'Son' and 'second Adam', reveals the meaning of the Fall and human sin in both personal and political terms. Augustine contrasts this new form of mediation that reveals God in human form as 'servant' and the Trinitarian form of the human made in God's image, to the deceptive mediations that characterise the imitation and worship of fallen spiritual powers. While some attention has been given to apocalyptic in Augustine's theology,[65] the overwhelming scholarly consensus – represented above all in the influential studies by Robert A. Markus – is that while eschatology is important for Augustine's political theology, it is in fact *anti*-apocalyptic.[66] Though political Augustinians such as Oliver O'Donovan and Robert Dodaro (among others) have developed criticisms of Markus's language of secular political 'neutrality' in characterising Augustine's position, they have generally avoided the characterisation of Augustine's political theology as apocalyptic, preferring to develop a sharp institutional dualism between Church and state in their differing spheres of authority, mediated above all by the political conscience of the 'Christian statesman'.[67]

Robert Dodaro has provided a lucid account of what is at issue here by outlining three different neo-Augustinian interpretations of Augustine's political thought, focusing especially on his understanding of the relationship between *ecclesia* (the role of bishop) and *res publica* (the role of statesman).[68] For Dodaro, the key to a proper understanding of Augustine's political theology is Christology, since for Augustine Christ is the divine mediator of justice who alone mediates true virtue to the soul (and thus to the statesman). Dodaro points out that Augustine was not preoccupied with the relationship between Church and *res publica* – that is a modern preoccupation, and thus stated it is a theoretical rather than spiritual question. (And yet Dodaro, like most political Augustinians, can't resist this framing for the sake of political relevance.) Dodaro argues that for Augustine, political justice is most crucially dependent upon freedom from the fear of death, which the humility of Christ and his vulnerability to death most fully mediates, in a manner that liberates human beings from the fallen desire for their own earthly glory. To explain this mediating capacity, Dodaro avers that Augustine brings together two Christological doctrines: 1) the unity of human and divine natures in one person (9.5–17) – a mystery of faith (not the *scientia* of our own *ratio*) that enables those who imitate Christ to participate in divine love, the true end and form of all virtues; and 2) the *totus Christus* teaching of Paul, whereby Christ as the head of the messianic body offers himself up sacrificially in the form of a servant in such a manner that the entire body participates liturgically in this sacrifice in which love of God and neighbour are realised (10.6, 20; 17.18).

What Dodaro overlooks is the apocalyptic background of Augustine's Christology – the cosmic conflict between the divine and the demonic that structures Augustine's mediation language in *City of God*, so closely connected to the language of worship and sacrifice in political theology. Dodaro pays attention to Christ's mediation, but not so much to the false mediation that Christ combats.[69] Not only does Augustine provide an apocalyptic demythologisation of Roman imperial ideology (see *City of God* 2.25–9, where Augustine identifies the problem as the libidinous imitation and worship of demonic examplars who foster division, deceit and conflict), he extends this demonic reading to the Platonic mediation of virtue in books 9 and 10, where he articulates the centrality of the above Christological doctrines for a critique of political idolatry in the more spiritual and intellectual registers of Platonic political virtue.

The warrior ethic of glorying in power (5.12–20) is rooted in a lie about divine glory and power, a lie perpetuated in the public media (theatre and civil religion) that focus on the love of power rather than the power of love. The powerful motivational correlative of such love of power is the fear of death.[70] Such a focus cannot bring the happiness of peaceable harmony rooted in the true justice of God that orders the good. To develop good judgement in 'seeing where true happiness (*felicitas*) lies, and where an empty show (*vanitas*) dwells entails 'the worship of the true God by true sacrifices and the service of good lives (*bonis moribus*)' (4.3). This shifts the focus from the earthly stage show of battling libidinous deities (both human and humanly projected) to the cosmic stage of divine providence. It also shifts the focus of attention from the divinity of human *virtus* to God's gift of virtue, which comes by *fides* – represented in the biblical statement that 'the just shall live by faith'.[71] Happiness and virtue are the gifts of God, and to receive them requires a proper spiritual orientation, not towards the moribund glory (the false immortality) of the earthly city but the eternal glory of the heavenly city (5.14; 19). It is in this context that one must interpret Augustine's statement in *City of God* 6.9: 'It is, strictly speaking, for the sake of eternal life alone that we are Christians' – it is here that human happiness is found, the life of the soul rooted in God, not on its own as an individual but in the community of worship, the messianic body of Christ.

Before elaborating his Christian apocalyptic interpretation of political judgement, however, Augustine develops a distinction between Roman civil theology and Platonic natural philosophy. In *City of God* 6.5 he introduces Varro's tripartite division of theology: mythical (based on the fables of the poets, which cater to pleasure), natural (based on philosophy, attuned to the eternal good that orders the world) and civil (the public cult of priests and citizens, focused on the city). While Varro praises the second, it is clear that he considers the third to be politically the most important and, furthermore, that the third and the first are really similar. The eternal order of divine good is abandoned for the human works of cities and theatres – which confirms Augustine's judgement that Varro really advocates the useful public worship of humanly fashioned gods, the gods of pleasure and coercive power, by turns flattering and threatening the citizens to behave. For this reason, the only natural theologian worthy of the name is Plato, who acknowledges the God who transcends the soul and gives blessedness (*beatitudo*, which goes beyond *felici-*

*tas*) to the rational soul through participation in God's unchanging and incorporeal light of wisdom (8.1). Only such an orientation offers moral insight into the true ordering of reality, in contrast to the deceptive external measures of the extension and duration of imperial power, in the service of which the deceptive rhetoric of Roman civil theology is marshalled. That is, only Plato's theology is truly theological, and therefore also effective in moving the political discussion from the rhetorical play of power to the love of wisdom. Socrates stands at the transition point of political philosophy from the study of external causality to spiritual causality: 'He believed that the first and highest cause exists in nothing but the will of the one supreme God; hence that the causation of the universe could be grasped only by a purified mind (*mundata mente*)' (8.3).

If Plato says that wisdom is found in the imitation, knowledge and love of this God, in the participation in whom is found true happiness, then, says Augustine, 'none come nearer to us than the Platonists' (8.5). Indeed, Plato's trinitarian structure in his philosophical theology – in God is found the *causa subsistendi* (the *principium* of all life and all being, 8.6), *ratio intelligendi* (the *logos*, the light of the mind that enables wise discernment, 8.7) and *ordo vivendi* (the discovery of happiness in the *summum bonum* to which all moral action is referred, 8.8) – suggests to Augustine the purest example of the natural revealed wisdom described by Paul in Romans 1:19–20 (8.10). The reference to Paul, however, signals the beginning of critique. It is a critique paralleled in the *Confessions* (book 7) – Platonic pride in the reputation for wisdom earned in the heroic disciplines of dialectical *paideia* and the intellectual virtues. Lacking here are the penitential tears of confession that purify the vision of the heart in a manner quite unlike anything found in Plato's dialogues. This is due to a very different principle of mediation in Paul – the word made flesh (mortal) in the 'form of a servant', whose death makes possible participation in the divine life itself (insofar as he remains also 'in the form of God').[72] Only this death makes possible the overcoming of the fear of death by faith in Christ as the one who is also raised up to God beyond death.

Equally important here is the model of imitation we are given to follow in Christ. Unlike a stage play, the model is not one of emotional catharsis in which one participates as an intellectually and emotionally engaged but inactive spectator. Unlike Plato's Socrates, the model is not an educative one of intellectual purification through the critical, dialectical expurgation of myths and conventional traditions. The key to spiritual causality is now to be found in an embodied model that nevertheless is claimed to be the very spiritual principle underlying all created reality, and this embodied model takes the form of a lowly servant, not an exalted ruler – political or philosophical or otherwise. It is an enactment in the most audacious terms of the principles of motion now brought into scandalous collision not only with political ideals but also intellectual and spiritual ones. It introduces a divine seriousness into the historical drama that compels recognition of God as not only the builder of the theatre (which is 'all the world') and the author of the script but also the primary actor in all agency as its personal, creative and moving principle. We learn what it means to take part in this divine agency when we follow the path of humble love (which cures our blinding pride) taken by God in the world, the *via caritatis*, and imitate its spiritual motion. For it is the divine Truth itself (*ipsa Veritas* and *ipsa Sapientia*), 'that Word through whom all things were made', that was made flesh so that God may dwell with us. 'Although he is our native country, he made himself also the way to that country.'[73]

As Augustine makes clear (see *Teaching Christianity* 1.12; *Trinity* 2.7) this divinely given spiritual motion by which God comes to dwell in God's own creation is not some form of space and time travel – God comes to where God already is. So also, therefore,

the motion of our return to God is not a spatio-temporal tradition to be studied or preserved any more than it is simply the motions of our psyche, but rather the fulfilment of
our created existence designed for eternal communion with God and our neighbours. The
cosmic spiritual drama in which we participate has its terms in the very shared life of the
divine Trinity. This is not something that can be worked out by human reasoning.[74] It can
only be accepted by faith as God's gift. So too the model of political authority, the rule
of Christ that reigns not only in the heavenly city but also in the hearts of the citizens of
the city of God on pilgrimage in the world. This is why Augustine introduces language of
divine agency as the central interpretive *principium* of political judgement in *City of God*:
one must understand human agency not in terms of stories of human beings or the gods
or other narrative accounts (which must themselves be measured by a larger good), but in
relation to God who has created human beings with the power to act (in God's image) and
therefore alone can measure it. As Augustine makes clear in *City of God* 8.20–5, the key
issue is mediation – the Platonic daemonic mediation (since 'no god mingles with human
beings')[75] is contrasted to messianic mediation as Augustine argues that only the God-
man can liberate human beings from bondage to the lordship of demonic powers with the
chains of their own disordered desires attached to false libidinous images (*simulacra*, 8.24).
Similitude to the true God is possible only by conformity in worship to the fully divine
yet fully human form of Christ. Only through the humility of Christ, the 'good mediator,
who reconciles enemies', can the human will be liberated from the 'evil mediator, who
separates loved ones' in the divisions of self-love (9.15). The universal path towards
the liberation of the 'whole human' (body, mind and spirit, 10.27) from the diabolical
dominion of injustice is the royal road (*via regalis*, 10.32) of the servant sovereign. The
apocalyptic terms of this spiritual and sociopolitical liberation are clearly spelt out in *City
of God* 14: the earthly city lives wholly oriented according to the diabolical lie that the
principle of mediation is found in my self, my own soul (the *similis diabolo* is a measure of
possession rooted in pride and envy, 14.3), whereas the heavenly city lives on pilgrimage
in the *saeculum* wholly oriented by the sacrifice to God that is the messianic body mediated by Christ, a sacrifice that heals the defective will of its deluded desires and enables it
to obey the divine will exemplified in the city's sovereign (14.13). Thus is the messianic
social body liberated from domination to Babylon, the diabolical/demonic order, to the
properly ordered will and *ordo amoris* of the *rex optimus* (17.16).

Insofar as the Church embodies the kenotic servant posture of Christ, and a vision of
justice that lives by faith, it adopts a martyrdom stance and not a heroic one. The *agon*
(*certamen*) of faith, in which fear of death is conquered, is seen pre-eminently in the holy
martyrs (*City of God* 13.4). The justice that defeats sin in the death of Christ and brings
with it participation in divine immortality (*Trinity* 13) overcomes the fear of death and
enables the martyrs to die rather than to sin.[76] In *City of God* 14 Augustine develops this
model of martyrdom further in terms of the will ordered *secundum spiritum* – a good will
is good and at rest in its desires when ordered by love of God. Here Augustine makes
reference to the Apostle Paul, that *vir optimus et fortissimus* (political terminology)[77] who
glories in his weakness. Again, the point is that fear of death is overcome not by the possession of virtue but by the gift of divine love given to the penitent heart. As Augustine
puts it in *City of God* 19.27:

> Our righteousness (*iustitia*) also, though true righteousness insofar as it is referred to the
> true ultimate good, is in this life only such as to consist in the forgiveness of sins rather
> than the perfection of virtues. This is borne out by the prayer of the whole City of God

during its pilgrimage in the world, which cries out to God in the voice of all its members: 'Forgive us our debts, as we forgive our debtors.'

This is a political and not merely private or spiritual vision and practice.[78] It is engaged
by the communal body that bears the mind of Christ, but only insofar as it worships the
true God in humility. Such worship, as *City of God* 10 makes clear, is both a spiritual and
a bodily sacrifice, communally offered and received in penitence.

History thus plays a role in Augustine's apocalyptic vision of spiritual causality and
political order that it does not in Plato, but history is not primarily about human agency.
The dramatic text that must be read in order for human beings to have their discernment
formed is the text of God's providential Trinitarian action into the Creation, ultimately by
sending the eternal form of divine wisdom itself into the temporal form humanly required
to discern it, the humble servant. The story of this providential agency is to be found in
Scripture, interpreted according to the rule of *caritas*. The second half of *City of God* develops its alternative account of political order through a figural reading of Scripture that, like
the New Testament, ends with an apocalyptic vision of the two cities that structures the
whole. This apocalypse represents the city on pilgrimage in the world as a community of
penitent martyrs who relate the earthly peace to the heavenly peace – but as pilgrims in
Babylonian exile (19.26). This pilgrim, diaspora vision of the Church's political service,
rooted in an apocalyptic understanding of political discernment, represents a different
vision of social conscience than that depicted in Dodoro's statesman, which is, I have
argued, still too individually and institutionally defined within a Church–state duality.

I have also argued elsewhere against treating the example of the political conscience
of the 'wise judge' proffered by Augustine in *City of God* 19.5–6 (cf. 14.28) as ethically
or politically 'normative' for thinking about Christian political responsibility in a secular
order. The context of this example is his debate with 'the philosophers' about the virtues
of the *sapientes* who are required to make political judgements under social conditions of
misery and sinful necessity in the earthly polis. But here it is important to take the whole
of book 19 into account, since the agonistic drama of virtue and vice is itself contextualised in the context of apocalyptic messianism – the cosmic liturgical contrast between
the *corpus mysticum* of the Eucharistic 'form of the servant' and the 'form of God' towards
which the former is being conformed through humility and obedience. Here *City of God*
book 19 may itself provide a helpful structure. Augustine is convinced that the same
existential relations of human love and justice hold true from the most intimate levels
of self-consciousness and household relations to the civic and international domains,
from the most visible bodily level to the cosmic spiritual context concerning the origin
and end of all things. No false, humanly imposed boundaries will enable us to sort this
out more simply – whether mythical or hypothetical.[79] This does not mean that divine
justice or judgement is transparent in the world, but it does mean that those ordered by
the liturgical practices of penitence and self-offering may not presume to mediate divine
judgement in anything but the servant form enacted therein. To the extent to which any
retributive judicial practices are devoted to the possessive and dominating 'order' of the
security state that claims to mediate a non-penitential justice, such practices are rooted in
sinful necessity and contribute to the 'lie' of a strictly human sovereignty. What is revealed
apocalyptically in the wisdom of the Word made flesh is a *libertas* and a peace tied not to
*imperium* – that secular commonwealth that buffers individual freedom of private properties and other *propria*/rights via the accumulation of wealth through political economic
domination and the 'enslavement' of lesser powers – but to the messianic 'form of the

servant' whose life is offered up as a sacrifice for the lives of others (both proximate and distant strangers) in the power of love, not the love of power. This too is a politics! And it reveals the terms whereby human beings may attain a just and happy life through the 'regeneration', and not the mere transcendence or humanly defined reconstruction, of the gift of creation offered to us as participation in the divine life itself.

# Notes

1. I offer an Augustinian critique of such political realism in P. Travis Kroeker, *Christian Ethics and Political Economy in North America: A Critical Analysis* (Montreal: McGill-Queen's University Press, 1995), pp. 133–43.
2. A more complete account of this is found in P. Travis Kroeker, *Messianic Political Theology and Diaspora Ethics: Essay in Exile* (Eugene, OR: Cascade Books, 2017. This essay especially draws upon chh. 1 and 3 of that volume, and I am grateful for permission to use material from my essay 'Augustine's Messianic Political Theology: An Apocalyptic Critique of Political Augustinianism', in *Augustine and Apocalyptic*, edited by John Doody, Kari Kloos and Kim Paffenroth (Lanham, MD: Lexington, 2014), pp. 129–49.
3. See the recent essay by Paul J. Griffiths, 'Secularity and the *Saeculum*', in *Augustine's City of God: A Critical Guide*, edited by James Wetzel (Cambridge: Cambridge University Press, 2012), pp. 33–54. The classic twentieth-century work is Robert A. Markus, *Saeculum: History and Society in the Theology of St. Augustine*, rev. ed. (Cambridge University Press, [1970] 1988).
4. For a fine summary account, see Michael J. S. Bruno, *Political Augustinianism: Modern Interpretations of Augustine's Political Thought* (Minneapolis: Fortress, 2014).
5. Carl Schmitt, *Politisches Theologie: Vier Kapitel zur Lehre von der Souveränität* (Berlin: Dunker und Humblot, [1922] 1934); published in English as *Political Theology: Four Chapters on the Concept of Sovereignty*, George Schwab (trans.) (Cambridge, MA: MIT Press, 1985).
6. Carl Schmitt, *The Leviathan in the State Theory of Thomas Hobbes: Meaning and Failure of a Political Symbol*, George Schwab (trans.) (Chicago: University of Chicago Press, 2008).
7. Schmitt, *Political Theology*, p. 15.
8. Schmitt, *Political Theology*, p. 36.
9. Carl Schmitt, *The Concept of the Political*, George Schwab (trans.) (Chicago: University of Chicago Press, 1996), pp. 26–37. See also Carl Schmitt, *The Nomos of the Earth in the International Law of the Jus Publicum Europaeum*, G. L. Ulmen (trans.) (New York: Telos Press, 2003): 'The ability to recognize a *justus hostis* [just enemy] is the beginning of all international law' (pp. 51–2).
10. Jennifer Rust, 'Political Theologies of the *Corpus Mysticum*: Schmitt, Kantorowicz, and de Lubac', in *Political Theology and Early Modernity*, edited by Graham Hammill and Julia Reinhard Lupton (Chicago: University of Chicago Press, 2012), pp. 102–23. See also Chad Pecknold, 'Migrations of the Host: Fugitive Democracy and the *Corpus Mysticum*', *Political Theology* 11 (2010): 77–101. Pecknold argues that Sheldon Wolin's 'fugitive democracy' critique of liberal democracy owes much to de Lubac's work because 'de Lubac imagined a 'mystical body politics' that was more inclusive, more humanising and ultimately more social than the isolating politics of the modern, liberal state' (p. 99), but that ultimately this cannot be detached from de Lubac's Augustinian ecclesiology of a visible, public messianic body. Wolin, like Schmitt and Kantorowicz, recognises that 'secular writers [including Rousseau's social contract conception of community] were not slow in perceiving the enormous emotional force that lay behind the idea of the *corpus mysticum*' in Sheldon Wolin, *Politics and Vision: Continuity and Innovation in Western Political Thought*, expanded edition (Princeton, NJ: Princeton University Press, 2004), p. 120.
11. Peterson's famous rejection of political theology is found in an essay that begins and ends with appeals to Augustine, 'Monotheism as a Political Problem' [1935], in *Theological Tractates*, Michael Hollerich (trans.) (Stanford: Stanford University Press, 2011), pp. 68–105: 'In this

way, not only was monotheism as a political problem resolved and the Christian faith liberated from bondage to the Roman Empire, but a fundamental break was made with every "political theology" that misuses the Christian proclamation for the justification of a political situation.' Peterson, *Theological Tractates*, p. 104. Schmitt's response is extensively and polemically articulated in *Political Theology II: The Myth of the Closure of any Political Theology*, Michael Hoelzl and Graham Ward (trans.) (Cambridge: Polity Press, 2008).

12. Jacob Taubes, *Political Theology of Paul*, Dana Hollander (trans.) (Stanford: Stanford University Press, 2004), p. 109; Jacob Taubes, *Occidental Eschatology*, David Ratmoko (trans.) (Stanford University Press, 2009), pp. 79–80, 86. Another recent version of this story is told by Michael S. Northcott, 'Revolutionary Messianism and the End of Empire', in *A Political Theology of Climate Change* (Grand Rapids: Eerdmans, 2013), esp. pp. 277ff.

13. Erik Peterson, 'Christ as *Imperator*', in *Theological Tractates*, Michael Hollerich (trans.) (Stanford: Stanford University Press, 2011), pp. 143–50: 147.

14. Oliver O'Donovan, *The Desire of the Nations: Rediscovering the Roots of Political Theology* (Cambridge: Cambridge University Press, 1996), p. 146.

15. Regarding O'Donovan's attempt to use Rom 13:1–5 as the Pauline authorisation of a new Christological grounding for the judicial role of the secular state, I find the following counter-reading (originally against Oscar Cullmann) by G. B. Caird useful: 'The powers of state are to be obeyed not because they have been made subject to Christ but simply because they exist, and because no authority can exist apart from God's decree . . . Paul achieves the universal centrality of Christ not by making the authority of the powers depend on the Cross but by declaring that Christ is God's agent in creation', in G. B. Caird, *Principalities and Powers: A Study in Pauline Theology* (Eugene, OR: Wipf and Stock, 2013), p. 25.

16. Giorgio Agamben, *The Kingdom and the Glory: For a Theological Genealogy of Economy and Government*, Lorenzo Chiesa (trans.) (Stanford: Stanford University Press, 2011).

17. Agamben, *The Kingdom and the Glory*, pp. 24–5. By contrast, see Bruno Blumenfeld, *The Political Paul: Justice, Democracy and Kingship in a Hellenistic Framework* (Sheffield: Sheffield Academic, 2001).

18. Blumenfeld's translation, *The Political Paul*, p. 138.

19. This is Hans Urs von Balthasar's account of Henri de Lubac's 'ecclesiocentrism' in *The Theology of Henri de Lubac: An Overview*, Joseph Fessio and Michael Waldstein (trans.) (San Francisco: Ignatius, 1991), pp. 115–20.

20. See especially Augustine, *City of God* 10.6 and 10.20. Cf. Augustine, *The Trinity* 14.22, where this same transformative process according the the 'form of a servant' is related to Romans 12. All quotations from Dyson's translation of *City of God*.

21. Henri de Lubac, *The Splendor of the Church*, Michael Mason (trans.) (San Francisco: Ignatius, 1999), p. 91. Cf. Henri de Lubac, *Corpus Mysticum: The Eucharist and the Church in the Middle Ages*, Gemma Simmonds (trans.) (Notre Dame, IN: University of Notre Dame Press, 2006), ch. 3.

22. Augustine, *City of God* 20.10.

23. de Lubac, *Corpus Mysticum*, pp. 248–56.

24. I fully agree with Lee's argument that *City of God* 19 requires the apocalyptic contextualisation of the earlier books to show that 'the difference between the two cities on the *summum bonum* is, in fact, the difference between heaven and hell'. Gregory W. Lee, 'Republics and Their Loves: Rereading *City of God* 19', *Modern Theology* 27:4 (2011), 553–81, p. 558. This is related to Lee's point that a better metaphor for interpreting Augustine's treatment of the relation between the two cities in *City of God* 19.17 than the authority of institutional political offices is Augustine's repeated comparison of the Christian situation to the Israelites in Babylonian captivity: 'Augustine's primary metaphor for the church's relation to the world is not citizenship but captivity' (p. 574).

25. Augustine, *City of God* 16.22; 17.5, 17, 20; 18.35; 20.10, 21.

26. For a very different reading of the figure of Melichizedek, see John Milbank, 'Augustine's Three

Cities', in *Beyond Secular Order: The Representation of Being and the Representation of the People* (Chichester: Wiley-Blackwell, 2013), pp. 228–30.

27. Augustine, *City of God* 1.29; in 1.10 he provides Paul's apocalyptic warrant for this ethic, given in 1 Cor. 7:31: 'make use of the world as if not (*hos me*) using it', for the form of this world is passing away.

28. Augustine, *City of God* 10.6. Augustine cites Romans 12:2.

29. Wendell Berry, *What Are People For?* (San Francisco: North Point, 1990), pp. 98ff.

30. Berry, *What Are People For?*, pp. 100, 136.

31. Berry, *What Are People For?*, p. 136.

32. 'We find it incomprehensible that theological ideas still inflame the minds of men, stirring up messianic passions that leave societies in ruins.' Mark Lilla, *The Stillborn God: Religion, Politics and the Modern West* (New York: Knopf, 2007), p. 3.

33. George Hunston Williams, *The Radical Reformation*, 3rd ed. (Kirksville, MO: Truman State University Press, 1995).

34. *Oikodomein*, an important verb for Paul, is primarily an apocalyptic and messianic concept, the *Theological Dictionary of the New Testament* tells us, vol. 5, p. 139. It is simultaneously theological as well as political and ethical.

35. Eric Gregory, *Politics and the Order of Love: An Augustinian Ethic of Democratic Citizenship* (Chicago: University of Chicago Press, 2008), p. 379; cf. pp. 256 and 269–70.

36. See Frederick C. Bauerschmidt, *Julian of Norwich and the Mystical Body Politic of Christ* (Notre Dame, IN: University of Notre Dame Press, 1999); David Aers, *Sin and Salvation: Augustine, Langland, and Fourteenth-Century Theology* (Notre Dame, IN: University of Notre Dame Press, 2009).

37. See Stanley Hauerwas, 'The End of Sacrifice: An Apocalyptic Politics', in *Apocalyptic and the Future of Theology*, edited by Joshua Davis and Douglas Harink (Eugene, OR: Cascade Books, 2012), pp. 354–68; David Aers, *Beyond Reformation? An Essay on William Langland's Piers Plowman and the End of Constantinian Christianity* (Notre Dame, IN: University of Notre Dame Press, 2015).

38. Gregory, *Politics and the Order of Love*, p. 91; cf. pp. 59, 138.

39. Charles Taylor, *A Secular Age* (Cambridge, MA: Harvard University Press, 2007).

40. See Taylor's discussion of 'hyper-Augustinianism' in Taylor, *A Secular Age*, pp. 105, 227, 231, 319, 511, 626, 651–4.

41. See Augustine, *The City of God* 13.23; 14.21; 21.12.

42. See, for example, Friedrich Nietzsche, *On the Genealogy of Morals*, Walter Kaufmann and R. J. Hollingdale (trans.) (New York: Vintage, 1967).

43. See Taylor, *A Secular Age*, pp. 737–43. Taylor also writes a very appreciative foreword to *The Rivers North of the Future: The Testament of Ivan Illich*, as Told to David Cayley (Toronto: Anansi, 2005).

44. Charles Taylor, *Sources of the Self: The Making of the Modern Identity* (Cambridge, MA: Harvard University Press, 1989), ch. 7. Nevertheless, I will take Taylor's position to be compatible with the political Augustinianism developed by Markus in *Christianity and the Secular* (Notre Dame, IN: University of Notre Dame Press, 2006). Markus himself makes the suggestion in his programmatic third chapter on 'Consensus in Augustine and the Liberal Tradition'.

45. John Milbank, 'A Closer Walk on the Wild Side', in *Varieties of Secularism*, edited by Michael Warner, Jonathan VanAntwerpen and Craig Calhoun (Cambridge, MA: Harvard University Press, 2010), p. 55.

46. Milbank, 'A Closer Walk on the Wild Side', p. 78.

47. Milbank, 'A Closer Walk on the Wild Side', p. 58.

48. Milbank, 'A Closer Walk on the Wild Side', pp. 80–2.

49. Illich, *Rivers*, p. 29.

50. Illich, *Rivers*, chh. 2, 14. Here is one of Illich's pithy formulations of what he means: 'The Anti-Christ, or, let's say, the *mysterium iniquitatis*, the mystery of evil, is the conglomerate of a series

of perversions by which we try to give security, survival ability, and independence from individual persons to the new possibilities that were opened through the Gospel by institutionalizing them' (p. 169). Compare Augustine's reflection on 2 Thess. 2 and the possible meaning of the *Antichristus* as the 'universal body' of the prince of apostasy, standing over against the messianic body as lie against truth (*City of God* 20.19).

51. Illich, *Rivers*, chh. 5, 15, 16.

52. See the valuable study by Johannes van Oort, *Jerusalem and Babylon: A Study into Augustine's 'City of God' and the Sources of His Doctrine of the Two Cities* (Leiden: Brill, 1991). He points up the problems (pp. 151–5) in Markus's anti-apocalyptic depiction of a possible political 'neutrality' between the two cities in the *saeculum*.

53. The reversal is that citizens of the earthly city, oriented towards their own self-pleasure, use the true peace of the heavenly city to enjoy earthly goods for themselves in the power game. See Augustine, *City of God* 14.1–4; 15.7; 19.17.

54. Van Oort points out the centrality of ch. 17 in book 19. Citizens of the heavenly city who live by faith 'make use of earthly and temporal things like pilgrims: they are not captivated by them, nor are they deflected by them from their progress towards God'. In this way do both kinds of citizens make *usus communis* of the necessities of life, in a 'cooperation of wills' (*compositionem voluntatum*) that are nevertheless oriented towards different ends (the *finis utendi* is divergent). It should be noted that the use and enjoyment language in *City of God* is introduced in 1.8ff., alongside the language of *peregrinatio* to denote in apocalyptic fashion the diaspora existence of the city of God on earth. In 1.10 Augustine provides a Pauline *hos me* apocalyptic warrant for his language of 'use' taken from 1 Cor. 7:31: make use of the world 'as if not using it', a making use of earthly goods (as Augustine puts it in 1.29) 'like pilgrims, without grasping after them' (*bonisque terrenis tamquam peregrina utitur nec capitur . . .*). In *City of God* 10.6 this kind of 'use' is related to the apocalyptic 'sacrifice' of the messianic body whose service in the world imitates the form of the servant.

55. Illich, *Rivers*, chh. 3–4.

56. Illich, *Rivers*, p. 65.

57. For Augustine's language of creation *ex nihilo* with regard to the logic of defection and 'fall', see *City of God* 12.6ff.; 14.11, 13; see also *Confessions* 12.7.7; 12.28.38; 12.29.40; 13.33.48. Importantly, therefore, for Augustine the human soul is also created *ex nihilo* and thus relies on God alone for its being and life (*City of God* 10.31).

58. Illich, *Rivers*, p. 49. See Augustine's language of divine causation in *City of God* 11.21–2; 12.26: all movement comes from God's hidden, intimate, yet pervasive power, so that 'if God were to withdraw His creative power, so to speak, from things, they would no more exist than they did before they were created' (22.24). Cf. *City of God* 10.15 and 9.22, where knowledge of the divine will, the most potent causality, is a matter of spiritual participation in the divine Word – i.e. love (*caritas*), not 'knowledge' (*scientia*, which is what the demons worship), in keeping with Paul's account in 1 Corinthians.

59. Illich, *Rivers*, pp. 51–2.

60. Illich, *Rivers*, p. 53. No reader of Augustine's *Confessions* and *The City of God* can fail to notice his repeated emphasis on the centrality of *misericordia* (misery) and *penitentia* (penance and forgiveness) in his account of the pilgrim Christian journey.

61. Illich, *Rivers*, p. 57.

62. See also Augustine's account of seminal causality rooted in invisible divine agency in *City of God* 12.26, a measure 'deemed fabulous' by those oriented according to external and technological measures of the real (12.24). Translation altered.

63. Edmund Hill's free but apt translation of Augustine, *The Trinity* 13.17.

64. Phillip Cary, *Augustine's Invention of the Inner Self: The Legacy of a Christian Platonist* (New York: Oxford University Press, 2000). Of course, what Cary (and others) locate in Augustine, others (like Daniel Boyarin) locate in Paul – namely, an otherworldly spiritualised conception of self and identity derived from disembodied Platonism.

65. See Van Oort, *Jerusalem and Babylon*, and Johannes van Oort, *History, Apocalypse, and the Secular Imagination*, Mark Vessey, Karla Pollmann, and Allen Fitzgerald (eds) (Bowling Green, OH: Philosophy Documentation Center, 1999).

66. Markus's basic claim in *Saeculum* is that like Tyconius, Augustine transposed the apocalyptic two cities language (interpreted in earlier African theology in more empirical sociological categories of Church and pagan society) into an eschatological key locating the tension in the individual human heart rather than public institutional embodiment. This paves the way for a greater recognition of ambiguity in the *saeculum*, an openness towards both cities reconfigured typologically rather than sociologically that ultimately precludes both triumphalist Christendom and apocalyptic sectarian forms of political theology. Markus, *Saeculum*, esp. pp. 55–71, 120–4 and ch. 7.

67. For O'Donovan the Church represents 'mercy' while the state represents 'judgment' – see *Desire of the Nations*, pp. 259–60. On the political virtue and conscience of the Christian statesman, where classical political virtues are transformed by 'true piety', see Robert Dodaro, *Christ and the Just Society in the Thought of Augustine* (Cambridge: Cambridge University Press, 2004), and Robert Dodaro, '*Ecclesia* and *Res Publica*: How Augustinian are Neo-Augustinian Politics?', edited by L. Boeve, M. Lamberigts and M. Wisse (Leuven: Peeters, 2009), pp. 237–71.

68. See Dodaro, '*Ecclesia* and *Res Publica*'. The three interpretations are 1) Peter Iver Kaufmann, *Incorrectly Political: Augustine and Thomas More* (Notre Dame, IN: University of Notre Dame Press, 2007), whose Augustine is characterised by a 'minimalist' approach where no real Christian transformation of political institutions is possible, only modest dispositional effects upon politicians (which for Dodaro is too pessimistic about the real effects of Christ's mediation in the conscience and particular ethical judgements of Christian statesmen); 2) Markus's 'secularist' account focusing on a reading of the consensus of wills rooted in common objects of love (*City of God* 19.17) in a neutral secular pluralist state (which ignores the substantive implications of Augustine's *totus Christus* for the mediation of a Christian politics); and 3) Milbank, the triumphalist ecclesiology that challenges modern liberal secularism in an idealist, conversionist Church (which ignores the limits of fallenness in Augustine's *ecclesia permixta* in which the pilgrim Church remains fallen and limited in its transformational powers).

69. Here again, it might be useful to compare the importance of the *totus Christus* of City of God 10.6, 20; 17.18 with the 'universal body' of the *Antichristus* in 20.19.

70. Augustine begins his lengthy deconstruction of Roman civil religion (which underlies its warrior domination model of political sovereignty and ethics, and which measures the strength of a regime by the extent of its empire), with the following remark (*City of God* 4.3): 'But I should like to preface the inquiry with a brief examination of the following question: Is it reasonable (*ratio*), is it sensible (*prudentia*), to glory in the extent and magnitude of empire, when you cannot show that men lived in happiness (*felicitas*), as they passed their lives in the midst of war, amid the shedding of men's blood – whether the blood of enemies or fellow-citizens – under the shadow of fear and amid the terror of ruthless passion (*cupiditas*)? The joy (*laetitia*) of such men may be compared to the fragile splendor of glass: they are horribly afraid that it may suddenly be shattered.' For an excellent discussion of Augustine's insight regarding fear of death as the basis of Roman political deception and ideology, see Robert Dodaro, 'Eloquent Lies, Just Wars and the Politics of Persuasion: Reading Augustine's *City of God* in a "Postmodern" World', *Augustinian Studies* 25 (1994): 77–138.

71. Hab. 2:4; Rom. 1:17; Gal. 3:11; Heb. 10:38.

72. See Augustine, *City of God* 9.15; 10.6, 20. This logic of mediation, taken from the Christological hymn in Phil. 2, is elaborated in extensive detail in *The Trinity* as the basic rule of interpretation, and it is closely linked by Augustine to 1 Cor. 15.

73. Augustine, *Teaching Christianity* 1.12–13, 34.

74. This is Augustine's point in criticising the cyclical process cosmologies in book 12 of *City of God* – the attempt to grasp immortality via human reason (cf. *Trinity* 13.12) leads one in circles (and indeed human attempts to 'close the circle' through human substitutions for the divine

gift of immortality that cannot be possessed). Such a rational disembodiment of the *logos* robs the *saeculum* of its significance, the beginnings and endings of which are in God's power and the revelation of which can only be accepted by faith, not rational sight.

75. *nullus Deus miscetur homini* (*City of God* 8.18, 20; 9.1, 16): the Platonic principle Augustine fastens upon from *Symposium* 203a, related to the principle of erotic mediation in *Symposium* 201e, where *eros* is described as neither divine nor human but 'between' (*metaxu*).

76. Indeed, the martyrs, like all Christians, realise that mortal human life itself is a 'race towards death' (*cursus ad mortem*, *City of God* 13.10) and that the death to the fleshly desire to cling to mortal life as if it were immortal is in fact to be liberated from bondage to the body of decay that is fallen human nature. This, however, is not entirely an intellectual or moral matter – it is a gift of faith. For a good discussion of how the various levels of justice are related to the disposition of the will and thus address the fear of death, see Basil Studer, 'Le Christ, notre justice, selon saint Augustin', *Recherches Augustiniennes* 15 (1980): 99–143.

77. Augustine calls Christ the *rex optimus* in *City of God* 17.16.

78. See Rowan Williams, 'Politics and the Soul: Reading the *City of God*', *On Augustine* (London: Bloomsbury, 2016), ch. 6. Williams offers a good critical rejoinder to Hannah Arendt's claim that Augustine subverts the public realm by focusing on the non-political and otherworldly virtue of *caritas*. What Augustine subverts is a vision of public virtue modelled on the warrior hero, but such a vision is itself based upon violence and disorder – it cannot produce civic peace, and it is not in fact public enough.

79. Here I'm referring to an often overlooked twentieth-century source for Augustinian political theology, Charles N. Cochrane, *Christianity and Classical Culture: A Study of Thought and Action from Augustus to Augustine* (New York: Oxford University Press, 1957): especially part 3, 'Regeneration' (and p. 477, where Cochrane calls Augustine's biblical theology of history 'indubitably apocalyptic'). See also the title essay in Charles N. Cochrane, *Augustine and the Problem of Power: The Essays and Lectures of Charles Norris Cochrane*, David Beer (ed.) (Eugene, OR: Cascade Books, 2017), ch. 1.

# Bibliography

Aers, David, *Beyond Reformation? An Essay on William Langland's Piers Plowman and the End of Constantinian Christianity* (Notre Dame, IN: University of Notre Dame Press, 2015).

Aers, David, *Sin and Salvation: Augustine, Langland, and Fourteenth-Century Theology* (Notre Dame, IN: University of Notre Dame Press, 2009).

Agamben, Giorgio, *The Kingdom and the Glory: For a Theological Genealogy of Economy and Government*, Lorenzo Chiesa (trans.) (Stanford: Stanford University Press, 2011).

Augustine, *The City of God against the Pagans*, R. W. Dyson (ed. and trans.) (Cambridge: Cambridge University Press, 1998).

Augustine, *Confessions*, Maria Boulding (trans.) (New York: New City Press, 1997).

Augustine, *Teaching Christianity*, Edmund Hill (trans.) (New York: New City Press, 1996).

Augustine, *The Trinity*, Edmund Hill (trans.) (New York: New City Press, 1991).

Balthasar, Hans Urs von, *The Theology of Henri de Lubac: An Overview*, Joseph Fessio and Michael Waldstein (trans.) (San Francisco: Ignatius, 1991).

Bauerschmidt, Frederick C., *Julian of Norwich and the Mystical Body Politic of Christ* (Notre Dame, IN: University of Notre Dame Press, 1999).

Berry, Wendell, *What Are People For?* (San Francisco: North Point, 1990).

Blumenberg, Hans, *Kontingenz: Die Religion in Geschichte und Gegenwart. Handwörterbuch für Theologie und Religionswissenschaft*, Kurt Galling (ed.), vol. 3 (Tübingen: Mohr, 1959).

Blumenfeld, Bruno, *The Political Paul: Justice, Democracy and Kingship in a Hellenistic Framework* (Sheffield: Sheffield Academic, 2001).

Bruno, Michael J. S., *Political Augustinianism: Modern Interpretations of Augustine's Political Thought* (Minneapolis: Fortress, 2014).

Caird, G. B., *Principalities and Powers: A Study in Pauline Theology* (Eugene, OR: Wipf and Stock, 2013).

Cary, Phillip, *Augustine's Invention of the Inner Self: The Legacy of a Christian Platonist* (New York: Oxford University Press, 2000).

Cochrane, Charles N., *Augustine and the Problem of Power: The Essays and Lectures of Charles Norris Cochrane*, David Beer (ed.) (Eugene, OR: Cascade Books, 2017).

Cochrane, Charles N., *Christianity and Classical Culture: A Study of Thought and Action from Augustus to Augustine* (New York: Oxford University Press, 1957).

de Lubac, Henri, *Corpus Mysticum: The Eucharist and the Church in the Middle Ages*, Gemma Simmonds (trans.) (Notre Dame, IN: University of Notre Dame Press, 2006).

de Lubac, Henri, *The Splendor of the Church*, Michael Mason (trans.) (San Francisco: Ignatius, 1999).

Dodaro, Robert, *Christ and the Just Society in the Thought of Augustine* (Cambridge: Cambridge University Press, 2004).

Dodaro, Robert, '*Ecclesia* and *Res Publica*: How Augustinian are Neo-Augustinian Politics?', in *Augustine and Postmodern Thought: A New Alliance Against Modernity?*, edited by L. Boeve, M. Lamberigts and M. Wisse (Leuven: Peeters, 2009), pp. 237–71.

Dodaro, Robert, 'Eloquent Lies, Just Wars and the Politics of Persuasion: Reading Augustine's *City of God* in a "Postmodern" World', *Augustinian Studies* 25 (1994): 77–138.

Gregory, Eric, *Politics and the Order of Love: An Augustinian Ethic of Democratic Citizenship* (Chicago: University of Chicago Press, 2008).

Griffiths, Paul J., 'Secularity and the *Saeculum*', in *Augustine's City of God: A Critical Guide*, edited by James Wetzel (Cambridge: Cambridge University Press, 2012), pp. 33–54.

Hauerwas, Stanley, 'The End of Sacrifice: An Apocalyptic Politics', in *Apocalyptic and the Future of Theology*, edited by Joshua Davis and Douglas Harink (Eugene, OR: Cascade Books, 2012), pp. 354–68.

Illich, Ivan, *The Rivers North of the Future: The Testament of Ivan Illich*, as told to David Cayley (Toronto: Anansi, 2005).

Kaufmann, Peter Iver, *Incorrectly Political: Augustine and Thomas More* (Notre Dame, IN: University of Notre Dame Press, 2007).

Kroeker, P. Travis, 'Augustine's Messianic Political Theology: An Apocalyptic Critique of Political Augustinianism', in *Augustine and Apocalyptic*, edited by John Doody, Kari Kloos and Kim Paffenroth (Lanham, MD: Lexington, 2014), pp. 129–49.

Kroeker, P. Travis, *Christian Ethics and Political Economy in North America: A Critical Analysis* (Montreal: McGill-Queen's University Press, 1995).

Kroeker, P. Travis, *Messianic Political Theology and Diaspora Ethics: Essay in Exile* (Eugene, OR: Cascade Books, 2017).

Lee, Gregory W., 'Republics and Their Loves: Rereading *City of God* 19', *Modern Theology* 27:4 (2011), 553–81.

Lilla, Mark, *The Stillborn God: Religion, Politics and the Modern West* (New York: Knopf, 2007).

Markus, Robert A., *Christianity and the Secular* (Notre Dame, IN: University of Notre Dame Press, 2006).

Markus, Robert A., *Saeculum: History and Society in the Theology of St. Augustine*, rev. ed. (Cambridge: Cambridge University Press, [1970] 1988).

Milbank, John, *Beyond Secular Order: The Representation of Being and the Representation of the People* (Chichester: Wiley-Blackwell, 2013).

Milbank, John, 'A Closer Walk on the Wild Side', in *Varieties of Secularism*, edited by Michael Warner, Jonathan VanAntwerpen and Craig Calhoun (Cambridge, MA: Harvard University Press, 2010).

Nietzsche, Friedrich, *On the Genealogy of Morals*, Walter Kaufmann and R. J. Hollingdale (trans.) (New York: Vintage, 1967).

Northcott, Michael S., *A Political Theology of Climate Change* (Grand Rapids: Eerdmans, 2013).

O'Donovan, Oliver, *The Desire of the Nations: Rediscovering the Roots of Political Theology* (Cambridge: Cambridge University Press, 1996).

Oort, Johannes van, *Jerusalem and Babylon: A Study into Augustine's 'City of God' and the Sources of His Doctrine of the Two Cities* (Leiden: Brill, 1991).

Pecknold, Chad, 'Migrations of the Host: Fugitive Democracy and the *Corpus Mysticum*', *Political Theology* 11 (2010): 77–101.

Peterson, Erik, 'Christ as *Imperator*', in *Theological Tractates*, Michael Hollerich (trans.) (Stanford: Stanford University Press, 2011), pp. 143–50.

Peterson, Erik, 'Monotheism as a Political Problem' [1935], in *Theological Tractates*, Michael Hollerich (trans.) (Stanford: Stanford University Press, 2011), pp. 68–105.

Rust, Jennifer, *The Body in Mystery: The Political Theology of the Corpus Mysticum in the Literature of Reformation England* (Evanston, IL: Northwestern University Press, 2014).

Rust, Jennifer, 'Political Theologies of the *Corpus Mysticum*: Schmitt, Kantorowicz, and de Lubac', in *Political Theology and Early Modernity*, edited by Graham Hammill and Julia Reinhard Lupton (Chicago: University of Chicago Press, 2012), pp. 102–23.

Schmitt, Carl, *The Concept of the Political*, George Schwab (trans.) (Chicago: University of Chicago Press, 1996).

Schmitt, Carl, *The Leviathan in the State Theory of Thomas Hobbes: Meaning and Failure of a Political Symbol*, George Schwab (trans.) (Chicago: University of Chicago Press, 2008).

Schmitt, Carl, *The Nomos of the Earth in the International Law of the Jus Publicum Europaeum*, G. L. Ulmen (trans.) (New York: Telos Press, 2003).

Schmitt, Carl, *Politisches Theologie: Vier Kapitel zur Lehre von der Souveranitat* (Berlin: Dunker und Humblot, [1922] 1934); published in English as *Political Theology: Four Chapters on the Concept of Sovereignty*, George Schwab (trans.) (Cambridge, MA: MIT Press, 1985).

Schmitt, Carl, *Political Theology II: The Myth of the Closure of any Political Theology*, Michael Hoelzl and Graham Ward (trans.) (Cambridge: Polity Press, 2008).

Studer, Basil, 'Le Christ, notre justice, selon saint Augustin', *Recherches Augustiniennes* 15 (1980): 99–143.

Taubes, Jacob, *Occidental Eschatology*, David Ratmoko (trans.) (Stanford University Press, 2009).

Taubes, Jacob, *Political Theology of Paul*, Dana Hollander (trans.) (Stanford: Stanford University Press, 2004).

Taylor, Charles, 'Foreword' to *The Rivers North of the Future: The Testament of Ivan Illich*, as told to David Cayley (Toronto: Anansi, 2005).

Taylor, Charles, *A Secular Age* (Cambridge, MA: Harvard University Press, 2007).

Taylor, Charles, *Sources of the Self: The Making of the Modern Identity* (Cambridge, MA: Harvard University Press, 1989).

Vessey, Mark, Karla Pollmann and Allen Fitzgerald (eds.), *History, Apocalypse, and the Secular Imagination* (Bowling Green, OH: Philosophy Documentation Center, 1999).

Williams, George Hunston, *The Radical Reformation*, 3rd ed. (Kirksville, MO: Truman State University Press, 1995).

Williams, Rowan, *On Augustine* (London: Bloomsbury, 2016).

Williams, Rowan, 'A Reading of the *City of God*', *Milltown Studies* 19/20 (1987): 55–72.

Wolin, Sheldon, *Politics and Vision: Continuity and Innovation in Western Political Thought*, expanded edition (Princeton, NJ: Princeton University Press, 2004).

# 14

# Globalisation after Empires

## *World Christianity and the Theological De-centring of Europe*

### *Kirsteen Kim*

## Introduction

The expansion of Christianity into lands beyond Europe was the main aim of the world missionary movements of the Catholic Church and Protestant churches in the colonial period. Those who observed the growth of mission-founded churches in Africa, Asia, Latin America, the Caribbean and the Pacific rejoiced and compared them to the early rise of Christianity in 'all nations' (Matt. 28:19). Nevertheless, most missionaries and Western Church leaders expected that the 'younger churches' would continue to need the tutelage of the 'older' ones for decades, even centuries to come. That these churches would one day rival those in the West was foreseen by very few. At the World Missionary Conference in Edinburgh in 1910, the organiser John Mott, a US American, made a particular point of inviting leaders of 'native churches' and giving them a platform at the conference. There was not much enthusiasm among the missions for this idea, and as a result there were only 19 among a total of 1,215 delegates. In the event, their speeches were among the most memorable but, as Brian Stanley shows, even the few who had hoped that Asian Christians (Africans were almost completely disregarded) would contribute new theological insight failed to recognise it, or to receive it, when it was presented to them.[1]

   This chapter explores several ways in which theologians from the majority world introduced new approaches into Western theology in the second half of the twentieth century, namely liberation theology, inculturation and dialogue, even though these were not overtly recognised or explicitly received, or were even actively resisted, by Western theologians. It does this by focusing on how theologians and issues from Africa, Asia, Latin America, the Caribbean and the Pacific impacted theological debates at three global gatherings in the 1970s: the Lausanne Congress on World Evangelisation in 1974, the Synod of Bishops on Evangelization in the same year, which was followed up in 1975 by Pope Paul VI's apostolic exhortation *Evangelii nuntiandi* and the World Council of Churches' General Assembly in Nairobi, also in 1975. The chapter will look at key background to these debates in the effects of decolonisation and globalisation, tracing the influence of these non-Western initiatives on Western theology to the end of the century. Finally, it will suggest that Western hermeneutics inhibited the reception of theological thinking from outside Europe and its integration into Western theology, and identify one theological initiative to address this difficulty.

## From Christian Empires to World Christianity

In the first half of the twentieth century, the enlarged meetings of the International Missionary Council (IMC), which continued the initiative of Edinburgh 1910, increasingly reflected the global nature of Christianity. Especially among the US Americans, who now dominated the world missionary movement, there was enthusiasm for 'one church for the world' or 'world Christianity'.[2] As national councils of churches were gradually admitted to the IMC, a sense of the 'universal fellowship' of Christians was created.[3] However, their inclusion as councils of churches, and not mission councils, revealed a model of mission 'from the West to the rest' in which the native churches were not expected to take the initiative. In the new world order, this colonial model proved unsustainable. Eventually in New Delhi in 1961 the IMC merged into the World Council of Churches (WCC). The WCC was already a coming together of Protestant Christianity with the Eastern and Oriental Orthodoxy of Eastern Europe and West Asia. One of the chief effects of the integration was to further internationalise the WCC and make it more representative of 'the world church'.[4] The WCC Theological Education Fund (TEF), launched in 1958, both strengthened theological education in formerly colonised countries and also linked together theologians from across the majority world. In the post-colonial and theologically liberal context of the 1960s and 70s, there was a flowering of 'Third World theologies'.[5]

Conspicuous by their absence in WCC circles were North American fundamentalists. Their interdenominational identity, independency and distrust of Europe did not incline them to join. Instead, they formed their own international bodies, such as Carl McIntyre's International Council of Christian Churches, founded in 1948, which defined themselves against the 'liberal' denominations and withdrew from public life. The resurrection of evangelicalism in the US from the 1950s by a network around the evangelist Billy Graham was a deliberate attempt to reverse 'the great reversal'.[6] The rise of evangelicalism was not only due to domestic matters but was also related to the Cold War context in which Christian faith – understood as adherence to certain doctrines – was seen as an ideological antidote to Communism. The first global conference of evangelicals organised by the Billy Graham Association and the *Christianity Today* magazine in 1966 was held, significantly, in Berlin at the height of the Cold War under the conviction that 'evangelism – the proclamation of the Gospel of Christ – is the only revolutionary force that can change our world'.[7]

In the Catholic Church, the Second Vatican Council (1962–5) was dominated by European theologians. However, the numerical growth since Vatican I of indigenous bishops from Africa, Asia, Latin America and the Pacific was conspicuous. Reflecting on this later, Karl Rahner claimed to have glimpsed a 'world Church'.[8] The development of this world Church was encouraged by such conciliar reforms as the redefinition of the Church as the people of God, the adoption of mission as an activity of the whole Church, the enabling of Mass in the vernacular, the stress on human dignity and freedom, the recognition of truth in other religions and the engagement with the modern world, which treated the Third World as part of the Church and raised issues affecting peoples beyond the West.[9] Although Vatican II further centralised the Church, its rising strength in Africa, Asia, Latin America, the Caribbean and the Pacific gradually led to greater representation in Rome, both in the universities and in the Curia. Furthermore, the council facilitated regional bishops' councils and global networks in which the views of theologians from other continents could be shared. The Ecumenical Association of Third World

Theologians (EATWOT), which was founded by Catholics in 1976, included Protestants as well. Collectively, Third World theologians increasingly articulated the need for contextualising theology and simultaneously decontextualising Western theology.[10]

The fact that Christianity is not inherently European became known by the shorthand of 'world Christianity', especially through the work of Andrew Walls at the University of Aberdeen from 1982 and later at the University of Edinburgh.[11] Walls described Christianity's polycentric origins and spread in Asia and Africa before European dominance. He pointed to both growth and decline and to ongoing 'shifts' in the religion's 'centre of gravity'.[12] The most recent demographic shift was that from about 1970, Christians in the majority world outnumbered those in Europe. Walls's erstwhile colleague in Aberdeen Lamin Sanneh drew attention to the role of the local people themselves in the translation of the message and attendant social transformation.[13] Walls, Sanneh and others showed that world Christianity is not merely a product of European colonialism. Nevertheless, it did create the conditions of globalisation in which the churches of the previously colonised world, Pentecostalism and other independent forms of Christianity thrived.[14] Since globalisation is not unidirectional, Christianity both contributed to globalisation during the twentieth century and was also changed by it.

While Walls and Sanneh were developing world Christianity as a historical discipline, the significance of the rise of 'world Christianity' for Western theology was barely recognised in the twentieth century. Despite the end of colonialism and the minority status of European Christianity, theology continued to be dominated by the historical and literary-critical methods that had been shaped during the imperial period. The Lausanne Congress, the Synod of Bishops on Evangelization and the Nairobi Assembly of the WCC are three examples of how European theology was challenged by theologians from the growing churches of the formerly colonised world. In each case the initiatives of Third World theologians were resisted mainly by Western theologians, although their ideas became influential in the long run.

## Social Responsibility at the Lausanne Congress on World Evangelisation, 1974

The Lausanne Congress on World Evangelisation, which was held in the eponymous Swiss city in 1974, was intended by Billy Graham as a follow-up to Berlin 1966 and as a more global gathering of evangelicals. More than 2,371 evangelical leaders from 143 countries attended. At the opening of the conference, Waldron Scott declared that 'Lausanne reflects the great new fact of our time . . . a *worldwide* Church.'[15] His view was substantiated by statistics, and Graham alerted the conference to the existence of missionary movements from the 'younger churches in Africa, Asia, and Latin America' who were said to have 'taken up the torch' and to be sending missionaries to other nations, including in the West.[16]

The choice of Lausanne, just 30 miles from the WCC headquarters in Geneva, positioned evangelicalism as an alternative to 'ecumenism'.[17] This was in the context of what Donald McGavran identified as 'the great debate in mission' over the relative importance of evangelism and social work.[18] Graham wanted the Lausanne Congress to pre-empt the World Council of Churches Assembly planned for 1975. He insisted that the congress should prioritise evangelism in the sense of personal repentance and faith in view of Christ's atoning work and target nominal Christians and hitherto 'unreached' groups in other parts of the world.[19] But his plans were complicated by evangelicals from the majority world led by Latin Americans René Padilla and Samuel Escobar, both leaders in student movements, who insisted that mission must be 'integral' (derived from the Spanish *integral*) or 'holistic'. According to Brian Stanley, 'Lausanne revealed the first clear signs of a radical de-centring of the geographical and cultural identity of Evangelicalism which has since become unmistakeable.'[20]

The Latin American intervention was provoked by a mission context that was significantly different from that of North American evangelicals. Although they also experienced communism as a threat, Latin Americans struggled additionally against US economic and cultural dominance. At the same time, evangelicals in the continent needed to address the growing problem of poverty and respond to the growing Catholic emphasis on justice and the 'option for the poor'. At Lausanne, Padilla directly attacked the 'culture Christianity' that saw the gospel as a product, and attitudes to world evangelisation that aimed 'to produce the greatest number of Christians at the least possible cost'.[21] Despite having received many criticisms of his previously circulated paper, Padilla insisted that calling for 'intellectual assent to a truncated Gospel' was not the way forward. Instead, like the liberation theologians, and drawing on much the same biblical material, he called attention to justice, economics, politics, ethics and the structural change of the Kingdom of God.[22] Escobar complained that, in the context of the Cold War, some tended to make Christianity the ideology of the West. Tasked with defining the relationship between evangelism and social justice, he stressed that salvation entailed a total transformation of a person's life; that conversion is into a community; that the Church is imperfect but growing; and that Christians share the aspirations of humans everywhere. Escobar also pushed back against critics by insisting that the 'good news to the poor' (Luke 4:18) should not be spiritualised but practised.[23]

Although the final version of the *Lausanne Covenant* (LC) produced by the congress, stated that 'In the Church's mission of sacrificial service evangelism is primary' (para. 6) and distinguished 'evangelism' from 'socio-political involvement', it also affirmed that both are 'part of our Christian duty' (para. 5).[24] The views of Padilla and Escobar received support from some Western evangelicals. John Stott, chair of the drafting committee of the LC, acknowledged that his opinion had been changed by interaction with them.[25] Largely due to their argument and insistence, an integral approach was clearly articulated in the *Manila Manifesto* produced by the Second Lausanne Congress in 1989, even though the phrase 'evangelism is primary', heavily qualified, was retained.[26] Integral mission became a defining characteristic of the Lausanne Movement, which distinguished it from other evangelical networks such as McIntyre's ICCC and the AD2000 movement that was launched by Luis Bush at the 1989 congress. Finally, at the third Lausanne congress in Cape Town in 2010, 'evangelism is primary' was dropped.[27]

In the judgement of Gregory Baum, theological dialogue with Marxism 'greatly enriched theology' in the twentieth century.[28] This took place not only in Europe but also in other continents, and Latin America's liberation theologians developed a distinctively biblical and economic approach. Although direct dialogue with Marxism was anathema to most evangelicals, through the work of Padilla, Escobar and others, some of the insights of liberation theology, such as the prophetic opposition to injustice, hearing the cry of the victims, the concepts of structural sin and praxis became part of evangelical theology globally.

## Inculturation at the Synod of Bishops on Evangelization, 1974

In the same year as the Lausanne Congress (1974), Pope Paul VI convened the third of the ordinary synods of bishops instigated in the wake of the Second Vatican Council which reviewed different topics. That year 'Evangelisation in the Modern World' was the chosen theme. In the decree *Ad gentes* (AG) of the council, 'evangelization' had been used synonymously with 'mission' to refer generally to 'spreading the good news'.[29] For a council in which at any one time a third to a half of the bishops were representing the South, and most of those were indigenous, this reframing was part of a deliberate attempt to move beyond colonial styles of mission.[30] The council put the responsibility for mission on the local bishop (AG, paras 5–6) and devoted significant attention to discussion of the local church (paras 15–22) which, 'endowed with the riches of its own nation's culture, should be deeply rooted in the people' (para. 15).

At the 1974 synod the proportion of bishops from the majority world was even larger than at Vatican II, and bishops of European descent were in a minority. The views of the bishops from the majority world were significant in the understanding of evangelisation that emerged.[31] The topic of liberation was dominant at the synod, and the local Church was also a key theme.[32] Those tasked with producing an official draft of the conclusions for the bishops to approve included D. S. Amalorpavadass, Director of the National Biblical Catechetical and Liturgical Centre in Bangalore, India. The latter was a pioneer of inculturation in India and had organised the All-India Consultation on Evangelisation the previous year at Patna.[33] At the council he produced a 'coherent, comprehensive, contextual theology of mission, drawing in both the bold new ventures of the majority and the questions of the cautionary minority'.[34] But such was the power of the Roman Curia that much of his contribution was written out of the version presented to the bishops. Realising this in time, Amalorpavadass circulated his own draft before the vote. When the bishops saw what had happened, the majority rejected the official document. Because it was not possible to agree a revised text before the end of the synod, Pope Paul himself presented his view of the deliberations in the apostolic exhortation *Evangelii nuntiandi* (EN) the following year.[35]

In the event, much of Amalorpavadass's text and other contributions from the majority-world bishops were included in EN by a pope who had listened attentively to the proceedings.[36] EN advocated an inculturation approach[37] in which, rather than 'preaching the Gospel in ever wider geographic areas or to ever greater numbers of people' (EN, para. 19), the emphasis was on the depth of evangelisation and its transforming effect on individuals, cultures and societies, whether in the West or in the majority world. This evangelisation of cultures (and not just individuals) was described as a dialogical relationship between gospel and culture (EN, para. 20). Furthermore, because the gospel is independent of any culture (EN, para. 20), the pope laid emphasis on the prophetic nature of the good news and on hearing the cries of the poor for liberation, as articulated by the bishops at the synod (EN, para. 29–38).

Despite the encouragement given by Vatican II and Paul VI to dialogue with cultures, inculturation remained contentious in the late twentieth century.[38] Those anxious to protect the Church and uphold tradition tended to have a one-sided approach by which gospel transformed culture but the effect of culture on gospel and Church was hardly recognised. After Karol Wojtyła, who had been one of the organisers of the 1974 synod, became John Paul II, he adopted a cautious approach to inculturation, which diverged from that of many non-Western theologians.[39] In his encyclical *Redemptoris missio* (RM,

1990), he revived the term 'mission' in order to safeguard the mission *ad gentes*, about which there was a crisis in the West, and reaffirmed the centrality of proclamation and church-planting to evangelisation.[40] RM was interpreted in India and elsewhere as an attack on the Indian theologies of inculturation which recognised the possibility of truth in other religions.[41] Although, as the millennium approached, John Paul II encouraged continental synods, he focused on 'compatibility with the gospel and communion with the universal Church' (RM, paras 52–4) rather than on cultural innovation. Furthermore, whereas Paul VI tried in EN to refer to the evangelisation of cultures (plural), John Paul II focused 'the new evangelisation' on the re-evangelisation of Europe.[42] It was not until the twenty-first-century intervention of Francis, a pope from the majority world, that bishops were once again encouraged to develop their understanding of mission locally.[43]

## Dialogue at the World Council of Churches' Fifth General Assembly, Nairobi, 1975

In retrospect, the fourth assembly of the WCC, in Uppsala, Sweden in 1968, marked the high point of WCC confidence in Western-led development to address issues of social justice and humanisation.[44] The fifth assembly of the WCC, which took place in Nairobi, Kenya, gave greater attention to criticism of the West, to liberation from unjust structures and also to human diversity.

The assembly took cognisance of both the LC and the previous year's synod of bishops.[45] In his report to the assembly, the moderator of the WCC central committee, M. M. Thomas, found convergences of these documents with the statement on 'Salvation Today' of the WCC conference on world mission and evangelism in Bangkok in 1973 in emphasising a holistic gospel and a comprehensive salvation.[46] At the same time, Thomas pointed to significant divergences, the deepest of which was in relation to interreligious dialogue and whether or not the Holy Spirit was at work in other faiths.[47]

Despite the interest in dialogue, Thomas, who was from South India, felt that none of the global bodies had yet developed a *theology* of dialogue with people of other faiths. In the WCC, a process towards that aim was under way through a subunit on 'Dialogue with People of Living Faiths and Ideologies' set up after Uppsala and led by Stanley Samartha, also South Indian. Samartha was anxious to move beyond the pre-war approach that had prevailed since the IMC meeting at Tambaram, India in 1938. Heavily influenced by the complicity of religion with German nationalism at that time, religions were regarded as mutually incommensurable and compromised by pagan culture.[48] In contrast, the unit prepared a report for the Nairobi assembly, 'Seeking Community: The Common Search of People of Various Faiths, Cultures, and Ideologies'.[49] This was initially rejected by the assembly because it was seen by some as a 'spiritual compromise' and opposed to the mission of the Church.[50] The opposition was from people whom Samartha described as motivated by 'fear' not 'love'.[51] Samuel Rayan, an Indian Catholic observer, was more specific. He saw the Nairobi debate as a clash between those (chiefly from Scandinavia, West Germany and England) who were opposed to dialogue on the grounds that Christians have the whole truth, and those (from Asia and Africa) who were shocked at the former's arrogance.[52] Rayan accused the opponents of dialogue as having a 'limited, clannish conception of God and Christ' that disregarded the experience of other Christians who lived with people of other faiths.[53] The opponents at Nairobi forced the addition of a preamble to the report containing what Samartha described as 'a cluster of warning signals'.[54] It pointed to an unresolvable 'tension' 'between belief in Jesus Christ and unbelief', the need for continuing world evangelisation, and the danger of syncretising different religious systems.[55] When the revised report was re-presented to the assembly, it was accompanied by pleas from two other theologians from the Indian subcontinent who urged Europeans to hear those who had more first-hand experience of living with people of other faiths, and it ultimately passed.[56]

Despite this initial setback, by the 1990s dialogue had become the unquestioned ecumenical approach to people of other faiths. Samartha had transformed the WCC approach from an intellectual one to a human one, and distanced it from evangelism. Dialogue was motivated by the pastoral responsibility of the Christian community to contribute to the wider multireligious community, the need for religious solidarity in the face of political and economic powers, and the danger of disruption of communities by religious tensions. It was explained as a lifestyle involving 'commitment' to one's own faith coupled with 'openness' to others that would guard against both exclusivism and relativism. Eventually in 1979 a set of guidelines for dialogue prepared by Samartha was adopted by the WCC.[57] Accompanying these were three theological foundations for interreligious harmony: God as the creator of all things and of all humankind', the life-giving work of the Spirit to all and the significance of the triune unity of God.[58] Dialogue also continued to be the official Catholic approach for the remainder of the century, and as tensions between religions increased, the argument for it only increased.[59]

## De-centring Europe in Theology

From our brief examination of these global events, we can note that three of the most influential theological developments of the late twentieth century – liberation theology, theology of inculturation and theology of dialogue – were all stimulated by issues that particularly concerned the churches of, and were articulated by theologians from, the majority world. During the Cold War, these innovations were mediated largely through Western missionaries, through global conferences and by students from other continents who studied in the West. As China opened and then the Soviet Union and the Communist Bloc fell, globalisation intensified. What was happening in other parts of world Christianity was communicated more directly, and in a more sustained way, by direct Church-to-Church links, the Internet and social media. Moreover, the reciprocal nature of globalisation was felt in the West as patterns of international migration increasingly brought Christians, and even whole Church communities, from Africa, Asia, Latin America, the Caribbean and the Pacific to the West. Such heightened contact stimulated identity politics which revealed that differences in theology might not only be attributable to different Church traditions or differences in Western philosophy but also to the varied racial, geopolitical, religious and cultural backgrounds of theologians.[60]

The influence of the theologians of the majority world was not often acknowledged in the text or footnotes of the work of the leading Western theologians.[61] Nevertheless, by the end of the century, theologies from Africa, Asia and Latin America were included in standard Protestant theological textbooks in English, although they were not integral to them.[62] While some claimed non-Western insights as their own and others overtly recognised theological diversity, most Western theologians continued to write as if European theology was normative for the rest of the Christian world. Even those who wanted to include theologies from other continents faced formidable obstacles of theological method. Whether intentionally or not, the historical-theological method and the linguistic-cultural turn in theology hindered global theological exchange.

The problem of historical theology was illustrated autobiographically by Richard Gaillardetz, who explained that his theological education had been limited to Europe because it was based on three main sources: theologians whose work paved the way for Vatican II (all European); the council and its reception (dominated by Europeans and European churches); and statements of the ecumenical movement (pertaining mainly to the historic churches of Europe). He saw that most of the Catholic theology of the last fifty years had continued to be similarly 'parochial'.[63] In this respect, the historical-theological approach stimulated by *ressourcement* theology, although it begins with the Bible and the Church Fathers, tends to privilege Western theology by taking a chronological line through Europe.

The Euro-centredness of theology is also part of a larger hermeneutical issue. Western philosophical hermeneutics as appropriated by European theology continues to rely on a Gadamerian approach which assumes a shared history of interpretation – a tradition, or culture, which is 'uniform, self-contained or inescapable'.[64] As Joshua Broggi explains, not only does this hermeneutic fail to consider the constructed nature of culture or the power questions around who defines it, Gadamer's *Truth and Method* assumes 'that a cyclical and interdependent relation between a text and reader will persist in an unbroken historical continuity'.[65] Hence, Gadamer cannot help Europeans to interpret texts which come from an external historical context (even though of course the Bible and the ancient creeds fall into that category). Nor does Gadamerian hermeneutics allow for what happens when a Christian text is read by someone, whether Christian or not, from a non-European tradition of interpretation.[66]

From this perspective, the postliberal theology of the late twentieth century exacerbated the problem and encouraged theological separatism, even European exceptionalism. Its classic exponent, George Lindbeck, found that the narrative mode of post or late modernity could be hospitable to the Christian story without having to compromise traditional doctrine as liberalism had done. He further theorised that religions were different forms of cultural-linguistic discourse which could only be truly understood from within and should be developed in their own terms.[67] Hence, postliberal theology seemed to isolate Christianity as a closed system from other faiths, other systems of thought and non-Western forms of Christianity.[68] Moreover, by suggesting that faiths were incommensurable, it also removed common ground for dialogue and could only seek to absorb the other into its world.[69] Lindbeck's system allowed for contextualised forms of European theologies but implied the priority of European Christianity. Kathryn Tanner responded that, although theology is a cultural product, it cannot and should not be limited by a narrowly Christian culture. Nor should Christian diversity be explained as entirely due to the contextualisation of Christianity in different cultures, because it is inherent in Christianity itself. Christian theology will always be contested and diverse in its expression because theology is creative and cannot be confined within any tradition.[70]

Taken together, the constraints of the historical-theological and the cultural-linguistic approaches were such that they increased the difficulty in the way of Europeans trying to engage with theologies from the majority world. But for the majority of the world's Christians, the question of whether their theological development could be accommodated within hermeneutical methods developed in Europe probably appeared irrelevant. After all, neither the Bible, nor the Creed of Nicaea, can be claimed as European. World Christianity is a problem for Western Christians because they risk being sidelined in global theological debates which will be increasingly driven by the issues from the majority world and addressed by theological initiatives from continents where there are large, young and growing Christian communities. Recognising the necessity of such engagement, in the early twenty-first century, Gaillardetz imagined a new *ressourcement* – this time in the form of engagement with contemporary sources from Africa, Asia and Latin America. These would be examined not primarily by the methods of historical and academic theology but by contextual and conciliar theologising.[71] However, unless and until contextual and conciliar theologising are also established as academically rigorous, European theology will continue to be normative (in the sight of Europeans at least).

There was one theological development from the late twentieth century which pointed a way towards establishing such a new *ressourcement* in the Western academy: intercultural theology. The term 'intercultural theology' was coined by Walter Hollenweger, Hans Margull and Richard Friedli in the 1970s as they reflected on the diversity of world Christianity.[72] From the mission perspective, Hollenweger and his colleagues were convinced that the non-Western forms of Christianity which they were documenting were discontinuous with European theology due to the social, political, cultural and religious diversity of their contexts.[73] From an ecumenical perspective, the catholicity or universality of Christianity was seen to admit, and even demand, an 'exchange of theologies' which would challenge churches, including in the West, that became too local or provincialised. Intercultural theology was an exercise in 'theological giving and receiving that characterises the history of Christianity in its post-colonial and polycentric period'.[74] In 1997, the US Catholic theologian Robert Schreiter suggested that an intercultural hermeneutics could contribute to 'a renewed and expanded concept of catholicity' as the theological response to the intensification of globalisation.[75] Such an intercultural theology would reflect on the unity and diversity of the Trinity, the asymmetrical power dynamics of the paschal mystery and the theme of reconciliation. Therefore, it would be marked by inclusion and intercultural exchange towards a fullness of faith.

The twentieth century saw the traumatic end of European empires and a tense transition to a globalised world in which people and cultures were increasingly de-territorialised. Significant Christian growth in the majority world brought new issues to the attention of theologians in the West and stimulated new theological developments. In this chapter, three such developments were examined in three different global Church forums. However, these initiatives tended to be resisted or sidelined by Western theologians who were developing theology only with reference to their particular tradition of discourse. By the end of the century, it was obvious that Christian theology was being done in many different contexts not regarded as Western, and there was a new historical perspective of 'world Christianity' which de-centred Europe and suggested that the future of Christianity lay outside the West. Some theologians schooled in the European tradition were beginning to search for a new academically credible tool for theologising which would facilitate constructive theological exchange and collaboration between theologians from other cultural contexts. Because there is no pure Christian reading uncontaminated by local factors, and also because of unequal power relations between Christian communities, there could not be a global theology. But there was the possibility of ongoing global theological conversation with others who claimed allegiance to Christ as an expression of Christian catholicity.[76]

# Notes

1. Brian Stanley, *The World Missionary Conference: Edinburgh 1910* (Grand Rapids: Eerdmans, 2009), pp. 91–131.

2. E.g. Kenneth Scott Latourette and William Richey Hogg, *Tomorrow Is Here* (New York: Friendship Press, 1948), p. 69.

3. IMC, *The Witness of a Revolutionary Church* (New York: IMC, 1947), pp. 9–22: 19.

4. W. A. Visser 't Hooft (ed.), *The New Delhi Report* (New York: Association Press, 1962), pp. 63–5.

5. John Parratt (ed.), *An Introduction to Third World Theologies* (Cambridge: Cambridge University Press, 2004), pp. 1–15.

6. See George M. Marsden, *Fundamentalism and American Culture*, 2nd ed. (New York: Oxford University Press, 2006), pp. 85–93.

7. Billy Graham, 'Opening Greetings', in *One Race, One Gospel, One Task: World Congress on Evangelism, Berlin 1966, Official Reference Volumes*, vol. 1, edited by Carl F. H. Henry and W. Stanley Mooneyham (Minneapolis: World Wide Publications, 1967), pp. 8–10: 8.

8. Karl Rahner, 'Towards a Fundamental Theological Interpretation of Vatican II', *Theological Studies* 40:4 (1979), 716–27.

9. Cf. Ian Linden, *Global Catholicism: Diversity and Change Since Vatican II* (New York: Columbia University Press, 2009), pp. 67–90.

10. E.g. Gerald H. Anderson and Thomas Stransky (eds), *Third World Theologies*, Mission Trends 3 (Grand Rapids: Eerdmans, 1976).

11. See William R. Burrows, Mark R. Gornik and Janice A. McLean (eds), *Understanding World Christianity: The Vision and Work of Andrew F. Walls* (Maryknoll, NY: Orbis, 2011).

12. See Andrew Walls, 'The Mission of the Church Today', *Word and World* 20:1 (Winter 2000), 17–21: 15–21.

13. Lamin Sanneh, *Translating the Message: The Missionary Impact on Culture* (Maryknoll, NY: Orbis, 1989).

14. For a contemporary account, see Harvey Cox, *Fire from Heaven: The Rise of Pentecostal Spirituality and the Reshaping of Religion in the Twenty-First Century* (Reading, MA: Addison-Wesley, 1994).

15. Waldron Scott, 'The Task before Us', in *Let the Earth Hear His Voice*, edited by J. D. Douglas (Minneapolis: World Wide, 1975), pp. 18–21: 18.

16. Billy Graham, 'Why Lausanne?', in *Let the Earth Hear His Voice*, edited by J. D. Douglas (Minneapolis: World Wide, 1975), pp. 22–36: 22.

17. Graham, 'Why Lausanne?' pp. 26–7.

18. Donald McGavran (ed.), *Eye of the Storm: The Great Debate in Mission* (Waco: Word Books, 1972).

19. Graham, 'Why Lausanne?'.

20. Stanley, Brian, '"Lausanne 1974": The Challenge of the Majority World to Northern-Hemisphere Evangelicalism', *The Journal of Ecclesiastical History* 64:3 (2013), 533–51.

21. René Padilla, 'Evangelism and the World', in *Let the Earth Hear His Voice*, edited by J. D. Douglas (Minneapolis: World Wide, 1975), pp. 116–46: 139.

22. Padilla, 'Evangelism and the World', pp. 143–5.

23. Samuel Escobar, 'Evangelism and Man's Search for Freedom, Justice, and Fulfilment', in *Let the Earth Hear His Voice*, edited by J. D. Douglas (Minneapolis: World Wide, 1975), pp. 303–26.

24. See J. D. Douglas (ed.), *Let the Earth Hear His Voice* (Minneapolis: World Wide, 1975), pp. 3–9.

25. John Stott and Christopher J. H. Wright, *Christian Mission in the Modern World*, 2nd ed. (Downers Grove, IL: InterVarsity, 2015), pp. 41–54. For Padilla's account see *Mission between the Times*, 2nd ed. (Carlisle: Langham, 2010), pp. 1–25.

26. Second Lausanne Congress, *The Manila Manifesto* (1989), accessed at www.lausanne.org/.

27. See Third Lausanne Congress, *The Cape Town Commitment* (2010), accessed at www.lausanne .org/.

28. Gregory Baum (ed.), *The Twentieth Century: A Theological Overview* (Maryknoll, NY: Orbis, 1999), p. 184.

29. *Ad gentes* (1974), accessed at www.vatican.va.

30. Noel Connolly, 'Ad gentes to Evangelii gaudium: Mission's Move to the Centre', The Australasian Catholic Record 92:4 (2015), 387–402: 390.

31. According to the eyewitness account of Archbishop Carter, 'The Synod of Bishops – 1974: An Assessment', International Review of Mission 64:255 (1975), 295–301: 298; cf. EN, para. 69.

32. Connolly, 'Ad gentes', p. 391; see also Carter, 'The Synod of Bishops', pp. 298–9.

33. Light and Life: We Seek to Share (Bangalore: Catholic Bishops' Conference of India, 1973); D. S. Amalorpavadass, Approach, Meaning and Horizon of Evangelization (Bangalore: NBCLC, 1973). This was one of many events in different continents in preparation for the synod. See James A. Kroeger, 'Exploring the Rich Treasures of Evangelii nuntiandi', SEDOS Bulletin 46:9–10 (2014), 227–34.

34. John Mansford Prior, 'Mission for the Twenty-First Century in Asia: Two Sketches, Three Flash-Backs and an Enigma', in Mission for the Twenty-First Century, edited by Stephen B. Bevans and Roger Schroeder (Chicago: CCGM Publications, 2001), pp. 68–109: 81.

35. Connolly, 'Ad gentes', p. 391. The papal exhortation in place of a synodal report set a precedent for future synods which arguably suppressed the voice of the majority world in the long run.

36. Prior, 'Mission for the Twenty-First Century'.

37. The actual term 'inculturation' does not appear in EN but became common currency afterwards. Aylward Shorter, Evangelization and Culture (London: Geoffrey Chapman, 1994), p. 32.

38. Shorter, Evangelization and Culture, pp. 26–54.

39. Shorter, Evangelization and Culture, p. 32. For example, the process for translation and adaptation of the liturgy was laborious and controlled in Rome; see Peter C. Phan, 'Liturgical Inculturation', in Liturgy in a Postmodern World, edited by Keith Pecklers (London: Continuum, 2003), pp. 55–91.

40. Francis Anekwe Oborji, Concepts of Mission: The Evolution of Contemporary Missiology (Maryknoll, NY: Orbis, 2006), pp. 7–11. Redemptoris missio (1990), accessed at www.vatican.va.

41. William R. Burrows (ed.), Redemption and Dialogue: Reading Redemptoris missio and Dialogue and Proclamation (Maryknoll, NY: Orbis, 1993), p. 244.

42. Paul Grogan and Kirsteen Kim (eds), The New Evangelization: Faith, People, Context and Practice (London: T&T Clark, 2015), pp. 1–14.

43. In Evangelii gaudium (2013), accessed at www.vatican.va, Pope Francis explicitly deferred to local bishops' conferences.

44. Martin E. Marty, 'The Global Context of Ecumenism 1968–2000', in A History of the Ecumenical Movement, vol. 3, 1968–2000, edited by John Briggs, Mercy Amba Oduyoye and Georges Tsetsis (Geneva: WCC Publications, 2004), pp. 3–22.

45. EN was released while the WCC assembly was taking place, so it could not be responded to directly, but Archbishop Samuel Carter, SJ, who had participated in the synod of bishops, addressed the WCC assembly, and Dr Philip Potter, general secretary of the WCC and a Caribbean colleague of Archbishop Carter, had addressed the synod.

46. M. M. Thomas, 'Report of the Moderator of the Central Committee', in Breaking Barriers: Nairobi 1975. The Official Report of the Fifth Assembly of the World Council of Churches, edited by David M. Paton (Geneva: WCC Publications, 1976), pp. 226–43. See also Commission on World Mission and Evangelism, Bangkok Assembly 1973 (Geneva: WCC Publications, 1973).

47. The LC appeared to say 'no', the synod said 'yes', and Bangkok gave a qualified 'yes'.

48. As articulated by Hendrik Kraemer, The Christian Message in a Non-Christian World (Grand Rapids: Kregel, 1938).

49. Nairobi Assembly, 'Seeking Community: The Common Search of People of Various Faiths, Cultures, and Ideologies', Breaking Barriers: Nairobi 1975. The Official Report of the Fifth Assembly of the World Council of Churches (Geneva: WCC Publications, 1976), pp. 70–85.

50. Nairobi Assembly, 'Seeking Community', p. 70.

51. Stanley J. Samartha, Courage for Dialogue: Ecumenical Issues in Inter-Religious Relationships (Geneva: WCC Publications, 1981), p. 49.

52. Samuel Rayan, 'The Ultimate Blasphemy?: On Putting God in a Box', *International Review of Mission* 65:257 (January 1976), 129–33.
53. Rayan, 'The Ultimate Blasphemy?', pp. 130–3.
54. Samartha, *Courage for Dialogue*, p. 49.
55. Nairobi Assembly, 'Seeking Community', p. 73.
56. Nairobi Assembly, 'Seeking Community', pp. 71–3.
57. WCC, *Guidelines for Dialogue* (Geneva: WCC Publications, 1979), accessed at www.oikoumene .org.
58. WCC, *Guidelines*, paras 3, 7–8, 12, 13.
59. E.g. Leonard Swidler, John B. Cobb Jr, Paul F. Knitter and Monika Hellwig, *Death or Dialogue? From the Age of Monologue to the Age of Dialogue* (London: SCM, 1990).
60. See Sebastian Kim and Kirsteen Kim, *Christianity as a World Religion: An Introduction*, 2nd ed. (London: Bloomsbury, 2016).
61. For the case of Jürgen Moltmann, see Susanne Hennecke, 'Related by Freedom: The Impact of Third-World Theologians on the Thinking of Jürgen Moltmann', *Exchange* 32:4 (2003), 292–309.
62. See for example David Ford (ed.), *The Modern Theologians*, 2nd ed. (Oxford: Wiley-Blackwell, 1997); Alister McGrath, *Christian Theology: An Introduction*, 3rd ed. (Oxford: Wiley-Blackwell, 2001).
63. Richard R. Gaillardetz, *Ecclesiology for a Global Church: A People Called and Sent* (Maryknoll, NY: Orbis, 2008), pp. xv–xvi.
64. Joshua D. Broggi, *Diversity in the Structure of Christian Reasoning* (Leiden: Brill, 2015), pp. 88–143; Henning Wrogemann, *Intercultural Hermeneutics*, vol. 1, Karl E. Böhmer (trans.) (Downers Grove, IL: InterVarsity, 2012), p. 59.
65. Broggi, *Diversity*, p. 127. Hans-Georg Gadamer, *Truth and Method*, translation revised by Joel Weinsheimer and Donald G. Marshall (London: Bloomsbury, 2013 [1975]).
66. Broggi, *Diversity*, pp. 127–9.
67. George Lindbeck, *The Nature of Doctrine: Religions and Theology in a Postliberal Age* (Louisville, KY: Westminster John Knox Press, 1984).
68. Cf. John Flett, *Apostolicity: The Ecumenical Question in World Christian Perspective* (Downers Grove, IL: InterVarsity Press Academic, 2016), pp. 48–9.
69. Marianne Moyaert, 'Absorption or Hospitality', in *Interreligious Hermeneutics*, edited by Catherine Cornille and Christopher Conway (Eugene, OR: Cascade, 2010), pp. 61–88.
70. Kathryn Tanner, *Theories of Culture: A New Agenda for Theology* (Minneapolis: Fortress, 1997), pp. 151–75.
71. Gaillardetz, *Ecclesiology for a Global Church*, pp. 68–83.
72. Walter Hollenweger, 'Intercultural Theology: Some Remarks on the Term', in *Towards an Intercultural Theology*, edited by Martha Frederiks, Meindert Dijkstra and Anton Houtepen (Zoetermeer: Meinema, 2003), pp. 89–95.
73. Werner Ustorf, 'The Cultural Origins of "Intercultural" Theology', in *Intercultural Theology: Approaches and Themes*, edited by Mark J. Cartledge and David Cheetham (London: SCM, 2011), pp. 11–28: 17.
74. Ustorf, 'The Cultural Origins', p. 14.
75. Robert Schreiter, *The New Catholicity: Theology between the Global and the Local* (Maryknoll, NY: Orbis, 1997), p. 127.
76. Cf. Tanner, *Theories of Culture*, p. 175; see also Kirsteen Kim, *The Holy Spirit in the World: A Global Conversation* (Maryknoll, NY: Orbis, 2007).

# Bibliography

*Ad gentes* (1974), accessed at www.vatican.va.
Amalorpavadass, D. S., *Approach, Meaning and Horizon of Evangelization* (Bangalore: NBCLC, 1973).

Anderson, Gerald H. and Thomas Stransky (eds), *Third World Theologies*, Mission Trends 3 (Grand Rapids: Eerdmans, 1976).

Baum, Gregory (ed.), *The Twentieth Century: A Theological Overview* (Maryknoll, NY: Orbis, 1999).

Broggi, Joshua D., *Diversity in the Structure of Christian Reasoning* (Leiden: Brill, 2015).

Burrows, William R. (ed.), *Redemption and Dialogue: Reading Redemptoris missio and Dialogue and Proclamation* (Maryknoll, NY: Orbis, 1993).

Burrows, William R., Mark R. Gornik and Janice A. McLean (eds), *Understanding World Christianity: The Vision and Work of Andrew F. Walls* (Maryknoll, NY: Orbis, 2011).

Carter, Samuel, 'The Synod of Bishops – 1974: An Assessment', *International Review of Mission* 64:255 (1975), 295–301.

Commission on World Mission and Evangelism, *Bangkok Assembly 1973* (Geneva: WCC Publications, 1973).

Connolly, Noel, 'Ad gentes to Evangelii gaudium: Mission's Move to the Centre', *The Australasian Catholic Record* 92:4 (2015), 387–402.

Cox, Harvey, *Fire from Heaven: The Rise of Pentecostal Spirituality and the Reshaping of Religion in the Twenty-First Century* (Reading, MA: Addison-Wesley, 1994).

Douglas, J. D. (ed.), *Let the Earth Hear His Voice* (Minneapolis: World Wide, 1975).

Escobar, Samuel, 'Evangelism and Man's Search for Freedom, Justice, and Fulfilment', in *Let the Earth Hear His Voice*, edited by J. D. Douglas (Minneapolis: World Wide, 1975), pp. 303–26.

*Evangelii gaudium* (2013), accessed at www.vatican.va.

Flett, John, *Apostolicity: The Ecumenical Question in World Christian Perspective* (Downers Grove, IL: InterVarsity Press Academic, 2016).

Ford, David (ed.), *The Modern Theologians*, 2nd ed. (Oxford: Wiley-Blackwell, 1997).

Gadamer, Hans-Georg, *Truth and Method*, translation revised by Joel Weinsheimer and Donald G. Marshall (London: Bloomsbury, 2013 [1975]).

Gaillardetz, Richard R., *Ecclesiology for a Global Church: A People Called and Sent* (Maryknoll, NY: Orbis, 2008).

Graham, Billy, 'Why Lausanne?', in *Let the Earth Hear His Voice*, edited by J. D. Douglas (Minneapolis: World Wide, 1975), pp. 22–36.

Graham, Billy, 'Opening Greetings', in *One Race, One Gospel, One Task: World Congress on Evangelism, Berlin 1966, Official Reference Volumes*, vol. 1, edited by Carl F. H. Henry and W. Stanley Mooneyham (Minneapolis: World Wide Publications, 1967), pp. 8–10.

Grogan, Paul and Kirsteen Kim (eds), *The New Evangelization: Faith, People, Context and Practice* (London: T&T Clark, 2015).

Hennecke, Susanne, 'Related by Freedom: The Impact of Third-World Theologians on the Thinking of Jürgen Moltmann', *Exchange* 32:4 (2003), 292–309.

Hollenweger, Walter, 'Intercultural Theology: Some Remarks on the Term', in *Towards an Intercultural Theology*, edited by Martha Frederiks, Meindert Dijkstra and Anton Houtepen (Zoetermeer: Meinema, 2003), pp. 89–95.

IMC, *The Witness of a Revolutionary Church* (New York: IMC, 1947).

Kim, Kirsteen, *The Holy Spirit in the World: A Global Conversation* (Maryknoll, NY: Orbis, 2007).

Kim, Sebastian and Kirsteen Kim, *Christianity as a World Religion: An Introduction*, 2nd ed. (London: Bloomsbury, 2016).

Kraemer, Hendrik, *The Christian Message in a Non-Christian World* (Grand Rapids: Kregel, 1938).

Kroeger, James A., 'Exploring the Rich Treasures of Evangelii nuntiandi', *SEDOS Bulletin* 46:9–10 (2014), 227–34.

Latourette, Kenneth Scott and William Richey Hogg, *Tomorrow Is Here* (New York: Friendship Press, 1948).

*Light and Life: We Seek to Share* (Bangalore: Catholic Bishops' Conference of India, 1973).

Lindbeck, George, *The Nature of Doctrine: Religions and Theology in a Postliberal Age* (Louisville, KY: Westminster John Knox Press, 1984).

Linden, Ian, *Global Catholicism: Diversity and Change Since Vatican II* (New York: Columbia University Press, 2009).

McGavran, Donald (ed.), *Eye of the Storm: The Great Debate in Mission* (Waco: Word Books, 1972).

McGrath, Alister, *Christian Theology: An Introduction*, 3rd ed. (Oxford: Wiley-Blackwell, 2001).

Marsden, George M., *Fundamentalism and American Culture*, 2nd ed. (New York: Oxford University Press, 2006).

Marty, Martin E., 'The Global Context of Ecumenism 1968–2000', in *A History of the Ecumenical Movement*, vol. 3, *1968–2000*, edited by John Briggs, Mercy Amba Oduyoye and Georges Tsetsis (Geneva: WCC Publications, 2004), pp. 3–22.

Moyaert, Marianne, 'Absorption or Hospitality', in *Interreligious Hermeneutics*, edited by Catherine Cornille and Christopher Conway (Eugene, OR: Cascade, 2010), pp. 61–88.

Nairobi Assembly, 'Seeking Community: The Common Search of People of Various Faiths, Cultures, and Ideologies', in *Breaking Barriers: Nairobi 1975. The Official Report of the Fifth Assembly of the World Council of Churches*, edited by David M. Paton (Geneva: WCC Publications, 1976).

Oborji, Francis Anekwe, *Concepts of Mission: The Evolution of Contemporary Missiology* (Maryknoll, NY: Orbis, 2006).

Padilla, René, 'Evangelism and the World', in *Let the Earth Hear His Voice*, edited by J. D. Douglas (Minneapolis: World Wide, 1975), pp. 116–46.

Padilla, René, *Mission between the Times*, 2nd ed. (Carlisle: Langham, 2010).

Parratt, John (ed.), *An Introduction to Third World Theologies* (Cambridge: Cambridge University Press, 2004).

Paton, David M. (ed.), *Breaking Barriers: Nairobi 1975. The Official Report of the Fifth Assembly of the World Council of Churches*, edited by David M. Paton (Geneva: WCC Publications, 1976).

Phan, Peter C., 'Liturgical Inculturation', in *Liturgy in a Postmodern World*, edited by Keith Pecklers (London: Continuum, 2003), pp. 55–91.

Prior, John Mansford, 'Mission for the Twenty-First Century in Asia: Two Sketches, Three Flash-Backs and an Enigma', in *Mission for the Twenty-First Century*, edited by Stephen B. Bevans and Roger Schroeder (Chicago: CCGM Publications, 2001), pp. 68–109.

Rahner, Karl, 'Towards a Fundamental Theological Interpretation of Vatican II', *Theological Studies* 40:4 (1979), 716–27.

Rayan, Samuel, 'The Ultimate Blasphemy?: On Putting God in a Box', *International Review of Mission* 65:257 (January 1976), 129–33.

*Redemptoris missio* (1990), accessed at www.vatican.va.

Samartha, Stanley J., *Courage for Dialogue: Ecumenical Issues in Inter-Religious Relationships* (Geneva: WCC Publications, 1981).

Sanneh, Lamin, *Translating the Message: The Missionary Impact on Culture* (Maryknoll, NY: Orbis, 1989).

Schreiter, Robert, *The New Catholicity: Theology between the Global and the Local* (Maryknoll, NY: Orbis, 1997).

Scott, Waldron, 'The Task Before Us', in *Let the Earth Hear His Voice*, edited by J. D. Douglas (Minneapolis: World Wide, 1975), pp. 18–21.

Second Lausanne Congress, *The Manila Manifesto* (1989), accessed at www.lausanne.org/.

Shorter, Aylward, *Evangelization and Culture* (London: Geoffrey Chapman, 1994).

Stanley, Brian, '"Lausanne 1974": The Challenge of the Majority World to Northern-Hemisphere Evangelicalism', *The Journal of Ecclesiastical History* 64:3 (2013), 533–51.

Stanley, Brian, *The World Missionary Conference: Edinburgh 1910* (Grand Rapids: Eerdmans, 2009).

Stott, John and Christopher J. H. Wright, *Christian Mission in the Modern World*, 2nd ed. (Downers Grove, IL: InterVarsity, 2015).

Swidler, Leonard, John B. Cobb Jr, Paul F. Knitter and Monika Hellwig, *Death or Dialogue? From the Age of Monologue to the Age of Dialogue* (London: SCM, 1990).

Tanner, Kathryn, *Theories of Culture: A New Agenda for Theology* (Minneapolis: Fortress, 1997).

Third Lausanne Congress, *The Cape Town Commitment* (2010), accessed at www.lausanne.org/.

Thomas, M. M., 'Report of the Moderator of the Central Committee', in *Breaking Barriers: Nairobi 1975. The Official Report of the Fifth Assembly of the World Council of Churches*, edited by David M. Paton (Geneva: WCC Publications, 1976), pp. 226–43.

Ustorf, Werner, 'The Cultural Origins of "Intercultural" Theology', in *Intercultural Theology: Approaches and Themes*, edited by Mark J. Cartledge and David Cheetham (London: SCM, 2011), pp. 11–28.

Visser 't Hooft, W.A. (ed.), *The New Delhi Report* (New York: Association Press, 1962).

Walls, Andrew, 'The Mission of the Church Today in Light of Global History', *Word and World* 20:1 (Winter 2000), 17–21.

WCC, *Guidelines for Dialogue* (Geneva: WCC Publications, 1979), accessed at www.oikoumene.org.

Wrogemann, Henning, *Intercultural Hermeneutics*, vol. 1, Karl E. Böhmer (trans) (Downers Grove, IL: InterVarsity, 2012).

# 15

# War and Peace

*Rachel Muers*

## Introduction

War and peace play a significant role in Christian theological tradition – far more significant than is recognised when the subject of 'war and peace' is consigned to a chapter of theological ethics. On the one hand, Christian theology is compelled to reckon with violence – if nothing else, because of its central commitment to the God revealed in a convicted criminal tortured and executed by an occupying army. On the other hand, Christian theology is also required to speak of and articulate the promise of peace that is integral to the scriptural and traditional language of God's blessing. Twentieth-century theology's distinctive engagements with questions of war and peace owe some of their distinctiveness to the particular character of the twentieth century's wars – and efforts towards peace; but they also reflect, as we shall see, wider debates in theology.

Christian Scripture and Christian theological tradition are permeated by the language and imagery of violence, and more specifically of warfare; and Christian history is and remains full of wars fought by Christians, with more or less explicit claims of divine sanction or blessing. It is important to note from the outset that the relationship between these two phenomena – the language and imagery of war and violence, and wars fought in real life – is far from straightforward.[1] Indeed, an important strand in twentieth-century Christian theology, in the aftermath of the enormously destructive European wars and of the recognition of the violence of Christian nations' imperialism, has involved rereadings of the scriptural and traditional 'war' texts to develop theological critiques of militarism.

We should note at this point that framing a discussion in terms of '*war* and peace' already represents a consequential decision – albeit a rather predictable one – about what forms of violence are of most concern for theology. There is a very long and well-known tradition of debate in Christian theology (and law and ethics) about the circumstances in which warfare is justified or indeed required. By contrast, there is little or no discussion, before the second half of the twentieth century, of violence within the family unit, or of male violence against women, as a significant issue for theology – despite the fact that, just as with warfare, both the language and symbolism and the practice are unquestionably present in Christian history.[2] There is a somewhat larger body of theological reflection on the use of violence or force in the name of law and order–- from Augustine's theological critique of the violence underlying the *pax Romana*, to the debates about the 'sword of the magistrate' in Reformation political theologies.[3] Even so, the ethics of, and the theological context for, warfare – with an emphasis on the activities and experiences of combatants, i.e. in the vast majority of cases men under the command of elite men – have tended to receive far more attention.[4] In the discussion that follows, while reflecting this feature of twentieth-century theology, I attempt to take a broad view of the many dimensions of 'war and peace' – attending, for example, to the connections, traced in certain key theological discussions, between warfare and patriarchal power.

I begin this discussion with a brief overview of some of the roles played by the symbolism of war and peace in twentieth-century Christian theology. I then focus on four themes in twentieth-century Christian theology related to war and peace, discussing them in relation to the concrete situations of warfare, violence and peacemaking in which they have been debated and developed. I engage with twentieth-century controversies around the question of 'redemptive violence', or the place of violence and warfare in the core narrative of Christian salvation history. I then consider the twentieth-century history of Christian nonviolence and pacifism, noting the important post-war shift towards active nonviolence and peacemaking, and the relationship between peace and justice in twentieth-century theology, with particular reference to questions arising in the theology of liberation. A final section, focusing on developments at the end of the century, considers the potential legacy of the twentieth century for theologies and practices of reconciliation.

## Symbolising War Theologically

What is theologically important or interesting about war? In most contexts where war is an explicit subject of discussion – for example in just war theory or in debates about pacifism – the answer is taken for granted; war is 'interesting' for theology because it raises questions about the theological justification (or lack of it) for violence, and in particular the deliberate taking of life. Looking at the wider scriptural and traditional context, however, the language and imagery of war appears under a wide range of doctrinal *loci*, in ways that draw attention to different features of the experience and practice of warfare.[5]

One obvious 'function' of war in the biblical texts is as a trial of strength between rulers, with the object of establishing sovereignty – so that, theologically, the language of warfare and conquest can be used to demonstrate how the sovereignty of God radically disrupts human claims to sovereignty. If kings and lords maintain their rule by commanding armies that can defeat any opposing force in battle, the 'king of kings and Lord of lords' overcomes all the armies and 'makes wars cease' (Rev. 19:16; Ps. 46:9). The overturning of existing power structures – God bringing down rulers from their thrones to establish God's own kingdom – can be represented as the overcoming of coercive force by superior force; and the core point is the contrast between *all* creaturely manifestations of power and the omnipotence of the creator.

Referring to 'rulers brought down from their thrones', however, draws attention to the fact that in Christian theology divine omnipotence is primarily understood through the history of salvation – that is, not as the theoretical 'power to do anything' but as the effective power to liberate and save, revealed in specific historical events. The establishment of God's sovereignty – which 'makes wars cease' – is not presented as a hypothetical threat to contemporary rulers, nor even as a consistent and relativising factor operating the background (*any* ruling power, just as such, is subject to divine power) but as a historical reality. This in turn brings the imagery of divine warfare, as a representation of the effective power of God made manifest, more clearly into the foreground. Twentieth-century theology saw intense interest in theologies of the Kingdom of God, particularly viewing the inauguration of God's kingdom as a dramatic reversal – spurred on in part by early twentieth-century rereadings of 'kingdom' language in the ministry of Jesus. In this context we should not be surprised to see renewed engagement with the *language* of divine warfare, even from those who associate the substantive reality of the Kingdom of God most closely with peace and nonviolence. Thus Albert Schweitzer – to give perhaps the most famous example of a (broadly) pacifist twentieth-century advocate of eschatological understandings of Jesus' message of the kingdom – concluded his study of successive quests for the historical Jesus by characterising the latter as an 'imperious ruler' in his promise to bring 'not peace, but a sword'.[6]

Twentieth-century theologies that emphasise the primacy and non-substitutability of biblical narrative as the core of divine revelation have to reckon – in some way – with the prominence of detailed narrative descriptions of warfare, not only in the Old Testament but also in parts of the New (most obviously in Revelation). On this point it is worth noting the critiques, developed in late twentieth-century Christian theology, of implicitly or explicitly anti-Jewish readings of the relationship between Old and New Testaments. To argue for example that the Old Testament depicts a violent God and the New Testament a nonviolent or peaceful God is not only a disturbingly selective reading of the texts, but also a convenient way of projecting all violent tendencies in Christian societies and Christian theologies on to the Jewish Other. The twentieth century's experiences of world war did much to call into question the assumptions about civilisational progress – including progress towards peace – that underlie at least some modern versions of supersessionism.[7]

Close attention to biblical narratives of war serve to highlight further theologically relevant features of warfare imagery – seeing war as more than a trial of strength between rulers. For example, in the Old Testament, war, and its effects on (what we would call) civilian populations, is at the centre of vivid depictions of humanly uncontrollable disaster, suffering and civilisational breakdown, associated not only with divine sovereignty but also with divine judgement. The theme of war as a sign of judgement – war experienced from the point of view not of those who wage it victoriously, but of those who experience its devastating effects – is, unsurprisingly, evident in twentieth-century theology. The most obvious example is the rise of dialectical theology – with its emphasis on the *krisis*, the radical divine judgement confronting any and every human action – after the First World War.[8] Even clearer in the way they connect the experience of twentieth-century warfare with the experience of being confronted with the reality of divine judgement on sin are P. T. Forsyth's 1916 'lectures for war-time on a Christian theodicy'.[9] In a somewhat different vein, Kazoh Kitamori, developing his theology from a post-war Japanese perspective, draws on the Old Testament images of post-war suffering – particularly from Jeremiah and Lamentations. He uses them as a starting-point for reflecting on the condition of human estrangement from God as the core not only of human suffering, but of the unity of divine wrath and love that he conceptualises as the 'pain of God', the pain of loving the object of wrath.[10]

It is important to counterbalance the discussion of war by noting twentieth-century developments in the interpretation of the biblical vocabulary and imagery of peace. The twentieth century saw a surge of theological interest in the biblical concept of *shalom*, and more broadly in the comprehensive and positive vision of peace that it is taken to convey. *Shalom*, the root of which in Hebrew relates to completeness or wholeness, when used in relation to a whole society, is taken to encompass both justice and peace – understanding both justice and peace positively, communally and in the context of God's relation to the reconciled and blessed creation.[11] Thus, for example, Pope John XXIII's encyclical *Pacem in terris* (1963) sets out clearly the theological vision, central to Catholic social teaching as it developed in the twentieth century, of a 'divinely established order' of justice and right relation that is inseparable from the promise of peace on earth. Interest in *shalom* in the twentieth century was unquestionably spurred to some extent by the development of social and political analyses of the connections between warfare and global economic injustice. It also, however, bespeaks a renewed commitment, particularly in the second half of the twentieth century, to serious engagement with Old Testament texts and theological emphases, including Old Testament eschatologies.

Making the theological connection between justice and peace, however, can further reinforce the sense that war – perhaps especially, for European theology, the First World War – reveals both the depths of human sin and the inescapability of divine judgement; war is both the outworking of pervasive injustice and a sign of judgement upon it.[12] Observing the link between war and divine judgement in scriptural texts, and applying it to twentieth-century experiences, obviously sharpens – without automatically answering – perennial theological questions about the appropriate way both to conceptualise and to imagine God's *salvific* action in history. Addressing these questions has in turn forced theology to engage in more detail with the question of how and whether divine 'warfare' or violence has a place in Christian theology – and, frequently, to focus this consideration on the central narratives of cross and resurrection.

## Violence and Redemption: Creation, Atonement and War in Twentieth-Century Theology

Critiques of Christian perpetuation of the 'myth of redemptive violence' – in brief, the idea that (divine or divinely sanctioned) violence is the prerequisite for peace – became particularly common in the second half of the twentieth century.[13] These critiques were propelled, sometimes explicitly, not only by concerns about the twentieth century's wars but also by evidence of continued belief in the 'redemptive' powers of violence in majority Christian countries (for example in the nuclear arms race, with the accompanying claim that that arms race was essential for world peace).[14]

One influential account of the 'myth of redemptive violence', and Christianity's response to it, takes up the legacy of nineteenth-century biblical criticism to draw out the (supposed) distinctiveness of Christian theologies of creation. Thus Walter Wink follows Karl Barth and others in reading Genesis, and hence Christian theologies of creation, as an explicitly 'non-mythological' narrative – a narrative that echoes, just in order to repudiate, the language of the mythological originary battle with evil forces in the Babylonian creation myth (the *Chaoskampf*), presenting a God who is *one* and hence has no evil rival or opponent to defeat in the act of creation.[15] Wink, however, goes beyond many twentieth-century theologians in emphasising the utter repudiation of the motif of the violent suppression of chaos, and drawing conclusions for contemporary Christian approaches to war and peace. Creation in Judaism and Christianity, as creation by the one God *ex nihilo* – so goes the narrative – is nonviolent; there is no primal conflict requiring mythological re-enactment.

A further implication of contrasting Christian theology with the 'myth of redemptive violence' is not only that there is an 'original peace' at the heart of Christianity, but also that this Christian 'original peace' is likely to be counter-cultural or even revolutionary. A nonviolent creation story stands in contrast to a deep-seated tendency both in human societies and in their various mythological (and ideological) justifications – the tendency to regard a good and just order as the precarious product of the violent subduing of chaos.[16]

Theology, on this approach, becomes a key resource for 'demythologising' persistent societal violence and militarism and challenging the ideologies that sustain it.

Various critical questions have been raised about the work that the 'nonviolent' creation *ex nihilo* is made to do in twentieth-century theology.[17] More importantly, however, assuming that we are content to work with some kind of account of protological or originary peace – even if there is debate about whether this is best served by a doctrine of creation *ex nihilo* – the bigger challenge for Christian theology in engaging with the rhetoric and reality of violence remains. Indeed, it is hinted at in Barth's handling of the *Chaoskampf* motif, in which he allows the 'nothingness' rejected at creation to remain a persistent and inexplicable threat to the creative purposes of God. How should Christian theology narrate how God overcomes and heals the sin that does violence to the peaceful creation? What is the relationship of violence to *redemption* proper?

Theologies of atonement came under particular scrutiny in the twentieth century, with critical interrogation of the ways in which they might normalize, or alternatively challenge, both the imagery and the practice of violence. The language of 'sacrifice' to describe violent death – language that is clearly part of scriptural and traditional attempts to understand the salvific centrality of the death of Christ – both came to the fore in the twentieth century and was subject to sustained critique. It came to the fore in memorialisations of the mass military casualties of the world wars – interpreting death in war as sacrificial death *for others* or *for a cause*, with a recognisable and sometimes explicit link to the death of Christ *pro nobis*; consider, for example, the frequent use on war memorials (particularly those for the 1914–18 war) of John 15:13.

The problems with the 'sacrificial' framing both of death in war and – for at least some twentieth-century theologians – of the death of Christ are powerfully evoked in British war poet Wilfred Owen's lyric on Abraham's sacrifice. In Owen's vision, the young soldiers in the trenches in 1914–18 are the bound victim, and Abraham, representing the leaders of the nations, refuses to stay his hand from the sacrifice:

'. . . Offer the Ram of Pride instead of him'.
But the old man would not so, but slew his son
And half the seed of Europe, one by one.[18]

Owen focuses his readers' attention on the figure of the one who *demands* sacrifices, or who forces others to sacrifice themselves; his alternative 'Abraham' is a repulsive and cruel father who lacks all paternal care. Accounts of the atonement that appear to make God demand the sacrifice of an innocent victim have often met with a similar repulsion – and not only in the twentieth century. It is probably no coincidence, however, that serious re-examination and critique – from within and not only from outside Christian theological tradition – of atonement theories and the terms in which they are conveyed gained traction in the aftermath of the twentieth century's experiences of mass slaughter.[19]

Additional impetus for the re-examination of the role of violence in atonement theory has come from sustained feminist and womanist theological critique of (certain) existing atonement theories. Famously, Joanne Carlson Brown and Rebecca Parker argued in a 1989 article that the pairing, in theological accounts of the atonement, of a divine Father demanding violent suffering and a divine Son willingly submitting to the violence created a picture of 'divine child abuse', with the potential to sustain 'a culture of abuse and [lead] to the abandonment of victims of abuse and oppression'.[20] Of particular concern for Carlson Brown and Parker were the gendered implications of such accounts – with the power of the father being associated with the power to inflict violence on a passive and accepting victim. Although not directly related to questions of 'war and peace', this discussion was placed in the context of a wider critical examination of the connections between Christian theology, violence and patriarchy. It had significant wider resonances with feminist and womanist work on the language and imagery of divine power – challenging Christian theology to break the persistent and pernicious association between power and violence and/or domination.[21]

It might seem ironic that an account of the atonement centred on the language of military victory has been put forward by many of its advocates as a key *alternative* to atonement theories that focused on a divine demand for sacrifice. Gustaf Aulén's 1931 study *Christus Victor* – the title of the book also being the term Aulén used for his preferred model of the atonement – argued on scriptural and traditional grounds that the salvific work of Christ on the cross ought primarily to be understood as a victory over the powers of evil. Rather than (primarily) satisfying *God's* justice or honour by his death, Jesus Christ breaks the *Devil's* hold on humanity. The death of Christ is still necessary for salvation – but its necessity is understood in a way that leaves no suggestion that God demands the violent death of the innocent.

Aulén himself described *Christus Victor* as dramatic and dualistic – centred on God's decisive action to conquer the powers of evil; it took up the scriptural and traditional narratives of 'divine violence' discussed in the previous section. This very feature, however, has in some cases made it particularly attractive to theologians developing critiques of militarism. Thus, for example, a review of *Christus Victor* in the 1980s focused on the 'mythological' or metaphorical language of the military victory in Aulén's account. Colin Gunton argued that the depiction of Christ as victor in battle was theologically defensible insofar as it forces a radical reappraisal, in Christocentric terms, of what 'victory' looks like, and that it was problematic insofar as it was used to provide symbolic support for military action, as paradigmatically in Constantine's interpretation of his vision of the cross.[22] The crucial point is that the 'victory' won in the atonement – the divine war to end all wars, as it were – is radically different *in kind*, and not merely in degree of power, from the wars fought by sinful humanity. Moreover, the difference can be, to some extent, specified – so this is not merely the general stricture against the literalisation of theological metaphors; the shape of God's 'victory in battle' is found in the identity and story of Jesus Christ.

A similar Christological focus in undoing or critiquing 'myths of redemptive violence' is suggested by the enormously influential and much-debated work of René Girard. Girard first suggests that mimetic violence – violence arising from rivalry that in turn arises from mimetic patterns of desire – is a persistent pattern in human societies.[23] Scapegoating contains and de-escalates cycles of mimetic violence, and hence preserves social order, by uniting the warring parties against an arbitrarily chosen victim. In many mythologies (including and perhaps especially contemporary ones), Girard argues, the idea that the victim needs to die or suffer in order to maintain social order is preserved – but the source of scapegoating in mimetic violence, and the innocence of the victim, is systemically forgotten. In the Bible, however, and centrally in the crucifixion of Jesus, the innocence of the victim is remembered and foregrounded – and the entrenched violence and injustice of the social 'order', the order that preserves itself by killing Jesus, is exposed for what it is. The attribution of guilt and blame that justifies or provokes the violent destruction of an 'offender', on this reading – organised violence against a common enemy – is not the necessary means to overcome social evil; it is part of the evil.

The most important aspect of Girard's theory for our purposes is that it functions not only as an account of the meaning of the crucifixion as a response to human sinfulness, but also – if we accept it – as an exposé of how certain strands of atonement theory are complicit in their own myths of redemptive violence. Theologians who draw on Girard in this area tend to focus, in particular, on accounts of the atonement in which the crucifixion is taken to fulfil the requirements of divine justice – whether as retributive punishment for sin or as satisfaction of God's honour. Even though, in both cases, the innocence of *this particular* victim of violence plays a central role, the critics will not tolerate the incorporation of violent retribution (in Girardian terms, mimetic violence) into divine justice.[24]

As I have suggested throughout this section, there are good reasons to hesitate before making assumptions about the connection between the theological language of violence and warfare, on the one hand, and the propensity of Christian societies to engage in warfare, on the other. The reasons are both descriptive (historically in practice, similar theological claims have been associated with different political practices) and normative (language is not univocally applied to God and to creatures). Nonetheless – if only given the centrality of the Incarnation – it is hard to avoid *all* 'points of contact' between theological accounts of God's encounters with violence and Christians' engagements with questions of war and peace. In the sections that follow, I begin with specific stories of twentieth-century Christians' practice in relation to war and peace, and trace their theological roots and implications.

## Rethinking Christian Nonviolence in the Twentieth Century

The twentieth century's world wars, along with its (violent and nonviolent) movements of popular resistance to colonial rule and to social injustice, created a distinctive context for theological reflection and practical action among members of Christian churches historically committed to nonviolence – principally the Mennonites and other inheritors of the Anabaptist tradition, and the Quakers.[25] Significant developments in the theological understanding of nonviolence were supported by participation in the global ecumenical movement by members of (what have come to be called in World Council of Churches contexts) the 'historic peace churches'. Particularly in the Mennonite case, a long tradition of commitment to living as the 'quiet in the land' – eschewing not only participation in war, but in many cases also active participation in political systems and structures – developed and diversified in the twentieth century, with new theological thought the influence of which extended well beyond confessional boundaries.

The pacifism of the 'historic peace churches' and their members was often understood and practised, in earlier centuries, as a matter of conscientious objection, by each individual, to taking part in the wars commanded by the state. Particularly in the case of the Anabaptists and their heirs, it was closely associated with the refusal to participate in many forms of state activity.[26] The (patchy and sporadic) legal recognition of 'conscientious objection' before and during the twentieth century framed the nonviolent stance both as a free decision of the individual conscience and as – in many cases – as valid insofar as the individual was part of a Church community committed to nonviolence.

The traditional Anabaptist commitment to nonviolence arises from the basic commitment to living as disciples of Jesus and in obedience to his commands, particularly the commands in the Sermon on the Mount – and being prepared, and indeed expecting, to incur the hatred of 'the world' as a result of this obedient discipleship. In the context of the twentieth century's wars – demanding a level of national mobilisation, and of state control of numerous aspects of 'civilian' life, rarely seen in previous centuries – it was perhaps inevitable that this collective negative commitment to nonresistance, nonviolence and nonparticipation would come to appear increasingly like a positive political commitment, grounded in the radically alternative 'politics of Jesus'.[27] Nonviolence became, in the work of Anabaptist and Anabaptist-influenced theologians, the clue to understanding the Church as an alternative political community not governed by the logic of domination. The refusal to extend power by force, or even to defend boundaries by force, marked the contrast between the Kingdom of God and the kingdoms 'of this world' – and the deep logic of the former is revealed in the resurrection, vindication and exaltation of the nonviolent victim of the world's violence.

Patience as a characteristic virtue of the disciple is articulated theologically, in this twentieth-century movement of peace theology, as resurrection hope – which despite all appearances is aligned, as Stanley Hauerwas puts it in one of his many influential articulations of the theology of nonviolence, 'with the grain of the universe'.[28] Beyond the potentially quietist emphasis on patience, however, the theological re-examination of nonviolence is also associated with a re-evaluation of another characteristic Anabaptist emphasis – on *witness* and selfless service of the neighbour. The counter-cultural community of disciples, in twentieth-century peace theologies, is the salt of the earth or the city on a hill – preserving their distinctive character not only *against* the world but *for the sake of* the world.

To identify the Church with the inbreaking Kingdom of God, from the perspective of a small religious minority, is not to claim political power for the Church but rather, in the first instance, to place oneself outwith all the struggles for domination that characterise the 'kingdoms of the world'; so it is a formal declaration of allegiance over against 'the world' rather than a developed political programme. The distinctive and innovative move of the twentieth century's peace theologies – both within and beyond the historic peace churches – was to begin from this declaration of allegiance to this nonviolent Kingdom of God and to develop an integrated account both of its theological framework and of its social and political implications.[29] Certainly this move, like many of the theological movements discussed in this chapter, has been influenced by social and political analyses of the relationships between violence, discrimination and economic injustice. It is rooted in the lived experience of visible commitment to nonviolence in a violent state, with all the personal and collective risks that implies – a subject to which I return in the next section. However, it is also influenced by the impetus to make the nonviolent elements in Christian theology *systematic* – that is, to make comprehensive theological sense of Jesus' command not to resist evil, and of his own life of active nonviolence. Just as Jesus' own obedience is an enactment of divine love for the sake of the world's abundant life, so too obedience to Jesus' commands has a *telos* and a pattern; it draws the individuals and the community into the enactment of self-sacrificial love for the world.[30]

If late twentieth-century theological reflections on peace reached beyond the narrow question of the 'ethics of war and peace' in the direction of systematic theology, they also put theology in ongoing conversation with a wide range of insights from the practice of peace work. The shift in peace theology towards the articulation of a positive counter-cultural politics has been associated with a flowering of Christian peace work and peace activism that extends beyond the refusal to take up arms. Christian contributions to the emerging body of literature and expertise on conflict resolution and conflict transformation draw on the work of peace activists whose witness extends to complex multilevel analysis of the causes of violence, and often creative and high-risk interventions in violent situations.[31]

The theological vision of nonviolence as defining the life of a counter-cultural community, however, also draws attention to the crucial and very visible role of active nonviolent protest in twentieth-century Christian political engagement – and this in turn poses sharp questions about how Christian theologians understand 'peace'. The challenge is seen perhaps most clearly in the life and work of Martin Luther King Jr – with his vision and enactment of a nonviolent struggle for civil rights that consistently repudiated a 'negative peace which is the absence of tension' in favour of 'a positive peace which is the presence of justice'.[32] King's theology and practice of nonviolent direct action centred on the link between peace and justice – and conversely between violence and injustice, drawing attention to the pervasive violence of white supremacy and its links to militarism. While linked in various ways to Gandhi's *satyagraha*, nonviolent direct action in the civil rights movement was for King more fundamentally an outworking of the Sermon on the Mount – read not simply as a call to 'nonresistance', but rather as an affirmation of agapeic love as the true 'resistance' to violence and injustice.[33]

Another twentieth-century Christian thinker whose life and work has become a focus for reflection on resistance to societal violence and injustice – in rather more controversial ways – is Dietrich Bonhoeffer. Bonhoeffer's interpretation of the Sermon on the Mount in the context of Nazi rule gave a clear Christological basis for Christian nonviolence – with the cross as the foundation for Christian obedience to the command to respond to evil not with retaliation but with 'suffering love'. Bonhoeffer later joined the circle of conspirators who attempted to assassinate Hitler in 1944, leading to his imprisonment and execution.[34] His unquestioned stature, both as a theologian and as a resister of Nazism, has made Bonhoeffer a particularly obvious and well-used – arguably, overused – 'test case' in debates about Christian pacifism and nonviolence since 1945.[35] For our purposes here, perhaps the most valuable outcome of this repeated re-examination of Bonhoeffer's life and writings is, once again, the recognition that attitudes to peace, violence and warfare cannot be isolated either from the larger theological framework from which they arise or from the specific circumstances in which they are worked out.[36]

## The Kingdom, the State, the Nation and the Revolution

The examples discussed in the previous section help to demonstrate, furthermore, that theological reflections on war and peace – whether or not they can be categorised as 'pacifist' or 'peace church' theologies – are likely to have implications for attitudes to the state. This is apparent whether we focus on the question of 'Constantinianism' – the term often used in twentieth-century Anabaptist-influenced theologies to critique ecclesial complicity in state power and hence state-sponsored violence – or on the question of the relationship between peace and justice and the possibilities for resistance to state injustice. Indeed, we should expect the connection between the two themes to be strong, given the association in influential twentieth-century theories of the state, between state power and the monopoly on the use of legitimate force.[37] This section looks at further twentieth-century examples of theological accounts of war and peace that position Christianity and the churches in different relations to state power.

Most students of twentieth-century European theology have heard of – although relatively few have read – the notorious 'Manifesto of the 93' intellectuals published in 1914 in support of the German invasion of Belgium, of German military strength and of the

'sacred' legacy of German civilisation. Signed by prominent Protestant and Catholic theologians among others, the letter acquired particular notoriety in the history of theology
(beyond the general notoriety it acquired outside Germany at the time of publication)
when Karl Barth cited it as a reason for his break with the liberal theological tradition
in which he had been trained.[38] For Barth, the key problem with the manifesto was
the explicit equation of nation and culture with the 'sacred'; but the link between this
Christianised nationalism and uncritical support, not only for the war itself but for every
aspect of the government's war policy, was clearly significant.

The case of the 'Manifesto of the 93' shows how the modern norm of *nation* states
– combining the 'imagined community' of a nation (associated with a shared culture,
language, history and so forth) with the state monopoly of force – brings the question
of theological attitudes to war and peace surprisingly close not only to Church–state
relations, but also to questions of theology and culture. It is perhaps not surprising, then,
that one of the twentieth century's major contributors on the latter issue – H. Richard
Niebuhr – should also be associated with (what was at least symbolically) a turning point
in theological discussions of war and peace in relation to the responsibilities of nation
states. This was the *Christian Century*'s publication of a debate between the Niebuhr
brothers, Reinhold and H. Richard, on the question of American attitudes to the Sino-
Japanese conflict. H. Richard's argument against military intervention, even in the context of (what was in the view of both brothers) obvious Japanese aggression, was framed
by his brother Reinhold as an 'apocalyptic' argument centred on 'ethical perfectionism'
that, while theoretically admirable, in practice stood in the way of responsible action to
secure 'human progress'.

Significantly for our purposes, H. Richard Niebuhr's approach in the *Christian Century*
debate centred to a large extent on a scaling back of ambitions to 'do something constructive' and a process of critical self-analysis by a nation as well as by individuals – taking
apart a national claim to 'righteous self-indignation' in the light of the disclosure in Christ
of the sinfulness of the *whole* world.[39] Reinhold's approach, focused on the responsibility of
a nation to act, points towards the 'Christian realism' that shaped his theological contributions to foreign policy as American national power increased – a realism that incorporated
the recognition that the state and its use of force would always be morally ambiguous.[40]
Many subsequent theological debates in the West about the place of nuclear deterrence in
'just war' theory – and more generally about Christian approaches to questions raised by
the 'Cold War' in the second half of the twentieth century – picked up the group of issues
around the responsible use, or non-use, of ever-growing state power.

Both the context and the content of theology in the twentieth century were shaped by
movements for national liberation in formerly colonised countries. I have already mentioned the influence of Gandhian *satyagraha*, from the Indian independence movement,
on Christian practices and theories of nonviolent resistance – but it is important also to
recognise the theological questions that arose from Christian involvement in liberation
movements not committed to nonviolent means. Some of these questions came to the
fore in a global ecumenical context in the second half of the twentieth century, as the
World Council of Churches' (WCC) Programme to Combat Racism developed its support for anti-apartheid movements in southern Africa, offering funding to organisations
(including the African National Congress) that were willing to use violent methods to
overthrow white minority rule. Theological debates in and around the WCC in the late
1960s and early 1970s focused, *inter alia*, on the structural violence of racism and colonial
oppression – and what the recognition of this structural violence meant for the theological

and ethical evaluation of violent 'combat' against racism. James Baldwin's speech to the WCC Assembly in Uppsala in 1968 linked the civil rights struggle in the US with anti-apartheid movements, and both with the figure of Jesus Christ, the 'criminal . . . put to death by Rome' for beginning a 'revolution' in which Christians were called to engage.[41]

Liberation theology in Latin America, from the 1960s and 70s onwards, was at times associated even more closely with the language and practice of revolution. The death of priest and liberation theologian Camilo Torres, killed when fighting Colombian government forces – and the associated image of the 'guerrilla Christ' – have focused critical attention, at the time and since, on the question of whether liberation theology's insistence that God sides with the oppressed can amount to a theological justification of revolutionary violence. Particularly controversial here – and in the Cold War context discussed above – was liberation theology's use of Marxist analysis, to extend (as the theologians themselves saw it) the moves made at Vatican II to connect economic and social justice with peace – and *injustice* with violence. The question was then whether the Marxist understanding of revolution – including revolutionary violence – also shaped theology's understanding of the process of human liberation.[42] In fact, as liberation theology developed – and came under critical pressure from various sources, including the Vatican – it increasingly kept revolutionary violence at arm's length both in theory and in practice, while continuing to denounce state oppression and to present Jesus Christ as a revolutionary figure.[43] The impossibility of peace without justice – at a societal or even a global level – remains a central theme of liberation theology even where revolutionary violence is not affirmed.

## Beyond the End of War: Theology and Reconciliation

A frequent refrain of this chapter has been that peace, in Christian theology and especially in twentieth-century Christian theology, is not simply the absence of war. A corollary of this must be that Christian 'peace work' and theological reflection on it is not limited to contexts in which warfare is a present danger. Christian involvement in reconciliation work within and between societies, and reflection on that work, is an important and often underrated dimension of theological engagement with themes of war and peace.

The practical implications of the theological theme of reconciliation came to prominence in the twentieth century in the light, *inter alia*, of major reconciliation initiatives in the wake of the Second World War, and of the development of theories and practices of restorative justice.[44] At the end of the twentieth century, however, South Africa's post-apartheid Truth and Reconciliation Commission (TRC) brought the practical and theological significance of Christian reconciliation work to global attention. The central role of Archbishop Desmond Tutu brought into the foreground the connections between the Commission's work and some basic themes of Christian theology – particularly of Christian theology in African contexts. The primacy of community solidarity and the interconnectedness of life – the principle of *Ubuntu* – was used, not least but not only by Tutu himself, to articulate the goal of the TRC process both theologically and politically.[45] Theologically, *Ubuntu* as solidarity and interconnectedness focuses soteriology – and hence accounts of the reconciliation achieved by God in Christ – on the restoration and re-formation of human community.

Forgiveness, or the willingness to forego vengeance, was one of the features of the Truth and Reconciliation Committee process that was most often attributed to its Christian theological antecedents. Theologically, the importance of forgiveness lay not only in the dominical command to forgive others (Matt. 6:14–15) but also in the wider call to the practice of reconciliation – life together in reconciled communities composed of former enemies – as a response to God's reconciling action in Christ. In the South African context Tutu and others were able to bring theologies of reconciliation to bear on the urgent task of nation-building. The TRC was designed, in Megan Shore's words, not only to ensure that individuals were enabled to tell their stories or to confess their wrongdoing, but rather to '[restore] relationships and [foster] the moral community that was broken with apartheid' – the strong underlying theological assumption being that humanity was created for community, a community that sin (and in this case apartheid's structural sin) had broken.[46] The specific post-apartheid context also exerted pressure on the theology of reconciliation. Thus, for example, in the aftermath of generations of structural injustice it became clear that talk of reconciliation without social and economic change was a failure fully to embody reconciled life. Reconciliation must entail 'restoring justice' – or perhaps rather *establishing* justice. This entailed not only the restoration of peaceful and nonviolent relationships but also the hearing and honouring of the stories of the victims of violence and injustice.[47]

All of these emphases in the practical work of reconciliation in turn have implications for theologies of war and peace – particularly in relation to how God's reconciling work is understood and narrated in relation to ecclesial and societal practices of reconciliation. Both in theology and in practice, the twentieth century leaves crucial questions open about Christian engagement with questions of war and peace. This chapter ends with the cautious hope that active peacemaking, reconciliation and an integral vision of peace and justice – worked through in their theological as well as their ethical implications – will form part of the twentieth century's enduring legacy.

## Notes

1. As Kathryn Tanner demonstrates, great circumspection – and close attention to the dynamics of specific examples – is required when proposing links between theological claims and political attitudes or actions. Kathryn Tanner, *The Politics of God: Christian Theologies and Social Justice* (Minneapolis: Fortress, 1992).
2. For a collective statement reflecting, and providing an overview of, international engagement with questions about violence against women in the late twentieth century, see Mary Grey, 'Final Statement of the "Women Against Violence" Dialogue', *Feminist Theology* 4:11 (1996), 46–54.
3. For the former, see for example Augustine, *City of God* 19.7. For an introduction to the latter, see the various articles on 'magistracy' and 'secular magistrate' in Hans J. Hillebrand (ed.), *Oxford Encyclopaedia of the Reformation* (Oxford University Press, 1996).
4. See for a contemporary critique of the male-dominated character of theological debates on war and peace, with attention to its implications for the Sri Lankan context, Anita Nesiah, *Towards Manushya Theology* (Moratuwa: Sarvodaya Vishva Lekha Publishers, 2005).
5. See for a further discussion of the various ways in which imagery of divine violence functions in the Bible, and its relationships to twentieth-century patterns of violence (including but not limited to warfare), Cheryl A. Kirk-Duggan, *Refiner's Fire: A Religious Engagement with Violence* (Minneapolis: Fortress, 2001).
6. Albert Schweitzer, *Quest of the Historical Jesus*, W. Montgomery (trans.) (London: A&C Black, [1906] 1910), p. 403.
7. See for a survey of anti-supersessionist theologies in the twentieth century – including some with an explicit focus on nonviolence – Peter Ochs, 'Judaism and Christian Theology', in *The Modern Theologians*, edited by David F. Ford and Rachel Muers (Oxford: Blackwell, 2005),

pp. 645–62; and for an early analysis of the structure of Christian anti-Judaism, including the projection of violent/nationalist 'particularism' on to Jews, Rosemary Radford Ruether, *Faith and Fratricide: The Theological Roots of Anti-Semitism* (New York: Seabury Press, 1974).

8. For which the *locus classicus* is Barth's prefaces to Romans, Karl Barth, *The Epistle to the Romans*, E. Hoskyns (trans.) (London: Oxford University Press, [1918] 1933).

9. P. T. Forsyth, *The Justification of God: Lectures for War-Time on a Christian Theodicy* (London: Duckworth, 1916), especially pp. 196–216.

10. Kazoh Kitamori, *Theology of the Pain of God* (Eugene, OR: Wipf and Stock, [1965] 2005), p. 61. Anri Morimoto argues in an introduction to the new edition that Kitamori's work bears few traces of wartime suffering; I suggest, in the light of Kitamori's use of the war-related texts on 'pain', that the picture is more complicated.

11. Examples of theological accounts of justice and peace centred on *shalom* include Letty M. Russell, *Human Liberation in a Feminist Perspective* (Philadelphia: Westminster, 1974); Nicholas Wolterstorff, *Until Justice and Peace Embrace* (Grand Rapids: Eerdmans, 1983).

12. For an example of this pattern of argument in relation to the First World War – taking the war as a reminder of judgement and an urgent call to do justice – see Charles Gore, *Christ and Society*, Halley Stewart Lectures 1927 (London: Allen and Unwin, 1928), pp. 146–9.

13. For the term 'myth of redemptive violence' see Walter Wink, *Engaging the Powers: Discernment and Resistance in a World of Domination* (Minneapolis: Fortress, 1992), p. 13.

14. There were – and are – of course a range of theological and ethical approaches to the specific issue of nuclear disarmament and nuclear deterrence. A notable example was Oliver O'Donovan, *Peace and Certainty: A Theological Essay on Deterrence* (Oxford: Clarendon Press, 1989), arguing against the policy of deterrence on the grounds that it substituted technological 'peacekeeping' for active peace*making* – and that relying on massive technological force for 'peace' was fundamentally idolatrous.

15. See Karl Barth, *Church Dogmatics*, vol. 3, part 1, G. W. Bromiley and T. F. Torrance (eds) (Edinburgh: T&T Clark, 1958), pp. 102–5.

16. In a similar vein, John Milbank, *Theology and Social Theory: Beyond Secular Reason* (Oxford: Blackwell, 1990), pp. 5–6, presents a Christian theological critique of (what he takes to be) the modern secular assumption of 'original violence'; in his work, Christian 'original peace' provides the counter-narrative to the Hobbesian myth of the battle of all against all.

17. Catherine Keller, for example, has argued that the *ex nihilo* itself can function ideologically, to repress and conceal the violence of a masculinist theology – that reduces the female/feminine 'chaos' to nothingness in order to establish 'absolute superiority' for the God depicted in masculine terms. Catherine Keller, *Face of the Deep: A Theology of Becoming* (London: Routledge, 2003), pp. 84–99.

18. Wilfred Owen, 'Parable of the Old Man and the Young'.

19. A particularly forceful – and controversial – articulation of the challenge, consciously located in the aftermath of the Sho'ah and the two world wars, is in Dorothee Sölle, *Suffering*, E. R. Kalin (trans.) (Philadelphia: Fortress, 1974), where a range of substitutionary accounts of the work of Christ are accused of producing 'theological sadism'.

20. Joanne Carlson Brown and Rebecca Parker, 'For God So Loved the World?', in *Christianity, Patriarchy, and Abuse: A Feminist Critique*, edited by Joanne Carlson Brown and Carole R. Bohn (New York: Pilgrim Press, 1989), pp. 1–30: 9.

21. See for example Emilie M. Townes, 'Living in the New Jerusalem', in *A Troubling in My Soul: Womanist Perspectives on Evil and Suffering*, edited by Emilie M. Townes (Maryknoll, NY: Orbis, 1993), pp. 78–90; Rita Nakashima Brock, *Journeys by Heart: A Christology of Erotic Power* (New York: Crossroad, 1989).

22. Colin Gunton, '*Christus Victor* Revisited: A Study in Metaphor and the Transformation of Meaning', *Journal of Theological Studies* 36:1 (1985), 129–45; note his concluding reference to 'the Church and the Bomb'. The reference to Constantine's vision also recalls George Lindbeck's famous example of the crusader whose battle cry, '*Christus est Dominus*', is untrue

(in Lindbeck's account) just insofar as it is used as a battle cry. George Lindbeck, *Nature of Doctrine: Religion and Theology in a Postliberal Age* (Louisville, KY: Westminster John Knox Press, 1984), p. 51.

23. See especially René Girard, *Violence and the Sacred*, Patrick Gregory (trans.) (Baltimore: Johns Hopkins University Press, 1977).

24. See, for a twenty-first-century example that picks up on earlier discussions, S. Mark Heim, *Saved from Sacrifice: A Theology of the Cross* (Grand Rapids: Eerdmans, 2006); and for an example of reading 'with and beyond' Girard on atonement, J. Denny Weaver, *Nonviolent Atonement* (Grand Rapids: Eerdmans, 2001). Problems remain, at least for some critics of 'redemptive violence' in atonement theory, with the apparent return to centring an innocent and passive victim in Girard's work; on feminist and womanist critiques of Girard, see Kirk-Duggan, *Refiner's Fire*, pp. 33–4.

25. I am indebted in what follows to members of the World Council of Churches Faith and Order Commission's study group on Moral Discernment, and in particular Anne-Cathy Graber. See Anne-Cathy Graber, 'In the Mennonite Tradition: From Passive Nonviolence to Active Nonviolence' (2017).

26. See Leo Drieger and Donald Kraybill, *Mennonite Peacemaking: From Quietism to Activism* (Scottdale, PA: Herald Press, 1994).

27. John Howard Yoder, *The Politics of Jesus* (Grand Rapids: Eerdmans, 1972). It is impossible to tell this story without citing Yoder's work, because he was in fact the major influence on this strand of Mennonite theology that has in turn been widely influential in English-language theology. It is also impossible to cite him without drawing attention to the fact that he was a serial sexual predator and abuser – and that it is likely that many Mennonite women theologians' voices are absent from the late twentieth-century conversation, on nonviolence and other topics, because of his actions. See Karen Guth, 'Doing Justice to the Complex Legacy of John Howard Yoder: Restorative Justice Resources in Witness and Feminist Ethics', *Journal of the Society of Christian Ethics* 35:2 (2015), 119–39.

28. Stanley Hauerwas, *With the Grain of the Universe: The Church's Witness and Natural Theology* (London: SCM Press, 2002); for the best-known example of his twentieth-century work on the subject, see *The Peaceable Kingdom: A Primer in Christian Ethics* (Notre Dame, IN: University of Notre Dame Press, 1983).

29. For examples from Catholic contexts see James W. Douglass, *The Non-Violent Cross: A Theology of Revolution and Peace* (New York: Macmillan, 1968); John Dear, *The God of Peace* (Maryknoll, NY: Orbis, 1994).

30. See James W. McClendon Jr, *Systematic Theology*, vol. 1, *Ethics*, 2nd ed. (Nashville: Abingdon Press, [1986] 2002), and subsequent volumes, for an example of systematic theology centred on active nonviolence.

31. See on conflict transformation John Paul Lederach, *Preparing for Peace: Conflict Transformation across Cultures* (Syracuse, NY: Syracuse University Press, 1996).

32. Martin Luther King Jr, 'Letter from Birmingham Jail' (1963), accessed at https://www.africa.upenn.edu/Articles_Gen/Letter_Birmingham.html.

33. See on this Jean Bethke Elshtain, 'Political Order, Political Violence and Ethical Limits', in *Bonhoeffer and King: Their Legacies and Import for Christian Social Thought*, edited by Willis Jenkins and Jennifer M. McBride (Minneapolis: Fortress, 2010), pp. 43–51; Larry Rasmussen, 'Life Worthy of Life: The Social Ecologies of Bonhoeffer and King', pp. 55–68 in the same volume.

34. Dietrich Bonhoeffer, *Discipleship*, Barbara Geen and Reinhard Krauss (trans.), Dietrich Bonhoeffer Works 4 (Minneapolis: Fortress, 2001), p. 137.

35. See for a discussion of this the foreword and introduction to Mark Thiessen Nation, *Bonhoeffer the Assassin? Challenging the Myth, Recovering His Call to Peacemaking* (Grand Rapids: Baker Academic, 2013), pp. xii–14.

36. For example in McClendon, *Ethics*, pp. 193–212.

37. Max Weber, 'Politics as a Vocation', in *The Vocation Lectures*, David Owen and Tracy B. Strong (eds), Rodney Livingstone (trans.) (Indianapolis: Hackett, 2004).
38. There is some dispute over the extent to which the publication of the Manifesto of the 93 was in fact, at the time, a turning point in Barth's thought – but what is clear is that Barth himself later remembered and described it as such. See George Hunsinger, *Disruptive Grace: Studies in the Theology of Karl Barth* (Grand Rapids: Eerdmans, 2000), pp. 319–20.
39. H. Richard Niebuhr, 'The Grace of Doing Nothing', *Christian Century* 49, 23 March 1932, pp. 378–80; Reinhold Niebuhr, 'Must We Do Nothing?', *Christian Century* 49, 30 March 1932, pp. 415–17.
40. Reinhold Niebuhr, *Christian Realism and Political Problems* (New York: Charles Scribner's Sons, 1953).
41. James Baldwin, 'White Racism or World Community?', *Ecumenical Review* 20:4 (1968), 371–6, p. 372. See also the discussion in Claude E. Welch Jr, 'Mobilizing Morality: The World Council of Churches and Its Program to Combat Racism, 1969–1994', *Human Rights Quarterly* 23:4 (2001), 863–910.
42. It is worth noting that Paul VI in *Populorum progressio* (1967) gave an implicit and limited sanction to revolution, in situations of 'longstanding tyranny'.
43. See, for discussion of the 'revolutionary Christ' alongside a range of other Christological responses to structural violence and revolutionary uprising in Latin American contexts, José Miguez Bonino, *Faces of Jesus: Latin American Christologies* (Maryknoll, NY: Orbis, 1984), pp. 1–6.
44. On the former, one influential example was the 'Cross of Nails' ministry and network centred on Coventry Cathedral. See Fraser Watts, 'Coventry Cathedral: A Theology of Society', *Theology* 118:6 (2015), 429–37.
45. Desmond Tutu, *Hope and Suffering* (Grand Rapids: Eerdmans, 1984). There is an extensive literature on the role of Christian theology in the Truth and Reconciliation Commission; see for example Megan Shore, *Religion and Conflict Resolution: Christianity and South Africa's Truth and Reconciliation Commission* (Aldershot: Ashgate, 2009).
46. Shore, *Religion and Conflict Resolution*, p. 109.
47. John de Gruchy, *Reconciliation: Restoring Justice* (Minneapolis: Fortress, 2002); Fanie Du Toit, 'Public Discourse, Theology and the TRC: A Theological Appreciation of the South African Truth and Reconciliation Commission', *Literature and Theology* 13:4 (1999), 340–57.

# Bibliography

Augustine, *The City of God Against the Pagans*, R. W. Dyson (ed. and trans.) (Cambridge: Cambridge University Press, 1998).
Aulén, Gustaf, *Christus Victor: A Historical Study of the Three Main Types of the Idea of Atonement*, A. G. Herber (trans.) (London: SPCK, 1931).
Baldwin, James, 'White Racism or World Community?', *Ecumenical Review* 20:4 (1968), 371–6.
Barth, Karl, *The Epistle to the Romans*, E. Hoskyns (trans.) (London: Oxford University Press, [1918] 1933).
Barth, Karl, *Church Dogmatics*, vol. 3, part 1, G. W. Bromiley and T. F. Torrance (eds) (Edinburgh: T&T Clark, 1958).
Bonhoeffer, Dietrich, *Discipleship*, Barbara Geen and Reinhard Krauss (trans.), Dietrich Bonhoeffer Works 4 (Minneapolis: Fortress, 2001).
Bonino, José Miguez (ed.), *Faces of Jesus: Latin American Christologies* (Maryknoll, NY: Orbis, 1984).
Brock, Rita Nakashima, *Journeys by Heart: A Christology of Erotic Power* (New York: Crossroad, 1989).
Brown, Joanne Carlson and Rebecca Parker, 'For God So Loved the World?', in *Christianity, Patriarchy, and Abuse: A Feminist Critique*, edited by Joanne Carlson Brown and Carole R. Bohn (New York: Pilgrim Press, 1989), pp. 1–30.

Dear, John, *The God of Peace* (Maryknoll, NY: Orbis, 1994).

Douglass, James W., *The Non-Violent Cross: A Theology of Revolution and Peace* (New York: Macmillan, 1968).

Drieger, Leo and Donald Kraybill, *Mennonite Peacemaking: From Quietism to Activism* (Scottdale, PA: Herald Press, 1994).

Du Toit, Fanie, 'Public Discourse, Theology and the TRC: A Theological Appreciation of the South African Truth and Reconciliation Commission', *Literature and Theology* 13:4 (1999), 340–57.

Elshtain, Jean Bethke, 'Political Order, Political Violence and Ethical Limits', in *Bonhoeffer and King: Their Legacies and Import for Christian Social Thought*, edited by Willis Jenkins and Jennifer M. McBride (Minneapolis: Fortress, 2010), pp. 43–51.

Forsyth, P. T. *The Justification of God: Lectures for War-Time on a Christian Theodicy* (London: Duckworth, 1916).

Girard, René, *Violence and the Sacred*, Patrick Gregory (trans.) (Baltimore: Johns Hopkins University Press, 1977).

Gore, Charles, *Christ and Society*, Halley Stewart Lectures 1927 (London: Allen and Unwin, 1928).

Graber, Anne-Cathy, 'In the Mennonite Tradition: From Passive Nonviolence to Active Nonviolence', paper presented to World Council of Churches Faith and Order Commission study group on Moral Discernment (2017).

Grey, Mary, 'Final Statement of the "Women Against Violence" Dialogue', *Feminist Theology* 4:11 (1996), 46–54.

Gruchy, John de, *Reconciliation: Restoring Justice* (Minneapolis: Fortress, 2002).

Gunton, Colin, '*Christus Victor* Revisited: A Study in Metaphor and the Transformation of Meaning', *Journal of Theological Studies* 36:1 (1985), 129–45.

Guth, Karen, 'Doing Justice to the Complex Legacy of John Howard Yoder: Restorative Justice Resources in Witness and Feminist Ethics', *Journal of the Society of Christian Ethics* 35:2 (2015), 119–39.

Hauerwas, Stanley, *The Peaceable Kingdom: A Primer in Christian Ethics* (Notre Dame, IN: University of Notre Dame Press, 1983).

Hauerwas, Stanley, *With the Grain of The Universe: The Church's Witness and Natural Theology* (London: SCM Press, 2002).

Heim, S. Mark, *Saved from Sacrifice: A Theology of the Cross* (Grand Rapids: Eerdmans, 2006).

Hillebrand, Hans J. (ed.), *The Oxford Encyclopaedia of the Reformation* (Oxford University Press, 1996).

Hunsinger, George, *Disruptive Grace: Studies in the Theology of Karl Barth* (Grand Rapids: Eerdmans, 2000).

Keller, Catherine, *Face of the Deep: A Theology of Becoming* (London: Routledge, 2003).

Kirk-Duggan, Cheryl A., *Refiner's Fire: A Religious Engagement with Violence* (Minneapolis: Fortress, 2001).

Kitamori, Kazoh, *Theology of the Pain of God* (Eugene, OR: Wipf and Stock, [1965] 2005).

Lederach, John Paul, *Preparing for Peace: Conflict Transformation across Cultures* (Syracuse, NY: Syracuse University Press, 1996).

Lindbeck, George, *The Nature of Doctrine: Religion and Theology in a Postliberal Age* (Louisville, KY: Westminster John Knox Press, 1984).

McClendon, James W., Jr, *Systematic Theology*, vol. 1, *Ethics*, 2nd ed. (Nashville: Abingdon Press, [1986] 2002).

Milbank, John, *Theology and Social Theory: Beyond Secular Reason* (Oxford: Blackwell, 1990).

Nation, Mark Thiessen, *Bonhoeffer the Assassin? Challenging the Myth, Recovering His Call to Peacemaking* (Grand Rapids: Baker Academic, 2013).

Nesiah, Anita, *Towards Manushya Theology* (Moratuwa: Sarvodaya Vishva Lekha Publishers, 2005).

Niebuhr, H. Richard, 'The Grace of Doing Nothing', *Christian Century* 49, 23 March 1932, pp. 378–80.

Niebuhr, Reinhold, 'Must We Do Nothing?', *Christian Century* 49, 30 March 1932, pp. 415–17.

Niebuhr, Reinhold, *Christian Realism and Political Problems* (New York: Charles Scribner's Sons, 1953).

Ochs, Peter, 'Judaism and Christian Theology', in *The Modern Theologians*, edited by David F. Ford and Rachel Muers (Oxford: Blackwell, 2005), pp. 645–62.

O'Donovan, Oliver, *Peace and Certainty: A Theological Essay on Deterrence* (Oxford: Clarendon Press, 1989).

Ramsey, Paul, *The Just War: Force and Political Responsibility* (New York: Scribner's, 1968).

Rasmussen, Larry, 'Life Worthy of Life: The Social Ecologies of Bonhoeffer and King', in *Bonhoeffer and King: Their Legacies and Import for Christian Social Thought*, edited by Willis Jenkins and Jennifer M. McBride (Minneapolis: Fortress, 2010), pp. 55–68.

Ruether, Rosemary Radford, *Faith and Fratricide: The Theological Roots of Anti-Semitism* (New York: Seabury Press, 1974).

Russell, Letty M., *Human Liberation in a Feminist Perspective* (Philadelphia: Westminster, 1974).

Schweitzer, Albert, *The Quest of the Historical Jesus*, W. Montgomery (trans.) (London: A&C Black, [1906] 1910).

Shore, Megan, *Religion and Conflict Resolution: Christianity and South Africa's Truth and Reconciliation Commission* (Aldershot: Ashgate, 2009).

Sölle, Dorothee, *Suffering*, E. R. Kalin (trans.) (Philadelphia: Fortress, 1974).

Tanner, Kathryn, *The Politics of God: Christian Theologies and Social Justice* (Minneapolis: Fortress, 1992).

Townes, Emilie M., 'Living in the New Jerusalem', in *A Troubling in My Soul: Womanist Perspectives on Evil and Suffering*, edited by Emilie M. Townes (Maryknoll, NY: Orbis, 1993), pp. 78–90.

Tutu, Desmond, *Hope and Suffering* (Grand Rapids: Eerdmans, 1984).

Watts, Fraser, 'Coventry Cathedral: A Theology of Society', *Theology* 118:6 (2015), 429–37.

Weaver, J. Denny, *The Nonviolent Atonement* (Grand Rapids: Eerdmans, 2001).

Weber, Max, 'Politics as a Vocation', in *The Vocation Lectures*, David Owen and Tracy B. Strong (eds), Rodney Livingstone (trans.) (Indianapolis: Hackett, 2004).

Welch, Claude E., Jr, 'Mobilizing Morality: The World Council of Churches and Its Program to Combat Racism, 1969–1994', *Human Rights Quarterly* 23:4 (2001), 863–910.

Wink, Walter, *Engaging the Powers: Discernment and Resistance in a World of Domination* (Minneapolis: Fortress, 1992).

Wolterstorff, Nicholas, *Until Justice and Peace Embrace* (Grand Rapids: Eerdmans, 1983).

Yoder, John Howard, *The Politics of Jesus* (Grand Rapids: Eerdmans, 1972).

# 16

# Race and Black Theology

*Anthony Bateza*

## Introduction

In his 1903 book *The Souls of Black Folk*, the sociologist, historian and activist W. E. B. DuBois begins his analysis of Black life in the United States by interrogating his own experiences with curious white people. Beneath their concern with the conditions facing Black people, DuBois detects a lurking, unacknowledged question: 'How does it feel to be a problem?' Through striking narratives and deep analysis, DuBois gives voice to the struggles and strivings of Black people. But DuBois does more than this. Instead of simply answering their questions, DuBois takes up the role of questioner, interrogating their tacit presuppositions that Black people represent a problem to be solved or an anomaly in want of an explanation. In effect, the structure and tone of his work asks whites about *their* problems. How does it feel to *make* Black people a problem? What half-truths – and complete falsehoods – does white supremacy require to continue the degradation of Black peoples? Are American and European whites ignorant of their whiteness as it is performed on the world stage where proclamations of freedom mask militaristic and colonial aspirations to mastery?[1]

While his writings are suffused with religious imagery and references, DuBois was not a theologian. Nevertheless, his example is instructive when we look at the paths followed by Christian thinkers across the twentieth century. In that century theologians and ethicists repeatedly plumbed the depths of racialised existence to draw out critical insights and resources for thinking, speaking and acting in response to Christian talk about God. They asked, and continue to ask, how the construction of 'whiteness', tied to projects of white supremacy and anti-Black racism, debases and destroys Christian thought and practice.[2]

In this chapter I address developments in the tradition of Black theology, focused on figures in the North American context. Because there already exists a wealth of resources for those wanting an introduction to the history and ideas within Black theology, and keeping with the goal of this volume to reconsider figures anew and to explore innovative and critical angles, what follows is largely a critical conversation with challenges and opportunities presented by the treatment of race within Black theology.[3] I argue that Black theology unites theological and ethical modes of enquiry in ways that provide a contextual account of theology wherein acknowledgement of context is more than a trivial acknowledgement of perspective. To support this argument, I begin by discussing the methodological framework of Black theology, the liberative norm and variegated sources upon which thinkers like James Cone and others have drawn. Then, in conversation with recent work in feminist standpoint theory, I address challenges the contextual approach faces with respect to the potential essentialisation of racial identity and the fragmentation of theological conversation into an incommensurate and relativistic morass.

Ultimately, I contend, Black theology can address these worries and provide critical and constructive resources for theological enquiry where attention to race is central and contestable. The consequences of this work are twofold. In the twentieth and twenty-first centuries, Black theology provides a rich account of Black religious thought and practice, including voices and drawing upon sources that were historically suppressed and remain marginalised in predominantly white theological conversations. Furthermore, Black theology goes beyond mere inclusion by challenging the formal and substantive claims of Christian thought. The terrain of theological enquiry is thereby expanded, its very aims and methods changed.

## Race, Norms and Contextual Theological Knowledge

Thinking about race, and out of one's racial identity and experiences, remains a core concern within the field of Black theology. While diverse in method and content, broadly speaking Black theologies share a commitment to the liberation of Black peoples from oppression, arguing that racialised patterns of thought and systems of power inflict innumerable harms on the religious, political, economic and affective lives of Black peoples. This means that, in the midst of vigorous disagreement and difference, Black theology advances a central normative claim about the task of theological enquiry: a theological project that fails to address this liberative aim fails to be properly theological. As we will see below, there are stronger and weaker versions of this claim, but amidst these variations race remains a crucial and not merely ancillary topic for all its theological endeavours.

This guiding liberative norm is powerfully articulated in the work of James Cone, widely recognised as one of the founding figures in Black theology, whose thought drove theological conversations about race through the second half of the twentieth century and into the twenty-first. Cone burst on to the theological stage in 1969 with *Black Theology and Black Power*, quickly followed by *A Black Theology of Liberation* the following year.[4] To be sure, the theological confrontation with race did not begin with Cone in the 1960s. Blacks in the Americas were well versed in the contradictions and possibilities of the Christian tradition as they gave birth to distinctive forms of Christian thought while enduring and overcoming centuries of domination and oppression at the hands of white Christians.[5] But in the twentieth century these efforts by Black peoples remained marginalised or forgotten by religious and academic communities dominated by whites. Cone upset this system, combining insights from the civil rights and Black Power movements in the United States with his own racial and religious experiences as a Black Christian nurtured within the Black Church and formed by classic theological training in the academy.[6] In response to the segregation of these communities and the glaring inattention to race among white Christians and white theological conversations, Cone offered strident criticism and a substantive alternative.

At the heart of Cone's project is a demand that theology work out and address the experience of oppressed peoples, making liberation not only the norm of Black theology but a criterion by which all good theology should be judged. Black theology is a better form of Christian theology because 'there can be no theology of the gospel which does not arise from an oppressed community'.[7] This norm is advanced on two fronts. First, Cone criticises the racialised, white readings of the Bible that proffer neutrality while perpetuating injustice. Second, in response he constructs an alternative that explicitly names the impact of race and builds upon the experiences of Black peoples in general and Black Christians in particular.

Framing theological enquiry by attending to the injustices created and maintained by racialised patterns of thought and systems of oppression intentionally blurs the ostensible boundaries between Christian theology and ethics. This does not mean that these disciplines lose their integrity, but Cone's programme does call into question disciplinary distinctions that readily lead to untenable divisions:

> The ethical question, 'What am I to do?' cannot be separated from its theological source, that is, what God has done and is doing to liberate the oppressed from slavery and injustice. Thus, Christian theology is the foundation of Christian ethics.[8]

While appreciative of and indebted to theological figures such as Rudolf Bultmann, Paul Tillich and Karl Barth, Cone wonders 'What could Karl Barth possibly mean for black students who had come from the cotton fields of Arkansas, Louisiana, and Mississippi, seeking to change the structure of their lives in a society that had defined *black* as nonbeing?'[9] Respect comes with disappointment in the tragic failures of theological figures such as these to see the tragic conditions facing Black people. Even Reinhold Niebuhr, who recognised the injustices of his time, called for patience and gradualism because the plight of Black people did not present a pressing challenge for Christian thought or practice. 'Niebuhr', Cone says, 'had "eyes to see" black suffering, but I believe he lacked the "heart to feel" it as his own.'[10]

When Cone criticises theologians and ethicists who have ignored or dismissed the experiential and political, he does so not only because morally they have failed to address an important social reality of their time, but because they have also failed at the theological task at hand. Cone uses the language of 'abstraction' to describe this problematically detached theological engagement. Abstraction does not refer to excessive intellectualism or academic pedantry, but instead captures an unacknowledged commitment to existing structures of domination. When 'theological discourse overlooks the oppressed and the hope given by Jesus Christ in their struggle, it inevitably becomes "abstract" talk, geared to the ideological justification of the status quo'.[11]

Cone maintains that 'American theology is racist; it identifies theology as dispassionate analysis of "the tradition", unrelated to the sufferings of the oppressed.'[12] The result is not only an eschewing of political or ethical responsibilities, but also a consistently ideological misinterpretation of Christian texts. As he describes it, the 'the liberation of people of color is at best a peripheral theme' among white Christians because they remain bound to white patterns of domination and exclusion, resulting in 'an ideological distortion of the gospel of Jesus'.[13] This move allows Cone to anticipate and address the complaint that Black theology is a 'mere reduction [of theology] to current black politics' by turning this potential criticism back on his interlocutors.[14] While a theology shaped by racial experience appears novel, it has in fact already been an ongoing feature of white theologies that 'have interpreted the gospel according to the cultural and political interests of white people'.[15]

The tight connection that Cone draws between social history and biblical interpretation places the meaning of the gospel into a dynamic relationship with racialised experience. As he views it, 'Black theology is biblical theology', which means that the sources of Black history and experience are shaping and being shaped by an encounter with the scriptural witness.[16] Cone argues that a proper reading of the gospel leads one to recognise a God of liberation, but this does not mean that the Bible 'makes decisions for us'.[17] It is the relationship between a reading community and the written text that Cone highlights, leaving open the possibility that other communities will draw different conclusions about the nature of the gospel. This potential openness does not diminish the strength of Cone's claims or invite relativistic abandon, but we will return to these challenges further below.

Black theology aims to make one's racialised identity and experiences an explicitly recognised, and potentially contestable, site of reflection. 'Theology', writes Cone, 'is not universal language; it is interested language and thus is always a reflection of the goals and aspirations of a particular people in a definite social setting'.[18] Similarly, J. Deotis Roberts offers the 'method of contextualization' as an amendment to Paul Tillich's language and method of correlation, where context 'will help shape the questions as well as the theological response'.[19] The contextual theologian will explicitly name their own context, acknowledging their location within different communities and identities, making clear how context shapes the theological questions that are raised, and the manner in which they are answered.

By explicitly naming and drawing from their own contexts, Cone, Roberts and others call into question the presumption of universality as nonparticularity that they see in white theologians and projects. Statements about the human condition or God's salvific work in which claims are taken to apply universally and univocally – i.e. as applying to all people and without potential variations in meaning and context – are viewed with critical suspicion as potentially dangerous abstractions and reductions.[20] This suggests that all theology, like all other modes of knowledge production, is contextual.[21] As Cone explains it, a stark difference marks the contexts out of which Black and white theology have developed:

> Like white American theology, black thought on Christianity has been influenced by its social context. But unlike white theologians, who spoke to and for the culture of the ruling class, black people's religious ideas were shaped by the cultural and political existence of the victims in North America. Unlike Europeans who immigrated to this land to escape from tyranny, Africans came in chains to serve a nation of tyrants. It was the slave-experience that shaped our idea of this land. And this difference in social existence between Europeans and Africans must be recognized if we are to understand correctly the contrast in the form and content of black and white theology.[22]

Taking the contextually situated experiences of Black peoples as a central feature of theological reflection invites a helpful comparison between the work of Black theology and the recent arguments advanced by feminist standpoint epistemologies. Standpoint epistemologies developed along several lines of enquiry, applying insights from Hegelian philosophy and Marxian criticism of ideology to the understanding of knowledge in the natural sciences, sociology, philosophy and theology.[23] Despite important debates and competing interpretations, there remains a shared commitment among feminist standpoint theorists to situate knowledge and interrogate the gendered social conditions within which knowledge is produced. Alessandra Tanesini succinctly identifies two unifying concepts among standpoint epistemologies:

> first, the notion of a standpoint or perspective; second, the notion that some perspectives are epistemically privileged. Thus, this sort of epistemology needs to establish that

there is a distinctive perspective which pertains to women or to feminists, and that this perspective is privileged.[24]

At first glance the notion of perspective or standpoint might appear mundane and trivial. We frequently expect that differently situated knowers possess relative epistemological advantages and disadvantages in virtue of their perspectives. For example, granting certain assumptions about my perceptual capacities such as decent eyesight and good lighting, it would be uncontroversial to claim that I am in a better position to know the contents of my office because I am currently sitting there and you, the reader, are not. By extension, we might grant that those who identify and are shaped by particular gendered or racialised experiences stand in a better position to give testimony to those experiences. A Black person, therefore, would presumably be better at describing the experience of being Black than their white-identified counterpart.

One response to the charge of triviality would note the *importance* of the issues on the table insofar as serious matters of justice and harm are at stake when dealing with racial identity and racist sociopolitical structures. Questions about the good and the right are weighty, moral questions, and so dismissing them as trivial strikes us as especially wrongheaded. Add to this acknowledgement that issues of race have a wide scope, that they affect broad swathes of our reality, and that our interlocking relations and judgements bound up with gendered or racialised ways of seeing and being in the world, and the importance of standpoint becomes potentially fundamental and not merely mundane. But there is still more at stake here.

We understand disagreements about the items on my desk when we occupy different positions, and we expect the possibility of agreement given our ability to take up the same position. You could enter my space, survey my surroundings, and come to form your own judgements and share in mine. Our differences are trivial, in some sense, because they can be resolved or reconciled relatively easily. In contrast, standpoint epistemologies problematise this possibility for shared judgements. The matters are not trivial, for epistemic reasons rather than moral ones, the challenges that standpoint poses for how knowledge is formed through particular and contingent histories, habits and differing evaluative criteria for questions of justification and validity. How this problematisation works out will be considered below when we turn to worries about incommensurability and relativism, but for now it is apparent that seemingly uncontroversial claims about perspective can quickly become contentious.

While thus far I have highlighted single knowers and perspectives, it must be noted that standpoint theorists warn us against individualist approaches. As Patricia Hill Collins observes when discussing standpoint theory and race, 'standpoint theory places less emphasis on individual experiences within socially constructed groups than on the social conditions that construct such groups'.[25] Collins argues that standpoint theories focus on groups because to do so allows one to analyse and explain power relationships and social inequality. Returning to Cone, we see a similar emphasis on the collective experiences of Black peoples as shared histories and present realities. The argument is not that Black people, as individuals, are just in a better position to understand Black experience, but that Black experience generally provides Black people as a group with a superior set of collective skills and abilities for understanding Christian religious experience when compared with the habits of thought, affect and practice that white racialised existence has established for whites. The normative claim of fit, of better and worse readings tied to better or worse capacities, requires a particular reading of the connection between text and context. As we saw above with Cone's claims about the gospel message and the views of Black interpretive communities, if one does not hold that gospel message is bound to certain claims about liberation, then the claim that Black peoples are well or better positioned to interpret Christian religious experience will seem questionable.

The resonance between standpoint epistemologies and the contextually articulated claims of Black theology brings up helpful conceptual analogues, but also similar substantive challenges. In what follows I take up two such challenges framed as persistent worries about race and Black theology, and by extension, most contextually situated theologies. The first is an essentialist worry, the concern that a racialised group experience reduces and fixes 'blackness' to a limited, and presumptively shared, normative meaning. This would repeat the fallacious logic of racist ideology by equating purported racial identity with some shared characteristic such as suffering or resistance. Attempts to account for the multiplicity and variety of Black experiences, collective or individual, generates a second worry about the infinite multiplication of identities. Granting radical particularity and plurality seems to create a fractured landscape of incommensurable claims, a terrain potted with relativistic indifference and the loss of shared values including a common commitment to truth.

## The Essentialist Worry: Racial Identity beyond Reduction

While the concept of blackness plays a central role in Black theology, the meaning of blackness and its utility are contested. For Cone, blackness carries on a double meaning. On the one hand it is a racial designation, one constructed over time by white oppressors but taken on by people of African descent in the Americas and beyond as a form of self-identification. On the other hand, 'blackness' becomes a symbol or cipher for any sociopolitically oppressed community. Admittedly, Cone shifts between these two meanings in his work, inviting potential confusion or misinterpretation. One example of this is found in his calls for repentance whereby white Christians might 'become black'. Cone characterises this as a conversion experience 'wherein they die to whiteness and are reborn anew in order to struggle *against* white oppression and *for* the liberation of the oppressed'.[26] Some conceptual ambiguity is generated by switching between the racialised experience of one community, a stance in relationship to that community and its oppression, and more generalised claims about oppression in a wide variety of contexts.

This shifting meaning of 'blackness', it could be argued, reflects ongoing debates about the meaning of race itself. Scholarly opinions in the twentieth century coalesced around a rejection of racial categories along naturalised, purportedly genetic lines of descent, favouring a constructivist interpretation that views racial categories as distinctly sociohistorical creations that draw upon, but are not defined by, phenotypic categories such as skin colour, hair texture or other physical descriptors.[27] While racial categories do not track biological reality, the impact of racialised categories on individuals and institutions remains persistent and, more often than not, pernicious. Race and racial identities are no longer taken as natural or essential, as given facts or states of affairs that correlate with genetic phenotypes or cranial topographies, but instead as beliefs, feelings and practices of identity formation that are fictions insofar as they are socially constructed and systemically reinforced patterns of thought and behaviour, as scripts or stories. These stories can be read as fictions, dynamic narratives that have been crafted and recrafted over time, but the effects of these stories remain real, particularly as they are linked to practices of resource allocation, broadly construed.[28] As Andrew Prevot observes, race is a fiction with real effects, as an assemblage of force relations, as an embodied subject-position in linguistic and historical spaces, as a materially reinforced symbol affecting the experiences and behaviors of groups and individuals, as a schema of perception more than mere sensation, as a set of scripted performances, as a story we tell ourselves.[29]

Granting that Cone's use of blackness as a category takes its cues from a constructivist account of racial identity and not the quasi-scientific categories of earlier racist paradigms, the challenge of essentialising racial identity remains. If blackness is a script and a story, then one wonders how many roles there are for Black peoples to play. In his critical appraisal of Black theology, Victor Anderson argues that even severed from the biological claims about race, Black theology remains tethered to what he calls 'ontological black-ness'. Anderson argues that

> under ontological blackness, the conscious lives of blacks are experienced as bound by unresolved binary dialectics of slavery and freedom, negro and citizen, insider and out-sider, black and white, struggle and survival. However, such binary polarities admit no possibility of transcendence or mediation.[30]

From Anderson's perspective, several problems converge when Black theology slips into ontological blackness. Viewed as a reactionary form of cultural apologetics, ontological blackness remains bound to the terms and patterns set by whiteness. Blackness is 'rei-fied into a totality or unity of black experience', which makes Black life 'fundamentally determined by black suffering and resistance to whiteness'.[31] The diversity of experiences had by Black peoples are easily overlooked, or worse, denied. Black religious and cultural voices that push back at this image of blackness risk being judged in terms of their authen-ticity or loyalty to the race.[32]

Anderson's criticisms push at a genuine vulnerability in the construction of blackness within Black theology, but the development of more expansive and inclusive visions of Black identity can ameliorate this concern. As Black theological projects have developed alongside and after Cone, it has become clear that a multitude of voices have articulated different approaches to blackness and the central concerns encountered by different Black communities. Successive generations of Black theologians and ethicists have followed in Cone's footsteps while critically pressing his arguments in new directions. First and foremost came the contributions of womanist thinkers who called into question Cone's inattention to the experiences and insights of Black women. Womanists, who took their name from the writings and thought of Alice Walker, responded to the exclusion of Black voices and concerns on multiple fronts.[33] Against the feminist movement, which was dominated by the interests of white, predominantly middle-class women, they insisted upon the central importance of race in experiences for understanding the particular chal-lenges Black women encountered. While authors like Cone made race central to their work, Black theology was proffered without including the voices or perspectives of Black women, revealing the enduring power of patriarchy within Black ecclesial spaces and Christian theological constructs.

In her pivotal 1985 essay 'The Emergence of Black Feminist Consciousness', Katie G. Cannon called for a Christian theology that addresses the particular forms of oppression encountered by Black women *as* Black women, drawing from their lived experiences, crit-ical reflections and persistent acts of endurance and resistance.[34] Cannon brought together critique and recovery, drawing from Black women authors and advancing a liberative interpretation of biblical texts. Cannon's work was quickly followed by others, such as Delores Williams, Emile Townes and M. Shawn Copland, to name but a few paradigmatic representatives. Over the course of his career, Cone increasingly employed an autobiographical voice and moved to engage non-traditional theological sources like Black Christian spirituals and literature, just as womanist authors have consistently made use of similarly literary, historical and ethnographic resources.[35] Rather than only filling out Black theology by incorporating these sources and Black feminine perspectives, Womanist thinkers pressed for novel methodological and doctrinal contributions overlooked by others. The question, as Jacquelyn Grant puts it, was 'What has Jesus to do with the status of women in the church and society?'[36] Stacy Floyd Thomas provides a clear summary of these efforts, describing four tenets of womanism as shared commitments to radical subjectivity, traditional communalism, redemptive self-love and critical engagement.[37] Several of these tenets warrant further brief exploration here.

'Radical subjectivity' involves attending to the dynamic character of Black women's experiences, picking out the dialectical interplay between women's lived experiences and formation through encounters within Black women in their families, communities and beyond. Important lessons about how to perceive and respond to the world are located within experiences that have, through passive neglect and active exclusion, been hidden from view by racist and masculinist structures. This does not mean that the experiences of Black women are forced to fit a preconceived narrative in which they must do the work of responding to Black suffering, to threats existential and otherwise. Instead, space is cleared in which to attend to Black women's stories and actions.[38] Moreover, Black people are themselves empowered to name their identities and experiences, making this work 'radical' in as much as a womanist 'claims her agency and has a subjective view of the world in which she is not a victim of circumstance, but rather is a responsible, serious, and in-charge woman'.[39] This work does not predetermine what counts as a legitimate expression of Black identity, but instead invites a robust conversation in which collective identities are worked out through their articulation, contestation and reflection.[40] Furthermore, while reacting against oppressive and dominating structures, womanists have pressed for fuller accounts of joy, freedom and human flourishing drawn from the lives and hopes of Black women, making blackness more than a merely reactionary concept.

A commitment to redemptive self-love is, in part, motivated by a resistance to both sociopolitical and theological forces. Womanists challenge cultural patterns that devalue the bodies and lives of Black women, and simultaneously critique the Christian constructions of love that highlight the dangers of pride or self-regard while commending only sacrifice, detachment and self-denigration.[41] Speaking of her own experiences, Kelly Brown Douglas describes redemptive self-love in rehearsing her discovery of womanism as affirming Black lives and as permission-giving:

> It let me know that it was all right to be black, female, and me . . . gave me a place from which to speak . . . It allowed me to stand with my black female sisters as they also struggled to find their way, their voice, and their place.[42]

The complexities of, and obstacles to, radical self-love persist in white subjects and structures and within Black communities as well. As Melanie Jones argues, attention to the aesthetics of Black women's bodies can be a liberative experience of agency and resistance or another instance of oppressive censure and surveillance, guided by a 'politics of respectability' whereby marginalised groups seek recognition and power by presenting themselves in ways deemed acceptable by dominant groups.[43]

These womanist insights and methodologies do not, of themselves, dispel the threat of essentialising blackness, or similar worries about essentialised categories of gender identity: such threats always exist when engaging in conceptual abstraction, and are especially acute when invoking dynamic and contested identity categories. What the womanist and Black theological approaches do is make this threat explicit and provide management strategies. While it is perhaps tempting to retreat into, or seek out, a decontextualised and purportedly neutral alternative, efforts at colourblind theological enquiry miss the complexities of both sources and interpreters. The superiority of the womanist approach comes in its ability to explicitly name these limitations and provide mechanisms for accounting for and negotiating differences. This occurs both indirectly, in the inclusion of wider areas of Black experience, and directly, through the arguments womanist and other Black thinkers have employed to resist constrictive renderings of 'Black'.[44] It could be said that this is how Black identity has functioned within Black communities for generations.[45]

Black theology continues to expand its landscape, including an ever-wider variety of Black experiences and contexts. This development can assuage fears about a narrowly and rigidly defined racial identity, lessening the worry about reductive and restrictive essentialism. But is there a cost? Does introducing a variety of identity claims indexed to blackness, to say nothing of other racialised and contextual identities, make theological conversation impossible? This takes us to our second global worry, namely, that contextual theology yields only manifold enclaves of untranslatable difference.

## The Relativistic Worry: Multiplying Incommensurate Identities

If the worry of essentialising Black identity is managed by expansive and inclusive approaches to racialised experience in general, and blackness in particular, then it might appear that one horn of a dilemma is avoided, only to be caught on the other. How are we to attend to contextual specificity when the relevant contexts themselves are admittedly unstable and appear to be proliferating? Ironically, perhaps, expanding the conversation risks making conversation itself impossible. Instead of a clear and uniting call for the shared experiences of Black peoples that fuelled the civil rights and Black Power movements and inspired James Cone's theology, are we left only with isolated pockets of difference? Theologically this generates problems for claims that in our talk about God we can be said to be, at a minimum, attempting to speak to the same reality. Practically this problem risks isolation and segregation, where those working out of different contexts find themselves unable or unwilling to speak to others.[46]

There are moments when Black theologians seem to invite this isolation. Cone, for example, at times emphasises that his writings emerged out of concern for, and are primarily directed at, Black Christians only. But a more careful reading of Cone's language and argument, to say nothing of his ongoing work as a scholar, teacher, activist and colleague, place these comments in their proper context. He pushes back on challenges to Black theology that come from white interlocutors, questioning 'the integrity of their objections' and the way that their arguments fail to engage Cone's thought and recreate efforts by whites to define what is or is not appropriate for Black communities.[47] The point is not to isolate Black theology but rather to question the motivations and criteria offered in criticism of it.[48] In point of fact, the response from Cone and others suggests that the isolationist tendency comes from noncontextual theologies, from a contraction of interest and the demarcation of boundaries historically constructed and structurally maintained to protect a limited range of proper theological questions determined by white figures past and present.

However, this back-and-forth debate about whose theological method is more isolating cannot be resolved by empirical claims. Simply noting which thinkers or traditions have traversed boundaries to facilitate conversations is beneficial, but this does not answer whether or not their practice is supported by their principles. Put differently, do the methodological commitments of Black theology permit such conversations?

The crux of this problem concerns the possibility of shared access to epistemic warrants. As Joseph Rouse observes with respect to standpoint theories in general, 'claims to differentiated warrants are self-defeating if they entail that knowers belong to self-enclosed, mutually inaccessible epistemic worlds, and thus cannot make recognisable *claims* upon one another'.[49] If one community of knowers can claim private access to knowledge, then their claims cannot be recognised, let alone contested, by others. With respect to race and theology, this would suggest that the deliverances of Black theology would be undeliverable, as it were, to other, differently situated knowers.

Given that this worry is common to standpoint theories, it is useful to call upon the work of Rebecca Kukla and Laura Ruetsche in feminist standpoint epistemology. Kukla and Ruetsche draw from Aristotle, Wilfrid Sellars, John McDowell and others to advance an argument that holds on to a species of objectivity and rationality. A gendered standpoint is cast as a 'second nature standpoint condition', a cultivated and established way of perceiving the world that yields 'access to results not available otherwise'.[50] But this does not commit the feminist standpoint theorist to what they term the 'demographic inaccessibility thesis', a claim 'that implies that it would never be rational for those outside the feminist standpoint to accept the rational deliverances issuing from women's second natures'.[51] To avoid this problematic conclusion, Kukla and Ruetsche chart a path that neither embraces the radical version of inaccessibility nor retreats to rarefied rationality that dismisses situated and historically contingent second natures. They key is to view second natures as plastic. To varying degrees, different second natures are to be viewed as capable of re-education. This 'training would be genuinely epistemological work, in that it would not just help people exercise the rational capacities they already had, but give them new ones, thereby giving them new access to genuine warrant'.[52]

These claims come with two important qualifications regarding the incompatibility and plasticity of second natures. Kukla and Ruetsche defend the position that a standpoint epistemology ought not entail that second natures 'give access to *incompatible* features of the world'.[53] They retain a commitment to an objective world where second nature capacities provide differential access to features of this one world. This is a stipulation or a regulative ideal, and such a theoretical commitment does not remove the practical reality of disagreement.[54] But the nature of this disagreement will turn upon our different judgements concerning the world, and concerning who is offering the better description of things, not upon a belief that there are different worlds we are describing.

Because second natures are formed by contingent experiences, they are by their very nature dynamic and changeable. But while all second natures are plastic, not all are optimally so, and not every aspect of our second natures is part of second nature rationality.[55] We might have developed tendencies to resist or exclude certain kinds of evidence, but this would represent either a deficiency or an example of irrationality insofar as it is not a practice 'of securing warrant and determining truth'.[56] Applied to race, this might mean that you are committed to the practice of excluding the testimony of Black peoples because you take them to be necessarily inferior or dishonest in virtue of their race. Notice that from *your* perspective this will be seen as an advantageous and rational stance, a protection against being deceived. And so, once again, we find ourselves thrown into the communal space of reasons, where judgements are offered and tested with others. Different educational and political interventions are required here, and simply pointing to an irrationality will be insufficient without reshaping a second nature disposition to notice and respond to different kinds of reasons.

To square these claims with the presuppositions concerning the epistemic and normative privileges claimed by contextual theologies generally, and by Black theology in particular, we must make clear what are often obscured presuppositions. If one grants that contingently formed standpoints have a bearing on our recognitional and epistemic capacities, there are two important but distinct claims being made within Black theology. The first is that theological discourse and reflection has been, and still remains, a predominantly white endeavour. This means that, as a rule, theology as practised in European and American contexts has excluded a potential source of knowledge through the exclusion of Black voices and perspectives. There are important moral questions here, criticisms about the unjust treatment of Black and other minoritised or marginalised subjects. But, approaching this matter solely as a moral question overlooks the distinctly epistemic question. That question asks whether or not there are forms of irrationality at work, practices born out of coloniality and commitments to white supremacy have successfully isolated white theological knowledge and have thereby failed to proceed in a rational manner. As an educational and political corrective, then, Black theology would invite and expect increased attention to these sources and a widening array of conversation partners as more excluded standpoints demand and win a hearing.

The second, and arguably stronger claim moves from the potential to the actual. Not only are the moral and epistemic practices of white-dominated theology faulty, but, Black theology contends, this has produced inferior *substantive* theological claims.[57] This means that Black theology provides important theological knowledge, judgements that will otherwise be lacking without its distinctive contributions and that are taken to be true and good. The epistemic privilege of Black standpoints is proven insofar as better arguments are offered, either by expansion or correction. If epistemic privilege is granted to situated Black subjects, this is by virtue of the complex relationship between their arguments *and* their racialised position, because knowledge and their context are interrelated. But notice, however, that agreement is not demanded solely because of racial identity, neither are any claims proffered as universal or uncontestable. There is not a claim that because Black people have suffered then what they say is, because of this suffering, necessarily true.[58] In fact, if Black theology took up such a position it would be difficult to explain vigorous and ongoing debate among Black thinkers. It would also call into question the aims of Black theology, which, as we have seen, always entail some effort to illuminate features of the world. Black theology shows its commitment to this process by rejecting absolute claims to normative superiority that would foreclose challenges, while simultaneously developing accounts and offering arguments that attempt to educate and explain their second nature contingent discoveries, making use of both critical and constructive strategies.[59]

On this reading, what might appear to be a relativistic loss of truth claims and a fracturing of the theological landscape is better understood as an extended and expanded summons to critical engagement. Instead of retreating into isolated discursive communities, Black theology and other contextual theologies are advancing against a historic isolated discursive community that has denied their potential contributions. The deliverances of Black thinkers and communities cannot be simply abstracted from their experiences, but this does not mean that only those with identical experiences can recognise, grasp and wrestle with these deliverances.

In the midst of disagreement, Black theologies strive to explain the connection between their perspectives and their propositions, while responding to ongoing conversations within the broad Christian tradition about classic *loci* and doctrines. With Cone we noted his argument about perilous inattention to Jesus' identity as one who works at the margins of society, with and for the oppressed. To this we could add numerous examples. Delores Williams's criticism of atonement theories continues to bear fruit in discussions about suffering and surrogacy in the Divine life and in human relationships.[60] JoAnne Terrell pushes back on conceptions of sin with an excessive focus on pride and an anemic account of self-love.[61] J. Kameron Carter argues for a Christological connection to modern conceptions of race in the recurring desire for purity and a resistance to letting go or trading against the benefits of whiteness. What is needed, he says, is a vision of Christian identity that calls us to holy 'impurity' and 'promiscuity' so as 'to enter into the misceginized or mulattic existence of divinisation (*theōsis*)'.[62]

Traci West confronts gender-based violence with a reconfigured account of Christian hope embodied in the anti-violent work of defiant solidarity, while Monica Coleman brings together process theology, womanism and postmodern commitments to describe soteriological possibilities for health and wholeness in body and mind.[63] Pamela Lightsey offers a theological reflection that brings together queer theory and womanist theology, unapologetically claiming her own context while also working 'to demonstrate, through experiential narratives and theological resources how the oppression of Black queer women harms the larger society'.[64] Attending to these arguments forces us to notice that race, in general, is doing less work than are particular claims about racialised experience. At issue is not blackness in the abstract but rather particular facets of racialised existence, rooted in but not reducible to a racialised identity category. At issue are particular and context-centred analyses that do not limit or relativise the conversation and claims made possible. In each of these instances we see intellectual and discursive association and not isolation, funded by a commitment to truth born out of contextualised experience and knowledge that embodies a determination to open and not foreclose conversation.

## A Concluding Worry: Displacement, Tragedy and Loss

We have seen how Black theology in the twentieth and twenty-first centuries has argued for the centrality of racialised existence and experience as valuable sites for theological reflection. Phrased this way, the claim is a soft invitation to consider the validity or utility of contextually situated and historically contingent knowledge. The inclusion of groups that have been, and remain, marginalised by racist systems and structures represents a genuine good for conversations and reflection about the highest good. But, as we have seen, Black thinkers in fact drive at a stronger position with more normative force: attending to race is not merely optional or beneficial for theology, but rather necessary. This necessity concerns the subjects counted as valid theological enquirers, the methodological recognition of theology's contextual nature, and particular theological claims regarding biblical interpretation and doctrinal articulation. To be clear, this is not to say that this attention to race alone is *sufficient* for theological enquiry, only that inattention represents a genuinely significant moral and intellectual loss.

I have argued that the epistemic privileges afforded to Black theology, as a representative of explicit contextual theology, are warranted. The warrants for this privilege, however, are varied. The historical and empirical claim is that white scholars and spaces are, on the whole, predisposed to denigrate or dismiss Black testimony and Black experience because of the effects of white supremacist structures and habits. The moral claim is that the unjust treatment of Black subjects, in theological conversations and the society at large, places a justifiable burden upon white subjects to respond and correct this treatment. The epistemic claim is connected to, but distinguishable from, both the historical and moral issues. A presumption is given that Black subjects are better situated to recognise and respond to certain features of the theological landscape in virtue of second nature recognitional capacities. These capacities are particular and not universal, they are articulated and defended within arguments about specific features and doctrines, and they remain open to contestation.

To some these interrelated claims about epistemic privilege provoke deep worries and suspicions. I must admit that, working as a Black scholar in a predominantly white field, it is tempting to dismiss these concerns as stemming from latent biases and prejudices against the inclusion of non-white figures and voices. Undoubtedly racial animus is alive and well in some instances of resistance to Black theology, and the lessons gleaned from the past decades and present sociohistorical moment have shifted the burden of proof from Black shoulders to white ones. Instead of expecting Black subjects to open conversations by defending their inclusion, it can be said that now white subjects have been asked to explain the exclusion of racially marked others. This shift, however, does not remove need for contestation and extended conversation. Black theologians must give an account of why race is a salient feature, but those who deny its saliency must also take up and respond to their arguments. Black Christian thinkers and practitioners have repeatedly risen to such challenges, inviting interrogation and reformatting their claims in the light of new questions. This highlights the value of engagement itself, the dignity and respect afforded when time and energy are spent receiving and responding to the claims of Black subjects.

The turn to race in Christian theology also represents a loss, but we must be careful how to articulate this loss. For some, attending to race is a loss because it abandons a shared Christian project to speak truthfully about God in favour of isolated and incommensurate conversations. I have argued that while this is possible, a properly conceived approach to contextual knowledge denies that this outcome is necessary or desirable. For others, attending to race is not properly theological, and when it comes to Black theology as an instance of contextual theology, it has been said that 'no one takes it seriously. Or if they do it is utterly tragic.'[65] Parsing these comments would prove difficult in this limited space, but two observations are worthy of note.

Practically speaking, giving greater space to racially identified and indexed conversations does displace other conversations that have previously occupied a central role. Without wholly embracing a narrative of scarcity, it can be said that contextual theological projects have received greater resources in recent decades. This certainly does not entail that other conversations and figures have themselves become marginalised, or that power has been seized from white figures and transferred to Black scholars. We might suspect that more work needs to be done teasing apart the difference between perceived losses and actual ones.

Theologically speaking, all of us take certain theological projects to be of greater value than others. Some may strike us as important and serious, but not particularly interesting, while others appear to be dead ends better off abandoned, faulty arguments labelled as historical aberrations or dangerous missteps to be avoided. No argument can be given, no rule can be laid down, that will ultimately settle debates about which paths are better left untrod. The invitation to reconsider, examine and explore new areas and aspects of theological reflection remains open. What can be offered are sustained arguments and extended conversation. In brief, I have endeavoured to show how Black theology does this work in self-critical and non-dominating ways, and how, as a consequence, new possibilities for reconceiving theological method and doctrine have been released.

## Notes

1. W. E. B. DuBois, *The Souls of Black Folk* (New York: Modern Library, [1903] 2003) and his essay 'The Souls of White Folk', in *Darkwater: Voices from within the Veil* (New York: Dover, [1920] 1999).

2. While the concept appears frequently in the literature, the meaning of 'whiteness' is contested, and its usage varies. I will follow the suggestions of the sociologist Ruth Frankenberg, who treats whiteness as describing three interlocking patterns with material and discursive dimensions: structural advantage, an epistemic standpoint or world view and a 'set of cultural practices that are usually unmarked and unnamed.' To this we could add Joe R. Feagin's insights about the 'white racial frame', an embedded script and way of perceiving, feeling and acting that sustains systemic racism. Franz Fanon's trenchant analysis on the cooperation of whiteness and coloniality, and their impact on Black subjects, adds psychological depth while demonstrating the shifting effects of whiteness within different sociohistorical contexts. Ruth Frankenberg, *White Women, Race Matters: The Social Construction of Whiteness* (Minneapolis, MN: University of Minnesota Press, 1993), Joe R. Feagin, *The White Racial Frame: Centuries of Racial Framing and Counter-Framing*, 2nd ed. (London: Routledge, 2013), Franz Fanon, *Black Skin, White Masks*, Richard Philcox (trans.) (New York: Grove Press, 1994).

3. For excellent critical and summative pieces, see M. Shawn Copland's 'Race', in *The Blackwell Companion to Modern Theology*, edited by Gareth Jones (Malden, MA: Blackwell, 2004), pp. 499–511, Emily M. Townes, 'Womanist Theology', in *The Encyclopedia of Women and Religion in North America*, edited by Rosemary Skinner Keller and Rosemary Radford Ruether (Bloomington, IN: Indiana University Press, 2006), pp. 159–76, and Andrew Prevot, *Theology and Race: Black and Womanist Traditions in the United States* (Leiden: Brill, 2018).

4. James H. Cone, *Black Theology and Black Power*, 50th anniversary edition (Maryknoll, NY: Orbis, 2019) and *A Black Theology of Liberation*, 40th anniversary edition (Maryknoll, NY: Orbis, 2010).

5. As one example, see Gayraud S. Wilmore's essay 'Historical Perspective', in *The Cambridge Companion to Black Theology*, edited by Dwight N. Hopkins and Edward P. Antonio (Cambridge: Cambridge University Press, 2012), pp. 19–32.

6. Cone later notes that the kind of liberative project he initiated in the 1960s emerged alongside the work of Latin American liberation theologians like Gustavo Gutiérrez, acknowledging that his inattention to these sources arose from simple ignorance of such work in his early career. This resulted in a regrettable inattention to global forms of oppression and sources of resistance. Importantly, Cone admits this shortcoming and brings it into his methodological commitment to do what all theologians must, to use what we have at our disposal while remaining open to critique and growth. For Cone's reflections on some of his early weaknesses, see the 1986 preface to *God of the Oppressed*, rev. ed. (Maryknoll, NY: Orbis, 1997), pp. xv–xxiv.

7. Cone, *A Black Theology of Liberation*, p. 5.

8. Cone, *God of the Oppressed*, p. 180.

9. Cone, *God of the Oppressed*, p. 5.

10. James H. Cone, *The Cross and the Lynching Tree* (Maryknoll, NY: Orbis, 2011), p. 41.

11. Cone, *God of the Oppressed*, pp. 117–18.

12. Cone, *A Black Theology of Liberation*, p. 19.

13. Cone, *God of the Oppressed*, p. 88.
14. Cone, *God of the Oppressed*, p. 87.
15. Cone, *God of the Oppressed*, p. 43.
16. Cone, *A Black Theology of Liberation*, p. 32.
17. Cone, *A Black Theology of Liberation*, p. 34.
18. Cone, *God of the Oppressed*, p. 36.
19. James Deotis Roberts, *Liberation and Reconciliation: A Black Theology* (Maryknoll, NY: Orbis, 2005), p. 15.
20. While I hew closely to the language found in Cone and others, the meaning of terms like 'abstraction' and 'universality' are notoriously slippery themselves. Onora O'Neill provides an important distinction between abstraction and 'idealization' that is valuable here. Abstraction, O'Neill argues, is a necessary and unobjectionable feature of our language use and reasoning, whereby general principles are drawn from particular details and cases. In contrast is 'idealization', excluding certain features of the world and offering others as the neutral standard of evaluation. 'If idealized descriptions are not simply abstracted from descriptions that are true of actual agents, they are not innocuous ways of extending the scope of reasoning . . . Idealizations may privilege certain sorts of human agent and life and certain sorts of society by covertly presenting (enhanced versions of) their specific characteristics as true of all human action and life . . . Idealization masquerading as abstraction yields theories that appear superficially to apply widely, but which covertly exclude those who do not match a certain ideal, or match it less well than others.' Onora O'Neill, *Bounds of Justice* (Cambridge: Cambridge University Press, 2000), p. 152.
21. For this reason, the category of contextual theology is recognised as a double-edged sword in that it could be read to imply that theologies not explicitly identified as contextual are somehow devoid of context.
22. James H. Cone, 'The Story Context of Black Theology', *Theology Today* 32:2 (1975), 144–50: 144.
23. Nancy Harstock, 'The Feminist Standpoint: Developing the Ground for a Specifically Feminist Historical Materialism', in *Discovering Reality: Feminist Perspectives on Epistemology, Metaphysics, Methodology, and Philosophy of Science*, edited by Sandra Harding and Merrill Hintikka (Boston, MA: D. Reidel, 1983), pp. 283–310, Sandra Harding, *The Science Question in Feminism* (Ithaca, NY: Cornell University Press, 1986), Dorothy Smith, *The Everyday World as Problematic: A Feminist Sociology* (Boston: Northeastern University Press, 1987), Patricia Hill Collins, *Black Feminist Thought: Knowledge, Consciousness, and the Politics of Empowerment* (Boston, MA: Unwin Hyman, 1990), Linda Alcoff and Elizabeth Potter (eds), *Feminist Epistemologies* (New York: Routledge, 1993), Donna Haraway, 'Situated Knowledges: The Science Question in Feminism and the Privilege of Partial Perspectives', *Feminist Studies* 14:3 (1998), 81–101, and Mary M. Solberg, *Compelling Knowledge: A Feminist Proposal for an Epistemology of the Cross* (Albany, NY: SUNY Press, 1997).
24. Alessandra Tanesini, *An Introduction to Feminist Epistemologies* (Malden, MA: Blackwell, 1999), pp. 138–9. See also Alison Wylie, 'Why Standpoint Theory Matters: Feminist Standpoint Theory', in *Philosophical Explorations of Science, Technology, and Diversity*, edited by Robert Figueroa and Sandra Harding (New York: Routledge, 2003), pp. 26–48.
25. Patricia Hill Collins, 'Comment on Hekman's "Truth and Method: Feminist Standpoint Theory Revisited": Where's the Power?', *Signs: Journal of Women in Culture and Society* 22:2 (1997), 375–81: 375.
26. Cone, *God of the Oppressed*, pp. 221–2. See also *A Black Theology of Liberation*, pp. 69–70.
27. For a helpful exploration of the history between scientific research and claims about race, see Angela Saini, *Superior: The Return of Race Science* (Boston, MA: Beacon Press, 2019). Attention to questions about population genetics, racial categories and biomedical research persist. See Pilar Ossario and Troy Duster, 'Race and Genetics: Controversies in Biomedical, Behavioral, and Forensic Sciences', *American Psychologist* 60 (2005), 115–28, and Michael Root, 'The

Use of Race in Medicine as a Proxy for Genetic Differences', *Philosophy of Science* 70 (2003), 1173–83 and Rick A. Kittles and Kenneth M. Weiss, 'Race, Ancestry, and Genes: Implications for Defining Disease Risk', *Annual Review of Genomics and Human Genetics* 4 (2003), 33–67.

28. Different accounts of racial categorisation, and the connections between such categories and racism, abound. Eduardo Bonilla-Silva contrasts idealist and structural views of racism. The idealist approach focuses on racism as a set of erroneous ideas or beliefs, suggesting that corrections to these beliefs at the individual, psychological level are the better course of action. In contrast, the structural view holds that racism is best understood as a racialised social system, a society in which 'economic, political, social, and ideological levels are partially structured by the placement of actors in racial categories or races'. Eduardo Bonilla-Silva, 'Rethinking Racism: Toward a Structural Interpretation', *American Sociological Review* 62:3 (1997), 465–80: 469. Howard Omi and Michal Winant's account of racial formation fits this structural approach. They argue that 'racial projects' become racist if and when they organise systems and resources in ways that create or reproduce 'structures of domination based on racial significations and identities'. Howard Omi and Michal Winant, *Racial Formation in the United States*, 3rd ed. (New York: Routledge, 2015), p. 125. While it risks reducing racism to emotional states, Jorge Garcia's volitional conception of racism contributes needed attention to the affective phenomena at work. Jorge Garcia, 'The Heart of Racism', *Journal of Social Philosophy* 27:1 (1996), 5–45. As Sara Ahmed and Paula Ioanide have persuasively shown, the persistence of racist affects reveals the problems in attempting flat-footed intellectual interventions. Sara Ahmed, 'A Phenomenology of Whiteness', *Feminist Theory* 8:2 (2007), 149–68, Paula Ioanide, *The Emotional Politics of Racism: How Feelings Trump Facts in an Era of Colorblindess* (Stanford, CA: Stanford University Press, 2015).

29. Prevot, *Theology and Race*, p. 4.

30. Victor Anderson, *Beyond Ontological Blackness: An Essay on African American Religious and Cultural Criticism* (New York: Continuum, 1995), p. 14.

31. Anderson, *Ontological Blackness*, pp. 91, 92.

32. Anderson, *Ontological Blackness*, p. 146.

33. Walker's clearest articulation of what 'womanism' means comes in her book *In Search of Our Mothers' Gardens: Womanist Prose* (San Diego, CA: Harcourt Brace Jovanovich, 1983), pp. xi–xxi.

34. First published in *Feminist Interpretation of the Bible*, edited by Letty M. Russell (Louisville, KY: Westminster Press, 1985), pp. 30–40, it was later included in *Katie's Canon: Womanism and the Soul of the Black Community* (New York: Continuum, 1995).

35. For greater depth on the use and value of ethnographic approaches, see Linda E. Thomas, *Living Stones in the Household of God: The Legacy and Future of Black Theology* (Minneapolis, MN: Fortress, 2004).

36. Jacquelyn Grant, *White Women's Christ and Black Women's Jesus: Feminist Christology and Womanist Response* (Atlanta: Scholars Press, 1989), p. 63.

37. Stacey Floyd-Thomas, *Mining the Motherlode: Methods in Womanist Ethics* (Cleveland, OH: Pilgrim Press, 2006).

38. As Eboni Marshall Turman notes, efforts at radical subjectivity 'are not directed toward the veracity and/or viability of ontic self-proclamation in the face of the threat of non-being', but instead ask fundamental questions about the presence and lives of women in historical events like the civil rights movement, where their involvement and actions have been ignored. See Eboni Marshall Turman, 'Of Men and [Mountain] Tops: Black Women, Martin Luther King Jr., and the Ethics and Aesthetics of Invisibility in the Movement for Black Lives', *Journal of the Society of Christian Ethics* 39:1 (2019), 57–73: 63.

39. Floyd Thomas, *Mining the Motherload*, pp. 8–9.

40. This is one way to understand the process of 'consciousness raising' or 'coming to voice', whereby women organised formal and informal ways to compare their lived experience in personal and political terms. Patricia Hill Collins prefers the language of 'self-defined standpoint because it ties

Black women's speech communities much more closely to institutionalized power relations'. See Catharine MacKinnon, 'Consciousness Raising', in *Towards a Feminist Theory of the State* (Boston, MA: Harvard University Press, 1989), pp. 83–105, bell hooks, *Talking Back: Thinking Feminist Thinking Black* (Boston, MA: South End Press, 1989), Patricia Hill Collins, *Fighting Words: Black Women and the Search for Justice* (Minneapolis, MN: University of Minnesota Press, 1998), p. 47.

41. See, for example, Delores Williams, *Sisters in the Wilderness: The Challenge of Womanist God-Talk* (Maryknoll, NY: Orbis, 2013), Grant, *White Women's Christ and Black Women's Jesus*, and JoAnne Marie Terrell, *Power in the Blood? The Cross in the African American Experience* (Maryknoll, NY: Orbis, 1998).

42. Kelly Brown Douglas, 'Twenty Years a Womanist: An Affirming Challenge', in *Deeper Shades of Purple: Womanism in Religion and Society*, edited by Stacey Floyd-Thomas (New York: New York University Press), p. 146.

43. Melanie C. Jones, 'The Will to Adorn: Beyond Self-Surveillance, Toward a Womanist Ethic of Redemptive Self-Love', *Black Theology* 16:3 (2018), 218–30.

44. While addressing different topics and sources, there are interesting connections here with Rahel Jaeggi's work on alienation. Jaeggi resists the essentialism of interiorising and romantic accounts of 'authenticity' that locate a person's real or genuine identity as a thing that exists within them or that needs to be 'found'. Social roles, like gender and, arguably, race, are not in themselves constraining simply because they are constructed. Indeed, it would be impossible to conceive of oneself without pregiven roles upon which to reflect and build. Alienation, she argues, is better understood 'as a disturbed relation of appropriation: alienation is impeded appropriation of world and self'. The work of appropriation involves both subjective and objective moments, and the normative criteria offered are pragmatic. Appropriation is an activity whereby one becomes familiar with oneself and the world, and this process can malfunction. 'Here the criteria for successful appropriation are located in this process itself, in the functioning of this process as a process . . . such a process is disturbed if it fails to "work" (or function) in a certain respect. An inadequate capacity for integration and problem solving, as well as a lack of openness and inclusivity in the process of appropriation are symptoms of such a functional deficiency.' Rahel Jaeggi, *Alienation*, Frederick Neuhouse and Alan E. Smith (trans.) (New York: Columbia University Press, 2014), pp. 151 and 153.

45. Examining the use of racial language among Black peoples to reflect and organise in the nineteenth century, Eddie Glaude notes that 'race understood as a biological category was not the basis of this solidarity. Instead, race as experienced by blacks was a sociological category, a consequence of a set of practices that demanded conjoint action on the part of person similarly situated.' Eddie Glaude, *Exodus! Religion, Race, and Nation in the Early Nineteenth-Century Black America* (Chicago, IL: Chicago University Press, 2000), p. 54.

46. The term 'ghettoising' is often brandished about, but the horrific realities behind this term, whether considering the treatment of Jews in Europe or of Black communities in the United States, makes using this language highly objectionable.

47. Cone, *God of the Oppressed*, p. 132; see also A *Theology of Black Liberation*, p. 130.

48. Cone maintained this openness to engaging criticism to the very end. See, for example, his chapter 'When He Put My Name on the Roll: Learning from my Critics', in his posthumously published *Said I Wasn't Gonna Tell Nobody: The Making of a Black Theologian* (Maryknoll, NY: Orbis, 2018).

49. Joseph Rouse, 'Standpoint Theories Reconsidered', *Hypatia* 24:4 (2009), 200–9: 202.

50. Rebecca Kukla and Laura Ruetsche, 'Contingent Natures and Virtuous Knowers: Could Epistemology be "Gendered"?', *Canadian Journal of Philosophy* 32:3 (September 2002), 289–418: 407.

51. Kukla and Ruetsche, 'Contingent Natures', p. 405.

52. Kukla and Ruetsche, 'Contingent Natures', p. 408.

53. Kukla and Ruetsche, 'Contingent Natures', p. 409.

54. Elsewhere Kukla points to Kant's views on aesthetic education, where she says that ideal

universal accessibility functions as 'a regulative presumption underlying communication and objective perception. Now if everyone had the perspective of the ideally educated, optimistically plastic inquirer, then, all warrant would in face be democratically accessible, or part of "common sense".' See Rebecca Kukla, 'Objectivity and Perspective in Empirical Knowledge', *Episteme* 3:1–2 (2006), 80–95: 92.

55. Kukla and Ruetsche, 'Contingent Natures', p. 411.
56. Kukla and Ruetsche, 'Contingent Natures', p. 411.
57. It should be noted, however, that the moral claims about errors in theological practice are predicated upon a shared moral language and the intelligibility this requires. To say that Black subjects have been treated unjustly is to expect a minimally accepted conception of justice. While this treatment of Black subjects might not have been known or acknowledged as unjust, the explication of the situation works in moments where shared ideals like the phrase 'all people are created equal' are shown to be inadequately realised in the histories and lives of Black people in the United States.
58. The phrase 'speak my truth' has become something of a commonplace when discussing contextual identities and arguing for a hearing about racialised experience. Read one way this phrase is ludicrous, as it would seem to hold that an individual can have their own 'truth' that cannot be accessed, understood or challenged by any other individual. But, read another way, this phrase is lucid. It can be read as a challenge to efforts at diminishing or denigrating particular individuals and experiences, a claim that one has been unjustly silenced and a refusal to allow such silencing to continue. Whether or not a truth has been offered remains an open question, insofar as the recipients of this testimony may or may not take it as true and give their assent to what is offered, in weaker and stronger ways, deferentially acceding or wholeheartedly embracing the claims.
59. Lest we forget, the natures and capacities here ought not to be construed in rigid and essentialist terms. Using Collins's language of the 'insider-outsider', which resonates with DuBois's 'double-consciousness', highlights the extent to which people can simultaneously occupy and transit between different standpoints.
60. Williams, *Sisters in the Wilderness*. See also Emilie M. Townes (ed.), *A Troubling in My Soul: Womanist Perspectives on Evil and Suffering* (Maryknoll, NY: Orbis, 1993). For a rich collection of historical material, see Anthony Pinn (ed.), *Moral Evil and Redemptive Suffering: A History of Theodicy in African-American Religious Thought* (Gainsville, FL: University Press of Florida, 2002).
61. Terrell, *Power in the Blood*.
62. J. Kameron Carter, *Race: A Theological Account* (Oxford: Oxford University Press, 2008), p. 192. Picking up this call, Brian Bantum draws on his own racial experiences to highlight the disciple-making functions of race. 'Race is not merely a form of social organization, but more significantly a form of religious expression and identity that shapes who a person is.' Mulatto bodies challenge racial binaries and boundaries, showing the tensions present in all racial performances which can be transformative, adaptable or interrupted. Bantum imagines a return to particular Christian liturgical practices, like baptism, as sites 'marked by continual transgression and transformation'. See Brian Bantum, *Redeeming Mulatto: A Theology of Race and Christian Hybridity* (Waco, TX: Baylor University Press, 2016), pp. 19 and 148 respectively.
63. Traci West, *Wounds of the Spirit: Black Women, Violence, and Resistance Ethics* (New York: New York University Press, 1999) and *Solidarity and Defiant Spirituality: Africana Lessons on Religion, Racism, and Ending Gender Violence* (New York: New York University Press, 2019); Monica A. Coleman, *Making a Way Out of No Way: A Womanist Theology* (Minneapolis, MN: Fortress, 2008).
64. Pamela Lightsey, *Our Lives Matter: A Womanist Queer Theology* (Eugene, OR: Wipf and Stock, 2015), p. xx.
65. John Milbank, Twitter post, 12 July 2020, 8.23 a.m., since deleted. This tweet remains available in Rubén Rosario Rodríguez's thoughtful blog post 'A "Themed Identity" Theologian Responds to John Milbank', *Political Theology Network*, 16 July 2020, accessed at https://politicaltheology .com/a-themed-identity-theologian-responds-to-john-milbank/.

# Bibliography

Ahmed, Sara, 'A Phenomenology of Whiteness', *Feminist Theory* 8:2 (2007): 149–68.

Alcoff, Linda and Elizabeth Potter (eds), *Feminist Epistemologies* (New York: Routledge, 1993).

Anderson, Victor, *Beyond Ontological Blackness: An Essay on African American Religious and Cultural Criticism* (New York: Continuum, 1995).

Bantum, Brian, *Redeeming Mulatto: A Theology of Race and Christian Hybridity* (Waco, TX: Baylor University Press, 2016).

Bonilla-Silva, Eduardo, 'Rethinking Racism: Toward a Structural Interpretation', *American Sociological Review* 62:3 (1997): 465–80.

Cannon, Katie G., 'The Emergence of Black Feminist Consciousness', in *Feminist Interpretation of the Bible*, edited by Letty M. Russell (Louisville, KY: Westminster Press, 1985), pp. 30–40.

Cannon, Katie G., *Katie's Canon: Womanism and the Soul of the Black Community* (New York: Continuum, 1995).

Carter, J. Kameron, *Race: A Theological Account* (Oxford: Oxford University Press, 2008).

Coleman, Monica A., *Making a Way Out of No Way: A Womanist Theology* (Minneapolis, MN: Fortress, 2008).

Cone, James H., *Black Theology and Black Power*, 50th anniversary edition (Maryknoll, NY: Orbis, 2019).

Cone, James H., *A Black Theology of Liberation*, 40th anniversary edition (Maryknoll, NY: Orbis, 2010).

Cone, James H., *The Cross and the Lynching Tree* (Maryknoll, NY: Orbis, 2011).

Cone, James H., *God of the Oppressed*, rev. ed. (Maryknoll, NY: Orbis, 1997).

Cone, James H., *Said I Wasn't Gonna Tell Nobody: The Making of a Black Theologian* (Maryknoll, NY: Orbis, 2018).

Cone, James H., 'The Story Context of Black Theology', *Theology Today* 32:2 (1975), 144–50.

Copland, M. Shawn, 'Race', in *The Blackwell Companion to Modern Theology*, edited by Gareth Jones (Malden, MA: Blackwell, 2004), pp. 499–511.

Douglas, Kelly Brown, 'Twenty Years a Womanist: An Affirming Challenge', in *Deeper Shades of Purple: Womanism in Religion and Society*, edited by Stacey Floyd-Thomas (New York: New York University Press, 2006), pp. 145–57.

DuBois, W. E. B., *Darkwater: Voices from within the Veil* (New York: Dover, [1920] 1999).

DuBois, W. E. B., *The Souls of Black Folk* (New York: Modern Library, [1903] 2003).

Fanon, Franz, *Black Skin, White Masks*, Richard Philcox (trans.) (New York: Grove Press, 1994).

Feagin, Joe R., *The White Racial Frame: Centuries of Racial Framing and Counter-Framing*, 2nd ed. (London: Routledge, 2013).

Floyd-Thomas, Stacey, *Mining the Motherlode: Methods in Womanist Ethics* (Cleveland, OH: Pilgrim Press, 2006).

Frankenberg, Ruth, *White Women, Race Matters: The Social Construction of Whiteness* (Minneapolis, MN: University of Minnesota Press, 1993).

Garcia, Jorge, 'The Heart of Racism', *Journal of Social Philosophy* 27:1 (1996), 5–45.

Glaude, Eddie, *Exodus! Religion, Race, and Nation in the Early Nineteenth-Century Black America* (Chicago, IL: Chicago University Press, 2000).

Grant, Jacquelyn, *White Women's Christ and Black Women's Jesus: Feminist Christology and Womanist Response* (Atlanta, GA: Scholars Press, 1989).

Haraway, Donna, 'Situated Knowledges: The Science Question in Feminism and the Privilege of Partial Perspectives', *Feminist Studies* 14:3 (1998), 81–101.

Harding, Sandra, *The Science Question in Feminism* (Ithaca, NY: Cornell University Press, 1986).

Harstock, Nancy, 'The Feminist Standpoint: Developing the Ground for a Specifically Feminist Historical Materialism', in *Discovering Reality: Feminist Perspectives on Epistemology, Metaphysics, Methodology, and Philosophy of Science*, edited by Sandra Harding and Merrill Hintikka (Boston, MA: D. Reidel, 1983), pp. 283–310.

Hill Collins, Patricia, *Black Feminist Thought: Knowledge, Consciousness, and the Politics of Empowerment* (Boston, MA: Unwin Hyman, 1990).

Hill Collins, Patricia, 'Comment on Hekman's "Truth and Method: Feminist Standpoint Theory Revisited": Where's the Power?', *Signs: Journal of Women in Culture and Society* 22:2 (1997), 375–81.

Hill Collins, Patricia, *Fighting Words: Black Women and the Search for Justice* (Minneapolis, MN: University of Minnesota Press, 1998).

hooks, bell, *Talking Back: Thinking Feminist Thinking Black* (Boston: South End Press, 1989).

Ioanide, Paula, *The Emotional Politics of Racism: How Feelings Trump Facts in an Era of Colorblindess* (Stanford, CA: Stanford University Press, 2015).

Jaeggi, Rahel, *Alienation*, Frederick Neuhouse and Alan E. Smith (trans.) (New York: Columbia University Press, 2014).

Jones, Melanie C., 'The Will to Adorn: Beyond Self-Surveillance, Toward a Womanist Ethic of Redemptive Self-Love', *Black Theology* 16:3 (2018), 218–30.

Kittles, Rick A. and Kenneth M. Weiss, 'Race, Ancestry, and Genes: Implications for Defining Disease Risk', *Annual Review of Genomics and Human Genetics* 4 (2003), 33–67.

Kukla, Rebecca, 'Objectivity and Perspective in Empirical Knowledge', *Episteme* 3:1–2 (2006), 80–95.

Kukla, Rebecca and Laura Ruetsche, 'Contingent Natures and Virtuous Knowers: Could Epistemology be "Gendered"?', *Canadian Journal of Philosophy* 32:3 (September 2002), 289–418.

Lightsey, Pamela, *Our Lives Matter: A Womanist Queer Theology* (Eugene, OR: Wipf and Stock, 2015).

MacKinnon, Catharine, *Towards a Feminist Theory of the State* (Boston, MA: Harvard University Press, 1989).

Omi, Howard and Michal Winant, *Racial Formation in the United States*, 3rd ed. (New York: Routledge, 2015).

O'Neill, Onora, *Bounds of Justice* (Cambridge: Cambridge University Press, 2000).

Ossario, Pilar and Troy Duster, 'Race and Genetics: Controversies in Biomedical, Behavioral, and Forensic Sciences', *American Psychologist* 60 (2005), 115–28.

Pinn, Anthony, *Moral Evil and Redemptive Suffering: A History of Theodicy in African-American Religious Thought* (Gainsville, FL: University Press of Florida, 2002).

Prevot, Andrew, *Theology and Race: Black and Womanist Traditions in the United States* (Leiden: Brill, 2018).

Roberts, James Deotis, *Liberation and Reconciliation: A Black Theology* (Maryknoll, NY: Orbis, 2005).

Root, Michael, 'The Use of Race in Medicine as a Proxy for Genetic Differences', *Philosophy of Science* 70 (2003), 1173–83.

Rouse, Joseph, 'Standpoint Theories Reconsidered', *Hypatia* 24:4 (2009), 200–9.

Saini, Angela, *Superior: The Return of Race Science* (Boston, MA: Beacon Press, 2019).

Smith, Dorothy, *The Everyday World as Problematic: A Feminist Sociology* (Boston: Northeastern University Press, 1987).

Solberg, Mary M., *Compelling Knowledge: A Feminist Proposal for an Epistemology of the Cross* (Albany, NY: SUNY Press, 1997).

Tanesini, Alessandra, *An Introduction to Feminist Epistemologies* (Malden, MA: Blackwell, 1999).

Terrell, JoAnne Marie, *Power in the Blood?: The Cross in the African American Experience* (Maryknoll, NY: Orbis, 1998).

Thomas, Linda E., *Living Stones in the Household of God: The Legacy and Future of Black Theology* (Minneapolis, MN: Fortress, 2004).

Townes, Emilie M. (ed.), *A Troubling in My Soul: Womanist Perspectives on Evil and Suffering* (Maryknoll, NY: Orbis, 1993).

Townes, Emily M., 'Womanist Theology', in *The Encyclopedia of Women and Religion in North America*, edited by Rosemary Skinner Keller and Rosemary Radford Ruether (Bloomington, IN: Indiana University Press, 2006), pp. 159–76.

Turman, Eboni Marshall, 'Of Men and [Mountain] Tops: Black Women, Martin Luther King Jr., and the Ethics and Aesthetics of Invisibility in the Movement for Black Lives', *Journal of the Society of Christian Ethics* 39:1 (2019), 57–73.

Walker, Alice, *In Search of Our Mothers' Gardens: Womanist Prose* (San Diego, CA: Harcourt Brace Jovanovich, 1983).

West, Traci, *Solidarity and Defiant Spirituality: Africana Lessons on Religion, Racism, and Ending Gender Violence* (New York: New York University Press, 2019).

West, Traci, *Wounds of the Spirit: Black Women, Violence, and Resistance Ethics* (New York: New York University Press, 1999).

Williams, Delores, *Sisters in the Wilderness: The Challenge of Womanist God-Talk* (Maryknoll, NY: Orbis, 2013).

Wilmore, Gayraud S., 'Historical Perspective', in *The Cambridge Companion to Black Theology*, edited by Dwight N. Hopkins and Edward P. Antonio (Cambridge: Cambridge University Press, 2012), pp. 19–32.

Wylie, Alison, 'Why Standpoint Theory Matters: Feminist Standpoint Theory', in *Philosophical Explorations of Science, Technology, and Diversity*, edited by Robert Figueroa and Sandra Harding (New York: Routledge, 2003), pp. 26–48.

# 17

# Sex and Gender

*Jane Barter*

In his revolutionary book of 1976, *The History of Sexuality: An Introduction*, Michel Foucault announced what is one of the most counterintuitive challenges to our conceptions of human identity. Sexuality, far from being a given, Foucault argued, is thoroughly constructed – it is the product of discursive regimes operating on the subject. Foucault's argument was an assault on the final stronghold of the Enlightenment subject, a subject understood to be autonomous and self-determining. For sexuality offered thinkers as diverse as Freudians and feminists, traditionalists and revolutionaries, a place to stand. Sexuality – and its concomitant conceptions of gender difference – afforded, it would seem, an unambiguously material and concrete starting point. Theologians of various stripes were keen to explore the new 'sciences' of sexuality,[1] and specifically to offer a uniquely theological framing of their discoveries. But what if sexuality is far less straightforward than it would seem? What if, for all its seeming self-evidence, sexuality serves as a cipher for other cultural anxieties and preoccupations? What if the final unveiling of sex's meaning leads to further concealment? Foucault puts it thus:

> Sex – that agency which appears to dominate us and that secret which seems to underlie all that we are, that point which enthralls us through the power it manifests and the meaning it conceals, and that which we ask to reveal what we are and to free us from what defines us – is doubtless but an idea point made necessary by the deployment of sexuality and its operation. We must not make the mistake of thinking that sex is an autonomous agency which secondarily produces manifold effects of sexuality over the entire length of its surface of contact with power. On the contrary, sex is the most speculative, most ideal, and most internal element in a deployment of sexuality organized by power in its grip on bodies and their materiality, their forces, energies, sensations and pleasures.[2]

Even if we wish to concede that there are material and biological data that can be read off human anatomy and experience, Foucault warns us that we should be cautious about the meaning that we attribute to these, and about the directives that theologians, like others, wish to mandate from the seemingly raw 'facts' of sexuality. Of specific concern for this essay are the heightened anthropological claims that sexuality appears to commend. This view – of sex as a subjectivising force, one in and through which the subject is revealed and made – became a central preoccupation of most of twentieth-century theology, Catholic, Orthodox and Protestant alike. This movement placed undue and novel emphasis upon both sex and gender as key categories in determining (and prescribing) the nature of human subjectivity. Because sexuality now marks the deepest, truest and most enigmatic part of the self, the differences between men and women are also seen to be laden with an irrepressible truth, which demands articulation and reinforcement. It is my contention that, with few exceptions, Christian theologians of the twentieth century heeded such demands.

In what follows, I will trace some of the major developments of Christian theologies of sex through several distinct theological sources. Because of the proliferation of official Catholic Church teaching on sex in the twentieth century, I have elected to focus on some of the major official pronouncements of the Vatican. Occasionally, I undertake a brief foray into Catholic theology proper as I consider the question of gender in twentieth-century Catholic theology. In my (all too brief) examination of Orthodox theology, I look to some of the ways in which theology was reformulated to address the dramatic changes of modernity, particularly as Trinitarian theology was enlisted to offer insight into status of sex and gender. Within Protestant theologies of the twentieth century, I look both to theologians' writings and Church debates, this time considering the vexed conversations surrounding homosexuality in the Anglican Communion. Given the range and influence of Karl Barth and given his disavowal of natural theology (for which he serves as a helpful counterpoint to Catholic teaching on sexuality), I engage his writing, particularly on the nature of sexual difference, in *Church Dogmatics*, vol. 3, part 4. I also examine feminist, womanist and queer theologies, which both conform to and trouble much the above. I end this essay with the child sexual abuse cases in the Catholic Church, a scandal that reveals some of the contradictions that inhere in theologies of sex during this century.

The discussion of each of these theologies is framed by Foucault's – and later Judith Butler's – insights into the changing significance accorded to sexuality and gender and the central role they are given in the making of subjects in the past century. Such theory is not intended as the foundation for a reconstructed theology of sex, but rather offers a critical heuristic, one which contextualises theological developments within a wider framework to which, as I argue, it generally conforms.

## The Twentieth Century: The Century of Sex

The twentieth century was marked by dramatic changes in sexual attitudes and mores in the West.[3] Technical advances in birth control in the latter half of the twentieth century gave women freedom from biological necessity, which in turn gave rise to the Second Wave of feminism. While the contraceptive pill assisted in uncoupling sex from marriage, the sexual revolution of the 1960s and 70s was especially intent upon lifting any repressive holds placed upon sex, including those issued by the Church. During the 'century of sex', sexuality became a chief concern within various disciplines as scholars of various stripes sought to unlock its mystery. In Foucault's terminology, sex became a 'discourse'; that is, a language that is contextually contingent, deployed by systems of power, while it is also prolifically generative of meaning: 'What is peculiar to modern societies, in fact, is not that they consigned sex to a shadow existence, but that they dedicated themselves to speaking of it *ad infinitum*, while exploiting it as *the* secret.'[4]

At the same time, attitudes towards gender began to shift dramatically. After the swell of the birth rate during the post-war baby boom, it gradually declined starting in 1960 in North America, from a high of 3.8 children per family to fewer than two in the late eighties.[5] Within the West, the majority of women continued to work after their children were born, with as many as two-thirds of women with children ages three and four employed outside the home by the century's end. The divorce rate also rose steadily, with almost 50 per cent of marriages ending in divorce by the turn of the millennium in the US.[6] Meanwhile, out-of-wedlock births increased fourfold.[7] It is little wonder that the churches grew anxious.

## Catholic Theology

Within Catholic theology, the response to such wide-scale change was largely conservative. However, it is not quite accurate to say that Catholic theology remained unmoved. While it continued to prohibit birth control, abortion and homosexuality, it nevertheless issued a vast array of teachings on sexuality and even transformed received theologies of marriage. Here, while the wider culture did not ultimately change official Church teaching on various ethical questions – such as divorce, abortion and contraception – sexuality was indeed reframed so that it was tied more thoroughly than before to expressive self-actualisation.[8]

In 1930, Pope Pius XI issued the encyclical *Casti connubii* ('Of Chaste Wedlock'). In it Pius affirmed the unitive function of marriage, but cast it as merely a secondary end, clearly subordinate to its procreative function. Consider how measured is its endorsement of sexuality as an expression of love:

> Nor are those considered as acting against nature who in the married state use their right in the proper manner although on account of natural reasons either of time or of certain defects, new life cannot be brought forth. *For in matrimony as well as in the use of the matrimonial rights there are also secondary ends, such as mutual aid, the cultivating of mutual love, and the quieting of concupiscence which husband and wife are not forbidden to consider so long as they are subordinated to the primary end and so long as the intrinsic nature of the act is preserved.*[9]

In this sense, *Casti connubii* fell in line with earlier Catholic teaching on sexuality insofar as sex itself was endowed with very little mystique. Pre-modern Catholic theology tended to regard sexuality within a narrowly biological frame, rather than as that which produced or expanded the subject. It is sex's natural end – procreation, rather than the expression of authentic selfhood – that guided Aquinas' theology of sex. For example, when commenting on the sin of fornication, Aquinas avers that lust is a violation not of the actors involved in the sexual act, but of potential posterity: 'The sin of fornication is contrary to the good of the human race, in so far as it is prejudicial to the individual begetting of the one man that may be born.'[10] Or, as Katie Grimes points out, for Aquinas, individual sins could be parsed out in accordance to sex's proper end, which is simply fecundity:

> [S]perm was thought to be the seed of a person that could grow and develop only when successfully deposited in the fertile soil of a woman's body; to deposit sperm any place in which it could not reach its potential was to misuse the sexual faculty and therefore sin.[11]

There is very little here that would encourage a view of sex as key to self-knowledge and fulfilment.

While *Casti connubii* upheld the received Catholic position on sexuality by foregrounding procreation, *Humanae vitae* ('Of Human Life') – issued in 1968 by Pope Paul VI

– shifted the ground somewhat. *Humanae vitae* refused to lift the ban on artificial con-traception, much to the chagrin of the Church's more progressive wing and in direct contradiction to the special commission Paul VI set up to study the moral permissibility of contraception;[12] nevertheless, it did make strides in reframing married sexuality as having equal and synergetic purposes, which are both procreation *and* union. Both of these ends were now considered to be equally 'inherent to the marriage act'.[13]

As others have argued,[14] the new emphasis upon the unitive dimension of the sex act has to do with the influence of a certain brand of personalism upon Catholic theology in the second half of the twentieth century. Eschewing notions of autonomous subjectivity, personalism sought to uphold the dignity and the responsibility of the human person as representative of the *imago Dei*. Within this framework, sex came to be seen as a form not only of exchange and mutuality, but also as a kind of self-knowledge and bearer of meaning. Charles Curran attributes much of the theology of *Humanae vitae* to the then Cardinal Karol Wojtyła, whose own brand of personalist philosophy insisted on the unity of procreation and love in each sexual act. As pope, Wojtyła/John Paul II would not only seek to tether the unitive and procreative dimensions of sex as a form of self-actualisation, but would also seek to plumb their gendered meaning: 'How indispensable is a thorough knowledge of the meaning of the body, in its masculinity and femininity, along the way of [its] vocation! A precise awareness of the nuptial meaning of the body, of its generating meaning, is necessary.'[15]

It is little surprise, then, that throughout his papacy John Paul II sought precisely this – 'a thorough knowledge on the meaning of the body' – in its 'masculinity and femininity'. The pronouncements that ensued on sexual difference – particularly on women's special 'dignity' – were prolific indeed. His 'Family in the Modern World' (1981), 'The Gospel of Life' (1985), *Mulieris dignitatem* ('On the Dignity of Women') (1988) and 'Letter to Women' (1995) all sought to promulgate a 'thorough knowledge of the meaning of the [gendered] body'. Between 1979 and 1984 the Pope gave no fewer than 129 lectures enti-tled 'Theology of the Body'. Here, the Pope claimed to advance a 'new feminism' based upon the special dignity of women as complementary to man:

> In our times the question of 'women's rights' has taken on new significance in the broad context of the rights of the human person. The biblical and evangelical message sheds light on this cause, which is the object of much attention today, by safeguarding the truth about the 'unity' of the 'two', that is to say the truth about that dignity and voca-tion that result from the specific diversity and personal originality of man and woman. Consequently, even the rightful opposition of women to what is expressed in the bibli-cal words 'He shall rule over you' (Gen. 3:16) must not under any condition lead to the 'masculinisation' of women. In the name of liberation from male 'domination', women must not appropriate to themselves male characteristics contrary to their own feminine 'originality'. There is a well-founded fear that if they take this path, women will not 'reach fulfillment', but instead will deform and lose what constitutes their essential richness.[16]

Pope John Paul II firmly sealed sexual difference into ontological categories that allowed no variation on the original design. Thus, sexual expression was limited to a very narrow set of experiences and desires – heterosexual, married and always potentially fecund. Complementarity was seen as the key to unlocking the mysteries of *imago Dei*: human beings, created in the image of God, were ontologically determined as male and female, each incomplete without the other. Although women and men are destined to play discrete roles within the Church and the wider society, they nevertheless are to be regarded as equal within their distinct spheres. Women's maternal role was particularly foregrounded, as their 'essential richness' is located within the particular role and vocation of motherhood.

It would be a mistake to suppose that the trope of complementarity was limited to official Church teachings and pronouncements. Catholic theologians affirmed the ontological grounding of sexual difference, and spoke not only to the essential nature of gendered humanity, but also of essential gender differences which inhere in God's relationship to humanity. Hans Urs von Balthasar foregrounds the nuptial mystery of Christ and the Church, but such analogy becomes prescriptive as he discusses Petrine and Marian offices in the Church. Indeed, Balthasar connects the nuptial mystery to highly gendered roles within Church life:

> The institution guarantees the perpetual presence of Christ the bridegroom for the Church, his Bride. So it is entrusted to men who, though they belong to the overall feminine modality of the Church, are selected from her and remain in her to exercise their office; their function is to embody Christ, who comes to the Church to make her fruitful.[17]

Thus, through a tersely allegorical reading of the nuptial mystery, Balthasar uses the seemingly natural categories of sexual difference to preclude women's participation in the office of priesthood. Women are to remain passively identified with the Church – a place of fecundity and receptivity, but never of leadership or of fullness.

The proliferation of discourses surrounding sexuality and gender in the Catholic Church had the effect not only of cementing the Church's position, but also of alienating many of its female members who had experienced some of the liberating effects of increased reproductive freedom after the advent of reliable means of birth control. In particular, its insistence that each sex act be open to conception won very few supporters.[18] Similarly, a heightened and over-determined preoccupation with gender difference served as a means of justifying the Church's continued ban of women from the priesthood. To many Catholic women, the 'new feminism' looked a good deal like the old patriarchy. In a world in which gender and sex norms were being questioned, Catholic theologies of sexuality seemed woefully out of step.

## Orthodox Theology

During the twentieth century, Orthodox theology began to engage more thoroughly with the Western Church than it had during the ten centuries of schism. This is due in part to the exodus of theologians fleeing persecution during the Bolshevik revolution and taking refuge in the West. The influence flowed both ways, with Western theology now engaging with unprecedented hospitality the deeply Trinitarian insights of the Eastern Church. In turn, the focus upon the self as the unique locus of God's revelation became a steady concern for Eastern theologians. This turn towards the subject was novel in the sense that the patristic sources upon which the Eastern Church depended were curiously reticent about these questions.[19] In terms of sexuality and gender, such exchange gave rise to a very similar position to that of Western Church on the manner in which sexuality was revelatory and gender was ontologically inscribed.

When it came to matters of sexuality and gender, Orthodox theology sought to address the sweeping changes that it encountered in the secular world through strong doctrinal formulations. The Russian school of sophiologists linked the relationship between fallen creation and the eternal God through the feminine concept of *Sophia*. *Sophia* was understood to be that power of Wisdom working in the world. Not only could *Sophia* stand as theological description of God's power in the world, but it also became a prescription for a theologically grounded conception of femininity. As Sergius Bulgakov (1871–1944) puts it:

> *In the Feminine are the mysteries of the world* . . . The generation of the world in Sophia is the operation of the whole Holy Trinity in each of its Hypostases which extends to the receptive essence, the Eternal Feminine. Through this she becomes the beginning of the world, as it were the *natura naturans*, forming the basis of the *natura naturata*, of the creaturely world.[20]

In Bulgakov's writing, sexual difference is naturalised, as *Sophia* is understood to be the receptive essence, the Eternal Feminine, who is identified primordially with the natural world. Thus, femininity is constrained ontologically to be a derivative and dependent power through which the masculine God is at work. Indeed, according the Bulgakov, sexual difference is fundamentally enshrined in the very being of God, as is women's subordination: 'Passive receptivity is proper to women; she is sensuality, generating but not initiating. Her power is her weakness.'[21]

While Orthodox theologians did not universally embrace sophiology, subsequent Orthodox positions offered similar ontologies of gender and exalted theologies of sexuality more generally. Developing his own physicalist version of complementarity, Paul Evdokimov looks to the bodily nature of man and woman to extrapolate generalities about them as ontologically distinct: 'While the "ecstatic" man resides essentially in the extension of himself in the world, "enstatic" woman exists within herself; she is turned inward into her own being.'[22]

Not surprisingly, these speculative ontologies of gender were also utilised to bar women from the priesthood. Evdokimov himself argued that women could not become priests without betraying ontology.[23] His position was representative of the consensus of the Orthodox world. One could ostensibly read off the male and female body the order of being. Women were to remain inwardly oriented and receptive, while men were enjoined to penetrate Church and world with their irreducible and ecstatic maleness.

## Protestant Theology

The rapid social changes to sexual morality also created an impetus for a uniquely Christian response among the Protestant churches. As in Catholicism and Orthodoxy, sexuality came to be seen in Protestant theology as uniquely revelatory, as capable of disclosing directly a concealed profundity of the human creature. While Protestant theology was not as encumbered in its treatment of sexuality by the Natural Law tradition, it nevertheless tended to treat the putatively natural data of human bodies as revelatory. Reading off female and male embodied difference as evidence of God's design, even theologians as anti-foundationalist as Karl Barth allowed for a good deal of essentialising when it came to gender. It is helpful to focus on Barth's work on sex and gender, for it is here that we see that, even in the eschewal of natural theology, the presupposition of an unmediated knowledge of sex and gender's meaning prevails.

Karl Barth helpfully uncoupled sexuality from conception. Recalling the messianic rupture of history in the coming of Christ the Messiah, Barth avers that humans no longer have an unconditional obligation to 'be fruitful and multiply' (Gen. 1:28).[24] This distances his theology of sexuality a good deal from the Catholic position. Nevertheless, the purpose and aim of sex remain similarly tied to self-actualisation, this time couched not in the terms of personalism, but in terms of obedience to the divine command.

Barth's commentary in *Church Dogmatics*, vol. 3, part 4, published in 1951, on the 'natural dualism'[25] of man and woman reveals a hardening of these categories according to their respective natures. Although Barth does not ontologise the subordination of woman to man, he roundly upholds it (as in the rather notorious A and B section of vol. 3, part 4),[26] and further characterises sexual difference as self-evident and unchanging. Commenting on Paul's injunction to women's silence in 1 Corinthians 14 he writes:

> The most essential point is that woman must always and in all circumstances be woman; that she must feel and conduct herself as such and not as a man; that the commandment of the Lord, which is for all eternity, directs both man and woman to their *own proper sacred place and forbids all attempts to violate this order*.[27]

In spite of Barth's general rejection of natural theology and of the Lutheran orders of creation, he manages to smuggle them in as he reads the biblical text. Women have a self-evident nature – 'she must feel and conduct herself as [a woman] and not as a man' – and this nature is supposedly self-evident.[28] Furthermore, this irrevocable distinction of the sexes foundationally orients the human subject to the world and to the other:

> [Man] cannot wish to liberate himself from the differentiation and exist beyond his sexual determination as mere man; for in everything that is commonly human he will always be in fact either the human male or the human female. Nor can he wish to liberate himself from the relationship and be man without woman or woman apart from man; for in all that characterizes him as man he will be thrown back upon woman, or as woman upon man . . . No other distinction between man and man goes as deep as that in which the human male and female are so utterly different from one another.[29]

It is little wonder, then, that homosexuality is a theological impossibility for Barth. Given the force of gender dualism in his thought, homosexuality can only be read as an aberration of nature.[30]

Indeed, in spite of the awareness of the joyous, gratuitous and non-teleological nature of sexuality in some of his writing,[31] Barth returns his theology of sex to a prescriptive view on marriage as the only legitimate expression of sexuality.[32] And though he frames marriage as the fulfilment of the divine command rather than as personalist self-realisation, sex nevertheless is understood in markedly similar ways. Sex is mysterious while it is also uniquely revelatory of what it is to be human as man and woman:

> Among the immediate data of existence there is certainly no greater riddle for man than the fact of the existence of woman and the question as to her nature . . . To live humanly means never to escape the astonishment of one's own sex at the other, and the desire of one's sex to understand the other.[33]

While Barth does not trouble sexual dualism based upon essential properties of man and woman, he nevertheless is less confident about the capacity of sexuality to be the self-evident datum of knowledge about the self. This perhaps has something to do with Barth's own ambiguous experience of sexuality in what he referred to as *die Sache* ('the matter'), which was the love triangle in which his marriage with Nelly Barth and his love for Charlotte von Kirschbaum was entwined. Barth's official work in the *Dogmatics* concerns marriage as the only legitimate expression of sexual love, and yet his letters to Kirschbaum point to the reality that God's revelation often exists at an angle to social orders such as marriage. Perhaps it is in his love letters (and indeed his love for Kirschbaum more generally) especially that his lingering natural theology is exploded, as sexuality represents a profound disruption to any knowledge that might be neatly conformed to in human life. As Barth confesses:

> The way that I am, I never could and still could not deny the reality of my marriage or the reality of my love. It is true that I am married, that I am a father and a grandfather. It is also true that I love. And it is true that these facts don't match. This is why that we after some hesitation at the beginning decided not to solve the problem with a separation on one or the other side.[34]

While feminist critics may chafe against Barth's characterisation of woman as a 'riddle' to man in her otherness, the fact that the desire to understand sexuality and sexual difference is never fully realised suggests a humbler position with respect to sexual knowledge in Barth's theology. Sex remains a riddle. It cannot serve as a foundation for an anthropology or for any neat analogy to God's purposive ends. If Barth's handing of *die Sache* is in any way illuminating, it offers a refusal to turn the riddle of sexuality into knowledge. In this sense (and in spite of his more confident pronouncements with respect to gender difference), Barth remained iconoclastic in a century that tended to domesticate sexuality into a mode of incessant enquiry and investigation.

## The Anglican Communion

Of all the denominations, Anglicanism was perhaps most profoundly affected by the challenges that the century of sex offered up. By the century's end Anglicanism was deeply fractured over the question of gay bishops and same-sex marriage. The dividing lines were also not as neat as North versus South or liberal versus conservative; rather, the disputes represented issues that far outstripped the sanctioning of same-sex love, including the legacy of British colonialism and Anglicanism's ambiguous ecclesiology.[35] Officially, the disputes about homosexuality did not become apparent until 1978, when Lambeth Conference called for a study of homosexuality, a call that was reissued in 1988. By Lambeth 1998, after much politicking, the bishops decreed that homosexual marriage was 'incompatible with scripture'.[36]

The willingness of some provinces to divide the Anglican Communion over this issue represented not merely conservativism, but a growing disinclination to allow the West to dominate the agenda for the Anglican Church worldwide. For many African bishops, the Church's tolerance of same-sex marriage and gay clergy amounted to the capitulation to secular values that they believed to be destroying the Church in the West, while the African Church flourished. This fundamental shift in power in the Anglican Communion unfortunately centred on questions of sexual orientation as opposed to more urgent ones within the African churches, such as the AIDS crisis, religious fundamentalism and the spread of neoliberal capitalism.[37]

In the midst of these debates, the future Archbishop of Canterbury, Rowan Williams, delivered one of the most influential lectures on homosexuality from an Anglican perspective. While this lecture did little to resolve Anglicanism's impasse, it did offer yet another layer of theological *gravitas* to theologies of sex.

'The Body's Grace' was first delivered in 1989 when Rowan Williams was Lady Margaret Professor of Divinity at Oxford. In this oft-cited lecture/essay, Williams links human sexuality with the inner triune life of God:

> The whole story of creation, incarnation and incorporation and fellowship of Christ's body tells us that God desires us, *as if we were God*, as if we were that unconditional response to God's giving that God's self makes in the life of the Trinity. We are created so that we may be caught up in this, so that we may grow into the wholehearted love of God by learning that God loves us as God loves God.[38]

According to Williams, human and divine life are analogically related. The inner triune life is one that is characterised by love, which spills over into the world incorporating human creatures into this boundless desire. The Church thus conceived is an erotic community – it is here in which members come to regard themselves as desirable because they are desired by God. Williams views the perception of lovers as a mutually enforcing bond, which allows us not only to perceive the beloved as an 'occasion of joy',[39] but the self as well.

While Rowan Williams's essay offers a good deal of theological legitimation of same-sex love (although, characteristically, in an indirect manner), and indeed of sexuality in general that moves beyond the confines of marriage, it nevertheless remained idealistic about the self-evident goodness of sex and its role in the shaping of subjects. Indeed, according to Williams it is *eros* that characterises the economy of salvation and even the inner life of God. While power and control are not absent from Williams's account of the sexual encounter, this idealised account of sex falls short of examining the manner in which the members of the Church seldom regard one another as 'desired', or as an 'occasion of joy'. Indeed, the Church remains a place in which encounter across difference is often translated into the disciplining of supposedly aberrant sexual subjects. Throughout the latter part of the twentieth century, the Anglican Communion was particularly prone to decreeing narrowly prescriptive accounts of sexuality against homosexuality, which, as Christopher Brittain and Andrew MacKinnon observe, served fundamentally as its chief 'symbolic boundary marker'.[40]

## Feminist Theology

Happily, feminist theology of the twentieth century troubled just about every normative and idealist theology of sex and gender. Sexuality and gender beyond hetero-patriarchy were disinhibited and explored. Feminist theologians came to see the Church's repressive theologies of sex and gender as the bulwark of patriarchy – both within the Church and the wider society. Not only did feminist theology offer a critical perspective on theology's treatment of sex and gender, it also offered a set of constructive proposals on how Christian theology might be reformed and foundationally transformed by feminist revision.

In discussing sex and gender, feminist theology was uniquely aware of the manner in which power and violence are at the very heart of sexual and gendered relationships within patriarchy. Drawing from the insights of radical feminist theory, feminist theologians deconstructed the 'texts of terror',[41] in the Bible, which were often used to sanction violence against women, as well as the role of a patriarchal Church in creating the ideological conditions and justification for women's and children's sexual abuse. In an anthology of essays titled *Christianity, Patriarchy, and Abuse*, published in 1989, leading feminist theologians critiqued Scripture and doctrine, and their role in perpetuating women's and children's abuse.[42] Marie Fortune's critical work on sexual abuse, including sexual abuse within the Church, was a very important source for practical theology,[43] as it shed light on the ideological deployment of theology in order to enact or perpetuate abuse.

In their critical theologies, feminist theologians, like secular feminists of the Second Wave, made a clear distinction between sex and gender. Feminists viewed gender as thoroughly constructed, always to the detriment of women. Sex, on the other hand, involved natural bodily difference. Thus, feminist theology rejected any theology which purported to speak of the 'true nature' of women. According to feminist theologies, Christianity served as an ideological weapon to guarantee a diminished role of women in Church and society. Indeed, most deployments of gender within theology were virtually impervious to critique, for they were immanent to an entire symbolic system. As Rosemary Radford Ruether writes:

> The male bias of Jewish and Christian theology not only affects the teaching about woman's person, nature and role, but also generates a symbolic universe based on the patriarchal hierarchy of male over female. The subordination of woman to man is replicated in the symbolic universe in the imagery of divine–human relations. God is imaged as a great patriarch over and against the earth or Creation, imaged in female terms. Likewise Christ is related to the Church as bridegroom to bride. Divine–human relations in the macrocosm are also reflected in the microcosm of the human being. Mind over body, reason over the passions, are also seen as images of the hierarchy of the 'masculine' over the 'feminine'. Thus everywhere the Christian and the Jew are surrounded by religious symbols that ratify male domination and female subordination as the normative way of understanding the world and God.[44]

According to Ruether, gender gets inscribed and reinscribed within religious symbolism and texts creating stark and hierarchalised ordering of God and Creation, man and woman, mind and body. For Ruether and other feminist theologians, one of the chief tasks of a critical feminist theology was to challenge and undermine such dualisms and propose 'a useable past' – which might point to alternative constructions of maleness and femaleness. Much of this work sought out examples of women's leadership in the Bible or in Church history that defied gendered stereotypes, thus 'recovering alternative histories for women in religion', which attempt to 'construct a new norm for the interpretation of the tradition'.[45]

However, there is difficulty in constructing a new norm that speaks to women's experience. Once gender is unmasked as a social construct, how does one come to define woman in ways that will not perpetuate stereotypes or – worse still – ontologies of gender? For many feminist theologians, the liberating unmasking of gender in patriarchal theology gave rise to the exploration of the seemingly more immediate category of experience itself as a source for theology. However, in turning to experience, some feminist theologians unwittingly prescribed equally narrow definitions of the category of woman. Consider this description of God as Mother by Sallie McFague:

Specifically, the critical experiences expressed most adequately in these [feminine] models are ones of rebirth, nurture, unmerited love, security in God alone, compassion, forgiveness, service. If we eliminate these experiences from the Christian relationship with God or substitute nonfeminine metaphors for expressing them, we will lose, I believe, essential aspects of that relationship.[46]

So, while these new models in theology represented a transversal of the values of patriarchal relations, they nevertheless left gender stereotypes – women as compassionate, serving, nurturing and maternal – intact. Indeed, McFague even veers close to complementarity as she posits the necessity of a supplementation of feminine metaphors within Christian language about God.

In part this has to do with the normative and uncritical role of experience within some early feminist theology. As womanist theologians and others have pointed out, women's experience is often deployed in feminist theology in a normative manner, which excludes a vast range of women's lives and priorities. As Jacquelyn Grant writes:

Of course, chief among the sources is women's experience. However what is often unmentioned is that feminist theologians' sources for women's experiences refer almost exclusively to White women's experience. White women's experience and Black women's experience are not the same. Indeed all experiences are unique to some degree. But in this case the difference is so radical that it may be said that White women and Black women are in completely different realms. Slavery and segregation have created such a gulf between these women, that White feminists' common assumption that all women are in the same situation with respect to sexism is difficult to understand when history so clearly tells a different story.[47]

By the turn of the century and the ushering in of a new millennium, critiques such as these began to challenge even the concept of woman itself within feminist theology. This marked a profound shift because much of feminist theology's energy derived from a belief that knowledge about gender would unmask the problems that have inhered within Christianity since its beginning, especially its exclusionary habits and hierarchical ordering.

While minority and two-thirds-world feminists would challenge the category of women's experience, the category of woman came under further scrutiny by yet another set of critics. This time, post-structuralism would seek to deconstruct any stable conception of the self, including the categories of man and woman. By the century's end, Foucault's insights into the discursive nature of sex received a feminist revision as Judith Butler published her magisterial and game-changing *Gender Trouble*. Arguing for the discursively constructed nature of both gender *and* sex, Butler dismantles essentialism, even in feminist form, and opens the gates for a veritable parade of non-binary, unessential gendered performance which will trouble all ontologies of sex, theological and otherwise:

[T]he ostensibly natural facts of sex [are] discursively produced in the service of other political and social interests . . . If the immutable character of sex is contested, perhaps this construct called 'sex' is as culturally constructed as gender; indeed, perhaps it was always already gender, with the consequence that the distinction between sex and gender turns out to be no distinction at all.[48]

Butler prompts her readers to reconsider the meaning of sexuality. Rather than disclosing hidden secrets about the subject, sex, like gender, is continually performed and is always already amenable to the myriad of discourses that shape it. The last stronghold of essentialism – the notion that women are united not by gender, but by sex, by the self-evident properties and desires marked by bodies – would come under attack to the degree that within the final years, the markers of male and female identity were replaced by conceptions of gender fluidity, non-binarity, and queerness.

## LGBTQ Theology

The 'queering' of gender has its roots not merely in the philosophy of post-structuralism, but more immediately within the LGBTQ community, where a proliferation of expressive and often parodic performances emerged, which troubled gender binaries and uprooted gender essentialism. This includes transgender, drag, bisexual and non-binary enactments of gender. As Butler points out, 'in imitating gender, drag implicitly reveals the imitative structure of gender itself – as well as its contingency'.[49]

Within the churches, new expressions of Christian faith developed helped to challenge gender essentialism. The Metropolitan Community Church (MCC) was founded in California in 1968, and eventually spread to thirty-seven countries. MCC saw its mission as being especially directed towards Christians who are lesbian, gay, bisexual, transgender and/or queer.[50] LGBTQ Christians also took up pastoral and spiritual issues, including the AIDS crisis, which deeply affected the community from the early 1980s to the turn of the century. While many denominations were asserting that AIDS was God's punishment,[51] gay Christians were on the forefront of offering care and advocacy. Within the Catholic Church, AIDS activism centred around challenging the intransigence of Catholic prohibition on condoms, even at the height of the crisis. Groups such as ACT UP and Dignity in the United States included (in addition to vocal opposition to Catholic teaching on homosexuality) direct outreach to AIDS patients.[52]

The queering of theology in the latter part of the twentieth century led to the unmasking of sexual identity – including gay identity – and argued that the sexual self is not fixed or static but is continually situated within multiple discourses. Against the modern subject, queer theology insisted upon the subject's plasticity – that gender, sex and sexual orientation included processes of self-transformation and non-identitarian positionality. The queering of theology represented a profoundly creative shift in which no doctrinal foundation was left unturned.[53]

## Sex Scandals and the Church

The obduracy of the Roman Catholic Church in matters of sexual ethics such as condom use during the AIDS crisis appeared especially duplicitous as the sexual abuse of young people under the Church's care came to light. From the late 1980s onward, repeated and discrete cases of pedophilia were uncovered and exposed throughout the globe.[54] Many of these cases stretched far back into the earlier decades of the century. It is ironic indeed, that in a century that was given over to the uncovering of sexuality as a matter of profound theological significance, the Church had so thoroughly covered up these multiple and sustained instances of sexual violence.[55]

Although data is difficult to obtain, studies suggest that between 2 and 8 per cent of priests in the United States were involved in the sexual abuse of minors. In Canada, 8.9

per cent of clergy were found to have sexually abused or to have had sexual contact with persons under nineteen years of age, while 2.3 per cent of clergy *admitted to* having sexually violated minors under thirteen years of age.[56] In Ireland, 4 per cent of priests were accused of abusing minors sexually.[57] Although other religious organisations have also exposed instances of sexual abuse, as have secular groups, the data suggest that the incidence of sexual abuse of minors is somewhat higher in the Catholic Church, and that the unique features of this abuse (by a homogeneous group of celibate men with institutional protection and authority who preyed overwhelmingly on boys) make these cases uniquely significant.[58] Boys comprised 84 per cent of the cases identified in the United States.[59] There is no evidence that homosexuality is linked to these cases.

The Vatican was silent on this issue throughout most of the twentieth century, in spite of the growing evidence of the existence and extent of these cases. It was not until 2001 that a pope openly condemned sexual abuse, when Pope John Paul II issued a letter declaring the sexual abuse of minors to be a *delictum gravius*, or grave sin. Catholic theologians, for the most part, were slow to respond to the crisis. It was feminist theology that was best equipped at this time to offer a theological response to the crisis, having long sounded alarms about the reality of sexual abuse in the Church. However, the voices of Catholic women theologians went largely unheeded.

What is certain is that the Church frequently mishandled or covered up abuses. Why is it the case that in a century in which sexuality was explored from every angle – including and especially as a theological source – these particular cases were so thoroughly and systematically hidden from view? Perhaps it has something to do with the fact that sexual violence of this nature and magnitude could not serve the overarching narrative of the 'theology of the body'. If sex is a straightforward gift from God – one that constitutes the human subject and is indeed iconic to divine life – then how do we account for it when it is manifestly sinful and violent? How to offer a theological account of bodies, gender and sexuality – and their role in the constitution of the subject – when subjects have been made into objects?

## Conclusion

The idealistic accounts of sex and gender as disclosive of theological meaning would have to give way once the extent and reach of sexual violence was more thoroughly uncovered and once the range and scope of sexual diversity and gender contingency was further explored. However, with few exceptions, a surprisingly common theme can be identified throughout twentieth-century theology. Sex and gender were seen to be fixed and stable entities from which we could read something revelatory about the true nature of humanity and of God's blessing upon it. It will take another generation of scholars – influenced by theorists like Butler and Foucault, but also shaken by the ubiquity of sexual violence and aware of the sheer diversity and contingency of gendered bodies – to nuance this idealised and stable picture of *homo sexualis*.

In the end, we may wonder along with Foucault how posterity will judge our chief preoccupation and what alternative energies may have claimed the Church's attention during what will surely be judged to be a brutal and dismal century. We may even chide ourselves for our endless production of sex, while at the same time overlooking its reality altogether:

Perhaps one day people will wonder at this. They will not be able to understand how a civilization so intent on developing enormous instruments of production and destruction found the time and the infinite patience to inquire so anxiously concerning the actual state of sex; people will smile perhaps when they recall that here were men – meaning ourselves – who believed that therein resided a truth every bit as precious as the one they had already demanded from the earth, the stars, and the pure forms of their thought; people will be surprised at the eagerness with which we went about pretending to rouse from its slumber a sexuality which everything – our discourses, our customs, our institutions, our regulations, our knowledges – was busy producing in the light of day and broadcasting to noisy accompaniment. And people will ask themselves why we were so bent on ending the rule of silence regarding what was the noisiest of our preoccupations.[60]

# Notes

1. Michel Foucault describes the emergence of the *scientia sexualis* as an apparatus, which 'put into operation an entire machinery for producing true discourses concerning it. Not only did it speak of sex and compel everyone to do so; it also set out to formulate the universal truth of sex. As if it suspected sex of harboring a fundamental secret. As if it needed this production of truth. As if it was essential that sex be inscribed not only in an economy of pleasure but in an ordered system of knowledge.' Michel Foucault, *The History of Sexuality: An Introduction*, vol. 1, Robert Hurley (trans.) (New York: Vintage Books, 1990), p. 69.
2. Foucault, *The History of Sexuality*, p. 155.
3. Of course there is much more to be said about the twentieth century than to label it as the 'century of sex'. One might think this a trivial characterisation when one considers the range of violence and suffering that humans inflicted upon themselves and the planet during this period. I do not think, however, that an emphasis on the centrality of the human as a sexual self is unrelated to the atrocities of the twentieth century. Foucault (and later, Giorgio Agamben) discusses how the control of life in all its forms characterises an ever widening range of political power. Such 'biopower' that controls citizens' bodies through tacit and perennial discipline, surveillance and abandonment clearly relates to the century's concern with sex. Indeed, one need only look to the Nazis' eugenic and sterilisation programmes to see how the new sciences of sexuality were deployed in concert with other forms of biopower.
4. Foucault, *The History of Sexuality*, p. 35.
5. Elaine Tyler May, 'Myths and Realities of the American Family', in *A History of Private Life: Riddles of Identity in Modern Times*, edited by Antoine Prost and Gérard Vincent (Cambridge, MA: Harvard University Press, 1991), pp. 539–92: 587.
6. May, 'Myths and Realities of the American Family', p. 583.
7. May, 'Myths and Realities of the American Family', p. 587.
8. Foucault writes of the 'generative principle of meaning' which frames sexuality within modern discourses: 'It is through sex . . . that each individual has to pass in order to have access to his own intelligibility (seeing that it is both the hidden aspect and the generative principle of meaning), to the whole of his body . . . to his identity.' Foucault, *History of Sexuality*, pp. 155–6.
9. Pius XI, *Casti connubii* (31 December 1930), accessed at www.vatican.va. Italics added.
10. Thomas Aquinas, *Summa theologica*, Fathers of the English Dominican Province (trans.) (New York: Benziger Brothers, 1911–25), IIa–IIae, q. 154, art. 3, res. 3.
11. Katie Grimes, 'Butler Interprets Aquinas: How to Speak Thomistically about Sex', *Journal of Religious Ethics* 42:2 (2014), 187–215: 200.
12. Many Catholic bishops and theologians roundly criticised *Humanae vitae* for its prohibition of birth control. As Charles Curran put it: 'No single church document has caused as much reaction throughout the Catholic world as *Humanae Vitae*.' Pope Paul VI was strenuously critiqued for overturning the recommendations of the Pontifical Study Commission on Family,

Population and Birth Problems, the vast majority of which commended the use of artificial birth control. Over six hundred theologians and clergy signed a document in protest against the Church's position on this issue. See Charles Curran, 'Humanae Vitae: Fifty Years Later', *Theological Studies* 79:3 (2018), 520–42.

13. Paul VI, *Humanae vitae* (25 July 1968), accessed at www.vatican.va.
14. Curran, 'Humanae Vitae: Fifty Years Later', p. 523.
15. John Paul II, *Theology of the Body* (Boston: Pauline Books, 1997), p. 89.
16. John Paul II, *Mulieris dignitatem* (15 August 1988), accessed at www.vatican.va.
17. Balthasar, *Theo-Drama III*, p. 354.
18. In a poll taken in the United States in 1968, only 28 per cent of Catholics agreed with *Humanae vitae*'s position against contraception; 54 disagreed with the pope, and the rest claimed to have no opinion. Lesley Woodcock Tentler, *Catholics and Contraception* (Ithaca, NY: Cornell University Press, 2004), p. 266.
19. See, for example, the anti-essentialist readings of Gregory of Nyssa in Lucian Turcescu's '"Person" versus "Individual", and Other Modern Misreadings of Gregory of Nyssa"', in *Re-Thinking Gregory of Nyssa*, edited by Sarah Coakley (Malden: Blackwell, 2003), pp. 97–110, and Sarah Coakley's 'Introduction: Gender, Trinitarian Analogies, and the Pedagogy of the Song', pp. 1–14 in the same volume.
20. Sergius Bulgakov, *The Unfading Light: Contemplations and Speculations*, Thomas Allen Smith (trans.) (Grand Rapids: Eerdmans, 2012), p. 218.
21. Bulgakov, *Unfading Light*, p. 320.
22. Paul Evdokimov, *Woman and the Salvation of the World: A Christian Anthropology on the Charisms of Women* (Crestwood, NY: St. Vladimir's Seminary Press, 1994), p. 63.
23. Sarah Hinlicky Wilson, *Woman, Women and the Priesthood in the Trinitarian Theology of Elizabeth Behr-Siegel* (New York: Bloomsbury T&T Clark, 2013), p. 144.
24. See Karl Barth, *Church Dogmatics*, vol. 3, part 4, G. W. Bromiley and T. F. Torrance (eds) (New York: T&T Clark, 2004), § 54, 1, p. 143 small print: 'In the Christian community, the problem of posterity and heirs can no longer have the specific importance which it had in Israel . . .'
25. Barth, *Church Dogmatics*, vol. 3, part 4, § 54, 1, p. 121.
26. See Barth, *Church Dogmatics*, vol. 3, part 4, § 54, 1, p. 169. 'Man and woman are an A and B, and therefore cannot be equated . . . A proceeds B, and B follows A. Order means succession. It means preceding and following. It means super- and sub-ordination.'
27. Barth, *Church Dogmatics*, vol. 3, part 4, § 54, 1, p. 156. Italics added.
28. Katherine Sonderegger helpfully reads Barth cautiously as an ally to feminists, in large part because of his challenge to natural theology and his persistence in naming the socially and historically mediated nature of human experience. Nevertheless, I think that certain sections of vol. 3, part 4, such as his commentary on 1 Corinthians, cast doubt as to his ability to get out from under the shadows of natural theology and Lutheran conceptions of the orders of creation when it comes to gender. See Katherine Sonderegger, 'Barth and Feminism', in *The Cambridge Companion to Karl Barth*, edited by John Webster (Cambridge: Cambridge University Press, 2000), pp. 258–73.
29. Barth, *Church Dogmatics*, vol. 3, part 4, § 54, 1, p. 118.
30. Barth, *Church Dogmatics*, vol. 3, part 4, § 54, 1, p. 166.
31. Katherine Sonderegger draws our attention to the 'sheer delight in embodied love and life' as she cites *Church Dogmatics*, vol. 3, part 4, p. 119: 'What else can stir him so much, bringing him as he thinks – whether he be a crude or highly cultivated person – into such ecstasy, such rapture, such enthusiasm, into what seem to be the depths and essence of all being . . .?' Sonderegger, 'Barth and Feminism', p. 269.
32. Barth, Church Dogmatics, III/4 §54, 1, p. 167.
33. Barth, *Church Dogmatics*, vol. 3, part 4, §54, 1, p. 167.
34. Karl Barth, 'Vorwort', xxii n. 3, letter of 1947, cited in Christiane Tietz, 'Karl Barth and Charlotte von Kirschbaum', *Theology Today* 74:2 (July 2017), 86–111.

35. Miranda K. Hassett, *Anglican Communion in Crisis: How Episcopal Dissidents and Their African Allies Are Reshaping Anglicanism* (Princeton, NJ: Princeton University Press, 2007).

36. See Jane Shaw, 'Conflicts within the Anglican Communion', in *The Oxford Handbook of Theology, Sexuality and Gender*, edited by Adrian Thatcher (Oxford: Oxford University Press), pp. 340–56: 348.

37. This is not to suggest that African churches were unanimous in condemning homosexuality. South Africa remained one of the most constant proponents of tolerance towards sexual difference. Likewise, other parts of the globe and whole segments of North American Anglicanism/ Episcopalianism expressed support of the contending African provinces. A statement on human sexuality was composed at the 1997 pre-Lambeth consultation of the 'Anglican Encounter in the South', which met in Kuala Lumpur, which upheld biblical teaching on marriage and called upon the Communion to 'reach a common mind before embarking on radical changes to Christian discipline and moral teaching'. Kevin Ward, *A History of Global Anglicanism* (Cambridge: Cambridge University Press, 2006), p. 309.

38. Rowan Williams, 'The Body's Grace', in *Theology and Sexuality: Classic and Contemporary Readings*, edited by Eugene F. Rogers Jr (Malden: Blackwell, 2002), pp. 309–21, p. 312.

39. 'The life of the Christian community has as its rationale – if not invariably its practical reality – the task of teaching us so to order our relation that humans may see themselves as desired, as the occasion of joy. It is not surprising that sexual imagery is freely used, in and out of the Bible, for this newness of perception.' 'The Body's Grace', p. 313.

40. Christopher Craig Brittain and Andrew McKinnon, 'Homosexuality and the Construction of "Anglican Orthodoxy": The Symbolic Politics of the Anglican Communion', *Sociology of Religion* 72:3 (Autumn 2011), 351–73.

41. Phyllis Trible, *Texts of Terror: Literary-Feminist Readings of Biblical Narratives* (Philadelphia: Fortress, 1984).

42. Joanne Carlson Brown and Carole R. Bohn, *Christianity, Patriarchy, and Abuse* (Ann Arbor: University of Michigan Press, 1989).

43. Marie M. Fortune, *Sexual Violence: The Unmentionable Sin* (New York: Pilgrim Press, 1983); Carol J. Adams and Marie M. Fortune (eds), *Violence against Women and Children: A Christian Theological Sourcebook* (New York: Continuum, 1995); Marie M. Fortune, *Is Nothing Sacred? When Sex Invades the Pastoral Relationship* (San Francisco: Harper San Francisco, 1992).

44. Rosemary Radford Ruether, 'The Feminist Critique in Religious Studies', *Soundings: An Interdisciplinary Journal* 64:4 (1981), 388–402: 390.

45. Ruether, 'The Feminist Critique in Religious Studies', p. 394.

46. Sallie McFague, *Metaphorical Theology: Models of God in Religious Language* (Philadelphia: Fortress, 1982), p. 177.

47. Jacquelyn Grant, *White Women's Christ and Black Women's Jesus: Feminist Christology and Womanist Response* (Atlanta: Scholars Press, 1989), pp. 195–6.

48. Judith Butler, *Gender Trouble* (New York: Routledge, 1999), pp. 10–11.

49. Butler, *Gender Trouble*, p. 187.

50. Metropolitan Community Churches, 'Who We Are'.

51. As late as 1993, eminent evangelist Billy Graham opined that he believed AIDS to be a judgement from God. Rick Warren responded to the AIDS crisis in the late twentieth century by launching an abstinence and monogamy within heterosexual marriage campaign, which became the basis of George W. Bush's policy. See Anthony Michael Petro, *After the Wrath of God: AIDS, Sexuality and American Religion* (Oxford: Oxford University Press, 2015).

52. One of Dignity's most publicised acts was its staged protest in St Patrick's Cathedral in 1987 after a group of gay Catholics was expelled from its parish at St Francis Xavier. At the very height of the AIDS crisis, the Church called upon police to forcibly remove and bar protesters from re-entry during the 'Cathedral Project'. See Thomas F. Rzeznik, 'The Church and the AIDS Crisis in New York City', *U.S. Catholic Historian* 34:1 (2016), 143–65.

53. See Robert Goss, *Jesus Acted Up: A Gay and Lesbian Manifesto* (San Francisco: Harper San Francisco, 1994).
54. In the United States, the exposure of the extent of sexual abuse within the Catholic Church did not occur until 2002, when the *Boston Globe* published a series of articles. In Canada, the widespread abuse of minors at Mount Cashel Orphanage in Newfoundland was exposed in 1988, and the case made its way to the Supreme Court of Canada in 2003, which ruled the Catholic Church to be 'vicariously liable'.
55. For the most part, these cases were handled at an episcopal level, and bishops regularly transferred offending priests to new and unsuspecting parishes. According the 'John Jay Report', only 27 per cent of priests who were subject to an allegation had their ministry restricted. National Review Board, *A Report on the Crisis in the Catholic Church in the United States* (27 February 2004), accessed at http://www.bishop-accountability.org/reports/2004_02_27_JohnJay/index.html.
56. Marie Keenan, *Child Sexual Abuse and the Catholic Church: Gender, Power, and Organizational Culture* (New York: Oxford University Press, 2012), p. 7.
57. Keenan, *Child Sexual Abuse and the Catholic Church*, p. 8.
58. Keenan, *Child Sexual Abuse and the Catholic Church*, p. 9.
59. Keenan, *Child Sexual Abuse and the Catholic Church*, p. 12.
60. Foucault, *The History of Sexuality*, p. 58.

# Bibliography

Adams, Carol J. and Marie M. Fortune (eds), *Violence against Women and Children: A Christian Theological Sourcebook* (New York: Continuum, 1995).

Aquinas, Thomas, *Summa theologica*, Fathers of the English Dominican Province (trans.) (New York: Benziger Brothers, 1911–25).

Balthasar, Hans Urs von, *Theo-Drama: Theological Dramatic Theory*, vol. 3: *The Dramatis Personae: The Person in Christ*, Graham Harrison (trans.) (San Francisco: Ignatius Press, 1992).

Barth, Karl, *Church Dogmatics*, vol. 3, part 4, G. W. Bromiley and T. F. Torrance (eds) (New York: T&T Clark, 2004).

Brittain, Christopher Craig and Andrew McKinnon, 'Homosexuality and the Construction of "Anglican Orthodoxy": The Symbolic Politics of the Anglican Communion', *Sociology of Religion* 72:3 (Autumn 2011), 351–73.

Brown, Joanne Carlson and Carole R. Bohn, *Christianity, Patriarchy, and Abuse* (Ann Arbor: University of Michigan Press, 1989).

Bulgakov, Sergius, *The Unfading Light: Contemplations and Speculations*, Thomas Allen Smith (trans.) (Grand Rapids: Eerdmans, 2012).

Butler, Judith, *Gender Trouble* (New York: Routledge, 1999).

Coakley, Sarah, 'Introduction: Gender, Trinitarian Analogies and the Pedagogy of the Song', in *Re-Thinking Gregory of Nyssa*, edited by Sarah Coakley (Malden: Blackwell, 2003), pp. 1–14.

Coakley, Sarah (ed.), *Re-thinking Gregory of Nyssa* (Oxford: Blackwell, 2004).

Curran, Charles, '*Humanae Vitae*: Fifty Years Later', *Theological Studies* 79:3 (2018), 520–42.

Evdokimov, Paul, *Woman and the Salvation of the World: A Christian Anthropology on the Charisms of Women* (Crestwood, NY: St. Vladimir's Seminary Press, 1994).

Fortune, Marie M., *Is Nothing Sacred? When Sex Invades the Pastoral Relationship* (San Francisco: Harper San Francisco, 1992).

Fortune, Marie M., *Sexual Violence: The Unmentionable Sin* (New York: Pilgrim Press, 1983).

Foucault, Michel, *The History of Sexuality: An Introduction*, vol. 1, Robert Hurley (trans.) (New York: Vintage Books, 1990).

Goss, Robert, *Jesus Acted Up: A Gay and Lesbian Manifesto* (San Francisco: Harper San Francisco, 1994).

Grant, Jacquelyn, *White Women's Christ and Black Women's Jesus: Feminist Christology and Womanist Response* (Atlanta: Scholars Press, 1989).

Grimes, Katie, 'Butler Interprets Aquinas', *Journal of Religious Ethics* 42:2 (2014), 187–215.

Hassett, Miranda K., *Anglican Communion in Crisis: How Episcopal Dissidents and Their African Allies Are Reshaping Anglicanism* (Princeton, NJ: Princeton University Press, 2007).

John Paul II, *Mulieris dignitatem* (15 August 1988), accessed at www.vatican.va.

John Paul II, *Theology of the Body* (Boston: Pauline Books, 1997).

Keenan, Marie, *Child Sexual Abuse and the Catholic Church: Gender, Power, and Organizational Culture* (New York: Oxford University Press, 2012).

McFague, Sallie, *Metaphorical Theology: Models of God in Religious Language* (Philadelphia: Fortress, 1982).

May, Elaine Tyler, 'Myths and Realities of the American Family', in *A History of Private Life: Riddles of Identity in Modern Times*, edited by Antoine Prost and Gérard Vincent (Cambridge, MA: Harvard University Press, 1991), pp. 539–92.

Metropolitan Community Churches, 'Who We Are', accessed at https://www.mcchurch.org/over view/.

National Review Board, *A Report on the Crisis in the Catholic Church in the United States* (27 February 2004), accessed at http://www.bishop-accountability.org/reports/2004_02_27_JohnJay/index .html.

Paul VI, *Humanae vitae* (25 July 1968), accessed at www.vatican.va.

Petro, Anthony Michael, *After the Wrath of God: AIDS, Sexuality and American Religion* (Oxford: Oxford University Press, 2015).

Pius XI, *Casti connubii* (31 December 1930), accessed at www.vatican.va.

Ruether, Rosemary Radford, 'The Feminist Critique in Religious Studies', *Soundings: An Interdisciplinary Journal* 64:4 (1981), 388–402.

Rzeznik, Thomas F., 'The Church and the AIDS Crisis in New York City', *U.S. Catholic Historian* 34:1 (2016), 143–65.

Shaw, Jane, 'Conflicts within the Anglican Communion', in *The Oxford Handbook of Theology, Sexuality and Gender*, edited by Adrian Thatcher (Oxford: Oxford University Press), pp. 340–56.

Sonderegger, Katherine, 'Barth and Feminism', in *The Cambridge Companion to Karl Barth*, edited by John Webster (Cambridge: Cambridge University Press, 2000), pp. 258–73.

Tentler, Lesley Woodcock, *Catholics and Contraception* (Ithaca, NY: Cornell University Press, 2004).

Thatcher, Adrian, *The Oxford Handbook of Theology and Sexuality* (Oxford: Oxford University Press, 2015).

Tietz, Christiane, 'Karl Barth and Charlotte von Kirschbaum', *Theology Today* 74:2 (July 2017), 86–111.

Trible, Phyllis, *Texts of Terror: Literary-Feminist Readings of Biblical Narratives* (Philadelphia: Fortress, 1984).

Turcescu, Lucian, '"Person" versus "Individual", and Other Modern Misreadings of Gregory of Nyssa', in *Re-Thinking Gregory of Nyssa*, edited by Sarah Coakley (Malden: Blackwell, 2003), pp. 97–110.

Ward, Kevin, *A History of Global Anglicanism* (Cambridge: Cambridge University Press, 2006).

Williams, Rowan, 'The Body's Grace', in *Theology and Sexuality: Classic and Contemporary Readings*, edited by Eugene F. Rogers Jr (Malden: Blackwell, 2002), pp. 309–21.

Wilson, Sarah Hinlicky, *Woman, Women and the Priesthood in the Trinitarian Theology of Elizabeth Behr-Siegel* (New York: Bloomsbury T&T Clark, 2013).

# 18

# Hope

*Judith Wolfe*

## Introduction

A guiding hypothesis of this series is that theology has opened up new ways of thinking about history which enable, indeed demand, a fresh consideration both of the development of theological thought and of its shaping role in the intellectual and public sphere at large. No subject within Christian theology is more explicitly concerned with the question of how to think about history than eschatology: that is, the Christian hope for 'the last things'. For most of Christian history, the biblical promise of Christ's Second Coming, followed by the resurrection of the dead, the Last Judgement and the advent of the heavenly Jerusalem, guided people's understanding both of their own actions and of the times they lived in. That promise had both a moral and a historical dimension. Morally, it set all actions within the purview of an omniscient judgement to come: regardless of current inequalities and deceptions, at the last the all-seeing God would weigh all deeds and judge all people equitably. Historically, the promise ordered all events within a divine drama leading through anguish to triumph: suffering, humiliation and persecution were no more than the biblically foretold birth pangs of the messianic kingdom. Throughout Christian history, religious conflicts arose from disagreements about how rightly to map biblical prophecy on to the present time: whether, for example, the pope should be understood as the vicar of Christ presiding over the thousand-year messianic reign preceding the Second Coming, or as the Antichrist beguiling the faithful. But these disputes did not touch the explanatory framework itself. The pressing religious question, in other words, was not whether the drama of life and history was plotted, but only what role each was playing in it.

The Enlightenment, challenging the reliability of revelation as a source of historical and metaphysical knowledge, inevitably changed this. After all, the last things were paradigmatically *revealed* knowledge. It was from the dominical sayings and actions, and from biblical (and sometimes extra-biblical) prophecy, that the divine plan of salvation and judgement was known. The Enlightenment crisis of revelation was therefore, as much as anything, a crisis of eschatology. From Kant and Schleiermacher onwards, theologians no longer felt able to rely solely on biblical testimony for their assessment of moral action or their expectation of the direction and end of history. Instead, they tried to find supposedly more reliable sources of knowledge about the last things (still framed in broadly biblical terms) in reason and experience. This led to a large-scale shift, shaping much of nineteenth-century thought, from understanding the eschatological kingdom foretold by Scripture as the act of a transcendent God judging his creation, to reading it as the outworking of an intrinsic movement of creation in which God was seen, to some extent, to be immanent as a guiding world spirit.

In the traditional view of an ordaining God, it had been questions of judgement that loomed largest in eschatology; in the imagination of an indwelling world spirit, it was questions of potentiality. Nineteenth-century eschatology, from Schleiermacher to Ritschl, was dominated by a theological optimism about the continuation of human progress beyond death or crisis, and a corresponding scepticism about traditional doctrines such as the eternal duration of post-mortal punishment in hell.[1] However, first shock waves went through this consensus towards the end of the century, and it irreparably broke amid the crisis of the First World War. They began with biblical scholars such as Franz Overbeck, Albert Schweitzer and the History of Religions School, who recalled their peers to the *disruptive* character of biblical eschatology: to the basic clash between the New Testament vision of Christ coming to defeat the forces of evil ravaging the world, and a meliorist understanding of life and history as moving towards a peaceable kingdom.

At first, this argument about biblical eschatology was mainly an academic one, in the sense that it seemed to have few practical implications. Most of the scholars who raised it regarded the biblical vision as untenable in the modern world, and concluded, if anything, that contemporary Christianity must leave its apocalyptic beginnings behind, not that it should return to them. But when the crises culminating in the First World War shattered Europeans' confidence in the upward movement of history, theologians returned to the disruptive vision of biblical eschatology out of more than merely academic interest. The question that twentieth-century eschatology saw itself as called upon to answer was whether and how God could be seen to work in history after theology's loss of faith both in divine intervention and in divine immanence.

## Eschatological Responses to the Crisis of Europe and the First World War

As just suggested, the late nineteenth- and early twentieth-century emphasis of the History of Religions School on the apocalyptic character of the New Testament was not, at least initially, motivated by a desire to retrieve it. Rather, it arose from a commitment to historicism. In engaging this commitment, English-language scholarship has a serious terminological problem, namely the translation as 'historicism' of two antithetical German concepts: *Historizismus* and *Historismus*. 'Historicism' in the first sense is a common description of Hegel's grand theory of history's dialectical progress towards the self-realisation of spirit. 'Historicism' in the second sense, by contrast, is the name of the philosophy of history emerging in the late nineteenth and early twentieth century as a repudiation of Hegelian and other strongly teleological accounts of historical development. Led by Wilhelm Dilthey, Wilhelm Windelband, Heinrich Rickert and others, historicists (in this second sense) stressed the unique contexts, pressures and actors of each historical era, which, they contended, made overarching theories of progress like Hegel's impossible.

When we speak of the historicism of the History of Religions School, it is in this second sense. Its aim was to uncover the particular circumstances of, actors within and influences on Christianity in its historical development. While Hegelian theologies tended to assert a historical trajectory culminating in an immanentised eschaton, 'eschatology' within historicist approaches was seen, rather, as a mark of the primitive apocalyptic mindset that irretrievably *separated* early Christianity from enlightened Christendom. For Johann

Weiss and Albert Schweitzer, for example, Jesus preached an imminent end of history which did not in fact arrive; later Christianity was forced to construct an institutional system of power, thought and ethics on the ruins of a disappointed eschatological expectation. Primitive eschatology or apocalypticism, for the History of Religions scholars, therefore merely confirmed the historicist thesis that even religions must be seen within their particular historical contexts, rather than as timeless deposits of faith or highways to the fulfilment of history.

The Roman Catholic Church soundly rejected the thesis of a disjunction between early apocalyptic expectation and later Church establishment in its 1907 syllabus of the errors of modernism, *Lamentabili*.[2] For the development of Protestant theology amid the crises attending and following the First World War, however, that thesis proved decisive. Most influential for this development was the formulation of the disjunction thesis put forward by the New Testament scholar Franz Overbeck (1837–1905). Overbeck had argued in his important (but now often forgotten) book *Über die Christlichkeit unserer heutigen Theologie* ('On the Christianness of Present-Day Theology', 1873, 2nd ed. 1902) that an absolute contrast prevailed between the ascetic apocalypticism of the earliest Christians, which represented a radical rejection of any hope of salvation within world and time, and the subsequent establishment of a Christian theology and Church, which 'secularised' and 'historicised' the Church. This later historicisation, he thought, was not only a departure from earliest Christian belief, but remained betrayal and self-deception, because it assumed the impossible possibility of a domestication of faith by reason, and of achieving within history what could only be attained by its End.[3]

What consequences Overbeck drew from this conclusion remained a matter of fierce debate among his readers. His philosophical admirers, including Friedrich Nietzsche (who was a close friend) and Martin Heidegger, understood him to have concluded that the Christian faith had, in the ruins of imminent eschatological expectation, simply become impossible. The young Karl Barth, by contrast, read Overbeck as having cleared the ground for a radical expectation of the inbreaking of God into the individual's life against and apart from all human securities and establishments. Whichever interpretation was more faithful, Overbeck's thesis crystallises the challenge of eschatology as it presented itself to theologians amid and after the First World War. History, they conceded, would not move confidently towards fulfilment. If there was to be eschatological judgement or fulfilment of any kind, therefore, it might resemble the apocalyptic vision of the Bible more than that of immanentist optimism. Eschatological fulfilment, in other words, must be seen not as completing but as *opposing* the flow of history: either by revolutionary force, or by eliding history altogether.

Between the wars, enormous theological energy was generated by the second, anti-political strategy of elision. The exegetical argument for the disruptive character of New Testament eschatology – its proclamation of an inbreaking God who would make 'all things new' – became a decisive theological resource for those who opposed the liberal theological establishment: emerging thinkers including Karl Barth, Eduard Thurneysen, Friedrich Gogarten and Rudolf Bultmann. In his commentary on the Epistle to the Romans of 1919 (2nd ed. 1922), Karl Barth, then still a young pastor in Switzerland, read Romans as a call for radical reorientation. In the second edition, revised largely in response to reading Overbeck,[4] he framed this call as a thoroughgoing eschatology. When the Kingdom of God came, he declared, it would bring about 'the dissolution of all things, the cessation of all becoming, the passing away of this world's time'.[5] As long as history continued, the 'end of time' analogously signified 'time's qualitative limitation through eternity' – the memorably phrased 'rock-face' of eternity always overhanging temporality.[6] This 'rock-face' demanded a surrender of human orders of being and knowing already in the now: an acknowledgement that humans had no ground to stand on and no language to speak of the God who was infinitely other, and who encountered humans perpendicularly to, rather than within, the worldly sphere.

The same year, Barth, Thurneysen and Gogarten launched a theological journal eschatologically entitled *Zwischen den Zeiten* (*Between the Ages*), deliberately opposing the liberally optimistic *Christliche Welt* (*Christian World*). In its issues, they and their colleagues developed what soon came to be known as dialectical theology, registering the irreducible dialectic articulated in Barth's commentary on Romans between eternity and time, God and humans, the content and method of theology. A particularly influential variant of these investigations was the New Testament exegesis of Rudolf Bultmann, who had been acquainted with Barth since before the war, and remained a collaborator until about 1930. In the late 1920s, he published a series of readings of the fourth gospel in *Zwischen den Zeiten*, most importantly 'The Eschatology of the Gospel of John' (1928). Here, Bultmann identified as the central impetus of John's Gospel an eschatological dynamic that eschewed the dramatic apocalypticism of other New Testament texts in favour of an 'eschatological now' which opened up – every moment anew – a possible new future. In his Gifford Lectures of 1954/5, Bultmann would distil this perspective in his famous declaration, 'In every moment slumbers the possibility of being the eschatological moment. You must awaken it.'

The dialectical theologians presented eschatology as both an affirmation and a radical revaluation of historicist relativism. History, in its determination by causal chains and the play and jostle of human wills, was separated by an 'infinite qualitative difference' from the eternal will of God, which could therefore manifest itself only as history's crisis, not as its redemption. The eschatological inbreaking of God, for them, effected the redemption of the individual from time, rather than the redemption of time. Bultmann would later state provocatively that with the cross, the definitive crisis of all reality, 'History has reached its end'. The Church 'is the community of the end-time, an eschatological phenomenon . . . The consciousness of being the eschatological community is at the same time the consciousness of being taken out of the still existing world.'[7]

This 'eschatology of the absolute moment', as Ernst Troeltsch critically described it,[8] remained a dominant paradigm for several decades. Its proponents took the anti-political stance demanded by their position seriously, and resolutely demonstrated its force in the face of the Nazi regime, erecting the Barmen Declaration and the Confessing Church against all political eschatologies. Nevertheless, their eschatology was accused, with justification, of taking too seriously the historicism of their time. One of their most incisive critics was Barth's friend Erik Peterson. To claim that eternity confronts humans perpendicularly to the relativities of history, Peterson contended, was not to overcome but rather to cede the battleground to historicism, surrendering the central Christian proclamation of a new age, and so abandoning the only position from which false political theologies could be effectively exposed and resisted.

Peterson (1890–1960) was one of Germany's most promising historical theologians, whose much-discussed conversion to Roman Catholicism in 1930 was hailed by the pontifical nuncio as the Church's gain of 'the best Catholic theologian of Germany'.[9] But the conversion lost Peterson his Chair of New Testament and Church History in Bonn, and despite constant writing and lecturing, he lived in poverty on the margins of academic theology until his appointment to a professorship in patristics at the Pontifical Institute for Christian Archaeology in Rome in 1947. Peterson's eschatology – directed equally against dialectical theology and against the political theology of his friend Carl Schmitt – has excited German scholars in recent decades, but has barely yet registered in English.[10]

Peterson's very different interpretation of Paul's Epistle to the Romans (published in 1925) announces a theological option that engages historicism head-on rather than affirming and revaluing it. It begins by explicitly rejecting the ahistorical eschatological community Bultmann envisions: 'We are not called, justified and glorified away from "history"', declares Peterson. If this were the case – 'if everything is eternally the same and unchanging, and human nature forever caught in the play of original sin' – then Christ need not have come in history. '[N]o old aeon need have ended nor a new aeon begun with Christ's enthronement.'[11] In fact, however, we are called precisely 'by the Christ who has inaugurated a new aeon'.[12]

This new aeon, for Peterson, is manifested in the 'eschatological publicity' of the Church, above all its celebration of the Eucharist as an anticipation of the eschatological feast of the Body of Christ. The anticipatory dimension is decisive here: the Church, though intended by Christ, is not simply identical with the messianic kingdom announced by Jesus, but always involves an 'eschatological reserve'.[13] This 'reserve' or 'not yet' is the inverse of Carl Schmitt's notorious *katechon*, the force of empire which, for Schmitt, keeps the Antichrist at bay.[14]

Political theologies like those discussed by Schmitt therefore amount, for Peterson, to false eschatologies. In Peterson's most influential tract, 'Monotheism as a Political Problem' (1935), he presents a historical study of patristic attitudes to the Roman Empire. Public theologians such as Eusebius and Ambrose praised the empire as the fulfilment of apocalyptic prophecies of the peace of the nations, transposing these from an eschatological into a historical and political register.[15] The empire, uniting the civilised world under a single ruler, seemed to them the proper earthly realisation and extension of the divine monarchy. For Peterson, this distorts both Christian monotheism and Christian eschatology. 'Monotheism', Peterson writes with portentous contemporary reference, here becomes 'a political imperative, a piece of *Reichspolitik*'.[16] In reality, he continues, Christian monotheism must forever be a '"revolt" in the metaphysical and political order': its Trinitarian form of unity 'ha[s] no correspondence in the created order', and therefore cannot be adduced to legitimate any political regime.[17] Accordingly, Augustine's two cities must remain distinct, and the eschatological peace be deferred until the full manifestation of the City of God.[18]

## Eschatological Hope after the Second World War

The attrition of the Second World War changed the character of eschatological thought. Early twentieth-century eschatologies had been propelled by a perceived gulf between the early Church and the present. In the concentration and prison camps of the 1930s and 40s, the experience of the earliest Christians – afflicted but not crushed, perplexed but not despairing, persecuted but not forsaken, carrying in the body the death of Jesus[19] – turned from irrecoverable 'then' to pressing 'now'.

In this context, the dominant mood of eschatology became hope, and its dominant theme the power of God's future to transform humanity's past and present. The leading theologians of this new generation were Jürgen Moltmann (b. 1926) and Wolfhart Pannenberg (1928–2014), both wartime converts to Christianity: one as a prisoner of war, the other through a teacher who had been part of the Confessing Church. Both Moltmann and Pannenberg built their accounts of history on the recognition that the 'eschatology of the absolute moment' of the dialectical theologians did not reject history per se, but history on its specifically historicist (*historistisch*) construction. They endeavoured not to confirm this history-denying eschatology, but to reimagine history as anticipatory of God's coming.[20]

Both Moltmann and Pannenberg, therefore, reverse the causal relationship between past and future, arguing that the future is not determined by past actions and happenings, but rather comes to determine the meaning of the past from its end. This claim is under-written by a belief in the biblical revelation of an eschatological kingdom, in which every tear will be wiped dry and God will be 'all in all'.[21] The retroactive power of this kingdom has been manifested in the resurrection of the crucified Christ, which revealed him as the Son of God and took up his ignominious death into the glory of God's salvation. Christ's resurrection is the promise and condition of the general resurrection to come, which will reveal those raised as adopted children of God and take up their perishable bodies into glory.[22]

Moltmann's and Pannenberg's approaches to this central conviction differed in char-acter. Moltmann's dominant philosophical influences were Left Hegelians and Marxists, especially Ernst Bloch, whose *Principle of Hope* (1954–9) became the model of Moltmann's epoch-defining *Theology of Hope* (1964). Against all Hegelians, however, Moltmann insisted that the future's power of transformation resulted not from the laws of history, but from the free act and promise of God. Resurrection may be dialectically related to death, but it does not emerge from it: rather, it is the gift of a sovereign God, who acts from beyond the range of immanent possibility.

The proper human response to this divine act and promise is hope resulting in action, overcoming paralysis. This hope is not (like Bloch's) utopian, but messianic:[23] it is directed not towards the unfolding of possibilities implicit in the present, but towards God's prom-ise to come, arousing our longing to 'go out' and meet him.[24] Such longing is a confession at once of need and of trust in the crucified Christ, who has already met us in the midst of suffering.[25] His eschatological kingdom is therefore not divorced from our experiences of defeat and weakness, but their transfiguration: 'The raised Christ is the crucified Christ and no other, but he is the crucified Christ in transfigured form (Phil 3.21).'[26]

Pannenberg's Hegelianism differs from Moltmann's, and his eschatology is concerned less with the dynamics of hope than the metaphysics of futurity. In the programmatic collection *Revelation as History* (1961), Pannenberg argues that divine revelation, though concentrated in particular words and events, encompasses nothing less than the whole of history. This is because God's revelation is not a matter of isolated information, but of self-communication, extending outward from his intra-Trinitarian relations to the free act of creation, whose completion will be the ingathering of creatures into communion with himself.

This consummation, like the initial act of creation, is not (*contra* Hegel) a dialectical process but a gift of divine love. Its outworking, though assured, is not predictable. This implies, among other things, that the meaning of history remains fragmentary and ambig-uous until it is gathered into God's kingdom. More radically, Pannenberg's prioritisation of eschatological consummation suggests that the nature of created realities, including humans, is not readily available in the present, but is determined by their end, which is reached through the drawing of God's love, and the voice of his calling.[27]

But, though not simply predictable, the consummation of God's self-revelation is already proleptically present in Christ, whose kenotic self-surrender unites divinity and humanity: it is an outworking, under human conditions, of his eternal submission to the Father's *monarchia*, as well as a disclosure of the human vocation to such obedience. That Pannenberg believes Christ's mode of divinity simultaneously to disclose perfected humanity indicates that he regards openness to God as the heart of human personhood. Indeed, Christ's life, death, resurrection and awaited return press an understanding of 'humanity' not as an intransigent, circumscribed 'nature', but as an eschatologically determined identity. As Paul suggests, human personhood will be fulfilled in eternal life with God, foreshadowed and enabled by Christ's resurrection: 'You have died, and your life is hidden with Christ in God. When Christ who is your life is revealed, then you also will be revealed with him in glory.'[28]

For both Moltmann and Pannenberg, in their different ways, the eschatological future is thus neither an extension of time nor perpendicular or parallel to it, but transforms time retroactively.

> When God comes in his glory . . . he will fill the universe with his radiance [and] swallow up death for ever. This future is God's mode of being in history. The power of the future is his power in time. His eternity is not timeless simultaneity; it is the power of his future over every historical time.[29]

Within this joint horizon, Pannenberg's emphasis is on the completion of identity, Moltmann's on the sublation of suffering. The sublating power of the Resurrection, Moltmann insists, transforms but does not erase the suffering of the cross: 'All Christian resurrection eschatology has the character of an *eschatologia crucis*.'[30] For both theologians, as for those who followed them, especially Robert Jenson,

> what is eschatologically new, itself creates its own continuity, since it does not annihilate the old but gathers it up and creates it anew. It is not that another creation takes the place of this one: '*this* perishable nature must put on the imperishable, and *this* mortal nature must put on immortality' (1 Cor 15.53).[31]

## Eschatological Prospects in the Late Twentieth Century

In the later twentieth century, movements of political and social emancipation, inflected by Moltmann's future-oriented eschatology, inspired Latin American, Black and other liberation theologies, which engaged eschatological promises as programmes of political and social transformation.[32] The vitality of these theologies continued into the twenty-first century, and has challenged traditional modes of exegesis, reasoning and communal action in the Church.

In the late twentieth century, academic theology (along with other cultural discourses) also began to take note on a wide scale of debates that had begun in the literary sphere earlier in the century.[33] Increasingly, ultimate matters that had been entirely out of human hands appeared practically possible, and threatened, or promised, to bring an end to the world as hitherto known. By the end of the twentieth century, these possibilities included unprecedented destruction: the devastation of the world through atomic weapons; depletion of resources or human-influenced climate change; the annihilation of cultures by economic, technological or medical disasters spreading unstoppably through a closely connected globe. Conversely, they promised a conceivable evolutionary leap: the inauguration of a 'brave new world' through death-defeating human enhancement or artificial superintelligence. The continuing advance of such possibilities engendered a widespread and inchoate apocalyptic imagination: a collective sense, marking politics, technology, art and common culture, of living at the far edge of familiar history.

Within these horizons, traditional Christian eschatology was apt to seem either insidious or obsolete. In the face of existential threats, the West's 'unquestioned orientation towards the future of its own projects'[34] was widely criticised as a failed project enabled by a Christian view of history as oriented towards a better future. As Christoph Schwöbel so memorably put it,

> The mood in the West was marked by the image of a planet threatened by the projects of its human inhabitants, who had striven to secure their future in ways that put under threat the conditions of having a future at all.[35]

Conversely, in the face of hitherto unimaginable possibility, the Christian promise of eternal happiness was dismissed by many as the immature first sketch of a mature secular achievement. Genetic engineering and other forms of bioenhancement, if extended to humans, would make it possible for them to transcend human boundaries that had so far been addressed primarily in a religious register. Alongside biotechnology, the progress of digital technology made conceivable the development of artificial superintelligence that would outstrip the limitations of organic existence altogether.

Late twentieth-century eschatology was thus shaped by the felt pressure of an urgent need for interdisciplinarity beyond the humanities. Rather than by questions of history and philosophy, theological responses were compelled by the challenges of biology, cosmology and technology. These responses largely abandoned the speculative reach of earlier twentieth-century accounts, and focused instead on clarifying the scope of theological claims vis-à-vis the expanding range of scientific and technological possibilities.[36] Conversely, ascendant speculative theologies largely sidelined eschatology: most thinkers associated with Radical Orthodoxy, for instance, dissolved eschatology into participationist accounts of creation in which eschatological fullness was already available in the present.[37] The dispersion of eschatology from systematic theology to the interdisciplinary arena (especially the growing field of science and religion, but also political theology) was balanced by a renewed interest in the concrete eschatology of the New Testament by biblical scholars.[38]

At the close of the twentieth century, academic theology had not yet risen to the challenge of responding to the generation's apocalyptic imagination in relevant and distinctly theological ways. The integration of earlier eschatological speculation, new scientific data and theories, and renewed attention to biblical eschatology was one of the challenges that defined eschatological work in the early twenty-first century.

## Notes

1. I have given a fuller account of nineteenth-century developments in Christian eschatology in Judith Wolfe, 'Eschatology', in *The Oxford Handbook of Nineteenth-Century Christian Thought*, edited by Joel Rasmussen, Judith Wolfe and Johannes Zachhuber (Oxford: Oxford University Press, 2017).
2. Pius X, *Lamentabili sane exitu* (Vatican, 1907), para. 52.
3. Franz Overbeck, *Über die Christlichkeit unserer heutigen Theologie* (Leipzig: C. G. Naumann, 1873); published in English as *How Christian Is Our Present-Day Theology?*, Martin Henry (trans.) (London: T&T Clark, 2005).

4. Karl Barth, *The Epistle to the Romans*, Edwyn C. Hoskyns (trans.), 6th ed. (Oxford: Oxford University Press, 1968), Preface, pp. 3–5.

5. Karl Barth, 'Biblische Fragen, Einblicke und Aussichten' (1920 address to the Aarau Student Conference), in *Die Anfänge der dialektischen Theologie*, edited by Jürgen Moltmann (Munich: C. Kaiser, 1962), vol. 1, pp. 49–76: 74; see also Bruce L. McCormack, *Karl Barth's Critically Realistic Dialectical Theology: Its Genesis and Development 1909–1936*, 2nd ed. (Oxford: Oxford University Press, 1997), p. 208.

6. Quoted in Jürgen Moltmann, *The Coming of God: Christian Eschatology*, Margaret Kohl (trans.) (London: SCM Press, 1996), p. 15.

7. Rudolf Bultmann, *History and Eschatology* (Edinburgh: Edinburgh University Press, 1957), p. 43.

8. Ernst Troeltsch, 'An Apple from the Tree of Kierkegaard', in *The Beginnings of Dialectical Theology*, edited by James M. Robinson, vol. 1 (Richmond, VA: John Knox Press, 1968), pp. 311–16.

9. Barbara Nichtweiß, *Erik Peterson: Neue Sicht auf Leben und Werk* (Freiburg: Herder, 1992), p. 726.

10. See esp. Kurt Anglet, *Messianität und Geschichte: Walter Benjamins Konstruktion der historischen Dialektik und deren Aufhebung ins Eschatologische durch Erik Peterson* (Berlin: Oldenbourg Akademieverlag, 1995); Barbara Nichtweiß (ed.), *Vom Ende der Zeit: Geschichtstheologie und Eschatologie bei Erik Peterson. Symposium Mainz 2000* (Münster: LIT Verlag, 2001); Roger Mielke, *Eschatologische Öffentlichkeit: Öffentlichkeit der Kirche und politische Theologie im Werk von Erik Peterson* (Göttingen: Vandenhoeck & Ruprecht, 2012); Christian Stoll, *Die Öffentlichkeit der Christus-Krise: Erik Petersons eschatologischer Kirchenbegriff im Kontext der Moderne* (Paderborn: Ferdinand Schöningh, 2017). English-language engagement with Peterson's eschatology has been sparse and conducted mainly in the context of Carl Schmitt scholarship, inspired mainly by Giorgio Agamben, *The Kingdom and the Glory: For a Theological Genealogy of Economy and Government*, Lorenzo Chiesa (trans.) (Stanford: Stanford University Press, 2011); see, for example, Miguel Vatter, 'The Political Theology of Carl Schmitt', in *The Oxford Handbook of Carl Schmitt*, edited by Jens Meierhenrich and Oliver Simons (Oxford: Oxford University Press, 2017), pp. 245–66.

11. Erik Peterson, *Der Brief an die Römer*, Barbara Nichtweiß (ed.), Ausgewählte Schriften 6 (Würzburg: Echter, 2012), p. 12.

12. Peterson, *Der Brief an die Römer*, p. 12.

13. In claiming this, Peterson makes constructive use of Alfred Loisy's provocative quip, 'Jésus annonçait le Royaume et c'est l'Église qui est venue'; see Erik Peterson, 'The Church' [1928–9], in *Theological Tractates*, Michael J. Hollerich (trans.) (Stanford: Stanford University Press, 2011), pp. 30–9; see also Kurt Anglet, *Der eschatologische Vorbehalt: Eine Denkfigur Erik Petersons* (Paderborn: Ferdinand Schoeningh, 2000).

14. See Carl Schmitt, *The Nomos of the Earth in the International Law of the Jus Publicum Europaeum*, G. L. Ulmen (trans.) (Candor, NY: Telos Press, 2006), pp. 59–60; Schmidt, 'The Return of the Katechon: Giorgio Agamben Contra Erik Peterson'. The term *katechon* is taken from 2 Thessalonians 2:6–7.

15. Erik Peterson, 'Monotheism as a Political Problem' [1935], in *Theological Tractates*, Michael J. Hollerich (trans.) (Stanford: Stanford University Press, 2011), pp. 68–105: 94–5.

16. Peterson, 'Monotheism as a Political Problem', p. 102.

17. Peterson, 'Monotheism as a Political Problem', pp. 103–4.

18. Peterson, 'Monotheism as a Political Problem', pp. 104–5.

19. See 2 Cor. 4:8–10.

20. See Jürgen Moltmann, *Theology of Hope: On the Ground and the Implications for a Christian Eschatology*, James W. Leitch (trans.) (London: SCM Press, 1967), pp. 45–51; see also Georg Essen, *Geschichtstheologie und Eschatologie in der Moderne: Eine Grundlegung* (Münster: LIT Verlag, 2011), p. 40.

21. See Rev. 21:4 and 1 Cor. 15:28.

22. See 1 Cor. 15:42–55 and Rom. 8:19.
23. See Judith Wolfe, 'Messianism', in *The Oxford Handbook of Theology and Modern European Thought*, edited by Nicholas Adams, George Pattison and Graham Ward (Oxford: Oxford University Press, 2013), pp. 301–23: 302.
24. See Jürgen Moltmann, 'Foreword', in M. Douglas Meeks, *Origins of the Theology of Hope* (Philadelphia: Augsburg Fortress, 1974), p. xiv.
25. See Jürgen Moltmann, *The Crucified God: The Cross of Christ as the Foundation and Criticism of Christian Theology*, R. A. Wilson and John Bowden (trans.) (London: SCM Press, 1973).
26. Moltmann, *The Coming of God*, p. 29.
27. Cf. T. S. Eliot, 'Little Gidding', V.240.
28. Col. 3:3–4.
29. Moltmann, *The Coming of God*, p. 24.
30. Moltmann, *Theology of Hope*, p. 83.
31. Moltmann, *The Coming of God*, p. 29; see also Robert Jenson, *Systematic Theology*, vol. 2 (Oxford: Oxford University Press, 1999), part 7.
32. See, for example, Gustavo Gutiérrez, *A Theology of Liberation: History, Politics and Salvation* (Maryknoll, NY: Orbis, 1973); James H. Cone, *Black Theology of Liberation* (Maryknoll, NY: Orbis, 1970), pp. 137–52; James H. Cone, *God of the Oppressed*, rev. ed. (Maryknoll, NY: Orbis, 1997); see also Vítor Westhelle, 'Liberation Theology', in *The Oxford Handbook of Eschatology*, edited by Jerry L. Walls (Oxford: Oxford University Press, 2007), pp. 311–27.
33. Mid-century examples include the debates between Olaf Stapledon, J. B. S. Haldane and C. S. Lewis on trans- and post-humanism. See e.g. Olaf Stapledon, *Last and First Men* (London: Methuen, 1930); J. B. S. Haldane, *Possible Worlds and Other Essays* (London: Chatto & Windus, 1927); C. S. Lewis, *That Hideous Strength* (Oxford: The Bodley Head, 1945). See also Aldous Huxley, *Brave New World* (London: Chatto & Windus, 1932).
34. Christoph Schwöbel, 'Last Things First? The Century of Eschatology in Retrospect', in *Future as God's Gift: Explorations in Christian Eschatology*, edited by David Fergusson and Marcel Sarot (Edinburgh: T&T Clark, 2000), pp. 217–41: 235.
35. Schwöbel, 'Last Things First?', p. 235.
36. See e.g. Polkinghorne and Welker (eds), *The End of the World and the Ends of God: Science and Theology on Eschatology* (London: Continuum, 2000).
37. See e.g. John Milbank, *Being Reconciled: Ontology and Pardon* (London: Routledge, 2003).
38. In very different forms, these included J. Christiaan Beker, J. Louis Martyn, Beverly Gaventa, Martinus C. de Boer, and N. T. Wright, further scholars following them in the early twenty-first century.

# Bibliography

Agamben, Giorgio, *The Kingdom and the Glory: For a Theological Genealogy of Economy and Government*, Lorenzo Chiesa (trans.) (Stanford: Stanford University Press, 2011).

Anglet, Kurt, *Der eschatologische Vorbehalt: Eine Denkfigur Erik Petersons* (Paderborn: Ferdinand Schoeningh, 2000).

Anglet, Kurt, *Messianität und Geschichte: Walter Benjamins Konstruktion der historischen Dialektik und deren Aufhebung ins Eschatologische durch Erik Peterson* (Berlin: Oldenbourg Akademieverlag, 1995).

Barth, Karl, 'Biblische Fragen, Einblicke und Aussichten' (1920 address to the Aarau Student Conference), (1920 address to the Aarau Student Conference), in *Die Anfänge der dialektischen Theologie*, edited by Jürgen Moltmann (Munich: C. Kaiser, 1962), vol. 1, pp. 49–76.

Barth, Karl, *The Epistle to the Romans*, Edwyn C. Hoskyns (trans.), 6th ed. (Oxford: Oxford University Press, 1968).

Bloch, Ernst, *The Principle of Hope*, Stephen Plaice, Paul Knight and Neville Plaice (trans.), 3 vols (Cambridge, MA: MIT Press, [1954–9] 1995).

Bultmann, Rudolf, *History and Eschatology* (Edinburgh: Edinburgh University Press, 1957).

Cone, James H., *Black Theology of Liberation* (Maryknoll, NY: Orbis, 1970).

Cone, James H., *God of the Oppressed*, rev. ed. (Maryknoll, NY: Orbis, 1997).

Eliot, T. S., *Four Quartets* (London: Faber & Faber, 2001).

Essen, Georg, *Geschichtstheologie und Eschatologie in der Moderne: Eine Grundlegung* (Münster: LIT Verlag, 2011).

Gutiérrez, Gustavo, *A Theology of Liberation: History, Politics and Salvation* (Maryknoll, NY: Orbis, 1973).

Haldane, J. B. S., *Possible Worlds and Other Essays* (London: Chatto & Windus, 1927).

Huxley, Aldous, *Brave New World* (London: Chatto & Windus, 1932).

Jenson, Robert, *Systematic Theology*, vol. 2 (Oxford: Oxford University Press, 1999).

Lewis, C. S., *That Hideous Strength* (Oxford: The Bodley Head, 1945).

McCormack, Bruce L., *Karl Barth's Critically Realistic Dialectical Theology: Its Genesis and Development 1909–1936*, 2nd ed. (Oxford: Oxford University Press, 1997).

Mielke, Roger, *Eschatologische Öffentlichkeit: Öffentlichkeit der Kirche und politische Theologie im Werk von Erik Peterson* (Göttingen: Vandenhoeck & Ruprecht, 2012).

Milbank, John, *Being Reconciled: Ontology and Pardon* (London: Routledge, 2003).

Moltmann, Jürgen, *The Coming of God: Christian Eschatology*, Margaret Kohl (trans.) (London: SCM Press, 1996).

Moltmann, Jürgen, *The Crucified God: The Cross of Christ as the Foundation and Criticism of Christian Theology*, R. A. Wilson and John Bowden (trans.) (London: SCM Press, 1973).

Moltmann, Jürgen, 'Foreword', in M. Douglas Meeks, *Origins of the Theology of Hope* (Philadelphia: Augsburg Fortress, 1974).

Moltmann, Jürgen, *Theology of Hope: On the Ground and the Implications for a Christian Eschatology*, James W. Leitch (trans.) (London: SCM Press, 1967).

Nichtweiß, Barbara, *Erik Peterson: Neue Sicht auf Leben und Werk* (Freiburg: Herder, 1992).

Nichtweiß, Barbara (ed.), *Vom Ende der Zeit: Geschichtstheologie und Eschatologie bei Erik Peterson. Symposium Mainz 2000* (Münster: LIT Verlag, 2001).

Overbeck, Franz, *Über die Christlichkeit unserer heutigen Theologie* (Leipzig: C. G. Naumann, 1873); published in English as *How Christian Is Our Present-Day Theology?*, Martin Henry (trans.) (London: T&T Clark, 2005).

Pannenberg, Wolfhart (ed.), *Revelation as History* (New York: Macmillan, [1961] 1968).

Peterson, Erik, 'The Church' [1928–9], in *Theological Tractates*, Michael J. Hollerich (trans.) (Stanford: Stanford University Press, 2011), pp. 30–9.

Peterson, Erik, *Der Brief an die Römer*, Barbara Nichtweiß (ed.), Ausgewählte Schriften 6 (Würzburg: Echter, 2012).

Pius X, *Lamentabili sane exitu* (Vatican, 1907).

Polkinghorne, John and Michael Welker (eds), *The End of the World and the Ends of God: Science and Theology on Eschatology* (London: Continuum, 2000).

Schmidt, Christoph, 'The Return of the Katechon: Giorgio Agamben contra Erik Peterson', *The Journal of Religion* 94:2 (2014), 182–203.

Schmitt, Carl, *The Nomos of the Earth in the International Law of the Jus Publicum Europaeum*, G. L. Ulmen (trans.) (Candor, NY: Telos Press, 2006).

Schwöbel, Christoph, 'Last Things First? The Century of Eschatology in Retrospect', in *Future as God's Gift: Explorations in Christian Eschatology*, edited by David Fergusson and Marcel Sarot (Edinburgh: T&T Clark, 2000), pp. 217–41.

Stapledon, Olaf, *Last and First Men* (London: Methuen, 1930).

Stoll, Christian, *Die Öffentlichkeit der Christus-Krise: Erik Petersons eschatologischer Kirchenbegriff im Kontext der Moderne* (Paderborn: Ferdinand Schöningh, 2017).

Troeltsch, Ernst, 'An Apple from the Tree of Kierkegaard', in *The Beginnings of Dialectical Theology*, edited by James M. Robinson, vol. 1 (Richmond, VA: John Knox Press, 1968).

Vatter, Miguel, 'The Political Theology of Carl Schmitt', in *The Oxford Handbook of Carl Schmitt*,

    edited by Jens Meierhenrich and Oliver Simons (Oxford: Oxford University Press, 2017),
    pp. 245–66.
Westhelle, Vítor, 'Liberation Theology', in *The Oxford Handbook of Eschatology*, edited by Jerry L.
    Walls (Oxford: Oxford University Press, 2007), pp. 311–27.
Wolfe, Judith, 'Eschatology', in *The Oxford Handbook of Nineteenth-Century Christian Thought*,
    edited by Joel Rasmussen, Judith Wolfe and Johannes Zachhuber (Oxford: Oxford University
    Press, 2017).
Wolfe, Judith, 'Messianism', in *The Oxford Handbook of Theology and Modern European Thought*,
    edited by Nicholas Adams, George Pattison and Graham Ward (Oxford: Oxford University Press,
    2013), pp. 301–23.

# Index